Research Methods in Psychology

Pearson

At Pearson, we have a simple mission: to help people make more of their lives through learning.

We combine innovative learning technology with trusted content and educational expertise to provide engaging and effective learning experiences that serve people wherever and whenever they are learning.

From classroom to boardroom, our curriculum materials, digital learning tools and testing programmes help to educate millions of people worldwide – more than any other private enterprise.

Every day our work helps learning flourish, and wherever learning flourishes, so do people.

To learn more, please visit us at **www.pearson.com/uk**

Research Methods in Psychology

Sixth Edition

Dennis Howitt Loughborough University
Duncan Cramer Loughborough University

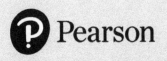 Pearson

Harlow, England • London • New York • Boston • San Francisco • Toronto • Sydney • Dubai • Singapore • Hong Kong
Tokyo • Seoul • Taipei • New Delhi • Cape Town • São Paulo • Mexico City • Madrid • Amsterdam • Munich • Paris • Milan

PEARSON EDUCATION LIMITED
KAO Two
KAO Park
Harlow CM17 9SR
United Kingdom
Tel: +44 (0)1279 623 623
Web: www.pearson.com/uk

First published 2005 (print)
Second edition published 2008 (print and electronic)
Third edition published 2011 (print and electronic)
Fourth edition published 2014 (print and electronic)
Fifth edition published 2017 (print and electronic)
Sixth edition published 2020 (print and electronic)

ISBN: 978-1-292-27670-0 (print)
978-1-292-27672-4 (PDF)
978-1-292-27671-7 (ePub)

British Library Cataloguing-in-Publication Data
A catalogue record for the print edition is available from the British Library

Library of Congress Cataloging-in-Publication Data
Names: Howitt, Dennis, author. | Cramer, Duncan, author.
Title: Research methods in psychology / Dennis Howitt, Loughborough
  University, Duncan Cramer, Loughborough University.
Other titles: Introduction to research methods in psychology
Description: Sixth Edition. | Hoboken : Pearson, 2020. | Revised edition of
  the authors' Introduction to research methods in psychology, [2017] |
  Includes bibliographical references and index. | Summary:
  "Comprehensive, clear, and practical, Introduction to Research Methods
  in Psychology, sixth edition is the essential student guide to
  understanding and undertaking quantitative and qualitative research in
  psychology. Revised throughout, this new edition includes a new chapter
  on 'Managing your research project'. This is the ideal guide for
  students just beginning and those moving on to more advanced research
  methods projects in psychology. New to this Edition New chapter
  'Managing your research project' provides practical suggestions to help
  students successfully manage the intellectual, organizational,
  emotional, and social demands of their research projects. New sections
  on multi-method research and the analysis of the big data generated by
  the digital media. Key features User-friendly boxed features and
  illustrations across the book help to bring the subject to life. These
  include: 'Research Examples' at the end of every chapter put research
  methods in a real-world context. 'Key ideas' are highlighted to help
  students grasp and revise the main topics and concepts. 'Talking Points'
  address some of the controversial issues to critically engage students
  with the debates in the field. 'Practical advice' boxes give handy hints
  and tips on how to carry out research in practice Examples of published
  research with 'how to' advice and guidance on writing up reports, helps
  students to develop a practical, as well as theoretical,
  understanding"-- Provided by publisher.
Identifiers: LCCN 2019046997 | ISBN 9781292276700 (paperback) | ISBN
  9781292276700 (epub)
Subjects: LCSH: Psychology--Research--Methodology.
Classification: LCC BF76.5 .H695 2020 | DDC 150.72/1--dc23
LC record available at https://lccn.loc.gov/2019046997

10 9 8 7 6 5 4 3 2 1
24 23 22 21 20

Front cover image © SEAN GLADWELL/Moment/Getty Images
Print edition typeset in 9.5/12pt Sabon LT Pro by Spi Global.

NOTE THAT ANY PAGE CROSS REFERENCES REFER TO THE PRINT EDITION

Brief contents

Contents

Companion Website

For open-access student resources specifically written to complement this textbook and support your learning, please visit **go.pearson.com/uk/he/resources**

Guided tour

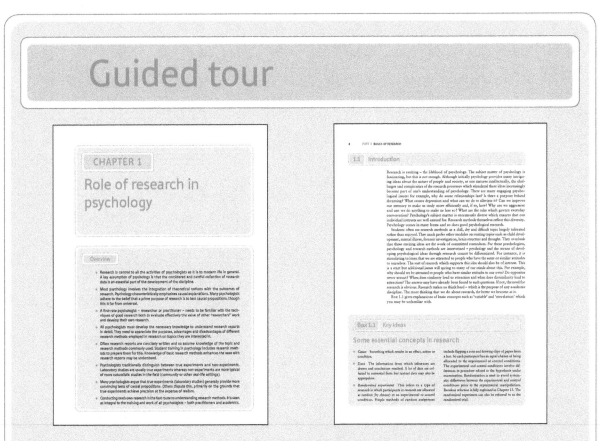

Clear Overview

Introduces the chapter to give students a feel for the topics covered

Key Ideas

Outlines the important concepts in more depth to give you a fuller understanding

Practical Advice

Gives you handy hints and tips on how to carry out research in practice

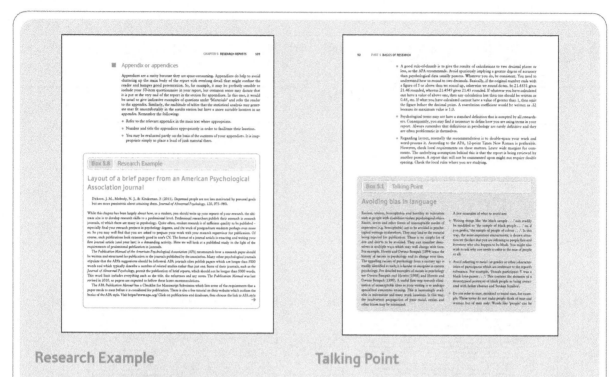

Research Example

Explores a real example of research being carried out, giving you an insight into the process

Talking Point

Investigates an important debate or issue in research

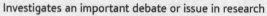

Conclusion/Key points

Each chapter has a conclusion and set of key points to help summarise chapter coverage when you're revising a topic

Activities

Each chapter concludes with activities to help you test your knowledge and explore the issues further

Introduction

Modern psychological research can seem daunting to the newcomer. This sixth edition of *Research Methods in Psychology* seeks to introduce a broad range of topics dealing with psychological research and analysis as currently practised. We cover statistical methods in psychology in a separate volume. Good research requires considerable thought, understanding, experience, and attention to detail. It is far from a simple rule-following exercise and to pretend otherwise is a great disservice to students. The incredible progress of modern psychology requires that teaching resources must struggle to be up to date and be appropriate for the variety of different educational experiences provided by different universities. We do not expect that this sixth edition will be read from beginning to end. Instead, choose what is appropriate for your needs from our sequence of largely self-contained chapters.

In *Research Methods in Psychology* you will find both quantitative and qualitative research covered in appropriate depth. These are commonly but, we think, wrongly seen as alternative and incompatible approaches to psychological research. For some researchers, there may be an intellectual incompatibility between the two. Increasingly, however, researchers appreciate that the two approaches can feed each other. Even if we are wrong about this, it is vitally important that students understand the intellectual roots of the two traditions, how research is carried out in these traditions, and what each tradition is capable of achieving. Armed with this understanding, students will be better placed to make intelligent and appropriate choices about the style of research appropriate to their chosen research questions. On its own, the qualitative material in this sixth edition effectively supports much of the qualitative research likely to be carried out today. There is as much detailed practical advice and theory on qualitative research methods as probably required. (If more is required, the book by Dennis Howitt (2019), *Introduction to Qualitative Research Methods in Psychology,* Harlow: Pearson Education, will probably meet your requirements.) But this is in addition to the quantitative coverage, which easily outstrips any competition in terms of variety, depth and authority. We have tried to provide students with resources to help them in ways largely ignored by most other texts. For example, Chapter 7 on literature searches is extremely comprehensive and practical. Similarly, Chapter 8 on ethics meets the most recent standards and deals with them in depth. Chapter 5 on writing research reports places report writing at the centre of the research process rather than as an add-on at the end. Writing a research report is highly demanding of a student's understanding of all of the elements of research. We provide practical help to this end by including chapters giving examples of quantitative and qualitative research which fail to meet the highest standards. You will also find some discussion of statistics in this book. For the most part, this is when dealing with topics which are missing from the popular SPSS-based statistics textbooks, simply because SPSS does not cover everything useful in psychological research. Statistics is a more controversial topic in psychology than struggling students may realise. So we have included a chapter on some of the more controversial aspects of statistics which may encourage a more mature understanding of the role of statistics in psychology. For the sixth edition, we have included new material on important but recent topics including multi-method research and data mining. The final chapter is new and is tips and hints which may help you cope better with the stresses and turmoil that planning and executing research may bring.

As far as is possible, we have tried to provide students with practical skills as well as the necessary conceptual overview of research methods in modern psychology. Nevertheless, there is a limit to this. The bottom line is that anyone wishing to understand research needs to read research, not merely plan, execute, analyse and write up research. Hence, almost from the start we emphasise that reading is not merely unavoidable but crucial. Without such additional reading, the point of this book is missed. It is not intended as a jumble of technical stuff too boring to be part of any module other than one on research methods. The material in the book is intended to expand students' understanding of psychology by explaining just how researchers go about creating psychology. At times this can be quite exciting as well as frustrating and demanding.

Acknowledgements

Authors' acknowledgements

Working with the team at Pearson on a book project is always a delight. Working without the team at Pearson on a book project is unimaginable. So we would like to offer our thanks to everyone involved for their kindness and hard work. But there are a few people that we would like to give a particular mention.

We have worked with Janey Webb for a good many years on numerous book projects. No matter what, she always gave 110% but, sadly, she has moved on from Pearson. It is difficult to describe the incredible support that she provided over all that time. Her official title was Publisher but she was just Janey to us. She is a remarkable person who will be missed. Partings of this sort are common in publishing but we also have said goodbye to Saraswati Banerjee who was Acquisition Editor for a while. She was also a rock and great support. We wish them both well wherever life leads them. This means that we can welcome Catherine Yates as the Publisher who has taken over from Janey.

We hope that you can tell a book by its cover as we think that the cover design, by Kelly Miller, is excellent and we wish her success after her departure from Pearson. Kevin Ancient took charge of the cover after this and did the all-important text design. He easily holds the record for the number of acknowledgements in our books.

The Project Manager is Sweda R who is just about the most helpful person imaginable. Unfortunately we never know whether to address her as Sweda or R. Maybe R sounds a bit too James Bondish. Perhaps all of us should be a letter.

Bincy Menon had overall responsibility for turning our manuscript into a fine looking book in her role as Content Producer. It never ceases to amaze us that a human being can oversee such a process yet remain charming and friendly.

The Copyeditor was Antonia Maxwell. Not only is she better at spotting our mistakes than even we are at making them, she imposed the text design on our manuscript with great aplomb. This cannot be easy for a book like this with its many elements. Even more remarkable is her ability not to appear irritated by the authors when surely she must have been.

Heather Ancient was the Proofreader for this edition. Proofreader is a word used to describe a very wise, very clever, very organized person with extremely high tolerance of boredom. Such qualities are not possible in just one human being which confirms our view that all proof readers are androids.

Finally, we should express our gratitude to Karen Mclaren who is the rhyming R&P Analyst at Pearson. R&P stands for Rights and Permissions. She stops us getting in big trouble with copyright holders. This makes us happy though sorting things out does not.

Dennis Howitt
Duncan Cramer

■ Publisher's acknowledgements

Text credits:

38 W. W. Norton & Company: Kelly, G. A. (1955). *The psychology of personal constructs. Volume 1: A theory of personality.* New York, NY: Norton; **41 American Psychological Association:** Byrne, D., & Blaylock, B. (1963). Similarity and assumed similarity of attitudes between husbands and wives. *Journal of Abnormal and Social Psychology, 67,* 636–640; **48 American Psychological Association:** Danziger, K., & Dzinas, K. (1997). How psychology got its variables. *Canadian Psychology, 38,* 43–48; **59–60 American Psychological Association:** Condon, J. W., & Crano, W. D. (1988). Inferred evaluation and the relation between attitude similarity and interpersonal attraction. *Journal of Personality and Social Psychology, 54,* 789–797; **82 Sage Publications:** Byrne, D., Gouaux, C., Griffitt, W., Lamberth, J., Murakawa, N., Prasad, M., Prasad, A., & Ramirez III, M. (1971). The ubiquitous relationship: Attitude similarity and attraction: A cross-cultural study. *Human Relations, 24,* 201–207; **110 American Psychological Association:** Dickson, J. M., Moberly, N. J., & Kinderman, P. (2011). Depressed people are not less motivated by personal goals but are more pessimistic about attaining them. *Journal of Abnormal Psychology, 120,* 975–980; **116 Elsevier:** Loftus, E. F., & Palmer, J. C. (1974). Reconstruction of automobile destruction: An example of the interaction between language and memory. *Journal of Verbal Learning and Verbal Behaviour, 13,* 585–589; **118 American Psychological Association:** Pickering, M. (1984). Elizabeth Loftus: An Appreciation. *Genuflecting Psychology Review, 29,* 29–43; **163–164 The British Psychological Society:** British Psychological Society (2011). *Code of human research ethics.* Leicester, UK: BPS. p. 5; **171 State University of New York Press:** Korn, J. H. (1997). *Illusions of reality: A history of deception in social psychology.* New York, NY: State University of New York Press; **180 Lawrence Erlbaum Associates:** Keith-Spiegel, P., & Koocher, G. P. (1985). *Ethics in psychology: Professional standards and cases.* Hillsdale, NJ: Lawrence Erlbaum Associates. p. 35; **181 Harper & Row:** Steffens, L. (1931). *Autobiography of Lincoln Steffens.* New York, NY: Harper & Row. p. 151; **235 Houghton Mifflin Company:** Campbell, D. T., & Stanley, J. C. (1963). *Experimental and quasi-experimental designs for research.* Boston, MA: Houghton Mifflin. p. 1; **236 Houghton Mifflin Company:** Cook, T. D., & Campbell, D. T. (1979). *Quasiexperimentation: Design and analysis issues for field settings.* Chicago, IL: Rand McNally. p. 295; **244 Taylor & Francis Group:** Pedhazur, E. J., & Schmelkin, L. P. (1991). *Measurement, design and analysis: An integrated approach.* Hillsdale, NJ: Lawrence Erlbaum Associates. pp. 44–45; **246 Elsevier:** Eagle, B. W., Miles, E. W., & Icenogle, M. L. (1997). Interrole conflicts and the permeability of work and family domains: Are there gender differences? *Journal of Vocational Behavior, 50,* 168–184; **251 Houghton Mifflin Company:** Cook, T. D., & Campbell, D. T. (1979). *Quasiexperimentation: Design and analysis issues for field settings.* Chicago, IL: Rand McNally; **255 American Psychological Association:** Baron, R. M., & Kenny, D. A. (1986). The moderator–mediator variable distinction in social psychological research: Conceptual, strategic, and statistical considerations. *Journal of Personality and Social Psychology, 51,* 1173–1182; **261 Sage Publications:** Fincham, F. D., Beach, S. R. H., Harold, G. T., & Osborne, L. N. (1997). Marital satisfaction and depression: Different causal relationships for men and women? *Psychological Science, 8,* 351–357; **271 Houghton Mifflin Company:** Hays, W. L. (1994). *Statistics* (5th ed.). New York: Harcourt Brace. p. 227; **271 Pearson Education:** Glass, G. V., & Hopkins, K. D. (1984). *Statistical methods in education and psychology* (2nd ed.). Englewood Cliffs, NJ: Prentice-Hall. p. 177; **271 Royal Anthropological Institute of Great Britain and Ireland:** Fisher, R. A. (1936b). "The coefficient of racial likeness" and the future of craniometry. *Journal of the Royal Anthropological Institute, 66,* 57–63. Retrieved February 6, 2016 from https://digital.library.adelaide.edu.au/dspace/handle/2440/15228; **274 Office for National**

Statistics: SOC: Archive Older versions of the UK Standard Occupational Classification, containing SOC 2000, Office for National Statistics, https://www.ons.gov.uk/methodology/classificationsandstandards/standardoccupationalclassificationsoc/socarchive#about-the-standard-occupational-classification-2000-soc2000; **280 American Psychological Association:** Hamby, S., & Turner, H. (2013). Measuring teen dating violence in males and females: Insights from the National Survey of Children's Exposure to Violence, *Psychology of Violence, 3,* 323–339; **284 American Psychological Association:** Wilkinson, L. (1999). Statistical methods in psychology journals: Guidelines and explanations. *American Psychologist, 54,* 594–604; **285 American Psychological Association:** American Psychological Association (2010). *Publication manual of the American Psychological Association* (6th ed.). Washington, DC: APA. p. 3,30; **286 No Starch Press, Inc:** Reinhart, A. (2015). *Statistics done wrong: The woefully complete guide.* San Francisco, CA: No Starch Press. p. 9; **286 Andy Field:** Field, A. (2005). Effect Size. www.statisticshell.com/docs/effectsizes.pdf; **289 No Starch Press, Inc:** Reinhart, A. (2015). *Statistics done wrong: The woefully complete guide.* San Francisco, CA: No Starch Press; **289 GraphPad Software, Inc:** Graphpad (2015). Interpreting the confidence interval of a mean. http://www.graphpad.com/guides/prism/6/statistics/index.htm?stat_more_about_confidence_interval.htm; **292 American Psychological Association:** Rosnow, R. I., & Rosenthal, R. (1989). Statistical procedures and the justification of knowledge in psychological science. *American Psychologist, 44,* 1276–1284; **296 Elsevier:** Pietschnig, J., Voracek, M., & Formann, A. K. (2010). Mozart effect–Shmozart effect: A meta-analysis. *Intelligence, 38,* 314–323; **298–299 Sage Publications:** Simmons, J. P., Nelson, L. D., & Simonsohn, U. (2011). False-positive psychology: Undisclosed flexibility in data collection and analysis allows presenting anything as significant. *Psychological Science, 22,* 1359–1366; **301 Sage Publications:** John, L. K., Loewenstein, G., & Prelec, D. (2012). Measuring the prevalence of questionable research practices with incentives for truth telling. *Psychological Science, 23,* 524–532; **306 American Psychological Association:** Atkinson, D. R., Furlong, M. J., & Wampold, B. E. (1982). Statistical significance, reviewer evaluations, and the scientific process: Is there a (statistically) significant relationship? *Journal of Counseling Psychology, 29,* 189–194; **328 Hogrefe Verlag:** Arribas-Aguila, D. (2011). Psychometric properties of the TEA Personality Test: Evidence of reliability and construct validity. *European Journal of Psychological Assessment, 27,* 121–126; **339-340 American Psychological Association:** Cronbach, L. J., & Meehl, P. E. (1955). Construct validity in psychological tests. *Psychological Bulletin, 52,* 281–302; **343-345 National Center for Biotechnology Information:** Ramo, D. E., Hall, S. M., & Prochaska, J. J. (2011). Reliability and validity of self-reported smoking in an anonymous online survey with young adults. *Health Psychology, 30,* 693–701; **369–370 Sage Publications:** Silverman, D. (1997). The logics of qualitative research. In G. Miller & R. Dingwall (Eds.), *Context and method in qualitative research* (pp. 12–25). London: Sage; **370 William M.K. Trochim:** Trochim, W. M. K. (2006). Positivism and post-positivism. http://www.socialresearchmethods.net/kb/positvsm.htm; **382 Oxford University Press:** Bryman, A. (2015). *Social research methods* (5th ed.). Oxford, UK: Oxford University Press; **393 Sage Publications:** Potter, J. (1997). Discourse analysis as a way of analysing naturally occurring talk. In D. Silverman (Ed.), *Qualitative research: Theory, methods and practice* (pp. 144–160). London, UK: Sage; **395–398 Kelly Benneworth:** Benneworth, K. (2004). A discursive analysis of police interviews with suspected paedophiles. Doctoral dissertation, Loughborough University, England, reprinted with permission from Kelly Benneworth-Gray; **399 Sage Publications:** O'Connell, D. C., & Kowal, S. (1995). Basic principles of transcription. In J. A. Smith, R. Harré, & L. van Langenhove (Eds.), *Rethinking methods in psychology* (pp. 93–105). London, UK: Sage; **405 Cambridge University Press:** Gee, D., Ward, T., & Eccleston, L. (2003). The function of sexual fantasies for sexual offenders: A preliminary model. *Behaviour Change, 20,* 44–60; **409 John Wiley & Sons:** Sheldon, K., & Howitt, D. (2007). *Sex offenders and the Internet.* Chichester, UK: Wiley; **412 Taylor & Francis:**

Braun, V., & Clarke, V. (2006). Using thematic analysis in psychology. *Qualitative Research in Psychology, 3,* 77–101; **420 Sage Publications:** Charmaz, K. (2000). Grounded theory: Objectivist and constructivist methods. In N. K. Denzin & Y. S. E. Lincoln (Eds.), *Handbook of qualitative research* (2nd ed.) (pp. 503–535). Thousand Oaks, CA: Sage; **424–426 Sage Publications:** Charmaz, K. (1995). Grounded theory. In J. A. Smith, R. Harré, & L. van Langenhove (Eds.), *Rethinking methods in psychology* (pp. 27–49). London, UK: Sage; **427 Sage Publications:** Strauss, A., & Corbin, J. (1999). Grounded theory methodology: An overview. In A. Bryman & R. G. Burgess (Eds.), *Qualitative research,* Vol. 3 (pp. 73–93). Thousand Oaks, CA: Sage; **430 Maggie O'Neil:** We are grateful to Maggie O'Neil and Jane Pitcher for help with this box; **431 Elsevier:** Potter, J. (1998). Qualitative and discourse analysis. In A. S. Bellack & M. Hersen (Eds.), *Comprehensive clinical psychology,* Vol. 3 (pp. 117–144). Oxford, UK: Pergamon; **432 Taylor & Francis:** Groom, R., Cushion, C., & Nelson, L. (2011). Delivery of video-based performance analysis by England youth soccer coaches: Towards a grounded theory. *Journal of Applied Sport Psychology, 23,* 16–23; **434 Sage Publications:** Strauss, A., & Corbin, J. (1999). Grounded theory methodology: An overview. In A. Bryman & R. G. Burgess (Eds.), *Qualitative research,* Vol. 3 (pp. 73–93). Thousand Oaks, CA: Sage; **437 Linguistic Society of America:** Tannen, D. (2007). Discourse analysis. Linguistic Society of America, http://www.lsadc.org/info/ling-fields-discourse.cfm; **438 Harvard University Press:** Austin, J. L. (1975). *How to do things with words.* Cambridge, MA: Harvard University Press; **438 Sage Publications:** Edley, N. (2001). Analysing masculinity: Interpretative repertoires, ideological dilemmas and subject positions. In M. Wetherell, S. Taylor, & S. J. E. Yates (Eds.), *Discourse as data: A guide for analysis* (pp. 189–228). London, UK: Sage; **438 Sage Publications:** Potter, J. (2004). Discourse analysis. In M. Hardy & A. Bryman (Eds.), *Handbook of data analysis* (pp. 607–624). London, UK: Sage; **438 Sage Publications:** Taylor, S. (2001). Locating and conducting discourse analytic research. In M. Wetherell, S. Taylor, & S. J. E. Yates (Eds.), *Discourse as data: A guide for analysis* (pp. 5–48). London, UK: Sage; **439 Cambridge University Press:** Searle, J. R. (1969). *Speech acts: An essay in the philosophy of language.* Cambridge, UK: Cambridge University Press; **441 Sage Publications:** Potter, J., & Wetherell, M. (1995). Discourse analysis. In J. A. Smith, R. Harré, & L. van Langenhove (Eds.), *Rethinking methods in psychology* (pp. 80–92). London, UK: Sage; **441 Sage Publications:** van Dijk, T. (2001). Principles of critical discourse analysis. In M. Wetherell, S. Taylor, & S. J. E. Yates (Eds.), *Discourse theory and practice: A reader* (pp. 300–317). London, UK: Sage; **442–443 Sage Publications:** Potter, J. (2004). Discourse analysis. In M. Hardy & A. Bryman (Eds.), *Handbook of data analysis* (pp. 607–624). London, UK: Sage; **443 Sage Publications:** Potter, J. (1997). Discourse analysis as a way of analysing naturally occurring talk. In D. Silverman (Ed.), *Qualitative research: Theory, methods and practice* (pp. 144–160). London, UK: Sage; **446 Sage Publications:** Taylor, S. (2001). Locating and conducting discourse analytic research. In M. Wetherell, S. Taylor, & S. J. E. Yates (Eds.), *Discourse as data: A guide for analysis* (pp. 5–48). London, UK: Sage; **445 Sage Publications:** Lovering, K. M. (1995). The bleeding body: Adolescents talk about menstruation. In S. Wilkinson & C. Kitzinger (Eds.), *Feminism and discourse: Psychological perspectives* (pp. 10–31). London: Sage; **456 Sage Publications:** Wooffitt, R. (2001). Researching psychic practitioners: Conversation analysis. In M. Wetherell, S. Taylor, & S. J. E. Yates (Eds.), *Discourse as data: A guide for analysis* (pp. 49–92). London: Sage; **457–458 Sage Publications:** Kitzinger, C., & Frith, H. (2001). Just say no? The use of conversation analysis in developing a feminist perspective on sexual refusal. In M. Wetherell, S. Taylor, & S. J. E. Yates (Eds.), *Discourse theory and practice: A reader* (pp. 167–185). London, UK: Sage; **465 Sage Publications:** Smith, J. A., & Osborn, M. (2003). Interpretative phenomenological analysis. In J. A. Smith (Ed.), *Qualitative psychology: A practical guide to research methods* (pp. 51–80). London, UK: Sage; **467 Sage Publications:** Robbins, B. D., & Parlavecchio, H. (2006). The unwanted exposure of the self: A phenomenological study of embarrassment. *The Humanistic*

Psychologist, 34(4), 321–345; **484 Elsevier:** Potter, J. (1998). Qualitative and discourse analysis. In A. S. Bellack & M. Hersen (Eds.), *Comprehensive clinical psychology*, Vol. 3 (pp. 117–144). Oxford, UK: Pergamon; **489 Academy of Management:** Pratt, M. G. (2009). From the editors: For the lack of a boilerplate: tips on writing up (and reviewing) qualitative research. *Academy of Management Journal, 52*, 856–862; **504 Springer:** Jaspal, R. (2015). The experience of relationship dissolution among British South Asian gay men: Identity threat and protection. *Sexuality Research and Social Policy, 12*, 34–46; **520 American Psychological Association:** Adapted from Haggbloom, S. J., Warnick, R., Warnick, J. E., Jones, V. K., Yarbrough, G. L., Russell, T. M., et al. (2002), The 100 most eminent psychologists of the 20th century, *Review of General Psychology, 6*, 139–152, American Psychological Association; **524 American Psychological Association:** Swann, W. B., Jr, Griffin, J. J., Predmore, S. C., & Gaines, B. (1987). The cognitive–affective cross-fire: When self-consistency confronts self-enhancement. *Journal of Personality and Social Psychology, 52*, 881–889.

Image credits:

148–150 Clarivate Analytics: Reprinted with permission from Clarivate Analytics. WEB OF SCIENCE, CLARIVATE, and CLARIVATE ANALYTICS & LOGO are trademarks of their respective owners and used herein with permission; **150 Ex Libris Ltd:** Reprinted with permission from Ex Libris Ltd; **150 Elsevier:** Sciencedirect; **151 Elsevier:** Elsevier; **152–153 American Psychological Association:** The PsycINFO® Database screenshot is reproduced with permission of the American Psychological Association, publisher of the PsycINFO database, all rights reserved. No further reproduction or distribution is permitted without written permission from the American Psychological Association; **152–153 EBSCO Information Services:** Reprinted with permission from EBSCO Information Services; **153 Ryan Tolman:** Original abstract from Tolman, 2017; **153 Loughborough University:** Reprinted with permission from Loughborough University; **157 Microsoft Corporation:** Screenshot of Microsoft.

PART 1

Basics of research

CHAPTER 1

Role of research in psychology

Overview

- Research is central to all the activities of psychologists as it is to modern life in general. A key assumption of psychology is that the considered and careful collection of research data is an essential part of the development of the discipline.

- Most psychology involves the integration of theoretical notions with the outcomes of research. Psychology characteristically emphasises causal explanations. Many psychologists adhere to the belief that a prime purpose of research is to test causal propositions, though this is far from universal.

- A first-rate psychologist – researcher or practitioner – needs to be familiar with the techniques of good research both to evaluate effectively the value of other researchers' work and develop their own research.

- All psychologists must develop the necessary knowledge to understand research reports in detail. They need to appreciate the purposes, advantages and disadvantages of different research methods employed in research on topics they are interested in.

- Often research reports are concisely written and so assume knowledge of the topic and research methods commonly used. Student training in psychology includes research methods to prepare them for this. Knowledge of basic research methods enhances the ease with research reports may be understood.

- Psychologists traditionally distinguish between true experiments and non-experiments. Laboratory studies are usually true experiments whereas non-experiments are more typical of more naturalistic studies in the field (community or other real-life settings).

- Many psychologists argue that true experiments (laboratory studies) generally provide more convincing tests of causal propositions. Others dispute this, primarily on the grounds that true experiments achieve precision at the expense of realism.

- Conducting one's own research is the fast route to understanding research methods. It is seen as integral to the training and work of all psychologists – both practitioners and academics.

1.1   Introduction

Research is exciting – the lifeblood of psychology. The subject matter of psychology is fascinating, but this is not enough. Although initially psychology provides many intriguing ideas about the nature of people and society, as one matures intellectually, the challenges and complexities of the research processes which stimulated these ideas increasingly become part of one's understanding of psychology. There are many engaging psychological issues: for example, why do some relationships last? Is there a purpose behind dreaming? What causes depression and what can we do to alleviate it? Can we improve our memory to make us study more efficiently and, if so, how? Why are we aggressive and can we do anything to make us less so? What are the rules which govern everyday conversation? Psychology's subject matter is enormously diverse which ensures that our individual interests are well catered for. Research methods themselves reflect this diversity. Psychology comes in many forms and so does good psychological research.

Students often see research methods as a dull, dry and difficult topic largely tolerated rather than enjoyed. They much prefer other modules on exciting topics such as child development, mental illness, forensic investigation, brain structure and thought. They overlook that these exciting ideas are the work of committed researchers. For these psychologists, psychology and research methods are intertwined – psychology and the means of developing psychological ideas through research cannot be differentiated. For instance, it is stimulating to learn that we are attracted to people who have the same or similar attitudes to ourselves. The sort of research which supports this idea should also be of interest. This is a start but additional issues will spring to many of our minds about this. For example, why should we be attracted to people who have similar attitudes to our own? Do opposites never attract? When does similarity lead to attraction and when does dissimilarity lead to attraction? The answer may have already been found to such questions. If not, the need for research is obvious. Research makes us think hard – which is the purpose of any academic discipline. The more thinking that we do about research, the better we become at it.

Box 1.1 gives explanations of basic concepts such as 'variable' and 'correlation' which you may be unfamiliar with.

Box 1.1   Key Ideas

Some essential concepts in research

- *Cause* Something which results in an effect, action or condition.

- *Data* The information from which inferences are drawn and conclusions reached. A lot of data are collected in numerical form but textual data may also be appropriate.

- *Randomised experiment* This refers to a type of research in which participants in research are allocated at random (by chance) to an experimental or control condition. Simple methods of random assignment

include flipping a coin and drawing slips of paper from a hat. So each participant has an equal chance of being allocated to the experimental or control conditions. The experimental and control conditions involve differences in procedure related to the hypothesis under examination. Randomisation is used to avoid systematic differences between the experimental and control conditions prior to the experimental manipulation. Random selection is fully explained in Chapter 13. The randomised experiment can also be referred to as the randomised trial.

● *Reference*   In psychology, this refers to the details of the book or article that is the source of the ideas or data being discussed. The reference includes such information as the author, the title and the publisher of the book or the journal in which the article appears.

● *Variable*   A variable is any concept that varies and can be measured or assessed in some way. Intelligence, height, gender and social status are simple examples.

1.2   The importance of reading

Reading research papers in detail is the best way of understanding psychological research methods. This can be slow at first but speeds up rapidly with practice. Textbooks can only provide an overview and reading some original papers will facilitate progress. Admittedly, some psychologists use unnecessary jargon in their writings so give priority to those who communicate clearly and effectively. University students spend only a small part of a working week being taught – they are expected to spend substantial time on independent study including reading and other work on assignments.

Glance through any textbook or lecture module's reading list and you will see the work of researchers cited. For example, the lecturer or author may cite the work of Byrne (1961) on attraction and similarity of attitude. Normally a list of the 'references' cited is provided. The citation provides information on the kind of work it is (e.g. what the study is about) and where it has been presented or published. The details are shown in the following way:

Unsworth, N. (2019). Individual differences in long-term memory. *Psychological Bulletin,* 145(1), 79–139.

In publications, nowadays this is usually followed by a DOI (digital object identifier) code which allows the publication to be rapidly found using a computer. The format is standard for a particular type of publication – a book may be referenced differently from a journal article and an Internet source is referenced differently still. For a journal article, the last name of the author is given first, followed by the year in which the paper was published. After this comes the title of the work. Like most research in psychology, Unsworth's study was published in a journal. The title of the journal is given next, together with the number of the volume in which the article appeared and the numbers of the first and last pages of the article. These references are generally listed alphabetically according to the last name of the first author in a reference list at the end of the journal article or book. Where there is more than one reference by the same author or authors, they will be listed according to the year the work was presented. This is known as the Harvard system or author–date system. More detail is given in the chapters about writing a research report (Chapters 5 and 6). We will cite references in this way in this book. However, we cite few references compared with psychology texts on other subjects, as many of the ideas we present have been generally accepted by authors (although usually not in the same way).

Many references cited by lecturers and textbooks refer to reports of research examining a particular question or small set of questions. Research studies are limited and selective in their scope – it is impossible to design a study to study everything. As already mentioned, research is primarily published in professional journals. These are organised into volumes usually published every year. Typically, a volume consists of several issues or parts which are published sequentially every three months or so. Each issue normally consists of several reports which are probably no more than 4000 or 5000 words in length, though it is not uncommon to find some of them 10,000 words long. Their shortness necessitates concise writing styles. Consequently, they can make for difficult reading and require careful reading in order to master them. Sometimes you may have to read additional studies for details which provide you with a better and more complete understanding.

One aim of this book is to provide the basic knowledge which you require to make sense of such publications – and even to write them. There are obstacles to obtaining necessary publications since, for example, there are too many different psychology journals and books for most libraries to stock physically on shelves. Your university or college library can borrow books from other libraries for use. Most journal articles, however, may be obtained by you in digital form (usually in Portable Digital Format or pdf). Your university or college almost certainly subscribes to digital versions of many different journals which will be readily available to you via your university library over the Internet. The chapter on searching the literature (Chapter 7) explains how to access publications not held in your own library. This is remarkably convenient and there are no overdue fines.

One rewarding aspect about studying psychology is that it is common for students to have questions about a topic which are not addressed in lectures or textbooks. For example, in the case of the research on liking and attitude similarity you may wonder whether the nature of the attitudes being shared affects the relationship. Are some attitudes more important than others and, if so, what are these? If you find yourself asking new questions while reading something then this is excellent. This sort of intellectual curiosity is required to become a good researcher. As your studies progress, you will probably become increasingly curious about what the latest thinking and research on the topic is. If you are interested in a topic, then wanting to know what other people are thinking about it is only natural. Your lecturers will certainly be pleased if you demonstrate such intellectual curiosity. There is a great deal to be learnt about how one can keep up with the latest developments in any academic discipline. Being able to discover what is currently happening and what has happened in a field of research is a vital skill. Chapter 7 discusses in detail how to search for the current publications on a topic.

1.3 Evaluating the evidence

So psychology is not simply about learning and accepting other people's conclusions about a particular research topic. It is more important to be able to carefully evaluate the evidence which has led to these conclusions. Why? Back to our example. What if you have always subscribed to the old adage 'opposites attract'? Would you suddenly change your mind simply because you read in a textbook that people with similar attitudes are attracted to each other? Most likely you would want to know a lot more about the evidence. For example, what if you found that the research in support of this idea was obtained simply by asking a sample of 100 people whether they believed that opposites attract? Actually, all that the researchers had really shown was that people generally thought it was true that people with similar attitudes tend to be attracted. But merely because people once believed the world was flat did not make it flat. It is interesting to know what people believe, but you would require different evidence to conclude that attraction actually is a consequence of attitude similarity. You might also wonder whether it is really true that people once believed the world to be flat. Frequently, in the newspapers and on television, one comes across startling findings from psychological research.

Is it wise simply to accept what the newspaper or television report claims, or would it be better to check the original research before deciding what to conclude?

We probably would be more convinced of the importance of attitude similarity in attraction if a researcher measured how attracted couples were to each other and then showed that those with the most similar attitudes were the most attracted. Even then we might still harbour some doubts. For example, just what do we mean by attraction? If we mean wanting to have a drink with the other person at a pub, then we might prefer the person with whom we might have a lively discussion, that is, someone who does not share our views. On the other hand, if willingness to share a flat with a person were the measure of attraction, then perhaps a housemate with a similar outlook to our own would be preferred. So we are beginning to see that the way in which we choose to measure a concept (or variable) such as attraction may affect the answers we get to our research questions. Notice that the stance of a researcher is somewhat sceptical – that is, they need to be convinced that something is the case.

Is it even more difficult to get a satisfactory measure of attitudes than attraction? There are many different topics that we can express attitudes about. So, would we expect attraction to be affected in the same way if two people shared the view that life exists on Mars compared with if they had similar religious views? Does it matter as much if two people have different tastes in music compared with if they had different views about openness in relationships? That is, some attitudes may be more important than others in determining attraction – perhaps similarity of some attitudes is irrelevant to the attraction between two people. One might study this by asking people about their attitudes on a variety of topics and then how important each of these attitudes is to them. (Importance is sometimes called salience.) Alternatively, if we thought that some attitudes are likely to be the most important then we might focus on these in some depth. All of this implies that the process of evaluating the research in a particular field is not a narrow, nit-picking exercise. Instead, it is a process by which new ideas are generated and new research stimulated.

The various propositions that we have discussed about the relationship between attraction and similarity are all examples of *hypotheses*. A hypothesis is merely a supposition or proposition which serves as the basis of further investigation, either through the collection of research data or through reasoning. The word hypothesis comes from the Greek word for foundation – perhaps confirming that hypotheses are the foundation on which psychology develops. Precision is an important characteristic of good hypotheses. So, our hypothesis that similarity of attitudes is related to attraction might benefit from refinement. It looks as if we might have to say something more about the attitudes that people have and what we mean by attraction, for that matter, if we are to pursue our basic research question further. If we think that the attitudes have to be important, then the hypothesis should be reformulated to read that *people are more attracted to those with similar attitudes on personally important topics*. If we thought attraction was based on having a similar attitude towards spending money, we should restate the hypothesis to say that *people are more attracted to those with similar attitudes towards spending money*.

The evaluation of research evidence involves examining the general assertion that the researcher is making about an issue and the information (data) relevant to this assertion. We need to check whether the evidence or data supports the assertion or whether the assertion goes beyond what could be confidently concluded. Sometimes, in extreme cases, researchers draw conclusions which seem not to be justified by their data. Any statement that goes beyond the data is speculation or conjecture and needs to be recognised as such. There is nothing wrong with speculation as such since hypotheses, for example, are themselves often speculative as they go beyond what is known already. However, speculation needs to be distinguished from legitimate inferences from data.

1.4   Inferring causality

The concept of *causality* has been important throughout most of the history of psychology. Other disciplines might consider it almost an obsession of psychology. The meaning of the term is embodied in the phrase 'cause and effect'. The idea is that things that happen in the world may have an effect on other things. So when we speak of a causal relationship between attitude similarity and attraction, we mean that attitude similarity is the cause of attraction to another person. Not all data allow one to infer causality with confidence. Sometimes researchers suggest that their research demonstrates a causal relationship when others would claim that it demonstrates no such thing – there may be a relationship but one thing did not cause the other. In strictly logical terms, some claims of a causal relationship can be regarded as an error since they are based on research methods which by their nature cannot prove causality with certainty. Frequently, research findings may be consistent with a causal relationship but they are, equally, consistent with other explanations.

A great deal of psychology focuses on causes of things even when the word 'cause' is not used directly. Questions such as why we are attracted to one person rather than another, why people become depressed and why some people commit violent crimes are typical examples of this. The sorts of explanation that are given might be, for example, that some people commit violent crimes because they were physically abused as children. In other words, physical abuse as a child is a *cause* of adult violent crime. There may be a relationship between physical abuse and violent crime, but does this establish that physical abuse is a cause? To return to our main example, suppose a study found that people who were attracted to each other had similar attitudes. Pairs of friends were compared with pairs of strangers in terms of how similar their attitudes were (see Figure 1.1). It emerged that the friends had more similar attitudes than pairs of strangers. Could we conclude from this finding that this study showed that attitude similarity causes people to be attracted towards one another? If we can conclude this, on what grounds can we do so? If not, then why not?

There are at least three main reasons why we cannot conclude definitively from this study that similar attitudes lead to people liking each other:

- Attraction, measured in terms of friendship, and similarity of attitudes are assessed once and at precisely the same time (see Figure 1.2). As a consequence, we do not know which of these two came first. Did similarity of attitudes come before friendship as it would have to if similar attitudes lead to liking? Without knowing the

Pairs of friends–
are their attitudes
similar?

Pairs of strangers–
are their attitudes
dissimilar?

| FIGURE 1.1 | Looking for causal relationships |

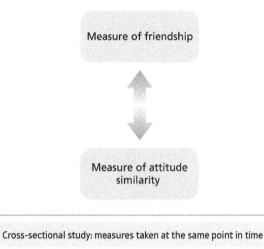

Measure of friendship

Measure of attitude similarity

FIGURE 1.2   Cross-sectional study: measures taken at the same point in time

temporal sequence, definitive statements about cause and effect are not possible (see Figure 1.3).

- Friendship may have preceded similarity of attitudes. In other words, perhaps friends develop similar attitudes because they happen to like one another for other reasons. Because this study measures both friendship and similarity of attitudes at the same time, we cannot tell which came first. In other words, we cannot determine which caused which (see Figure 1.4).

- The development of attraction and similarity may be the result of the influence of a third factor. For example, if one moves to university, one begins to be attracted to new people and, because of the general influence of the campus environment, attitudes begin to change. In these circumstances, the relationship between attraction and similarity is

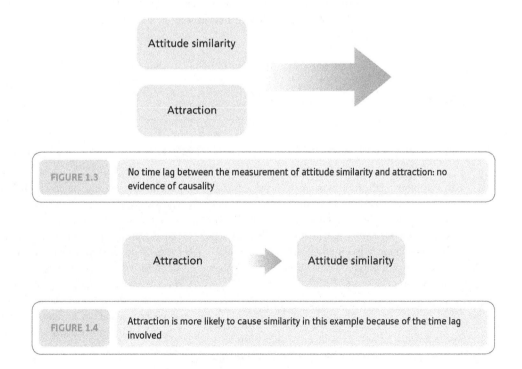

Attitude similarity

Attraction

FIGURE 1.3   No time lag between the measurement of attitude similarity and attraction: no evidence of causality

Attraction   Attitude similarity

FIGURE 1.4   Attraction is more likely to cause similarity in this example because of the time lag involved

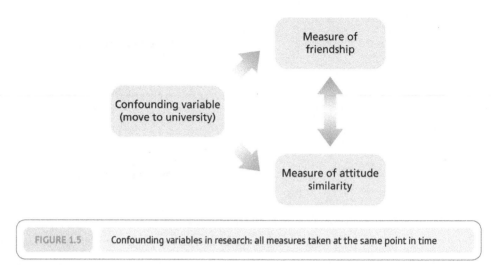

FIGURE 1.5 Confounding variables in research: all measures taken at the same point in time

not causal (in either direction) but the result of a third factor, which is the effect of the move to campus (see Figure 1.5).

Care needs to be taken here. This research in question is not worthless simply because it cannot definitively establish a causal relationship. The research findings are clearly compatible with a causal hypothesis and one might be inclined to accept the possibility that it is causal with increased confidence. Nevertheless, one cannot be certain and may find it difficult to argue against someone who rejects the idea. Such divergences of opinion sometimes become controversies in psychology which is a positive thing when it leads to new research designed to resolve the disagreement.

Some of psychology's most characteristic research methods are geared towards addressing the issue of causality. Most of these will be outlined in due course. Most importantly, the contrast between randomised experiments so familiar to psychologists in the form of laboratory experiments and research outside the laboratory has this issue at its root.

The role of causality in psychology is a controversial topic. See Box 1.2 for a discussion of this.

Box 1.2 Talking Point

Causal explanations: psychology's weakest link?

It is well worth taking the time to study the history of psychology. This will help you to identify the characteristics of the discipline (e.g. Hergenhahn, 2001; Leahy, 2004). What is very obvious is that psychology has been much more concerned about causality than many related disciplines – sociology is a good example. There are a number of reasons for this:

● Psychology was much more influenced by the philosophies of positivism and logical positivism than these other disciplines. Broadly speaking, positivism is a description of the methods of the natural sciences

such as physics and chemistry. It basically holds that knowledge is obtained through observation. So the more focused and precise the empirical observation, the better. Hence, a precisely defined cause and an equally precisely defined effect would be regarded as appropriate. Positivism is a concept originating in the work of the French sociologist Auguste Comte (1798–1857). It refers to the historical period when knowledge was based on science rather than, say, religious authority. Logical positivism is discussed in some detail later in this book (Chapter 18).

● Psychology has traditionally defined itself as much as a biological science as a social science. Consequently, methods employed in the natural sciences have found profoundly influenced psychology. In the natural sciences, laboratory studies (experiments) in which small numbers of variables at a time are controlled and studied are common, as they have been in psychology. The success of other disciplines, especially physics in the nineteenth century and later, encouraged psychologists to emulate this approach.

● By emulating the natural sciences approach, psychologists have tended to seek general principles of human behaviour just as natural scientists believe that their laws apply throughout the physical universe. Translated into psychological terms, the implication is that findings from the laboratory are applicable to situations outside the psychological laboratory. Randomised laboratory experiments tend to provide the most convincing evidence of causality – that is what they are designed to do but at the cost of artificiality.

Modern psychology is much more varied in scope than ever in the past. The issue of causality is not seen as crucial as it once was. There is a great deal of research that makes a positive contribution to psychology which eschews issues of causality. For example, the forensic psychologist who wishes to predict suicide risk in prisoners does not have to know the causes of suicide among prisoners. So if research shows that being in prison for the first time is the strongest predictor of suicide, then this may have policy implications. It is irrelevant whether the predictor is in itself the direct cause of suicide. There are a multitude of research questions which are not about causality.

Many modern psychologists regard the search for causal relationships as somewhat counterproductive. It may be a good ideal in theory, but in practice it may have a negative influence on the progress of psychology. One reason for this is that the procedures which can help establish causality can actually result in highly artificial and contrived situations, with the researcher focusing on fine detail rather than obtaining a broad view, and the findings of such research are often not all that useful in practice. One does not have to study psychology for long before it becomes more than apparent that there is a diversity of opinion on many matters.

1.5   Types of research and the assessment of causality

In this section, we will describe a number of different types of study in order to achieve a broad overview of research methods in psychology. There is no intention to prioritise them in terms of importance or sophistication. They are:

● Correlational or cross-sectional studies

● Longitudinal studies

● Experiments – or studies with randomised assignment.

As this section deals largely with these in relation to the issue of causality, all of the types of research discussed below involve a minimum of two variables examined in relation to each other. Types of study which primarily aim to describe the characteristics of things are dealt with elsewhere, for example, surveys (Chapter 13) and qualitative methods in depth (Chapters 18–26).

Correlational or cross-sectional studies

Correlational (or cross-sectional) studies are a very common type of research. Basically what happens is that a number of different variables (see Box 1.1) are measured more or less simultaneously for a sample of individuals (see Figure 1.6). Generally in psychology, the strategy is to examine the extent to which these variables measured at a single point in time are associated (i.e. correlated) with one another. A correlation coefficient is a statistical index or test which describes the degree and direction of the relationship between two characteristics or variables. To say that there is a correlation between two characteristics merely means that there is a relationship between them.

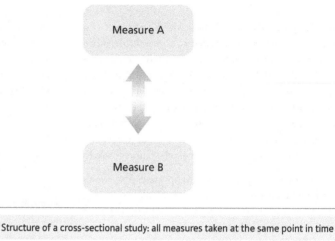

FIGURE 1.6   Structure of a cross-sectional study: all measures taken at the same point in time

The correlation coefficient is not the only way of testing for a relationship. There are many other statistical techniques which can be used to describe and assess the relationship between two variables. For example, although we could correlate the extent to which people are friends or strangers with how similar their attitudes are using the correlation coefficient, there are other possibilities. An equivalent way of doing this is to examine differences. This is not done as commonly in this kind of study. One would look at whether there is a difference in the extent to which friends are similar in their attitudes compared with how similar random pairs of strangers are. If there is a difference between the two in terms of degrees of attitude similarity, it means that there is a relationship between the variable 'friends/strangers' and the variable 'similarity of attitudes'. So a test of differences (e.g. the *t*-test) can be applied rather than a correlation coefficient. A more accurate term for describing these studies is cross-sectional in that they measure variables at one point in time or across a slice or section of time. This alternative term leaves open how we analyse the data statistically, since it implies neither a test of correlation nor a test of differences in itself. Issues related to this general topic are discussed in depth later (Chapter 4).

Correlational or cross-sectional studies are often carried out in psychology's subdisciplines of social, personality, developmental, educational, and abnormal or clinical psychology. In these areas such research designs have the advantage of enabling the researcher to measure a number of different variables simultaneously. Any of these variables might possibly explain why something occurs. It is likely that anything that we are interested in explaining will have a number of different causes rather than a single cause. By measuring a number of different variables at the same time, it becomes possible to see which of the variables is most strongly related to what it is we are seeking to explain.

Confounding variables

A major reason why we cannot infer causality is the possible influence of unconsidered variables. Sometimes this is referred to as the third variable problem. For example, it could be that both friendship and similarity of attitudes are determined by the area, or kind of area, in which you live (such as a campus, as mentioned earlier). You are more likely to make friends with people you meet, who are more likely to live in the same area as you. People living in the same area also may be more likely to have the same or similar attitudes. An example of this might be that northerners are attracted to other northerners and that they share characteristics largely because they are from the north. Variables

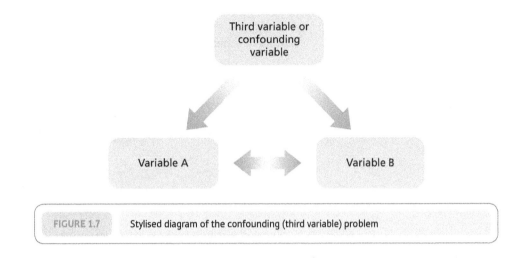

FIGURE 1.7   Stylised diagram of the confounding (third variable) problem

which either wholly or partially account for the relationship between two other variables are known as *confounding* variables. Area, or type of area, could be a confounding variable which we may need to check (see Figure 1.7).

One could try to hold constant in several ways the area from which people come. For example, one could select only people from the same area. In this way the influence of different areas is eliminated. If you did this, then there may still be other factors which account for the fact that people are attracted to others who have similar attitudes to them. It is not always obvious or easy to think what these other factors might be. Because we have to study a sample of several friendships, it is likely that these pairs of friends differ in many ways from other pairs. It would be very difficult to hold all of these different factors constant. One such factor might be age. Pairs of friends are likely to differ in age. Some pairs of friends will be older than other pairs of friends. It could be that any association or relationship between being friends and having similar attitudes is due to age. People are more likely to be friends with people who are similar in age to them. People of a similar age may have similar attitudes, such as the kind of music they like or the kinds of clothes they wear. So age may determine both who becomes friends with whom and what their attitudes are. The easiest way to control for confounding variables is to try to measure them and to control for them statistically. There is another way, which we will mention shortly.

Longitudinal studies

Supposing we measured both friendship and similarity of attitudes at two (or more) different points of time, could we then determine whether friendship led to having similar attitudes? This kind of study is known as a longitudinal study as opposed to a cross-sectional one. It is more difficult to organise this kind of study, but it could be and has been done. We would have to take a group of people who did not know each other initially but who would have sufficient opportunity subsequently to get to know each other. Some of these people would probably strike up friendships. One possible group of participants would be first-year psychology students who were meeting together for the first time at the start of their degree. It would probably be best if any participants who knew each other before going to university or came from the same area were dropped from the analysis. We would also need to measure their attitudes towards various issues. Then after a suitable period of time had elapsed, say, three or more months, we would find out what friendships had developed and what their attitudes were (see Figure 1.8).

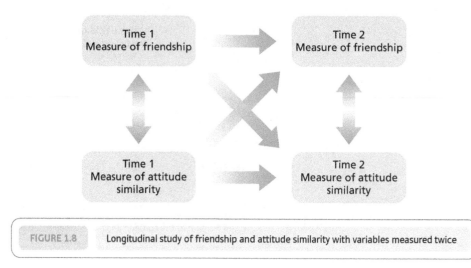

FIGURE 1.8   Longitudinal study of friendship and attitude similarity with variables measured twice

Supposing it were found that students who subsequently became friends started off as having the same or similar attitudes and also had the same or similar attitudes subsequently, could we then conclude that similar attitudes lead to friendship? In addition, suppose that those who did not become friends started off dissimilar in attitudes and were still dissimilar three months later. This situation or analysis is illustrated in Figure 1.9 in the left-hand column. Well, it is certainly stronger evidence that similarity of attitudes may result in friendship than we obtained from the cross-sectional study. Nevertheless, as it stands, it is still possible for the sceptic to suggest that there may be other confounding variables which explain both the friendships and the similarity in attitudes despite the longitudinal nature of our new study. This association between friendship and attitude similarity possibly could be explained in terms of confounding variables (see Figure 1.10). For example, the idea was discussed earlier that people who come from similar kinds of areas may be the most likely to become friends as they find out they are familiar with the same customs or have shared similar experiences. They may also have similar attitudes because they come from similar areas. Thus similarity of area rather than similarity of attitudes could lead to friendships, as illustrated in Figure 1.10.

As with cross-sectional studies, statistical methods of controlling these confounding variables are used in longitudinal studies. Longitudinal studies provide more information than cross-sectional ones. In our example, they will tell us how stable attitudes

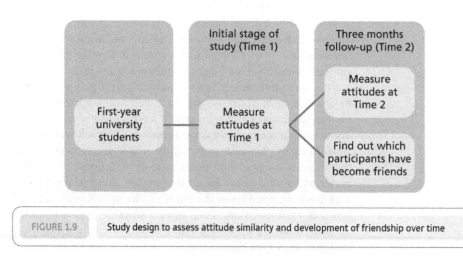

FIGURE 1.9   Study design to assess attitude similarity and development of friendship over time

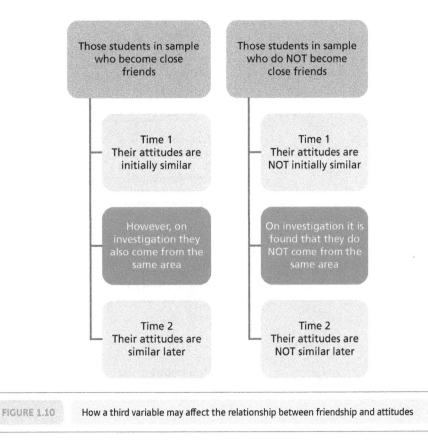

FIGURE 1.10   How a third variable may affect the relationship between friendship and attitudes

are over time. If attitudes are found not to be very stable and if similarity of attitudes determines friendships, then in theory friendships should not be very stable. Because longitudinal studies involve more complex relationships, their analysis is more complicated and requires more effort to understand. As with cross-sectional studies, the major problem is the difficulty of considering every confounding factor that potentially affects the results. If one could guarantee to deal with every possible confounding variable, longitudinal research would be an ideal type of approach. Unfortunately, there can be no such guarantee.

Studies with randomised assignment – experiments

We have now identified a basic problem. Researchers simply do not and cannot know what other variables affect their key measures. Is there any way of taking into account every confounding variable when we do not know what those variables are? For some psychologists, the answer to this fundamental problem lies in randomisation. Imagine a study in which two groups of participants are given the opportunity to interact in pairs and get to know each other better. For one group, the pairs are formed by choosing one member of the pair at random and then selecting the other member at random from the participants who had similar attitudes to the first member of the pair. In the other condition, participants are selected at random but paired with another person dissimilar in attitude to them, again selected at random. By allocating participants to similarity and dissimilarity conditions by chance, any differences between the conditions cannot be accounted for by these confounding variables. By randomising in this way, similarities and dissimilarities in the areas from which the participants come, for example,

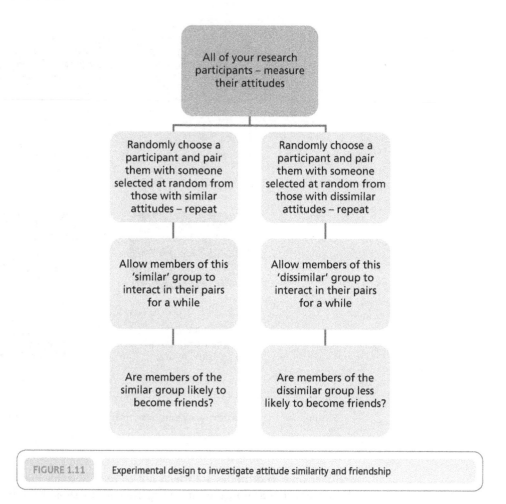

All of your research participants – measure their attitudes

Randomly choose a participant and pair them with someone selected at random from those with similar attitudes – repeat

Randomly choose a participant and pair them with someone selected at random from those with dissimilar attitudes – repeat

Allow members of this 'similar' group to interact in their pairs for a while

Allow members of this 'dissimilar' group to interact in their pairs for a while

Are members of the similar group likely to become friends?

Are members of the dissimilar group less likely to become friends?

FIGURE 1.11   Experimental design to investigate attitude similarity and friendship

would be expected to be equalised between groups. This particular example is illustrated in Figure 1.11 and the more general principles of experimental design are shown in Figure 1.12.

A simple method of randomisation to use in this example is to allocate participants to the different conditions by tossing a coin. We would have to specify before we tossed the coin whether a coin landing heads facing upwards would mean that the person was paired with a person with the same attitude as them or with a different attitude from them. If we tossed a coin a fixed number of times, say, 20 times, then it should come up heads 10 times and tails 10 times on average in the long run. If we had decided that a head means meeting someone with the same attitude, approximately 10 people will have been chosen to meet someone with similar attitudes and approximately 10 people someone with different attitudes. Such a procedure is referred to as random assignment. People can be randomly assigned to different situations which are usually called conditions, groups or treatments or levels of treatment. (Actually, we have not solved all of the difficulties, as we will see later.)

If half the people in our study came from, say, Bristol and half from Birmingham, then approximately half of the people who were randomly assigned to meeting a person with the same attitude as them would be from Bristol and the remaining half would be from Birmingham. The same would be true of the people who were randomly assigned to meeting a person with a different attitude from them. About half would be from Bristol and the remaining half would be from Birmingham. In other words, random assignment should control for the area that people came from by ensuring that there are roughly equal numbers of people from those areas in the two groups. This will hold true for any factor

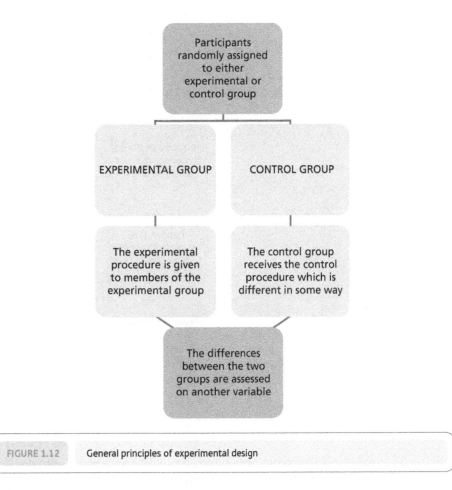

General principles of experimental design

such as the age of the person or their gender. In other words, random assignment ensures that all confounding factors are held constant – without the researcher needing to know what those confounding factors are. While this is true, it only applies in the long run and biased outcomes can occur if only a few cases are involved.

Sampling error

The randomised study is not foolproof. Sampling error will always be a problem. If a coin is tossed any number of times, it will not always come up heads half the time and tails half the time. It could vary from one extreme of no heads to the other extreme of all heads, with the most common number of heads being half or close to half. In other words, the proportion of heads will differ from the number expected by chance. This variability is known as sampling error and is a feature of any study. A sample is people (or units) that are being studied. The smaller the sample, the greater the sampling error will be. A sample of 10 people will have a greater sampling error than one of 20 people. Although you may find doing this a little tedious, you could check this for yourself in the following way. Toss a coin 10 times and count the number of heads (this is the first sample). Repeat this process, say 30 times in total, which gives you 30 separate samples of coin tossing. Note the number of times heads comes up for each sample. Now do this again but toss the coin 20 times on each occasion rather than 10 times for each sample. You will find that the number of heads is usually closer to half when tossing the coin 20 times on each occasion rather than 10 times (see Figure 1.13). Many studies will have as few as 20 people in each group or condition, because it is thought that the sampling error for such numbers

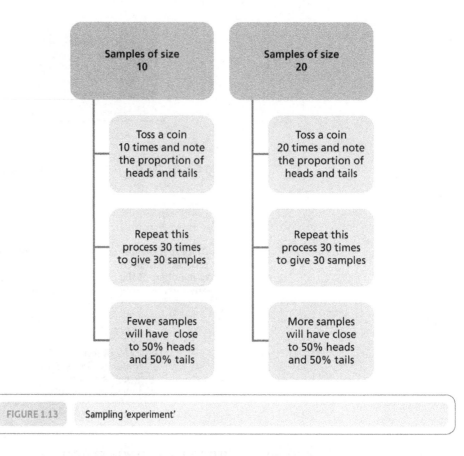

Samples of size 10	Samples of size 20
Toss a coin 10 times and note the proportion of heads and tails	Toss a coin 20 times and note the proportion of heads and tails
Repeat this process 30 times to give 30 samples	Repeat this process 30 times to give 30 samples
Fewer samples will have close to 50% heads and 50% tails	More samples will have close to 50% heads and 50% tails

FIGURE 1.13   Sampling 'experiment'

is acceptable. See our companion statistics text, *Understanding statistics in psychology with SPSS* (Howitt & Cramer, 2020), for a more detailed discussion of sampling error.

Intervention or manipulation

So, in many ways, if the purpose of one's research is to establish whether two variables are causally related, it is attractive to consider controlling for confounding variables through random assignment of participants to different conditions. To determine whether similar attitudes lead to friendship, we could randomly assign people to meet strangers with either similar or dissimilar attitudes to their own, as we have already described. Remember that we have also raised the possibility that people's attitudes are related to other factors such as the area or kind of area they come from. Assuming that this is the case, participants meeting strangers with the same attitudes as theirs might be meeting people who come from the same area or kind of area as theirs. On the other hand, participants meeting strangers with different attitudes from theirs may well be meeting people who come from a different area or kind of area from theirs. In other words, we still cannot separate out the effects of having the attitude similarity from the possible confounding effects of area similarity. It is clear that we need to disentangle these two different but interrelated factors. It is not possible to do this using real strangers because we cannot separate the stranger from the place they come from.

Let's consider possible approaches to this difficulty. We need to ensure that the stranger expresses similar attitudes to those of the participant in the same-attitudes condition. That is, if they did not share attitudes with a particular participant, they would nevertheless pretend that they did. In the different-attitudes condition, then, we could ensure that the stranger always expresses different attitudes from those of the participant. That is, the stranger pretends to have different attitudes from those of the participant. See Table 1.1

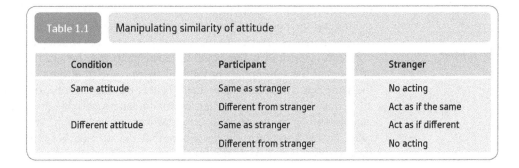

Table 1.1	Manipulating similarity of attitude	
Condition	**Participant**	**Stranger**
Same attitude	Same as stranger	No acting
	Different from stranger	Act as if the same
Different attitude	Same as stranger	Act as if different
	Different from stranger	No acting

for an overview of this. In effect, the stranger is now the accomplice, confederate, stooge or co-worker of the researcher with this research design.

The number of times the stranger does not have to act as if they have a different attitude from the one they have is likely to be the same or similar in the two conditions – that is, if participants have been randomly allocated to them. This will also be true for the number of times the stranger has to act as if their attitude is different from the one they have.

Unfortunately, all that has been achieved by this is an increase in complexity of the research design for no other certain gain. We simply have not solved the basic problem of separating similarity of attitude from area. This is because in the same attitude condition some of the strangers who share the same attitude as the participant may well be attractive to the participant actually because they come from the same area as the participant – for example, they may speak with similar accents. Similarly, some of the participants in the different-attitudes condition will not be so attracted to the stranger because the stranger comes from a different area. Quite how this will affect the outcome of the research cannot be known. However, the fact that we do not know means that we cannot assess the causal influence of attitude similarity on attraction with absolute certainty.

We need to try to remove any potential influence of place entirely or include it as a variable in the study. Probably the only way to remove the influence of place entirely is by not using a real person as the stranger. One could present information about a stranger's attitude and ask the participant how likely they are to like someone like that. This kind of situation might appear rather contrived or artificial. We could try to make it less so by using some sort of cover story such as saying that we are interested in finding out how people make judgements or form impressions about other people. Obviously the participants would not be told the proposition that we are testing in case their behaviour is affected by this information. For example, they may simply act in accordance with their beliefs about whether or not people are attracted to others with similar attitudes. If they are not given this information, they may still come to their own conclusions about what the study is about and, perhaps, act accordingly.

Participants may not realise what the researcher wants to test because they take part in only one of the two conditions of the study (unless they talk to other people who have already participated in the other condition of the study). We could further disguise the purpose of our study by providing a lot more information about the stranger over and above their attitudes. This additional information would be the same for the stranger in both conditions – the only difference is in terms of the information concerning attitude similarity. In one condition attitudes would be the same as those of the participant, while in the other condition they would be different.

If (a) the only difference between the two conditions is whether the stranger's attitudes are similar to or dissimilar from those of the participant, and (b) we find that participants are more attracted to strangers with similar than with dissimilar attitudes, then this difference in attraction must be due to the only difference between the two conditions, that is the influence of the difference in attitudes. Even then, there are problems in terms of how to interpret the evidence. One possibility is that the difference in attraction is not directly due to differences in attitudes themselves but to factors which participants associate with differences in attitudes. For example, participants may believe that people with the same attitudes as themselves may be more likely to come from the same kind of area or be of the same age. Thus it would be these beliefs which are responsible for the differences in attraction. In other words, when we manipulate a variable in a study we may, in fact, inadvertently manipulate other variables without realising it. We could try to hold these other factors constant by making sure that the stranger is similar to the participant in these respects, or we could test for the effects of these other factors by manipulating them as well as similarity of attitude.

This kind of study where:

- the presumed cause of an effect is manipulated,

- participants are randomly assigned to conditions, and

- all other factors are held constant

was called a *true experiment* by Campbell (1957) and Campbell and Stanley (1963). In a later revision of their book, the term 'true' was replaced by 'randomised' (Shadish, Cook, & Campbell, 2002, p. 12) although others used this term much earlier (Kempthorne & Barclay, 1953, pp. 611, 613). This design can also be described as a randomised trial. If any of the three requirements listed above do not hold, then the study may be described as a *non-experiment* or *quasi-experiment*. These terms will be used in this book. True or randomised experiments are more common in psychology's sub-disciplines such as perception, learning, memory and biological psychology where it is easier to manipulate the variables of interest. The main attraction of true experiments is that they can provide logically more convincing evidence of the causal impact of one variable on another. There are disadvantages which may be very apparent in some fields of psychology. For example, the manipulation of variables may result in very contrived and implausible situations, as was the case in our example. Furthermore, exactly what the nature of the manipulation of variables has achieved may not always be clear. Studies are often conducted to try to rule out or to put forward plausible alternative interpretations or explanations of a particular finding. We will have more confidence in a research finding if it has been confirmed or replicated a number of times, by different people, using different methods and adopting a critical approach.

So the legitimacy of assertions about causal effects depends on the research design that has been used to study them. If we read claims that a causal effect has been established, then we might be more convinced if we find that the studies in question which showed this effect were true experiments rather than quasi-experiments. Furthermore, how effectively the causal variable was manipulated must also be considered. Is it possible, as we have seen, that other variables were inadvertently varied at the same time? The nature of the design and of any manipulations that have been carried out are described in journal articles in the section entitled 'Method'.

These and other designs are discussed in more detail in subsequent chapters. Few areas of research depend solely on a single method. Nevertheless, certain methods are more characteristic of certain fields of psychology than others. In 1999, a random sample of studies published in the electronic database PsycINFO were found to be dominated by experimental studies though a variety of research designs were represented (Bodner, 2006a). These findings are summarised in Figure 1.14. Unfortunately this sort of study is infrequent but a glance at relevant journals should give you some idea of the up-to-date situation. Knowing about the strengths and weaknesses of research designs should help you to be in a better position to critically evaluate their findings. There is more on design considerations in later chapters. A comparison of the main research designs is given in Figure 1.15.

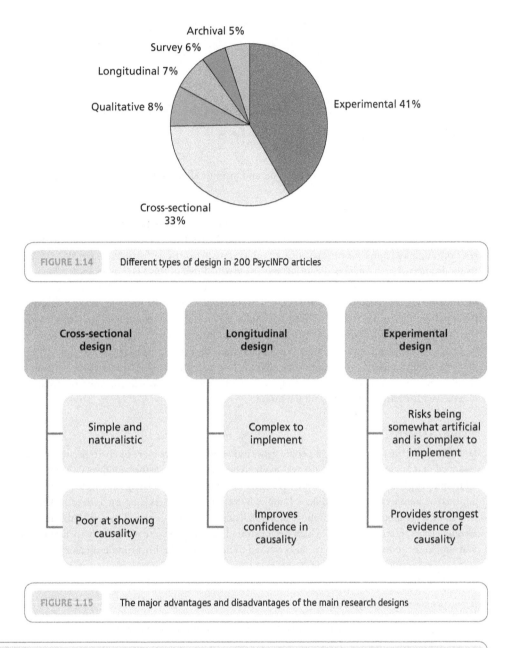

FIGURE 1.14   Different types of design in 200 PsycINFO articles

FIGURE 1.15   The major advantages and disadvantages of the main research designs

1.6   Practice

The empirical testing of research ideas is important in much psychology. Consequently, doing research is required in the vast majority of psychology degrees. For example, to be recognised by the British Psychological Society as a practising psychologist you are required to have a basic understanding of research methodology and the skills to carry it out. This is the case even if you do not intend to carry out research in your profession. Practising psychologists like educational or clinical psychologists simply cannot rely on academic psychologists to carry out all of the necessary research to benefit their psychological practice. The modern idea of the practitioner–researcher means that practitioners such as occupational psychologists and forensic psychologists should carry out research to advance practice in their field of work. To be brutally frank, a student who is not prepared to develop their research skills is doing themselves and the discipline of psychology no favours at all.

A true (i.e. randomised) experiment on the effect of attitude similarity on liking

Byrne, D. (1961). Interpersonal attraction and attitude similarity. *Journal of Abnormal and Social Psychology, 62,* 713–715.

As a newcomer to psychological research you are beginning a process during which you will become increasingly familiar with the major findings of psychological research and the methods which generate these findings. Textbooks summarise research findings, but a more sophisticated understanding of these findings comes with the realisation that research methods and research findings are intractably intertwined. All of this takes time and effort. Reading research studies is an important aspect of this. Through reading, we learn of the reasoning behind research and how the process of research involves making crucial decisions at each and every stage about how the research will be done. Most chapters of this book present illustrative research studies which describe in some detail interesting and worthwhile research pertinent to the chapter in question. For this first chapter, we have chosen to give details of some of the work of Donn Byrne which is fundamental to the discussion in the main body of the text for this chapter.

We have also included the author's suggestions for further research. This serves as a reminder that a research study should not be seen as definitive but merely part of a longer process which encompasses what has been done in the past together with what might be done in the future.

Background

Donn Byrne's (1961) idea was that people with similar attitudes are more likely to be attracted towards one another. He reasoned that having similar attitudes was likely to be rewarding since they confirmed the person's view of their world. In addition, people with similar attitudes were more likely to be seen as being intelligent, knowledgeable, moral and better adjusted. A number of non-experimental studies by various researchers supported the idea. They showed that the attitudes of friends were more similar than those of non-friends. The possible causal nature of this relationship was suggested by a couple of experimental studies which demonstrated that people were more likely to accept and to like a stranger who had similar attitudes to them. Byrne also wanted to determine whether attitude similarity caused or led to attraction.

Hypotheses

Byrne proposed three hypotheses:

1. Strangers with similar attitudes are better liked than strangers with dissimilar attitudes;

2. Strangers with similar attitudes are judged to be more intelligent, better informed, more moral and better adjusted than strangers with dissimilar attitudes; and

3. Strangers with similar attitudes on important issues and dissimilar attitudes on unimportant issues are evaluated more positively than strangers with dissimilar attitudes on important issues and similar attitudes on unimportant attitudes.

Based on a small-scale or pilot study, Byrne selected 26 topics which varied in importance from extremely important (such as believing in racial integration or in God) to less important (such as an interest in classical music or politics).

Method

Participants

A class of 36 male and 28 female introductory psychology students were asked to report their attitude on these topics. They also had to indicate which were the 13 most important and 13 least important issues to them so that the similarity on these two types of issues could be varied to test the third hypothesis. Two weeks later, these students were told that another class had also filled in this questionnaire. They were to be given a questionnaire completed by a person of the same gender from the other class in a study of how much students could learn about the other person from the information in their questionnaire.

Procedure

The students were randomly assigned to one of four conditions in which they received a 'bogus' questionnaire which had actually been made up by the researcher to create four different conditions. In other words, the students had been deceived about the procedure and that the questionnaire had not actually been completed by another student. The four versions of the questionnaire were:

1. The other student held opinions which were exactly the same as their own.

2. The other student held opinions which were exactly the opposite of their own.

3. The other student held opinions which were similar on the most important issues and dissimilar on the least important ones.

4. The other student held opinions which were dissimilar on the most important issues and similar on the least important ones.

So, underlying this was the fact that two variables were manipulated: (1) the similarity of the attitude (same vs opposite) and (2) the importance of the attitude (most vs least important). These variables can also be termed the *independent variables* as they are manipulated independently of other variables (see Chapters 2 and 3). The design is summarised in Figure 1.16.

After reading the supposed answers of the other student, participants in the research had to rate their opinion of the other person on six characteristics. Two characteristics assessed how much they liked the other person. The two questions were how well they felt they would like this person and whether they believed they would enjoy working with them in an experiment. The other four characteristics were how they evaluated the intelligence, knowledge of current affairs, morality and adjustment of the other student. These variables are known as the *dependent variables* as their values are thought to depend on the independent variables.

Results

Byrne used the statistical technique known as the unrelated *t*-test to test his three hypotheses, as there are two different groups of participants (e.g. he compared two groups of strangers – one group had similar attitudes to those of the participants and the other group had dissimilar attitudes to those of the participants). Liking was measured on a scale which makes it a score variable.

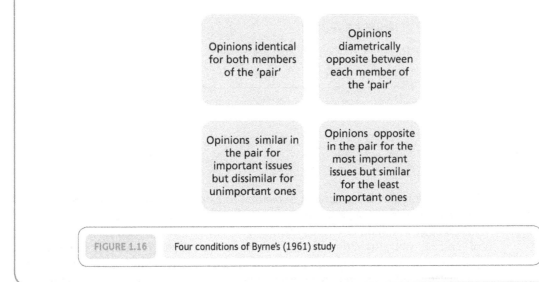

| FIGURE 1.16 | Four conditions of Byrne's (1961) study |

1. The first hypothesis was confirmed. Those who were given the questionnaire of someone with exactly the same attitudes as their own thought they would like this person significantly more. They believed that they would enjoy working with them significantly more than those who were presented with the questionnaire of someone with exactly the opposite attitudes to theirs.

2. The second hypothesis was also confirmed in that those who were presented with the questionnaire of someone with exactly the same attitudes as their own rated that person as being significantly more intelligent, knowledgeable, moral and adjusted than those who were presented with the questionnaire of someone with exactly the opposite attitudes to theirs.

3. The third hypothesis was only partially confirmed. Those who were presented with the questionnaire of someone with similar attitudes on the most important issues and dissimilar attitudes on the less important issues thought they would like this person significantly more and rated them as being significantly more moral and better adjusted than those who were presented with the questionnaire of someone with dissimilar attitudes on the most important issues and similar attitudes on the least important issues. However, this hypothesis was not confirmed in every respect in that there was no statistically significant difference between these two groups in whether they believed they would enjoy working with this other person or rated them as more intelligent or knowledgeable.

The four groups were found to be similar in their attitudes in that they did not differ significantly on any of the 26 topics. This is important in that the results of this study may have been more difficult to interpret if the groups had differed in terms of their initial attitudes. For example, if the opinions of the second group had been found to be more extreme than those of the first group, then the difference between these two groups in positive evaluation of the stranger may have been due to the difference in extremeness rather than the difference in disagreement.

An alternative explanation

Byrne considered an alternative explanation to that of attitude similarity for his two confirmed hypotheses. He thought that as the students generally had similar attitudes to one another, they may have been reacting to others with dissimilar attitudes as being deviant or unusual rather than as dissimilar. To test this idea, he formed two groups which had the most usual and the least usual attitudes. He then seems to have compared these two groups for those with similar and dissimilar attitudes and found that they did not differ. Presumably if the deviancy hypothesis was to be confirmed, then those with more usual attitudes should evaluate those who were dissimilar to them (and more deviant) as more negative than those with less usual attitudes. This was not found to be the case. We have described Byrne's analysis and reasoning cautiously, because it is not absolutely clear from his rather brief description of them exactly what he did. (This lack of clarity is not unusual in research reports, so be careful not to assume without more reason that you are at fault rather than the author.)

Author's suggestions for future research

Byrne briefly suggested that less extreme attitude differences could be investigated as well as other variables that might interact with attitude differences.

1.7   Conclusion

Most psychological ideas develop in relation to empirical data. Propositions are made, tested and emerge through the process of collecting and analysing data. The dissemination of ideas and findings as they emerge out of the research process is a crucial activity of most psychologists. Primarily this is done through papers (articles) in academic and practitioner journals. Another important means by which new ideas and research are disseminated is academic and practitioner conferences at which new and ongoing research is presented. Academic books also have a role but to a lesser extent. These various forms of publication and presentation serve a dual purpose:

- To keep psychologists abreast with the latest thinking and developments in their fields of activity.

- To provide psychologists with detailed accounts of developing research ideas and theory so that they may question and evaluate their value.

Although causality is not quite so central to psychological research currently as it was, it remains a defining concern of psychology unlike in related disciplines. Causality is about the basic question of whether particular variables cause or bring about a particular effect. Many psychologists still argue that 'true' experiments in which participants are assigned to different manipulated conditions are the best way of testing causal propositions. Even then, there is considerable room for doubt as to what variable has been manipulated in a true experiment. It is important to check out the possibility that the experimental manipulation has not created effects quite different from the ones that were intended. Alternative interpretations of the findings should always be a concern of psychologists. The archetypal true experiment is the conventional laboratory experiment. However, there are many variables which simply cannot be manipulated by the researcher: for example, it is not possible to manipulate variables such as schizophrenia, gender, social economic status or intelligence for the convenience of testing ideas.

Many psychologists enjoy the added variety and stimulation of using the more naturalistic or realistic approaches. Often these are the only feasible choice in field settings. Sometimes these are described as non-experimental designs which, from some points of view, might be regarded as a somewhat pejorative term. It is a bit like describing women as non-men. It implies that the randomised experiment is the right and proper way of doing psychology. The truth is that there is no single right and proper way of intellectual progress. The development of psychology is *not* dependent on any single study but on the collective activity of a great many researchers and practitioners. Until there is widespread acceptance and adoption of an idea, it is not possible to judge its value.

Key points

- As a research-based discipline, psychology requires a high degree of sophistication regarding research and research methods, even as part of the training of psychologists. Crucially, this includes reading research articles or papers published in academic journals. All psychologists should be able to critically, but constructively, evaluate and benefit from reading such publications.

- Research articles take some time to read as they will refer to other research as well as principles of research methodology with which one at first may not be familiar. As one becomes more familiar with the research in an area and with the principles of doing research, the importance of the contents of research papers becomes much quicker and easier to appreciate.

- One major feature of a research study is the design that it uses. There are various designs. A very basic distinction is between what has been called a true or randomised experiment and everything else which can be referred to as non-experimental.

- True experiments involve the deliberate manipulation of what is presumed to be the causal variable, the random assignment of participants to the conditions reflecting that manipulation and the attempt to hold all other factors constant. Whether or not true experiments should hold a hallowed place in psychology is a

→

matter of controversy. Many researchers and practitioners never have recourse to their use or even to the use of their findings.

- Even if their value is accepted, the use of true experiments is not straightforward. The manipulation of the presumed causal variable and holding all other factors constant are often very difficult. Consequently, a study is never definitive in itself, since it requires further research to rule out alternative interpretations of the manipulation by allowing for particular factors which were not held constant in the original study.

- Psychologists generally favour the true experiment because it appears to be the most appropriate way for determining causal effects. If you have manipulated only one variable, held all else constant and found an effect, then that effect is likely to be due to the manipulation. At the same time, however, this is also a potential fatal flaw of true experiments. In real life, variables do not operate independently and one at a time, so why should research assume that they do?

- Furthermore, it is not always possible to manipulate the variable presumed to be a cause or to manipulate it in a way which is not contrived. Anyway, not all psychologists are interested in testing causal propositions. Hence there is a trend for psychologists to increasingly use a wide variety of non-experimental research designs.

- Because of the centrality of research to all aspects of psychology, psychology students are generally required and taught to carry out and write up research. This experience should help them understand what research involves. It also gives them an opportunity to make a contribution to a topic that interests them.

ACTIVITIES

1. Choose a recent study that has been referred to either in a textbook you are reading or in a lecture that you have attended. Obtain the original publication. Were the study and its findings correctly reported in the textbook? Do you think that there were important aspects of the study that were not mentioned in the text or the lecture that should have been? If you do think there were important omissions, what are they? Why do you think they were not cited? Did the study test a causal proposition? If so, what was this proposition? If not, what was the main aim of this study? In terms of the designs outlined in this chapter, what kind of design did the study use?

2. Either choose a chapter from a textbook or obtain a copy of a single issue of a journal. Work through the material and for every study you find, classify it as one of the following:

   - Correlational or cross-sectional study

   - Longitudinal study

   - Experiment – or study with randomised assignment.

   What percentage of each did you find?

CHAPTER 2

Aims and hypotheses in research

Overview

- Different research methods are effective at doing different things. There are methods which are particularly good at describing a phenomenon in some detail, estimating how common a particular behaviour is, evaluating the effects of some intervention, testing a causal proposition or statistically summarising the results of a number of similar studies. No method is satisfactory for all research.

- The aims and justification of the study are invariably presented in the first section or introduction to a report or paper. All research should have clear objectives and needs careful justification given the expenditure of time and effort involved. Procedures for carrying out the research also need a rationale.

- In their simplest form, hypotheses propose that a relationship exists between a minimum of two variables.

- Hypotheses are a key component of mainstream psychological research. Hypotheses are usually formally, clearly and precisely stated. Your hypotheses should also be justified and a case made for putting them forward.

- Alternatively, the general aims and objectives of the research can be summarised if your research is not particularly conducive to presentation using hypotheses.

- Hypotheses are the basic building blocks of much of psychology. Some research attempts to test hypotheses, other research attempts to explore hypotheses, and yet other research seeks to generate hypotheses. There is an important distinction between research hypotheses (which guide research) and statistical hypotheses (which guide statistical analyses). Research hypotheses are evaluated in a range of different ways, including statistics. Statistical hypothesis testing employs a very restricted concept of hypothesis.

→

- Frequently a researcher has an idea of what the relationship is likely to be between two variables. That is, the variables are expected or predicted to be related in a particular way or direction. So wherever possible, state clearly the nature (or direction) of the relationship together with the reasons for this expectation.

- The variable that is manipulated or thought to be the cause of an effect on another variable is the independent variable. The variable that is measured or thought to be the effect of the influence of another variable is the dependent variable.

- The terms 'independent' and 'dependent' are sometimes restricted to true experiments where the direction of the causal effect being investigated is clearer. Their use with other types of research can cause confusion, since a variable may be independent or dependent according to circumstances.

- The hypothetico-deductive method describes a dominant view of how scientists go about their work. From what has been observed, generalisations are proposed (i.e. hypotheses), which are then tested, ideally by using methods which potentially could refute the hypothesis. The scientist then would either reformulate their hypothesis or test the hypothesis further, depending on the outcome.

2.1   Introduction

By now, it should be clear that research is an immensely diverse activity with many different objectives and purposes as well as topics for investigation. In psychology, these are very varied. This chapter looks in some detail at the keystones of most research in psychology: the aims and hypotheses underlying a study.

Research is a thoughtful, rational process. It does not proceed simply by measuring variables and finding out what the relationship is between them. Instead, research is built on a sense of purpose on the part of the researcher who sees their work as fitting in with, and building on, established psychological knowledge in their chosen field. This sense of direction does not simply happen; it has to be worked at and worked towards. The idea of research is not simply to create new information or facts but to build on, expand, clarify and illuminate what is already known. Collecting data with no sense of direction or purpose might be referred to, cruelly, as mindless or rampant empiricism. Merely collecting data does not constitute research in any meaningful sense.

The sense of purpose in research has to be learnt. Most of us develop it slowly as part of learning to appreciate the nature of psychology itself. Until we have understood that psychology is more than just a few facts to learn, good research ideas are unlikely. There are a number of aspects to this, especially:

- It is vital to understand how real psychologists (not just textbook authors) go about psychology. The only way to achieve this is to read and study in depth the writings of psychologists – especially those who are interested in the sorts of things that you are interested in.

- The way in which real psychologists think about their discipline, their work and the work of their intellectual colleagues has to be studied. Throughout the writings of psychologists, one will find a positive but sceptical attitude to theory and research. In a sense, good psychologists regard all knowledge as tentative and even temporary – the feeling that, collectively, psychologists could always do better.

2.2 Types of study

One useful way of beginning to understand the possible aims of psychological research is to examine some broad research objectives in psychology and decide what each of them contributes. We will look at the following in turn:

● Descriptive or exploratory studies

● Evaluation or outcome studies

● Meta-analytic studies.

◼ Descriptive or exploratory studies

An obvious first approach to research in any field is simply to describe in detail the characteristics and features of the thing in question. Without such descriptive material, it is difficult for research to progress effectively. For example, it is hard to imagine research into, say, the causes of schizophrenia without a substantial body of knowledge which describes the major features and types of schizophrenia. Descriptions require that we categorise in some way the observations we make. Curiously, perhaps perversely, psychology is not replete with famous examples of purely descriptive studies. Later in this book (Part 4), we discuss in detail qualitative research methods. That type of research typically uses textual material which is rich in detail and may include descriptive analyses as well as analytic interpretations. But significant interest in qualitative work of this sort only emerged in psychology the last 30 years.

Case studies are reports that describe a particular case in detail. They are common in psychiatry though, once again, relatively uncommon in modern psychology. An early and often cited instance of a case study is that of 'Albert' in which an attempt was made to demonstrate that an 11-month-old boy could be taught or conditioned to become frightened of a rat when he previously was not afraid (Watson & Rayner, 1920). Whether or not this is a purely descriptive study could probably be argued either way. Certainly the study goes beyond a mere description of the situation; for example, it could also be conceived as investigating the factors that can create fear.

In some disciplines (such as sociology and media studies), one sort of descriptive study, known as *content analysis,* is common. The main objective of this is to describe the contents of the media in a systematic way. So, content analyses describing features of television's output are plentiful. For example, the types of violence contained in television programmes could be recorded, classified and counted in order to establish how much of each there is. Actually, we have already seen a good example of content analysis. One aim of the study by Bodner (2006a) mentioned in Chapter 1 was to find out the characteristics of studies published in 1999 in PsycINFO (an electronic bibliographic database described in Chapter 7). It assessed the different types of methods employed in the research reported in a sample of articles.

◼ Evaluation or outcome studies

Other research aims to test the effectiveness of a particular feature or intervention. Not every such study seeks to test theoretical propositions or develop theory. Many simply have purely empirical objectives. Good examples of an intervention into a situation are studies of the effectiveness of psychotherapeutic treatments. Ideally in such studies participants are randomly assigned to the different treatments or conditions and, usually, one or more non-treated or control conditions. These studies are sometimes referred to as evaluation or outcome studies. Especially when used to assess the effectiveness of a clinical treatment like psychotherapy, evaluation studies are known as randomised controlled trials. Usually evaluation studies assess whether the intervention overall is effective. Rarely is it possible to assess which aspects of the intervention are producing the observed changes. Since interventions usually take place over an extended period of time, holding other factors constant is more difficult than in laboratory studies lasting just a few minutes.

So evaluation studies often seek to examine whether an intervention has had its intended effect of causing the expected change. However, explanations about why the intervention was successful are secondary or disregarded, as the primary objective is not theory development.

Meta-analytic studies

A meta-analysis aims to statistically summarise and analyse the results of all available studies investigating a particular topic meeting particular criteria. Of course, any review of studies tries to integrate their findings. Meta-analysis does this but in a systematic and structured way quantitatively. Using statistical techniques, it combines and differentiates between the findings of a number of data analyses. This makes it a powerful integrative tool. For example, is cognitive behaviour therapy more effective in treating phobias or intense fears than no treatment. By collecting reports of studies investigating this question, we can gather together information about the statistical trends found in each study. These trends are usually expressed statistically as *effect sizes*. This is merely a measure of the size of the trend in the data; depending on the measure used, this may then be adjusted for the variability in the data.

There are several different measures of effect size. For example, in Chapter 35 of the companion volume *Understanding statistics in psychology with SPSS* (Howitt & Cramer, 2020), we describe the procedures using the correlation coefficient as a measure of effect size. As the correlation coefficient is a common statistical measure, it is familiar to most researchers. There are other measures of effect size. For example, we can calculate the difference between the two conditions of the study and then standardise this by dividing by a measure of the variability in the individual scores. Variability can either be the standard deviation of one of the conditions (as in Glass's Δ) or the combined standard deviation of both conditions of the study (as in Cohen's d) (see Rosenthal, 1991). We can calculate the average effect size from any of these measures. Because this difference or effect size is based on a number of studies, it provides a clearer assessment of the typical effects found in a particular area of research.

We can also see whether the effect size differs between studies with different characteristics. For example, some of the studies may have been carried out on student volunteers for a study of the treatment of phobias. Because these participants have not sought professional treatment for their phobias, these studies are sometimes referred to as analogue studies. Other studies may have been conducted on patients who sought professional help for their phobias. These studies are sometimes referred to as clinical studies. It may be easier to treat phobias in students because they may be less severe. That is, the effect size may be greater for studies using students. If there are differences in the effect size for the two kinds of study, we should be more cautious in generalising from analogue studies to clinical ones. Actually, any feature of studies reviewed in the meta-analysis may be considered in relation to effect size, even, for example, such things as the year of publication. The results of earlier research may be compared with later research.

When reading the results of a meta-analysis, check the reports of at least a few of the studies involved. This will help you familiarise yourself with specifics of their designs. Some social scientists have argued against the use of meta-analyses because they combine the results of well-designed studies with poorly designed ones. Furthermore, the results of different types of studies might also be combined. For example, they may use studies in which participants were randomly assigned to conditions together with ones in which this has not been done (Shadish & Ragsdale, 1996). Differences in the quality of design are more likely to occur in evaluation studies which are more difficult to conduct without adequate resources. However, one can compare the effect size of these two kinds of studies to see whether the effect size differs. If the effect size does not differ (as has been found in some studies), then the effect size is unlikely to be biased by the more poorly designed studies. Sometimes, meta-analytic studies use ratings by researchers of the overall quality of each of the studies involved. In this way, it is possible to investigate the relationship between the quality of the study and the size of the effects found. None of this amounts to a justification for researchers conducting poorly designed studies.

While few students contemplate carrying out a meta-analysis (though it is difficult to understand this reluctance), meta-analytic studies are increasingly carried out in psychology. One big problem is the need to obtain copies of the original studies from which to extract aspects of the original analysis. An example of a meta-analytic study is given later in this book (Chapter 7).

2.3   Aims of research

Already it should be abundantly clear that psychological research is an intellectually highly organised and coherent activity. Research, as a whole, does not proceed willy-nilly at the whim of a privileged group of dilettante researchers. The research activities of psychologists are primarily directed at other psychologists. In this way, individual researchers and groups of researchers are contributing to a wider, collective activity. Research which fails to meet certain basic requirements is effectively excluded. Research which has no point, has a bad design, or is faulty in some other way has little chance of being published, heard about and read. The dissemination of research in psychology is subject to certain quality controls which are largely carried out by a peer review process in which experts in the field recommend whether or not a research report should be published and what improvements need to be made to it before doing so.

Researchers have to account for the research they do by justifying key aspects of their work. Central to this is the requirement that researchers have a good, sound purpose for doing the research that they do. In other words, researchers have to specify the *aims* of their research. This is twofold:

● Researchers need a coherent understanding of the purposes their research will serve and the likelihood of achieving these. Anyone unable to see the point of their research is likely to be a dispirited, bad researcher. Student researchers doing research under time pressure to meet course requirements are at risk of this. So clarity about their research aims is, primarily, an obligation of researchers to themselves.

● Researchers need to be able to present their study's aims clearly enough to justify the research to interested, but critical, others. Research reports always include justifications of this sort, but it is imperative, for example, in applications for research funds to outside bodies.

Clearly stated aims are essential means of indicating what a study can contribute. They also help clarify just why the research was done in a particular way. By clarity, we mean a number of things. Of course it means that the aims are presented as well-written, grammatical sentences. More importantly, research aims must be clearly justified by their rationale. The case for the stated research aims are to be found in the report's introduction. Justifications can involve the following:

- Explaining how the research is relevant to what is already known about the topic including previous theoretical and empirical advancements in the field. For many psychological topics, the previous research literature may be copious. This can be daunting to newcomers. A later chapter on searching the literature (Chapter 7) describes how to become efficient and effective at becoming familiar with the relevant research literature. Examples of the sorts of reasons that can justify doing research on a particular topic are discussed in Chapter 28.

- Reference to the wider social context for research. Psychological research often responds to society's broader concerns exemplified by government, social institutions such as the legal and educational systems, business, and so forth. Substantial quantities of publications emanate from government sources including statistical information, discussion documents and the like. Generally these are not the work of psychologists but are relevant to their activities.

2.4   Research hypotheses

The use of hypotheses is far more common in psychological research than in disciplines such as sociology, economics and other related disciplines. The concept of hypotheses derives from natural sciences such as physics, chemistry and biology which influenced mainstream psychology especially strongly. The aims of a great deal of psychological research (but by no means all) may be formulated in terms of one or more working suppositions about the possible research findings. These are known as hypotheses. So hypotheses are working assumptions or propositions expressing expectations linked to the aims of the study. Hypotheses do not have to be true, since the point of research is to examine the empirical support or otherwise for them.

In practice, it is fairly easy to write hypotheses once we have clarified our expectations. Since a hypothesis is merely a statement which describes the relationship expected between two (or more) variables, at a minimum we need to identify which two variables we are interested in and propose that there is a relationship between the two. We could go one step further and specify the direction of that relationship. Taking the idea, introduced in Chapter 1, that people with similar attitudes tend to be attracted to each other, what would the hypothesis be? The two variables derived from this might be 'attitude similarity' and 'attraction'. The hypothesised relationship between the two is that the greater the attitude similarity, then the greater the attraction. Expressed as a hypothesis, this might read something like: 'Higher levels of attitude similarity lead to higher levels of attraction'. However, there are many ways of writing the same thing, as the following short list of alternatives demonstrates:

- People with more similar attitudes will be more attracted to each other than people with less similar attitudes.

- Greater attitude similarity will be associated with greater interpersonal attraction.

- Attitude similarity is *positively* linked with interpersonal attraction.

The terms 'positive' and 'negative' relationship or association are fundamental concepts in research. It is important to understand their meaning, as they are very commonly used phrases:

- A positive or direct association is one in which *more* of one quality (attitude similarity) goes together with *more* of another quality (interpersonal attraction).

- A negative or inverse association is one in which *more* of one quality (attitude similarity) goes together with *less* of another quality (interpersonal attraction).

So an example of a negative or inverse association is that greater attitude similarity is associated with *less* attraction. This is *not* the hypothesis we are testing, though some might consider it a reasonable hypothesis – after all, there is an old saying which suggests that opposites attract. Both past research and theory have led us to the expectation that similarity leads to attraction. If that did not exist, then we would have little justification for our choice of hypothesis. In the absence of justification for the direction of the relationship, we can only hypothesise that there will be a relationship of some sort, positive or negative.

The precise phrasing of a hypothesis is guided by considerations of clarity and precision. Inevitably, different researchers will use different ways of saying more-or less-the same thing.

Hypotheses can be somewhat more complex than the above example. For instance, a third variable could be incorporated into our hypothesis. This third variable might be the importance of the attitudes to the individual. So it might be suggested that the more important the attitude is to the person, the more they will be attracted to someone with a similar attitude. So this hypothesis actually contains three variables:

- 'Attitude importance'

- 'Attitude similarity'

- 'Interpersonal attraction'.

In this case, the hypothesis might be expressed along the lines of the following: 'The relationship between attitude similarity and attraction will be greater when the attitudes are important'. This is quite a technically complex hypothesis to test. It requires a degree of sophistication about aspects of research design and statistical analysis. This type of hypothesis was the third hypothesis tested in the study of Byrne (1961), described in Chapter 1. So, at this stage, we will confine ourselves to simpler hypotheses involving just two variables.

Few researchers do research which has a single aim. Usually studies involve several interrelated aims. This helps the researcher to take advantage of economies of time and other resources. A study which tests several hypotheses at the same time also potentially has more information on which to base conclusions. Another advantage is that there is a better chance that the researcher has something more interesting and more publishable (but see Chapter 14). Of course, studies carried out as part of training in psychological research methods may be equally or more effective for teaching purposes if a single hypothesis is addressed.

2.5 Four types of hypothesis

The distinction between relationships and causal relationships is important. Hypotheses should be carefully phrased in order to indicate the causal nature or otherwise of the relationships being investigated.

The statement that attitude similarity is associated with attraction is an example of a non-causal hypothesis. It indicates that we believe that the two variables are interrelated but does *not* imply that one variable has a causal effect on the other. An association between two variables is all that we can infer with confidence when we measure two variables at the same time. Some psychologists would argue that, strictly speaking, hypotheses should be presented in a non-causal form when a non-experimental design is used. When a true experimental design is used, the use of terms which refer directly or indirectly to a causal relationship is appropriate. True experimental designs involve the manipulation of the causal variable, participants are randomly assigned to conditions and all else is held constant. Expressing the hypothesis of a true experiment in a non-causal form fails to give credit to the main virtue of this design.

A range of terms is used which indicate that a causal relationship is being described or assumed. Some of these are illustrated in Figure 2.1. These phrases are so associated with questions of causality that they are best reserved for when causality is assumed, to avoid confusion.

The direction of the expected relationship should be incorporated into the wording of the hypothesis if at all possible. But this is not a matter of whim and there should be good reasons for your choice. Hypotheses which indicate direction could be:

- Greater attitude similarity will lead to greater attraction.

- Greater attitude similarity will be associated with greater interpersonal attraction.

Since such hypotheses indicate the direction of the relationship expected, they are referred to as *directional hypotheses*. There are circumstances in which we may not be able to make predictions as to the direction of the relationship with any confidence. For example, there may be two different, but equally pertinent, theories which lead us to expect contradictory results from our study. For example, social learning theory predicts that watching aggression should lead to greater aggression, whereas the idea of catharsis predicts that it should lead to less aggression. Of course, it is not always possible to pin a direction to a relationship. Sometimes hypotheses have to be stated without specifying

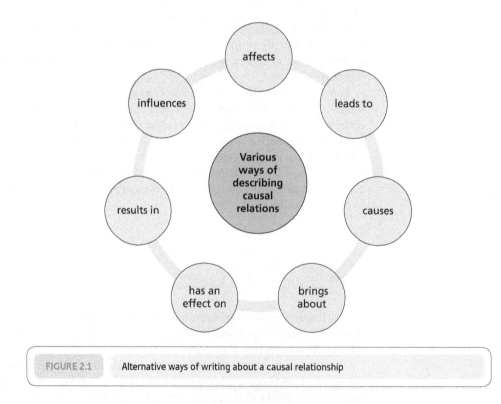

FIGURE 2.1   Alternative ways of writing about a causal relationship

a direction, simply because there are reasonable arguments to expect either outcome and there is no strong reason to predict a particular direction of outcome. There are important issues connected with the statistical analyses of such hypotheses. These are discussed in Box 2.1.

Box 2.1 Key Ideas

Direction, hypotheses and statistical analysis

It is important to differentiate between:

- assessing the adequacy of what has been called the research hypothesis (e.g. Cohen & Hyman, 1979) or scientific hypothesis (e.g. Bolles, 1962; Edwards, 1965) which underlies the research study in question; and

- testing the null hypothesis and alternate hypothesis in significance testing (or statistical inference) as part of the statistical analysis.

These are frequently confused. The hypothesis testing model in statistical analysis deals with a very simple question: are the trends found in the data simply the consequence of chance fluctuations due to sampling? Statistical analysis in psychology is guided by the Neyman–Pearson hypothesis testing model, although it is rarely referred to as such and seems to be frequently just taken for granted. This approach had its origins in the 1930s (e.g. Neyman & Pearson, 1933a). In the Neyman–Pearson hypothesis testing model, two statistical hypotheses are offered:

- That there is no relationship between the two variables that we are investigating – this is known as the null hypothesis.

- That there is a relationship between the two variables – this is known as the alternate hypothesis.

The researcher is required to choose between the null hypothesis and the alternate hypothesis. They must accept one of them and reject the other. Since we are dealing with probabilities, we do not say that we have proven the hypothesis or null hypothesis. In effect, hypothesis testing assesses the hypothesis that any trends in the data may be reasonably explained by chance due to using samples of cases rather than all of the cases. The alternative is that the relationship found in the data represents a substantial trend which is not reasonably accountable for on the basis of chance.

To put it directly, statistical testing is only one aspect of hypothesis testing. We test research hypotheses in other ways in addition to statistically. There may be alternative explanations of our findings which perhaps fit the data even better, there may be methodological flaws in the research that statistical analysis is not intended to, and cannot, identify, or there may be evidence that the hypotheses work only with certain groups of participants, for example. So significance testing is only a minimal test of a hypothesis – there are many more considerations when properly assessing the adequacy of our research hypothesis.

Similarly, the question of direction of a hypothesis comes up in a very different way in statistical analysis. Once again, one should not confuse direction when applied to a research hypothesis with direction when applied to statistical significance testing. One-tailed testing and two-tailed testing are discussed in virtually any statistics textbook; for example, Chapter 17 of our companion statistics text *Understanding statistics in psychology with SPSS* (Howitt & Cramer, 2020) is devoted to this topic. Quite simply, one-tailed testing is testing a directional hypothesis, whereas two-tailed testing is for testing non-directional hypotheses. However, there are exacting requirements which need to be met before applying one-tailed testing to a statistical analysis:

- There should be very strong theoretical or empirical reasons for expecting a particular relationship between two variables.

- The decision about the nature of the relationship between the two variables should be made in ignorance of the data. That is, you do not check the data first to see which direction the data are going in – that would be tantamount to cheating.

- Neither should you try a one-tailed test of significance first and then try the two-tailed test of significance in its place if the trend is in the incorrect direction.

→

These requirements are so demanding that very little research can justify the use of one-tailed testing. Psychological theory is seldom so well developed that it can make precise enough predictions about outcomes of new research, for example. Previous research in psychology has a tendency to manifest very varied outcomes. It is notorious that there is often inconsistency between the outcomes of ostensibly similar studies in psychology. Hence, the difficulty of making precise enough predictions to warrant the use of one-tailed tests.

One-tailed (directional) significance testing will produce statistically significant findings more readily than two-tailed testing – so long as the outcome is in the predicted direction. As a consequence, there is a need for caution about the incorrect use of one-tailed significance testing, since we are applying a less stringent test if these requirements are violated. Two-tailed testing should be the preferred method in all but the most exceptional circumstances as described above. The criteria for one- and two-tailed types of significance are presented in Figure 2.2.

The distinction between a research or scientific hypothesis (which is evaluated in a multitude of ways) and a statistical hypothesis (which can be evaluated statistically only through significance testing) needs to be remembered. Any researcher who evaluates the worth of a research hypothesis merely on the basis of statistical hypothesis testing has only partially completed the task.

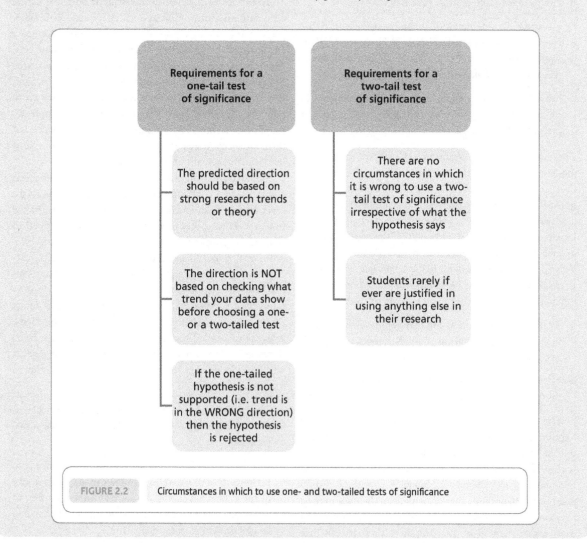

FIGURE 2.2   Circumstances in which to use one- and two-tailed tests of significance

Figure 2.3 summarises the four possible types of hypothesis which can be generated by considering the causal versus non-causal and directional versus non-directional distinctions. The letters A and B refer to the two variables. So A could be attitude similarity and B interpersonal attraction or any other variables, for that matter.

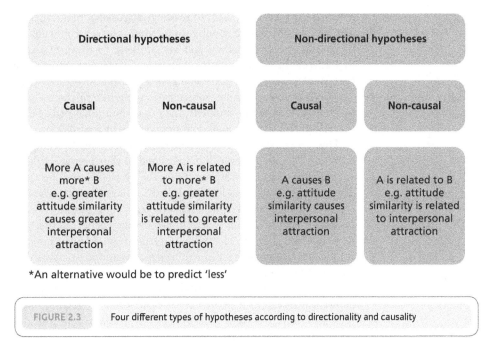

*An alternative would be to predict 'less'

FIGURE 2.3   Four different types of hypotheses according to directionality and causality

Without a rationale for a hypothesis based on theory or previous research, the case for examining the relationship between two variables is weakened. This means that identifying the reasons which justify researching the relationship between two variables must be a priority. Given the billions of potential variables that could be available to psychologists, why choose variable 2 743 322 and variable 99 634 187 for study? Research is *not* about data collection and analysis for its own sake. Research is part of a systematic and coordinated attempt to understand its subject matter. Until one understands the relationship between research and advancement of understanding, research methods will probably remain a mass of buzzing confusion.

The aims and hypotheses of a study are its driving force. Once the aims and hypotheses are clarified, other aspects of the research fall into place much more easily. They give us a focus when reading the pertinent published literature since aims and hypotheses help indicate what is most relevant. In turn, the salient material in what we read can be used to strengthen and make more convincing the aims and hypotheses. The aims and hypotheses clarify what variables need to be measured. Similarly, the aims and hypotheses help guide the researcher towards an appropriate research design. The data will support or not support the hypotheses, either wholly or partially. Finally, the discussion of the results will primarily refer back to the aims and hypotheses. It is hardly surprising, then, to find that a study's aims and hypotheses are the lynchpin that holds a report together. If they are incoherent and confused, little hope can be offered about the value of the study.

2.6   Difficulties in formulating aims and hypotheses

The aims or objectives of published studies are usually well defined and clear. They are, after all, the final stage of the research process – publication. It is far more difficult to be confident about the aims and hypotheses of a study that you are planning for yourself as someone new to research. Refining one's tentative research ideas into aims and hypotheses is demanding – there is a lot of reading, discussing, planning and other work to be done. You will usually have a rough idea of what research you want to do, but initially because of your limited experience you are unlikely to think explicitly in terms of aims and hypotheses. Take some comfort in personal construct theory (Kelly, 1955) which suggests that humans act like scientists and construct theories about people and the nature of the world. You may recognise yourself behaving like this when you catch yourself thinking in ways such as 'if this happens, then that should happen'. For example, 'If I send a text message then he might invite me to his party in return'.

This kind of statement is not different from saying 'if someone has the same attitude as someone else, then they will be attracted to that person' or 'the more similar someone's attitude is to that of another person, the more they will be attracted to that individual'. These are known as conditional propositions and are clearly not dissimilar from hypotheses. This kind of thinking is not always easy to recognise. Take, for example, the belief or statement that behaviour is determined by one's genes. At first sight this may not appear to be a conditional or 'if . . . , then . . . ' proposition. However, it can be turned into one if we restate it as 'if someone has the same genes as another person, they will behave in the same way' or 'the more similar the genes of people are, the more similarly they will behave'.

There is another fundamental thing about developing aims and hypotheses for psychological research. If people are natural scientists testing out theories and hypotheses, they also need to have a natural curiosity about people and the world. In other words, good research ideas in psychology will only come to those interested in other people and society. Research can effectively be built on your interests and ideas just so long as you remember that these must be integrated with what others have achieved, starting with similar interests. In psychology the hypothetico-deductive method was once dominant and is discussed in Box 2.2.

| Box 2.2 | Key Ideas |

Hypothetico-deductive method

The notion of the hypothesis is deeply embedded in psychological thinking and it is also one of the first ideas that psychology students learn about. However, it is a mistake to think that the testing of hypotheses is the way in which psychological research must invariably proceed. The process of hypothesis testing, however, particularly exemplifies the approach of so-called scientific psychology. Karl Popper (1902–1994), a philosopher, is generally regarded as the principal advocate and populariser of the hypothetico-deductive method, although some have suggested that it has its origins in the work of the nineteenth-century academic William Whewell and others that this is a misleading claim (e.g. Snyder, 1999). One of the earliest uses of the term in psychology was in the mid-1930s (Brown, 1935, 1936, 1937). Crucial to Popper's contribution is the stress on the importance of falsification – a hypothesis

which cannot be shown to be incorrect is not worthwhile (e.g. Popper, 1935/1959). The foundation of the method, which is really a description of how scientists do their work, is that scientists build from the observations they make through the process of inductive reasoning. Induction refers to making generalisations from particular instances. These inductions in the scientific method are referred to as hypotheses, which comes from a Greek word meaning 'suggestion'.

Thus when scientists develop hypotheses they are merely making a suggestion about what is happening in general based on their observations. Notice that induction is a creative process and that it is characteristic of much human thinking, not just that of scientists.

In the scientific method, hypotheses are tested to assess their adequacy. There are two main ways of doing this: (1)

by seeking evidence which confirms the hypothesis; and (2) by seeking evidence which refutes the hypothesis. There are problems in using confirmatory evidence, since this is a very weak test of a hypothesis. For example, take Sigmund Freud's idea that hysteria is a 'disease' of women. We could seek confirmatory evidence of this by studying women and assessing them for hysteria. Each woman who has hysteria does, indeed, confirm the hypothesis. The women who do not have hysteria do not refute the hypothesis, since there was no claim that all women suffer hysteria. However, by seeking confirmatory evidence, we do not put the hypothesis to its most stringent test. What evidence would refute the hypothesis that hysteria is a disease of women? Well, evidence of the existence of hysteria in men would undermine the hypothesis, for example. So a scientist seeking to evaluate a hypothesis by looking for disconfirming evidence might study the incidence of hysteria in men. Any man found to have hysteria undermines the stated hypothesis. In other words, a negative instance logically should have much greater impact than any number of confirmatory instances. So, the word 'deductive' in 'hypothetico-deductive' method refers to the process of deducing logically a test of a hypothesis (which, in contrast, is based on inductive reasoning).

In this context, one of Karl Popper's most important contributions was his major proposal about what it is that differentiates scientific thinking from other forms of thinking. This is known as demarcation, since it concerns what demarcates the scientific approach from non-scientific approaches. For Popper, an idea is scientific only if it is falsifiable and, by implication, a theory is scientific only if it is falsifiable. So some ideas are intrinsically non-scientific, such as the view that there is a god. It is not possible to imagine the evidence which disconfirms this, so the idea is not falsifiable. Popper criticised the scientific status of the work of Sigmund Freud because Freud's theories, he argued, were often impossible to falsify.

The hypothetico-deductive method can be seen as a process, as illustrated in Figure 2.4. Disconfirmation of a hypothesis should lead to an upsurge in the creative process as new hypotheses need to be developed which take account of the disconfirmation. On the other hand, finding support for the hypothesis does not imply an end to the researcher's attempts to test the hypothesis, since there are many other possible ways of disconfirming the hypothesis. This is part of the reason why psychologists do not speak or write of a hypothesis as being proven but say that it has been supported or confirmed.

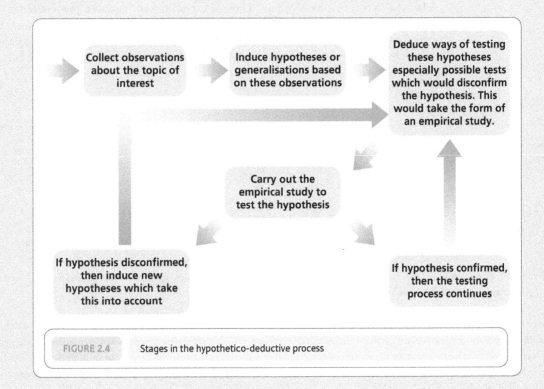

FIGURE 2.4   Stages in the hypothetico-deductive process

■ Comparative method

Characteristically, hypotheses in psychology imply a comparison between two or more groups. Sometimes this comparison is taken for granted in the expression of hypotheses, so is not overtly stated. Unless one recognises such implicit comparisons in hypotheses, it may prove difficult to formulate satisfactory ones and, furthermore, it may not be obvious that the appropriate research design should involve a comparison of two or more groups. Suppose we are interested in physical abuse in romantic relationships. One possible reason for such abuse is that one or both of the partners in the relationship is very possessive of the other person. So the violence may occur whenever a partner feels threatened by what the other person does or does not do. The research we carry out examines whether or not abusive partners are possessive. So the hypothesis is that abusive partners are possessive. We give out questionnaires measuring possessiveness to 50 people known to have physically abused their partner. Suppose we find that 70 per cent of people in abusive relationships are possessive. What can we conclude on the basis of this? Well, it is certainly true that most abusive people are possessive. However, we do not know how many people not in abusive relationships are also possessive. That is, when it is suggested that abusive people are possessive, there is an implication that non-abusive people are *not* possessive.

The problem does not stem from how we have tested our hypothesis but from our understanding of the hypothesis itself. What the hypothesis implies is that abusive partners are *more* possessive than non-abusive partners. Just by looking at abusive partners we cannot tell whether they are more possessive than non-abusive partners. It could be that 70 per cent or even 90 per cent of non-abusive partners were possessive. If this were the case, abusive partners are not more possessive than non-abusive partners. They may even be less possessive than non-abusive partners.

Had the hypothesis been put as 'There is a relationship between possessiveness and abuse', then the comparison is built in but may still not be entirely obvious to those starting research for the first time. Probably, the best rule-of-thumb is the assumption that psychological hypotheses almost invariably include or imply comparisons between groups of people.

Box 2.3	Research Example

Non-experimental cross-sectional study of attitude similarity and liking

Byrne, D., & Blaylock, B. (1963). Similarity and assumed similarity of attitudes between husbands and wives. *Journal of Abnormal and Social Psychology, 67*, 636–640.

One of the things which you will learn is that there is no single perfect way of doing research. Furthermore, psychologists have different preferences in terms of the research methods which they will employ. Most psychologists engage in a variety of styles of research in their careers and very few adhere to just one. Each way of doing research has its own advantages and disadvantages and it is an important part of the researcher's task to make choices between the feasible alternatives.

When reviewing past research, the researcher is extremely conscious of the fact that interpretation of research findings can be significantly affected by the choice of methods used in that research. Hence, you will find psychologists contesting the meaning of the findings of important research studies. We have seen (Chapter 1, Box 1.3) how Byrne (1961) studied attitude similarity and liking using experimental methods. In this box, we will see how Byrne tackled his research question using non-experimental methods.

Background

Donn Byrne and Barbara Blaylock (1963) thought that people who liked each other were more likely to have similar attitudes about issues because having such attitudes would be mutually rewarding in that they would help confirm their view of the world. Although they reported there had been a few studies at the time which had found that wives and husbands had similar attitudes towards communism, they wanted to see whether this held for more general political attitudes. In addition, they wanted to see whether spouses would assume that their attitudes were more similar than they actually were, as suggested by various consistency theories. Consistency theories argue that the elements of our thinking and behaviour will tend to be consistent (i.e. congruent) with each other. According to these theories, people who are attracted towards others are more likely to see their attitudes as being similar or to change them to be more similar, so that there is greater consistency between their attitudes and relationships. Consistency theories suggest that attraction can lead to actual or perceived attitude similarity, as well as attitude similarity leading to attraction. Byrne and Blaylock reported that there was considerable experimental evidence to suggest that such changes in attitudes took place.

Hypotheses

There were two hypotheses:

- Hypothesis 1 was 'married individuals are similar in their general political attitudes' (Byrne & Blaylock, p. 637).

- Hypothesis 2 was 'assumed similarity of political attitudes is greater than actual similarity of political attitudes for married couples' (p. 637).

Both these hypotheses are directional in that they state what the direction of the results is expected to be. Rather than simply proposing that there is a relationship between being married and attitude similarity, a directional hypothesis rejects the possibility, in this case that married couples have less similar attitudes, and instead makes the prediction that the relationship will be in terms of greater similarity. The hypotheses are also non-causal in that they do not specify what variables are thought to be causal ones. The two variables are described as being related to one another rather than as one variable causing the other one.

Method

Participants

The participants consisted of 36 married couples who had been married for a period of 4 months to 37 years with a median of 2.5 years. Twenty-four of the husbands were students.

Procedure

The design of the research is summarised in Figure 2.5. Husbands and wives completed the questionnaires separately, first, in terms of what their own opinions were and second, in terms of what they assumed their spouse's opinions were.

Political attitudes were measured by three scales developed by Milton Rokeach (1960). These were Left Opinionation, Right Opinionation and a slightly revised Dogmatism Scale. Byrne and Blaylock did not describe in more detail what these scales measured. In order to find this out, one needs to check other references such as the one they give to Rokeach (1960). Briefly, Left Opinionation and Right Opinionation refer to left- and right-wing beliefs, respectively. Dogmatism refers to having closed beliefs which are proclaimed by authority figures and which are intolerant of others.

→

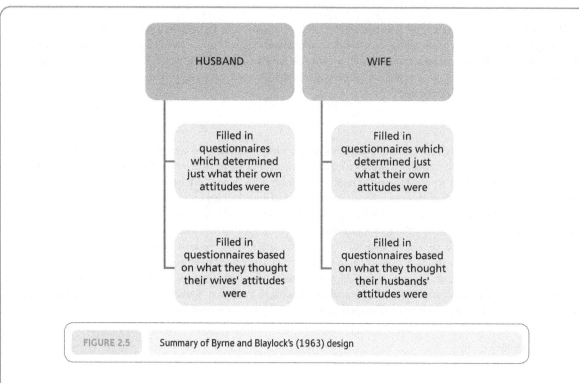

FIGURE 2.5   Summary of Byrne and Blaylock's (1963) design

Results

Pearson (product-moment) correlations were used to determine the actual similarity between the attitudes of husbands and wives and the similarity between the spouse's own attitude and what they thought their spouse believed. The latter analysis was done for husbands and wives separately.

Discussion

The first hypothesis that husbands and wives had similar political attitudes was confirmed in that there was a small but significant positive correlation between their actual attitudes. The correlations ranged from .30 for Left Opinionation to .44 for Right Opinionation. In other words, higher scores on political attitudes in one spouse went with higher scores on the same political attitudes in the other spouse. (Correlation coefficients range from 0, which means no or no linear relationship, to 1, which means a perfect relationship. The coefficient can take a positive or a negative value to indicate the direction of the relationship. Correlations of .30 and .44 are modest ones, implying a relationship but one which is far from perfect.)

The second hypothesis, that the similarity between the spouse's own attitude and what they assumed their spouse's attitude to be would be greater than the similarity between the spouses' own attitudes, was also confirmed. This hypothesis was tested in two steps. First, correlations were calculated between the spouse's own attitudes and what they assumed their spouse's attitude to be. All these correlations were high and significantly positive. They varied from .69 (for Right Opinionation between the husband's own views and what they assumed their wife's views to be) to .89 (for Right Opinionation between the wife's own views and what they thought their husband's views were). Correlations as big as these are very strong relationships and approach the maximum values obtained in psychological research. The second step was to determine whether the correlation between the spouse's own view and what they assumed their spouse thought was significantly higher than the correlation between the husband's and wife's own views. This comparison was made with a modified *t*-test. All six comparisons were statistically significant, so supporting the hypothesis.

Authors' suggestions for future research

Byrne and Blaylock briefly suggested that where dissimilarity in personality may be rewarding such as in terms of dominance, partners may assume dissimilarity to be greater than it actually is.

2.7   Conclusion

It is almost a truism to suggest that the aims and hypotheses of research should be clear. This may seem difficult early on and perseverance is needed. Since research is one way by which psychological knowledge and ideas develop, it is almost inevitable that aims and hypotheses go through a process of refinement. Reformulation of one's aims and objectives commonly occurs in the research planning stage, and sometimes after. All research is guided by aims, but hypotheses are only universal in certain types of research – especially true experiments – where it is possible to specify likely outcomes fairly precisely. Hypotheses are best included wherever possible, since they represent the distillation of the researcher's thoughts about the subject matter. Sometimes, for non-experimental studies, the formulation of hypotheses becomes too cumbersome to be of value. Hence, many excellent studies in psychology will not include hypotheses.

The true experiment (e.g. the laboratory experiment) has many advantages in terms of the testing of hypotheses: (a) its ability to randomise participants to conditions, (b) the requirement of manipulating the independent variable rather than using already existing variables such as gender, and (c) the control over variables. Although we have largely discussed the testing of a single hypothesis at a time, very little research is so restricted. Most research studies have several aims and several hypotheses, because we are usually interested how several different variables may be related to one another. Economies of time and effort result by considering several hypotheses in one study.

The penultimate section of this book on qualitative research methods shows how valuable research can proceed using a quite different approach in which the idea of specified aims and hypotheses is something of an anathema. Nevertheless, much research in mainstream psychology either overtly or tacitly subscribes to hypothesis testing as an ideal. Later (Chapter 18) we present an overview of the theoretical basis to these different approaches to research.

Key points

- Research studies have different general aims. Most seem to be concerned with testing causal propositions or hypotheses. Others may describe a phenomenon or intervention in detail, estimate how common a behaviour is in some population, evaluate the effects of interventions, or statistically summarise the results of similar studies. The aim or aims of a study should be clearly and accurately stated.

- Studies which test causal propositions should describe clearly and accurately what these propositions are.

- The research study should make a contribution to the topic. While research usually builds on previous research in an area, the contribution of the study should be original to some extent in the sense that the particular question addressed has not been entirely investigated in this way before.

- A hypothesis describes what the relationship is expected to be between two or more variables. The hypothesis should be stated in a causal form when the study is a true experiment. It should be stated in a non-causal form when the study is a non-experiment.

- When suggesting that variables may be related to one another, we usually expect the variables to be related in a particular way or direction. When this is the case, we should specify in the hypothesis what this direction is.

→

- The variable thought to be the cause may be called the independent variable and the variable presumed to be the effect the dependent variable. Some researchers feel that these two terms should be restricted to the variables in a true experiment. In non-experiments, the variable assumed to be the cause may be called the predictor and the variable considered to be the effect the criterion.

ACTIVITIES

1. Choose a recent study that has been referred to either in research you are reading or in a lecture that you have attended. What kind of aim or aims did the study have in terms of the aims mentioned in this chapter? What were the specific aims of this study? What kinds of variables were manipulated or measured? If the study involved testing hypotheses, were the direction and the causal nature of the relationship specified? If the hypothesis was stated in a causal form, was the design a true (i.e. randomised) one?

2. You wish to test the hypothesis that we are what we eat. How could you do this? What variables could you measure?

CHAPTER 3

Variables, concepts and measures

Overview

- The variable is a key concept in psychological research. A variable is anything which varies and can be measured. There is an important distinction between a concept and how it is measured.

- Despite its centrality and apparent ubiquity, the concept of variables was imported into psychology relatively late on from statistics. The dominance of 'variables' in psychology has been criticised for placing emphasis on measurement rather than theoretical and other conceptual refinements of basic psychological concepts.

- In psychology, the distinction between independent and dependent variables is important. Generally, the independent variable is regarded as having an influence on the dependent variable. This is especially so in terms of experimental designs which seek to identify cause-and-effect sequences by manipulating the independent variable.

- Nominal variables allocate cases to categories. Binomial means that there are two categories, multinomial means more than two categories. A quantitative variable is one in which a numerical value or score is assigned to indicate the amount of a characteristic an individual demonstrates.

- Stevens' theory of measurement suggests that variables can be measured on one of four different measurement scales – nominal, ordinal, interval and ratio. Different mathematical and statistical procedures are applicable to each. However, generally in psychological research data are collected in the form of numerical scores and analysed assuming that the interval scale of measurement underlies the scores.

- Operational definitions describe psychological concepts in terms of the procedures or processes used to measure them. This idea is borrowed from the physical sciences and seeks to objectify the definition of concepts. Operational definitions risk emphasising measurement at the expense of careful understanding and reification of concepts.

→

● Mediator variables intervene between two variables and can be regarded as responsible for the relationship between those two variables. Moderator variables, on the other hand, simply show that the relationship between an independent and a dependent variable is not consistent but may be different at different levels of the moderator variable. For example, the relationship between age and income may be different for men and women. In this case, gender would be the moderator variable.

● Hypothetical constructs are not variables but theoretical or conceptual inventions which explain what we can observe.

3.1 Introduction

In this chapter, we will explore the idea of *variables* in some depth. Variables are what we create when we try to measure concepts. So far, we have used the term variable without detailed discussion. Yet variables are at the heart of much psychological research. Hypotheses are often stated using the names of the variables involved, together with a statement of the relationship between them.

A variable is any characteristic or quality that has two or more categories or values. Of course, what that characteristic or quality is has to be defined in some way by the researcher. Saying that a variable has two or more categories or values simply reminds us that a variable must vary by definition, otherwise it is a *constant*. Researchers refer to a number of different types of variable, as we will discuss in this chapter. Despite the apparent ubiquity of the idea of variables in psychology textbooks, the centrality of the concept of variables in much of modern psychology should be understood as applying largely to quantitative mainstream psychology. The concept is not normally used in qualitative psychology. Furthermore, historically, the concept of a variable is a relatively modern import into psychology from statistics.

Variables are the things that we measure; they are not exactly the same thing as the concepts that we use when trying to develop theories about something. In psychological theories, we talk in terms of concepts: in Freudian psychology, a key concept is the ego; in social psychology, a key concept is social pressure; in biological psychology, a key concept might be pheromones. None of these, in itself, constitutes a variable. Concepts are about understanding things – they are not the same as the variables we measure. Of course, a major task in research is to identify variables which help us measure concepts. For example, if we wished to measure social influence, we might do so in a number of different ways, such as the number of people in a group who disagree with what a participant in a group has to say.

3.2 History of the variable in psychology

The concept of the 'variable' has an interesting history in that psychology managed without reference to variables for the first 50 or so years of the discipline's modern existence (Danziger & Dzinas, 1997). The beginnings of modern psychology are usually dated from the 1870s when Wilhelm Wundt (1832–1920) set up the first laboratory for psychological research at the University of Leipzig in 1879. Search through the work of early psychologists such as Sigmund Freud (1856–1939) and you find that they discuss psychological phenomena and not variables. The term 'independent variable', so familiar to all psychology students nowadays, was hardly mentioned at all in psychology publications before 1930. Most psychologists now use the term without questioning it and it is probably one of the first pieces of psychological jargon that students experience and use. Psychology textbooks almost invariably discuss studies, especially laboratory experiments, in terms of *independent* and *dependent variables;* these terms are used instead of the names of the psychological phenomena or concepts that are being studied.

Variables, then, were latecomers in the history of psychology. It probably comes as no surprise to learn that the term 'variable' has its origins in nineteenth-century mathematics, especially the field of statistics. It was introduced into psychology from the work of Karl Pearson (1857–1936), who originated the idea of the correlation coefficient (Pearson, 1900). By the 1930s, psychologists were generally aware of important statistical ideas, so familiarity with the term 'variable' had become common.

Edward Tolman (1886–1959), who is probably best remembered for his cognitive behavioural theory of learning and motivation, was the first to make extensive use of the word 'variable' in the 1930s when he discussed independent and dependent variables together with his new idea of *intervening variables*. The significance of this can be understood better if one tries to discuss Freudian psychology, for example in terms of these three types of variable. The id, repression, cathexis and other important Freudian concepts cannot readily be written about in terms of variables – independent, dependent or intervening. Once one tries to do so, the importance and nuances of Freudian ideas are lost. In other words, the notion of variables favours or facilitates certain ways of looking at the psychological world.

Danziger and Dzinas (1997) studied the prevalence of the term 'variable' in four major psychological journals published in 1938, 1949 and 1958. In the early journals, there is some use of the term 'variable' in what Danziger and Dzinas describe as the 'softer' areas of psychology, such as personality, abnormal and social psychology; surprisingly, laboratory researchers were less likely to use the term. The increasing use of the word 'variable' did not follow from an increase in the use of statistics in published articles, since this was virtually universal in published research from 1938 onwards. It is also not accounted for by an increase in references to the term 'intervening variable' since it was rarely mentioned in empirical research papers though it was mentioned in theoretical discussions.

The concepts of independent and dependent variables, however, were actively encouraged by experimental psychologists to replace the terminology of stimulus and response. Robert Woodworth (1869–1962), a prominent and highly influential author of a major psychology textbook of the time (Woodworth, 1934), adopted the new terminology and others followed his lead (Winston, 1988). Perhaps influenced by this, there was a substantial increase in the use of the terms 'independent variable' and 'dependent variable' during the time period the journals were studied by Danziger and Dzinas.

Danziger and Dzinas argue that 'variables' gained prominence because psychologists effectively reconstrued psychological phenomena which would require precise definition and explication as being the same as statistical variables. In this way and by doing so, psychological phenomena became merely mathematical entities or, at least, the distinction between the psychological phenomenon and its mathematical representation was obscured. Thus, psychologists write of personality variables when discussing aspects of personality which have not yet even been measured (as they would have to be to become statistical variables). This amounts to a 'prestructuring' or construction of the psychological world in terms of variables and the consequent assumption that psychological research simply seeks to identify the variables involved. Consequently variables ceased to be merely a technical aspect of how psychological research is carried out but became a statement or theory of the nature of psychological phenomena:

> When some of the texts we have examined here proceeded as if everything that exists psychologically exists as a variable they were not only taking a metaphysical position but they were also foreclosing further discussion about the appropriateness of their procedures to the reality being investigated.

> (Danziger & Dzinas, 1997, p. 47)

So do any areas of psychology not use the concept of variable? Well, it is very difficult to find references to variables in qualitative research, for example. Furthermore, it might be noted that facet theory (Canter, 1983; Shye & Elizur, 1994) regards the measures that we use in research simply as aspects of the world we are trying to understand. The analogy is with cutting precious stones. There are many different possible facets of a diamond depending on the way in which it is cut. Thus our measures simply reflect aspects of reality which are incomplete and less than the full picture of the psychological phenomena in which we are interested. In other words, our measures are only a very limited sample of possible measures of whatever it is we are interested in theoretically. So the researcher should avoid confusing the definition of psychological concepts with how we measure them, but explore more deeply the definition of the concept at the theoretical level.

3.3 Types of variable

There are numerous different types of variable in psychology, perhaps indicative of the centrality of the concept in psychology. Some of these are presented in Table 3.1, which also shows aspects of the relationships between the different types. Notice how some of the meanings are of theoretical and conceptual interest, whereas others are primarily statistical in nature. Of course, given the close relationship between psychology and statistics, some types of variable are a mixture of the two. This is sometimes because psychologists have taken statistical terminology and absorbed it into their professional vocabulary to refer to slightly different things.

There is an implication of Table 3.1 which may not appear immediately obvious. That is, how easy it is to fall into the trap of discussing psychological issues as if they are really statistical issues. This is best exemplified when psychologists seek to identify causal influences of one variable on another. The only way in which it is possible to establish that a relationship between two variables is causal is by employing an appropriate research design to do this. The randomised experiment is the best example of this by far. The statistical analysis employed cannot establish causality in itself – nor is it intended to do so.

Table 3.1	Some of the main types of variable	
Type of variable	Domain – psychological or statistical	Comments
Binomial variable	Statistical	A variable which has just two possible values.
Causal variable	Psychological	It is not possible to establish cause-and-effect sequences simply on the basis of statistics. Cause and effect can be established only by the use of appropriate research designs.
Confounding variable	Psychological	A general term for variables which cause confusion as to the interpretation of the relationship between two variables of interest.
Continuous variable	Statistical	A variable for which the possible scores have every possible value within its range. So any decimal value, for example, is possible for the scores.
Dependent variable	Both	The variable assumed to be affected by the independent variable.
Discrete variable	Statistical	A variable for which the possible scores have a limited number of 'discrete' (usually whole number) values within its range – that is, not every numerical value is possible.
Dummy variable	Statistical	Used to describe the variables created to convert nominal category data to approximate score data.
Hypothetical construct	Psychological	Not really a form of variable but an unobservable psychological structure or process which explains observable findings. See Box 3.2.
Independent variable	Both	The variation in the independent variable is assumed to account for all or some of the variation in the dependent variable. As a psychological concept, it tends to be assumed that the independent variable has a causal effect on the dependent variable. This is not the case when considered as a statistical concept. See Chapter 5, Box 5.4.
Interval variable	Statistical	Variables measured on a numerical scale where the unit of measurement is the same size irrespective of the position on the scale.
Intervening variable	Primarily psychological but also statistical	More or less the same as a mediator variable. It is a variable (concept) which is responsible for the influence of variable A on variable B. In other words, it intervenes between the effect of variable A on variable B.
Mediator variable	Primarily psychological but also statistical	A variable (concept) which is responsible for the influence of variable A on variable B. In other words, it mediates the effect of variable A on variable B. See Box 3.1.
Moderator variable	Statistical	A variable that changes the character of the relationship between two other variables. See Box 3.1.
Multinomial variables	Statistical	A nominal variable which has more than two values.
Nominal (category or categorical) variable	Statistical	Any variable which is measured by allocating cases to named categories without any implications of quantity.
Ordinal variable	Statistical	A variable which is measured in a way which allows the researcher to order cases in terms of the quantity of a particular characteristic. Derives from Stevens' theory of measurement.
Score variable	Statistical	Any variable which is measured using numbers which are indicative of the quantity of a particular characteristic.
Suppressor variable or masking variable	Statistical	A variable which hides (reduces) the true relationship between two other variables of interest.
Third variable	Statistical	A general term for variables which in some way influences the relationship between two variables of interest.

3.4   Independent and dependent variables

The concept of independent and dependent variables is common in psychological writings. The distinction between the two is at its clearest when we consider the true experiment and, ideally, would be limited to laboratory and similar true experiments. The variable which is manipulated by the researcher is known as the independent variable. Actually, it is totally independent of any other variable in a true experimental design, since purely random processes are used to allocate participants to the different experimental treatments. Nothing in the situation, apart from random processes, influences the level of the independent variable. The variable which is measured (rather than manipulated) is the dependent variable, since the experimental manipulation is expected to influence how the participants in the experiment behave. In other words, the dependent variable is thought to be subject to the influence of the independent variable.

The concepts of independent and dependent variables would appear to be quite simple, that is, the independent variable is the manipulated variable and the dependent variable is the measured variable which is expected to be influenced by the manipulated variable. It becomes rather confusing because the distinction between independent and dependent variables is applied to non-experimental designs. For example, the term independent variable is applied to comparisons between different groups. So if we were comparing men and women in terms of their computer literacy, then gender would be the independent variable. Computer literacy would be the dependent variable.

Of course, gender cannot be manipulated by the researcher – it is a fixed characteristic of the participant. Variables which cannot be or were not manipulated and which are characteristic of the participant or subject are sometimes called *subject variables*. They include things like how old, intelligent, and anxious the participant is. Variables like these are described as the independent variable by some researchers. But how can a variable be the independent variable if the causal direction of the relationship is not known? In non-experiments, it may be better to use more neutral terms for these two types of variable such as *predictor variable* for the independent variable and *criterion variable* for the dependent variable. In this case, we are trying to predict what the value of the criterion variable is from the values of the predictor variable(s).

Things get a little complicated, since in non-experimental designs the independent variable for one analysis can become the dependent variable for another, and vice versa. This may be all the more reason for confining the independent–dependent variable distinction to experimental designs.

3.5   Measurement characteristics of variables

Measurement is the process of assigning individuals to the categories or values of a variable. Different variables have different measurement characteristics which need to be understood in order to plan and execute research effectively. The most important way in which variables differ is in terms of nominal versus quantitative measurement. These are illustrated in Figure 3.1.

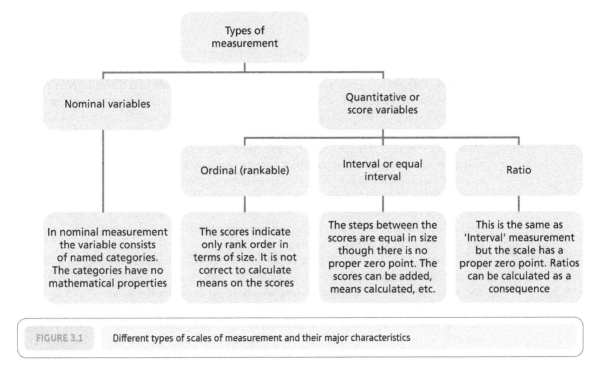

FIGURE 3.1   Different types of scales of measurement and their major characteristics

◼ Nominal variables (also known as qualitative, category or categorical variables)

Nominal variables are ones in which measurement consists of categorising cases in terms of two or more named categories. The number of different categories employed is also used to describe these variables:

- *Dichotomous, binomial or binary variables*   These are merely variables which are measured using just two different values. (The term dichotomous is derived from the Greek, meaning equally divided or cut in two: *dicho* is Greek for apart, separate or in two parts; while '*-ous*' is Latin for characterised by.) For example, one category could be 'friend' while the other category would be anyone else (i.e. non-friend).

- *Multinomial variables*   When a nominal variable has more than two values, it is described as a multinomial, polychomous or polytomous variable (*poly* is Greek for many). We could have the four categories of 'friend', 'family member', 'acquaintance' and 'stranger'.

Each value or category of a dichotomous or multinomial variable needs to be identified or labelled. For example, we could refer to the four categories friend, family member, acquaintance and stranger as category A, category B, category C and category D. We could also refer to them as category 1, category 2, category 3 and category 4. The problem with this is that the categories named in this way have been separated from their original labels – friend, family member, acquaintance and stranger. This kind of variable may be known as a nominal, qualitative, category, categorical or frequency variable. Numbers are simply used as names or labels for the different categories. We may have to use numbers for the names of categories when analysing this sort of data on a computer, but that is a matter of practicality since numbers merely symbolise the categories in this case. The only arithmetical operation that can be applied to dichotomous and multinomial variables is to count the frequency of how many cases fall into the different categories.

■ Quantitative variables

When we measure a quantitative variable, the numbers or values we assign to each person or case represent increasing levels of the variable. These numbers are known as scores, since they represent amounts of something. A simple example of a quantitative variable might be social class (socio-economic status is a common variable to use in research). Suppose that social class is measured using the three different values of lower, middle and upper class. Lower class may be given the value of 1, middle class the value of 2 and upper class the value of 3. Hence, higher values represent higher social status. The important thing to remember is that the numbers here are being used to indicate different quantities of the variable 'social class'. Many quantitative variables (such as age, income, reaction time, number of errors or the score on a questionnaire scale) are measured using many more than three categories. When a variable is measured quantitatively, the range of arithmetic operations that can be carried out is extensive – we can, for example, calculate the average value or sum the values.

The term 'dichotomous' can be applied to certain quantitative variables as it was to some nominal variables. For example, we could simply measure a variable such as income using two categories – poor and rich, which might be given the values 1 and 2. Quite clearly the rich have greater income than the poor, so the values clearly indicate quantities. However, this is true of any dichotomous variable. Take the dichotomous variable sex or gender. For example, females may be given the value of 1 and males the value of 2. These values actually indicate quantity. A person who has the value 2 has more maleness than a person given the value 1. In other words, the distinction between quantitative and qualitative variables is reduced when considering dichotomous variables.

Box 3.1   Key Ideas

Mediator versus moderator variables

Conceptually, modern psychologists speak of the distinction between mediator and moderator variables. These present quite different views of the roles for third variables in relationships between two variables (e.g. the independent and dependent variables). Mediator and moderator variables are conceptual matters more important to research design and methodology than to statistical analysis as such. In the relationship between the independent and dependent variables, a *mediator* variable is a variable which is responsible for this relationship. For example, the independent variable might be age and the dependent variable may be scores on a pub quiz or some other measure of general knowledge. Older people do better on the general knowledge quiz. Age, itself, is not directly responsible for higher scores on the pub quiz. Perhaps older people have greater general knowledge because they have had more time in their lives to read

books and newspapers, watch television, and undertake other educational experiences. It is these learning experiences which are responsible for age's relationship to general knowledge. In this instance, then, these educational experiences are a mediator variable for the age-general knowledge relationship.

Another way of describing this is that there is an indirect effect of age on the scores on the pub quiz. Of course, there may be more than one mediator variable in the relationship between an independent and a dependent variable. There is no substantial difference between a mediator variable and an intervening variable other than that intervening

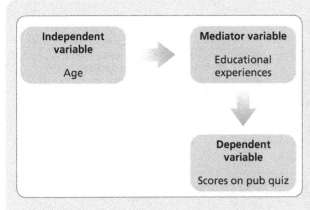

variables are regarded as hypothetical variables, whereas mediator variables seem not to be regarded as necessarily hypothetical.

A moderator variable is very different. A moderator variable is one which shows that the independent-dependent variable relationship is not consistent throughout the data. For example, imagine that a researcher investigates the relationship between age and scores on a pub quiz but considers the relationship for men and women separately.

They may find that the relationship between the two is different for men and women. Perhaps there is a strong correlation of .70 between age and scores on the pub quiz for women but a weak one of .20 between age and scores on the pub quiz for men. Thus the relationship is different for different subparts of data. Different conclusions are needed for men and for women. So we can say that gender moderates the relationship between age and scores on the pub quiz. Having established that gender is a moderator variable in this case does not explain in itself why the relationship is different for men and women. One possibility is that the pub quiz in question had a gender bias such that most of the questions were about topics which are of interest to women but not to men. Consequently, we might expect that the relationship would be reduced for men.

The interpretation of moderator variables is dependent on whether or not the independent variable in the independent variable – moderator variable – dependent variable chain is a randomised variable or not. Only where it is randomised can the researcher be sure of the causal sequence, otherwise there is uncertainty about what is causing what.

3.6   Stevens' theory of scales of measurement

The previous section describes the measurement principles underlying variables in the most useful and practical way possible. However, there is another approach which is common in textbooks. Research methods textbooks are full of ideas which appear to be the uncontroversial bedrock of the discipline. A good example of this is the theory of scales of measurement put forward by the psychologist Stanley Stevens (1906–1973) in an article in the journal *Science* (Stevens, 1946). You may have heard of other ideas of his, but that of the different scales of measures already discussed in this chapter is probably the most pervasive one. Probably few psychologists nowadays could name Stevens as the originator of the idea of nominal, ordinal, interval and ratio scales, though they would all know about these different scales. Remarkably, his ideas are surrounded by controversy in specialist statistical publications, but one would be forgiven for thinking that they are indisputable 'facts' given their uncritical presentation presented in research methods and statistics textbooks. So in this section we will look at Stevens' theory in a somewhat critical way, unlike other sources that you will find. You might be glad of the enlightenment.

By measurement, Stevens means the allocation of a number (or symbol) to things using some consistent rule. So, for example, we could measure sweets in a number of different ways: (a) we could allocate a colour (blue, red, yellow are linguistic symbols, of course) to each sweet; (b) we could measure each sweet's weight as a number of grams; or (c) we could grade them in terms of how good they taste. Measurement, conceptually,

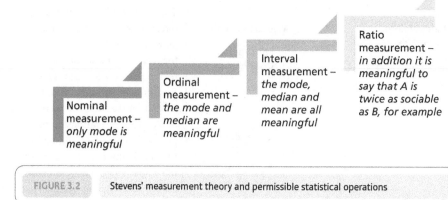

Stevens' measurement theory and permissible statistical operations

amounts to quite a simple process, as these examples illustrate. Clearly these three ways of measurement are rather different in terms of how the measurement would be carried out. Stevens argued that there are four different types of measurement which have somewhat different mathematical properties. This means that the mathematical procedures that can be applied to each type of measurement differ. The mathematical operations which are appropriate for one type of measurement may be inappropriate for another. One consequence of this is that the sort of statistical analysis that is appropriate for one sort of variable may be inappropriate for another sort. Choosing a statistical technique appropriate to the sort of measurement one has is one of the skills needed when using statistics.

Stevens' four types of measurement are usually put in the order nominal, ordinal, interval and ratio scales of measurement (see Figure 3.2). This is actually a hierarchy from the least powerful data to the most powerful data numerically. The later in the series the scale of measurement is, the more information is contained within the measurement. Thus variables measured in a manner indicative of a ratio scale are at the highest level of measurement and contain more information, all other things being equal. The different measurement scales are often referred to as different levels of measurement which, of course, in itself implies a hierarchy. Let us take each of these in turn, starting with the highest level of the hierarchy.

1. *Ratio measurement scales*   The key feature of a ratio measurement scale is that it should be possible to calculate a meaningful ratio between two things which have been measured. This is a simpler idea than it sounds, because we are talking ratios when we say things like Grant is twice as tall as Michelle. So if we measure the weights of two chocolates in grams, we can say that the coffee cream chocolate was 50 per cent heavier than the strawberry truffle chocolate. In order to have a ratio measurement scale, it is necessary for there to be a zero point on the scale which implies zero quantity for the measurement. Weights do have a zero point – zero grams means that there is no weight. So weight is a ratio measurement scale. A common measurement that does not have a proper zero (implying zero quantity) is temperature measured in degrees Celsius or Fahrenheit. To be sure, if you look at a thermometer you will find a zero point on both the Celsius and Fahrenheit scales, but this is not the lowest temperature possible. Zero on the Celsius scale is the freezing point of water, but it can get a lot colder than that. What this means is that for temperature, it is not possible to say that something is twice as hot as something else using any of the familiar temperature scales. Thirty degrees Celsius cannot be regarded as twice as hot as 15 degree Celsius. Any statistical procedure can be applied to ratio data. For example, it is meaningful to calculate the mean of ratio

data – as well as ratios. There is another feature of ratio measurement scales, that there should be equal intervals between points on the scale. However, this requirement of equal intervals is also a requirement of the next measurement scale – the interval measurement scale – as we shall see.

2. *(Equal) interval measurement scale* This involves assigning real numbers (as opposed to ranks or descriptive labels) to whatever is being measured. It is difficult to give common examples of interval measures which are not also ratio measures. Let us look on our bag of sweets: we find a sell-by date. Now the sell-by date is part of a measurement scale which measures time. If a bag of sweets has the sell-by date of 22 February, then this is one day less than a sell-by date of 23 February. Sell-by date is being measured on an equal interval measure in which each unit is a day and that unit is constant throughout the scale of measurement, of course. However, there is not a zero point on this scale. We all know that the year 0 is not the earliest year that there has ever been, since it is the point where BCE changes to CE. We could, if we wanted to, work out the average sell-by date on bags of sweets in a shop. The average would be meaningful because it is based on an equal-step scale of measurement. There are many statistical techniques which utilise data that are measured on interval scales of measurement. Indeed, most of the statistical techniques available to researchers can handle interval-scale data. Conceptually, there is a clear difference between interval-scale measurements and ratio-scale measurements though in most instances it makes little difference, say, in terms of the appropriate statistical analysis – it is only important when one wishes to use ratios which, in truth, is not common in psychology.

3. *Ordinal measurement scales* This involves giving a value to each of the things being measured that indicates their relative order on some sort of characteristic. For example, you might wish to order the chocolates in a box of chocolates in terms of how much you like each of them. So you could put the ones that you most like on the left-hand side of a table, the ones that you like a bit less to the right of them, and so forth until the ones that you most dislike are on the far right-hand side of the table. In this way, the chocolates have been placed in order from the most liked to the least liked. This is like ordinal measurement in that you have ordered them from the most to the least. Nothing can really be said about how much more you like, say, the hazelnut cluster from the cherry delight, only that one is preferred to the other because you put them at different points on the table. It is not possible to say how much more you like one of the chocolates than another. Even if you measured the distance between where you put the hazelnut cluster and where you put the cherry delight, this gives no precise indication of how much more one chocolate is liked than another. Ordinal numbers (first, second, third, fourth, . . . , last) could be applied to the positions from left to right at which the chocolates were placed. These ordinal numbers correspond to the rank order. The hazelnut cluster might be eighth and the cherry delight might be ninth. However, it still remains the case that although the hazelnut cluster is more liked than the cherry delight, how much more it is liked is not known. Ordinal measurements, it is argued, are not appropriate for calculating statistics such as the mean. This is certainly true for data that have been converted to ranks, since the mean rank is totally determined by the number of items ranked. However, psychologists rarely collect data in the form of ranks but much more often in the form of scores. In Stevens' measurement theory, any numerical score which is not on a scale where the steps are equal intervals is defined as ordinal. Stevens argued that the mode and the median are more useful statistics for ordinal data and that the mean is inappropriate. Ordinal measurements are frequently analysed using what are known as non-parametric or distribution-free statistics. They vary, but many of these are based on putting the raw data into ranks.

4. *Nominal (or category/categorical) measurement scales*   This measurement scale involves giving labels to the things being measured. It is illustrated by labelling sweets in an assorted bag of sweets in terms of their colour. Colour names are linguistic symbols, but one could use letters or numbers as symbols to represent each colour if one so wished. So we could call red Colour A and blue Colour B, for instance. Furthermore, we could use numbers purely as symbols, so that we could call red Colour 1 and blue Colour 2. Whether we use words, letters, numbers or some other symbol to represent each colour does not make any practical difference. It has to be recognised that if we use numbers as the code, then these numbers do not have mathematical properties any more than letters would have. So things become a little more complicated when we think about what numerical procedures we can perform on these measurements. We are very restricted. For example, we cannot multiply red by blue – this would be meaningless. Actually, the only numerical procedure we could perform in these circumstances would be to count the number of red sweets, the number of blue sweets, and the number of yellow sweets, for example. By counting we mean the same thing as calculating the frequency of things, so we are able to say that red sweets have a frequency of 10, blue sweets have a frequency of 5, and yellow sweets have a frequency of 19 in our particular bag of sweets. We can say which is the most frequent or typical sweet colour (yellow) in our bag of sweets but little else. We cannot meaningfully calculate things such as the average red sweet, the average blue sweet and the average yellow sweet, based on giving each sweet a colour label. So in terms of statistical analysis, only statistics that are designed for use with frequencies could be used. Confusion can occur if the symbols used for the nominal scale of measurement are numbers. There is nothing wrong with using numbers as symbols to represent things so long as one remembers that they are merely symbols and that they are no different from words or letters in this context.

It is not too difficult to grasp the differences between these four different scales of measurement. The problem arises when one tries to apply what has been learnt to the vast variety of different psychological measures. It will not have escaped your attention how in order to explain interval and ratio data physical measurements such as weight and temperature were employed. This is because these measures clearly meet the requirements of these measurement scales. When it comes to psychological measures, it is much more difficult to find examples of interval and ratio data that everyone would agree about. There are a few examples but they are rare. Reaction time (the amount of time it takes to respond to a particular signal) is one obvious exception, but largely because it is a physical measure (time) anyway. Examples of more psychological variables which reflect the interval and ratio levels of measurement are difficult to find. Take, for example, IQ (intelligence quotient) scores. It is certainly possible to say that a person with an IQ of 140 is more intelligent than a person with an IQ of 70. Thus we can regard IQ as an ordinal measurement. However, is it possible to say that a person with an IQ of 140 is twice as intelligent as someone with an IQ of 70, which would make it a ratio measurement? Are the units that IQ is measured in equal throughout the scale? Is the difference between an IQ of 70 and an IQ of 71 the same difference as that between an IQ of 140 and an IQ of 141? They need to be the same if IQ is being measured on an equal-interval scale of measurement. One thing that should be pointed out is that one unit on our measure of IQ is in terms of the number involved being the same no matter where it occurs on the scale. The problem is that in terms of what we are really interested in – intelligence – we do not know that each mathematical unit is the same as each psychological unit. If this is not clear, then consider using electric shocks to cause pain. The scale may be from zero volts to 6000 volts. This is clearly both an interval scale and a ratio scale in terms of the volts, but in terms of the resulting pain this is not the case. We all know that touching the terminals of a small battery has no effect on us, which means that at the low voltage levels no pain is caused, but this is not true at higher voltage levels. Thus, in terms of pain, this scale is not equal interval.

Not surprisingly, Stevens' theory of measurement has caused many students great consternation, especially given that it is usually taught in conjunction with statistics, which itself is a difficult set of ideas for many students. The situation is that anyone using the theory – and it is a theory – will generally have great difficulty in arguing that their measures are on either an interval or a ratio scale of measurement, simply because there is generally no way of specifying that each interval on the scale is in some way equal to all of the others to start with. Furthermore, there are problems with the idea that a measure is ordinal. One reason for this, as already mentioned, is that psychologists rarely simply gather data in the form of ranks as opposed to some form of score. These scores therefore contain more information than that implied merely by a rank, though the precise interpretation of these scores is not known. There is no way of showing that these scores are on an equal-interval scale, so they should be regarded as ordinal data according to Stevens' theory. Clearly this is entirely unsatisfactory. Non-parametric statistics were frequently advocated in the past for psychological data, since these do not assume equality of the measurement intervals. Unfortunately, many powerful statistical techniques are excluded if one adopts the strategy of using non-parametric statistics.

One argument, which we find convincing, is that it is not the psychological implications of the scores that are important but simply the mathematical properties of the numbers involved. In other words, so long as the scores are on a numerical scale, they can be treated as if they are interval-scale data (and, in exceptional circumstances where there is a zero point, as ratio-scale data). The truth of the matter, and quite remarkable given the dominance of Stevens' ideas about measurement in psychology, is that researchers usually treat any measures they make involving scores as if they were interval data. This is done without questioning the status of their measures in terms of Stevens' theory. Actually there are statistical studies which partly support this in which ordinal data are subject to statistical analyses which are based on the interval scale of measurement. For many statistics, this makes little or no difference. Hence, in that sense, Stevens' theory of measurement leads to a sort of wild goose chase.

| Box 3.2 | Key Ideas |

Hypothetical constructs

Hypothetical constructs were first defined by Kenneth MacCorquodale (1919–1986) and Paul E. Meehl (1920–2003) in 1948. They are not variables in the sense we have discussed in this chapter. Essentially a hypothetical construct is a theoretical invention which is introduced to explain observable facts. It is something which is not directly observable but nevertheless is useful in explaining things such as relationships between variables found in a research study. There is a wide variety of hypothetical constructs in psychology. Self-esteem, intelligence, the ego, the id and the superego are just some examples. None of these things is directly observable, yet they are discussed as explanations of any number of observable phenomena. Some of them, such as intelligence, might at first sight seem to be observable things but usually they are not, since they are based on inferences rather than observation. In the case of the hypothetical construct of intelligence, we use observables such as the fact that a child is top of their class, is a chess champion and has a good vocabulary to infer that they are intelligent. Perhaps more crucially, the Freudian concept of the id is not observable as such but is a way of uniting observable phenomena in a meaningful way which constitutes an explanation of those observables.

3.7   Operationalising concepts and variables

There is a crucial distinction to be made between a variable and the measure of that variable. Variables are fundamentally concepts or abstractions which are created and refined as part of the advancement of the discipline of psychology. Gender is not a tick on a questionnaire, but we can measure gender by getting participants to tick male or female on a questionnaire. The tick on the questionnaire is an *indicator* of gender, but it is not gender. Operationalisation (Bridgman, 1927) is the steps (or operations) that we take to measure the variable in question. Percy Williams Bridgman (1882–1961) was a physical scientist who, at the time that he developed his ideas, was concerned that concepts in the physical sciences were extremely poorly defined and lacked clarity. Of course, this is frequently the case in the softer discipline of psychology too. Operationalism was, however, introduced into psychology largely by Stanley Stevens (1935), whom we have earlier discussed in terms of measurement theory. For Bridgman, the solution was to argue that precision is brought to the definition of concepts by specifying precisely the operations by which a concept is measured. So the definition of weight is through describing the measurement process, for example the steps by which one weighs something, using some sort of measurement scale. Of course, operationalising concepts is not guaranteed to provide precision of definition unless the measurement process is close to the concept in question and the measurement process can be precisely defined. So, for example, is it possible to provide a good operational definition of a concept like love? By what operations can love be measured is the specific question. One possible operational definition might be to measure the amount of time that a couple spends in each other's company in a week. There are obvious problems with this operational definition, which suggests that it is not wholly adequate. It has little to do with our ideas about what love is. Imagine the conversation: 'Do you love me?' 'Well, I spend a lot of time with you each week, don't I?' This should quickly paint a picture of the problem with such an operational definition.

Nevertheless, some researchers in psychology argue that the best way of defining the nature of our variables is to describe how they are measured. For example, there are various ways in which we could operationalise the concept or variable of anxiety. We could manipulate it by putting participants in a situation which makes them anxious and compare that situation with one in which they do not feel anxious. We could assess anxiety by asking them how anxious they are, getting other people to rate how anxious they seem to be, or measuring some physiological index of anxiety such as their heart rate. These are different ways of operationalising anxiety, though none of them is anxiety itself. If they all reflect what we consider to be anxiety, we should find that these different methods are related to one another. So we would expect participants in a situation which makes them anxious to report being more anxious, be rated as being more anxious and to have a faster heart rate than those in a situation that does not make them anxious. If these methods are not related to one another, then they may not all be measuring anxiety.

Operationalisation has both benefits and drawbacks. The benefit is that by defining a concept by the steps involved in measuring it, the meaning of the concept could not be more explicit. The costs include that operationalisation places less onus on the researcher to make explicit the nature of their concepts and encourages the concentration on measurement issues rather than conceptual issues. Of course, ultimately any concept used in research has to be measured using specific and specified operations. However, this should not be at the expense of careful consideration of the nature of what it is that the researcher really is trying to understand – the theoretical concepts involved. Unfortunately, we cannot escape the problem that operational definitions tend to result in a concentration on measurement in psychology rather to the detriment of the development of the ideas embedded in psychological theory.

Study of the relationship between attitude similarity and liking being mediated by assuming the other person likes us

Condon, J. W., & Crano, W. D. (1988). Inferred evaluation and the relation between attitude similarity and interpersonal attraction. *Journal of Personality and Social Psychology, 54*, 789–797.

Unravelling what is going on in our research can be very complex, as we will illustrate using another research study on attitude similarity and liking. The variables that we include systematically and deliberately in our studies may be underpinned by processes that are rather different from what we first envisaged when we originally planned our research. That is, no matter the hypothesis that we begin our research with, the best interpretation of the relationships we find can be rather different. This is where the issues discussed in this chapter become more salient and more interesting. Research rarely follows a straight line and can be full of surprising convolutions before our understanding is sufficiently clear.

Background

This study by John Condon and William Crano (1988) was primarily concerned with whether Byrne's (1961) relationship between having similar attitudes to someone and liking them could be explained by people assuming that the other person was more likely to like them if they had similar rather than dissimilar attitudes. In other words, the authors were interested in determining to what extent the relationship between attitude similarity and liking was mediated by people's inferences about what the stranger felt towards them. This is a different explanation from that of Elliot Aronson and Philip Worchel (1966) who thought that liking a stranger was solely determined by whether that stranger liked the person and not by how similar their attitudes were to theirs. Aronson and Worchel's research seemed to support that idea. The view that the relationship between attitude similarity and liking may be mediated by being liked also differed from that of Donn Byrne and Ray Rhamey (1965) who suggested and showed that being liked by a stranger may be more rewarding than having similar attitudes. In other words, Byrne and Rhamey thought that both attitude similarity and being liked could be interpreted in terms of the single variable of how rewarding these two aspects were.

Hypothesis

The hypothesis of this study was not explicitly stated as such. It is best encapsulated by the first sentence of the Abstract which stated that 'This research examines the possibility that the relation between attitude similarity and attraction is mediated by people's attribution of the other's evaluation of them' (Condon & Crano, p. 789). Part of the last sentence in the Introduction to the paper also suggests the hypothesis as being 'a more clear and compelling test of the critical question of the mediation of the similarity–attraction association' (p. 791).

Method

Design

The design of this study was fairly complicated (see Figure 3.3). Only its main features, which are concerned with testing the mediating effects of being liked, will be described. A large sample of 226 introductory psychology students were first asked to indicate their attitudes on 12 topics. They were then randomly assigned to the supposed attitude of another student on these topics which varied in terms of how much they agreed with them. They were also randomly assigned to one of two conditions in which either they were positively evaluated by the supposed student or they received no

→

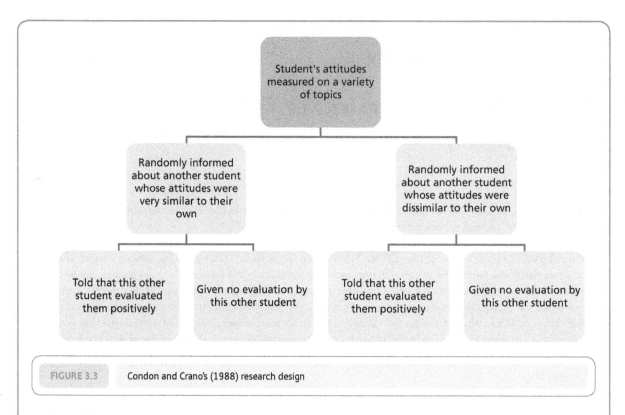

Condon and Crano's (1988) research design

evaluation. There was no third condition in which they were negatively evaluated by this student, as this manipulation was thought to be unethical. The second condition, in which they received no evaluation from the supposed student, was thought to be the most critical for testing the mediation hypothesis, because they were given no information about how the supposed student felt about them.

The extent to which the students thought the other student liked them was based on two questions. These two questions were similar to the two questions that were used to assess the extent to which the participant students liked the other student, with the exception that the subject and object of the questions were reversed. These two questions or statements were 'This person would probably like(dislike) me very much' and 'I believe that this person would very much like(dislike) working with me in an experiment' (p. 792).

The extent to which the students thought that the other student had similar attitudes to theirs was measured with a single question assessing this.

Mediation results

Only the results for the students in the no-evaluation condition will be presented here, to keep the presentation brief and because these findings were thought by the authors to be the most critical to their study. However, the results for the positive-evaluation group were very similar to those for the no-evaluation condition. The single-item measure of student's perception of agreement was found to be moderately positively and significantly correlated with the two-item measure of the student's liking for the supposed student. In other words, attitude similarity was positively related to attraction as expected. This means that the more students saw the other student as agreeing with them, the more they liked the other student. The size of this correlation was .64, which indicates a relatively substantial relationship but one which is far from perfect.

To determine if this similarity–attraction association was mediated by how much the students thought the other student liked them, a statistical procedure known as partial correlation was carried out. Partial correlation removes the influence of a third variable from the relationship between the two main variables. In this instance, how much the students thought the other student liked them was removed or 'partialled out' from the association between attitude similarity and attraction. If the association between attitude similarity and liking was not mediated by how much the other student was assumed to like them, the partial correlation between attitude similarity and attraction should differ little from the non-partial correlation between them. In other words, it should be close to .64. The smaller the positive partial correlation was compared to the non-partial correlation, the greater is the mediating effect of assuming the other student liked them. The partial correlation between attitude similarity and liking, removing the effect of liking, was .18. In other words, it was substantially smaller than the non-partial correlation of .64 between attitude similarity and attraction. This reduction suggests that the association between attitude similarity and attraction is largely mediated by how much the other student was assumed to like them.

This partial correlation can easily be calculated as shown later (Chapter 11). To do this, you also need to know the correlation between assumed liking and attitude similarity, which was .70, and the correlation between assumed liking and liking, which was .81.

Authors' suggestions for future research

Condon and Crano made several suggestions about future work. One suggestion was that research should investigate what kind of information people look for when evaluating others and how they use that information.

3.8 | Conclusion

Perhaps the key thing to have emerged in this chapter is that some of the accepted ideas in psychological research methods are not simply practical matters but were important philosophical contributions to the development of the methods of the discipline. A concept such as a variable has its own timeline, is not universal in the discipline, and brings to psychology its own baggage. Although some of these ideas seem to be consensually accepted by many psychologists, it does not alter the fact that they are not the only way of conceptualising psychological research, as later parts of this book will demonstrate. While the idea of operational definitions of concepts pervades much of psychology, once again it should be regarded as a notion which may have its advantages but also can be limiting in that it encourages psychologists to focus on measurement but not in the context of a thorough theoretical and conceptual understanding of what is being measured.

The concept of a variable has many different ramifications in psychology. Many of these are a consequence of the origins of the concept in statistics. Intervening variables, moderator variables, mediating variables, continuous variables, discrete variables, independent variables, dependent variables and so forth are all examples of variables but all are different conceptually. Some have more to do with statistics than others.

Measurement theory introduced the notions of nominal, ordinal, interval and ratio measurement. While these ideas are useful in helping the researcher not to make fundamental mistakes such as suggesting that one person is twice as intelligent as another when such statements require a ratio level of measurement, they are actually out of step with psychological practice in terms of the statistical analysis of research data.

Key points

- The concept of the variable firmly ties psychology to statistics, since it is a statistical concept at root. There are many different types of variable which relate as much to theoretical issues as to empirical issues. For example, the distinction between independent and dependent variables and the distinction between moderator and mediating variables relate to explanations of psychological phenomena and not simply to empirical methods of data collection.

- Stevens' measurement theory has an important place in the teaching of statistics but is problematic in relation to the practice of research. Nevertheless, it can help prevent a researcher from making totally erroneous statements based on their data. Most research in psychology ignores measurement theory and simply assumes that data in the form of scores (as opposed to nominal data) can be analysed as if they are based on the interval scale of measurement.

- Psychologists stress operational definitions of concepts in which theoretical concepts are defined in terms of the processes by which they are measured. In the worst cases, this can encourage the concentration of easily measured variables at the expense of trying to understand the fundamental concept better at a conceptual and theoretical level.

ACTIVITIES

1. Try to list the defining characteristics of the concept 'love'. Suggest how love can be defined using operational definitions.

2. Could Stevens' theory of measurement be applied to measures of love? For example, what type of measurement would describe classifying relationships as either platonic or romantic love?

CHAPTER 4

Problems of generalisation and decision-making in research

Chance findings and sample size

Overview

- Psychological research is best regarded as a complex decision-making process which is irreducible to a simplistic formula or rules-of-thumb.

- Several factors are especially influential on limiting the generalisability of any data including the statistical significance of the findings. Psychologists over-generalise because of the discipline's tendency towards universalism, which assumes that what is true of one group of people is true of all people.

- Psychological research (unlike psychological practice) usually involves samples of people rather than specific individuals. This encourages the consideration of general trends at the expense of neglecting idiosyncratic aspects of individuals.

- Samples are often selected because they are convenient for the researcher to obtain. These are generally called convenience samples. Random sampling from a clearly specified population is much more expensive in time and other resources.

- Characteristically, much psychological research studies general principles of human behaviour. They are assumed to be true of people in general so representative sampling is ignored.

- Statistical analysis frequently addresses the basic question of how safe it is to generalise from a particular study or sample of data (null-hypothesis testing). The usual statistical testing model in psychology deals with what would happen if the null hypothesis were true and compares this with what the research actually found.

→

- The probability of accepting that the study's results are not due to chance sampling if the null hypothesis were true is usually set at the 5 per cent or .05 level. This means that the probability of the finding being due to chance when the null hypothesis is in fact true is five times out of 100, or less. Results that meet this criterion are called statistically significant, otherwise they are statistically non-significant.

- The larger the sample, the more likely it is that the results will be statistically significant – all other things being equal. Consequently, it is necessary to look at the size of the finding as well as its statistical significance when evaluating its importance.

- Research should not use more resources than is necessary to address the research questions to be asked. For that reason, it is increasingly common for researchers to estimate the size of the smallest sample needed in order for the research findings to demonstrate a relationship where there is in fact a relationship. Equally one should not squander resources by employing such a small sample that an important trend in the data cannot be statistically significant.

4.1   Introduction

The process of generalising from research findings can be problematic. Are we justified in making statements about our research findings which apply beyond the circumstances and setting of the research itself? For example, research findings which only apply in laboratory settings are of little interest in general. What are the limitations on the generalisability of our research? At least three important issues warrant consideration:

- The lack of limitations placed on generalisation by the universalism of much psychological theory.

- The limitations placed on generalisation by the sampling methods used.

- The limitations placed on generalisation by the strictures of statistical significance testing.

We will deal with each of these in turn. Each has a different influence on the extent to which a researcher is wise or correct to generalise beyond the immediate setting and findings of their research. Statistical considerations are more than technical matters and can have a bearing on conceptual issues. For example, you might be less likely to generalise when your measures of concepts or variables are relatively weak or ineffective. This will lead to low correlations between such variables and others – hence we cannot be confident in generalising from such findings. However, statistics can also indicate what the correlations would be if the measures were strong and reliable. On the basis of this, you may revise your opinion of what can be claimed on the basis of your data. See Figure 4.1 for a summary of some of the aspects of generalisation.

Issues such as the generalisability of data are components of decision-making involved in research. The researcher's task is to reach a balanced judgement at every stage of their research based on the information they have before them together with a reasoned evaluation of the choices available at that time. This decision-making process cannot be reduced to a few rules-of-thumb. No matter how appealing such a recipe might seem, it distorts the reality of research. So even significance testing which is often reduced to a formula in statistics textbooks actually involves judgement. Research is not simply a

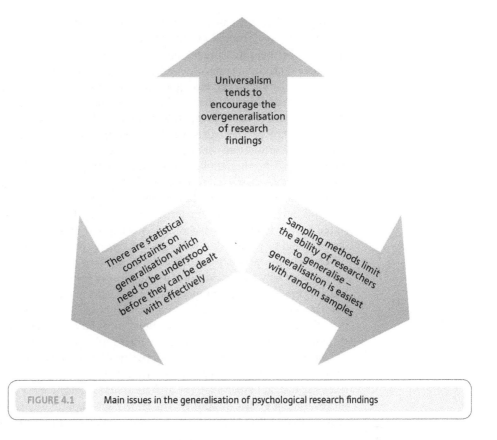

FIGURE 4.1   Main issues in the generalisation of psychological research findings

matter of deciding whether a hypothesis is supported by one's data or not. Other important issues include:

- On the basis of one's research findings, is it desirable to develop further questions for future related research in the area?

- Is the most important next step to establish whether one's findings apply in very different circumstances or with very different groups of participants or using very different methods?

- How confident should one be in one's research findings?

There are other questions, of course, such as the desirability of abandoning this particular line of research. Again, this is not simply a matter of failing to find support for a hypothesis in a particular study, but a decision-making process based on much fuller considerations than statistical significance alone. Much finer judgements than decisions about statistical significance need to be made when deciding whether the hypothesis had been given a fair chance in the study.

4.2   Universalism

One of the characteristics of psychology is its tendency towards *universalism*. This is the fundamental assumption that the principles of psychology will not vary. Psychological findings will apply anywhere and are the same for all people irrespective of their society and their culture. So when psychologists propose a hypothesis, there is an implicit assumption that it is true of all people – rarely is it stated or implied that the principle applies only to restricted groups of people. In other words, psychologists in practice appear to be interested in making generalisations about behaviour largely unrestrained by context and circumstances. Psychological principles are assumed to be laws of human behaviour anywhere. Increasingly, however, psychologists are questioning this idea of universalism and arguing that a culturally specific approach to psychology is more realistic and productive (Owusu-Bempah & Howitt, 2000). Historically, many of the principles put forward by psychologists were assumed to apply to animals and not just people. So it was only natural that studies of basic processes were carried out on animals and the findings applied to human beings. Classic examples of this include classical conditioning theory famously based on research with dogs (Pavlov, 1927) and operant conditioning theory (Skinner, 1938), based on research with rats and pigeons.

While universalism is characteristic of much psychological thinking, it is rarely, if ever, stated as such in modern psychology. Any psychologist making such a claim without evidence would be regarded as naïve. Nowadays psychologists are likely to be aware of the problems of universalism but fail to build this into their research practices. Universalism operates covertly but reveals itself in a number of different ways – such as when university students are used unquestioningly as participants in a great deal of academic research as if what were true for university students will be true for every other grouping and sector in society. Seldom do psychologists build into their research a variety of groups of participants specifically to assess whether their findings apply throughout.

Universalism, however, is uncharacteristic of qualitative research which usually adopts a relativist perspective, rejecting the idea of a single reality that can be discovered through research. Instead, qualitative researchers assume that there is a multiplicity of viewpoints on reality. This basic supposition is clearly incompatible with universalism and is discussed in more detail in Part 4 of this book on qualitative research methods.

4.3   Sampling and generalisation

Many criticisms have been made of psychology for its restricted approach to sampling. A common one is that psychology is the psychology of psychology students or sophomores (Rosenthal & Rosnow, 1969, p. 59) (a sophomore is a second-year undergraduate in the USA). This criticism is only meaningful if the idea of universalism is being questioned, otherwise the laws of human behaviour could just as well be determined from studies using psychology students as any other group of participants. Whatever the group used, it would reveal the same universal laws. The emphasis of psychology on the processes involved in human behaviour and interaction is a strength of the discipline which, it could be argued, has relatively little to do with the issue of sampling. So, although psychology's sampling methods may be lacking to some extent, this is not the entire story by any means.

Not all research has or needs a sample of participants. The earliest psychological research tended to use the researcher themselves as the principal or only research participant. Consequently, experimental psychologists would explore phenomena on themselves. This was extremely common in introspectionism (or structuralism), which was the dominant school of psychology at the start of modern psychology until it was eventually replaced by behaviourism early in the twentieth century. Similarly, and famously, Ebbinghaus (1913) studied memory or forgetting on himself. There are circumstances in which a single case may be an appropriate unit for study. Some psychologists advocate using single cases or relatively few cases in order to investigate changing a particular individual's behaviour (Barlow & Hersen, 1984) and this is common in qualitative research too.

A single-case experimental study in quantitative research involves applying the independent variable at different random points in time. If the independent variable is having an effect, then the participant should respond differently at the points in time that the independent variable is applied than when it is not. The obvious important advantage of the single-case study is that it can be helpful when the particular sort of participant is very rare. For example, if a particular patient has a very unusual brain condition, then a single-case study provides a way of studying the effect of that condition. Clinical researchers working with a particular patient might consider this style of research.

The problems with the approach include the high demands on the participant's time. It also has the usual problems associated with participants being aware of the nature of the design – it is somewhat apparent and obvious what is happening – which may result in the person being studied cooperating with what they see as the purpose of the study. Although the single-case method is rare in mainstream psychology but apparently becoming less so (Forsyth, Kollins, Palav, Duff, & Maher, 1999), its use questions the extent to which researchers always need substantial samples for their research to be worthwhile or effective.

Representative samples and convenience samples

Most research studies use more than a few participants. The mean number of participants per study in articles published in 1988 in the *Journal of Personality and Social Psychology* was about 200 (Reis & Stiller, 1992). This is quite a substantial average number of participants. So:

- How big should a sample be in order for us to claim that our findings apply generally?

- How should samples be selected in order for us to maximise our ability to generalise from our findings?

If everyone behaved in exactly the same way in our studies, we would only need to select one person to investigate the topic in question – everyone else would behave exactly the same. The way in which we select the sample would not have any bearing on the outcome of the research, because there is no variability. We only need sampling designs and statistics, for that matter, because of this variability. Psychology would also be a very boring topic to study.

Fortunately, people vary enormously. Take, for example, something as basic as the number of hours people say they usually sleep a day. Differences between people and within a person are common, just as one might suppose. While most people claim to sleep between seven and eight hours, others claim that they sleep less than six hours and others that they sleep more than 10 hours (Cox et al., 1987, p. 129). In other words, there is considerable variation in the number of hours claimed. Furthermore, how much sleep a person has varies from day to day – one day it may be six hours and the next day eight hours. Sampling adds a different type of variability – that due to sampling itself.

The necessary size of the samples used in research should be commensurate with the consequences of the findings of the research. Research for which the outcome matters crucially demands larger samples than research for which the outcome, whatever it is, is less important. For example, what size sample would one require if the outcome of the study could result in counselling services being withdrawn by a health authority? What size sample would one require if a study is just part of the training of psychology students – a practical exercise? What size sample would one require for a pilot study prior to a major investigation? While psychologists might disagree about the exact sample size to use, probably they would all agree that larger samples are required for the study that might put the future of counselling services at risk. This is because they know that a larger sample is more likely to demonstrate a trend in the study if there is one in reality (i.e. all things being equal, a larger sample is more likely to produce statistically significant findings).

As we have mentioned, many psychologists also tend to favour larger sample sizes because they believe that this is likely to result in greater precision in their estimates of what is being measured. For example, it is generally the case that larger samples are employed when we are trying to estimate the frequency, or typical value, of a particular behaviour or characteristic in the population. If we wanted an estimate of the mean number of reported hours of sleep in, say, the elderly, then we are likely to use a rather substantial sample. What this means is that it is possible to claim that the average number of hours of sleep has a particular value and that there is only a small margin of error involved in this estimate. That is, our estimate is likely to be pretty close to what the average is in reality. On the other hand, if we want to know whether the number of hours slept is related to mental health, then we may feel that a smaller sample will suffice. The reason for this is that we only need to establish that sleep and mental health are related – we are less concerned about the precise size of the relationship between the two.

If the aim is to produce an estimate of some characteristic for the population, then we will have more confidence in that estimate if the sample is selected in such a way that it is representative of the population. The usual way of doing this is to draw samples at random. Ways of selecting a representative sample will be discussed in detail later (Chapter 13) along with other sampling methods. The more representative we can assume our sample to be, the more confidence we can have in our generalisations based on that sample. Probably most sampling in psychological research is what is termed *convenience samples*. These are *not* random samples of anything, but groups of people that are relatively easy for the researcher to recruit. In the case of university lecturers and students, the most convenient sample typically consists of students – often psychology students. What is convenient for one psychologist may not be convenient for another, of course. For a clinical psychologist, psychotherapy patients may be a more convenient sample than undergraduate students. Bodner (2006a) noted that for a random sample of 200 studies selected from the electronic bibliographic database PsycINFO in 1999, only 25 per cent of them used college students, ranging from as low as 5 per cent in clinical or health psychology to as high as 50 per cent in social psychology.

Convenience samples are usually considered to be acceptable for much psychological research. Given that psychological research often seeks to investigate whether there is a relationship between two or more variables, a precisely defined sample may be unnecessary (Campbell, 1969, pp. 360–362). Others would argue that this is very presumptuous about the nature of the relationship between the two variables, and especially that it is consistent over different sorts of people. For example, imagine that watching television violence is related to aggressiveness in males but inversely related to aggressiveness in females. By taking a sample of psychology students, who tend to be female, a convenience sample of university students will actually stack things in favour of finding that watching television is associated with lower levels of aggressiveness.

Whether it is possible to generalise from a sample of psychology students, or even students as a whole, to the wider population is obviously an empirical question for any research topic. It is also a matter of credibility, since studying post-partum depression using a general convenience sample of university students would not be sensible. There are research topics for which it would seem perverse to study students, though it does happen. For example, if the research is on the comprehensibility of the police caution, then using university students is less appropriate than employing a sample of people with poor educational attainment. The use of students for a study has its advantages if the context is their education and training; on the other hand, students are bad proxies for other groups. Getting the balance right is a matter for the research community in general, not just students learning to do psychology.

Often it is difficult to identify the population that the researcher has in their mind. Although common sense would suggest that the population is that which is represented by the actual participants in the research, researchers seem to regard it differently. Probably because psychologists tend to see research questions as general propositions about human behaviour rather than propositions about a particular type of person or a specific population, they have a tendency to generalise beyond the population represented by their research sample. The difficulty is, of course, just when the generalisation should stop – if ever. Similarly, there tends to be an assumption that propositions are true not just at one point in time but across a number of points in time. For example, psychological processes first identified more than a lifetime ago are still considered relevant today and into the future. Gergen (1973) has argued for the historical relativity of psychological ideas which Schlenker (1974) has questioned.

So there appears to be a distinction between the *population of interest* and the population defined by the sample actually used in the research. Of course, it would be possible to limit our population in time and space. We could say that our population is all students at Harvard University in 2019. However, it is almost certain that having claimed this, we would readily generalise the findings that we obtain to students at other universities, for example. We may not directly state this but we would write in a way suggestive of this. Furthermore, people in our research may be samples from a particular group simply because of the resource constraints affecting our options. For example, a researcher may decide to select some, but not all, 16-year-olds at a particular school to take part in research. Within this school, participants are selected using a random procedure from the school's list of 16-year-olds. While this would be a random sample from the school and can be correctly described as such, the population as defined by the sample would be very limited. Because the initial selection of schools was extremely limited (in this example just one school), the study's results may be less informative than a study which did not employ random selection but used a wider variety of schools.

The appropriateness of the samples used in most psychological research can be questioned. Psychological researchers rarely use random sampling from a clearly defined population. Almost invariably some sort of convenience sample of participants is employed – where randomisation is used it mostly takes the form of random allocation to the conditions of an experiment or a participant's sequence of taking part in the different conditions. This is as true of the best and most influential psychological research as of more mundane research. In other words, if precise sampling were the criterion for good research, psychology textbooks may just as well be put through the shredder. This is not to say that sampling in psychological research is good enough – there is a great deal to be desired in terms of current practices. However, given that the major justification for typical current practice lies in the assumed generality of psychological principles, things probably will not change materially in the near future.

Another factor needs to be considered is that participation rates in many sorts of research are very low. Participation rates refer to the proportion of people who take part in the research compared with the number asked to take part in the research, that is, the proportion who supply usable data. Random sampling is considerably undermined by poor participation rates; it cannot be assumed that those who do *not* participate are a random sample of the people approached. Presumably they do not participate for various reasons, which in turn may lead to non-participants having different characteristics from participants. These reasons may be systematically related to the research topic – maybe some potential participants are simply uninterested in the topic of the research. Alternatively, there may be more technical reasons why participation rates are low. A study which involves the completion of a questionnaire is likely to result in less literate potential participants declining to take part. So sampling requires constant attention, consideration and vigilance by researchers when planning, analysing and evaluating research. The issues are complex and it is impossible to provide rules-of-thumb to deal with every situation.

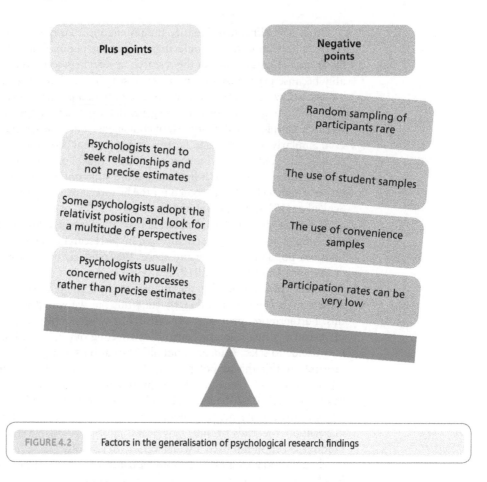

Plus points

Negative points

Random sampling of participants rare

Psychologists tend to seek relationships and not precise estimates

The use of student samples

Some psychologists adopt the relativist position and look for a multitude of perspectives

The use of convenience samples

Psychologists usually concerned with processes rather than precise estimates

Participation rates can be very low

FIGURE 4.2   Factors in the generalisation of psychological research findings

The lesson is that merely using random selection methods does not ensure a random sample. In these circumstances, convenience samples may be much more attractive propositions than they at first appear to be – if poor participation rates systematically distort the sample then what is to be gained by careful sampling? Figure 4.2 displays some points about the kinds of samples typically used by psychologists.

4.4   Statistics and generalisation

Statistical analysis serves many important roles in psychology – as some students will feel they know to their cost. There are numerous statistical techniques that help researchers explore the patterns in their data, for example, which have little or nothing to do with what is taught in introductory statistics courses. Most students, however, are more familiar with what is known as 'inferential statistics' or, more likely, the concept of 'significance testing'. Significance testing is only one aspect of research but is a crucial one in terms of a researcher's willingness to generalise the trends found in their data. While students are encouraged to believe that statistical significance is an important criterion, it is just one of two really important things. The other is the size of the trend, difference, effect or relationship found in the research. The bigger these are, the more important is the relationship. Statistical significance is only one criterion by which to evaluate research. One needs a fuller picture than just that when reaching decisions about your data.

Moreover, given the tendency of psychologists to emphasise statistical significance, the consequences of failing to identify a real trend in their data can be overlooked. This is as serious as thinking that there is a trend in the data when, in reality, no trend exists because our sample has capitalised on chance. For example, what if the study involves an innovative treatment for autism? It would be a tragedy if the researcher decided that the treatment did not work simply because the sample size used was far too small for the statistical analysis to be statistically significant. Essentially this boils down to the need to plan research in the light of the significance level selected, the minimum size of the effect or trend in your data that you wish to detect, and the risk that you are prepared to take of your data not showing a trend when in reality there is a trend. With these things decided, it is possible to calculate, for example, the minimum sample size that your study will need to be statistically significant for a particular size of effect. This is a rather unfamiliar area of statistics to most psychologists, known as statistical power analysis. It is included in the statistics textbook which accompanies this book (e.g. Howitt & Cramer, 2020).

◼ Chance findings and statistical significance

When studying a research question, the decision about what sample size is appropriate is probably made largely on the size of the effect or association expected. The bigger the effect or association is, the smaller the sample can be in purely statistical terms. Bigger effects are more likely to be statistically significant with small sample sizes. A statistically significant finding is one that is large enough that it is unlikely to be the result of chance fluctuations due to sampling. (It should be stressed that the calculation of statistical significance is normally based on the hypothetical situation defined by the null hypothesis that there is no trend in the data.) The conventionally accepted level of significance is the 5 per cent or .05 level. This means that a finding as big as ours can be expected to occur by chance on five or fewer occasions if we tested that finding on 100 occasions (and assuming that the null hypothesis is in fact true). A finding or effect that is likely to occur on more than five out of 100 occasions by chance is described as being statistically non-significant or not statistically significant. Note that the correct term is 'non-significant', *not* that it is statistically 'insignificant', although authors sometimes use this term which reviewers or editors fail to correct. Insignificant is a misleading term, since it implies that the finding is not statistically important – but that simply is not what is meant in significance testing. The importance of a finding lies in the strength of the relationship between two variables or in the size of the difference between two samples. To summarise, statistical significance testing merely refers to the question whether the trend is sufficiently large in the data so that it is unlikely that it could be the result of chance factors due to the variability inherent in sampling, that is, there is little chance that the null hypothesis of no trend or difference is correct.

Too much can be made of statistical significance if the size of the trend in the data is ignored which is a mistake. For example, it has been argued that with very large samples, virtually any relationship will be statistically significant though the relationship may itself be minute. That is, in some circumstances a statistically significant relationship may, in fact, represent only a very small trend in the data. Put another way, very few null hypotheses are true *if* one deals with very large samples and one will accept even the most modest of trends in the data. So small trends found in a very large sample are not likely to generalise to small samples.

The difference between statistical significance and psychological significance is at the root of the following question: *Which is better: a correlation of .06 which is statistically significant with a sample of 1000 participants, or a correlation of .8 that is statistically significant with a sample of six participants?* This is a surprisingly difficult question for many psychologists to answer.

While the critical value of 5 per cent or .05 or less is an arbitrary cut-off point, nevertheless it is a widely accepted one. It is not simply the point for rejecting the null hypothesis but also the point at which a researcher is likely to wish to generalise their findings. However, there are circumstances in which this arbitrary criterion of significance may be replaced with an alternative value:

● The significance level may be set at a value other than 5 per cent or .05. If the finding had important consequences and we wanted to be more certain that it was not due to chance, we might set it at a more stringent level. For example, we may have developed a test that we found was significantly related at the 5 per cent level to whether or not someone had been convicted of child abuse. Because people may want to use this test to help determine whether someone had committed, or was likely to commit, child abuse, we may wish to set the critical value at a more stringent or conservative level, because we would not want to wrongly suggest that someone would be likely to commit child abuse. Consequently, we may set the critical value at, say, 0.1 per cent or .001, which is 1 out of 1000 times or less. This is a matter of careful assessment and judgement, not merely one of applying rules.

● Where a number of effects or associations are being evaluated at the same time, this critical value may need to be set at less than the 5 per cent or .05 level. For example, if we were comparing differences between three groups, we could make a total of three comparisons altogether. We could compare group 1 with group 2, group 1 with group 3, and group 2 with group 3. If the probability of finding a difference between any two groups is set at 5 per cent or .05, then the probability of finding any of the three comparisons statistically significant at this level is three times as big, in other words 15 per cent or .15. Because we want to maintain the overall significance level at 5 per cent or .05 for the three comparisons, we could divide the 5 per cent or the .05 by 3, which would give us an adjusted or corrected critical value of 1.67 per cent (5/3 = 1.666) or .017 (.05/3 = .0166). This correction is known as a Bonferroni adjustment. (See our companion statistics text, *Understanding statistics in psychology with SPSS*, Howitt & Cramer, 2020, for further information on this and other related procedures.) That is, the value of, say, the *t*-test would have to be significant at the 1.67 per cent level according to the calculation in order to be reported as statistically significant at the 5 per cent level.

● For a pilot study using a small sample and less than adequate measuring instruments, the 5 per cent or .05 level of significance may be an unnecessarily stringent criterion. The size of the trends in the data (relationship, difference between means, etc.) is possibly more important. For the purposes of such a pilot study, the significance level may be set at 10 per cent or .1 to the advantage of the research process. There may be other circumstances in which we might wish to be flexible about accepting significance levels of 5 per cent or .05. For example, in medical research, imagine that researchers have found a relationship between taking hormone replacement therapy and the development of breast cancer. Say that we find this relationship to be statistically significant at the 8 per cent or .08 level; would we willingly conclude that the null hypothesis is preferred or would we be unwilling to take the risk that the hypothesis linking hormone replacement therapy with cancer is in fact true? Probably not. Significance testing is not at fault here, but a researcher who takes too mechanical an approach to significance testing is not taking the totality of the research into consideration. Once we have obtained our significance level, a whole range of factors need to be brought into play. Research is an intellectual process requiring substantial careful thought and consideration in order to make what otherwise appear to be straightforward decisions on the basis of statistical significance testing.

However, students are well advised to stick with the 5 per cent or .05 level as a matter of routine. One would normally be expected to make the case for varying this, but this may prove difficult to do in the typical study undertaken by students.

4.5   Directional and non-directional hypotheses again

Directional and non-directional hypotheses were discussed earlier in this book (Box 2.1), but there is more to be added. When hypotheses are being developed, researchers usually have an idea of the direction of the trend, correlation or difference that they expect. For example, who would express the opinion that there is a difference between the driving skills of men and women without expressing an opinion as to what that difference is such as women are definitely worse drivers? In everyday life, a person who expresses such a belief about women's driving skills is likely to be expressing prejudices about women or joking or being deliberately provocative – they are unlikely to be a woman. Researchers, similarly, often have expectations about the likely outcome of their research – that is, the direction of the trend in their data. A researcher would not express such a view on the basis of a whim or prejudice, but they would make as strong an argument as possible built on supportive evidence. In some cases there will be sound reasons for expecting a particular direction or trend in the data, whereas in other circumstances no sound grounds are possible. Research works best when the researcher articulates coherent, factually based and convincing grounds for their expectations.

So research hypotheses often will be expressed in a directional form. In statistical testing, a similar distinction is made between directional and non-directional tests but the justifications are required to be exacting and reasoned (see Box 2.1). In a statistical analysis (as we saw in Chapter 2), there are tough requirements before a directional hypothesis can be offered. These requirements are that there are very strong empirical or theoretical reasons for expecting the relationship to go in a particular direction and that researchers are ignorant of their data before making the prediction. It would be silly to claim to be making a prediction if one is just reporting the trend observed in the data. These criteria are so exacting that it questionable whether any student research should employ directional *statistical* hypotheses. Probably the main exceptions are where a student researcher is replicating the findings of a classic study, which has repeatedly been shown to demonstrate a particular trend.

The reason why directional statistical hypotheses have such exacting requirements is that conventionally the significance level is adjusted for the directional hypothesis. Directional hypothesis testing is referred to as one-tailed significance testing. Non-directional hypothesis testing is referred to as two-tailed significance testing. In two-tailed significance testing, the 5 per cent or .05 chance level is split equally between the two possibilities – that the association or difference between two variables is either positive or negative. So, if the hypothesis is that cognitive behaviour therapy has an effect, this would be supported by cognitive behaviour therapy either being better in the highest 2.5 per cent or .025 of samples or worse in the lowest 2.5 per cent or .025 of samples. In one-tailed testing the 5 per cent is piled just at one extreme – the extreme which is in the direction of the one-tailed hypothesis. Put another way, a directional hypothesis is supported by weaker data than would be required by the non-directional hypothesis. The only satisfactory justification for accepting a weaker trend is that there is especially good reason to think that it is correct, that is, either previous research has shown much the same trend or theory powerfully predicts a particular outcome. Given the often weak predictive power of much psychological theory, the strength of the previous research is probably the most useful of the two.

If a hypothesis is directional, then the significance level is confined to just one half of the distribution – that is, the 5 per cent is just at one end of the distribution (not both), which means, in effect, that a smaller trend will be statistically significant with a directional test. There is a proviso to this: that the trend is in the predicted direction. Otherwise it is very bad news, since even big trends are not significant if they are in the wrong direction! The problem with directional hypotheses is, then, what happens when the researcher gets it wrong, that is, the trend in the data is exactly the reverse of what is suggested in the hypothesis. There are two possibilities:

● That the researcher rejects the hypothesis.

● That the researcher rejects the hypothesis but argues that the reverse of the hypothesis has been demonstrated by the data.

The latter is rather like having one's cake and eating it, statistically speaking. If the original hypothesis had been supported using the less stringent requirements then the researcher would claim credit for that finding. If, on the other hand, the original hypothesis was actually substantially reversed by the data, then this finding would now find favour. The reversed hypothesis, however, was deemed untenable when the original decision to offer a directional hypothesis had been taken. So how can it suddenly be favoured when it was previously given no credence with good reason? The only conclusion must be that the findings were chance findings.

So the hypothesis should be rejected. The temptation, of course, is to forget about the original directional hypothesis and substitute a non-directional or reverse directional hypothesis. Both of these are totally wrong but who can say when even a researcher will succumb to temptation?

Consequently, one could argue that possibly the only circumstances in which a student should employ directional *statistical* hypotheses is when conducting fairly exact replication studies. In these circumstances, the direction, of the hypothesis is justified by the findings of the original study. If the research supports the original direction then the conclusion is obvious. If the replication actually finds the reverse of the original findings, the researcher would be unlikely to claim that the reverse of the original findings is true since it would apply only to the replication study. The situation is one in which the original findings are in doubt and so are the new findings, since they are diametrically opposite to these.

One- versus two-tailed significance level

Splitting the 5 per cent or .05 chance or significance level between the two possible outcomes is usually known as the two-tailed significance level, because two outcomes (directions of the trend or effect) in both a positive and a negative direction are being considered. We do this if our hypothesis is non-directional, as we have not specified which of the two outcomes we expect to find. Confining the outcome to one of the two possibilities is known as the one-tailed significance level because only one outcome is predicted. This is what we do if our hypothesis is directional, where we expect the results to go in one direction.

To understand what is meant by the term 'tailed', we need to plot the probability of obtaining each of the possible outcomes that could be obtained by sampling *if the null hypothesis is assumed to be true*. This is the working assumption of hypothesis testing, and reference to the null hypothesis is inescapable if hypothesis testing is to be understood. The technicalities of working out the distribution of random samples if the null hypothesis is true can be obtained from a good many statistics textbooks. The 'trick' to it all is employing the information contained in the actual data. This gives us information about the distribution of scores. One measure of the distribution of scores is the *standard deviation*. In a nutshell, this is a sort of average of the amount by which scores in a sample differ from the mean of the sample. It is computationally a small step from the standard deviation of scores to the standard error of the means of samples. Standard error is a sort of measure of the variation of sample means drawn from the population defined by the null hypothesis. Since we can calculate the standard error quite simply, this tells us how likely each of the different sample means are. (Standard error is the distribution of sample means.) Not surprisingly, samples very different from the outcome defined by the null hypothesis are increasingly uncommon the more different they are from what would be expected on the basis of the null hypothesis.

This is saying little more than that if the null hypothesis is true, then samples that are unlike what would be expected on the basis of this null hypothesis are likely to be uncommon.

4.6 More on the similarity between measures of effect (difference) and association

Often measures of the effect (or difference) in experimental designs are seen as unlike measures of association. This is somewhat misleading. Simple basic research designs in psychology are often analysed using the *t*-test (especially in laboratory experiments) and the Pearson correlation coefficient (especially in cross-sectional or correlational studies). The *t*-test is based on comparing the means (usually) of two samples and essentially examines the size of the difference between the two means relative to the variability in the data. The Pearson correlation coefficient is a measure of the amount of association or relationship between two variables. Generally speaking, especially in introductory statistics textbooks, they are regarded as two very different approaches to the statistical analysis of data. This can be helpful for learning purposes. However, they are actually very closely related.

A *t*-test is usually used to determine whether an effect is significant in terms of whether the mean scores of two groups differ. We could use a *t*-test to find out whether the mean depression score was lower in the cognitive behaviour therapy group than in the no-treatment group. A *t*-test is the mean of one group subtracted from the mean of the other group and divided by what is known as the standard error of the mean:

$$t = \frac{\text{mean of one group} - \text{mean of other group}}{\text{standard error of the mean}}$$

The standard error of the mean is a measure of the extent to which sample means are likely to differ. It is usually derived from the extent to which scores in the data differ, so it is also a sort of measure of the variability in the data. There are different versions of the *t*-test. Some calculate the standard error of the mean and others calculate the standard error of the difference between two means.

The value of *t* can be thought of as the ratio of the difference between the two means to the degree of the variability of the scores in the data. If the individual scores differ widely, then the *t* value will be smaller than if they do not differ much. The bigger the *t* value is, the more likely it is to be statistically significant. To be statistically significant at the two-tailed .05 level, the *t* value has to be 2.00 or bigger for samples of more than 61 cases. A statistically significant *t* value will be slightly less than 2.00 for bigger samples. The minimum value that *t* has to exceed to be significant at this level is 1.96, which is for an infinite number of cases. These figures can be found in the tables in some statistics texts such as *Understanding statistics in psychology with SPSS* (Howitt & Cramer, 2020).

Bigger values of *t* generally indicate a bigger effect (a bigger difference between the sample means relative to the variability in the data). However, this is affected by the sample size, so this needs to be taken into consideration as well. Bigger values of *t* also tend to indicate increasingly significant findings if the sample size is kept constant.

The Pearson's correlation shows the size of an association between two quantitative variables. It varies from −1 through 0 to 1:

● A negative value or correlation means that lower values on one variable go together with higher values on the other variable.

● A positive value or correlation means that higher values on one variable go together with higher values on the other variable.

● A value of zero or close to zero means that there is no relationship or no linear relationship between the two groups and the outcome measure.

Note that Pearson's correlation is typically used to indicate the association between two quantitative variables. Both variables should consist of a number of values, the frequencies of which take the shape of a bell approximately. The bell-shaped distribution is known as the normal distribution. (See the companion book *Understanding statistics in psychology with SPSS,* Howitt & Cramer, 2020, or any other statistics textbook for a detailed discussion of precisely what is meant by a normal distribution.) Suppose, for example, we are interested in what the relationship is between how satisfied people are with their leisure time and how satisfied they are with their work. Suppose the scores on these two measures vary from 1 to 20 and higher scores indicate greater satisfaction. A positive correlation between the two measures means that people who are more satisfied with their leisure time are also more satisfied with their work. It could be that these people are generally positive, or that being satisfied in one area of your life spills over into other areas. A negative correlation indicates that people who are more satisfied with their leisure time are less satisfied with their work. It is possible that people who are dissatisfied in one area of their life try to compensate in another area.

A correlation of zero or close to zero shows that either there is no relationship between these two variables or there is a relationship but it does not vary in a linear way. For example, people who are the most and least satisfied with their leisure may be less satisfied with work than people who are moderately satisfied with their lives. In other words, there is a curvilinear relationship between leisure and work satisfaction. The simplest and the most appropriate way of determining whether a correlation of zero or close to zero indicates a non-linear relationship between two variables is to draw a scattergram or scatterplot as shown in Figure 4.3. Each point in the scatterplot indicates the position of one or more cases or participants in terms of their scores on the two measures of leisure time and work satisfaction.

The *t* values which compare the means of two unrelated or different groups of cases can be converted into a Pearson's correlation or what is sometimes called a point–biserial correlation, which is the same thing. The following formula is used to convert an unrelated *t* value to a Pearson's correlation, denoted by the letter *r* (*n* is, of course, the sample size):

$$r = \sqrt{\frac{t^2}{t^2 + n - 2}}$$

Alternatively, we could calculate the value of *r* directly from the data. Suppose higher values on the measure of depression indicate greater depression and that the cognitive behaviour therapy group shows less depression than the no-treatment group. If we code or call the no-treatment group 1 and the cognitive behaviour therapy group 2, then we will have a negative correlation between the two groups and depression when we calculate the Pearson correlation value.

Because of the interchangeability of the concepts of correlation and tests of difference as shown, it should be apparent that we can speak of a difference between two groups or alternatively of a correlation or an association between group membership and another variable. This is quite a sophisticated matter and important when developing a mature understanding of research methods.

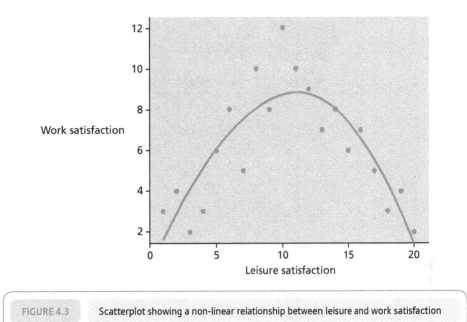

FIGURE 4.3   Scatterplot showing a non-linear relationship between leisure and work satisfaction

4.7   Sample size and size of association

Now that we have provided some idea as to what statistical significance is and how to convert a test of difference into a correlation, we can discuss how big a sample should be in order to see whether an effect or association is statistically significant. The bigger the correlation is, the smaller the sample can be for that correlation to be statistically significant. For purposes of illustration, in Table 4.1 we present 11 correlations decreasing in size by .10 from ± 1.00 to 0.00 and the size that the sample has to exceed to be significant at the one-tailed 5 per cent or .05 level. So, for example, if we expect the association to be about .20 or more, we would need a sample of more than 69 for that association to be statistically significant. It is unusual to have an overall sample size of less than 16. The size of an effect may be expected to be bigger when manipulating variables as in an experiment rather than simply measuring two variables as in a cross-sectional study. This is because the researcher, normally, does everything possible to reduce extraneous sources of variation in an experiment using procedural controls such as standardisation – this is another way of saying that error variance is likely to be less in a true experiment. Consequently, sample sizes are generally smaller for true experiments than for non-experiments.

When dealing with two groups, it is important that they are roughly equal in size. If there were only a few cases in one of the groups (very disproportionate group sizes), we cannot be so confident that our estimate of the population characteristics based on these is reasonably accurate. The conversion of a t value into a Pearson's correlation presupposes that the variation or variance in the two groups is also similar in size. Where there is a big disparity, the statistical outcome is likely to be somewhat imprecise. Where there are only two values, as in the case of two groups, one should ensure, if possible, that the two groups are roughly similar in size. So it is important that the researcher should be aware of exactly what is happening in their data in respect of this

A correlation of zero is never significant no matter how big the sample – since that is the value which best supports the null hypothesis. Correlations of 1.00 are very unusual, as they represent a perfect straight-line or linear relationship between two variables. This would happen if we correlated the variable with itself either intentionally or by accident. You need

Table 4.1	Size of sample required for a correlation to be statistically significant at the two-tailed 5 per cent or .05 level		
Correlation(r)	Verbal label for the size of correlation according to Cohen (1988)	Minimum sample size to be significant (n)	Percentage of variance shared r²%
±1.0	Perfect		100%
±.9	Large	5	81
±.8	Large	7	64
±.7	Large	9	49
±.6	Large	12	36
±.5	Large	16	25
±.4	Medium	25	16
±.3	Medium	44	9
±.2	Medium	97	4
±.1	Small	384	1
0.0	None	Cannot be significant	0

to have a minimum sample of four to determine the statistical significance of a correlation using a two-tailed test, though we would not suggest that you adopt this strategy, since the size of the relationship would have to be rather larger than we would normally expect in psychological research. Thus, a correlation of .99 or more would be significant at the two-tailed 5 per cent or .05 level if the sample was four. Consequently, no sample size has been given for a correlation of 1.00. These sample sizes apply to both positive correlations and negative ones. It is the size of the correlation that matters when determining statistical significance and not its sign (unless you are carrying out a directional test).

Size of an association and its meaning

The size of a correlation is often described in words as well as in numbers. One common system is that of Cohen (1988) which describes a correlation of .5 as large, one of .3 as medium, and a correlation of .1 as small. We might get a large correlation, say, if we measured the same variable on two occasions twice – depression might give a large correlation, for example. Medium correlations would typically be found when two different variables, such as depression and social support, are measured on the same or different occasions. The meaning of the size of a correlation is better understood if we square the correlation value – this gives us something called the *coefficient of determination*. So a correlation of .20 when squared gives a coefficient of determination of .04. This value represents the proportion of the variation in a variable that is shared with the variation in another variable. Technically, this variation is measured in terms of a concept or formula called variance. The way to calculate variance can be found in a statistics textbook such as the companion book, *Understanding statistics in psychology with SPSS* (Howitt & Cramer, 2020).

A correlation of 1.00 gives a coefficient of determination of 1.00, which means that the two variables are perfectly related. A correlation of zero produces a coefficient of determination of zero, which indicates that the variables either are totally separate or do not have a straight-line relationship such as the relationship between work and leisure satisfaction in Figure 4.3. These proportions may be expressed as a percentage, which

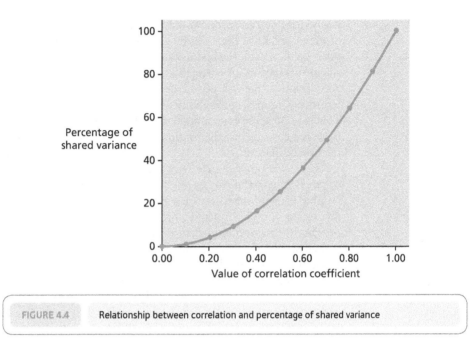

FIGURE 4.4   Relationship between correlation and percentage of shared variance

may be easier to understand. We simply multiply the proportion by 100, so .04 becomes 4 (.04 × 100). The percentage of the variance shared by the correlations in Table 4.1 is shown in the final column of that table.

If we plot the percentage of variance shared against the size of the correlation as shown in Figure 4.4, we can see that there is not a straight-line or linear relationship between the two but what is called an exponential relationship. The percentage of variance increases at a faster rate at higher than at lower correlations. As the size of a correlation doubles, the corresponding size of the percentage of shared variance quadruples. To give an example of this, a correlation of .40 is twice as big as one of .20. If we express these correlations as the percentage of shared variance, we can see that a percentage of 16 is four times as big as one of 4. This should tell you that it is helpful to consider the amount of variation explained by a correlation and not simply the numerical size. A correlation of .40 is not twice as good as a correlation of .20, because in terms of the amount of variation (variance) explained, the larger correlation accounts for *four* times the amount of variation. Table 4.1 gives the figures for the amounts of variation explained.

Justification for the use of these labels might come from considering just how many variables or factors may be expected to explain a particular kind of behaviour. Racial prejudice is a good example of such behaviour. It is reasonable to assume that racial prejudice is determined by a number of factors rather than just a single factor. The tendency towards holding authoritarian attitudes has a correlation of .30 with a measure of racial prejudice (Billig & Cramer, 1990). This means that authoritarian attitudes share 9 per cent of its variance with racial prejudice. On the face of things, this is not a big percentage of the variance. What if we had, say, another 10 variables that individually and independently explained (accounted for) a similar proportion of the variance? Then we could claim a complete account of racial prejudice. The problem in psychology is finding out what these other 10 variables are – or whether they exist. Actually a correlation of .30 is not unusual in psychological research and many other variables will explain considerably less of the variance than this.

There is another way of looking at this issue. That is to ask what the value is of a correlation of .30 – a question which is meaningless in absolute terms. In the above example, the purpose of the research was basically associated with an attempt to theorise about the nature of racial prejudice. In this context, the correlation of .30 would seem to imply that one's resources would be better applied to finding more effective explanations of racial prejudice than can be offered on the basis of authoritarian attitudes. On the other hand, what if the researcher was interested in using cognitive behaviour therapy in suicide prevention? A correlation of .30 between the use of cognitive behaviour therapy and decline in the risk of suicide is a much more important matter – it amounts to an improvement in the probability of suicide prevention from .35 to .65 (Rosenthal, 1991). This is in no sense even a moderate finding: it is of major importance. In other words, there is a case against the routine use of labels when assessing the importance of a correlation coefficient.

There is another reason why we should be cautious about the routine application of labels to correlations or any other research result. Our measures are not perfectly reliable or valid measures of what they are measuring (see Chapter 16 for a detailed discussion of reliability and validity). Because they are often relatively poor measures of what they are intended to measure, they tend usually to underestimate the true or real size of the association. There is a simple statistical procedure for taking into account the unreliability of the measures, called the correction for attenuation (see the companion book, *Understanding statistics in psychology with SPSS,* Howitt & Cramer, 2020, Chapter 37). Basically it gives us an idealised version of the correlation between two variables as if they were perfect measures. The formula for the corrected correlation is:

$$\text{corrected correlation} = \frac{\text{correlation between measures 1 and 2}}{\sqrt{\text{measure 1 reliability} \times \text{measure 2 reliability}}}$$

If the correlation between the two measures is .30 and their reliability is .75 and .60 respectively, the corrected correlation is .45:

$$\text{corrected correlation} = \frac{.30}{\sqrt{.75 \times .60}} = \frac{.30}{\sqrt{.45}} = \frac{.30}{\sqrt{.67}} = .45$$

This means that these two variables share about 20 per cent of their variance. If this is generally true, we would only need another four variables to explain what we are interested in. (Although this is a common view in the theory of psychological measurement, the adjustment actually redefines each of the concepts as the *stable* component of the variables. That is, it statistically makes the variables completely stable (reliable). This obviously is to ignore the aspects of a variable which are unstable, for example, why depression varies over time, which may be as interesting and important to explain as the stable aspects of the variable.)

How do we know what size of effect or association to expect if we are just setting out on doing our research?

● Psychologists often work in areas where there has already been considerable research. While what they propose to do may never have been done before, there may be similar research. It should be possible from this research to estimate or guesstimate how big the effect is likely to be.

● One may consider collecting data on a small sample to see what size of relationship may be expected and then to collect a sample of the appropriate size to ensure that statistical significance is achieved if the trend in the main study is equal to that found in the pilot study. So, if the pilot study shows a correlation of .40 between the two variables we are interested in, then we would need a minimum of about 24 cases in our main study. This is because by checking tables of the significance of the correlation coefficient, we find that .40 is statistically significant at the 5 per cent level (two-tailed test) with a sample size of 24 (or more). These tables are to be found in many statistics textbooks – our companion statistics text, *Understanding statistics in psychology with SPSS* (Howitt & Cramer, 2020), has all you will need.

- Another approach is to decide just what size of relationship or effect is big enough to be of interest. Remember that very small relationships and effects are significant with very large samples. If one is not interested in small trends in the data, then there is little point in depleting resources by collecting data from very large samples. The difficulty is deciding what size of relationship or effect is sufficient for your purposes. Since these purposes vary widely, no simple prescription may be offered. It is partly a matter of assessing the value of the relationship or effect under consideration. Then the consequences of getting things wrong need to be evaluated. (The risk of getting things wrong is higher with smaller relationships or effects, all other things being equal.) It is important not simply to operate as if statistical significance is the only basis for drawing conclusions from research.

It is probably abundantly clear by now that purely statistical approaches to generalisation of research findings are something of an impossibility. Alongside the numbers on the computer output is a variety of issues or questions that modify what we get out of the statistical analysis alone. These largely require thought about one's research findings and the need not to simply regard any aspect of research as routine or mechanical.

Box 4.1	Research Example

Cross-cultural study on attitude similarity and liking

Byrne, D., Gouaux, C., Griffitt, W., Lamberth, J., Murakawa, N., Prasad, M., Prasad, A., & Ramirez III, M. (1971). The ubiquitous relationship: Attitude similarity and attraction: A cross-cultural study. *Human Relations*, 24, 201–207.

It has been a common criticism of psychology that it assumes the universality of research findings without providing the evidence for this universality. Although the research findings of physics and chemistry might be expected to show universality, psychology is not physics or chemistry and painstaking work is needed to establish where and when our research findings apply. Similarly, the dependence of psychological research substantially on student samples has been seen as an unfortunate tendency. The generality of one's research findings should not be assumed and it is always a good idea to move one's research into new populations and even new geographical locations. This does not mean that initial research based on a very restricted sampling of possible recruits is of no value, but it does mean that when research findings are beginning to cohere, then it is incumbent on researchers to test the research findings in diverse settings. This may involve using systematically different samples and methodologies. In this example, we see how Byrne extended his work on attitude similarity and liking by replicating it in a systematically varied selection of countries and cultures.

Background

A number of studies in the United States using the same methodology in various groups of people have found that we evaluate more positively a stranger with similar attitudes than one with dissimilar attitudes. The aim of this study by

Donn Byrne and his colleagues (1971) was to see whether this relationship was restricted to the United States or occurred more generally in some other countries.

Hypothesis

This aim was not expressed as a specific hypothesis but as a general question, which was 'The question to be answered is whether the response to attitude similarity–dissimilarity represents a specifically American characteristic or a general characteristic of mankind' (Byrne et al., 1971, p. 202).

If this question was phrased as a hypothesis, it would be non-directional and non-causal. It is non-directional in the sense that it is not even stated whether a difference is expected. It is non-causal in that it does not say what aspect of a culture affects whether there is a difference.

Method

Procedure

To test this aim, students were selected from two countries with highly developed economies and two countries with less-developed economies. The highly developed countries were the United States and Japan. The two less-developed countries were Mexico and India. In addition, there was a sample of Chinese American and Japanese Americans in Hawaii who were thought to represent a mid-point between the two continents of America and Asia. Figure 4.5 shows the research design.

Groups of students were asked to indicate their attitude on 15 topics. They were then given what they were told were the attitudes of another student of the same gender and similar age. They were provided with one of two sets of responses. In one set, the responses were exactly the opposite of that in the other set. For example, in one set the student enjoyed reading novels and disliked dogs as pets, whereas in the other set, they disliked reading novels and liked dogs as pets. It was not stated why two sets were used, but presumably this may have been to increase the likelihood of disagreement being found. Finally, they had to evaluate the stranger on six characteristics such as how intelligent they thought the stranger was and how much they would like the stranger. The measure of attraction was based on the two questions of how much they would like the other person and how much they would enjoy working with them.

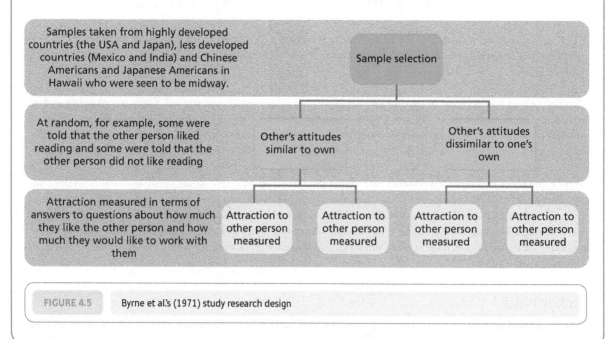

FIGURE 4.5   Byrne et al.'s (1971) study research design

Results

To test whether there were differences in how positively the stranger was evaluated in the different countries, students were first roughly divided into three groups in terms of the proportion of attitudes which were similar to the stranger's. The proportion of similar attitudes varied from 0 to 40 per cent in the first group, from 47 to 60 per cent in the second group and from 67 to 100 per cent in the third group.

Then a two-way analysis of variance (a statistical technique which is capable of analysing the effect of two variables on a dependent variable in the same analysis) was conducted on the measure of attraction in which one factor was the three levels of agreement and the other factor was the five countries. To show there was an effect of similarity on attraction, this effect needs to be statistically significant, which it was at p being equal to or less than .0001, which is very statistically significant. Looking at the mean levels of attraction in the three similarity conditions presented in their paper, we can see that attraction was highest in the most similar condition and lowest in the least similar condition.

To demonstrate that this similarity effect varied according to country, there needs to be a significant interaction between the two factors of similarity and country, which there was not. An interaction means that the effect was not the same for different types of country. Note that if there were a significant interaction effect, then the variable of country could be described as being a moderator effect. As there was no significant interaction effect, it can be concluded that this study provided no evidence for the similarity–attraction effect varying with type of country.

Authors' suggestions for future research

Byrne and his colleagues suggested that finding out what leads us to denigrating others who disagree with us may help us learn about what leads us to be more tolerant of others who disagree with us.

4.8 Conclusion

Psychologists are often interested in making generalisations about human behaviour that they believe to be true of, or apply to, people in general, though they will vary in the extent to which they believe that their generalisations apply universally. If they believe that the generalisation they are testing is specific to a particular group of people, they will state what that group of people is. Because all people do not behave in exactly the same way in a situation, many psychologists believe that it is necessary to determine the extent to which the generalisation they are examining holds for a number, or sample, of people. If they believe that the generalisation applies by and large to most people and not to a particular population, they will usually test this generalisation on a sample of people that is convenient for them to use.

The data they collect to test this generalisation will be either consistent or not consistent with it. If the data are consistent with the generalisation, the extent to which they are consistent will vary. The more consistent the data are, the stronger the evidence will be for the generalisation. The process of generalisation is not based solely on simple criteria about statistical significance. Instead it involves considerations such as the nature of the sampling, the adequacy of each of the measures taken and an assessment of the value or worth of the findings for the purpose for which they were intended.

Key points

- Psychologists are often concerned with testing generalisations about human behaviour that are thought to apply to all human beings. This is known as universalism, since it assumes that psychological processes are likely to apply similarly to all people no matter their geographical location, culture or gender.

- The ability of a researcher to generalise from their research findings is limited by a range of factors and amounts to a complex decision-making process. These factors include the statistical significance of the findings, the representativeness of the sample used, participation and dropout rates, and the strength of the findings.

- Participants are usually chosen for their convenience to the researcher, for example, because they are easily accessible. A case can be made for the use of convenience samples on the basis that these people are thought for theoretical purposes to be similar to people in general. Nonetheless, researchers are often expected to acknowledge this limitation of their sample.

- The data collected to test a generalisation or hypothesis will be either consistent with it or not consistent with it. The probability of accepting that the results or findings are consistent with the generalisation is set at 5 per cent or .05. This means that these results are likely to be due to chance five times out of 100 or less. Findings that meet this criterion or critical value are called statistically significant. Those that do not match this criterion are called statistically non-significant.

ACTIVITIES

1. Choose a recent quantitative study that has been referred to either in research you are reading or in a lecture that you have attended. What was the size of the sample used? Was a one- or a two-tailed significance level used and do you think that this 'tailedness' was appropriate? What could the minimum size of the sample have been to meet the critical level of significance adopted in this study? What was the size of the effect or association, and do you think that this shows that the predictor or independent variable may play a reasonable role in explaining the criterion or dependent variable? Are there other variables that you think may have shown a stronger effect or association?

2. Choose a finding from just about any psychological study that you feel is important. Do you think that the principle of universalism applies to this finding? For example, does it apply to both genders, all age groups and all cultures? If not, then to which groups would you be willing to generalise the finding?

CHAPTER 5

Research reports

The total picture

Overview

- Research reports are the most important means of communication for researchers. Laboratory reports, projects, master's and doctoral dissertations and journal articles all use a similar and relatively standard structure. Research reports are more than an account of how data were collected and analysed. They describe the entire process by which psychological knowledge develops.

- Research reports have certain conventions about style, presentation, structure and content. This conventional structure aids communication once the basics have been learnt.

- The research report should be regarded as a whole entity, not a set of discrete parts. Each aspect – title, abstract, tables, text and referencing – contributes something important but different.

- This chapter describes the detailed structure of a research report and offers practical advice on numerous difficulties.

5.1 Introduction

Research is not just about data collection and analysis without rhyme or reason. Its major purpose is to advance theory, concepts and information concerning psychological processes. The research report describes the role that a particular study plays in achieving these ends. A research report gives an account of the process of developing understanding and knowledge. Not surprisingly, writing a research report is a demanding and sometimes confusing business.

There are many different types of research report (laboratory report, dissertation, thesis, journal article, etc.), but generally they all adopt a broadly standard structure. Accounts of research found in psychology journals – journal articles – are the professional end of the continuum. At the other end are the research reports or laboratory reports written by undergraduate students. In between there is the final-year project, the master's dissertation and the doctoral dissertation. An undergraduate laboratory or practical report is probably 2000 words, a journal article 5000 words, a final-year project 10 000 words, a master's dissertation 20 000–40 000 words and a doctoral dissertation in Europe 80 000 words but shorter where the programme includes substantial assessment of taught courses. Conference presentations may also adopt this standard format. The common structure facilitates comprehension and absorption of the study's details. Nevertheless, it should be regarded as flexible enough to cope with different contingencies. Psychology is a diverse field of study, so it should come as no surprise to find conflicting ideas about research reports. Some of the objections to the standard approach are discussed in the chapters on qualitative methods (Chapters 18–26). Writing the research report should be seen as a constructive process which can usefully begin even at the planning stage of the research. That is, the research report is not the final stage of the research but is integral to the process. If this seems curious then perhaps you should consider what many qualitative researchers do when analysing their textual data. They begin their analysis and analytic note-taking as soon as the first data become available. Such forethought and planning are difficult to fulfil, but you should regard them as an ideal to be aimed at.

There are two main reasons why research reports can be difficult to write:

● The research report is complex with a number of different elements, each of which requires different skills. The skills required when reviewing the previous theoretical and empirical studies in a field are not the same as those involved in drawing conclusions from statistical data. The skills of organising research and carrying it out are very different from the skills required to communicate the findings of the research effectively.

● When students first start writing research (laboratory) reports they are unlikely to have read other research reports such as journal articles. There is something of a chicken-and-egg problem here. Until students have understood some of the basics of psychological research and statistics, they will find journal articles very difficult to follow. At the same time, they are being asked essentially to write a report using much the same structure as a journal article. Hopefully, some of the best students will be the next generation of professional researchers writing the journal articles.

This chapter on writing the research report comes early in this book. Other books have it tucked away at the end. But reading and understanding research papers is helped if one appreciates how and why research reports are structured as they are. Remember, writing a report should not be regarded as an afterthought but part of the process of doing research. Apart from training and educational reasons, there is little point in doing research which is not communicated to others. Regard the structure of the research report as, more-or-less, a blueprint of the entire research process, though perhaps a little more organised and systematic than the actual research itself. For example, the review of previous research (literature review) would appear to be done first, judging by most research reports – it follows the title and summary (abstract), after all. The assumption is that the new research question and hypotheses are built on the literature review. Nevertheless, most researchers would admit that they read relevant publications even while writing the final draft of their report. The research report actually prioritises what should be done in research. In contrast, for example, increasing numbers of researchers (see Chapter 24) reject the idea that the literature review should come first – some claim that only after the data have been collected and analysed should the previous research be examined to assess its degree of compatibility with the new findings. This is not sloppiness or laziness on their part. Instead, it is a desire to analyse data unsullied by preconceptions, but it does mean that building on previous research is not central to this alternative formulation. Put another way, a research report is largely the way it is because the methodology of psychology is the way it is. Departures from the standard practice serve to emphasise the nature and characteristics of the mainstream psychological method.

The conventional report structure, then, provides the building blocks of mainstream research. Good researchers integrate all of the elements into a whole – a hotchpotch of unrelated thoughts, ideas and activities is *not* required. At the same time, research reports do not give every last detail of the process but give a clear synthesis of its major and critical aspects. A research report contains a rather tidy version of events, of course, and avoids the messy details in favour of presenting the key stages logically and coherently.

Something as complex as a research report is likely to be subject to a degree of inconsistency. The requirements of different journals are not identical and often journals publish detailed style instructions for those submitting material. The American Psychological Association (APA) describes its requirements for the journals it publishes in a very substantial manual known as the *Publication Manual of the American Psychological Association* (APA, 2010). This includes the structure and writing style to be employed. Its recommendations are frequently adopted by other publishers. This helps to provide some consistency. The manual addresses all aspects of the author's manuscript including writing style, referencing style, type-face and so forth. The requirements can be a little daunting at first. You may find it helpful to study the examples of manuscripts provided by the APA which you can find at https://www.apa.org/. Click on 'Publications and databases', then choose the link to 'APA style', choose 'All topics' and then sample papers. More generally, the APA has a website with helpful resources https://www.apa.org/. Click on 'Publications and databases', then choose the link to 'APA style'. There are tutorials available on various aspects of the style aimed at students and these are well-worth looking at. (Google 'American Psychological Association style tutorial' to find them). Of course, your university may have its own recommended style for writing reports probably based on the APA style perhaps modified. Follow the recommended style for your department. Wherever practicable, we have used the style guidelines of the APA. This helps prepare students for a possible future as users and producers of psychological and other research.

5.2　Overall strategy of report writing

Structure

Reports are organised into a number of sections. The sections are generally preceded by a main heading – that is, a heading centred on the page. Do not use bold or italics for these and do not use all italics. You may use subheadings to denote subsections of each section. These subheadings are on the left hand of the page. In APA style, a psychological research report normally consists of the following sections:

- *Title page*   This is the first page and contains the title, the author and author details such as their address, e-mail address, and so forth. For a student report, this will be replaced with details such as student ID number, degree programme name and module name.

- *Abstract*   This is the second page of the report and in the APA style the heading Abstract is used.

- *Title*   This is another new page – the title is repeated from the first page but no details as to authorship are provided this time. This is to make it easier for editors to send out the manuscript for anonymous review by other researchers. The title is used in an abbreviated form if necessary as the running heading for the paper.

- *Introduction*   This continues on the same page but normally the heading 'Introduction' is omitted. It is an introduction to the problem the research study addresses. According to the APA (2010), it should explain why the problem is important, describe the relevant research and theory and give the hypotheses and how they are addressed by the research design.

- *Method*   This is a heading but usually followed by a number of secondary headings (or subheadings) such as the following as appropriate:

  - Participants – give appropriate detail of the broad characteristics of the sample

  - Materials, measures and apparatus

  - Design and procedure.

- *Results*   This heading is used in the text. The results section includes the findings from statistical analyses, tables and diagrams.

- *Discussion*   This heading is used in the text. This goes into a detailed explanation of the findings presented under results. It can be quite conjectural. In the APA style, the Conclusions you draw from your study are included under the Discussion heading. You could use a subheading within the Discussion section if you wish.

- *References*   This heading is used in the text. The reference list starts on a new page using APA style. It is an alphabetical (then chronological if necessary) list of the sources that one has cited in the body of the text.

- *Appendices*   This heading is used in the text. This is an optional section and is relatively rare in professional publications. Usually they contain material which is helpful but confusing if incorporated into the main body of the text.

This is the basic, standard structure which underlies the majority of research reports. However, sometimes other sections are included where appropriate. Similarly, sometimes sections of the report are merged *if* this improves clarity. The different sections of the structure are presented in detail later in this chapter. Figure 5.1 gives the basic structure of a psychological report.

Although these different components may be regarded as distinct elements of the report, their integration into a whole is a characteristic of a skilfully written report. In practice, this means that even the title should characterise the entire report. With only a few words at your disposal for the title, this is difficult, but nevertheless quite a lot can be done. Similarly, the discussion needs to integrate with the earlier components such as the introduction to give a sense of completeness and coherence. The title is probably the first thing read and so should orientate the reader to the report's content. The abstract (summary) overviews

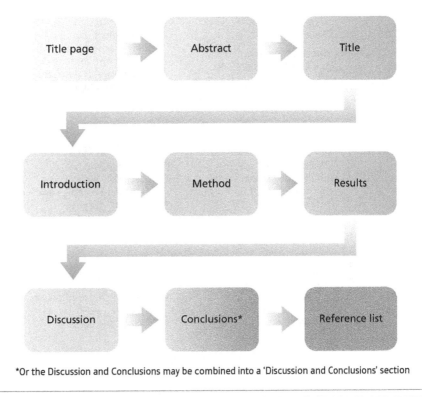

*Or the Discussion and Conclusions may be combined into a 'Discussion and Conclusions' section

FIGURE 5.1   Basic structure of a psychological report

key aspects of the research, so clarity not only creates a good impression but also helps reassure the reader that the report and the research it describes are of a high quality.

As your writing skills develop, you might wish to consult the *Publication Manual of the American Psychological Association* (2010) especially Tables 1 to 4 in its appendix (pp. 247–252), which provides lists of the information that should be included in different types of research report.

Overall writing style

Clarity is essential given the complexity of the information the report contains. Its content should be geared to the report's major themes. This is particularly the case with the introduction in which the research literature is reviewed. For example, do not simply review the research in the chosen field but, instead, choose to discuss studies most relevant to the issues directly raised by your research. Bear in mind the following points concerning style (as summarised in Figure 5.2):

- Keep sentences short and as simple as possible. Sentences of 8–10 words are the optimum for readability. Check carefully for sentences over, say, 20 words in length. The reader will have forgotten the beginning of the sentence by the time the end is reached! With modern word processing, it is possible to check for sentence length. In Microsoft Word, for example, the spelling and grammar checker can do this and it is possible to get readability statistics by selecting the appropriate option. If you have concerns about sentence length then you should consider using this facility. (Readability statistics are based on such features as average sentence length. As such they provide a numerical indication of stylistic inadequacies.)

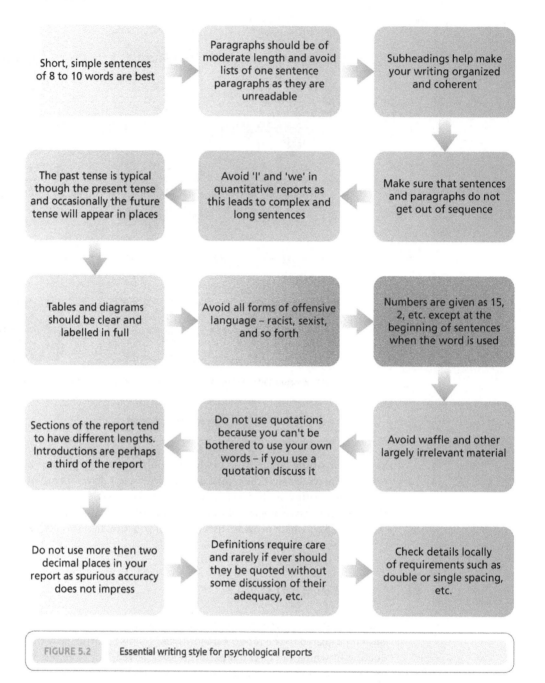

FIGURE 5.2   Essential writing style for psychological reports

- Paragraphing needs care and thought. A lack of paragraphing makes a report difficult to read. Ideally a paragraph should be no more than about half a printed page. Equally, numerous one-sentence paragraphs make the report incoherent and unreadable. Take a broad look at your work. Break up any very long paragraphs. Combine very short paragraphs, especially those of just one or two sentences.

- Subheadings are often useful in addition to the conventional main headings. Subheadings should indicate precisely what is contained within that section – and what should not be. Even if you delete the subheadings before submitting the final report, using them as provisional signposts will help you to write a report in which the material is in a meaningful order. If you think that your draft report is unclear, try to put in subheadings. This can also help you spot whether any material is out of order.

- Make sure that sentences are in a logical order. It is easy to allow them to get slightly out of order.

- It is normally regarded as inappropriate to use personal pronouns such as 'I' and 'we' in a research report, as it creates an overly wordy style. For example: 'We gave the participants a questionnaire to complete.' However, care is needed here, as simply avoiding the personal pronoun might result in the following equally unwieldy version: 'Participants were given a questionnaire to complete'. It is preferable and neater to reframe the sentence using the active voice: 'Participants completed a questionnaire.' Using the active voice rather than the passive is neater, saves words and has greater impact on the reader.

- The dominant tense in a research report will be the past tense. This is because the bulk of the report describes completed activities in the past (e.g. 'The questionnaire measured two different components of loneliness'). That is, the activities completed by the researcher when collecting, analysing and interpreting data take place in the past and are no longer ongoing. Other tenses are, however, sometimes used. The present tense is often used to describe the current beliefs of researchers (e.g. 'It is generally considered that loneliness consists of two major components . . .'). Put this idea into the past tense and the implications are clearly different (e.g. 'It was generally considered that loneliness consists of two major components . . .'). The future tense is also used sometimes (e.g. 'Clarification of the reasons for the relationship between loneliness and lack of social support will help clinicians plan treatment strategies').

- Remember that the tables and diagrams included in the report need to communicate as clearly and effectively as the text. Some readers will focus on tables and diagrams before reading the text, since these give a quick overview of what the research and the research findings are about. Too many tables and diagrams are not helpful and every table and diagram should be made as clear as possible by using headings and clear labels.

- Avoid racist and sexist language, and other demeaning and otherwise offensive language about minority groups. The inclusion of this in a professional research report may result in the rejection of the article or substantial revision to eliminate such material (see Box 5.1). The APA style tutorial gives various examples of language to avoid.

- Numbers should be expressed as figures, e.g. 27, 35, 42, etc., in most of the text except where they occur as the first words of the sentence or are less than 10. The APA recommends avoiding beginning sentences with figures for reasons of clarity. In this case, we would write 'Twenty-seven airline pilots and 35 cabin crew completed the alcoholism scale'.

- Keep your report reasonably compact. Do not waffle or put in material simply because you have it available. It is not desirable to exceed word limits, so sometimes material has to be omitted. Excess length can be trimmed simply by judicious editing. A quarter or even a third of words can be edited out if necessary while retaining key content.

- Do *not* include quotations from other authors except when it is undesirable to omit them (see Box 5.7). For example, you may wish to question what a previous writer has written and only by quoting directly can its nuances be communicated.

- Generally, introductions are the longest section of a research report. Some authorities suggest about a third of the available space should be devoted to the introduction but adjustments may be needed according to circumstances. Research that collects data on numerous variables may need more space devoted to the results section.

- A good rule-of-thumb is to give the results of calculations to two decimal places or less, as the APA recommends. Avoid spuriously implying a greater degree of accuracy than psychological data usually possess. Whatever you do, be consistent. You need to understand how to round to two decimals. Basically, if the original number ends with a figure of 5 or above then we round up, otherwise we round down. So 21.4551 gives 21.46 rounded, whereas 21.4549 gives 21.45 rounded. If whatever you have calculated can have a value of above one, then any calculation less than one should be written as 0.45, etc. If what you have calculated cannot have a value of greater than 1, then omit the figure before the decimal point. A correlation coefficient would be written as .32 because its maximum value is 1.0.

- Psychological terms may not have a standard definition that is accepted by all researchers. Consequently, you may find it necessary to define how you are using terms in your report. Always remember that definitions in psychology are rarely definitive and they are often problematic in themselves.

- Regarding layout, normally the recommendation is to double-space your work and word-process it. According to the APA, 12-point Times New Roman is preferable. However, check local requirements on these matters. Leave wide margins for comments. The underlying assumption behind this is that the report is being reviewed by another person. A report that will not be commented upon might not require double spacing. Check the local rules where you are studying.

| Box 5.1 | Talking Point |

Avoiding bias in language

Racism, sexism, homophobia and hostility to minorities such as people with disabilities violate psychological ethics. Racist, sexist and other forms of unacceptable modes of expression (e.g. homophobic) are to be avoided in psychological writings as elsewhere. They may lead to the material being rejected for publication. There is no simple list of dos and don'ts to be avoided. They can manifest themselves in multiple ways which may well change with time. For example, Howitt and Owusu-Bempah (1994) trace the history of racism in psychology and its change over time. The appalling racism of psychology from a century ago is readily identified as such; it is harder to recognise in current psychology. For detailed examples of racism in psychology see Owusu-Bempah and Howitt (1995) and Howitt and Owusu-Bempah (1990). A useful first-step towards elimination of unacceptable ideas in your writing is to undergo specialised awareness training. This is increasingly available in universities and many work locations. In this way, the inadvertent propagation of your racial, sexist, and other biases may be minimised.

A few examples of what to avoid are:

- Writing things like 'the black sample . . .' can readily be modified to 'the sample of black people . . .' or, if you prefer, 'the sample of people of colour . . .'. In this way, the most important characteristic is drawn attention to: the fact that you are referring to people first and foremost who also happen to be black. You might also wish to ask why one needs to refer to the race of people at all.

- Avoid referring to racial (or gender or other) characteristics of participants which are irrelevant to the report's substance. For example, 'Female participant Y was a black lone-parent . . .'. This contains the elements of a stereotypical portrayal of black people as being associated with father absence and 'broken families'.

- Do not refer to man, mankind or social man, for example. These terms do not make people think of man and woman but of men only. Words like 'people' can be substituted. Similarly, referring to 'he' contributes to the invisibility of women.

Careful thought and consideration should be given when writing about any group that is disadvantaged or discriminated against. People with disabilities should be treated with dignity in the choice of language and terms used. So, for example, the phrase 'disabled people' is not acceptable and should be replaced with 'people with disabilities'. The APA website contains in-depth material on these topics – race and ethnicity, gender and disabilities. Should your report touch on any of these, you are well advised to consult the Association's guidance. The APA website is found at https://www.apa. org/. Click on 'Publications and databases', then choose the link to 'APA style', choose 'All topics' and then 'Bias-free language'.

5.3   Sections of the research report in detail

■ Title

The title is *not* used as a heading or subheading. Often it is given twice – once on the separate title page and again just before the introduction.

The title of a research report serves two main purposes:

- To attract the attention of potential readers. This is especially the case for professional research reports, since the potential reader becomes aware of the research by seeing the title in a database or by browsing through the contents of a journal.

- To inform the reader of the major features of the research paper. In other words, it summarises the report in 12 words or less (although 20 words might be used if necessary). This includes any subheading.

A good understanding of your research is needed in order to write a good title. Try writing your title as soon as you can even prior to completing your data collection. This first attempt is likely to be clumsy and too wordy and so needs honing into shape. Anyone familiar with your research plan may be able to reformulate your initial effort if necessary. The following suggestions may help you write a clear and communicative title for your work:

- Phrases such as 'A study of . . .', 'An investigation into . . .' and 'An experiment investigating . . .' would normally not be included in well-written titles, since they are not really informative and take up precious words.

- Avoid clever or tricky titles which, at best, merely attract attention. So titles like 'The journey out of darkness' for a report on the effectiveness of therapy for depression fails the informativeness test. It may be excellent for your first novel but not any of your psychology research reports. Better titles might include 'Effectiveness of cognitive behavioural therapy in recovery from depression during long-term imprisonment'. It tells us that the key dependent variable is depression, that the population being researched is long-term prisoners, and that the main independent variable is cognitive behavioural therapy. Occasionally, you may come across a title which is tricky or over-clever but nevertheless communicates well. For example, one of us published a paper with the title 'Attitudes do predict behaviour – in mails at least'. The first four words clearly state the overriding theme of the paper. The last four words do not contain a misprint but an indication that the paper refers to letter post. Another example from another study is 'Deception among pairs: "Let's say we had lunch and hope they will swallow it!"' The best advice is to avoid being this smart.

- If all else fails, one can concentrate on the major hypothesis being tested in the study (if there is one). Titles based on this approach would have a rudimentary structure something like 'The effects of [variable A] on [variable B]' or 'The relationship between [variable A] and [variable B]'. A published example of this is 'The effects of children's age and delay on recall in a cognitive or structured interview'. The basic structure can be elaborated as in the following published example: 'Effects of pretrial juror bias, strength of evidence and deliberation process on juror decisions: New validity evidence of the juror bias scale scores'. The phrase 'Effects of . . .' may create some confusion. It may mean 'the causal effect of variable A on variable B' but not necessarily so. Often it means 'the relationship between variable A and variable B'. 'The effects of' and 'the relationship between' are sometimes used interchangeably. It is preferable to restrict 'Effects of' to true experiments and 'Relationships between' to non-experiments.

Abstract

The abstract is probably best given this heading in a student's report, and it is recommended in the APA publication manual for professional writing. Since the abstract is a summary of major aspects of the research report, normally it is written after the main body of the report has been drafted. This helps prevent the situation in which the abstract refers to things *not* actually in the main body of the report. Since the abstract is crucially important, expect to write several drafts before it takes its final shape. The brevity of the abstract is one major reason for the difficulty. The key thing is that the abstract is a (fairly detailed) summary of *all* major aspects of the research report. The maximum number of words allowed varies but limits of 150–250 words are typical for journal articles. With space available for only 10–20 short sentences, inevitably the abstract has to be selective. Do *not* cope with the small number of words available to you by concentrating on just one or two aspects of the whole report; for example, the hypotheses and the data collection method used would be insufficient on their own. When writing an abstract, you should take each of the major sections of the report in turn and summarise the key features of each. There is an element of judgement in this, but a well-written abstract will give a good overview of the contents of the report.

It is increasingly common to find 'structured abstracts'. The structure may vary but a good structure would be the following four subheadings:

- Purpose

- Method

- Results

- Discussion (perhaps concentrating on the main conclusions).

This structure ensures that the abstract covers the major components of the research. You could use it to draft an abstract and delete these headings after they have served their purpose of concentrating your mind on each component of the research. Box 5.2 summarises these important points.

Although this does not apply to student research reports, the abstract (apart from the title) is likely to be all that potential readers have available in the first instance. Databases of publications in psychology and other academic disciplines usually include just the title and the abstract together with details of the publication. Hence, the abstract is very important in a literature search – it is readily available to the researcher, whereas obtaining the actual research report can take some time. Computer data base searches are very quick and easy and often the article may be quickly downloaded. However, having a summary in the form of an abstract is far quicker to read than the original article though

Box 5.2   Practical Advice

Important points to summarise in the abstract

Ideally, the following should be outlined in the abstract. Normally, subheadings are *not* used except in structured abstracts, though this rule may be broken if necessary. They are given here simply for purposes of clarity.

- *Introduction* This is a brief statement justifying the research and explaining the purpose, followed by a short statement of the research question or the main hypotheses. The justification may be in terms of the social or practical utility of the research, its relevance to theory, or even the absence of previous research. Probably no more than 30 per cent of the abstract will be such introductory material.

- *Method* This is a broad orientation to the type of research that was carried out. Often a simple phrase will be sufficient to orient the reader to the style of research in question. So phrases like 'Brain activity was studied using PET (positron emission tomography) and FMRI (functional magnetic resonance imaging) . . .', 'A controlled experiment was conducted . . .', 'The interview transcripts were analysed using discourse analysis . . .' and 'A survey was conducted . . .' suggest a great deal about the way in which the research was carried out without being wordy.

- *Participants* This will consist of essential detail about the sample(s) employed, for example, 'Interview data from an opportunity sample consisting of young carers of older relatives was compared with a sample of young people entering the labour market for the first time, matched for age'.

- *Procedure* This should identify the main measures employed, for example, 'Loneliness was assessed using the shortened UCLA loneliness scale. A new scale was developed to measure social support'. By stipulating the important measures employed, one also identifies the key variables. For an experiment, in addition it would be appropriate to describe how the different conditions were created (i.e. manipulated), for example, 'Levels of hunger were manipulated by asking participants to refrain from eating or drinking for one hour, three hours and six hours prior to the experiment'.

- *Results* There is no space in an abstract for elaborate presentations of the statistical analyses that the researcher may have carried out. Typically, however, broad indications are given of the style of analysis, for example, 'Factor analysis of the 20-item anxiety scale revealed two main factors', 'The groups were compared using a mixed-design ANOVA' or 'Binomial logistic regression revealed five main factors which differentiated men and women'. Now these statistical techniques may be meaningless to you at the moment but they will not be to most researchers. They refer to very distinct types of analysis, so the terms are very informative to researchers. In addition, the major findings of the statistical analysis need to be reported. Normally, this will be the important, statistically significant features of the data analysis. Of course, sometimes the lack of significance is the most important thing to draw attention to in the abstract. There is no need and usually no space to use the succinct methods of the reporting of statistics in the abstract. So things like $[t(17) = 2.43, p < .05]$ are rare in abstracts and best omitted.

- *Discussion* In an abstract, the discussion (and conclusions) need to be confined to the main things that the reader should take away from the research. As ever, there are a number of ways of doing this. If you have already stated the hypothesis, then you need do little other than confirm whether or not this was supported, given any limitations you think are important concerning your research, and possibly mention any crucial recommendations for further research activity in the field.

it is not a substitute for eventually reading that article. A badly written abstract may deter some researchers from reading the original research report and may cause others to waste effort obtaining a report which is not quite what they expected it to be.

Since the abstract provides a summary of the entire paper, having read the abstract, the reader will know what to expect in the report and this speeds up and simplifies the task of reading. First impressions are important, so writing the abstract should not be

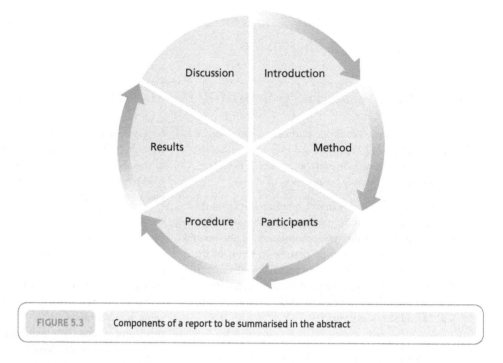

FIGURE 5.3   Components of a report to be summarised in the abstract

regarded as drudgery but as a way of giving an impression of how good your full report is likely to be. Get it wrong, and the reader may get the impression that you are confused and muddled – bad news if that person is giving you a grade or possibly considering your work for publication.

You will find examples of abstracts in any psychology journal. Figure 5.3 shows the aspects of a report to be summarised in the abstract.

Introduction

Usually, the introduction to a report is *not* given a heading or subheading – to do so merely states the obvious. The introduction sets the scene for the research, the analysis and discussion which follow it. In effect, it explains why your chosen research topic deserves researching and the importance of the particular aspect of the topic you have chosen to focus on. Just being interested in the topic is not a good or sufficient reason for doing research in academic terms. Normally you should make the intellectual case for doing the research, not your personal reasons. Justifications for a particular research topic include the following:

- There is a need to empirically test ideas that have been developed in theoretical discussions of the topic. In other words, the advancement of theory may be offered as full or partial reasons for engaging in research.

- There is a pressing concern over a particular issue which can be informed by empirical data. Often social research is carried out into issues of public concern, but the stimulus may, instead, come from the concerns of organisations such as health services, industry and commerce, the criminal justice system and so forth.

- There is an unresolved issue arising out of previous research on a topic which may be illuminated by further research – especially research which constructively replicates the earlier research.

The introduction contains a *pertinent* review of previous research and publications on the topic in question, partly to justify or contextualise the new research. One explains the theoretical issues, the problems with previous research, or even the pressing public interest by reference to what other researchers have done and written before. Research is regarded as part of a collective enterprise in which each individual contribution is part of and builds on the totality. The keyword is *pertinent* – or relevant – previous research and publications. Just writing vaguely about the topic of the research using any material that is to hand is not appropriate. Incorporate things which directly lead to your research as it is described later in the report. In other words, the literature review needs to be in tune with the general thrust of your research. That it is vaguely relevant is not a good reason for the inclusion of anything, and you may well find that such an unfocused review is counterproductive as it may imply that your literature search is inadequate.

Secondary sources, for example a description given in a textbook, may sometimes cause students problems. Secondary sources often contain insufficient detail about, say, a particular study or theory. Consequently, students lack the necessary detail to incorporate into their writings. Sometimes they introduce errors through reading into the secondary source things they would not if they had consulted the original. There is no easy way around this other than reading sources that cover the topic in depth. Ideally this will be the original source but some secondary sources are better than others.

The introduction should consistently and steadily lead to a statement of the aims of your research and to the hypotheses (though there is some research for which hypotheses are either not possible or inappropriate). There is a difference between the aims and the hypotheses. Aims are broad, hypotheses more specific. For example, 'the aim of this study was to investigate gender differences in conversation', but a hypothesis used in the paper might be 'Males will interrupt more than females in mixed-gender dyads'.

It is generally but not always the case that the introduction is written in the past tense. The past perfect tense describes activities which were completed in the past. *I ran home, the car broke down, the CD finished playing,* are all examples of the past tense. Unfortunately, the past tense cannot always be used – sometimes to do so would produce silly or confusing writing. For example, the sentence 'The general consensus among researchers is that loneliness is a multifaceted concept' is in the present tense. The past tense cannot convey the same meaning. 'The general consensus among researchers was that loneliness is a multifaceted concept' actually implies that this is no longer the general consensus. One needs to be aware of such pitfalls. However, since most of the material in the introduction refers to completed actions in the past, most of it will be in the past tense. Sentences like 'Smith and Hardcastle (1976) showed that intelligence cannot be adequately assessed using motor skills alone' refer to past events. Similarly, 'Haig (2004) argued for the inclusion of "waiting list" control groups in studies of the effectiveness of counselling' cannot be expressed well using a different tense.

Putting all of this together, a typical structure of an introduction is as follows:

- A brief description of the topic of the research.

- Key concepts and ideas explained in some detail or defined if this is possible.

- Criticisms given of aspects of the relevant research literature together with synthesis where the literature clearly leads to certain conclusions.

- A review of the most important and relevant aspects of the research literature.

- A discussion of theory pertinent to the research.

- A description and discussion of the key variables to be explored in your research.

List your aims and hypotheses as summary statements at the end of the introduction. Box 5.3 discusses the use of abbreviations.

Box 5.3   Talking Point

Abbreviations

Abbreviations should be used with caution in a research report. Their main advantage is brevity. Before the days of computerisation, typesetting was very expensive, and the use of abbreviations saved some considerable expense. This is no longer the case. Student writing rarely benefits from the use of abbreviations. If they are used badly or inappropriately, they risk confusing the reader, who may then feel that the student is confused.

The major disadvantage of abbreviations is that they hamper communication and readability. Ss, DV, *n*, SD and SS are examples of abbreviations that were sometimes included in reports. The trouble is that we assume that the reader knows what abbreviations refer to. Stating the meaning of an abbreviation early in the report (for example,

'The dependent variable (DV) was mental wonderment (MW)') does not entirely solve this problem. The reader may not read your definition or they may forget the meaning of the abbreviation the next time it appears. Acronyms for organisations can similarly tax readers unnecessarily. Acronyms are commonly used by those inside an organisation but outsiders may be unfamiliar with them. The APA (2010) in the *Publications Manual* recommends the use of abbreviations only in circumstances where their use helps communication. So things which are usually abbreviated, and thus are familiar in an abbreviated form, should be abbreviated – such as when you succinctly report your statistical findings (for example, $t(27) = 2.30$, $p = .05$).

■ Method

This is a major heading. The method section can be tricky to write, since the overall strategy is to provide sufficient information for another researcher to replicate your study precisely. Nevertheless, space constraints mean that the minutiae of your procedure cannot be included. Clearly getting the balance between what to include and what to omit is difficult. Too much detail and the report becomes dense, unclear and difficult to read. Too little detail and significant aspects of the research may be difficult for other researchers to reproduce. Sufficient detail will mean that the reader has a clear understanding of what you did – they could probably replicate the research, more or less. In a sense, it is rather like a musical score: broadly speaking, the musicians will know what and how to play, but they will have to fill in some of the detail themselves. Inevitably, the method section contains a greater density of detail than most other sections, which tend to summarise and present an overview.

The method section may include as many as six or more sub-sections if the procedures are especially complex. These include:

- Participants (sometimes archaically referred to as subjects)

- Materials or apparatus (or even both)

- Procedure (always)

- Design (possibly)

- Stimuli (if these require detailed description)

- Ethical considerations (recommended).

Of these, design and stimuli would only be used when they are not simple or straightforward; it is a matter of judgement whether to include them or not. One approach would be to include them in the early draft of your report. If they seem unnecessary

Box 5.4	Key Ideas

Independent and dependent variables

In student research reports, quite commonly independent variables (IV) and dependent variables (DV) are identified although this is rare in professional research reports. It is probably useful for students new to research to do this. One problem in professional research is that the independent variables and dependent variables are often interchangeable. This is especially the case in regression analyses. There is no necessary assumption that there is a causal link at all. The value of the independent variable is merely expected to be related to affect that of the dependent variable. However, in controlled experiments (see Chapter 9), the independent variable is always the variable(s) defined by the experimental manipulation(s).

So, if the level of anger in participants is manipulated by the experimenter, anger level is the independent variable. In an experiment, any variable that might be expected to be affected by, for example, varying the level of anger is called a dependent variable. The dependent variable is the one for which we calculate the means and standard deviations, etc. In a controlled or randomised experiment, the independent variable is expected to have a direct effect on the scores of the dependent variable, i.e. it is a causal relationship. This is not the case with non-randomised research, where all that can be established is whether there is an association or relationship between the independent and the dependent variables.

or if you write very little under them (just a few sentences) then they can be combined quickly with a few mouse clicks on the word processor. An ethical considerations section is becoming increasingly common and is required in some professional writings. Students should only carry out research which uses well-established, ethically sound procedures. Including an ethics section demonstrates that the ethical standing of the research has been considered.

Normally, the methods heading is given as a centred major title but not in italics or bold in the APA system. The section subheadings are subheadings and are aligned to the left margin. It is usual to go straight from the methods heading to the participants subheading with no preamble.

Participants

This sub-section should contain sufficient information so that the reader knows how many participants you had in total in each condition of the study. Sufficient detail about the characteristics of the participants is needed to make clear the likely limitations on generalising the findings. Given that much student research is conducted on other students, often the description will be brief in these cases. It is old-fashioned (and misleading; see Box 5.5) to refer to those taking part in your research as subjects. Avoid doing so. Once in a while the word subjects will occur in relation to particular statistical analyses which traditionally used the term (e.g. within-subjects analysis of variance). It is difficult to change this usage.

We would normally expect to include the following information to describe the participants:

- The total number of participants.

- The numbers of participants in each of the groups or conditions of the study.

- The gender distribution of the participants.

- The average age of the participants (group by group if they are not randomly allocated to conditions) together with an appropriate measure of the spread of the characteristic (for example, standard deviation, variance or standard error – these are equally understandable to most researchers and more or less equivalent in their implications).

- Major characteristics of the participants or groups of participants. Often this will be university students, but other research may have different participant characteristics, for example, preschool children, visitors to a health farm, etc. These may also be presented in numerical form as frequencies.

- How the participants were contacted or recruited initially.

- How the participants were selected for the research. Rarely are participants formally sampled using random sampling in psychological research. Convenience sampling is much more common (see Chapter 13).

- It is good practice, but not universal, to give some indication of refusal rates and dropout rates for the participants. Refusal rates are the numbers of people asked to take part in the research but refusing or otherwise failing to do so. Dropout rates are the numbers who initially take part but nevertheless fail to complete all of the stages. Sometimes this is known alarmingly as 'the mortality rate' or the 'experimental mortality'.

- Any inducements or rewards given to participants to take part in the study. So, for example, giving the participants monetary rewards or course credits would be mentioned.

■ Materials or apparatus

The materials or apparatus section describes psychological tests, questionnaires, laboratory equipment and other such resources involved in the research. Once again, the idea is to supply enough detail so that another researcher could essentially replicate the study and the reader gains a clear impression of the questionnaires, tests and other equipment used. The amount of detail needed is a matter of judgement but this will improve with practice and reading professional research reports. The degree of detail provided should

---

Box 5.5   Talking Point

No subjects – just participants

One of the most misleading psychological terms ever was the 'subject'. Monarchs have subjects, psychologists do not. In the early days, terms such as reactors, observers, experimentees and individuals under experiment were used. Then the researchers frequently used other professors, students and friends which may explain the absence of the somewhat negative term 'subjects' (Danziger, 1985). Although the term 'subjects' had a long history in psychological writings, it gives a false, misleading picture since it construes a powerful researcher and a manipulated subject. Research long ago dispelled this myth – research participants are not passive but actively involve themselves in the research process. They form hypotheses about the researcher's hypotheses, for example. In the 1990s, psychological associations such as the APA and the British Psychological Society recommended or insisted on the modern term 'participant' for their journals.

be sufficient to help the reader understand your procedure but not so much that the wood cannot be seen for the trees. Usually trivial or irrelevant details such as the make of the stopwatch used, the colour of the pen given to participants, and the physical dimensions of the research setting are omitted unless especially pertinent. For example, in a study of the effects of stress on feelings of claustrophobia then the physical dimensions of the laboratory would be very important and ought to be given. Provide details of the manufacturers of specialised laboratory equipment which is not generally available.

It is also usual to give details of any psychological tests and measures employed. This would probably include the official name of the test, the number of items used in the measure, broadly what sorts of items are employed, the response format, basic information that is available about its reliability and validity, and any adjustments or alterations you may have made to it. Of course, you may have constructed a psychological measure yourself (see Chapter 15), in which case, more detail should be provided about the items included in the questionnaire and so forth. It is unlikely that you would include the full test or measure in the description, though this may be included in an appendix if space is available. The method section is normally the place where one outlines how questionnaires, etc., were quantified (scored) or coded.

Remember that the materials and apparatus in a sense operationalise the variables being measured and give some insight into the procedures employed. Hence, the importance of a clearly structured description of materials and apparatus. Jumble this and your reader will have trouble reaching a clear understanding.

Procedure

The procedure subsection describes the essential sequence of events through which you put participants in your research. The key word is sequence and this implies a chronological order. It may help to make a list of the major steps in your research separately before beginning to write the procedure. Make sure that you put down the key stages in order – and to allocate space proportional to their importance. Provide the instructions given to participants in the research together with variations in their content (e.g. between experimental and control group). Do not forget to include debriefing and similar aspects of the research in this section.

Also you should mention any randomisation that was involved – random allocation to conditions, for example, or randomisation of the order of presentation of materials or stimuli. A true experimental design will always include randomisation.

Recommending a length for the procedure section is difficult as studies vary enormously in their complexity. A complex laboratory experiment may take rather more space to describe than a simple study of the differences in mathematical ability in male and female psychology students. Given that published studies may use procedures very similar to your own, you should gain a better idea of what to include and exclude by reading these – though this is not an invitation to plagiarise the work of others.

Finally, it may be appropriate to describe broadly the strategy of the statistical analysis especially, for example, if specialised computer programs or statistics are employed. This is in order to give an overview should one seem necessary.

Design

This optional subheading may be helpful for complex research designs. A diagram may be appropriate if it is difficult to explain in words alone. The design subheading may be desirable when one has a between-subjects or repeated measures design, for example (see Chapters 9 and 10).

Results

This is a major, centred heading, not in italics or bold. Written largely in the past tense, the results section mainly concerns the outcome of the statistical analysis. Statistical outcomes from research are *not* the same as the psychological interpretation of your statistical findings. Your statistical analyses should then normally be reported without conjecture about their psychological meaning – simply write what the findings are. So if you find that there is a significant difference between two groups of participants, in the results section you draw no further inferences other than that there is a statistical difference. Since the statistical analysis is often related to the hypotheses, one appropriate writing strategy is to present the results hypothesis by hypothesis and indicate whether the statistical evidence supports each hypothesis.

The results section will vary in length according, in part, to the numbers of variables and the type of statistical analysis employed. It is not usual to go into a detailed description of the statistical tests used – just the outcome of applying them. There is no need to mention how the computations were done whether using a statistical package such as SPSS or a calculator. Nevertheless, if unusual software or a very uncommon statistical technique is used then provide essential details. Sometimes this would be put in the methods section but not necessarily so.

One common difficulty occurs when writing about research not involving hypothesis or theory testing, that is, largely, when carrying out non-experimental research. Separating the results section from the following section (the discussion) sometimes is problematic. Ultimately, clarity of communication has to take precedence over the standard conventions and some blurring of the boundaries of the standard structure for reports may be necessary.

Statistical analyses, almost without exception in psychology, consist of two components:

- *Descriptive statistics* which describe the characteristics of your data, for example, the means and standard deviations of all of your variables, where appropriate.

- *Inferential statistics* which indicate whether your findings are statistically significant in the sense that they are unlikely to be due to chance. The correlation coefficient and *t*-test are examples of the sorts of inferential statistics that beginning researchers use.

Both descriptive and inferential statistics should be included in the results section, though not to the extent that they obstruct clarity. The statistical analysis is not a description of everything that you did with the data but the crucial steps in terms of reaching the conclusions that you draw.

Conventionally, the raw, unprocessed data are *not* included in the results section. The means, standard deviations and other characteristics of the variables are given instead. This convention is difficult to justify other than on the basis of the impracticality of including large datasets in a report. Students should always consider including their raw data in an appendix, most conveniently as a computer file. All researchers should remember the ethical principle of the APA which requires that they should make their data available to any other researcher who has a legitimate reason to verify their findings.

Tables and diagrams are common in the results section. They are not decorations. They are a means of communicating one's findings to others. We suggest a few rules-of-thumb for consideration:

- Keep the number of tables and diagrams to a minimum. If you include too many, they become confusing. Worse still, they become irritating. For example, giving separate tables for many very similar variables can exhaust the reader. Far better to have fewer tables and diagrams but ones which can allow comparisons, say, between the variables in your study. In the analysis of your data, you may have produced many different tables, graphs and the like, but those were for the purpose of exploring and analysing the data and many of them will be of little interest to anyone other than the researcher. So do not try to include tables and diagrams which serve no purpose in the report.

- Always take care about titling and labelling your tables and diagrams. If the title and labels are unclear, the whole table or diagram may become meaningless. It is easy to use misleading or clumsy titles and labels. Revise them if necessary.

- Some readers will look at tables and diagrams before reading your text, so for them the quality of the tables and diagrams is even more important. Those used to statistical analyses will be drawn to such tables, as they are often more quickly absorbed than what is written in the text.

- Tables and diagrams should be numbered in order of appearance.

- Tables and diagrams must be referred to in your text. At the very least you need to say what the table or diagram indicates – the important features of the table or diagram.

- Tables and diagrams are readily created in SPSS, Excel and other computer programs. The difficulty is that the basic versions (the default options) of tables and diagrams are often unclear or in some other way inadequate. Tables may need simplifying to make them more accessible to the reader. They need editing and consolidation to achieve clarity. Much student work is spoilt by the use of computer-generated tables and diagrams without modification. Think very carefully before using any unmodified output from a computer program in your report.

A glance at any psychology research journal will indicate that very little space is devoted to presenting each statistical analysis. Succinct methods are used which provide the key elements of the analysis simply and clearly. These are discussed in detail in the companion book *Understanding statistics in psychology with SPSS,* Chapter 17 (Howitt & Cramer, 2020). Basically the strategy is to report the statistical test used, the sample size or the degrees of freedom, and the level of statistical significance. So you will see things like:

$$t(14) = 1.55, p < .14$$
$$(t = 2.37, N = 16, p < .05)$$
$$(t = 2.37, df = 14, p = 5\%)$$

All of these are much the same. The first is in APA style. They all give the statistic used, an indication of the sample size(s) or degrees of freedom (df), and the level of statistical significance.

Discussion

This is a main heading without italics or bold. The past tense will dominate the discussion section, but the present and future tenses can occur depending on what is being discussed. The material in the discussion should not simply rehash that in the introduction. You may need to move material between the introduction and the discussion sections to ensure this. A previous study may be put in the discussion rather than the introduction. A research report is no place for repetition.

If your study tested a hypothesis, then the discussion is likely to begin with a statement indicating whether or not your hypothesis was supported by the statistical analysis (i.e. the results). Remember that most statistical analyses are based on samples, so the findings are probabilistic, not absolute. Consequently, researchers can only find their hypotheses to be supported or not supported. Research based on samples (i.e. most research) cannot definitely establish the truth or falsity of the hypothesis, since a different sample might produce different outcomes. Consequently, it grates to read that the hypothesis was 'proved' or 'not proved'. This suggests that the writer does not fully understand the nature of statistical inference.

The discussion section will include your new findings as well as ones from previous research. Your research findings should be compared to those of previous research which they may completely, partially or not support. The differences between your research and past research should be described alongside the similarities. Hopefully, previous research findings may help cast light on your findings. Where there is a disparity between the new findings and previous findings, attempts should be made to explain the disparity. Different types of sample, for example, may be the explanation, though it may not be as simple as that. The task is to explain how our knowledge is extended, enhanced or complicated by the new findings.

Of course, different methodological features may explain disparities between studies. Notice that we use the term methodological features rather than methodological flaws. The influence of methodological differences cuts both ways – different studies may have different strengths and weaknesses. Try to identify what these may be. Describe the role of different methodological features as accurately and precisely as possible – merely pointing out that the samples are different is not very helpful. Better to explain the ways in which the sample differences could produce the differences in the findings. And, of course, it is ideal if you can recommend improvements to your methodology.

Avoid including routine commonplaces. The inclusion of phrases such as 'A larger sample size may result in different findings' is not much of a contribution, especially when you have demonstrated large trends in your data.

The discussion should also include any theoretical implications which may be consequent on your findings. Perhaps the theory is not quite as rigorous as you initially thought. Your findings may have wider implications and suggesting further research or practical applications desirable. Suggest further research or practical applications wherever possible.

Finally, the discussion should lead to your conclusion. This should be the main things that the reader should take away from your research. In APA style there is no requirement for a separate *Conclusions* subheading. It can seem clumsy or awkward to do so, especially in non-experimental research. But this is a matter of choice – and judgement which improves with experience.

References

This major heading should start on a fresh page. Academic disciplines consider it important to provide evidence in support of all aspects of the argument that you are making. The research evidence itself and your interpretation of it are perhaps the most striking component of this. However, your report will make a lot of claims over and above this based on the research and writings of others. You will claim that the relevant theory suggests something, that previous studies indicate something else, and so forth. In order for your report's reader to be in a position to check the accuracy or truth of your claims, it is essential to refer them to the sources of information and ideas that you use. Simply suggesting that 'research has found that' or 'it is obvious that' is not enough. So it is necessary to identify the source of your assertions. This includes two main components:

- You cite your sources in the text as, say, (Wolf & Richards, 2019). 'Wolf & Richards' gives the names of the authors and 2019 is the work's year of publication (dissemination). There are many systems in use for giving citations, but in psychology it is virtually universal to use this author–date system. It is known as the Harvard system and we will use the American Psychological Association's version of this, which is employed throughout the world by psychological associations and others.

● You provide an alphabetical list of references by the surname of the first author. There is a standard format for the references, though the detail varies whether it is a book, a journal article, an Internet source, etc. The reference contains sufficient information for a reader to track down and, in most cases, obtain a copy of the original document.

■ The citation

While the citation in the text seems to be very straightforward, there are a number of things that you need to remember:

● The citation should be placed adjacent to the idea which it supports. Sometimes confusion can be caused because the citation is placed at the end of a sentence which contains more than one idea which is misleading as to which ideas the citation concerns. So think very carefully about where you insert the citation. You may choose to put it anywhere appropriate within the sentence. The best choice depends on the sentence's structure and its complexity.

● Citations should be to your source of information. So, if you read the information in Smith (2020) then you should really cite this as the source. The trouble is that Smith (2020) may be a secondary source which is explaining, say, Freud's theory of neurosis, Piaget's developmental stages, or the work of some other theorist or researcher.

● Students rarely have time or resources to read all of the original publication from which the idea came, although it is a good idea to try to read some of it. So, although uncommon in professional report writing, student research reports will often contain citations such as (Piaget, 1953, as cited in Atkinson, 2018). In this way, the ultimate source of the idea is acknowledged but the actual source is also given. To attribute to Atkinson ideas which the reader might recognise as those of Piaget might cause some confusion and would be misleading anyway. The *Publication Manual of the American Psychological Association* indicates that you should give the reference to Atkinson (2018) but not Piaget (1953).

● Citations with three to five authors should give all the authors' names the first time the reference is cited. Subsequently, only the first author need be given followed by 'et al.' which is plural. Citations of references with six or more authors should always give the first author's name followed by 'et al.'. If there are several references with the same lead author, you may need to add the second (and third, etc.) author's name to avoid confusion. The 'et al.' should be followed by a full stop to indicate an abbreviation. In the past, et al. was in italics to indicate a foreign word or phrase but, increasingly, this is not done. APA style does not italicise et al. though it does so generally for foreign words.

● Student writing (especially the literature review) can become very stilted, because they write things like 'Brownlow (1989) argued that children's memories are very different from those of adults. Singh (1996) found evidence of this. Perkins and Ottaway (2002) confirmed Singh's findings in a group of 7-year-olds'. The problem with this is that the sentence structure is repetitive and the person whom you are citing tends to appear more important than their ideas. It is a good idea to keep this structure to a minimum and bring their contributions to the fore instead. For example: 'Memory in children is different from that of adults (Brownlow, 1989). This was initially confirmed in preschool children (Singh, 1996) and extended to seven-year-olds by Perkins and Ottaway (2002)'. Both versions contain similar information but the second illustrates a greater range of stylistic possibilities.

● When you cite several sources at the same time (Brownlow, 1989; Perkins & Ottaway, 2002; Singh, 2002, 2003), do so in alphabetical order (and then date order if necessary).

- Sometimes an author (or authors) has published more than one thing in a particular year and you want to cite all of them. There may be two papers by Kerry Brownlow published in 2009. To distinguish them, the sources would be labelled Brownlow (2009a) and Brownlow (2009b). The order of the title of the books or articles in the report determines which is 'a' and which is 'b'. In the references, we include the 'a' and 'b' after the date so that the sources are clearly distinguished. Remember to do this as soon as possible to save you from having to reread the two sources later to know which contains what. If you were citing both sources then you would condense things by putting (Brownlow, 2009a, b).

- It is important to demonstrate that you have read up-to-date material. However, do not try to bamboozle your lecturers by inserting citations which you have not read in a misguided attempt to impress (see Box 5.7). Your lecturer will not be taken in. There are many tell-tale signs such as citing obscure sources which are virtually impossible to obtain.

Some of the problems associated with citations and reference lists can be avoided by using reference and citation bibliographic software such as RefWorks, Endnote or Mendeley (see Chapter 7). These are basically databases in which you enter essential details such as the authors, the date of publication, the title of the publication, and the source of the publication. One can also insert notes as to the work's contents. It is also possible to download details of publications directly from some Internet databases of publications, which can save a lot of typing. If you do this properly and systematically, it is possible to use the programs in conjunction with a word processing program to insert citations at appropriate places and to generate a reference list. Even more useful is that the software will do the citations and reference list in a range of styles to suit different journal requirements, etc. The researcher can easily change the references to another style should this be necessary.

The main problem with these programs may be their cost. Bona fide students may get heavily discounted rates. Increasingly, universities have site licences for this sort of bibliographic software, so check before making any unnecessary expenditure. They are obviously most useful to professional researchers who may use the same references in a number of different publications.

Box 5.6	Talking Point

Citing what you have not actually read!

The basic rules of citations are clear. You indicate the source of the idea in the text just like this (Conqueror, 1066) and then put where the information was found in the reference list. What do you do if you have not read Conqueror (1066) but got the information from a secondary source such as a textbook because you were not able to get your hands on Conqueror (1066)? Now one could simply cite the textbook from which the information came, but this has problems. If one cites the secondary source, it can read as if the secondary source was actually responsible for the idea, which they were not. So what does the student do?

There are three, probably equally acceptable, ways of doing this in student work:

- In the main body of the text, give the original source first, followed by 'as cited in' and then the secondary source (Conqueror, 1066, as cited in Bradley, 2004). Then in the reference list simply list Bradley (2004) in full in the usual way. This has the advantage of keeping the reference list short. This is the procedure that the American Psychological Association (2010) recommends.

- In the main body of the text, give the original source (Conqueror, 1066). Then in the reference list insert:

Conqueror, W. (1066). Visual acuity in fatally wounded monarchs. *Journal of Monocular Vision Studies, 5,* 361–372. Cited in Bradley, M. (2004). *Introduction to Historical Psychology.* Hastings: Forlorn Hope Press.

This method allows one to note the full source of both the primary information and the secondary information.

- In the main body of the text, give the original source (Conqueror, 1066). Then in the reference list insert:

Conqueror, W. (1066). Cited in Bradley, M. (2004). *Introduction to Historical Psychology.* Hastings: Forlorn Hope Press.

This is much the same as the previous version, but the full details of the original source are not given.

It might be wise to check which version your lecturer/supervisor prefers. Stick to one method and do not mix them up in your work.

■ Reference list

References will be a main heading at the end of the report. There is a difference between a list of references and a bibliography. The reference list only contains the sources which you cite in the main body of your report. A bibliography lists everything that you have read which is pertinent to the research report – even if it is not cited in the text. Normally, just include the references you cite, unless it is indicated to you to do otherwise.

Items in reference lists are *not* numbered in the Harvard system (APA style); they are merely given in alphabetical order by surname of the author.

One problem with reference lists is that the structure varies depending on the original source. The structure for books is different from the structure for journal articles. Both are different from the structure for Internet sources. Unpublished sources have yet another structure. In the world of professional researchers, this results in lengthy style guides for citing and referencing. Fortunately, the basic style for references boils down to just a few standard patterns. However, house styles of publishers differ. The house style of Pearson Education, for example, differs slightly from the APA style recommended and used in this book. We would recommend that you obtain examples of reference lists from journal articles and books which correspond to the approved style in your department. These constitute the most compact style guide possible.

Traditionally, journal names were underlined, as were book titles. This was a printer's convention to indicate that emphasis should be added. In the final printed version, it is likely that what was underlined appeared in *italics*. When preparing a manuscript for publication, this convention is generally no longer followed. If it is a report or thesis, then it is appropriate for you to use italics for emphasis instead of the underline. Do not use underlining in addition to italics. The use of italics has the advantage of being less cluttered and has a positive advantage for readers with dyslexia, as underlining often makes the text harder to read. Actually, avoid underlining throughout.

The following indicates the style you should adopt for different kinds of source.

Books

Author's family name, comma, author's initials or first name, year of publication in brackets, stop/period, title of book in lower case except for the first word (or words where the first letter is usually capitalised) as in the following example, stop/period, place of publication, colon, publisher details:

Howitt, D. (2015). *Forensic and criminal psychology* (5th ed.). Harlow: Pearson.

Journal articles

Author's family name, comma, author's initials or first name, year of publication in brackets, stop/period, journal article title in lower case except for the first word, stop/period, title of journal in italics or underlined, with capitals on first letter of first word and significant parts of the title, comma, volume of journal in italics, comma, first and last page of journal article not italicised. Issue numbers are not required unless each issue starts with the page numbered 1 which is unusual. Without the issue number, it is unclear where the paper is located. Issue numbers are also useful for journal websites where the issue numbers but not the page numbers are given:

Schopp, R. F. (1996). Communicating risk assessments: Accuracy, efficacy, and responsibility. *American Psychologist, 9,* 939–944.

The latest version of the APA's *Publication Manual* recommends that the number that is used to identify the electronic source of an article (a DOI or Digital Object Identifier) should be presented at the end of the reference where it is available. However, this may not be necessary for student work. With the DOI added, the above reference would read as follows:

Schopp, R. F. (1996). Communicating risk assessments: Accuracy, efficacy, and responsibility. *American Psychologist, 9,* 939–944 doi:10.1037/0003-066X.51.9.939

Web sources

Material which is sourced from the Internet basically needs the source identified using the http (hypertext transfer protocol) address. So for a book or other material to be found on the Internet the following style would be adopted:

Williams, F. (2002). Communications made clear. Retrieved from http://www.23232221222

Box 5.7   Talking Point

Use of quotations

The most straightforward approach to quotations is *never* to use them. It is generally best to put things in your own words. The use of quotations tends to cause problems, because they are often used as a substitute for explaining and describing things oneself. The only legitimate use of quotations, we would suggest, is when the wording of the quotation for some reason does not lend itself to being put in your own words. Sometimes the nuances of the wording are essential. The use of a quotation really should always be accompanied by some commentary of your own. This might be a critical discussion of what the quoted author wrote.

Quotations should always be clearly identified as such by making sure that they appear in quotation marks and indicating just where they appear in the original source. There are two ways of doing this. One is simply to put the page number into the citation: (Smith, 2004: 56). This means that the quotation is on page 56 of Smith (2004). Alternatively, the pages can be indicated at the end of the quotation as (pp. 45–46) or (p. 47). This latter style is favoured by the APA.

■ Appendix or appendices

Appendices are a rarity because they are space-consuming. Appendices do help to avoid cluttering up the main body of the report with overlong detail that might confuse the reader and hamper good presentation. So, for example, it may be perfectly sensible to include your 50-item questionnaire in your report, but common sense may dictate that it is put at the very end of the report in the section for appendices. In this case, it would be usual to give indicative examples of questions under 'Materials' and refer the reader to the appendix. Similarly, the multitude of tables that the statistical analysis may generate may fit uncomfortably in the results section but have a more suitable location in an appendix. Remember the following:

● Refer to the relevant appendix in the main text where appropriate.

● Number and title the appendices appropriately in order to facilitate their location.

● You may be evaluated partly on the basis of the contents of your appendices. It is inappropriate simply to place a load of junk material there.

> ## Box 5.8   Research Example
>
> # Layout of a brief paper from an American Psychological Association journal
>
> Dickson, J. M., Moberly, N. J., & Kinderman, P. (2011). Depressed people are not less motivated by personal goals but are more pessimistic about attaining them. *Journal of Abnormal Psychology, 120,* 975–980.
>
> While this chapter has been largely about how, as a student, you should write up your reports of your research, the ultimate aim is to develop research skills to a professional level. Professional researchers publish their research in research journals, of which there are many in psychology. Quite often, student research is of sufficient quality to be published – especially final-year research projects in psychology degrees, and the work of postgraduate students perhaps even more so. So you may well find that you are asked to prepare your work with your research supervisor for publication. Of course, such publications look extremely good in one's CV. The format of a journal article is exacting and writing your first journal article (and your last) is a demanding activity. Here we will look at a published study in the light of the requirements of professional publication in journals.
>
> The *Publication Manual of the American Psychological Association* (APA) recommends how a research paper should be written and structured for publication in the journals published by the association. Many other psychological journals stipulate that the APA's suggestions should be followed. APA journals often publish papers which are longer than 5000 words and which typically describe a number of related studies rather than just one. Some of their journals, such as the *Journal of Abnormal Psychology*, permit the publication of brief reports, which should not be longer than 5000 words. This word limit includes everything such as the title, the references and any notes. The *Publication Manual* was last revised in 2010, so papers are expected to follow these latest recommendations.
>
> The APA *Publication Manual* has a Checklist for Manuscript Submission which lists some of the requirements that a paper needs to meet before it is considered for publication. There is also a free tutorial on their website which outlines the basics of the APA style. Visit https://www.apa.org/. Click on 'Publications and databases', then choose the link to 'APA style'
>
> →

and use the search facility to find the tutorial. Not all of the requirements are explicitly listed in this checklist, so other sources need to be consulted. One of the checklist specifications is that each paragraph should be longer than a single sentence but not longer than a double-spaced page (which is shorter than from the start of this box to here). The length of text on a page, of course, is governed by the size of the margins, the font style and the font size, so we need information on these in order to follow this guideline. The margin is specified in the checklist as being at least 1 inch (2.54 cm) wide and in the *Publication Manual* (p. 229) as being that wide all round. However, the font style and font size are not presented in the checklist. One font style recommended both in the fifth slide of the basics tutorial and in the *Publication Manual* is Times New Roman. The *Publication Manual* (p. 228) specifies the preferred font size as being 12 point.

The general structure of psychological quantitative research papers has remained fairly consistent over a number of decades. However, how authors write their paper and what journal editors and reviewers want in them vary, so how these papers are presented may also differ somewhat. Because the *Publication Manual* has recently been revised and because most students are going to write research reports of about 5000 words, a brief paper recently published in an APA journal has been selected as a research example. This study was carried out by Joanne Dickson and two collaborators and was published in 2011 in the *Journal of Abnormal Psychology*. You might like to download a copy via your university library.

The title is expressed as a sentence which describes the main finding. It consists of 16 words, which is slightly more than the 12 recommended in the checklist and the *Publication Manual* (p. 23). The title is 'Depressed people are not less motivated by personal goals but are more pessimistic about attaining them'. A shorter alternative title might have been 'Depression and personal goal motivation'. This simply lists the main variables of the study and is appropriate for a non-experimental study, which was the type of study carried out. This kind of title had been used by the first author in two previous papers cited and illustrates its use. The title is written in upper and lower case with the first letter of the major words capitalised (or in upper case) as described in the *Publication* Manual.

The Abstract is 198 words long, which is within the 150–250-word limit suggested in the checklist. The *Publication Manual* (p. 27) acknowledges that, although the length of the Abstract typically ranges from 150 to 250 words, it varies according to the journal, and the guidelines for the journal should be followed.

The paper is divided into five main sections. The approximate percentage of each of these sections is 26 for the Introduction, 27 for the Method, including the three footnotes, 17 for the Results, including the tables, 14 for the Discussion and 16 for the References. Each paragraph is indented. The indentation is specified as being half an inch (1.27 cm) in the basics tutorial and in the *Publication Manual* (p. 229). The first section is the Introduction or Background to the study. The hypotheses are stated in the final paragraph of the Introduction. The remaining four sections have centred subheadings, which are in bold as specified in the basics tutorial and the *Publication Manual* (pp. 62–63). This is the first level of headings. The seventh slide of the basics tutorial and the Publication Manual describes the format of five levels of headings.

The Method section is divided into three subsections entitled Participants, Materials and Procedure. This is the second level of headings. These are flush with the margin (also called flushed left, left aligned and left justified) and are in bold and in upper and lower case. The Results section is also subdivided into subsections, which is optional. The subheadings in this section represent the analyses of the different variables such as the 'Number and Importance of Goals' and the 'Goal Outcome Likelihood'.

The Participants and Materials subsections of the Method section are further subdivided into sections which reflect a third level of headings. These are paragraph headings which are indented, in bold, and end with a period or full stop. The first letter of the first word and of names is capitalised (or in upper case) and the rest of the word is in lower case. The Participants section has two of these third-level headings, 'Depressed group.' and 'Control group.' The Materials section has four of them such as 'Goal task.' and 'Goal ratings.'

The final section is the References and lists 25 references. They are presented in what is called the hanging indent paragraph style where the first line of the reference is flush with the margin and the remaining lines are indented. A DOI (Digital Object Identifier) is given at the end of each journal article, such as in the following:

Dickson, J. M., & MacLeod, A. K. (2004b). Anxiety, depression and approach and avoidance goals. *Cognition and Emotion, 18*, 423–430. DOI: 10.1037/a0023665

The *Publication Manual* (p. 175) states that when there are between three and five authors, all the authors should be listed the first time they are mentioned. Subsequently, only the first author need be mentioned followed by 'et al.'. This rule is followed apart from one reference which is referred to only once and is presented as 'Pizzagalli et al.'.

There are two tables in this paper. They are consecutively numbered with Arabic numerals and the tables are referred to in the text. The first line of the title of the table is simply 'Table' followed by the number of the table and is not italicised. The second line of the title is italicised and is in upper and lower case. There are no vertical lines in the table and each column has a heading.

5.4   Conclusion

Writing effective research reports requires a range of skills and so is one of the most exacting tasks that any researcher can undertake. In truth, few professional researchers would have all of the style detail committed to memory and some aspect or other will regularly have to be checked. The complexity, initially, can be very daunting for students who may feel overwhelmed by having so much to remember. It takes time to become skilled at writing research reports. The key points are as follows:

- Make sure that the text is clearly written with attention paid to spelling and grammar.

- Keep to the conventional structure (title, abstract, introduction, method, etc.) as far as is possible at the initial stages.

- Ensure that you cite your sources carefully and include all of them in the list of references.

- Carefully label and title all tables and diagrams. Make sure that they are helpful and that they communicate effectively and efficiently.

- Remember that reading some of the relevant research literature will not only improve the quality of your report but also quickly familiarise you with the way in which professionals write about their research.

Box 5.9   Practical Advice

Some essentials of the research report at a glance

Title

- This is normally centred and is often emphasised in bold.

- It should be informative about the study.

- It is usually of no more than 12 words but is sometimes longer.

- Avoid uninformative phrases such as 'A study of'.

- A good title will orient the reader to the contents of the research report.

→

Abstract or summary

- Usually 100–200 words long but this may vary.

- The abstract is a summary of all key aspects of the report. It should include key elements from the introduction, method, findings and conclusions.

- The abstract is crucial in providing access to your study and needs very careful writing and editing.

Introduction

- This is not normally given a heading in research reports, unless it is a very long thesis.

- It should be a focused account of why the research was needed. All material should be pertinent and lead to the question addressed by the research.

- It should contain key concepts and ideas together with any relevant theory.

- Avoid using quotations unless their content is to be discussed in detail. Do not use them as a substitute for writing in your own words.

- Consider using subheadings to ensure that the flow of the argument is structured. They can easily be removed once the report is complete.

- Make sure that the argument leads directly to the aims of your research.

Method

- This is a centred, main heading.

- Sections should include participants, materials or apparatus, procedure, design where not simple, stimuli and (recommended) ethical considerations.

- It is difficult to judge the level of detail to include. Basically the aim is to provide enough detail that another researcher could replicate the study in its essence.

- Do not regard the structure as too rigid. It is more important to communicate effectively than to include all sections no matter whether they apply or not.

Results

- This is a centred, main heading.

- The results are intended to be the outcomes of the statistical analysis of the data. Quite clearly, this is not appropriate for many qualitative studies.

- Do not evaluate the results or draw general conclusions in the results section.

- Remember that tables and diagrams are extremely important and need to be very well done. They help provide a structure for the reader. So good titles, labelling and general clarity are necessary.

- Do not leave the reader to find the results in your tables and diagrams. You need to write what the results are – you should not leave it to the reader to find them for themselves.

Discussion

- This is a centred, main heading.

- This is the discussion of the results. It is not the discussion of new material except in so far as the new material helps in understanding the results.

- Do not regurgitate material from the Introduction here.

- Ensure that your findings are related back to previous research findings.

- Methodological differences between your study and previous studies which might explain any disparities in the findings should be highlighted. Explain why the disparities might explain the different outcomes.

- The discussion should lead to the conclusions you may wish to draw.

References

- This is a centred, main heading.

- It is an alphabetical list of the sources that you cite in the text of the report.

- A bibliography is not normally given. This is an alphabetical list of all the things that you have read when preparing the report.

- The sources are given in a standard fashion for each of journal articles, books, reports, unpublished sources and Internet sites. Examples of how to do this are given in the subsection on the Reference list above.

- Multiple references by the same author(s) published in a single year are given letters, starting with 'a', after the date to distinguish each (e.g. 2004a, 2004b).

- If you wish to cite sources which you have only obtained from secondary sources (i.e. you have not read the original but, say, read about it in textbooks) then you must indicate this. Box 5.6 gives several ways of doing this.

Appendix

- Appendix (or appendices) is a centred, main heading usually beginning on a fresh page.

- These are uncommon in published research reports largely because of the expense. However, they can be a place for questionnaires and the like. For student reports, they may be an appropriate place for providing the raw data.

- The appendices should be numbered (Appendix 1, Appendix 2, etc.) and referred to in the main text. For example, you may refer to the appropriate appendix by putting it in brackets: '(see Appendix 5)'.

- As much work should go into the appendices as other components of the report. They should be clear, carefully structured and organised.

Tables and diagrams

- Tables and diagrams should be placed in the text at appropriate points and their presence indicated in the text (with phrases such as 'see Table 3'). In work submitted for publication, tables and diagrams are put on separate pages after the references. Their approximate location in the text is indicated by the phrase 'Insert Table 5 about here' put in the text and centred.

- Tables and diagrams are key features of an effectively communicating report. There should be a balance between keeping their numbers low and providing sufficient detail.

- They should be numbered and given an accurate and descriptive title.

- All components should be carefully labelled, for example, axes should be given titles, frequencies indicated to be frequencies, and so forth.

- Avoid using a multitude of virtually identical tables by combining them into a clear summary table or diagram.

- Remember that well-constructed tables and diagrams may be helpful to the reader as a means of giving an overview of your research.

Key points

- The research report draws together the important features of the research process and does not simply describe the details of the empirical research. As such, it brings the various aspects of the research process into an entirety. It is difficult to write because of the variety of different skills involved.

- There is a basic, standard structure that underlies all research reports, which allows a degree of flexibility. The detail of the structure is too great to remember in full, and style manuals are available even for professional researchers to help them with this.

- Although quality of writing is an important aspect of all research reports, there are conventions which should be followed in all but exceptional circumstances. For example, most of the report is written in the past tense, avoids the personal pronoun, and uses the active, not passive, voice.

- A research report needs to document carefully the sources of the evidence supporting the arguments made. Citations and references are the key to this and should correspond to the recommended format.

- All parts of the report should work to communicate the major messages emerging from the empirical research. Thus, the title and abstract are as important in the communication as the discussion and conclusions.

ACTIVITIES

1. Photocopy or print an article in a current psychology journal held in the library. Draw up a list of any disparities between this article and the conventional structure described in this chapter. Why did the author(s) make these changes?

2. Find a recent practical report that you have written. Using the material in this chapter, list some of the ways in which your report could be better.

CHAPTER 6

Improving your quantitative write-up

Overview

- The complex business of writing a research report takes time and much thought and practice. It involves the full range of knowledge and skills employed by research psychologists. So there is a limit to speeding up the process by reducing it to a set of 'rules' to follow. Nevertheless, this chapter provides easy-access practice in thinking about report writing.

- A fictitious laboratory report is provided concerning a study essentially replicating Loftus and Palmer's (1974) classic research into the effect of questioning on memory for an eye-witnessed incident.

- This should be read in conjunction with Chapter 5 which systematically explains the important features of a good research report. If you wish to check back as you read through this fictitious research study, Box 5.9 may be especially useful.

- Problems with the report are indicated.

- A 'model' write-up of the same study is given. This is not intended as 'perfection' but as a way of indicating some of the features of better than average work. This write-up gives a clear impression of a student who is on top of the research that they conducted, understands the basics of report writing, and can accurately communicate ideas.

- Whenever you are working on a research report, try to have a pertinent published article as a model for your work. It serves as a guide to how things are done. Make sure that the selected article is from a core psychology journal which follows APA guidelines.

6.1　Introduction

The bottom line is that writing an entirely satisfactory research report is far from easy, as we saw in Chapter 5. Each new study you do throws up new writing problems, often little like those you have encountered previously. Most professional researchers find research report writing demanding because of its complexity and the need to condense so many things into one relatively brief document. Not surprisingly, then, students who may have never read a journal article find the process problematic. Although everyone will improve with practice, problems will remain no matter how sophisticated one becomes. The novice researcher will almost certainly be daunted by the task of reading research reports in psychology journals. However, these are the work of seasoned professionals and have been through the high level quality-checking procedures known as peer-review. In this, referees (respected researchers) comment upon manuscripts submitted to journals. Usually there are two such experts who will identify problems and may insist that they are corrected, for example, prior to publication. Worse still, they may reject the manuscript. Student work is largely their own unaided effort and lecturers do not review drafts before submission for marking.

In this chapter, there is a sample research report which contains numerous errors and inadequacies but also some good features for you to learn by. Your task is to spot the good and bad elements. You may identify more than we mention – there is always a subjective aspect to the assessment of any academic work. Although we considered giving a real example from student work, this is unlikely to demonstrate a sufficiently wide range of problems. So, instead, we have written a report which features problems in various areas to illustrate the kinds of error that can occur as well as some of the good points. You should do your best to identify what these problems are and to make suggestions about how to correct them. We have indicated many problem areas in the research report by the use of superscript numbers which hint at where we think there are problems. You may well find additional problems overlooked by us. Our ideas as to how the report could be improved follow the report. It is unlikely that your own research reports will have such detailed feedback as we have provided for this example, so if the assessor of your report has not commented on aspects of it, do not assume that these parts cannot be improved.

One classic study in modern psychology is Elizabeth Loftus's study of memory (Loftus & Palmer, 1974) in which participants were shown a video of a vehicle accident and then asked one of a variety of questions such as 'About how fast were the cars going when they smashed each other?'. Other participants were given words such as hit, collided, bumped or contacted instead of smashed. Participants gave different estimates according to the particular version of the question asked. Those who were asked about the speed when the cars 'contacted' gave an average estimate of 31 miles per hour, but those asked about cars which 'smashed' estimated a speed 10 miles per hour faster than this, on average. The argument is, of course, that this study demonstrates that memory can be modified by the kind of question asked after the event.

We have decided to write up a fictional study which replicates Loftus and Palmer's study but with some variations. The report is brief compared with, say, the length a journal article would be, and in parts it is truncated as a consequence. Nevertheless, it is about 2000 words in length, which is probably in the middle of the range of word-lengths that lecturers demand. Of course, it would be too short for a final-year project/dissertation. Nevertheless, many of the points we make here would apply to much more substantial pieces of writing.

It would be wise to familiarise yourself with the contents of Chapter 5 on writing research reports before going further. Then read through the following practical report, carefully noting what you believe to be the problems and the good qualities of the report. Finally, make suggestions about how the report could be improved. It is easier to spot problems than to identify good elements, so you will find that the former dominate in our comments. Remember that the superscript numbers shown at various points of the report roughly indicate the points at which we have something to comment on. Notice that our research report introduces a novel element into the study which was not part of the Loftus and Palmer original. It is a variation on the original idea which might have psychological implications. Depending on the level of study, the expectation of originality for a student's work may vary. Introductory-level students are more likely to be given precise instructions about the research that they are to carry out, whereas more advanced students may be expected to introduce their own ideas into the research that they do. We have taken the middle ground in which the student has been encouraged to replicate an earlier study, introducing some relevant variation in the design. This is often referred to as a constructive replication.

You will find it helpful to have a copy of a relevant journal article to hand when you write your own reports. You may find such an article helpful when studying our fictitious report. It would be a good idea to get hold of Loftus and Palmer's original report, though this may have variations from what is now the accepted style of writing and presenting research reports. Of course, whichever journal article you use should reflect the mainstream psychology style of writing reports. So make sure that you use an article from a core psychology journal, as other disciplines often have different styles. Remember, too, that research reports in the field in which you carry out your research will be good guides for your future research reports. Of course, the important thing is to use them as 'guides' or 'models' – do not copy the material directly, as this is bad practice which is likely to get you into trouble for plagiarism (see Chapter 8).

6.2   Poorly written quantitative report

Particular issues are flagged with numbers in the report and then explained in detail in the analysis that follows. As you are not familiar with this report, it may be better to read it first before deciding what is wrong with it. However, if you notice what are obvious errors on first reading, do make a note of them.

Practical Report

A smashing study: Memory for accidents[1]

Ellie Simms

Abstract

This was an investigation of the way in which people remember accidents after a period of time has elapsed.[2] Seventy-six subjects took part in the study in which they were shown a video of a young man running down the street and colliding with a pushchair being pushed by a young woman.[3] Following this, the participants were given one of two different questionnaires. In one version, the participants were asked a number of questions, one of which they were asked was 'How fast was the young man running when he injured the baby in the pushchair?' and in the other condition subjects were asked 'How fast was the young man running when he bumped into the pushchair?'[4] Participants were asked to estimate the speed of the runner in miles per hour. The data was analysed[5] using the SPSS computer program which is a standard way of carrying out statistical analyses of data. The data estimated speeds were put in one column of the SPSS spreadsheet.[6] The difference between the conditions was significant at the 5 per cent level of significance with a sample size of 76 participants.[7] So the null hypothesis was disproven and the alternate hypothesis proved.[8]

→

Introduction

I wanted to carry out this study because eyewitness evidence is notoriously unreliable. There are numerous cases where eyewitness evidence has produced wrong verdicts. It has been shown that most of the cases of false convictions for crimes have been established by later DNA evidence involved eyewitness testimony.[9] Loftus and Palmer (1974) carried out a study in which they asked participants questions about an accident they had witnessed on a video. The researchers found that the specific content of questioning subsequently had an influence on how fast the vehicle in the accident was going at the time of the collision.[10] Much higher speeds were reported when the term 'smashed' was used than when the term 'contacted' was used. Numerous other researchers have replicated these findings (Adamson et al, 1983; Wilcox and Henry (1982); Brown, 1987; Fabian, 1989).[11] However, there have been a number of criticisms of the research such as the artificial nature of the eyewitness situation which may be very different from witnessing a real-life accident which is likely to be a much more emotional experience. Furthermore, it is notoriously difficult to judge the speed of vehicles.[12] In addition, participants may have been given strong clues as to the expectations of the researchers by the questions used to assess the speed of the impact. While Loftus and Palmer conclude that the content of the questions affected memory for the collision, it may be that memory is actually unaffected and that the influence of the questioning is only on the estimates given rather than the memory trace of the events.

Rodgers (1987)[13] argued that the Loftus and Palmer study had no validity in terms of eyewitness research. Valkery and Dunn (1983) stated that the unreliability of eyewitness testimony reflects personality characteristics of the eyewitness more than the influence of questioning on memory. Eastwood, Marr and Anderson, 1985 stated that memory is fallible under conditions of high stress. Myrtleberry and Duckworth, 1979 recommend that student samples are notoriously unrepresentative of the population in general and should not be used in research into memory intrusions in order to improve ecological validity. Pickering (1984) states that 'Loftus and Palmer have made an enormous contribution to our understanding of memory phenomenon in eyewitness research'.[14]

Loftus and Palmer's study seems to demonstrate that the wording of a question can influence the way in which memories are reported.[15] In order to make the research more realistic, it was decided to replicate their study but with a different way of influencing recall of the events. It was reasoned that memory for events such as accidents may be influenced by the consequence of an accident such as whether or not someone was injured in the accident. Does the consequence of an accident influence the way in which it was perceived?[16] This was believed to be a more realistic aspect of eyewitness behaviour than the rather unsubtle questioning manipulation employed in the Loftus and Palmer's research.[17]

It was hypothesised that an accident which results in injury to an individual will be regarded as involving more dangerous behaviour. The null hypothesis states that accidents which result in injury to individuals will be regarded as involving less dangerous behaviour.[18]

Participants[19]

Seventy-six students at the University were recruited to participate in the study using a convenience sampling method. Those who agreed to take part were allocated to either the experimental ($n = 29$) or control condition ($n = 47$).[20]

Materials and apparatus

A specially prepared video of an accidental collision between a running man and a woman pushing a pushchair with what appeared to be a baby in it. The video lasted two minutes and shows the man initially walking down a street but then he begins to run down what is a fairly crowded street. Turning a corner, he collides with the woman pushing the pushchair. The video was filmed on a digital video camera by myself with the help of other students. A Pananony S516 camera was used which features a $15 \times$ zoom lens and four megapixels image resolution. It was mounted on a Jenkins Video Tripod to maximise the quality of the recording.

The participants were given a short self-completion questionnaire including two versions of the critical question which comprised the experimental manipulation. The first version read 'How fast do you think the man was running in miles per hour when he collided with the woman with the pushchair and the baby was injured?' The second version read 'How fast do you think the man was running in miles per hour when he collided with the woman with the pushchair and baby?' The questionnaire began with questions about the gender of the participant, their age and what degree course they were taking. The critical questions were embedded in a sequence of five questions which were filler questions designed to divert the participant's attention from the purpose of the study. These questionnaires were 'What colour was the man's shirt?', 'How many people saw the collision occur?', 'What was the name of the shop outside of which the accident occurred?', 'Was the running man wearing trainers?' and 'Was the woman with the pushchair wearing jeans?'

Procedure

Participants were recruited from psychological students on the university campus.[21] They were recruited randomly.[22] It was explained to them that the research was for an undergraduate project and that participation was voluntary and that they could withdraw from the study at any stage they wished. The participants in the research were offered a bonus on their coursework of 5 per cent for taking part in three different pieces of research but that does not appear to have affected their willingness to take part in the research. Students failing to participate in research are referred to the Head of Department as it is part of their training. Participants were taken to a small psychological laboratory in the Psychology Department. A data projector was used to show them the short video of the running man and his collision with the woman with a pushchair. The video was two minutes long and in colour. After the video had been shown, the participants were given the questionnaire to complete. Finally they were thanked for their participation in the research and left.

Ethics

The research met the current British Psychological Society ethical standards and complied with the University Ethical Advisory Committee's requirements.[23] The participants were free to withdraw from the research at any time and they were told that their data would be destroyed if they so wished. All participants signed to confirm that they agreed to these requirements.

Results

Group Statistics[24]

	group	N	Mean	Std Deviation	Std Error Mean
speed	1.00	29	4.7138	1.66749	.30964
	2.00	47	3.1500	1.37161	.20007

The scores on ERS[25] were compared between the two groups using the Independent Samples t-test on SPSS.[26] SPSS is the internationally accepted computer program for the analysis of statistical data.[27] The t-test is used where there are two levels of the independent variable and where the dependent variable is a score.[28]

The mean scores for the two groups are different with the scores being higher where the baby was injured in the collision.[29] The difference between the two means was statistically significant at the .000[30] level using the t-test.[31]

$$t = 4.443^{[32]}, df = 74, p = .000^{[33]}$$

Thus the hypothesis was proven and the null hypothesis shown to be wrong.[34]

Independent Samples Test[35]

→

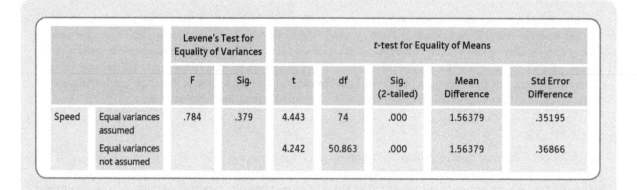

		Levene's Test for Equality of Variances		t-test for Equality of Means				
		F	Sig.	t	df	Sig. (2-tailed)	Mean Difference	Std Error Difference
Speed	Equal variances assumed	.784	.379	4.443	74	.000	1.56379	.35195
	Equal variances not assumed			4.242	50.863	.000	1.56379	.36866

Discussion and conclusions

This study supports the findings of Loftus and Palmer (1974) in that memory is affected by being asked questions following the witnessed incident.[36] Memory can be changed by events following the incident witnessed. Everyone will be affected by questions which contain information relevant to the witnessed event and their memories will change permanently.[37] In addition, it is clear that memory is not simply affected by asking leading questions of the sort used by Loftus and Palmer, but perceptions of the events leading to the incident are affected by the seriousness of the consequences of those actions.

It is not clear why serious consequences should affect memory in this way but there are parallels with the Loftus and Palmer research. When asked questions about vehicles smashing into each other then this implies a more serious consequence than if the vehicles had only bumped. This is much the same as the present research in which memories of events are affected by the injury to the baby which is an indication of the seriousness of the accident. The faster the man ran then the more likely it is that someone would get hurt.

The study provides support for the view that eyewitness evidence is unreliable and cannot be trusted. Many innocent people have spent years in prison for crimes that they did not commit because judges have not paid attention to the findings of Loftus and Palmer and many other researchers.[38]

There are a number of limitations on this study. In particular, the use of a more general sample of participants than university students would be appropriate and would provide more valid data.[39] A larger sample of participants would increase the validity of the research findings.[40] It is suggested that a further improvement to the research design would be to add a neutral condition in which participants simply rated the speed of the runner with no reference to the accident. This could be achieved by having a separate group estimate the speed of the runner.

It was concluded that eyewitness testimony is affected by a variety of factors which make its value difficult to assess.[41]

References

Adamson, P. T., & Huthwaite, N. (1983). Eyewitness recall of events under different questioning styles. *Cognitive and Applied Psychology*, 18, 312–321.[42]

Brown, I. (1987). *The gullible eyewitness*. Advances in Criminological Research.[43]

Myrtleberry, P. I. E., & Duckworth, J. (1979). The artificiality of eyewitness research: Recommendations for improving the fit between research and practice. *Critical Conclusions in Psychology Quarterly*, 9, 312–319.[44]

Eastwood, A. Marr, W. & Anderson, P. (1985). The fallibility of memory under conditions of high and low stress. *Memory and Cognition Quarterly*, 46, 208–224.[45]

Fabian (1989). *The Fallible Mind*. London: University of Battersea Press.[46]

Howitt, D., & Cramer, D. (2017). *Introduction to SPSS in psychology* (7th edn). Harlow: Pearson.[47]

Loftus, E. F., & Palmer, J. C. (1974). Reconstruction of automobile destruction: An example of the interaction between language and memory. *Journal of Verbal Learning and Verbal Behaviour*, 13, 585–589.

Pickering, M. (1984). Elizabeth Loftus: An Appreciation. *Genuflecting Psychology Review, 29*, 29–43.[48]

Rodgers, T. J. (1987). The Ecological Validity of Laboratory-based Eyewitness Research. *Critical Psychology and Theory Development, 8* (1), 588–601.[49]

Valkery, Robert, O., Dunn, B. W. (1983). The unreliable witness as a personality disposition. *Personality and Forensic Psychology, 19* (4), 21–39.[50]

Wilcox, A. R., and Henry, Z. W. (1982). *Two hypotheses about questioning style and recall.* Unpublished paper, Department of Psychology, University of Northallerton.[51]

6.3 Analysis of the report

▪ Title

1 The title is clever but not very informative as to the research you are describing. Make sure that your title contains as much information as possible about the contents of your report. Loftus and Palmer themselves entitled their study 'Reconstructions of automobile destruction: An example of the interaction between language and memory'. This is more informative but probably could be improved on, since all of the useful information is in the second part of the title. A better title might be 'The relation between memory for witnessed events and later suggestive interviewing'. This would also be a good title for our study, though it might be better as 'The influence of later suggestive interviewing on recall of witnessed events: A constructive replication of Loftus and Palmer's classic study'. An alternative title might be 'The effect of question wording on eyewitness recall'. Using the term 'effect' suggests that the study employs a true or randomised design. Note that it is not necessary to preface this title with a phrase such as 'An experimental study of' or 'An investigation into' because we can assume that the report is of a study and so this phrase is redundant.

▪ Abstract

2 The description of the purpose of the study is not accurate and precise enough. The study concerns the influences of leading questioning on memory for events, not the recall of eye-witnessed events over a period of time, as such. This may confuse the reader, as it is inconsistent with what is described in the rest of the report.

3 *Subjects* is an old-fashioned and misleading term for participants, which is the modern and accurate way of characterising those who take part in research, though you sometimes still see it. Also note that the abstract says little about who the participants were. Finally, often there are tight word limits for abstracts, so shortening sentences is desirable where possible. Changing the sentence to read 'Seventy-six undergraduates watched a video of a young man running down the street and colliding with a pushchair' corrects these three main errors and so is more acceptable.

4   The wording of these two sentences could be improved. At present the second sentence could be read to suggest that participants given the second version of the questionnaire were asked only one question, which was not the case. One way of rewriting these two sentences is as follows: 'They were then given a questionnaire consisting of six questions in which the wording of a question about how fast the man was running was varied. In one version, the baby was described as injured while in the other version there was no mention of this'.

5   The word 'data' is plural, so this should read 'data were'.

6   There is a lot of unnecessary detail about SPSS and data entry which adds nothing to our understanding of the research. This could be deleted without loss. By doing so, space would be freed for providing more important information about the study which is currently missing from the abstract. This information would include a clear description of what the hypothesis was.

7   The findings of the study are not very clear from this sentence and the reader would have to guess what was actually found. A better version would be 'The speed of the runner was estimated to be significantly faster when the baby was injured $(t(74) = 4.43, p < .001)$'. This contains more new information and presents the statistical findings in a succinct but professional manner. However, statistical values such as t and probability levels are not usually presented in abstracts mainly because of the shortness of abstracts. It is important to state whether the results being presented are statistically significant and this can be done by using the adjective 'significant' or the adverb 'significantly'. Note that the sample size is mentioned twice in the original, which is repetitive and wastes words which are tight in an abstract.

8   Hypotheses can be supported, confirmed or accepted but they cannot be proven (or disproved for that matter). It would be better to say that the research provided support for the hypothesis. But notice that the writer has not said what the hypothesis was, so how meaningful to the reader is this part of the write-up? Ideally, the main aim or hypothesis of a study should be described earlier on in the abstract. If this had been done, then we would know what the hypothesis was, in which case it would not be necessary to repeat it here. Also, the reader is left without a clear idea of what the researcher has concluded from this study. Leaving it as simply a test of a hypothesis fails to place the study in its wider context. While significance testing is usually taught in terms of the null and the alternate hypotheses, the results of research are generally more simply described in terms of whether the (alternate) hypothesis was confirmed or not. In other words, it is not necessary to mention the null hypothesis. If the alternate hypothesis is confirmed, then we can take as read that the null hypothesis has been disconfirmed.

◾ Introduction

9   There are a number of problems with these first few lines of introduction: (a) it is not the convention to write in the first person; (b) what has been written is not particularly relevant to the research that was actually carried out and so is something of a waste of space; (c) the sources of the statement are not cited, so the reader does not know where the information came from; and (d) these statements mislead the reader into thinking that the research to be described is about the fallibility of eyewitness evidence. It is not. Of course, the extent to which relevance is an issue depends on the space available and what comes later in the report. If the researcher is arguing that most of the fallibility of eyewitnesses is because of the intrusive effects of later questioning, then these introductory lines become more relevant.

10 This sentence is inaccurately expressed. The question asked did not affect the actual speed of the car. It affected the estimated speed of the car.

11 There are a number of problems with these citations: (a) they are not in alphabetical order; (b) they are not separated consistently by a semi-colon; (c) 'et al' should have a full stop after 'al' but as this is the first occurrence of the citation it would be more usual to list the authors in full; and (d) the citations are quite dated and the impression is created that the student is relying on a fairly elderly textbook for the information.

12 Not only is this comment not documented with a citation, but also it is not clear what the argument is. If we assume that the comment is true, in just what way does it imply a criticism of the original study? As it stands, the comment seems irrelevant to the point being made. It would, therefore, be better deleted.

13 It is good to indent the first line of every paragraph. This gives a clear indication as to the paragraph structure of the report. Without these indentations, it is not always clear where one paragraph ends and another begins, which makes the report harder to read. This is especially a problem where one paragraph ends at the right-hand margin at the very bottom of one page and the new paragraph begins at the start of the new page. Without the indentation the division between the two paragraphs is not clear.

14 This entire paragraph is stylistically clumsy, since it consists of the name of a researcher followed by a statement of what they did, said, wrote or thought. It is then succeeded by several sentences using exactly the same structure. The entire paragraph needs rewriting, so that the issues being discussed are the focus of the writing. Generally, avoid citing an authority at the beginning of sentences, as this poor style is the result. Discuss their idea and then cite them at the end. But there are other problems. The paragraph seems to be a set of unconnected notes which have been gleaned from some source or other without much attempt to process the material into something coherent. Just how each point contributes to the general argument being made in the report is unclear. Furthermore, be very careful when using direct quotations. The writer, in this case, has failed to give the page or pages from where the quotation was obtained. Also, it needs to be questioned just what purpose using the quotation serves. The writer could probably have said it just as clearly in their own words and there is obviously no discussion of the quotation – it is just there and serves no particular purpose. Quotations may be used, but there needs to be a good reason for them, such as where a report goes on to discuss, question or criticise what is in the quote in some way. A more minor point is that the references to Eastwood, Marr and Anderson and to Myrtleberry and Duckworth should have the date or year in brackets.

15 Why is the phrase 'seems to' used? If the study does not demonstrate what the researchers claim of it, then its validity should be questioned as part of the discussion of the material.

16 This is an interesting idea, but is it really the case that there is no relevant research to bring in at this point? Certainly no citations are given to research relevant to this point. One would look for previous research on whether the consequences of events are taken into account when assessing the seriousness of the behaviours which led to these events.

17 It is not clear how the questions used by Loftus and Palmer were unsubtle. The ways in which their question manipulation is unsubtle need to be explained. It is good to see a critical argument being used, but the presentation of the argument could be clearer.

18 The hypothesis is not stated sufficiently clearly or accurately. It might be better to begin by describing the hypothesis more generally as 'It was hypothesised that memory for a witnessed event will be affected by later information concerning the consequences of that

event'. It might be preferable to try to formulate it in a way which relates more closely to what was actually tested. For example, we might wish to hypothesise that 'The estimated speed of an object will be recalled as faster the more serious the impact that that object is later said to have had'. The null hypothesis as presented here reveals a misunderstanding of the nature of a null hypothesis. A null hypothesis is simply a statement that there is *no* relationship between two variables. It does not imply a relationship between the two variables in question. The null hypothesis is not usually presented in reports, as it is generally assumed that the reader knows what it is. It is also better to describe the hypothesis in terms of the independent and dependent variables and to state what the direction of the results is expected to be, if this can be specified. For example, we could say that 'Participants who were informed that the baby was injured were predicted to give faster estimates of running time than those who were not told this'.

■ Method

19   The main section following the Introduction is the Method section and should be titled as such. This overall title is missing from the report. The Method section is broken down into subsections which in this case start with Participants and end with Ethics. You may wish to make the distinction between sections and subsections clearer by centring the titles of the sections.

20   (a) Numbers such as 76 are written in words if they begin a sentence. (b) The way in which participants were allocated to the conditions should be clearly stated. It is not clear whether this was done randomly, systematically or in some other way. (c) Which condition is the experimental one and which condition is the control should be described clearly, as this has not been done previously. To work out which are the experimental and control groups requires that we search elsewhere in the report, which makes the report harder to read. (d) More information should be given about the participants. It should be indicated whether the sample consisted of both men and women and, if so, how many of each gender there were. In addition, the mean age of the sample should be given as well as some indication of its variability. Variability is usually described in terms of standard deviation, but other indices can be used, such as the minimum and maximum age.

21   The students were not psychological. They were psychology students.

22   In the Participants subsection, it was stated that participants were a convenience sample, which means that they were recruited at the convenience of the researcher, not randomly or systematically. In psychology, the term 'random' or 'randomly' has a specific technical meaning and should be used only when a randomised procedure is employed. If such a procedure has been used, it is necessary to describe what the population consisted of (e.g. all psychology undergraduates at that university), what the target sample was (e.g. 10 per cent of that population) and what the selection procedure was (e.g. numbering the last name of each psychology undergraduate alphabetically, generating 100 numbers randomly and then approaching the students given those numbers). When a random or systematic procedure has not been used, as seems to be the case in this study, it is not necessary to describe the selection procedure in any detail. It may be sufficient simply to state that 'An e-mail was sent to all psychology undergraduates inviting them to participate in the study' or 'Psychology undergraduates in practical classes were invited to take part in the study'.

23   This sentence is inaccurate, as the research did not meet all the ethical requirements of the BPS. For example, it is not stated that the participants were debriefed at the end of their participation, which they should have been. The previous paragraph

describes several ethically dubious procedures which the writer does not appear to acknowledge.

◼ Results

24 (a) All tables need to be given the title 'Table' followed by a number indicating the order of the tables in the report. As this is the first table in the report, it would be called Table 1. (b) The table should have a brief label describing its contents. For example, this table could be called 'Descriptive statistics for estimated speed in the two conditions'. (c) In general, it is not a good idea to begin the Results section with a table. It is better to present the table after the text which refers to the content of the table. In this case, this would be after the second paragraph where the mean scores are described. (d) SPSS tables should not be pasted into the report, because generally they contain too much statistical information and are often somewhat unclear. For example, it is sufficient to describe all statistical values apart from probability levels to two decimal places. Values for the standard error of the mean need not be presented. Notice that the table does not identify what Group 1.00 is and what Group 2.00 is. (e) Tables should be used only where doing so makes it easier to understand the results. With only two conditions it seems preferable to describe this information as text. For example, we could report the results very concisely as follows: 'The mean estimated running speed for those told the baby was injured ($M = 4.71, SD = 1.67$) was significantly faster, unrelated $t(74) = 4.43$, two-tailed $p < .001$, than for those not told this ($M = 3.15, SD = 1.37$).' (In order to be able to write this, we need to know which group in the table is Group 1.00 and which is Group 2.00.) The Results section will be very short if we report the results in this way, but this concise description of the results is sufficient for this study. There is no need to make it longer than is necessary. If our sample included a sufficient number of men and women, we could have included the gender of the participants as another variable to be analysed. If this were the case, we could have carried out a 2(condition) $\times$ 2(gender) unrelated analysis of variance (ANOVA).

25 It is generally better not to use abbreviations to refer to measures when writing up a study. If you do use abbreviations, you need to give the full unabbreviated name first, followed by the abbreviation in brackets when the measure is first mentioned. In this case, we have to guess that ERS refers to 'estimated running speed', as it has not previously been mentioned.

26 As we have discussed under number 24, we can describe the results of this study in a single sentence. The term 'unrelated t' refers to the unrelated t-test which SPSS calls the Independent Samples t-Test. In our summary sentence, it is clear that we are using the unrelated t-test to compare the mean of the two groups, so it is not necessary to state this again. We do not have to state how the t-test was calculated. We generally do not need to mention the type of statistical software used for this kind of analysis. We may only need to do this if we are carrying out some more specialist statistics such as structural equation modelling or hierarchical linear modelling that employs less familiar software than SPSS, which is unlikely for student work.

27 As we discussed under number 26, we do not usually need to mention the statistical software we used, so this sentence should be omitted. The sentence basically gives superfluous detail anyway.

28 As the t-test should be very familiar to psychologists, there is no need to describe when it should be used.

29 If it is thought advisable to present a table of the mean and standard deviation of esti-mated speed for the two groups, we need to refer to this table in the text. At present, the table is not linked to the text. We could do this here by starting this sentence with a phrase such as 'As shown in Table 1' or 'As can be seen from Table 1'. It would also be more informative if the direction of the difference was described in this sentence rather than simply saying that the means differ. Notice that this is the first sentence in the report that enables us to identify which condition is associated with the highest scores.

30 The level of statistical significance or probability can never be zero. Some readers would see a probability of .000 as being zero probability. This figure is taken from the output produced by SPSS which gives the significance level to three decimal places. What this means is that the significance level is less than .0005. For most purposes, it is sufficient to give the significance level to three decimal places, in which case some psychologists would round up the third zero to a 1. In other words, the significance level here is .001. Strictly speaking, the significance level is equal to or less than a particular level such as .001, although the symbol for this ($\leq$) is rarely used.

31 We have previously stated that the *t*-test was used, so it is not necessary to state it again.

32 It is sufficient to give statistical values other than the significance level to two decimal places. In this case, we can write that $t = 4.44$.

33 As presently displayed, these statistical values appear to hang on their own and seem not to be part of a sentence. They should be clearly incorporated into a sentence. We have already shown under number 24 how this can be concisely done by placing these values within commas.

34 As discussed under number 8, hypotheses cannot be proven or shown to be wrong. Saying that a hypothesis has been proved or disproved implies that other results are not possible. Another study might find that there is no difference between the two conditions or that the results are in the opposite direction to that found here. Con-sequently, when the results are consistent with the hypothesis, it is more accurate to describe them as being confirmed, accepted or supported rather than proved. When the results are not consistent with the hypothesis, it is better to describe them as not confirmed, not accepted or not supported rather than disproved. It is not necessary to mention the null hypothesis. If we know the results for the alternate hypothesis, we will know the results for the null hypothesis.

35 As previously mentioned under number 24, we need to label any tables to indicate what they refer to. Also, we should not simply copy or paste in tables from SPSS output. We have been able to describe succinctly the results of our analysis in a single sentence which includes the essential information from this table, so there is no need to include the table. If you want to show the results of your SPSS output, then it is better to append this to your report rather than include it in the Results section.

Discussion

36 It is usual to begin the Discussion section by reporting what the main findings of the study are. In this case, it would be saying something along the lines that 'The hypoth-esis that the memory of a witnessed event is affected by later information about the consequences of that event was supported, in that participants who were informed

that the baby was injured estimated the speed of the man running into the pushchair as significantly faster than those not told this'.

37 This assertion is not supported by any evidence. No information is presented to show that everyone was affected, let alone will be affected, or that the change was permanent.

38 No evidence is cited to support this statement. It would be difficult to test this assertion. How can we determine whether someone is innocent when the evidence is often circumstantial? How can we show that these wrong convictions were due to the way in which the witnesses were questioned? These are not easy questions to test or to carry out research on. It would be much easier to find out how familiar judges were with research on eyewitness testimony and whether this knowledge affected the way in which they made their judgements. Unless evidence can be found to support this assertion, it would be better to describe it as a possibility rather than a fact. In other words, we could rewrite this sentence as follows: 'Many innocent people may have spent years in prison for crimes that they did not commit because judges may have not paid attention to the findings of Loftus and Palmer and many other researchers'.

39 It would be better to say in what way the data would be more valid if a more general sample of participants was used. For example, we might say that the use of a more general sample would determine the extent to which the findings could be replicated in a more diverse group of people.

40 It is not stated how a larger sample would improve the validity of the findings. This would not appear to be the case. As the size of sample used in this study produced significant findings, we do not have to use a larger sample to determine the replicability of the results. However, it would be more informative if we could suggest a further study that would help our understanding of why this effect occurs or the conditions under which it occurs rather than simply repeat the same study.

41 No evidence is presented in the discussion of a variety of factors affecting eyewitness testimony, so this cannot be a conclusion. As it stands, it is a new idea introduced right at the end of the report. It is also unclear what the term 'value' means, so the writer needs to be more specific. If eyewitness testimony has been shown to be affected by various factors, it is unclear why this makes its value difficult to assess. One or more reasons need to be given to support this assertion.

References

42 It is important to use a consistent style when giving full details of the references. It is usual to italicise the title and volume number of journals. As this is done for the other journals, it should be done here.

43 Although this may not be immediately obvious, there seem to be three errors here. It is usual to italicise the names of books and journals and the titles of unpublished papers. The name of a book is followed by the place of publication and the name of the publisher. As this was not done here, it implies that the subsequent title refers to the name of a journal. If this is the case, then (a) the title of the paper should not be italicised, (b) the title of the journal should be italicised and (c) the volume number and the page numbers of the journal should be given for that paper.

44 This reference has not been placed in the correct alphabetical order of the last name of the first author. It should come after Loftus and Palmer.

45 Underlining is usually used to indicate to publishers that the underlined text is to be printed in italics. This convention was developed when manuscripts were written with manual typewriters. As it is easy to italicise text in electronic documents, there is less need for this convention. As the journal titles of the other references have not been underlined, this title should not be underlined and should be italic.

46 The initial or initials of this author are missing. The titles of books are often presented in what Microsoft Word calls 'sentence case'. This means that the first letter of the first word is capitalised but the first letters of the subsequent words are not, unless they refer to a name.

47 Although we hope that the student has used this book to help them analyse their results, they have not cited it and so it should not be listed as a reference.

48 The titles of journal papers are usually presented in sentence case. The first letter of 'Appreciation' should be in lowercase.

49 The title of this journal paper should be in sentence case, like most of the titles of the other papers. It is considered important that you are consistent in the way you present references. The number of the issue in which the paper was published is given. This is indicated by the number in brackets after the volume number. This is not usually done and in this paper is not generally done, so decide what you want to do and do it consistently.

50 The ampersand sign (&) indicating 'and' is missing between the two authors. It is usually placed between the initials of the penultimate author and the last name of the last author. First names of authors are not usually given and have not been given for the other authors listed here, so should not be shown here.

51 'and' is used instead of '&' to link the names of the two authors. Once again, you need to be consistent in how you do this. The American Psychological Association uses '&' while some other publishers use 'and'.

6.4   Improved version of the report

While a lot may be learnt by studying examples of below-par work, it is helpful to have a good example to hand, so a better write-up of the study follows. This is not to say that the report is perfect – you may well find that problems remain – but that it is an improvement over the previous version. Look through this version and see what you can learn from it. We would suggest that you take note of the following:

- Notice how the reader is given clear information in both the title and the abstract. These summarise the research very well and give the reader a good idea of what to expect in the main body of the text. Put another way, they give a good impression of the competence of the writer.

- This version of the report is a big improvement, since a fairly coherent argument runs all the way through it. The writing is not episodic but fairly integrated throughout.

- Just the right amount of information is provided in a logical and coherent order.

- While the results section is very short, it contains all the detail that the reader needs. At no point is it unclear quite what the writer is referring to. This is achieved by carefully stating the results in words, using succinct statistical reporting methods, and by making sure that any table included is a model of clarity.

- All of the arguments are justified throughout the report, and the discussion and conclusions section makes pertinent points throughout which have a bearing on the research that had been carried out.

- Finally, the reference section is well ordered and consistent. The writer has found up-to-date work relevant to the new study which creates the impression of a student who is actively involved in their studies rather than someone who simply does what is easiest. A good touch is that the writer shows honesty by indicating where they have not read the original publication. This has been done by indicating the actual source of the information.

Practical Report

Effect of later suggestive interviewing on memory for witnessed events

Ellie Simms

Abstract

The influence of leading questioning on memory for events was investigated in a constructive replication of the Loftus and Palmer (1974) study. It was hypothesised that memory for a witnessed event will be affected by later information concerning the consequences of that event. Thirty-four male and 42 female undergraduates watched a video of a young man running down the street and colliding with a pushchair. They were then given a questionnaire consisting of six questions in which the wording of a question about how fast the man was running was varied. In one version the baby was described as injured while in the other version there was no mention of this. It was found that the estimated running speed was significantly greater where the consequences of the action was more serious. Thus the hypothesis was supported.

Introduction

This study explored the effect of the seriousness of the consequences of events on memory for those events. In a classic study, Loftus and Palmer (1974) investigated the influences of later questioning on memory for events that had been witnessed. Participants in their research were asked questions about an accident they had witnessed on a video. The researchers found that the specific content of questioning influences estimates of how fast the vehicle in the accident was going at the time of the collision. Much higher average speeds were reported when the term 'smashed' was used than when the term 'contacted' was used. Numerous other researchers have replicated these findings (Adamson & Huthwaite, 1983; Brown, 1987; Edmonson, 2007; Fabian, 1989; Jacobs, 2014; Wilcox & Henry, 1982). However, there have been a number of criticisms of the research such as the artificial nature of the eyewitness situation which may be very different from witnessing a real-life accident, which is likely to be a much more emotional experience (Slatterly, 2016). Furthermore, it is notoriously difficult to judge the speed of vehicles (Blair & Brown, 2017). In addition, participants may have been given strong clues as to the expectations of the researchers by the questions used to assess the speed of the impact. While Loftus and Palmer conclude that the content of the questions affected memory for the collision, it may be that memory is actually unaffected and that the influence of the questioning is only on the estimates given rather than on the memory trace of the events (Pink, 2011).

The validity of Loftus and Palmer's research in terms of its relevance to eyewitness evidence in real-life situations has been questioned by Rodgers (1987) who argues that the study has poor validity. Furthermore, student populations may be unrepresentative of the more general population and should be avoided to improve the ecological validity of research in this field (Myrtleberry & Duckworth, 1979). These views are not shared by all researchers, thus Pickering (1984) writes of the important contribution that the Loftus and Palmer study has made to our understanding of eyewitness memory.

→

Loftus and Palmer demonstrated that the form of questioning following a witnessed event can influence the way in which that event is later recalled. However, there is evidence that evaluations of crime are influenced by the consequences of the crime rather than the criminal actions involved (Parker, 2001). So, for example, a burglary which results in the victim having subsequent psychological problems is judged to be more serious than an identical crime which led to no serious consequence. It was reasoned that memory for events such as accidents may be influenced by the consequence of an accident such as whether or not someone was injured in the accident. Does the consequence of an accident influence the way in which the events leading up to the accident are recalled?

Based on this, it was hypothesised that memory for a witnessed event will be affected by later information concerning the consequences of that event. In particular, it was predicted that where the consequences of the event were more severe, the events leading up to the accident would be perceived as more extreme than when the consequences were less severe.

Method

Participants

Thirty-four male and 42 female psychology students at the University were recruited to participate in the study using a convenience sampling method which involved inviting them in lectures and elsewhere to participate in the research. Those who agreed to take part were randomly allocated to either the experimental ($n = 29$) or the control condition ($n = 47$). There were 15 male and 14 female participants in the experimental group and 19 male and 28 female participants in the control group. The mean age of participants was 20.38 years ($SD = 1.73$).

Materials and apparatus

A specially prepared two-minute video of an accidental collision between a running man and a woman pushing a push-chair with what appeared to be a baby in it was shown. Initially, the young man is seen walking down a street, but then he begins to run down what is a fairly crowded street. Turning a corner, he collides with the woman pushing the push-chair. The video was filmed using a good-quality digital video camera mounted on a tripod with a high degree of image resolution by myself with the help of other students. A data projector was used to show the video.

The participants were given a short self-completion questionnaire including two versions of the critical question which comprised the experimental manipulation. The first version, which was given to the experimental group, read 'How fast do you think the man was running in miles per hour when he collided with the woman with the pushchair and the baby was injured?'. The second version, which was given to the control group, read 'How fast do you think the man was running in miles per hour when he collided with the woman with the pushchair and baby?'. These questions were embedded in the questionnaire among other questions which started with ones concerning the gender of the participant, their age and what degree course they were taking. The critical questions were placed at the end of five questions which were filler questions designed to divert the participants' attention from the purpose of the study. These questions were 'What colour was the man's shirt?', 'How many people saw the collision occur?', 'What was the name of the shop outside which the accident occurred?', 'Was the running man wearing trainers?' and 'Was the woman with the pushchair wearing jeans?'.

Design and procedure

The study employed an experimental design in which participants were randomly assigned to these conditions on the basis of the toss of a coin. The experimental group witnessed events which led to the serious consequence of an injury to a baby, and the control group witnessed the same events but with no serious consequence.

Participants took part in the study individually in a small psychology laboratory on the University campus. Prior to showing the video, it was explained to them that the research was for an undergraduate project, that participation was voluntary and that they could withdraw from the study at any stage if they wished. Psychology students are encouraged to volunteer as participants in other students' studies for educational reasons, though there is no requirement that they should do so. A data projector was used to show them the short video of the running man and his collision with the woman with a pushchair. The video was two minutes long and in colour. After the video had been shown, the participants were given one of the two different versions of the questionnaire to complete. Finally, they were thanked for their participation in the research, debriefed about the study and given an opportunity to ask questions. Participants were asked if they wished to receive a brief summary of the research findings when these were available.

Ethics

The research met the current British Psychological Society ethical standards and complied with the University Ethical Advisory Committee's requirements. In particular, the voluntary nature of participation was stressed to participants and care was taken to debrief all participants at the end of their involvement in the study. All data were recorded anonymously. All participants signed to confirm that they had been informed of the ethical principles underlying the research.

Results

Table 1 gives the mean estimates of the running speed in the video for the serious consequence and the no-consequence conditions. The mean estimated running speed for those told the baby was injured ($M = 4.71$, SD $= 1.67$) was significantly faster, $t(74) = 4.43$, two-tailed $p < .001$, than for those not told this ($M = 3.15$, SD $= 1.37$).

Table 1	Descriptive statistics on estimated running speed in the two conditions		
Condition	**Sample size**	**M**	**SD**
Serious consequence	29	4.71	1.67
No consequence	47	3.15	1.37

This finding supports the hypothesis that memory for a witnessed event will be affected by later information concerning the consequences of that event.

Discussion and conclusions

This study supports the findings of Loftus and Palmer (1974) in that memory was affected by the nature of questions asked following the witnessed incident. Memory can be changed by events following the incident witnessed. For those who believed that the incident had led to a serious injury, there was a tendency to estimate that the runner who was responsible for the accident was running faster than for members of the control group. This is important, because it illustrates that the consequences of an action may influence the perceptions of the characteristics of that action.

However, the study does not explain why the serious consequences of an incident should affect memory in this way, but there are parallels with the Loftus and Palmer research which may be helpful. Asking questions about vehicles 'smashing' into each other implies a more serious consequence than if the vehicles had only 'bumped'. This is much the same as the present research in which memories of events were affected by the injury to the baby, which is an indication of the seriousness of the accident. The faster the man ran, the more likely it was that someone would get hurt.

There are implications of the study for the interviewing of witnesses. In particular, the research raises the question of the extent to which the police should give additional information unknown to the witness during the course of an interview. In real life, an eyewitness may not know that the victim of an accident had, say, died later in hospital. Is it appropriate that the police should provide this information in the light of the findings of the present study?

There are a number of limitations on this study. In particular, the use of a more representative sample of the general population would provide an indication of the generalisability of the findings of the present sample. A further improvement would be to add a neutral condition in which participants simply rated the speed of the runner with no reference to the accident. This could be achieved by having a separate group estimate the speed of the runner without any reference to a collision in the question. Finally, the speed of the runner is not the only measure that could be taken. For example,

→

questions could be asked about the reason why the man was running, whether he was looking where he was running, and whether the woman pushing the pushchair was partly responsible for the collision.

It is concluded that memory for eye-witnessed events is affected by information about the consequences of those events. This may have implications for police interviews with eyewitnesses and the amount of information that the police supply in this context.

References

Adamson, P. T., & Huthwaite, N. (1983). Eyewitness recall of events under different questioning styles. *Cognitive and Applied Psychology, 18*, 312–321.

Blair, A., & Brown, G. (2017). Speed estimates of real and virtual objects. *Traffic Psychology, 23*, 21–27.

Brown, I. (1987). The gullible eyewitness. *Advances in Criminological Research, 3*, 229–241.

Edmonson, C. (2007). Question content and eye-witness recall. *Journal of Criminal Investigations, 5*, 31–39. Cited in D. Smith (2008), *Introduction to cognition*. Lakeside, UK: Independent Psychology Press.

Fabian, G. (1989). *The fallible mind*. London: University of Battersea Press.

Jacobs, D. (2014). Eyewitness evidence and interview techniques. *Forensic Investigation Quarterly, 21*, 48–62.

Loftus, E. F., & Palmer, J. C. (1974). Reconstruction of automobile destruction: An example of the interaction between language and memory. *Journal of Verbal Learning and Verbal Behaviour, 13*, 585–589.

Myrtleberry, P. I. E., & Duckworth, J. (1979). The artificiality of eyewitness research: Recommendations for improving the fit between research and practice. *Critical Conclusions in Psychology Quarterly, 9*, 312–319.

Parker, V. (2001). Consequences and judgement. *Applied Cognitive Behavior, 6*, 249–263.

Pickering, M. (1984). Elizabeth Loftus: An appreciation. *Genuflecting Psychology Review, 29*, 29–43.

Pink, J. W. (2011). What changes follow leading interviews: The memory or the report of the memory? *Essential Psychology Review, 22*, 142–151.

Rodgers, T. J. (1987). The ecological validity of laboratory-based eyewitness research. *Critical Psychology and Theory Development, 8*, 588–601.

Slatterly, O. (2016). Validity issues in forensic psychology. *Criminal and Forensic Research, 2*, 121–129.

Wilcox, A. R., & Henry, Z. W. (1982). *Two hypotheses about questioning style and recall*. Unpublished paper, Department of Psychology, University of Northallerton.

| Box 6.1 | Research Example |

Study on the effect of question words on speed estimation and recall

Loftus, E. F., & Palmer, J. C. (1974). Reconstruction of automobile destruction: An example of the interaction between language and memory. *Journal of Verbal Learning and Verbal Behaviour, 13*, 585–589.

The research report discussed in this chapter was based on the work of Elizabeth Loftus. You might find it useful to have more details of her research and how she went about answering her research question. Unlike the version presented in this chapter, the original research publication contains more than one study. This is common in research publications. Sometimes this is because the initial study leaves some unanswered questions or has an obvious weakness which the later studies attempt to deal with. Reading a journal article requires a lot more than just an ability to read. One has to understand the protocol of research reports as well as technicalities such as different research methods or statistical techniques. Few readers of most journal articles will fully appreciate their contents in one reading. It is good practice to study the title and abstract first of all. The more that one can get from these, the easier will be reading the full publication. When you start reading journal articles, you may feel overwhelmed and somewhat daunted by the task. It does get easier with practice but never is it easy, like reading a novel, say. Try to be active in your reading by taking notes and highlighting what you see as the significant details. Also mark parts which seem important but are difficult to follow on first reading. You can go back to these later. Of course, you can only do this with photocopies or copies that you have downloaded for your study purposes.

Background

Elizabeth Loftus and John Palmer (1974) described the results of two studies which looked at the way the word used to describe the impact of two cars, such as 'hit' or 'smashed', affected the estimate of the speed at which the two cars were travelling. That such words may have an effect was based on the fact that people varied widely in their estimation of car speeds and the suggestion that these words implied different speeds.

Study 1

In the first study, 45 students were shown seven films of two cars crashing into each other. After each film, they were asked various questions, including the critical question about how fast the cars were going. There were five conditions of nine students each, in which one of five different words was used to describe the collision for the question in that group. These words were contacted, hit, bumped, collided and smashed. Loftus and Palmer found a significant analysis of variance effect for the five conditions, although they did not test for differences between pairs of conditions. The slowest speed estimate was for the word 'contacted' (31.8 mph) and the highest for the word 'smashed' (40.8 mph). This effect suggested that the word used to describe the impact may affect a witness's estimate of speed. It should be noted that it was not said that students were randomly assigned to the five conditions and that they were similar in how accurate they were at judging speeds. If they had been randomly assigned to the five conditions, they would more probably have been similar in their accuracy of estimating speeds.

Study 2

The second study was the more important one and was designed to test two interpretations of this finding. One interpretation was that the word used only biased the estimate when people could not decide between two speeds. The second interpretation was that the word used also affected their recall of other aspects of the accident that did not occur but that would be consistent with faster speeds, such as whether or not glass was broken.

There were three conditions in which 150 students watched the same one-minute film of a multiple car accident. After watching the film, they were asked various questions. In one condition, they were asked how fast the cars were going when they smashed into each other. In another condition, they were asked how fast the cars were going when they hit each other. In the third condition, they were not asked about the speed of the cars. Once again, it is not stated whether students were randomly assigned to one of the three conditions, which would eliminate the possibility that the participants in the three conditions were systematically different from each other.

One week later they were asked 10 questions about the accident, one of which was whether they saw any broken glass. There had not been any broken glass in the film. Until this point in the paper, no formal hypotheses had been stated, although they are implied. At this stage, the authors state that they expected subjects who had been asked the 'smashed' question to say more often that they saw broken glass. The authors carried out a 2×3 chi-square analysis, which was statistically significant. This analysis showed that more students in the 'smashed' condition (16) said there was broken glass than in the 'hit' (7) or the control (6) condition. This result suggests that people are more likely to recall events which did not occur but which are consistent with how they were described at the time.

Authors' suggestions for future research

Loftus and Palmer did not suggest any future lines of research in their brief Discussion section.

6.5 Conclusion

A good research report should provide a strong and convincing argument for the research. To be convincing, the argument has to be clear, otherwise the reader will not be able to follow it. It also has to be accurate. You should try to ensure that what you write is an accurate description of what you are writing about. When you refer to the work of others, it is important that you are familiar with their work so that you know in what way their work is relevant to your own. In writing your report, it is important to check it carefully sentence by sentence to make sure that it makes sense and is clearly and accurately articulated. It is sometimes difficult for us to evaluate our own work, because we often interpret what we have written in terms of what we know but have not mentioned in the report itself. Although we may be able to find other people to check what we have written, we cannot always be sure how thoroughly or critically they will do this. They may not want to offend us by being critical, or they may not be sufficiently interested in having a thorough grasp of what we have done and in questioning what we have written. Consequently, we need to check what we have written ourselves. It is often useful to leave the work for a few days and to return to it when we are less familiar with it. It may then be easier to spot anything that is not as clear as it should be.

Key points

- Writing research reports is a complex task. We need to have a clear idea of what we want to say and to say it clearly. We need to present a strong and convincing argument as to why we believe our research is important and how exactly it makes a contribution to what is already known about the topic we are studying.

- A research report consists of the following major parts: a title, an abstract, an introduction, a method section, a results section, a discussion section and a list of references. All of these components of a report are important and deserve careful consideration. It is a pity to spoil an otherwise good report with a clumsy title or an insufficiently detailed abstract.

- It is useful to bear in mind what the main aims or hypotheses of your study are and to use these to structure your report. These should be clearly stated. They are generally stated and restated in various parts of the report. When doing this, it is important to make sure that you do not change what they are, as this will cause confusion. They should be most fully described in the introduction and should form the basis of the discussion section. They should be briefly mentioned in the abstract, and it should be clear in the results section how they were analysed and what the results of these analyses were.

- We need to describe the most relevant previous research that has been carried out on the topic and to show how this work is related to what we have done and how it has not addressed the question or questions that we are interested in.

- The abstract is written last. It may be useful to have a working title which you may change later on, so that it captures in as few words as possible what your study is about.

- Your views on what you write may change as you think more thoroughly about what you have done and as you become more familiar with your research and your understanding of it improves. You should expect to have to revise what you have already written in terms of what you choose to say in a subsequent draft. For example, writing about your findings in the discussion section may lead you to carry out further analyses or to change or add material to the introduction.

● If you are having difficulty in writing any part of your report, look at how authors of published research have handled this part of their report. This is usually best done by looking at journal articles which are the most relevant or most strongly related to your own research.

● Writing the report is ultimately your own responsibility. You need to read and reread it carefully a number of times. It is often a good idea to let some time elapse before rereading your report so that you can look at it again with a fresh mind.

ACTIVITIES

1. Find a paper that interests you and read it carefully. Could the title be made more informative and, if so, how? Pick out a statement which provides supporting evidence for some information. Check the references cited. Do they support the statement and, if so, in what way? Find a statistical analysis that you are not very familiar with. Try and learn more about it. How would you carry out that analysis using SPSS? What suggestions are made for further research? Can you think of any other suggestions? Could you, and if so, how would you carry out a further study on this topic?

2. You might like to offer to read and to provide constructive criticism of a report written by one of your fellow students. Where appropriate, you could ask them to clarify or to better substantiate what they are saying or to suggest an alternative way of saying it.

CHAPTER 7

Literature search

Overview

- Literature searches are an integral part of the research process. The pertinent research and theoretical papers identified in this way provide an overview of up-to-date thinking and research on a topic. Searches may be time-consuming, but they are essential to developing ideas about issues to be addressed or further explored.

- Literature searches start broadly but move as rapidly as possible to a more focused strategy. One common approach would be to firstly concentrate on recent research and writings on the topic. These contain the fruits of other researchers' literature searches as well as up-to-date information of where current research has taken us and what remains to be done in the field. Of course, the problem is that current publications may omit earlier relevant research sometimes without justification.

- Computerised databases are the most efficient way of searching the research literature (e.g. Web of Science and PsycINFO). Among a lot of other information, they provide a brief abstract or summary of the publication. These come from the article itself in the case of Web of Science, whereas PsycINFO may provide their own.

- Well written abstracts contain a degree of detail about the research in question and its theoretical context. Usually abstracts have enough information to help the reader decide whether to obtain the original article or report. Almost certainly, local college and university libraries can only physically have a small fraction of these in stock. The use of electronic versions of journals by libraries is changing that situation. Otherwise, the material may have to be obtained from elsewhere. There are various ways of doing this, including visiting other libraries, e-mailing the author of the article or getting your library to obtain a copy or photocopy.

- You need the original article for a number of reasons. For example, it may be the only way of obtaining sufficient detail of the methods and procedures employed. Sometimes you may have doubts about the soundness of the conclusions drawn and may wish to evaluate, say, possible flaws in the statistical analysis.

- Keep a careful record of publications that you consider important to your research. Although time-consuming initially, it is far less frustrating in the long run. There are a number of ways of doing this, including computerised personal databases (such as RefWorks, EndNote or Mendeley), simple hand-written index cards, or computer files to which material may be copied and pasted.

7.1   Introduction

How a literature search is conducted depends a little on one's starting point. A professional researcher with a well-established reputation will have much of the previous research and theory readily at their command. Of course, professional researchers regularly keep up to date, perhaps searching the new literature on a monthly basis. If one knows very little about a topic, a sensible first stage is to read introductory material such as that found in textbooks. A relatively recent textbook is likely to cover fairly up-to-date thinking on the topic, although in brief overview form. Textbooks are likely to provide fairly rapid access to a field in general which is especially useful when students are learning to do research for the first time in practical classes. When you need to dig more deeply into the published research, materials in the college or university library or accessible from the Internet are likely to be your first port of call. Obtaining material not available locally can take a little time and cause you time management problems like failing to meet submission deadlines.

Bear in mind that professional researchers are part of complex social and professional networks in which they share ideas and interests. As such, information flows through a variety of informal channels and few researchers would rely exclusively on the sources described in this chapter. Keeping other researchers abreast of one's new research even prior to publication cuts down the inevitable delay of a year or two between the completion of the research and it being published. Conference presentations and circulating pre-publication drafts are ways of speeding research dissemination. E-mail has allowed researchers to easily circulate early versions of their papers to those working in the same field of research. Increasingly, journals publish on the Internet before they publish in hard-copy journal form. Yet other journals now are Internet-only and simply do not publish as physical volumes which speeds up the publication process.

Searching one's college or university library normally involves using its electronic catalogue system via computer terminals or your own computer. As there are a number of such systems, these may differ across universities. Many British university libraries use the OPAC (Online Public Access Catalogue) system. Leaflets or online information about using the local system are likely to be available from the library. Induction or training sessions for new library users or simply seeking help from a member of the library staff are among the other options. If you have, say, a specific book in mind then entering its title and author into the electronic cataloguing system will help you quickly discover its location in the library.

However, if you are simply searching with a general keyword such as 'memory' or 'intelligence', then you are likely to find lots of entries or hits – perhaps too many. Sometimes it is worthwhile simply going to the section of the library where items with particular keywords are likely to be held, though this is less systematic and others on the course or module may have beaten you there. The general principles of the library classification systems need to be understood if one is to use this sort of method.

Box 7.1 discusses an advanced form of literature review known as the systematic review.

> ## Box 7.1   Key Ideas
>
> # The systematic review
>
> One of the strange things about studying psychology is that some things you are taught while other things you are simply expected to be able to do. The literature review is a good example of the latter. Very little help is available to assist you carry out a literature review itself as opposed to handling bibliographic software. Even having read this chapter, you may feel uncomfortable about the process of reviewing the literature. You may have the basics about how to search a database, but there is clearly more to it than that. Doing a literature review feels like engaging in a somewhat unfocused, haphazard process. You will find many instances of literature reviews by different authors but on the same topic producing somewhat conflicting conclusions. Sometimes, even the research studies selected for the review fail to overlap substantially. Even the most straightforward tasks involved in a literature review can prove to be problematic. For example, just what search terms should be used? There is no foolproof way of selecting these but they have a profound influence on what research studies are found which, in turn, determines the conclusions drawn. Many of the problems with the traditional research review are avoided by using the methodology of the systematic review. Systematic reviews were first developed around the 1970s and 1980s. Since then, a substantial literature has emerged describing the processes involved (e.g. Bettanysalikov & McSherry, 2016; Boland, Cherry, & Dickson, 2013; Gough, Oliver, & Thomas, 2017; Jesson, 2011; Petticrew & Roberts, 2006 – none of these is specifically for psychologists). Students are unlikely to ever perform a systematic review but professional researchers may be required to carry out such a review in order to obtain funding for their research.
>
> Just what is a systematic review? The key thing is that a systematic review is a highly structured and exacting set of procedures designed to effectively address important topics using the findings of pertinent research. Underlying the systematic review approach is a desire to serve the need of social policy makers in government and elsewhere for thorough and convincing accounts of research findings on a particular topic. That is, how can the extant research literature inform policy, practice, and possibly guide future research funding? Of course, policy-makers will have a preference for highly structured, relatively objective methods on which to base their initiatives. They certainly would not wish to be embroiled in public disputes between researchers about what the research literature has to say about the topic in question. Systematic reviews facilitate research-based professional
>
> practice of all sorts. You will come across some so-called systematic reviews aimed at a purely academic audience and some which hardly warrant the description 'systematic review'. Areas where psychologists are likely to be involved in systematic reviews include clinical psychology (such as when asked to review the research evidence on the effectiveness of cognitive behaviour therapy) and forensic psychology (such as when asked to review the evidence of the effects of Internet pornography on the criminal sexual behaviours of teenagers). Nevertheless, enter the search term 'systematic review' into the PsycINFO data base and you will see systematic reviews on a wide variety of topics. Usually the requirements for a student literature review are modest in comparison to those involved in a systematic review. A systematic review is not needed, for example, when a student is given an essay assignment to compare two different theories in a particular area. Of course, for post-graduate dissertations a systematic review might be appropriate.
>
> It is possible to differentiate three main types of literature review:
>
> - *The traditional or narrative literature review*   The use of the term narrative review is a little odd since all types of literature review include a narrative. This sort of literature review pervades the entirety of every psychological journal. It is governed by few if any explicit rules though vague criteria such as comprehensive, thorough, balanced, critical and so forth are bandied about. It is almost entirely in the hands of the researcher how the process is conducted. Readers may be in no position to judge just how diligent the researcher has been or how skilled they are in digital data retrieval methods. Such reviews are subject to the vagaries of the researcher's writing. Every psychology student will produce a number of narrative reviews during the course of their studies.
>
> - *Systematic review*   As we have described, systematic reviews involve a highly structured reviewing process usually carried out by a varied team of researchers and consultants. For good reason, an expert in bibliographic methods will usually be part of the team, since systematic reviews cover a variety of databases which may be unfamiliar to the rest of the team. Remember that systematic reviews may be conducted to aid social policy initiatives so basing one on a single discipline like psychology may be too restrictive. In this chapter, only the

Web of Science and PsycINFO are discussed, but there are many more databases for other disciplines available. There is a general view that systematic reviews are robust in the sense that their outcome is the product of a precisely structured set of procedures and, as a consequence, will be more-or-less independent of the personnel staffing the team.

● *Meta-analytic review or synthesis* These are studies of studies as the word meta-analysis implies. But so are systematic reviews. Meta-analysis focuses primarily on the use of specialist statistical techniques for combining together the outcomes of different research studies on a topic. It can show, for example, that certain sorts of studies (e.g. laboratory experiments) exhibit stronger statistical relationships than other sorts of study. Often, meta-analysis and systematic reviews are both employed

by a research team reviewing research on a particular topic. Actually, systematic reviews were a development from the meta-analytic approach. Both require much the same diligence in tracking down material for inclusion. Howitt and Cramer (2020) present an easy but workable introduction to meta-analysis.

Systematic reviews differ from traditional narrative reviews in a number of crucial ways. Most importantly, systematic reviews exhibit a high degree of transparency which ensures that key features of the review process are readily apparent to the reader. In contrast, the traditional literature review is a somewhat mysterious process. Systematic reviews are expected to be definitive because of the exacting processes involved so they should never need redoing – only updating with more recent research. Traditional narrative reviews and systematic reviews are compared in Figure 7.1.

Systematic review	Traditional narrative review
• Involves a well-established, transparent process • The process follows standard procedures • Draws upon the expertise of practitioners in the field • Involves a substantial research team including bibliographic and statistics specialists • The method specifically identifies possible biases in the research literature • The choice of databases to search is clearly explained and articulated • The objective is to contribute to social policy on the topic in question • The expectation is that the systematic review is the best possible and relatively unaffected by the particular personnel involved – new research simply needs to be added to a systematic review which need not be repeated in its entirety • The objective character of the systematic review makes it attractive to government and other bodies • Tends to exclude peripheral research which may have something to contribute • Too demanding of resources to be an attractive methodology to students • Requires a highly organised approach on the researcher which helps cope with the mass of information available such as the systematic coding of research study characteristics • Dissemination of research findings to practitioners in the field is an integral part of the plan for the review	• The process is poorly described and informal • The process is haphazard with no clear plan • There is no assumption that the expertise of practitioners should be consulted • Conducted by a small number of researchers as part of a wider project • Some likelihood that the researcher will introduce personal biases • Usually the databases searched are not identified • Simply provides background relevant to the research question • Merely one of the possible reviews and not necesarily cumulative – new research necessitates new narrative reviews • May be the focus of controversy between researchers and so may not be considered safe for policy initiatives • Can quite easily incorporate peripheral research and ideas • Required in student work at all levels • The researcher is faced with a mass of material which is difficult to manage • Dissemination beyond the research community is rare

FIGURE 7.1   Comparison of traditional narrative and systematic reviews

Systematic reviews involve teamwork between professionals with relevant experience, knowledge, and skills. They do not all have to be researchers or academics especially when the systematic review concerns social policy matters. Indeed, the involvement of potential users of the systematic review at all stages of the research is a recommended feature. Their inclusion helps ensure the usefulness of the review to practitioners. The precise make-up of the research team depends to an extent on the review's topic. Needless to say, expertise in using digital information retrieval systems is one essential as is perhaps specialist statistical advice. Just as it can be frustrating to search the Internet for information, using digital data base searches well is far from easy. Hitting on the best search terms to use can be a struggle and may require multiple attempts and trials. Even when we have good search terms, we may be overwhelmed with an incredible number of hits. It may take an inordinate amount of time to sieve out the reports which turn out to be irrelevant to the research topic. Just like the Internet, we may have doubts about the value or trustworthiness of the publications we obtain. Here is where an expert in research methodology can be important. Having decided

what is the best quality material, the tasks of summarising it effectively and integrating it with other valuable material remain. Of course, creating a list of potential research for inclusion in the systematic review is one thing, storing and retrieving copies of these research reports is demanding in other ways. Figure 7.2 summarises how articles are found and checked against inclusion/exclusion criteria.

Systematic reviews can be thought of as being much the same as any research and subject to much the same strictures. Various authors have described their versions of the steps involved though they boil down to much the same thing (EPPI Centre, 2008; Centre for Reviews and Dissemination, 2008; Petticrew & Roberts, 2006). The following are some important steps in the process:

- Policy makers, practitioners, or researchers begin to recognise a need for a definitive review of research on a particular topic. Reduplication of effort is to be avoided so if a high quality systematic review already exists then this should be extended. Any stakeholder in the topic may instigate a systematic review and enable the provision of funding. A coherent case for

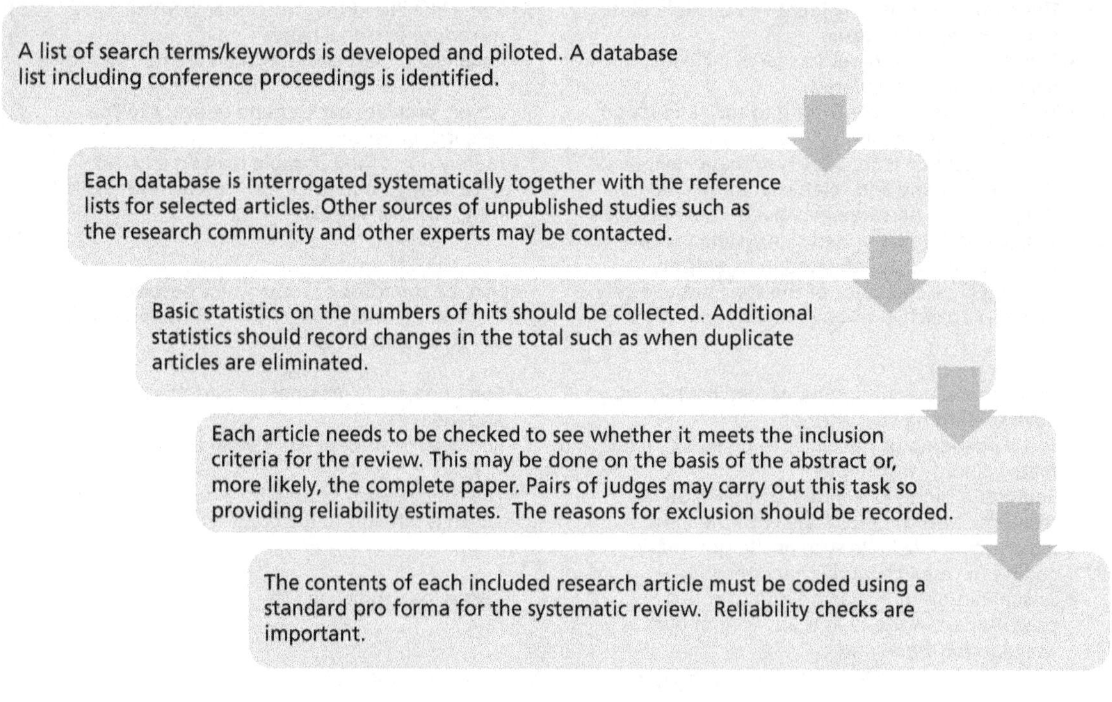

A list of search terms/keywords is developed and piloted. A database list including conference proceedings is identified.

Each database is interrogated systematically together with the reference lists for selected articles. Other sources of unpublished studies such as the research community and other experts may be contacted.

Basic statistics on the numbers of hits should be collected. Additional statistics should record changes in the total such as when duplicate articles are eliminated.

Each article needs to be checked to see whether it meets the inclusion criteria for the review. This may be done on the basis of the abstract or, more likely, the complete paper. Pairs of judges may carry out this task so providing reliability estimates. The reasons for exclusion should be recorded.

The contents of each included research article must be coded using a standard pro forma for the systematic review. Reliability checks are important.

FIGURE 7.2   Process of identifying material for inclusion in the systematic review

the review should be developed. Among the possible justifications include that a new social policy initiative needs to be research led, that there is a lack of clarity or agreement about the interpretation of the existing research literature, that a synthesis of research findings is needed, and that a topic has become the subject of social concern, for example.

- A systematic review follows a preliminary exploratory study which shows that there is a substantial body of research on a particular topic requiring synthesis. This preliminary process may also indicate the resources of time, staffing, premises, and so forth required. At the same time, the broad parameters of the review need to be identified to optimise the usefulness of the final review. For example, consultation with practitioners may widen the perspective of the review. Furthermore, what subpopulations of research participants should be included? So, for example, should a systematic review of the effects of social media include studies of adults in addition to those involving teenagers?

- The formal support structure for the review needs establishing. This includes the roles of staff on the project as well as advisors. Consultants outside of the research community are expected to be involved. The day-to-day staffing for the project is likely to involve expertise in things like statistics, methodology, use of bibliographic resources, and so forth.

- A detailed plan for the work of the project should be approved by all involved parties. It should define precisely the topic of the review. Exclusion and inclusion criteria for the review need to be determined. For example, a plan may stipulate that only randomised trials (controlled experiments) are to be reviewed. These are bespoke parameters fitting the particular research topic. In other words, it is the sampling plan.

- The database search will find more studies than will be retained for review. Being driven by keywords or search terms, the literature search inevitably generates a substantial number of hits some of which may turn out to be irrelevant. Sifting these out can be very time consuming.

- The data collection phase of a systematic review is the literature search. Within the parameters of the systematic review, all pertinent research should be identified. This requires expertise with all sorts of databases. Nowadays, electronic databases will be the first port of call although a thorough search will almost certainly be

wider. Electronic databases may omit books and book chapters, pertinent research studies may only have been published in conference proceedings, and some research may never have been published. Considerable effort is involved to find this more obscure material. Among the various techniques for doing this is contacting researchers in the broad field about unpublished studies of which they are aware. Searching through the reference lists of published research may also uncover this sort of material.

- There is a lot of busy work associated with the systematic review. Copies of the papers for possible inclusion in the review will have to be obtained. Many will be available for download but some will have to be obtained in hard copy form. Hence the skills of an expert librarian may be beneficial. There will be a lot of material to organise or catalogue. Not to have a system is counterproductive because it will be hard to retrieve a particular paper from the archive.

- Every paper identified in the literature search must be carefully assessed in terms of whether it meets the review's inclusion criteria. A high proportion of irrelevant material is likely to be found. Some irrelevant papers might be weeded out by examining the paper's abstract. Two members of staff may make these decisions about inclusion/exclusion independently so allowing for reliability checks. In some cases, the entire research paper will need reviewing in order to decide.

- Preliminary plans must be made for the synthesis of the retained material. In particular, just what procedures will be used to evaluate the research studies for features such as the quality of the studies, the methodology employed, and so forth.

- Each retained research paper will be coded in terms of a pre-agreed coding schedule which has been developed as part of the project. Typical of the possible codings are the specific type of research methodology employed, the size and nature of the sample of participants, the statistical methods employed, and the main findings from the study.

- Assessment of a research paper's quality is important in a systematic review. This can be overall ratings or ratings of several specific parts of the report such as the thoroughness of sampling or the adequacy of the statistical analysis. Quality and most codings are probably best assessed by having pairs of raters evaluate each research paper independently which

→

allows for reliability to be measured. But there are alternatives. For example, the quality ratings could be based on the frequency that the paper is cited by other researchers or the esteem of the journal in which it was published. Of course, it is always important to be aware of the possible biases of the raters. For example, if researchers were known anti-pornography activists then their judgements of the methodological adequacy of a study may be dependent on what the study concludes.

- The potential for bias in research papers is a concern. There are many aspects to this. Publication bias, for example, is the tendency of researchers to only submit for publication research showing statistical significance or journal editors to prefer to publish research demonstrating significant findings. However, there are other types of bias. For example, certain types of methodology are more likely to lead to particular conclusions. If the outcome measures in the included studies were all based on self-reports rather than researcher observation, serious questions might be asked about the objectivity of the evidence.

- One aspect of the analysis stage of the systematic review involves summarising the characteristics of the sample of research studies used. This information is based largely on the codings of the research papers described earlier. Some sort of statistical or tabular presentation of the overall trends is expected.

- The review process accumulates a mass of data on the selected body of research including details of the findings from each of the included research studies as well more general information about each study. The next step is to develop a synthesis of the included research. Some aspects of the data may be in need of reanalysis. If the research team had simultaneously carried out a meta-analysis, this is an appropriate stage to incorporate its findings. The report of the systematic review will provide detail of how the synthesis was achieved. Writing the report will normally overlap with the synthesis stage as is common in research.

- The basic principles of systematic reviews include a stress on the dissemination of the findings of the review. The review plan will normally stipulate the target audience for its findings. The research team are responsible for ensuring that the target audience are made aware of their findings. This is helped by the wide variety of consultants involved in the research. Dissemination should not be regarded as an afterthought but as integral with the development of the project.

These are the bare bones details of systematic reviews. There are many more in-depth accounts which you may consult (e.g. McLeroy, Northridge, Balcazar, Greenberg, & Landers, 2012; Petticrew & Roberts, 2006). You may also find it worthwhile to read examples of systematic reviews, especially by psychologists (e.g. Häggman-Laitila, Salokekkilä, & Karki 2018; Rogers, Webb, & Jafari, 2018). Unlike much psychological work, good quality systematic reviews are regarded as being definitive. This may seem a little over confident but the thorough, highly structured process of a systematic review is clearly far superior to an ad hoc traditional literature review. Not every study described as a systematic review actually reaches the high standards because they are systematic reviews in name only.

Although a full-scale systematic review is beyond the scope of students at the beginning of their careers, being aware of some of the shortcomings of the traditional narrative review is a positive thing. It is possible that you can incorporate some of the better aspects of the systematic review into your traditional literature review. For example, using a coding schedule to describe each of the research reports you select for inclusion would allow you to present some of your review in a systematic form including tables and diagrams. Unfortunately, the lack of resources means that your review will have to be limited in scope. The sheer quantity of research on some topics is daunting to professional researchers, for students it may seem an unsurmountable mountain. The methodology of the systematic review may stimulate in you some thoughts about how to deal with the information overload. Not every literature review has to be a systematic review, of course, but they are becoming more the norm in some types of research. Medical science is a good example. Areas of psychology closest to health studies in medicine are probably most likely to adopt the systematic review approach.

7.2 Library classification systems

The important thing is to know how to find books in your library, but understanding the basics of classification systems may be helpful. Two main systems for classifying and arranging non-fiction (mostly) books in libraries:

- The Dewey Decimal Classification (DDC) system was developed by Melvil Dewey in 1876 and is reputedly the world's most widely used library classification system, although not necessarily in university libraries (Chan & Mitchell, 2003; Dewey Services, n.d.). Each publication is given three whole numbers followed by several decimal places as shown in Figure 7.3. These numbers are known as *call numbers* in both systems. The first of the three whole numbers indicates the classes, of which there

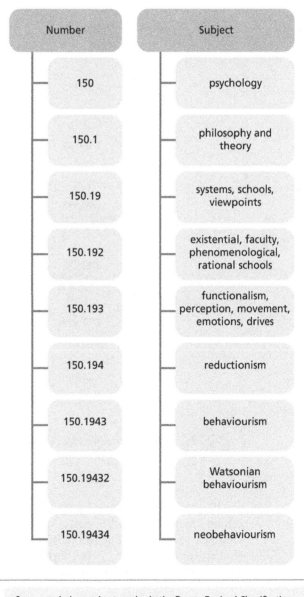

Number	Subject
150	psychology
150.1	philosophy and theory
150.19	systems, schools, viewpoints
150.192	existential, faculty, phenomenological, rational schools
150.193	functionalism, perception, movement, emotions, drives
150.194	reductionism
150.1943	behaviourism
150.19432	Watsonian behaviourism
150.19434	neobehaviourism

FIGURE 7.3   Some psychology subcategories in the Dewey Decimal Classification

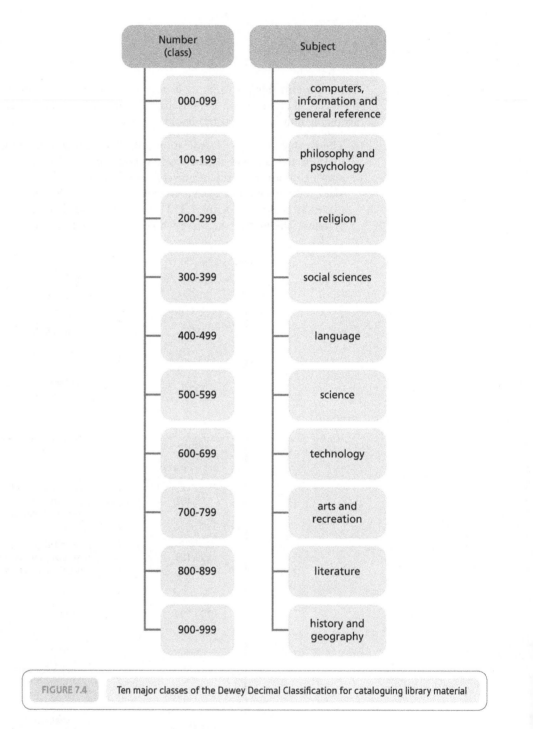

Number (class)	Subject
000-099	computers, information and general reference
100-199	philosophy and psychology
200-299	religion
300-399	social sciences
400-499	language
500-599	science
600-699	technology
700-799	arts and recreation
800-899	literature
900-999	history and geography

FIGURE 7.4   Ten major classes of the Dewey Decimal Classification for cataloguing library material

are 10, as shown in Figure 7.4. So psychology mainly comes under 1 _ _, although certain areas fall into other classes. For example, abnormal or clinical psychology is classified under 6 _ _. The second whole number shows the divisions. Much of psychology comes under 15 _. The third whole number refers to the section. The decimal numbers indicate further subdivisions of the sections.

- The Library of Congress classification system (Chan, 1999; Library of Congress Classification Outline, n.d.), developed by that library in the United States. Each publication is assigned one or two letters, signifying a category, followed by a whole number between 1 and 9999. There are 21 main categories labelled A to Z but excluding I, O, W, X and Y. These categories are shown in Table 7.1. Psychology largely comes under BF. Some of the numbers and categories under BF are presented in Table 7.2.

Table 7.1	Twenty-one major categories of the Library of Congress classification system for cataloguing non-fiction		
Letter (category)	**Subject**	**Letter (category)**	**Subject**
A	General works	M	Music
B	Philosophy, psychology, religion	N	Fine arts
C	Auxiliary sciences of history	P	Language and literature
D	History: (general) and history of Europe	Q	Science
		R	Medicine
E	History: America	S	Agriculture
F	History: America	T	Technology
G	Geography, anthropology, recreation	U	Military science
		V	Naval science
H	Social sciences	Z	Bibliography, library science, information resources
J	Political science		
K	Law		
L	Education		

Table 7.2	Some psychology subcategories in the Library of Congress classification system	
Letter (category)	**Number (subcategory)**	**Subject**
BF	1–1999	Psychology, parapsychology, occult sciences
	1–990	Psychology
	38–64	Philosophy, relation to other topics
	173–175.5	Psychoanalysis
	176–176.5	Psychological tests and testing
	180–198.7	Experimental psychology
	203	Gestalt psychology
	207–209	Psychotropic drugs and other substances
	231–299	Sensation, aesthesiology
	309–499	Consciousness, cognition

7.3   Electronic databases

Using the library catalogue for a literature search is haphazard in the sense that it depends entirely on what your particular library stocks. Consequently you may prefer to use electronic databases which list what has been published. Several different electronic databases list information relevant to psychology. Generally, libraries have to pay for you to access these, but without them research and scholarship would be severely hampered. Your library's web pages will usually provide details about what electronic databases are available to you at your university or college. For databases only available on the web, you will need a username and password which your library or computer centre may supply or maybe some other arrangement is used locally. Two databases are especially useful for psychology – *Web of Science* and *PsycINFO*. PsycINFO is short for Psychological Information and is produced by the American Psychological Association. Both have different strengths and weaknesses so try to become familiar with both of them (and others). Both PsycINFO and Web of Science are archives of summaries of publications. These summaries are known as abstracts. They provide probably the most complete summary of the contents of journal articles.

PsycINFO is more comprehensive than Web of Science in its coverage of psychology journals (and others especially relevant to psychology). Originally it was published in print form as *Psychological Abstracts*. It summarises psychology books and sometimes individual chapters, but primarily PsycINFO deals with journal articles. For books, it goes back as far as 1597. Abstracts of books and chapters make up 11 per cent of its database (PsycINFO Database Information, n.d.). However, it also includes abstracts of postgraduate dissertations, called *Dissertation Abstracts International*, which constitute a further 12 per cent of items listed. These abstracts are based on postgraduate work which has not been specially reviewed for publication, unlike the vast majority of published research reports. The dissertations themselves are often the length of a short book and rather difficult to get access to – certainly they are difficult to obtain in a hurry. Consequently, their use is problematic when normal student submission deadlines are considered.

Web of Science contains the abstracts of articles published since 1945 for science articles and since 1956 for social science articles. It covers only those in journals that are thought to be the most important in a discipline (Clarivate Analytics, n.d.). It ranges through a number of disciplines not just psychology. Moreover, like PsycINFO it may be linked to the electronic catalogue of journals held by your library. If so, it will inform you about the availability of the journal from your library. This facility is very useful, as there are a large number of psychology journals and your library will subscribe to only some of them.

■ Using Web of Science

Web of Science can be directly accessed online. The home or opening appears as in Figure 7.5. It is not possible in the limited space available here to show you all its different facilities. Once you have tried out one or two basic literature searches, you may wish to explore its other capabilities. Find out from your college library whether you can access it and, if so, how to do so.

Box 7.2	Practical Advice

Psychology of the literature search

Carrying out literature searches can be daunting, especially as a newcomer to a research area. Professional researchers and academics are more likely to update a literature search than carry out a completely new one. Students sometimes seem overwhelmed when their attempts at a literature search initially do not go well. Furthermore, carrying out a literature search can involve a lot of time and there is no absolute certainty that it will be fruitful. The following may be of help to keep the task of searching the literature manageable:

● As a student you will only have a limited amount of time to devote to the literature search. It is better to concentrate on material published in recent years, since this demonstrates that you are aware of up-to-date research, is more easily obtainable, and is likely to contain discussions of and references to the older material, some of which remains important in your field of interest or has been forgotten but perhaps warrants reviving.

● Literature searches on topics rising out of a student's general knowledge of psychology are less likely to present problems than where the idea being pursued is not already based on reading. Where the student has an idea based on their novel experiences, difficulties tend to arise. For one reason, the appropriate terminology may elude the student because their common-sense terminology is not what is used in the research literature. For example, a common-sense term may be 'remembering' whereas the appropriate research literature might refer to 'reminiscence'. Finding appropriate search terms can be difficult and often a matter of trial and error.

● Many students avoid carrying out a proper literature search because the cost of obtaining the material seems prohibitive. However, nowadays authors can be contacted by e-mail and many of them are delighted to e-mail you copies of their articles. This is without cost, of course, and often very quick. This does not apply to obtaining copies of books, for obvious reasons.

● Most databases count the number of hits that your search terms have produced. If this number is large (say, more than 200) and they appear to be largely irrelevant,

then you need to try more restricted search terms which will produce a manageable number of pertinent publications. If the database yields only a small number of articles (say, less than 10), this can be equally problematic, especially where they are not particularly relevant to your interests. You need to formulate searches which identify more papers.

● There may be research areas that you are interested in which have only a rudimentary or non-existent research base. In these cases, your search may well be fruitless. The trouble is that it can take some time to determine whether or not this is the case, since it could be your search terms which are at fault.

● Most databases contain advanced search options which can be used to maximise the number of hits you make on relevant material and may reduce the number of times you find irrelevant material. Usually it is advantageous to confine your search to the titles or abstracts sections rather than to, say, anywhere on the database.

● When you find articles which are relevant to your interests, examine their database entries in order to get clues as to the sorts of keywords or terms you should be searching for to find articles like the one you are looking for. Furthermore, as many databases now include the full reference list from the original article, these should be perused as they are likely to contain other references pertinent to your interests.

● The articles which the database identifies on the basis of your search need to be examined in order to decide whether they are actually pertinent. It is probably best to restrict this on-screen to the article's title. Reading a lot of abstracts on the computer in one sitting can become very tiring. Once potential articles have been selected on the basis of their title, you should then save the details of the article, including the abstract, for later perusal. This can often be done by ticking a box on screen and e-mailing the text to yourself or by employing a cut-and-paste procedure to put the text into a file. It is then much easier to carefully select the articles you wish to follow up.

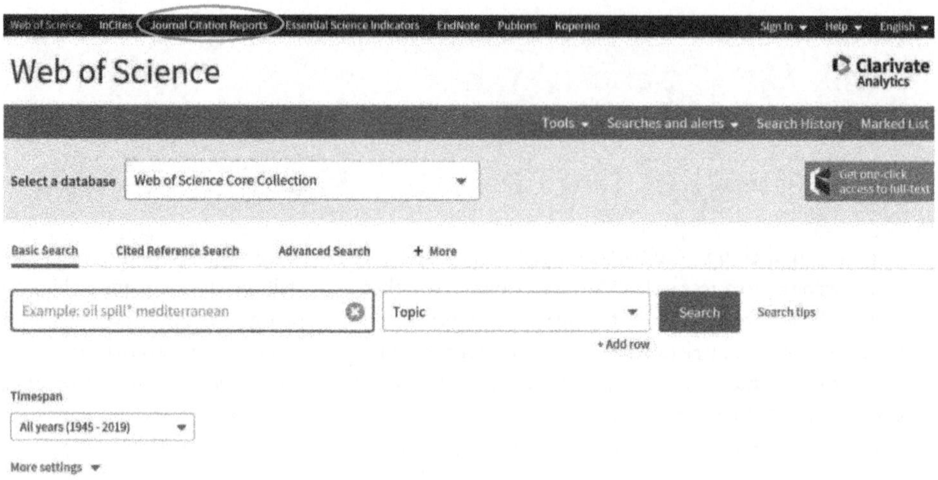

FIGURE 7.5   Web of Science home page (Source: Clarivate Analytics)

FIGURE 7.6   Web of Science home page with two topics added (Source: Clarivate Analytics)

A 'Basic Search' by 'Topic' is sufficient in most cases. Enter the keywords or terms that describe the topic on which you want to conduct the search. If too many references are found, limit your search by adding further keywords. There is a *Help* facility if you want more information on what to do. Suppose you want to find out what articles there are on the topic of interpersonal attraction together with attitude similarity. You type in these terms in the 'Topic' box provided, combining them with the word or search operator 'and'. Then press the *Return* key or select the *Search* option.

The first part of the first page of the results of this search is shown in Figure 7.6. Of course, if you search using these terms now, you may get newer publications than these, as this example was done in January 2019. Articles are listed in order of the most recent ones shown in the *Sort by:* box in Figure 7.7. If you sort them in order of the highest relevance of the keywords, articles listed first contain more of these terms and presented closer together.

Four kinds of information are provided for each article listed in the results:

● The title of the article

● The last and first name of the authors

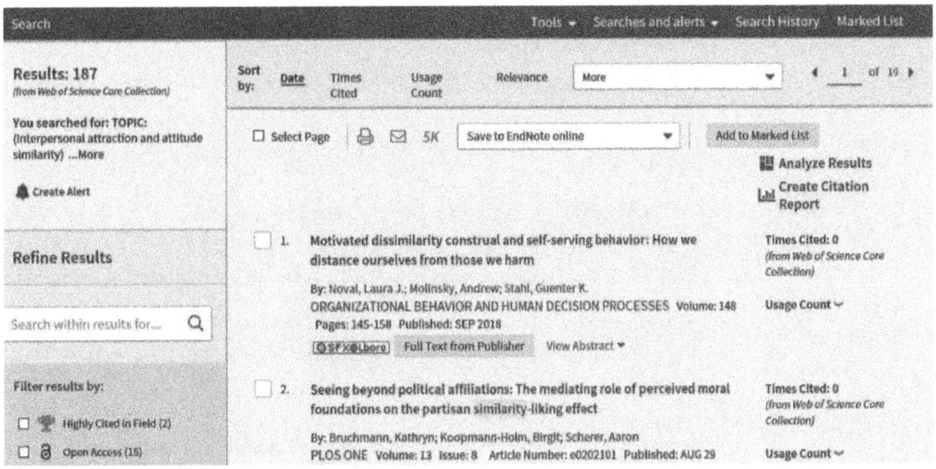

FIGURE 7.7   Web of Science first summary page of the results of search (Source: Clarivate Analytics)

- The name of the journal together with the volume number, the issue number, the first and last page numbers of the article, its Digital Object Identifier (DOI) and the month and year the issue was published

- The number of times the article has been cited in other papers.

If your library has this software, just below this last entry may be the *SFX* icon (see Figure 7.7). Selecting this icon enables you to find out whether your library has this journal as described later.

For the first article shown in Figure 7.7, its title is 'Motivated dissimilarity construal and self-serving behavior: How we distance ourselves from those we harm'. The authors are Noval, Molinsky and Stahl. The journal is *Organizational Behavior and Human Decision Processes.*

The title alone may tell us whether the paper is directly relevant to our interests. If it seems irrelevant, we can ignore it. If relevant, click on (select) the title, which produces the full record. The keywords are highlighted. From the Abstract it is understood that this paper is not directly concerned with interpersonal attraction and attitude similarity, so you are probably best off looking at some of the other references.

Web of Science includes the references the paper cites. To look at the references, select the number of references immediately above 'Cited References' under 'Citation Network'. The first two cited references are shown in Figure 7.8.

If available, select the *SFX* icon in Figure 7.7 just below the title of the original paper to find out whether your library has this paper. *SFX* may produce the kind of web page shown in Figure 7.9. Clearly Loughborough University Library has access to the electronic version of this paper. If you select *Go* for either entry, the window in Figure 7.10 appears. You can now download and read the PDF file (Figure 7.11).

There are several ways of saving Web of Science information. Perhaps easiest is moving the cursor to the start of the information you want to save, hold down the left button of the mouse and drag the cursor down the page until you reach the end of the required

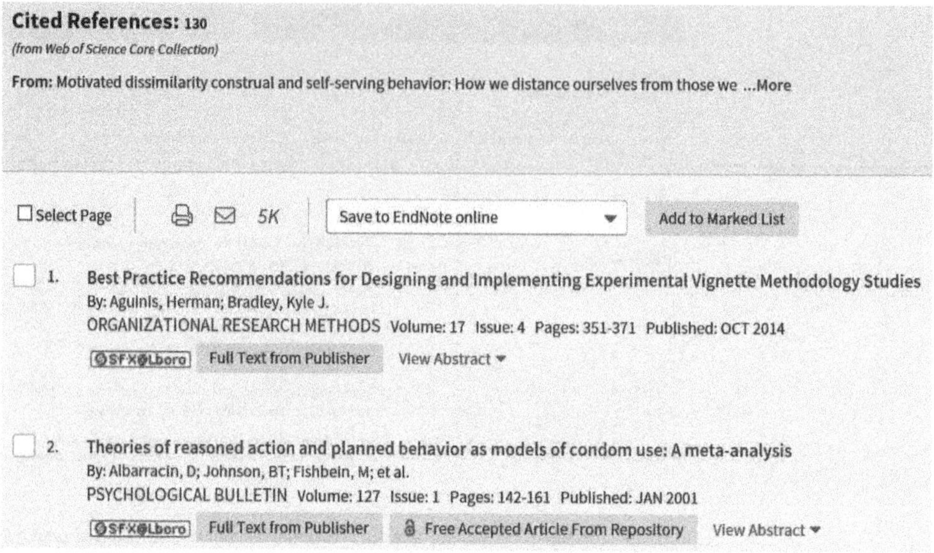

Cited References: 130

(from Web of Science Core Collection)

From: Motivated dissimilarity construal and self-serving behavior: How we distance ourselves from those we ...More

☐ Select Page   🖨 ✉ 5K | Save to EndNote online ▾ | Add to Marked List

☐ **1.**   **Best Practice Recommendations for Designing and Implementing Experimental Vignette Methodology Studies**
By: Aguinis, Herman; Bradley, Kyle J.
ORGANIZATIONAL RESEARCH METHODS   Volume: 17   Issue: 4   Pages: 351-371   Published: OCT 2014
🔗SFX@Lboro   Full Text from Publisher   View Abstract ▾

☐ **2.**   **Theories of reasoned action and planned behavior as models of condom use: A meta-analysis**
By: Albarracin, D; Johnson, BT; Fishbein, M; et al.
PSYCHOLOGICAL BULLETIN   Volume: 127   Issue: 1   Pages: 142-161   Published: JAN 2001
🔗SFX@Lboro   Full Text from Publisher   🔓 Free Accepted Article From Repository   View Abstract ▾

FIGURE 7.8   Web of Science cited references of an article (Source: Clarivate Analytics)

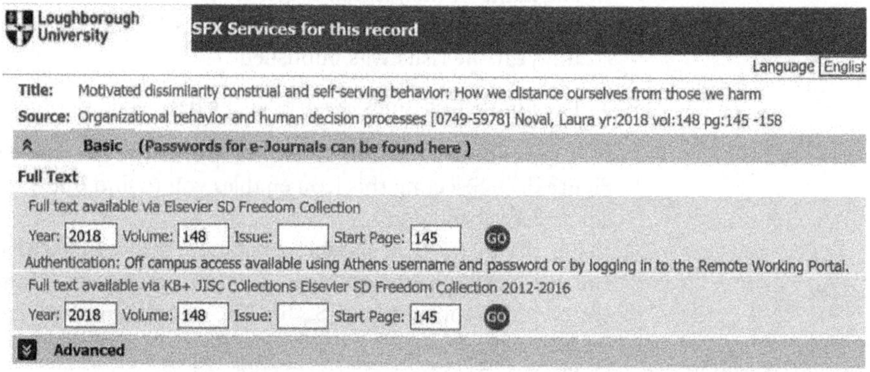

Loughborough University   **SFX Services for this record**

Language | English

Title: Motivated dissimilarity construal and self-serving behavior: How we distance ourselves from those we harm

Source: Organizational behavior and human decision processes [0749-5978] Noval, Laura yr:2018 vol:148 pg:145 -158

   Basic   (Passwords for e-Journals can be found here)

Full Text

Full text available via Elsevier SD Freedom Collection
Year: 2018   Volume: 148   Issue: Start Page: 145   **GO**
Authentication: Off campus access available using Athens username and password or by logging in to the Remote Working Portal.
Full text available via KB+ JISC Collections Elsevier SD Freedom Collection 2012-2016
Year: 2018   Volume: 148   Issue: Start Page: 145   **GO**

Advanced

FIGURE 7.9   SFX window (Source: Ex Libris Ltd)

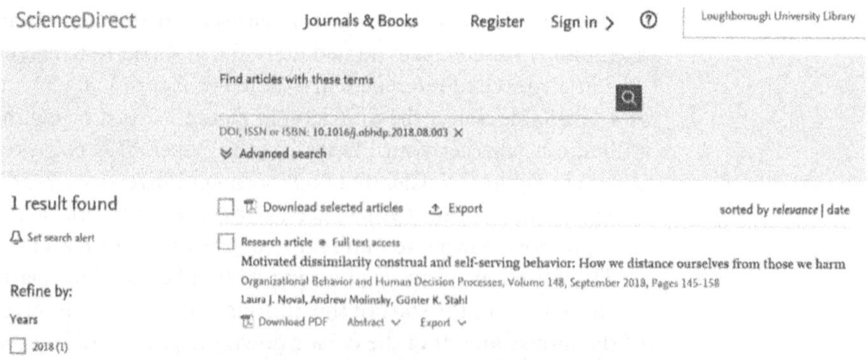

ScienceDirect   Journals & Books   Register   Sign in ›   ⑦   Loughborough University Library

Find articles with these terms   🔍

DOI, ISSN or ISBN: 10.1016/j.obhdp.2018.08.003 ✕
⌄ Advanced search

1 result found

🔔 Set search alert

Refine by:

Years

☐ 2018 (1)

☐ 🔲 Download selected articles   ⬆ Export   sorted by *relevance* | date

☐ Research article ● Full text access
Motivated dissimilarity construal and self-serving behavior: How we distance ourselves from those we harm
Organizational Behavior and Human Decision Processes, Volume 148, September 2018, Pages 145-158
Laura J. Noval, Andrew Molinsky, Günter K. Stahl
🔲 Download PDF   Abstract ⌄   Export ⌄

FIGURE 7.10   Electronic access to a full article (Source: ScienceDirect)

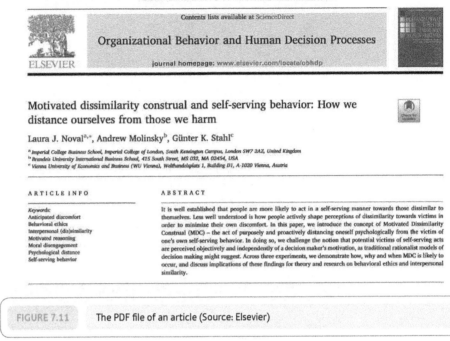

Organizational Behavior and Human Decision Processes 148 (2018) 145–158

Contents lists available at ScienceDirect

Organizational Behavior and Human Decision Processes

journal homepage: www.elsevier.com/locate/obhdp

Motivated dissimilarity construal and self-serving behavior: How we distance ourselves from those we harm

Laura J. Noval[a,*], Andrew Molinsky[b], Günter K. Stahl[c]

[a] Imperial College Business School, Imperial College of London, South Kensington Campus, London SW7 2AZ, United Kingdom
[b] Brandeis University International Business School, 415 South Street, MS 032, MA 02454, USA
[c] Vienna University of Economics and Business (WU Vienna), Welthandelsplatz 1, Building D1, A-1020 Vienna, Austria

ARTICLE INFO

ABSTRACT

Keywords:
Anticipated discomfort
Behavioral ethics
Interpersonal (dis)similarity
Motivated reasoning
Moral disengagement
Psychological distance
Self-serving behavior

It is well established that people are more likely to act in a self-serving manner towards those dissimilar to themselves. Less well understood is how people actively shape perceptions of dissimilarity towards victims in order to minimize their own discomfort. In this paper, we introduce the concept of Motivated Dissimilarity Construal (MDC) – the act of purposely and proactively distancing oneself psychologically from the victim of one's own self-serving behavior. In doing so, we challenge the notion that potential victims of self-serving acts are perceived objectively and independently of a decision maker's motivation, as traditional rationalist models of decision making might suggest. Across three experiments, we demonstrate how, why and when MDC is likely to occur, and discuss implications of these findings for theory and research on behavioral ethics and interpersonal similarity.

FIGURE 7.11   The PDF file of an article (Source: Elsevier)

information. The address is useful if you want to contact the authors. This area will be highlighted. Select the *Edit* option on the bar at the top of the screen, which will produce a dropdown menu. Select *Copy* from this menu. Then paste this copied material into a Word file. You could also download the PDF file and save it.

Using PsycINFO

PsycINFO has the best coverage of psychology publications so it is essential to know how to use it. It is generally accessed online, which is the version we will illustrate. You may need to contact your college library to see whether you can access it and, if so, how. After you have selected PsycINFO, you may be presented with a window like that shown in Figure 7.12, which is that provided by EBSCO. EBSCO is an acronym for Elton B. Stephens Co.

We will again search using the terms 'interpersonal attraction' and 'attitude similarity' by entering them into the first two boxes as shown in Figure 7.13 and restrict the search to words in the Abstract. To select 'Abstract', select the button on the relevant row of the rightmost box, when a menu will appear as shown in Figure 7.13. 'Abstract' is the ninth keyword on this list. Then press the *Return* key or select *Search*. This will produce the kind of list shown in Figure 7.14. Your list will, of course, be more up to date than the one shown. It is also somewhat different from that for Web of Science shown in Figure 7.7. However, the same three kinds of information are provided for each record or reference – the title of the reference, the authors and where it was published. You can restrict what publications are listed by selecting, for example, *Academic Journals* (on the left under *Refine Results*) if you want to see the results for just those journals.

If you want to see the full abstract for an item, select the title. This is a dissertation, the abstract of which is presented in Figure 7.15. Note that references cited can be obtained

| New Search | Thesaurus | Cited References | Indexes | | Sign In | 📁 Folder | Preferences | Languages |

EBSCOhost

Searching: **PsycINFO** | Choose Databases

| | Select a Field (optional) ▾ | **Search** |

AND ▾ | | Select a Field (optional) ▾ | Clear ⑦

AND ▾ | | Select a Field (optional) ▾ | ⊕ ⊖

Basic Search   Advanced Search   Search History

FIGURE 7.12 | PsycINFO search home page (EBSCO) (Source: The PsycINFO® Database screenshot is reproduced with permission of the American Psychological Association, publisher of the PsycINFO database, all rights reserved. No further reproduction or distribution is permitted without written permission from the American Psychological Association and reproduction with permission from EBSCO Information Services)

| New Search | Thesaurus | Cited References | Indexes | | Sign In | 📁 Folder | Preferences | Languag |

EBSCOhost

Searching: **PsycINFO** | Choose Databases

interpersonal attraction | Select a Field (optional) ▾ | **Search**

AND ▾ | attitude similarity |

Select a Field (optional)
TX All Text
TI Title
AU Author
AF Author Affiliation
SU Subjects
DE Subjects [exact]
MJ Word in Major Subject Heading

AND ▾ |

Basic Search   Advanced Search   Search History

Search Options

FIGURE 7.13 | PsycINFO search (Source: The PsycINFO® Database screenshot is reproduced with permission of the American Psychological Association, publisher of the PsycINFO database, all rights reserved. No further reproduction or distribution is permitted without written permission from the American Psychological Association and reproduction with permission from EBSCO Information Services)

by selecting *Cited References* on the left under *Detailed Record* and the references citing this paper by selecting *Times Cited in this Database*. Checking the references citing the paper may be useful in alerting you to other similar studies carried out subsequently which may have cited this paper. To keep a copy of the details of a search, select and copy the information you want and then paste it into a Word file as described for Web of Science.

If you have details of the authors, date of publication, title and journal name, volume and page numbers of a paper that you want to obtain an electronic copy of, then you can enter some key or all aspects of this information into Web of Science and PsycINFO to see if the paper is available to you. For example, in PsycINFO you could put one of the authors under *AU Author* in the first field, the year of publication under *DT Date of Publication* in the second field and a word from the title under *TI Title* in the third field. However, sometimes it is quicker to paste in some of these details into Google Scholar (and sometimes Google) to see if you can obtain papers in this way. You can

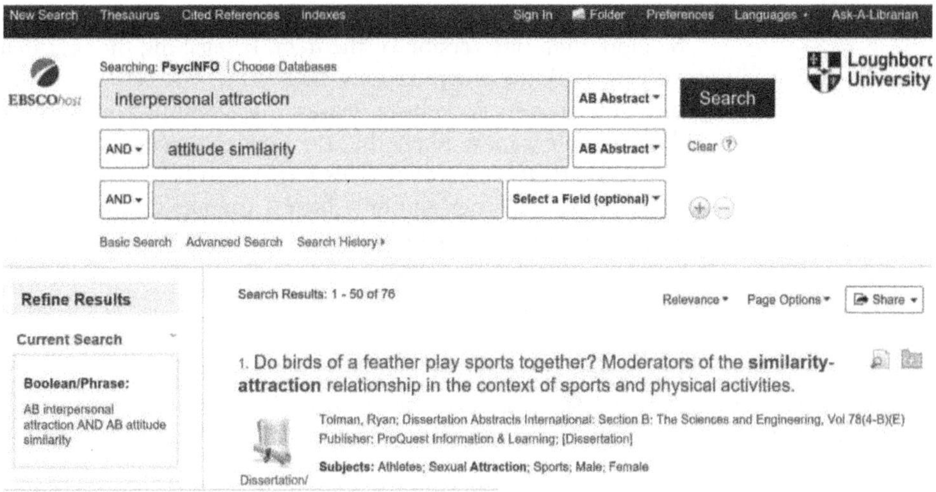

EBSCO*host*

Searching: **PsycINFO** | Choose Databases

🏛 **Loughborc**
University

interpersonal attraction | AB Abstract ▾ | Search

AND ▾   attitude similarity | AB Abstract ▾ | Clear ⑦

AND ▾ | Select a Field (optional) ▾ | ⊕⊖

Basic Search   Advanced Search   Search History ▸

Refine Results

Current Search

Boolean/Phrase:

AB interpersonal
attraction AND AB attitude
similarity

Search Results: 1 - 50 of 76

Relevance ▾   Page Options ▾   📤 Share ▾

1. Do birds of a feather play sports together? Moderators of the **similarity-attraction** relationship in the context of sports and physical activities.

Tolman, Ryan; Dissertation Abstracts International: Section B: The Sciences and Engineering, Vol 78(4-B)(E)
Publisher: ProQuest Information & Learning; [Dissertation]

Subjects: Athletes; Sexual **Attraction**; Sports; Male; Female

Dissertation/

FIGURE 7.14

PsycINFO results (Source: The PsycINFO® Database screenshot is reproduced with permission of the American Psychological Association, publisher of the PsycINFO database, all rights reserved. No further reproduction or distribution is permitted without written permission from the American Psychological Association and reproduction with permission from EBSCO Information Services)

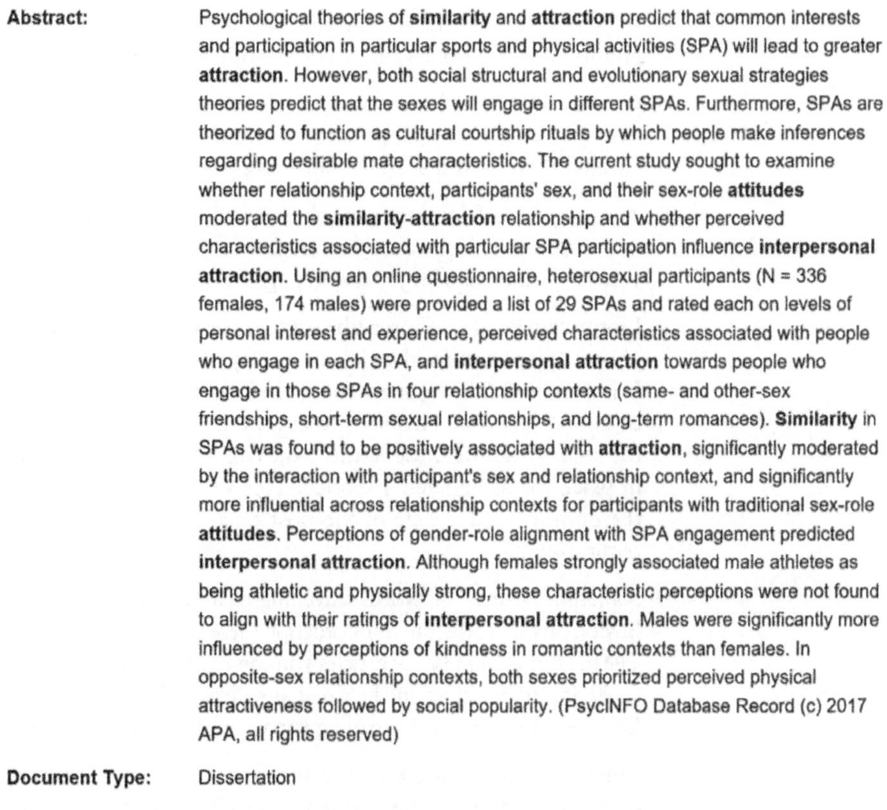

Abstract:

Psychological theories of **similarity** and **attraction** predict that common interests and participation in particular sports and physical activities (SPA) will lead to greater **attraction**. However, both social structural and evolutionary sexual strategies theories predict that the sexes will engage in different SPAs. Furthermore, SPAs are theorized to function as cultural courtship rituals by which people make inferences regarding desirable mate characteristics. The current study sought to examine whether relationship context, participants' sex, and their sex-role **attitudes** moderated the **similarity-attraction** relationship and whether perceived characteristics associated with particular SPA participation influence **interpersonal attraction**. Using an online questionnaire, heterosexual participants (N = 336 females, 174 males) were provided a list of 29 SPAs and rated each on levels of personal interest and experience, perceived characteristics associated with people who engage in each SPA, and **interpersonal attraction** towards people who engage in those SPAs in four relationship contexts (same- and other-sex friendships, short-term sexual relationships, and long-term romances). **Similarity** in SPAs was found to be positively associated with **attraction**, significantly moderated by the interaction with participant's sex and relationship context, and significantly more influential across relationship contexts for participants with traditional sex-role **attitudes**. Perceptions of gender-role alignment with SPA engagement predicted **interpersonal attraction**. Although females strongly associated male athletes as being athletic and physically strong, these characteristic perceptions were not found to align with their ratings of **interpersonal attraction**. Males were significantly more influenced by perceptions of kindness in romantic contexts than females. In opposite-sex relationship contexts, both sexes prioritized perceived physical attractiveness followed by social popularity. (PsycINFO Database Record (c) 2017 APA, all rights reserved)

Document Type: Dissertation

FIGURE 7.15

PsycINFO abstract (Source: PsycINFO is a registered trademark of the American Psychological Association (APA). Reprinted with permission of the American Psychological Association and Ryan Tolman)

also search for specific phrases used by putting them in inverted commas. There may be more than one version of the item. If selecting the first item does not produce the article, check the other versions. In general, it is better to do this while you are logged into your university website just as you would if you were using these bibliographic databases. It is more likely that the university has access to the journal websites than you as a private individual. This might also help you if you have lost or mislaid the full details of a paper and only have a fragment such as the authors or the title. It is surprising how often you can locate the full details simply by typing what you have into an Internet search engine.

7.4 Obtaining articles not in your library

A large number of journals are published relevant to psychology. As the budgets of libraries are limited, your library will subscribe to only a fraction in hard copy. Furthermore, it may not have a complete set of a journal. Inevitably, some of the articles you are interested in reading will not be available in your library. There are at least six different courses of remedy:

- Many journals now have a web-based electronic version which you may be able to access. Information about this may be available on your library's website. If your library subscribes to the electronic version of a journal, this is very good news indeed, since you can obtain virtually instant access to it from your computer, which allows you to view it on the screen, save a copy and print it.

- It is possible that the article is freely available on the web. To see whether this is the case, you could type some of the major details of the article in a search engine such as Google Scholar and see whether it is present.

- You may have friends at other universities or there may be other universities near to where you live. You can check in their catalogue to see whether they have the journal volume you need using the web pages of your local library in many cases.

- Libraries provide an inter-library loan service through which you can obtain either a photocopy of a journal article or a copy of the issue in which the article was published. It is worth obtaining the issue if there is more than one article in that issue which is of interest to you. This service is generally not free and you may be expected to pay for some or all of these loans. You will need to check locally what arrangements are in place for using such a service. This service is relatively quick and you may receive the photocopied article in the post or an e-mailed electronic copy within a week of requesting it.

- Sometimes it may be worth travelling to a library such as the British Lending Library at Boston Spa in Yorkshire to photocopy these yourself. You need to order articles in advance. The maximum number of articles you can request in a day at this library is currently restricted to 10. It is worth checking before going. You will find contact details on https://www.bl.uk/. Choose 'Visit' and then 'Reading rooms' and the 'Boston Spa Reading Room' option.

- You may write to or e-mail the author (or one of the authors if there is more than one) of the paper and ask them to send you a copy of it. E-mail is best. Authors usually have an electronic version of their paper which they can send to you as an attachment. Some authors may have copies of their papers which you can download from their website. Perhaps the easiest way to find an author's e-mail address is to find out where they currently work by looking up their most recently published paper. This is readily done in Web of Science or PsycINFO. Then use an Internet search engine such as Google by typing in their name and the name of the institution. Include your postal address in your e-mail so that authors know where to send the paper should they not have an electronic copy. Remember to be courteous when wording your e-mail by thanking them for their help.

Box 7.3   Talking Point

Judging the reputation of a publication

There is a form of pecking-order for research journals in all disciplines, including psychology. To have an article published in *Nature* or *Science* signals something of the importance of one's work. Researchers are attracted to publishing in the most prestigious journals for professional notice and advancement. Virtually every journal has a surfeit of material submitted to it, so very good material may sometimes be rejected. The rejection rate of articles submitted for publication in journals is relatively high. In 2017, rejection rates varied from 34 per cent for *Experimental and Clinical Pharmacology* to 90 per cent for *Journal of Applied Psychology*, with an average of 70 per cent across the non-divisional journals published by the leading American Psychological Association (American Psychological Association, 2018). Not unexpectedly, agreement between referees or reviewers about an article's quality may be considerably less than perfect in psychology (Cicchetti, 1991; Munley, Sharkin, & Gelso, 1988) and in other disciplines such as medicine (Callaham, Baxt, Waeckerle, & Wears, 1998). Quality, after all, is a matter of judgement. Authors often find that an article rejected by one journal will be accepted by the next journal they approach.

The impact factor is a measure of the frequency with which the average article in a journal has been cited within a particular period. This may be regarded as a useful indicator of the quality of the journal. More prestigious journals should be more frequently cited than less prestigious ones. Clarivate Analytics, which produces Web of Science, also publishes *Journal Citation Reports* annually in the summer following the year they cover (encircled in blue in Figure 7.5). The impact factor of a particular journal may be found using these reports. The period looked at by *Journal Citation Reports* is the two years prior to the year being considered (Institute for Scientific Information, 1994). For example, if the year being considered is 2019, the two years prior to that are 2017 and 2018. The impact

factor of a journal in 2019 is the ratio of the number of times in 2019 that articles published in that journal in 2017 and 2018 were cited in that and other journals to the number of articles published in that journal in 2017 and 2018:

$$\text{journal's impact factor 2019} =$$
$$\frac{\text{citations in 2019 of articles published in journal in } 2017 - 2018}{\text{number of articles published in journal in } 2017 - 2018}$$

So, for example, if the total number of articles published in 2017 and 2018 was 200 and the number of citations of those articles in 2018 was 200, the impact factor is 1.00. The impact factor excludes what are called self-citations where authors refer to their previous articles.

Taking into account the number of articles published in a particular period controls for the size of the journal. If one journal publishes more articles than another journal, the former is more likely to be cited simply for that reason, if all else is equal. This correction may not be necessary, as it was found by Tomer (1986) that the corrected and the uncorrected impact factors correlate almost perfectly (.97).

The impact factors for a selection of psychology journals for the years 2013 to 2017 are presented in Table 7.3. The impact factor varies across years for a journal. For example, for the *British Journal of Social Psychology* it increased from 1.69 in 2016 to 1.78 in 2017. It also differs between journals. For these journals in 2017, the highest impact factor was 5.73 for the *Journal of Personality and Social Psychology* and the lowest was 1.23 for the *Journal of Social Psychology*. An impact factor of about 1.00 means that the average article published in that journal was cited about once in the previous two years, taking into account the number of articles published in that journal in

→

Table 7.3	Impact factors for some psychology journals for 2017 to 2013				
Journal	2017	2016	2015	2014	2013
British Journal of Social Psychology	1.78	1.69	1.80	1.91	1.51
Journal of Personality and Social Psychology	5.73	5.02	4.74	5.03	5.51
Journal of Psychology	1.52	1.64	1.25	1.73	0.97
Journal of Social and Personal Relationships	1.70	1.43	1.46	1.16	1.08
Journal of Social Psychology	1.23	0.84	0.77	0.98	0.71
Personality and Social Psychology Bulletin	2.50	2.50	2.56	2.91	2.52
Social Psychology Quarterly	2.34	1.90	1.46	1.41	1.65

those two years. Web of Science includes only those journals that are considered to be the most important (Clarivate Analytics, n.d.).

However, even the Institute for Scientific Information, which introduced the impact factor measure, says that the usefulness of a journal should not be judged only on its impact factor but also on the views of informed colleagues or peers (Institute for Scientific Information, 1994). The impact factor is likely to be affected by a number of variables such as the average number of references cited in a journal or the number of review articles that are published by a journal. The relationship between the citation count of a journal and the subjective judgement of its standing by psychologists has not been found to be strong. For example, Buss and McDermot (1976) reported a rank-order correlation of .45 between the frequency of citations for 64 psychology journals in the period 1973–1975 and a five-point rating made of those journals by the chairs or heads of 48 psychology departments in the United States based on an earlier study by Mace and Warner (1973). This relationship was stronger at .56 when it was restricted to the 10 most highly cited journals. In other words, agreement was higher when the less highly cited journals were excluded. Rushton and Roediger (1978) found a Kendall's tau correlation of .45 between the ratings of these journals by these departmental heads and their impact factors. Chairs of departments are an influential group of people in that they are often responsible for selecting, giving tenure and promoting academic staff. However, it is possible that nowadays chairs are more aware of impact factors and so the relationship between the impact factor and the rating of the journal may be higher.

There appears not to be a strong relationship between the number of times a published paper is cited by other authors and either the quality or the impact of the paper as rated by about 380 current or former editors, associate editors and consulting editors of nine major psychology journals who had not published papers in those journals (Gottfredson, 1978). Because the distribution of the number of citations was highly skewed with most articles not being cited, the logarithm of the citation number was taken. The correlation between this transformed number was .22 for the quality scale and .36 for the impact scale. The number of times a paper is cited is given by both Web of Science and PsycINFO (*Cited References* under *PDF Full Text*). The number of times a paper is cited in these two databases is likely to differ as their coverages differ. Provided that the number of citations is not zero, if you select *Cited References* in PsycINFO or the number of references immediately after it in Web of Science, you will see details of the papers that have cited this reference.

The lack of agreement about the quality of published papers was dramatically illustrated in a study by Peters and Ceci (1982) in which 12 papers which had been published in highly regarded American psychology journals were resubmitted to them 18–32 months later using fictitious names and institutions. Of the 38 editors and reviewers who dealt with these papers, only three realised that they were resubmissions. Of the nine remaining papers, eight of these previously published papers were rejected largely on the grounds of having serious methodological flaws. This finding emphasises the importance of the reader being able to evaluate the worth of a paper by themselves and not relying entirely on the judgements of others.

7.5   Personal bibliographic database software

There are several bibliographic database software packages that enable you to quickly store the details of references of interest to you from electronic databases such as Web of Science and PsycINFO. These include EndNote, RefWorks and Mendeley. If you look at the Web of Science screenshot in Figure 7.8, you will see that there is an option to *Save to EndNote online* (RefWorks is on the drop-down menu). For example, we could save the details of the reference by Noval, Molinsky and Stahl in Mendeley as shown in Figure 7.16. Mendeley is free at the time of writing. The easiest way of saving this is to move this PDF to the box under *All Documents*. You can also use this kind of software to write out the references that you cite in your work in a particular style such as that recommended by the American Psychological Association. For example, we could format the Noval, Molinsky and Stahl reference in terms of the 6th edition of the APA *Publication Manual* using Mendeley's *Citation Plugin* as presented in Figure 7.17. Once you have chosen this style and inserted all your citations (i.e. Noval, Molinsky and Stahl) in a Microsoft Word or LibreOffice document using *Insert Citation* (as encircled in blue in Figure 7.17), you simply select *Insert Bibliography* (also encircled in blue in Figure 7.17). You still have to familiarise yourself with the details of this particular style, as it is necessary to check whether the reference list matches the chosen style.

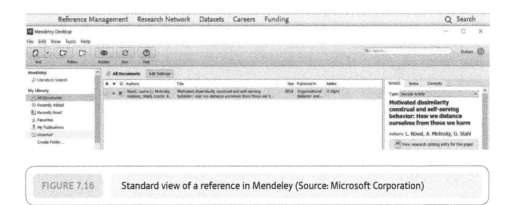

FIGURE 7.16   Standard view of a reference in Mendeley (Source: Microsoft Corporation)

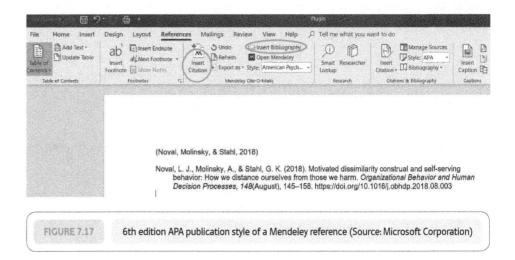

FIGURE 7.17   6th edition APA publication style of a Mendeley reference (Source: Microsoft Corporation)

Box 7.4   Research Example

Meta-analysis of the relation between the five-factor model of personality and academic performance

Poropat, A. E. (2009). A meta-analysis of the five-factor model of personality and academic performance. *Psychological Bulletin, 135*, 322–338.

One modern version of the literature review is known as meta-analysis. Primarily, it differs from the regular literature analysis in that statistical methods are used to combine the data across a range of studies to establish overall (meta-) trends. Although meta-analyses can look extremely technical, it is not too difficult to produce a worthwhile meta-analysis using relatively simple methods, as we demonstrate in Howitt and Cramer (2020). Unfortunately, this is not a topic tackled by the ubiquitous statistical package SPSS, though naturally meta-analysis programs are available. However, if you understand a few very basic statistical ideas such as effect size, then it is not too difficult to incorporate ideas from meta-analysis into your research review. Effect size is simply the size of the effect (trend) expressed in a standardised form so that all studies can be compared irrespective of how key variables were measured. One measure of effect size – the correlation coefficient – you are probably aware of, but there are others. So maybe the difference between your experimental group and control group means is 5.2. This can actually be turned into a correlation coefficient, but it can also be turned into another measure of effect size (e.g. Cohen's *d*) in a way not too dissimilar from calculating the *t*-value in a *t*-test or *z*-score. The important thing at this point is to understand that the results of a wide range of studies can be meaningfully combined. Often students complain that even similar studies of the same thing can produce contradictory findings. Meta-analysis provides methods of making sense of this confusion.

A thorough and up-to-date literature review is important for all quantitative research but particularly for meta-analyses which seek to provide an overall statistical summary of published and often unpublished studies. Including unpublished studies is considered useful because they may not have found statistically significant findings and may as a consequence be less likely to be submitted for publication or be published if submitted.

Background

Arthur Poropat (2009) conducted a meta-analysis of studies which had investigated the relationship between the five-factor model of personality and academic performance (see Figure 7.18). These five factors were Agreeableness (such as being likeable and friendly), Conscientiousness (such as being dependable and keen to achieve), Emotional Stability (such as being calm and relaxed), Extraversion (such as being active and sociable) and Openness (such as being imaginative

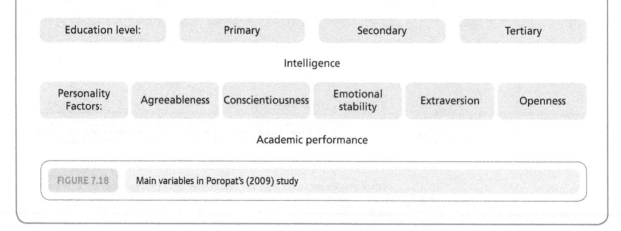

| Education level: | Primary | Secondary | Tertiary |

Intelligence

| Personality Factors: | Agreeableness | Conscientiousness | Emotional stability | Extraversion | Openness |

Academic performance

FIGURE 7.18   Main variables in Poropat's (2009) study

and broad-minded). Among the reasons given for carrying out such a meta-analysis were that previous studies had not restricted themselves to the five factors, did not use a consistent measure of academic performance, did not control for the relationship of personality with intelligence and did not test for moderator effects.

Literature search

Five electronic databases were used to search for research publications on the relation between personality and academic performance. These were PsycINFO (covering psychological publications), ISI Web of Science (covering science, social science and arts and humanities publications), MEDLINE (covering life sciences and biomedical publications), ERIC (covering educational publications) and ProQuest Dissertations and Theses (covering unpublished doctoral and thesis research). These databases were searched using the following terms and the Boolean operators OR and AND: (academic OR education OR university OR school) AND (grade OR GPA OR performance OR achievement) AND (personality OR temperament). GPA stands for Grade Point Average. (Search engines often use Boolean logic, which means that if you ask them to search for, say, hats, coats and umbrellas then each of these three terms will be looked for and, in addition, all possible combinations of the three search terms. You have to use the Boolean logic 'hats OR coats OR umbrellas' to just deal with these individually.) There were three sets of bracketed terms. The terms within brackets were separated by the Boolean operator OR. The three sets of terms were combined with the Boolean operator AND. For a publication to be selected, it must contain one term from each of the three sets of terms. This search apparently identified 80 research reports which presumably were included in the meta-analysis. However, in the References there were 86 research reports which are indicated with an asterisk as having been included in the meta-analysis.

Some findings

A research report may contain more than one sample of participants, so the number of samples that was included was greater than the number of research papers that was covered. The largest number of samples that looked at the relationship between personality and academic performance was 138 for Conscientiousness. The total number of participants in these samples was 70 926 individuals, which represents a very large total sample. The five-factor personality variable having the strongest correlation with academic achievement was Conscientiousness. This correlation, corrected for sample size, was small at .19. When the correlation was corrected for both sample size and the internal alpha reliability of the measures, it was slightly higher at .22. This small positive correlation means there is a weak tendency for more conscientious individuals to perform better academically.

Conscientiousness was very weakly negatively correlated with intelligence, so there was a very small tendency for more conscientious individuals to be less intelligent. When intelligence was controlled by partialling out its relation with academic performance, the partial correlation between Conscientiousness and academic performance was slightly higher at .24. As there were only 47 samples that included a measure of intelligence, the maximum number of samples this partial correlation was based on was 47. These 47 samples contained 31 955 individuals, which is a large total sample.

Another question that was looked at was whether the relationship between personality and academic performance varied according to whether participants were in primary, secondary or tertiary education, in other words, whether the relationship between personality and academic performance was moderated by level of education. This was not found to be the case for the relationship between Conscientiousness and academic performance. The correlation between Conscientiousness and academic performance was similar for the three levels of education. The correlation, corrected for sample size and scale reliability, was .28 at primary level, .21 at secondary level and .23 at tertiary level.

Author's suggestions for future research

Poropat made several suggestions as to what further research on the relationship between personality and academic performance should include. One of these suggestions was that studies should report the standard deviations of their measures, so that this could be taken into account when comparing studies. Studies which have measures with smaller or restricted standard deviations may report lower correlations between personality and academic performance than those with larger standard deviations. As standard deviations were not available for the personality variables in nearly two-thirds of the studies included in this meta-analysis, the potential effect of restricted standard deviations was not taken into account.

7.6 Conclusion

The development of any discipline is the collective effort of numerous researchers acting to a degree independently but overall in cooperative networks of those with similar interests. It is necessary for researchers to communicate their findings and ideas in publications such as journal articles. Similarly, researchers need to be able to access the work of other researchers in order to make an effective contribution to developing the field of research in question. Effectively searching the literature involves a number of skills. In this chapter, we have concentrated on efficient searches of available databases. Of course, professional researchers have a wider variety of information sources available. For example, they go to conferences and hear of new work there, they get sent copies of reports by colleagues doing research elsewhere, and they have an extensive network of contacts through which news of research elsewhere gets communicated. Students have fewer options at first.

Searching the literature on a topic takes time and unless this is taken into account, students may have problems fitting it into their schedule. No one can expect that all materials will be available in their university or college library. There are ways of obtaining material which are increasingly dependent on the World Wide Web. If you are unfamiliar with the research on a particular topic, it may be helpful to find a recently published book which includes an introduction to that topic to give you some idea of what has been done and found. Electronic databases such as Web of Science and PsycINFO are also a very convenient way to find out what has been published on a particular topic. These electronic databases provide short abstracts or summaries of publications which should give you a clearer idea of whether the publication is relevant to your needs. You may not always realise the importance or relevance of a paper when you first come across it. Consequently, it may be better to make a note of a paper even if it does not appear immediately relevant to your needs. This is easily done with the copy and paste functions of the computer software you are using. You need to learn to judge the value of a research paper in terms of what has been done rather than simply accepting it as being important because it has been published or has been published in what is reputedly a good journal.

Key points

- The key to carrying out a successful literature search in any discipline lies in using the various available sources of information. Of these, modern research is most heavily dependent on the use of electronic databases such as Web of Science and PsycINFO. These are generally available in universities and elsewhere. Students will find them useful, but often the materials available via their library catalogue will take priority because of their ease of availability.

- The major databases essentially consist of abstracts or summaries of research publications, including both journal articles and books. An abstract gives a fairly detailed summary of the research article and is an intermediate step to help the reader decide whether or not the complete article or book is required. In addition, these databases frequently contain enough information to enable the author to be contacted – often including an e-mail address.

- Databases are not all the same and one may supplement another. Furthermore, there may well be other sources of information that some researchers can profitably refer to. For example, the fields of biology, medicine, sociology and economics might provide essential information for researchers in some fields of psychology. Knowledge of these builds up with experience.

- Abstracts and other information may be copied and pasted on your computer. In this way, it is possible to build up a record of the materials you feel will be useful to you.

- There are additional ways of obtaining published research. The Internet and e-mail are an increasingly rich source. It can be surprisingly easy to get in touch with academics all over the world. Many are quite happy to send copies of their work either in the mail or electronically.

ACTIVITIES

1. If you do not already know this, find out what electronic databases are available in your library and how to access them. The best way of checking how good a system is and how to use it is to try it out on a topic that you are familiar with. It should produce information you are already aware of. If it does not do this, then you can try to find out how to locate this information in this system. Try out a few systems to see which suits your purposes best.

2. Many university libraries provide training in the use of their resources and systems. These are an excellent way of quickly learning about the local situation. Enquire at your library and sign up for the most promising. Afterwards, try to turn your effort into better grades by conducting a more thorough search as preparation for your essays, practical reports and projects. Using information sources effectively is a valuable skill, and should be recognised and rewarded.

CHAPTER 8

Ethics and data management in research

Overview

- Psychological ethics are moral principles governing the work of psychologists. Research ethics apply these broader principles to research. Occasionally unresolvable conflicts arise between ethical principles – these are known as ethical dilemmas.

- Psychology's professional bodies publish detailed ethical guidelines. This chapter is based on the most recent revisions of these.

- However, most institutions employing psychologists (including universities) have research committees vetting research carried out under its aegis. This bureaucratic process often shares underlying principles with the professional bodies.

- Deception, potential harm, informed consent and confidentiality are commonly the focus of ethical concerns. However, ethical issues stretch much more widely to include the law, publication, plagiarism and data fabrication.

- Ethics apply equally to students as professional researchers.

- It is increasingly the norm that researchers obtain formal consent from their participants that they are agreeing to participate on an informed basis.

- Data management involves ways of storing and handling personal data collected from research participants which protect their confidentiality. Data items which are truly anonymous are exempt from legislation.

8.1   Introduction

Quite simply, ethics are the moral principles by which we conduct ourselves. Psychological ethics, then, are the moral principles by which psychologists conduct themselves. Research ethics, similarly, is a term referring to 'the moral principles guiding research from its inception through to completion and publication of results' (British Psychological Society, 2011, p. 5). Ethics are not merely the rules or regulations governing psychologists' conduct. Psychological work is far too varied and complex to allow it to be policed by a few rules. Ethical dilemmas involve conflicts between different principles of moral conduct. Consequently, psychologists may differ in terms of their position on a particular matter. Ethical behaviour is not merely each individual psychologist's responsibility alone but a matter for the entire psychology community. Monitoring the activities of fellow psychologists, seeking the advice of other psychologists when ethical difficulties come to light and collectively advancing ethical behaviour in their workplace are all mutual concerns that all psychologists should have concerning professional conduct. Equally, psychological ethics cannot be entirely separated from personal morality.

The American Psychological Association's most recent ethical code, *Ethical Principles of Psychologists and Code of Conduct,* came into effect on 1 June 2003 with amendments made in 2010. The second edition of the British Psychological Society's *Code of Human Research Ethics* was published in 2014 and covers all forms of psychological research with human participants. This society published guidelines for the day-to-day activities of psychologists in 2018 as *Code of Ethics and Conduct.* Other professional associations for psychologists will have their own ethical guidelines. Psychologists' private conduct is not covered by these ethics where they are distinct. Nevertheless the codes are far-reaching. The American Psychological Association's code stipulates, for example, that in terms of teaching, for example, that psychology courses should accurately reflect the current state of knowledge. Ethical codes apply to students just as much as professional psychologists. So all psychology students need a full and mature understanding of the ethical principles governing the profession. Ignorance of the relevant ethical standards is no defence for unethical conduct and neither is the failure to understand the standards properly.

What is the purpose of ethical codes? The self-evident answer that psychologists should know how to conduct themselves properly is only part of the reason. One of the characteristics of professions is their desire to retain autonomy. This is well illustrated by the history of the medical profession during the nineteenth century (Howitt, 1992a). Autonomy implies self-regulation of the affairs of members by the professional body. It is impossible to be autonomous if a profession is under the detailed control of legislation. So professions must stipulate and police standards of conduct. Another reason why psychology seeks to maintain high ethical standards is the good reputation of the discipline among the general public. If psychologists collectively had a reputation for being dishonest, exploitative and prurient liars, then few would employ their services or willingly participate in their research. Public trust in the profession is essential.

Failure to adhere to sound ethical principles may result in complaints to professional bodies. Sanctions may be imposed on those violating ethical principles. Ultimately, the final sanction is ending the individual's membership of the professional body, which may result in the individual being unable to practise professionally. However, there is a wider range of sources of control on ethics in research (see Figure 8.1).

Many organisations, including universities, have ethics committees that supervise both the research carried out by employees but also that of other researchers wishing

The ethical environment of psychology

to do research within the organisation. While this does provide a measure of protection for all parties (including the researcher), it is not to be regarded as the final guarantee of good ethical practices in research. Research ethics committees in universities, hospitals and other institutions monitor the good ethical standards of the research of its employees and outsiders who may wish to research within those institutions. A research ethics committee (REC) is 'a multidisciplinary, independent body responsible for reviewing research proposals involving human participants to ensure that their dignity, rights and welfare are protected. The independence and competence of a REC are based upon its membership, its rules regarding conflicts of interest and on regular monitoring of and accountability for its decisions' (British Psychological Society, 2011, p. 5).

The research ethics committee is the main guardian of standards that psychologists, including students, will be exposed to. Psychologists and students in universities will have to submit their proposed research to a general research ethics committee. This needs to be factored into your research plans as bureaucratic procedures like these slow down or even halt the progress of research. Of course, a great deal of research presents little or nothing by way of ethical issues. Research committees usually recognise this and may employ a fast-track system to identify quickly and approve straightforward cases. There are at least two ways of doing this:

● By granting general approval to research conforming to a particular protocol. This usually means initially going through the full research approval process to obtain generic approval for the protocol but then research involving that protocol no longer needs specific approval although the committee may require that it is informed that the research will take place.

● By employing some sort of checklist to identify the research which is potentially ethically problematic for further scrutiny. Research for which no problems are identified by the checklist is then automatically approved.

The upshot of all this is that there has been a major shift in emphasis which places responsibility first of all in the hands of the ethics committee of the institution and then, by extension, in the hands of managers, supervisors and so forth. In short, it is unlikely that you would ever be in a position to carry out research which has not been approved by the ethics committee. Ethical violations would be the consequence of not following the procedures laid down by the institution. So long as you consult with academic staff, follow their suggestions and do what the institution requires, you will almost certainly go through the necessary checks on your planned research. While institutional research committees do publish their own documentation about acceptable ethical standards which may be similar to professional ethical codes, they are not necessarily the same in every respect. Most ethical principles tend to follow those employed in medical research to a degree – hardly surprising, as ethically unacceptable practices by the medical profession led to the development of the first ethical codes. You need to find out about the procedures at your institution in good time so that you may seek permission in instances where there might be a problem, for example, in things like research on children or prisoners. This amounts to potential extra pressure on the time management of your studies. Of course, your supervisor or another member of staff should be able to provide you with appropriate information on how things work where you are studying.

We will focus on the American Psychological Association's ethical guidelines and those of the British Psychological Society, as probably the most comprehensive available. Legislation is also relevant, of course, and the particular impact of data protection legislation constitutes the best example of this. Few, if any, psychology students will have contact with research animals. Box 8.3 discusses the legal and ethical principles involved in animal research in psychology.

8.2   Ethics: general principles

Both the APA and the BPS ethical codes formulate their general principles which are given in Figure 8.2. The principles are expressed somewhat differently by the two organisations but overlap quite substantially. The point of principles is that ethics are not 'rules', since they require discretion and interpretation when applied. A rule suggests that it is the same irrespective of circumstances; principles suggests that circumstances often dictate what is appropriate. Knowing the principles underlying ethics means that the researcher can judge each situation independently and come to a conclusion led by the principles rather than a rule. Although the principles are somewhat different, their importance is as much that they lead to thinking about issues and provide a means of doing so as that they provide definitive 'rules' for ethical conduct in research. The basic ethical issues in research are not too difficult to grasp, but adopting a too formulaic approach to ethics is to potentially overlook serious issues when they arise.

8.3   Research ethics

The ethical procedures affecting research are discussed below in the approximate order in which they are likely to occur. So we begin with the preparatory stage of planning research and finish with publication.

AMERICAN PSYCHOLOGICAL ASSOCIATION RESEARCH ETHICS PRINCIPLES	BRITISH PSYCHOLOGICAL SOCIETY RESEARCH ETHICS PRINCIPLES
Principle A: Beneficence and non-maleficence Psychologists seek to benefit and avoid harm to those whom they engage with professionally. Psychologists should both be aware of and guard against those factors which may result in harm to others. The list of factors is long and includes financial, social and institutional considerations. This principle also includes the animals used in research.	**Principle 1: Respect for the autonomy and dignity of persons:** This is very similar to Principle E of the APA code. The implication is that psychologists should be more than keen to explain the research that they are asking someone to take part in. The psychologist will ensure that personal privacy and so forth will not be compromised in any way by their research, including respecting confidentiality. The psychologist will be willing to respect the voice of those taking part in the research.
Principle B: Fidelity and responsibility In their professional work, psychologists are in relationships of trust with people. They are thus required to take responsibility for their actions, adhere to professional standards of conduct, and make clear exactly their role and obligations in all aspects of their professional activities. In relation to research and practice, psychologists are not merely concerned with their own personal activities but with the ethical conduct of their colleagues (widely defined). It is worthwhile quoting word for word one aspect of the professional fidelity ethic: 'Psychologists strive to contribute a portion of their professional time for little or no compensation or personal advantage.'	**Principle 2: Scientific value:** Badly designed and conducted research is a waste of resources. The scientific value of a study refers to the way in which the design and conduct of research should be such that the contribution of the research to the development of knowledge and understanding is ensured. The ethical implication of this is that the standards of their research are defensible and robust in the face of criticism.
Principle C: Integrity – accuracy, honesty, truthfulness Psychologists are expected to manifest integrity in all aspects of their professional work. One possible exception to this is circumstances in which the ratio of benefits to harm of using deception is large. Nevertheless, it remains the duty of psychologists even in these circumstances to seriously assess the possible harmful consequences of the deception including the ensuing distrust. The psychologist has a duty to correct these harmful consequences. The problem of deception is discussed in more detail in the text.	**Principle 3: Social responsibility:** Psychology exists in the context of society and its collective duty is the welfare of other human beings and non-human beings. The ethical consequence of this is that psychological research should be used for beneficial purposes for society. It also involves being aware of and admitting the problematic nature of the process of interpreting psychological research findings.
Principle D: Justice – equality of access to the benefits of psychology Psychologists should exercise careful judgement and take care in order that all people experience just and fair psychological practices. Psychologists should be aware of the nature of their biases (potential and actual). They should not engage in, or condone, unjust practices and need to be aware of the ways in which injustice may manifest itself.	**Principle 4: Maximising benefit and minimising harm:** This is similar to Principal A Beneficience and non-maleficence of the APA ethical code. It is the responsibility of psychology to consider research from the position of the participant in research. The aim is to serve the interests of the well-being of participants including their personal values and dignity. Ethically researchers need to be aware of the possible impact in this way of their research and try to minimise or obviate such risks.
Principle E: Respect for people's rights and dignity Individuals have the rights of privacy, confidentiality and self-determination. Some individuals manifest vulnerabilities which make it hard for some individuals to make autonomous decisions. Children are an obvious example. The principle also requires psychologists to be aware of and respect differences among cultures, individuals and roles such as age, culture, disability, ethnicity, gender, gender identity, language, national origin, race, religion, sexual orientation and socio-economic status. Psychologists should avoid and remove biases related to these differences but be vigilant for, and critical of, those who fail to meet this standard.	

FIGURE 8.2   Comparison of the ethical principles of the APA and BPS

■ Institutional approval

To summarise, much research takes place in organisations such as the police, prisons, schools and health services. Many, if not all, of these require formal approval for research carried out by members of the organisation or outside researchers needing access to that organisation. Sometimes this is the responsibility of an individual (e.g. a headteacher) but, more likely, a committee. In the case of universities, almost universally permission is needed from a general ethics committee or Institutional Review Board (IRB). There is no way of avoiding at least part of this process. Furthermore, the research proposal put forward for approval must be transparent in the sense that the information provided about the research should accurately reflect the nature of the research. It should be perfectly clear what procedures the researcher intends to employ and what precautions will be taken. So any form of deceit or sharp practice such as lies, lying by omission and partial truths is unacceptable. Finally, the research when it is carried out should follow the protocol for the research which has been approved. Material changes are not permissible and, if unavoidable, may require additional approval. Research ethics committees are not beyond criticism as discussed by Hoecht (2011). For example, most ethical codes are based on ones originally developed for medical research, which may mean that they do not effectively deal with some research of a non-medical nature.

■ Informed consent to research

Undue pressure, fear, coercion and the like should not be present or implied in an ethical study. Taking part in research should be a freely made decision by the participant who has been made aware of just what they are subjecting themselves to. Otherwise, there is a risk that they may inadvertently agree to participate in something which they would have declined to do had they known. The general principle of informed consent applies widely and includes assessment, counselling and therapy as well as research. People have the right to have prior knowledge of just what they are agreeing to before agreeing to it. The nature of the research should be explained to potential participants in terms which they could reasonably be expected to understand. So the way things are explained to a child may need to be different from that for a university student. Later we will discuss exceptional circumstances in which informed consent is not required.

The following need to be in place to demonstrate informed consent:

- The purpose, procedures and approximate duration of the research should be provided to potential participants.

- Participants are made aware that they are free to refuse to take part in the research and withdraw from the research at any stage. This includes the right to withdraw any data already provided. Shredding questionnaires and the recordings are ways of doing this, or they may simply be given to the participant to dispose of as they wish.

- Any possible outcomes or consequences of refusing to participate or withdrawing from research should be explained. For example, some organisations require clients to take part in research in the voluntary 'contract' between the organisation and client. Not to participate may be construed as non-cooperation. A sex offender undergoing treatment who declines to take part in research might be regarded as lacking in contrition. Such judgements may have implications for the client's future. The original contract is not the responsibility of the researcher, but they should be aware of these (subtle) pressures to participate and stress the voluntary nature of participation.

- Participants should be told about aspects of the research which might influence their decision to participate. These include discomforts, risks and adverse outcomes inherent in the research. For example, research in which pornographic images will be shown may offend the moral and/or social sensibilities of some participants.

- Similarly, benefits from taking part should be clarified including benefits for academic research, benefits for the community, and even benefits for the individual participant. Otherwise, these considerations may not be obvious to the participant.

- Explain to participants any limits to the confidentiality of information they provide during the research. Normally, researchers ensure data anonymity but this is not always possible. For example, prison authorities may require that researchers inform them of any offences mentioned in interviews which were previously undisclosed to the authorities. In these circumstances, the appropriate course of action might be to pre-warn the participant offender that this is the case.

- Incentives for participation should be described. Some people agree to take part as an act of kindness or because they believe that research is important. If they are unaware of a cash payment, they may feel that their good intentions are being compromised when the payment is eventually offered.

- Contact details of someone whom may be approached for further details about the research and the rights of participants in the research should be provided. This allows participants to ask for more details or clarification. Furthermore, it helps establish the legitimacy of the research. For example, if the contact is a professor at a university, then this would help establish the bona fides of the research.

- Special provisions apply to experimental research involving potentially beneficial treatments which may not be offered to all participants (see Box 8.1).

Box 8.1   Talking Point

Informed consent in intervention experiments

When a psychologist conducts *intervention research* there may be issues of informed consent. This does not refer to every experiment but those in which there may be significant advantages to receiving the treatment and significant disadvantages in *not* receiving the treatment. The treatment, for example, might be a therapeutic drug, counselling or therapy. In these circumstances most participants probably would prefer to receive the treatment rather than no treatment. In psychological research, someone may continue to suffer debilitating depression simply because they are allocated to the control group not receiving treatment. Owing to these possibilities, the researcher in these circumstances should do the following:

- The experimental nature of the treatments should be explained at the outset of the research.

- The services or treatments which will *not* be available to participants allocated to the control condition should be made clear.

- The method of assignment to the experimental or the control conditions should be explained. If the method of selection for the experimental and control conditions is random, this should be made clear.

- The nature of the services or treatments available to those who choose not to take part in the research should be explained.

- Financial aspects of participation should be clarified. For example, the participant may be paid for participation, but it is conceivable that they may be expected to contribute to the cost of their treatment.

One infamous study violating the above principles is known as the Tuskegee Experiment (Jones, 1981). Significantly, the study involved only black people as participants. They were suffering from syphilis in the 1930s, a time when this was a killer disease. The researchers, unbeknown to the participants, allocated them to experimental and control conditions. Hence those in the control group had effective treatment withheld, so were at a serious health risk as a consequence. This may have been bad enough, but there was worse. Even when it had become clear that the treatment was effective, the members of the control group were left to suffer from the disease because the researchers also wished to study its natural progression!

◼ Informed consent for recordings and photography

Taking voice recordings, videos or photographs of participants is subject to the usual principle of informed consent. However, exceptions are stipulated in the US ethical code:

● Informed consent is not necessary if the recording or photography takes place in a public place and is naturalistic (i.e. there is no experimental intervention). This is ethical only to the extent that there is no risk of the inadvertent participants being identified personally or harmed by the recording or photography.

● If the research requires deception (and that deception is ethical), then consent for using the recording may be obtained retrospectively during the debriefing session in which the participant is given information about the research and an opportunity to ask questions. Deception is discussed below.

◼ Circumstances in which informed consent may not be necessary

The ethical guidelines do not impose an invariant requirement of informed consent. They suggest limited circumstances in which it may be permissible to carry out research without prior consent of this sort. The overriding requirement is that the research could not be expected to (i.e. *not* likely to) cause distress or harm to participants. Additionally, at least *one* of the following should apply to the research in question:

● The study uses anonymous questionnaires or observations in a natural setting or archival materials. Even then, such participants should not be placed at risk of harm of any sort (even to their reputation) and confidentiality should be maintained.

● The study concerns jobs or related organisational matters in circumstances where the participant is under no risk concerning employment and the requirements of confidentiality are met.

● The study concerns 'normal educational practices, curricula or classroom management methods' in a context of an educational establishment.

Research need not employ informed consent *if* the law or institutional regulations permit research without it. This ethics provision may cause some consternation. Most of us probably have no difficulty with the principle that psychologists should keep to the law in terms of their professional activities. Stealing from clients, for example, is illegal as well as unethical. However, there is a distinction to be made between what is permissible in law and what is ethical. A good example of this is the medical practitioner who has consenting sex with a patient. In some countries, this may not be illegal and no crime is committed. However, it is unethical for a doctor to do so, and the punishment imposed by the medical profession is severe: possible removal from the register of medical practitioners. There may be a potential conflict between ethics and the law. It seems to be somewhat lame to prefer the permission of the law rather than the constraints of the ethical standards.

◼ Research with individuals in a less powerful or subordinate position to the researcher

Psychologists are often in a position of power relative to others. A university professor of psychology has power over his or her students. Clients of psychologists are dependent on the psychologists for help or treatment. Junior members of research staff are dependent on senior research staff and subordinate to them. Individuals may suffer adverse consequences as a result of refusing to take part in research or may be under undue pressure to participate simply because of this power differential. Holaday and Yost (1995) found that the most frequent root of ethical problems were the demands of supervisors and others involved in managing research. Any psychologist in such a position of power has an ethical duty to protect these vulnerable individuals from such adverse consequences. Sometimes, participation in research is a requirement of particular university courses, or inducements may be given to participate in the form of additional credit. In these circumstances, the ethical recommendation is that fair alternative choices should be made available for individuals who do not wish to participate in research.

Inducements to participate

Financial and other encouragements to participate in research are subject to the following requirements:

- Psychologists should not offer unreasonably large monetary or other inducements (e.g. gifts) to potential participants in research. In some circumstances such rewards can become coercive. One simply has to take the medical analogy of offering people large amounts of money to donate organs in order to understand the undesirability of this. While acceptable levels of inducements are not stipulated in the ethics, one reasonable approach might be to limit payments where offered to out-of-pocket expenses (such as travel) and a modest hourly rate for time. Of course, this provision is probably out of the question for student researchers.

- Sometimes professional services are offered as a way of encouraging participation in research. These might be, for example, counselling or psychological advice of some sort. In these circumstances, it is essential to clarify the precise nature of the services, including possible risks, further obligations and the limitations to the provision of such services. A further requirement, not mentioned in the APA ethics, might be that the researcher should be competent to deliver these services. Once again, it is difficult to imagine the circumstances in which students could be offering such inducements.

Use of deception in research

The fundamental ethical position is that deception should *not* be used in psychological research procedures. There are *no* circumstances in which deception is acceptable if there is a reasonable expectation that physical pain or emotional distress will be caused. However, it is recognised that there are circumstances in which the use of deception may be justified. If the proposed research has 'scientific, educational or applied value' (or the prospect of it), then deception may be considered. The next step is to establish that no effective alternative approach is possible which does not use deception. These are not matters on which individual psychologists should regard themselves as their own personal arbiters. Consultation with disinterested colleagues is an appropriate course of action.

If the use of deception is the only feasible option, it is incumbent on the psychologist to explain the deception as early as possible. This is preferably immediately after the data have been collected from each individual, but it may be delayed until all of the data from all of the participants have been collected. The deceived participant should be given the unfettered opportunity to withdraw their data. Box 8.2 discusses how deception has been a central feature of social psychological research. The ethics of the British Psychological Society indicate that a distinction may be drawn between deliberate lies and omission of particular details about the nature of the research that the individual is participating in.

Box 8.2 Talking Point

Deception in the history of social psychology

Deception has characterised the work of social psychologists more than in any other branch of psychological research. In his account of the history of deception in social psychology, Korn (1997) argues that this was the almost inevitable consequence of using laboratory methods to study social phenomena. Deception first occurred in psychological research in 1897 when Leon Solomons studied how we discriminate between a single point touching our skin and two points touching our skin at the same time. Some participants were led to believe that there were two points and others that there was just one point. Whichever they believed made a difference to what they perceived. Interestingly, Solomons told his participants that they might be being deceived before participation.

In the early history of psychology, deception was indeed a rare occurrence, but so was any sort of empirical research. There was a gradual growth in the use of deception between 1921 and 1947. The *Journal of Abnormal and Social Psychology* was surveyed during this period. Fifty-two per cent of articles involved studies using misinformation as part of the procedure, while 42 per cent used 'false cover stories' (Korn, 1997). Little fuss was made about deception at this time. According to a variety of surveys of journals, the use of deception increased between 1948 and 1979 despite more and more criticisms being raised. Of course, the purpose of deception in many cases is simply to hide the true purpose of the experiment. Participants threatened with a painful injection might be expected to behave differently if they believe it is necessary for a physiological experiment than if they know that the threat of the injection is simply a way of manipulating their stress levels.

Many famous studies in social psychology used deceit of some sort or another. These did not necessarily involve trivial matters. In Milgram's studies of obedience in which participants were told that they were punishing a third party with electric shock, it appeared at one stage that the victim of the shock had been severely hurt. All of this was a lie and deception (Milgram, 1974). Milgram tended to refer to his deceptions euphemistically as 'technical illusions'. In studies by other researchers, participants believed that they were in an emergency situation when smoke was seeping into a laboratory through a vent – again a

deliberate deception (Latane & Darley, 1970). Deception was endemic and routine in social psychological research. It had to be, given the great stress on laboratory experimentation in the social psychology of the time. Without the staging of such extreme situations by means of deception, experimental social psychological research is difficult, if not impossible.

Sometimes the deceptions seem relatively trivial and innocuous. For example, imagine that one wished to study the effects of the gender of a student on the grades that they get for an essay. Few would have grave concerns about taking an essay and giving it to a sample of lecturers for marking, telling half of them that the essay was by a man and the other half that it was by a woman. It would seem to be important to know through research whether or not there is a gender bias in marking. Clearly there has been a deception but it probably does not jeopardise in any way the participants' psychological well-being. However, believing that you have endangered someone's life by giving them dangerous levels of electric shock is not benign but may fundamentally affect a person's ideas about themselves. In some studies, participants have been deceitfully abused about their abilities or competence in order to make them angry (Berkowitz, 1962).

How would studies like these stand up to ethical scrutiny? Well, deception as such is not banned by ethical codes. There are circumstances in which it may be justifiable. Deception may be appropriate when the study has, or potentially has, significant 'scientific, educational or applied value', according to the APA ethical principles. Some might question what this means. For example, if we wanted to study the grieving process, would it be right to tell someone that the university had been informed that their mother had just died? Grief is an important experience and clearly it is of great importance to study the phenomenon. Does that give the researcher *carte blanche* to do anything?

Deception is common in our society. The white lie is a deception, for example. Does the fact that deception is endemic in society justify its use in research? Psychologists are professionals who as a group do not benefit from developing a reputation as tricksters. The culture of deception in research may lead to suspicion and hostility towards participation in the research.

This is essentially the distinction between lying by omission and lying by commission. You might wonder if this distinction is sufficient justification of anything. The British Psychological Society indicates that a key test of the acceptability is the response of participants at debriefing when the nature of the deception is revealed. If they express anger, discomfort or otherwise object to the deception, then the deception was inappropriate and the future of the project should be reviewed. The BPS guidelines do not specify the next step, however.

■ Debriefing

As soon as the research is over (or the essential stages are complete), debriefing should be carried out. This involves a mutual discussion between researcher and participant to fully inform the participant about matters such as the nature of the results, the results of the research and the conclusions of the research. The researcher should try to correct the misconceptions of the participant that may have developed about any aspect of research. Of course, there may be good scientific or humane reasons for withholding some information – or delaying the main debriefing until a suitable time. For example, it may be that the research involves two or more stages separated by a considerable interval of time. Debriefing participants after the first stage may considerably contaminate the results at the second stage.

Debriefing cannot be guaranteed to deal effectively with the harm done to participants by deception. Whenever a researcher recognises that a particular participant appears to have been (inadvertently) harmed in some way by the procedures, reasonable efforts should be made to deal with this harm. It should be remembered that researchers are not normally qualified to offer counselling, and other forms of help and referral to relevant professionals may be the only appropriate course of action. There is a body of research on the effects of debriefing (e.g. Epley & Huff, 1998; Sharpe & Faye, 2009; Smith & Richardson, 1983). Box 8.4 later in this chapter gives details of Epley and Huff's study as a research example.

Box 8.3	Talking Point

Ethics and research with animals

Nowadays, few students have contact with laboratory animals during their education and training. Many universities simply do not have any facilities for animal research. However, many students have active concerns about the welfare of animals and so may be particularly interested in the ethical provision for such research in psychology. The British Psychological Society, for example, published details in *Guidelines for Psychologists Working with Animals* (Standing Advisory Committee on the Welfare of Animals in Psychology, 2007). The American Psychological Association similarly has published *Guidelines for Ethical Conduct in the Care and Use of Nonhuman Animals in Research*' which is available at http://www.apa.org/science/leadership/care/care-animal-guidelines.pdf.

It needs to be stressed that this is an area where the law in many countries has exacting requirements that may be even more stringent than those required ethically. The first principle is that psychologists involved in research with animals must adhere to the pertinent laws and regulations. This includes the means by which laboratory animals are acquired, the ways in which the animals are cared for, the ways in which the animals are used and the ways in which laboratory animals are disposed of or retired from research.

Some further ethical requirements are as follows:

● Psychologists both experienced and trained in research methods with laboratory animals should adopt a supervisory role for all work involving animals. Their responsibilities include consideration of the 'comfort, health and humane treatment' of animals under their supervision.

- It should be ensured that all researchers using animals have training in animal research methods and the care of animals. This should include appropriate ways of looking after the particular animal species involved and the ways in which they should be handled. The supervising psychologist is responsible for this.

- Psychologists should take appropriate action in order that the adverse aspects of animal research should be minimised. This includes matters such as the animal's pain, comfort, freedom from infection and illnesses.

- While in some circumstances it may be ethically acceptable to expose animals to stress, pain or some form of privation of its bodily needs, this is subject to requirements. There must be no alternative way of doing the research. Furthermore, it should be done only when it is possible to justify the procedure on the basis of its 'scientific, educational or applied value'.

- Anaesthesia before and after surgery is required to minimise pain. Techniques which minimise the risk of infection are also required.

- Should it be necessary and appropriate to terminate the animal's life, this should be done painlessly and as quickly as possible. The accepted procedures for doing so should be employed.

One suspects that many will regard this list as inadequate. The list makes a number of assumptions – not the least being that it is ethically justifiable to carry out research on animals in certain conditions. But is this morally acceptable? Some might question whether cruelty to animals (and the unnecessary infliction of pain is cruel) is defensible in any circumstances. Others may be concerned about the lack of clarity in terms of when animal research is appropriate. Isn't any research defensible on the grounds of scientific progress? What does scientific progress mean? Is it achieved by publication in an academic psychology journal?

8.4   Ethics and publication

The following few ethical standards for research might have particular significance for student researchers.

Ethical standards in reporting research

It is ethically wrong to fabricate data. Remember that this applies to students. Of course, errors may inadvertently be made in published data. These are most likely to be computational or statistical errors. The researcher, on spotting the error, should take reasonable efforts to correct it. Among the possibilities are corrections or retractions in the journal in question.

Plagiarism

Plagiarism is using the work of another person without acknowledgement and as if it were one's own work. Psychologists do *not* plagiarise. Ethical principles hold that merely occasionally citing the original source is insufficient to militate charges of plagiarism. So, copying chunks of other people's work directly is inappropriate even if the authors are occasionally cited during this procedure. Of course, quotations clearly identified as such by the use of quotation marks, attribution of authorship, and citation of the source are normally acceptable. Even then, quotations should be kept short and within the limits set by publishers, for example.

■ Proper credit for publications

It is ethically inappropriate to stake a claim on work which one has not actually done or in some way contributed to substantially. This includes claiming authorship on publications. The principal author of a publication (the first-named) should be the individual who has contributed the most to the research. Of course, sometimes such a decision will be arbitrary where contributions cannot be ranked. Being senior in terms of formal employment role should not be a reason for principal authorship. Being in charge of the research unit is no reason for being included in the list of authors. Sometimes an individual makes a contribution but less than a significant one. This should be dealt with by a footnote acknowledging their contribution or some similar means. Authorship is not the reward for a minor contribution of this sort.

It is of particular importance to note that publications based on the dissertations of students should credit the student as principal (first) author. The issue of publication credit should be raised with students as soon as practicable by responsible academics.

■ Publishing the same data repeatedly

When data are published for the second or more time, the publication should clearly indicate the fact of republication. This is acceptable. It is not acceptable to repeatedly publish the same data as if for the first time.

■ Availability of data for verification

Following the publication of the results of research, they should be available for checking or verification by others competent to do so. This is not *carte blanche* for anyone to take another person's data for publication in some other form – that would require agreement. It is merely a safeguard for the verification of substantive claims made by the original researcher. The verifying psychologist may have to meet the costs of supplying the data for verification. Exceptions to this principle of verification are:

- Circumstances in which the participants' confidentiality (e.g. anonymity) cannot be ensured.

- Situations in which the data may not be released because another party has proprietary rights over the data because they financed it.

8.5 How to obtain a participant's consent

It is commonplace nowadays that the researcher both provides the potential participant with written information about the nature of the study and obtains their agreement or consent to participation in the study. Usually these include a statement of the participant's rights and the obligations of the researcher. The things which normally would go into this sort of documentation are described separately for the information sheet or study description and the consent form. It is important that these are geared to your particular study, so what follows is a list of things to consider for inclusion rather than a ready-made form to adopt.

■ Information sheet or study description

The information sheet or study description should be written in such a way that it communicates effectively to those taking part in the study. It should therefore avoid complex language and, especially, the use of jargon which will be meaningless to anyone not trained in psychology. The following are the broad areas which should be covered in what you write. Some of these things might be irrelevant to your particular study:

- The purpose of the study and what it aims to achieve
- What the participant will be expected to do in the study
- Indications of the likely amount of time which the participant will devote to the study
- The arrangements to deal with the confidentiality of the data
- The arrangements to deal with the privacy of any personal data stored
- The arrangements for the security of the data
- A list of who would have access to the data
- The purposes for which the data will be used
- Whether participants will be personally identifiable in publications based on the research
- That participation is entirely voluntary
- That it is the participant's right to withdraw themselves and the data from the study without giving a reason or explanation (possibly also a statement that there will be no consequences of doing so, such as the withdrawal of psychological services, if the context of the research requires this)
- The benefits that participation in the research might bring to the individual and others
- Any risks or potential harm that the research might pose to those participating
- If you wish to contact the participant in future for further participation in the research, it is necessary to get their permission to do so at this stage. If you do not, you cannot contact them in the future, under the terms of data protection legislation in the UK and elsewhere.
- Details of the research team or your supervisor if you are a student, from which the participant can obtain further information if necessary, and the contact details of the relevant Ethics Committee in case of issues which cannot be dealt with by the research team or the supervisor.

■ Consent form

The consent form provides an opportunity for the participants to indicate that they understand the arrangements for the research and to give their agreement to take part in the research in the light of these. The typical consent form probably should cover the following points, though perhaps modified in parts:

- The title of the research project
- I have been informed about and understand the nature of the study.   *Yes/No*
- Any questions that I had were answered to my satisfaction.   *Yes/No*
- I understand that I am free to withdraw myself and my data from the research at any time with no adverse consequences.   *Yes/No*

- No information about me will be published in a form which might
  potentially identify me.   *Yes/No*

- My data, in an anonymous form, may be used by other researchers.   *Yes/No*

- I consent to participate in the study as outlined in the information sheet. *Yes/No*

- Space for the signature of the participant, their name in full, and the date
  of the agreement.

8.6   Data management

The rise of digital technologies brought about legislation designed to protect personal
data. Most recently, the European Union's *General Data Protection Directive* of 2018
has evolved data protection. Individual countries may have made small changes to this
when enacting it into law. Broadly speaking, individuals received new rights to know what
personal information is held about them and organisations were put under closer regimes
for handling personal data. Data management includes some issues very closely related to
ethical matters; however, it is different. Ethical matters, as we have seen, are not driven
primarily by legislation, whereas data management issues have a substantial basis in legislation. Information stored in filing cabinets is covered just as much as information held by the
digital social media. Data protection is not mainly or substantially about data in research;
it is far wider than that. It covers any personal data which are held by an organisation for
whatever purpose. It covers things such as application forms, work and health records, and
much more – anything which involves personal data, period. There are exemptions, but the
legislation is likely to apply to all of your professional activities and even as a student of
psychology. Research is treated positively in data protection legislation in the UK.

The good news is that data protection legislation does not apply if the personal data
are in anonymous form. Essentially this means that the data should be anonymous at the
point of collection. This could be achieved, for example, by not asking those completing a
questionnaire to give their name or address or anything like that. It might be wise to avoid
other potentially identifiable information in order to be on the safe side – for example, just
ask for their year of birth rather than the precise date if the latter risks identifying individual
participants. Giving random numbers for participants to use may be a good strategy so long
as you do not keep a list of the names associated with each number. All of this needs some
thought. While it is sensible advice to use anonymised data make sure that individuals cannot
be identified even having done that. These procedures obviously impose some limits on what
you can do – for example, you could not contact the participant to take part in a follow-up
to the study and you cannot supplement the data that you have with additional information
from other sources. But most of the time you would not want to do these things anyway.
You would need specific agreement from a participant to include them in a future follow-up
study together with satisfactory arrangements for storing and protecting their data.

Of course, some data inevitably will allow for the identification of a research participant.
Just because they are not named does not mean that they are not identifiable. For example,
videoed research participants may well be identifiable, and individuals with a particular job
within an organisation may also be identifiable by virtue of that fact. So it is possible that
data protection legislation applies. It is immaterial in what form the data are stored – hard
copy, digital recording media, or what-have-you: if the data are personal and the person is
identifiable, then the Act applies. What follows will be familiar from parts of the previous
section. Data protection requires that the researcher must give consideration to the safe keeping of identifiable personal data. So it includes the question of which people have access to
the data. Probably this is all that you need to know about data protection, but organisations
will have their own data protection officers from whom you may seek advice if necessary.

Effect of negative feedback and debriefing on the evaluation of a psychology experiment involving deception

Epley, N., & Huff, C. (1998). Suspicion, affective response, and educational benefit as a result of deception in psychology research. *Personality and Social Psychology Bulletin, 24,* 759–768.

Most ideas about ethics are based on moral considerations and not on research. But, not surprisingly, psychologists have researched a number of ethical issues, as in the following example. Not only does this research involve serious questions about ethically sensitive procedures, but at the same time it involves the same ethically sensitive procedures. So not only is it a good example of how researchers deal with ethical issues in their research, but also the research itself provides food for thought about the assumptions behind ethical guidelines.

Background

Psychologists need to consider the ethics of using deception and negative feedback in psychological research. There is non-experimental evidence that participants report few negative feelings about being deceived and say they enjoyed and learned more from participating in research involving deception than from non-deception. This research suggests that participants may view deception more positively than some psychologists and many institutional ethical committees have assumed. The aim of this study by Nicholas Epley and Chuck Huff (1998) was to investigate how participants felt about taking part in an experiment which involved receiving false feedback about themselves and being debriefed about this. They also looked at how suspicious participants felt after having been deceived. There were no explicit research hypotheses as such.

Method

The study used a factorial design in which there were two independent or manipulated variables which were combined or crossed with one other. The two variables each consisted of two conditions. The variables and conditions were negative versus positive performance feedback and full versus partial debriefing. These two variables formed four groups: (1) negative feedback and full debriefing; (2) negative feedback and partial debriefing; (3) positive feedback and full debriefing; and (4) positive feedback and partial debriefing (see Figure 8.3). A total of 39 female and 18 male students were randomly assigned to one of these four groups.

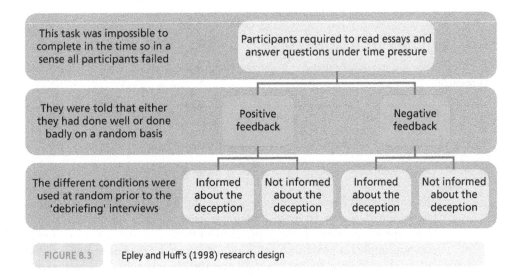

FIGURE 8.3   Epley and Huff's (1998) research design

Participants were given the impossible task of reading six undergraduate essays in seven minutes and answering questions on them. This was done so that they would not be able to estimate how well they had performed. After the seven minutes, they were given either negative or positive feedback about their performance. To check that the manipulation of the feedback had worked, they were asked to report what it was. Next, about half the participants were informed about the deception while the other half were not informed about it. Both debriefings were similar in how long they took.

Before leaving, the participants completed measures to assess the dependent variables. There were two questions, measuring how suspicious they would be of the experimenter in the future and how trustworthy and honest they thought psychologists were. There was one question on how much they had benefited educationally from participating in this research. There were seven questions on how positively they felt about their experience of taking part in this psychology experiment.

Participants were asked to return three to five days later, when they were asked about the experiment. After this they were all fully debriefed about the research. About three months later they were contacted by phone to complete the three dependent measures again.

Some results

All participants correctly reported the feedback they had received, showing that the feedback manipulation had worked.

Positive feelings

In terms of the seven-item index of how positively they felt about taking part in the experiment, participants generally reported they felt positively about the experience. On a seven-point scale where points of above 4 indicate they felt positively about it, participants who received negative feedback reported significantly less positive feelings at both points in time ($M = 5.42$) than those who received positive feedback ($M = 5.86$). Participants also felt significantly more positively about the experience three months later ($M = 5.80$) than they did initially ($M = 5.41$). Debriefing had no effect on how positively they felt.

Suspiciousness

A significant difference in how suspicious participants were of psychologists was only found for the first item about how suspicious they would feel in future. Participants who were initially given a full debriefing were significantly more suspicious ($M = 3.63$) than those given a partial debriefing ($M = 4.75$), where points of below 4 on a seven-point scale indicate feeling suspicious. This suspiciousness was still present three months later at the time of the second assessment of the dependent variables.

Educational benefits

In terms of the single question of whether they felt they had benefited educationally from the experience, participants felt that they had. They had a mean score of 5.32 where points of above 4 indicate educational benefit. There were no significant differences on this question for the different debriefing or feedback conditions.

Authors' suggestions for future research

Epley and Huff briefly suggested it would be useful to investigate whether suspicion affects the way participants behave in subsequent research.

8.7 Conclusion

Research ethics cover virtually every stage of the research process. The literature review, for example, is covered by the requirements of fidelity, and other stages of the process have specific recommendations attached to them. It is in the nature of ethics that they do not simply list proscribed behaviours. Frequently, they offer advice on which aspects of research require ethical attention and the circumstances in which exceptions to the generally accepted standards may be considered. They impose a duty on all psychologists to engage in consideration and consultation about the ethical standing of their research as well as that of other members of the psychology community. Furthermore, the process does not end prior to the commencement of data collection but requires attention and vigilance throughout the research process, since new information may indicate ethical problems where they had not been anticipated.

Importantly, ethics require a degree of judgement in their application. It is easy for students to seek rules for their research. For example, is it unethical to cause a degree of upset in the participants in your research? What if your research was into experiences of bereavement? Is it wrong to interview people about bereavement knowing that it will distress some of them? Assume that you have carefully explained to participants that the interviews are about bereavement. Is it wrong then to cause them any distress in this way? What if the research was just a Friday afternoon practical class on interviewing? Is it right to cause distress in these circumstances? What if it were a Friday workshop for trainee clinical psychologists on bereavement counselling? Is this any more acceptable? All of this reinforces the idea that ethics are fine judgements, not blanket prohibitions for the most part. Of course, ethics committees may take away some of this need for fine judgement from researchers.

The consideration of ethics is a fundamental requirement of the research process that cannot be avoided by any psychologist – including students at any level. It starts with not fiddling the data and not plagiarising. And what if your best friend fiddles the data and plagiarises?

Key points

- Psychological associations such as the American Psychological Association and the British Psychological Society publish ethical guidelines to help their members behave with propriety in their professional work. Self-regulation of ethics is a characteristic of professions.

- Ethics may be based on broad principles, but frequently advice is provided in guidelines about their specific application, for example, in the context of research. So one general ethical principle is that of integrity, meaning accuracy, honesty and truthfulness. This principle clearly has different implications for the use of deception in research from those when reporting data.

- Informed consent is the principle that participants in research should willingly consent to taking part in research in the light of a clear description by the researcher about what the research entails. At the same time, participants in research should feel in a position to withdraw from the research at any stage with the option of withdrawing any data that have already been provided. There are exceptions where informed consent is not deemed necessary – especially naturalistic observations of people who might expect to be observed by someone since they are in a public place.

- Deception of participants in research is regarded as problematic in modern psychology despite having been endemic in some fields, particularly social psychology. Nevertheless, there is no complete ban on deception, only the requirements that the deception is absolutely necessary since the research is important and there is no effective alternative deception-free way of conducting it. The response of participants during debriefing to the deception may be taken as an indicator of the risks inherent in that deception.

- The publication of research is subject to ethical constraints. The fabrication of data, plagiarism of the work of others, claiming the role of author on a publication to which one has only minimally contributed, and the full acknowledgement by first authorship of students' research work are all covered in current ethical guidelines.

- Increasingly, there are more formal constraints on researchers, such as those coming from ethics committees and the increased need to obtain research participants' formal consent. Although data protection legislation can apply to research data, data in a truly anonymous or unidentifiable form are exempt from the legislation.

ACTIVITIES

Are any principles of ethical conduct violated in the following examples? What valid arguments could be made to justify what occurs? These are matters that could be debated. Alternatively, you could list the ethical pros and cons of each before reaching a conclusion.

1. Ken is researching memory and Dawn volunteers to be a participant in the research. Ken is very attracted to Dawn and asks for her address and mobile phone number, explaining that she may need to be contacted for a follow-up interview. This is a lie, as no such interviews are planned. He later phones her up for a date.

2. A research team is planning to study Internet sex offenders. They set up a bogus Internet pornography site – 'All tastes sex'. The site contains a range of links to specialised pages devoted to a specific sexual interest – bondage, mature sex, Asian women and the like. Visitors to the site who press these links see mild pornographic pictures in line with the theme of the link. The main focus of the researchers is on child pornography users on the Internet. To this end they have a series of links labelled '12-year-olds and under', 'young boys need men friends', 'schoolgirls for real', 'sexy toddlers' and so forth. These links lead nowhere but the researchers have the site programmed such that visitors to the different pages can be counted. Furthermore, they have a 'data miner' which implants itself in the visitor's computer and can extract information from that computer and report back to the researchers. They use this information in order to send out an e-mail questionnaire concerning the lifestyle of the visitor to the porn site – details such as their age, interests, address, and so forth, as well as psychological tests. To encourage completion, the researchers claim that in return for completing the questionnaire, they have a chance of being selected for a prize of a Caribbean holiday. The research team is approached by the police, who believe that the data being gathered may be useful in tracking down paedophiles.

3. A student researcher is studying illicit drug use on a university campus. She is given permission to distribute question-naires during an introductory psychology lecture. Participants are assured anonymity and confidentiality, although the researcher has deliberately included questions about demographic information such as the participants' exact date of birth, their home town, the modules they are taking and so forth. However, the student researcher is really interested in personality factors and drug taking. She gets another student to distribute personality questionnaires to the same class a few weeks later. The same information about exact date of birth, home town, place of birth and so forth is collected. This is used to match each drug questionnaire with that same person's personality questionnaire. However, the question-naires are anonymous, since no name is requested.

4. Professor Green is interested in fascist and other far-right political organisations. Since he believes that these organisa-tions would not permit a researcher to observe them, he poses as a market trader and applies for and is given member-ship of several of these organisations. He attends the meetings and other events with other members. He is carrying out participant observation and is compiling extensive notes of what he witnesses for eventual publication.

5. A researcher studying sleep feels that a young man taking part in the research is physically attracted to him. She tries to kiss him.

6. Some researchers believe that watching filmed violence leads to violence in real life. Professor Jenkins carries out a study in which scenes of extreme violence taken from the film *Reservoir Dogs* are shown to a focus group. A week later, one of the participants in the focus group is arrested for the murder of his partner on the day after seeing the film.

7. A discourse analyst examines President Bill Clinton's television claim that he did not have sexual intercourse with Monica Lewinsky, in order to assess discursive strategies that he employed and to seek any evidence of lying. The results of this analysis are published in a psychology journal.

8. 'Kitty Friend complained to an ethics committee about a psychologist she read about in the newspaper who was doing research on evoked potentials in cat brains. She asserted that the use of domesticated cats in research was unethi-cal, inhumane and immoral' (Keith-Spiegel & Koocher, 1985, p. 35). The ethics committee chooses not to consider the complaint.

9. A psychology student chooses to investigate suicidal thoughts in a student population. She distributes a range of personality questionnaires among her friends. While scoring the test, she notices that one of her friends, Tom, has scored heavily on a measure of suicide ideation and has written at the end of the questionnaire that he feels desperately depressed. She knows that it is Tom from the handwriting, which is very distinctive.

10. Steffens (1931) described how along with others he studied the laboratory records of a student of Wilhelm Wundt, generally regarded as the founder of the first psychological laboratory. This student went on to be a distinguished professor in America. Basically, the student's data failed to support aspects of Wundt's psychological writings. Steffens (p. 151) writes:

    [The student] must have thought . . . that Wundt might have been reluctant to crown a discovery which would require the old philosopher [Wundt] to rewrite volumes of his lifework. The budding psychologist solved the ethical problem before him by deciding to alter his results, and his papers showed how he did this, by changing the figures item by item, experiment by experiment, so as to make the curve of his averages come out for instead of against our school. After a few minutes of silent admiration of the mathematical feat performed on the papers before us, we buried sadly these remains of a great sacrifice to loyalty, to the school spirit, and to practical ethics.

PART 2

Quantitative research methods

CHAPTER 9

Basic laboratory experiments

Overview

- Laboratory experiments have a key role in psychological research. They allow the investigation of causal relationships (i.e. cause-and-effect sequences).

- The essence of experiments is the systematic variation of a variable that is thought to have a causal effect and measuring this effect while holding other variables constant.

- The simplest experimental design used by psychologists consists of two conditions. One condition (the experimental condition) has a different level of the manipulated variable than the other condition (the control condition). These two conditions are (levels of) the independent variable. The researcher assesses whether the scores on the measured variable differ between the two conditions. The measured variable is often termed the dependent variable.

- If the size of the effect differs significantly between the two conditions and all variables other than the manipulated variable were held constant, then this difference is most likely due to the manipulated variable.

- Researchers try to hold variables other than the independent and dependent variables constant in various ways. These include randomly assigning participants to the different conditions (which ensures equality in the long run), carrying out the study in the controlled setting of a laboratory where hopefully other factors are constant, and generally making the conditions as similar as possible for all participants except in so far as they are in the experimental or the control condition.

- In between-subjects designs, participants are randomly assigned to just one of the conditions of the study. In within-subjects designs, the same participants carry out all conditions. Rather than being randomly assigned to just one condition, they are randomly assigned to the different orders in which the conditions are to be run.

→

- Random assignment of participants only guarantees that in the long run the participants in all conditions start off similar in all regards. For any individual study, random assignment cannot ensure equality. Consequently, some experimental designs use a prior measure of the dependent variable (the measured variable) which can be used to assess how effective the random assignment has been. The experimental and control groups should have similar (ideally identical) mean scores on this pre-measure, which is known as the pre-test. The measurement after the experimental manipulation is known as a post-test in this sort of design. The difference between the pre-test and the post-test provides an indication of the change in the measured variable.

- Disadvantages of the basic laboratory experiment include the obvious artificiality of the laboratory experiment compared with naturalistic settings. Furthermore, practicalities mean the number of variables that may be manipulated in a single experiment is limited, which can be frustrating when one is studying a complex psychological process.

9.1   Introduction

Used appropriately, the randomised laboratory experiment is one of the most powerful research tools. This simply means that the laboratory is an appropriate environment for studying many psychological processes – particularly physiological, sensory or cognitive processes. However, it is not always or even often ideal, nor is it every researcher's preferred method. The use of the laboratory to study social processes, for example, is not greeted with universal enthusiasm. Nevertheless, true or randomised laboratory experiments are commonplace. Any psychologist, even if they never carry out a laboratory experiment in their professional career, needs to understand the basics of laboratory experimental research, otherwise much psychological research might fly over their heads.

It is essential to differentiate between two major sorts of laboratory experimental designs (Grice, 1966; see Figure 9.1) which are common:

- Experiments in which different participants take part in different conditions are known variously as between-subjects, between-participants, independent-groups, unrelated-groups or uncorrelated-groups designs. Figure 9.2a shows a simple between-subjects design with only two conditions.

- Designs in which the same participants take part in all (or sometimes some) of the various conditions are called within-subjects, within-participants, repeated-measures, dependent-groups, related-groups or correlated-groups designs. Figure 9.2b shows a simple within-subjects design with only two conditions.

An example of a between-subjects design would be a study comparing the number of errors made entering data into a computer spreadsheet for a sample of people listening to loud popular music with the number of errors made by a different control sample listening to white noise at the same volume. That is to say, two different groups of people are compared. An example of a within-subjects design would be a study of the number of keyboard errors made by a group of 20 secretaries, comparing the number of errors when music is being played with the number when music is not being

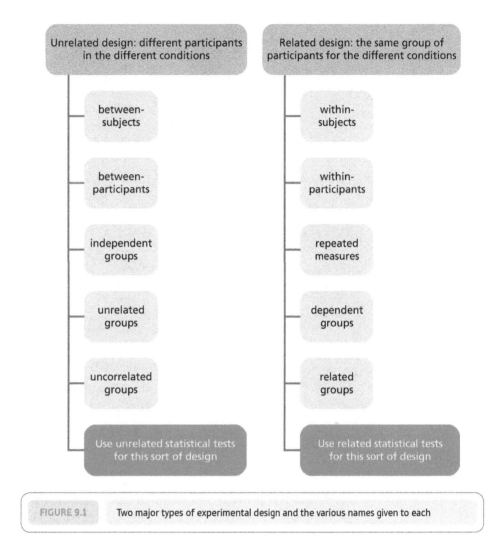

FIGURE 9.1   Two major types of experimental design and the various names given to each

played. Thus, the performance of one group of people is compared in two different circumstances.

One important reason to distinguish between these two broad types of design is that they use rather different methods of statistical analysis. The first design, which uses different groups of participants for each condition, would require an unrelated statistical test (such as the unrelated or uncorrelated t-test). The second design, in which the same group of participants take part in every condition of the experiment, would require a related statistical test (such as the related or correlated t-test). In brief, the reason for this is that the related design helps to control for the variation between individuals which affects their performance in the different conditions. In other words, there is less unaccounted for variation. Strictly speaking, the scores in the different conditions should correlate if a correlated or related test of significance is used, but this is generally not mentioned by psychologists in their reports. However, computer programs such as SPSS do actually provide the required statistics to make this judgement as part of the output for correlated tests. This is discussed in greater detail in Howitt and Cramer (2020).

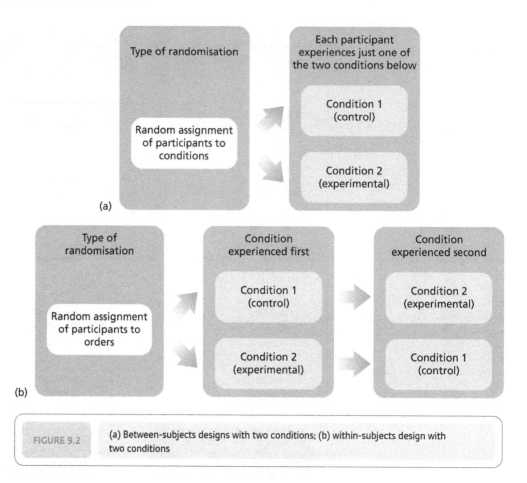

FIGURE 9.2   (a) Between-subjects designs with two conditions; (b) within-subjects design with two conditions

Although it is perfectly feasible to do experiments in a wide variety of settings, a custom-designed research laboratory is usually preferred. There are two main reasons for using a research laboratory:

- *Practicalities*   A study may require the use of equipment or apparatus that may be too bulky or too heavy to move elsewhere, or needs to be kept secure because it may be expensive or inconvenient to replace.

- *Experimental control*   In an experiment, it is important to try to keep all factors constant other than the variable or variables that are manipulated. This is obviously easier to do in a room or laboratory that is custom-designed for the task and in which all participants take part in the study. The lighting, the temperature, the noise and the arrangement of any equipment can all be kept constant. In addition, other distractions such as people walking through or talking can be excluded. You will often find great detail about the physical set-up of the laboratory where the research was done in reports of laboratory experiments.

The importance of holding these extraneous or environmental factors constant depends on how strong the effect of the manipulated variable is on the measured variable. Unfortunately, the researcher is unlikely to know in advance what their effect is. To the extent that the extraneous variable seems or has been shown not to influence the key variables in the research, one may consider moving the research to a more appropriate or convenient research location. For example, if you are carrying out a study in a school, it is unlikely that that school will have a purpose-built psychology laboratory for you to use. You may find yourself in a room which is normally used for other functions. If it is important that you control the kind or the level of noise in the room, which will vary throughout the day as this is a school location, you could do this by playing what is called 'white noise' through earphones worn by each participant. If it is essential that the study takes place in a more carefully controlled setting, then the pupils will need to come to your laboratory.

Inevitably although researchers may aim for perfection, most research is something of a compromise between various considerations. The perfect research study has probably never been designed and is probably an oxymoron. That should not stop you trying for the best possible, but it should be remembered when you seem not to be able to reach the highest standard in your research.

Because of the important role it plays in psychological research, we introduced the concept of a true experiment early in this book (Chapter 1). As we saw, studies employing a true or randomised experimental design are the commonest type of psychological research (Bodner, 2006a). They constituted 41 per cent of all the studies sampled in 1999. The percentage of true or randomised experimental designs was highest in areas such as learning, perception, cognition and memory. These are areas of research which were traditionally called experimental psychology because of their heavy use of this design.

9.2   Characteristics of the true or randomised experiment

The most basic laboratory experiment is easily demonstrated. Decide on an experimental and control group and allocate participants to one or other on the basis of a coin toss. Put the experimental group through a slightly different procedure from that of the comparison (control) group (Coover & Angell, 1907; Hahn & Thorndike, 1914; Kottenkamp & Ullrich, 1870; Solomon, 1949). This is known as the experimental manipulation and corresponds to a variable which the researcher believes might affect responses on another variable called the dependent variable. After the data have been collected, the researcher examines the average score for the two conditions to see whether they differ substantially. For many purposes, such a simple design will work well.

There are three essential aspects which need to be understood in order to design effective experiments (see Figure 9.3):

- Experimental manipulation of independent variable

- Standardisation of procedures – that is, the control of all variables other than the independent variable

- Random assignment to conditions or order of conditions.

Each of these is described in the following sections in turn.

Experimental manipulation

Only the variable that is assumed to cause or affect another variable is manipulated (varied) by the researcher in the simplest experiments. This manipulated variable is often referred to as the *independent variable* because it is assumed to be varied independently of any other variable (Winston, 1988; Woodworth, 1934). If it is not manipulated independently, then any effect that we observe may in fact be due to those other variables. An example of an independent variable is amount of alcohol. It is a reasonable expectation to think that alcohol can increase the number of mistakes we make on tasks, so it is a worthwhile issue for a researcher to investigate. In such a study, alcohol (or more strictly speaking, the level or amount of alcohol) is the independent variable which would be

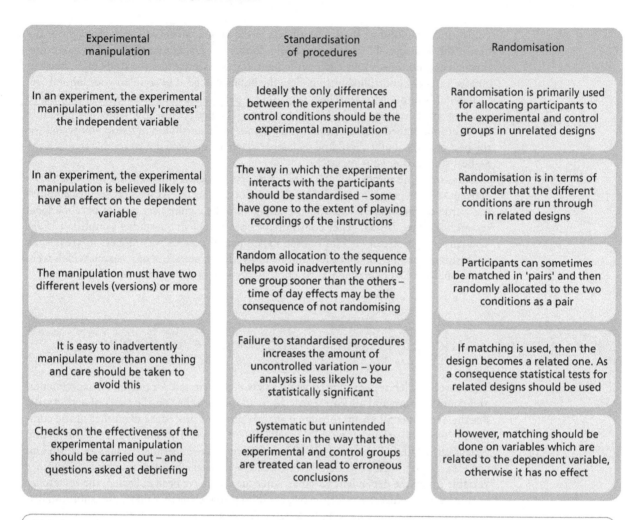

Experimental manipulation	Standardisation of procedures	Randomisation
In an experiment, the experimental manipulation essentially 'creates' the independent variable	Ideally the only differences between the experimental and control conditions should be the experimental manipulation	Randomisation is primarily used for allocating participants to the experimental and control groups in unrelated designs
In an experiment, the experimental manipulation is believed likely to have an effect on the dependent variable	The way in which the experimenter interacts with the participants should be standardised – some have gone to the extent of playing recordings of the instructions	Randomisation is in terms of the order that the different conditions are run through in related designs
The manipulation must have two different levels (versions) or more	Random allocation to the sequence helps avoid inadvertently running one group sooner than the others – time of day effects may be the consequence of not randomising	Participants can sometimes be matched in 'pairs' and then randomly allocated to the two conditions as a pair
It is easy to inadvertently manipulate more than one thing and care should be taken to avoid this	Failure to standardised procedures increases the amount of uncontrolled variation – your analysis is less likely to be statistically significant	If matching is used, then the design becomes a related one. As a consequence statistical tests for related designs should be used
Checks on the effectiveness of the experimental manipulation should be carried out – and questions asked at debriefing	Systematic but unintended differences in the way that the experimental and control groups are treated can lead to erroneous conclusions	However, matching should be done on variables which are related to the dependent variable, otherwise it has no effect

FIGURE 9.3   Essential features in a simple experimental design summarised

manipulated. The measured variable (errors) that is presumed to be affected by the independent or manipulated variable is called the *dependent variable* because it is thought to be dependent on the independent variable. In this example, the dependent variable is the number of mistakes made in a task such as walking along a straight line.

In the most basic true or randomised experiment, we would have only two *conditions* (also known as *levels of treatment* or *groups;* Baxter, 1941; Fisher, 1935). In one condition, a lower amount of alcohol would be given to the participant, while in the other condition the participant receives a higher level of alcohol. The amount of alcohol given would be standard for all participants in a condition. So, in condition 1, the amount might be standardised as 8 millilitres (ml). This is about the amount of alcohol in a glass of wine. In the second condition, the amount may be doubled to 16 ml. If the size of the effect varies directly with the amount of alcohol given, then the more the two groups will differ on the measured variable. That is, the effect will be bigger.

Why did we choose to give *both* groups alcohol? After all, we could have given the experimental group alcohol but the control group no alcohol at all. By giving both groups alcohol, we hope that participants in both groups are aware that they have consumed alcohol. Participants receiving alcohol probably realise that they have been given alcohol. Unless the quantity of alcohol was very small, participants may detect it. So two things have happened – they have been given alcohol and they are also aware that they have been given alcohol. However, if one group received no alcohol then, unless we deliberately misled them, members of this group will not believe that they have taken alcohol. So we would not know whether the alcohol or the belief that they had been given alcohol was the key causal variable. Since the effects of alcohol are well known, participants believing that they have taken alcohol may behave accordingly. By giving both groups alcohol, both groups will believe that they have taken alcohol. The only thing that varies is the key variable of the amount of alcohol taken. In good experimental research the effectiveness of the experimental manipulation should be evaluated. This is discussed in Box 9.1. In our example, at the end of the study in a debriefing interview, participants in the experiment might be asked about whether or not they believed that they had taken alcohol.

| Box 9.1 | Key Ideas |

Checks on the experimental manipulation

It can be a grave mistake to assume that simply because an experimental manipulation has been introduced by the researcher, the independent variable has actually been effectively manipulated. It might be argued that if the researcher finds a difference between the experimental and control conditions on the dependent variable, the manipulation must have been effective, but things are not that simple. The experimental manipulation may have affected the participants but not quite in the expected way.

Assume that we are investigating the effects of anger on memory. In order to manipulate anger, the researcher deliberately says certain pre-scripted offensive comments to the participants in the experimental group, whereas nice things are said to the participants in the control group. It is very presumptuous to assume that this procedure will work effectively without subjecting it to some test to show that that is the case.

For example, the participants might well in some circumstances regard the offensive comments as a joke rather than an insult, so the manipulation may make them happier rather than angrier. Alternatively, the control may find the nice comments of the experimenter to be patronising and become somewhat annoyed or angry as a consequence. So there is always some uncertainty as to whether or not the experimental manipulation has actually worked. One relatively simple thing to do in this case would be to get participants to complete a questionnaire about their mood containing a list of various emotional states, such as angry, happy and sad, for the participant to rate their own feelings on in the study. In this way, it is possible to assess whether the experimental group was indeed angrier than the control group following the anger manipulation.

Alternatively, at the debriefing session following participation in the experiment, the participants could be asked about how they felt after the experimenter said the offensive or nice things. This check would also demonstrate that the manipulation had a measurable effect on the participants' anger levels.

Sometimes it is appropriate, as part of pilot work trying out one's procedures prior to the study proper, to establish the effectiveness of the experimental manipulation. This makes establishing the effectiveness of the experimental manipulation a distinct step in the research. Researchers should not assume, without further evidence, that simply obtaining statistically significant differences between the experimental and control conditions is evidence of the effectiveness of their experimental manipulation. If the experimental manipulation has had an effect on the participants but not the one intended, it is vital that the researcher knows this, otherwise the conceptual basis for their analysis may be inappropriate. For example, they may be discussing the effects of anger when they should be discussing the effects of happiness.

In our experience, checks on the experimental manipulation are not common in published research and are probably even rarer in student research. Yet such checks seem to be essential. As we have seen, the debriefing session can be an ideal opportunity to interview participants about this aspect of the study along with its other features. The most thorough researchers may also consider a more objective demonstration of the effectiveness of the manipulation, as described above when the participants' mood was assessed. Using both would be the optimum.

The condition of having the lower quantity of alcohol is referred to as the *control condition*. The condition of having the higher quantity of alcohol may be called the *experimental condition*. The purpose of the control condition is to see how participants behave when they receive a lower level of the variable that is being manipulated.

In theory, if not always in practice, the experimental and control conditions should be identical in every way but for the variable being manipulated. It is easy to overlook differences and the researcher needs to constantly be aware of this possibility. So, in our alcohol experiment participants in both groups should be given the same total quantity of liquid to drink. But it is easy to overlook this if the low-alcohol group are given, say, one glass of wine and the high-alcohol group two glasses of wine. If the participants in the control condition are not given the same amount to drink, then alcohol is not being manipulated independently of all other factors. Participants in the experimental condition would have been given more to drink, while participants in the control condition would have been given less to drink. If we find that reaction time was slower in the experimental condition than in the control condition, then this could be due to either the alcohol or the amount of liquid drunk. Despite this being superficially very pernickety, it is possible that dehydration through having less liquid may have an effect on behaviour, or the participant may find it difficult to concentrate because they need to go to the toilet! The point of the laboratory experiment is that we try to control as many factors as possible despite the difficulty involved in doing this. Of course, variations in the volume of liquid drunk could be introduced into the research design in order to discover what the effect of varying volume is on errors. This might be seen as a worthwhile improvement to the research design.

Standardisation of procedures

A second essential characteristic of the true experiment is implicit in the previous characteristic. That is, all factors should be held constant apart from the variable(s) being investigated. This is largely achieved by standardising all aspects of the procedures employed. Only the experimental manipulation should vary. To standardise procedures perfectly is, of course, somewhat of an impossibility, but it is an ideal to aim for. The less variation due to factors other than the manipulated variable in a study, the better, as this extraneous variation can swamp the influence of the manipulated variable. We saw the importance of this in our alcohol study when we stressed that the two conditions should be identical apart from the amount of alcohol taken. So participants in both conditions were made aware that they would be given alcohol and they are given the same amount of liquid to drink.

Other factors needing to be held constant are not so obvious: the time of day the study is carried out, the body weight of the participants, how long it is since they last ate, and so forth. Standardisation is not always easy to achieve. For example, what about variations in the behaviour of the experimenter during an experiment? If this differs systematically between the two groups, then experimenter behaviour and the effects of the independent variable will be confounded. We may confuse the variability in the behaviour of the experimenter with the effects of different quantities of alcohol. Some experiments have used an automated procedure in which there is no experimenter present in the laboratory. As an illustration, audio-recorded instructions could be played to participants through loudspeakers in the laboratory ensuring that all participants hear identical presentations.

Standardisation of procedures is part of the gold standard for the laboratory experiment though easier said than done. At a minimum, details such as the instructions to participants would usually be written out as a guide for the experimenter when running the experiment. However, the procedures used in experiments vary greatly which makes it impossible to offer advice that would apply in every case. Because of the difficulty in standardising all aspects of the experiment, it is desirable to randomly order the running of the experimental and control conditions. For example, we know that cognitive functions vary according to the time of day. It is very difficult to standardise the time of day at which an experiment is run. Hence it is desirable to decide randomly which condition the participant who arrives at 2.30 p.m. will be assigned to, and so forth. In this way, there will be no systematic bias for one of the conditions of the experiment to be run at different times of the day from the other conditions.

■ Random assignment

Random assignment is the third essential feature of an experiment (Fisher, 1925, p. 264; Hall, 2007). There are two main procedures according to the type of experimental design:

- Participants are put in the experimental or the control condition at random using a proper randomisation procedure. This may be simply the toss of a coin – heads the experimental group, tails the control group. Other methods of randomisation will be discussed later. Random assignment to conditions is used when the participants take part in only one condition.

- Alternatively, if participants undertake more than one condition (in the simplest case both the experimental and the control conditions), then they are randomly assigned to the different orders of those two conditions. With just two conditions there are just two possible orders – experimental condition first followed by control condition second, or control condition first followed by experimental condition second. Of course, with three or more conditions, there is a rapidly increasing number of possible orders.

It is easy to get confused about the term 'random'. The word should never be used carelessly by psychologists and its formal meaning should always be applied. Random assignment requires the use of a proper random procedure. This is not the same thing at all as a haphazard or casual choice. By random we mean that each possible outcome has an equal chance of being selected. We do not want a selection process which systematically favours one outcome rather than another. (e.g. the toss of a coin is normally a random process but it would not be if the coin has been doctored to land heads up mostly.)

There are a number of random procedures that may be employed. We have already mentioned the toss of a coin but will include it again in the list of possibilities, as it is a good and simple procedure:

- With two conditions or orders, you can toss a coin and assign the participant to one of them if the coin lands 'heads' up and to the other if it lands 'tails' up.

- Similarly, especially if there are more than two conditions, you could throw a die.

- You could write the two conditions or orders on two separate index cards or slips of paper, shuffle them without seeing them and select one of them.

- Computers can be used to generate a sequence of random numbers. Try searching on the Internet using the term 'random number generator' and you will find sites that provide you with a random sequence of numbers which you could use for random allocation. There are apps which allow you to do much the same on your mobile phone.

- You could use random number tables where, say, even numbers represent one condition or order and odd numbers represent the other one. These tables can be found in some statistics textbooks.

You could either go through one of these randomisation procedures for each successive participant or draw up a list in advance for the entire experiment. However, there are two things you need to consider:

- You may find that you have 'runs' of the same condition, such as six participants in sequence all of whom are in, say, the control group. If you get runs like this, you may find, for example, that you are testing one condition more often at a particular time of day. That is, despite the randomisation, the two conditions are not similar in all respects. For example, these six participants may all be tested in the morning rather than spread throughout the day.

- Alternatively, you may find that the number of participants in the two conditions or orders is very different. There is even a remote possibility that all your participants are assigned to one condition or order.

Randomisation only equates things in the long run. In the short run, it merely guarantees that there is no systematic bias in the selection. In the short term, chance may nevertheless lead to differences between the conditions.

There is no need to go into technical details, but if it is possible to have equal numbers in each condition of an experimental design, then you should try to do so. However, you will find that computers will give you statistical output even where the sample sizes are uneven. Equal sample sizes generally give you the optimum test of significance. Nevertheless, if equal numbers are impossible, then so be it. One can ensure that there are equal numbers of participants in each condition in various ways. For example, one can employ *matched* or *block randomisation*. That is, the first participant of every pair of participants is assigned at random using a specified procedure, while the second participant is assigned to the remaining condition or order. So, if the first participant has been randomly assigned to the control condition, the second participant will be allocated to the experimental condition. If you do this, the result will be equal numbers of participants in the two conditions or orders if you have an even number of participants. Box 9.2 discusses how you can pair off participants to ensure that the different groups have similar characteristics.

In the between-subjects design (in which participants serve in just one condition of the experiment), any differences between the participants are usually controlled by random assignment. The prime purpose of this is to avoid systematic biases in the allocation of participants to one or other condition. If the experimenter merely decided on the spot which group a participant should be in, then all sorts of 'subconscious' factors may influence this choice and perhaps affect the experiment's outcome as a consequence. For example, without randomisation a researcher might allocate mainly males to the experimental group and females to the control group – and not even notice what they have done. If there is a gender difference on the dependent variable, the results of the experiment may confuse the experimental effect with the bias in participant selection.

Conceptually, randomisation can be regarded in rather more complex ways and the language which researchers use needs to be carefully understood. When referring to randomisation in between-subjects randomised experiments (what we called the unrelated design earlier) we usually say something like participants were randomly assigned to what we variously call treatments, conditions or groups. In effect, however, we randomly vary the order of the treatments and assign participants sequentially to those treatments (e.g. Schulz & Grimes, 2002). As we cannot usually administer all treatments simultaneously, we use a random procedure to decide the order in which the conditions are run and then we allocate the first participant to the first condition in that sequence. Next we allocate the second participant to a second condition in that sequence, and so on. Note this second condition may be the same as the first condition in a random order just as we can flip two heads or two tails in a row.

This procedure is somewhat analogous to Fisher's (1935) agricultural field experiments in which the plots of earth were randomly ordered and then the seed varieties were allocated to them. Strictly speaking, if participants had actually been randomly assigned to the treatment, then the order of the treatments would also have to be randomly varied. Obviously we would not want the extreme case where all of one treatment were run first, followed by all of another treatment, and so on. Ideally the order would be random.

If we had randomly assigned participants to treatments, we would have to carry out two randomisations. First, we would have to randomly allocate participants to treatments and then we would have to randomly vary the order of treatments because we cannot usually run all treatments at the same time. This double randomisation procedure would be more complicated and unnecessary. So, it would seem more accurate to say that participants were allocated to a random order of the treatments in a between-subjects randomised experiment but it remains to be seen whether this more seemingly accurate phraseology will be adopted.

If there is more than one experimenter carrying out a randomised experiment (McGuigan, 1963), then experimenters should also be randomly assigned to conditions as any two experimenters may potentially differ as much as any two participants. We would like to control for these experimenter differences through randomisation. In clinical trials where there is more than one clinician, the clinician should be randomly assigned to treatments (e.g. Michelson, Mavissakalian, & Marchione, 1985; Vernmark et al., 2010) as clinicians also vary. However, this may not be possible where the particular expertise of the clinician is tied to and therefore confounded with the treatment. For example, if we were comparing behaviour therapy with psychoanalytic therapy, then we could not really expect the same therapists to be equally experienced in both therapies and so it would not be appropriate to allocate them to the two treatments, regardless of whether we did this randomly. Many randomised clinical trials unfortunately do not describe in sufficient detail the randomisation procedure used making it difficult to evaluate the procedure employed (e.g. Matar, Almerie, Al Marhi, & Adams, 2009). Given that randomisation is one of the key defining features of a true experiment, it is important to describe it as fully as other key features of a randomised experiment. This is not usually done.

Box 9.2   Key Ideas

Matching

One way of ensuring that the participants in the experimental and control groups are similar on variables which might be expected to affect the outcome of the study is to use matching. Participants in an experiment will vary in many ways, so there may be occasions when you want to ensure that there is a degree of consistency. For instance, some participants may be older than others unless we ensure that they are all the same age. However, it is difficult, if not impossible, to control for all possible individual differences. For example, some participants may have had less sleep than others the night before or gone without breakfast, some might have more familiarity than others with the type of task to be carried out, and so on.

We could try to hold all these factors constant by making sure, for example, that all participants were female, aged 18, weighed 12 stone (76 kilograms), had slept seven hours the night before, and so on. But this would be difficult. It is generally much more practicable to use random assignment. To simplify this illustration, we will think of all these variables as being dichotomous (i.e. having only two categories) such as female/male, older/younger, heavier/lighter and so on. If you look at Table 9.1, you will see that we have arranged our 24 possible participants in order and that they fall into sets of individuals who have the same pattern of characteristics on these three variables. For example, the first three individuals are all female, older and heavier. This is a matched set of individuals. We could choose one of these three at random to be in the experimental condition and another at random to be in the control condition. The third individual would not be matched with anyone else, so they cannot be used in our matched study in this case. We could then move on to the next set of matched participants and select one of them at random for the experimental condition and a second for the control condition.

→

Table 9.1	Gender, age and weight details for 24 participants		
Number	**Gender**	**Age**	**Weight**
1	female	older	heavier
2	female	older	heavier
3	female	older	heavier
4	female	older	lighter
5	female	older	lighter
6	female	older	lighter
7	female	younger	heavier
8	female	younger	heavier
9	female	younger	heavier
10	female	younger	lighter
11	female	younger	lighter
12	female	younger	lighter
13	male	older	heavier
14	male	older	heavier
15	male	older	heavier
16	male	older	lighter
17	male	older	lighter
18	male	older	lighter
19	male	younger	heavier
20	male	younger	heavier
21	male	younger	heavier
22	male	younger	lighter
23	male	younger	lighter
24	male	younger	lighter

You might like to try this with the remaining cases in Table 9.1 using the information given concerning the gender, age and weight of the 24 people we are going to randomly assign to the two groups.

Matching is a useful tool in some circumstances. There are a few things that have to be remembered if you use matching as part of your research design:

- The appropriate statistical tests are those for related data, so a test like the related *t*-test, the Wilcoxon matched pairs test or the related ANOVA would be appropriate.

- Variables which correlate with both the independent and the dependent variables are needed for the matching variables. If a variable is unrelated to either or both of the independent or dependent variables, there is no point in using it as a matching variable. It could make no difference to the outcome of the study.

- The most appropriate variable to match on is probably the dependent variable measured at the start of the study. This is not unrelated to the idea of pre-testing (see below), though in pre-testing, participants have already been allocated to the experimental and the control conditions. But pre-testing, you've guessed it, also has its problems.

9.3   More advanced research designs

This chapter has stressed throughout that there is no such thing as a perfect research design that can be used irrespective of the research question and circumstances. If there were then not only would this book be rather short but also research would probably rank in the top three most boring jobs in the world. Research is intellectually challenging because it is problematic. The best research that any of us can do is probably a compromise between a wide range of different considerations. In this chapter, we are essentially looking at the simplest laboratory experiment in which we have a single independent variable. But even this basic experimental design gathers levels of complexity as we try to plug the holes in the simple research design we plan. So even the simplest research design has problems. For example, if a single study is to be relied on, then the more certain we are that the experimental and control conditions are similar prior to the experimental manipulation, the better. One way to achieve this is obvious: assess the two groups prior to the experimental manipulation to see whether they are similar on the dependent variable. This is a good move but, as we will see, it brings with it further problems to solve. It should be stressed that none of what you are about to read reduces the importance of using random allocation procedures for participants in experimental studies.

Pre-test and post-test sensitisation effects

The pre-test is a way of checking whether random assignment has, in fact, equated the experimental and control groups on the dependent variable prior to the experimental manipulation which is crucial. Otherwise it is not possible to know whether the differences following the experimental manipulation are due to the experimental manipulation or to pre-existing differences between the groups on the dependent variable.

The number of mistakes is the dependent variable in our alcohol-effects example. If members of one group make more mistakes than do members of the other group *before* drinking alcohol, they are likely to make more mistakes *after* drinking alcohol. For example, if the participants in the 8 ml alcohol condition have a tendency to make more errors regardless of whether or not they have had any alcohol, they may make more mistakes after drinking 8 ml of alcohol than the participants who have drunk 16 ml.

This situation is illustrated in Figure 9.4. In this graph, the vertical axis represents the number of mistakes made. On the horizontal axis are two marks which indicate participants' performance before and after drinking alcohol. The measurement of the participants' performance before receiving the manipulation is usually called the *pre-test*

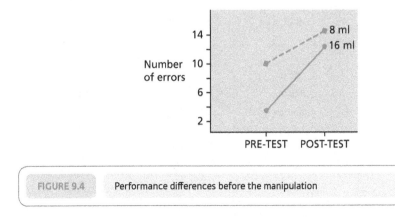

| FIGURE 9.4 | Performance differences before the manipulation |

and the measurement after receiving the manipulation the *post-test*. The results of the post-test are usually placed after those of the pre-test in graphs and tables, as time is usually depicted as travelling from left to right.

Without the pre-test measure, there is only the measure of performance after drinking alcohol. Just looking at these post-test measures, people who drank 8 ml of alcohol made more mistakes than those who drank 16 ml. In other words, drinking more alcohol seems to have resulted in making *fewer* mistakes, not more mistakes as we might have anticipated. This interpretation is incorrect since, by chance, random assignment to conditions resulted in the participants in the 8 ml condition being those who tend to make more mistakes. Without the pre-test we cannot know this, however.

It is clearer to see what is going on if we calculate the difference between the number of mistakes made at pre-test and the number made at post-test (simply by subtracting one from the other). Now it can be seen that the increase in the number of mistakes was greater for the 16 ml condition ($12 - 4 = 8$) than for the 8 ml condition ($14 - 10 = 4$). In other words, the increase in the number of mistakes made was greater for those drinking more alcohol.

We can illustrate the situation summarised in Figure 9.4 with the fictitious raw data in Table 9.2 where there are three participants in each of the two conditions. Each participant is represented by the letter P with a subscript from 1 to 6 to indicate the six different participants. There are two scores for each participant – the first for the pre-test and the second for the post-test. These data could be analysed in a number of different ways. Among the better of these would be the mixed-design analysis of variance. This statistical test is described in some introductory statistics texts such as the companion book *Understanding statistics in psychology with SPSS* (Howitt & Cramer, 2020). However, this requires more than a basic level of statistical sophistication. If you are already familiar with analysis of variance, essentially you would be looking for an interaction effect between time (pre-test/post-test) and the independent variable. A simpler way of analysing the same data would be to compare the differences between the pre-test and post-test measures for the two conditions. An unrelated *t*-test would be suitable for this.

Experimental designs which include a pre-test are referred to as a pre-test–post-test design, while those without a pre-test are called a post-test-only design. There are two main advantages of having a pre-test:

- As we have already seen, it enables us to determine whether randomisation has worked in the sense of equating the groups on the dependent variable prior to the experimental

Table 9.2	Fictitious data for a pre-test–post-test two-group design		
	Participant	Pre-test	Post-test
Condition 1	P_1	9	13
	P_2	10	15
	P_3	11	14
Sum		30	42
Mean		30/3 = 10	42/3 = 14
Condition 2	P_4	3	12
	P_5	4	11
	P_6	5	13
Sum		12	36
Mean		12/3 = 4	36/3 = 12

manipulation. If the pre-test scores are not similar, then we can make them the same statistically by carrying out an analysis of covariance (ANCOVA) in which we covary and hold constant the pre-test scores.

● It allows us to determine whether or not there has been a change in performance between pre-test and post-test. If we just have the post-test scores, we cannot tell whether there has been a change in those scores and what that change is. For example, the post-test scores may show a decline from the pre-test. Without the pre-test, we may suggest incorrectly that the independent variable is increasing the scores on the dependent variable.

In order to understand why a pre-test may be useful, look at the data shown in the graph in Figure 9.5. Concentrate on the post-test scores and ignore the pre-test. That is, pretend that we have a post-test-only design for the moment. Participants who had drunk 16 ml of alcohol made more errors than those who had drunk 8 ml. From these results, we may conclude that drinking more alcohol increases the number of mistakes made. If the pre-test number of errors made were as shown in Figure 9.5, this interpretation would be incorrect. If we know the pre-test scores, we can see that drinking 16 ml of alcohol decreased the number of errors made ($10 - 14 = -4$), while drinking 8 ml of alcohol had no effect on the number of errors ($6 - 6 = 0$). Having a pre-test enables us to determine whether or not randomisation has been successful and what, if any, was the change in the scores. (Indeed, we are not being precise if we talk of the conditions in a post-test-only study as increasing or decreasing scores on the dependent variable. All that we can legitimately say is that there is a difference between the conditions.)

Whatever their advantages, pre-tests have disadvantages. One common criticism of pre-test designs is that they may alert participants to the purpose of the experiment and consequently influence their behaviour. That is, the pre-test affects or sensitises participants in terms of their behaviour on the post-test (Lana, 1969; Solomon, 1949; Wilson & Putnam, 1982). Again, we might extend our basic research design to take this into account. We need to add to our basic design groups which undergo the pre-test and other groups which do not. Solomon (1949) called this a four-group design, since at a minimum there will be two groups (an experimental and a control group) that include a pre-test and two further groups that do not have a pre-test, as shown in Figure 9.6.

One way of analysing the results of this more sophisticated design is to tabulate the data as illustrated in Table 9.3. This contains fictitious post-test scores for three participants in each of the four conditions. The pre-test scores are *not* given in Table 9.3. Each participant is represented by the letter P with a subscript consisting of a number ranging from 1 to 12 to denote there are 12 participants.

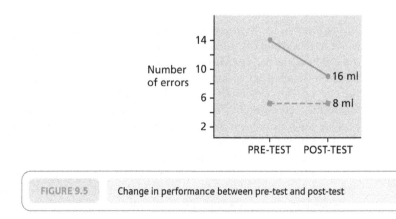

| FIGURE 9.5 | Change in performance between pre-test and post-test |

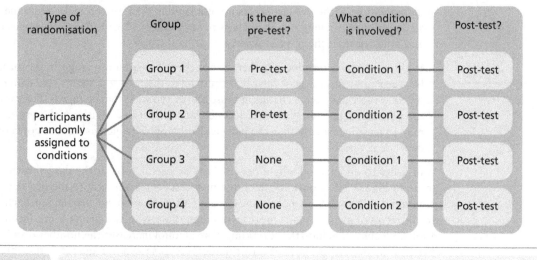

FIGURE 9.6   Solomon's (1949) four-group design

Table 9.3	Fictitious post-test scores for a Solomon four-group design

	Had pre-test	Had no pre-test	
Condition 1	$P_1 = 4$	$P_7 = 0$	
	$P_2 = 5$	$P_8 = 1$	
	$P_3 = 6$	$P_9 = 2$	
Sum	15	3	Row total = 18
Cell mean	$15/3 = 5$	$3/3 = 1$	Row mean = $18/6 = 3$
Condition 2	$P_4 = 10$	$P_{10} = 2$	
	$P_5 = 11$	$P_{11} = 3$	
	$P_6 = 12$	$P_{12} = 4$	
Sum	33	9	Row total = 42
Cell mean	$33/3 = 11$	$9/3 = 3$	Row mean = $42/6 = 7$
Column sums	48	12	
Column means	$48/6 = 8$	$12/6 = 2$	

The analysis of these data involves combining the data over the two conditions. That is, we have a group of six cases which had a pre-test and another group of six cases which did not have the pre-test. The mean score of the group which had a pre-test is 8, whereas the mean score of the group which had no pre-test is 2. In other words, we are ignoring the effect of the two conditions at this stage. We have a pre-test sensitisation effect if the means for these two (combined) conditions differ significantly. In our example, there may be a pre-test sensitisation effect, since the mean score of the combined two conditions with the pre-test is 8, which is higher than the mean score of 2 for the two conditions without the pre-test combined. If this difference is statistically significant, we have a pre-test sensitisation effect. (The difference in the two means could be tested using an unrelated t-test. Alternatively, one could use a two-way analysis of variance. In this case, we would look for a pre-test–no pre-test main effect.)

Of course, it is possible that the pre-test sensitisation effect is different for the experimental and control conditions (conditions 1 and 2):

- For condition 1, we can see in Table 9.3 that the difference in the mean score for the group with the pre-test and the group without the pre-test is $5 - 1 = 4$

- For condition 2, we can see that the difference in the mean score for the group with the pre-test and the group without the pre-test is $11 - 3 = 8$

In other words, the mean scores of the two conditions with the pre-test and the two conditions without the pre-test appear to depend on, or interact with, the condition in question. The effect of pre-test sensitisation is greater for condition 1 than for condition 2. The difference between the two in our example is quite small, however. This differential effect of the pre-test according to the condition in question would be termed a pre-test or condition interaction effect. We could test for such an interaction effect using a two-way analysis of variance. How to do this is described in some introductory statistics texts such as the companion volume *Understanding statistics in psychology with SPSS* (Howitt & Cramer, 2020). If the interaction between the pre-test and the experimental condition is statistically significant, we have a pre-test sensitisation interaction effect.

If you are beginning to lose the plot in a sea of numbers and tables, perhaps the following will help. Pre-test sensitisation simply means that participants who are pre-tested on the dependent variable tend to have different scores on the post-test from the participants who were not pre-tested. There are many reasons for this. For example, the pre-test may simply coach the participants in the task in question. However, the pre-test or condition interaction means that the effect of pre-testing is different for the experimental and the control conditions. Again, there may be many reasons why the effects of pre-testing will differ for the experimental group. For example, participants in the experimental group may have many more clues as to what the experimenter is expecting to happen. As a consequence, they may change their behaviour more in the experimental condition than in the control condition.

Pre-test sensitisation in itself may not be a problem, whereas if it interacts with the condition to produce different outcomes it is problematic:

- A pre-test sensitisation interaction effect causes uncertainties in interpreting the results of a study. We simply do not know with certainty whether the effect is different in the different conditions. Further investigation would be needed to shed additional light on the matter. If we are interested in understanding this differential effect, we need to investigate it further to find out why it has occurred.

- A pre-test sensitisation effect without a pre-test sensitisation interaction effect would not be a problem if we are simply interested in the relative effect of an independent variable and not its absolute effect. For example, it would not be a problem if we just wanted to know whether drinking a greater amount of alcohol leads to making more errors than drinking a smaller amount. The size of the difference would be similar with a pre-test to without one. On the other hand, we might be interested in the absolute number of errors made by drinking alcohol. For example, we may want to recommend the maximum amount of alcohol that can be taken without affecting performance as a driver. In these circumstances, it is important to know about pre-test sensitisation effects if these result in greater errors. In this case, we would base our recommendation on the testing condition which resulted in the greater number of errors.

Various techniques may help to reduce pre-test sensitisation to a minimum when using a pretest:

- Try disguising the pre-test by embedding it in another apparently unrelated task or context.

- Increase the time between the pre-test and the manipulation so that the pre-test may have less effect on the post-test. So if the pre-test serves as a practice for the post-test measure, a big interval of time may result in a reduced practice effect.

● Where the experimental manipulation is likely to have only short-lived effects, one could administer the 'pre-test' *after* the post-test! For example, in a study of alcohol's effects, the participants could be tested again a few hours later when its effects had worn away. The two groups could be tested to see whether they made similar numbers of errors once the effects of alcohol had dissipated.

While there are many studies which use a pre-test and a post-test measure fruitfully, the Solomon four-groups design is rarely used. That is, while it is important to be aware of pre-test sensitisation effects, we know few published studies which actually tested for them.

Within-subjects design

Where the same participants take part in all conditions, this effectively controls for differences between participants. For example, a participant may make numerous errors irrespective of the experimental condition. Because this person is in every experimental condition, their pre-existing tendency to make many errors applies equally to all conditions. The effect of alcohol will be additional to their pre-existing tendencies. The within-subjects design provides a more sensitive test for differences between conditions by controlling individual differences. Having a more sensitive test and having the same participants take part in all conditions means that, ideally, fewer participants are needed in a within-subjects than in a between-subjects design.

This is dependent on there being a correlation between the scores in the experimental and control conditions. Statistical tests appropriate for within-subjects designs often indicate the extent of this correlation as well as the statistical significance of the difference between the two conditions. This is discussed in more detail in Chapter 13 of our companion statistics text, *Understanding statistics in psychology with SPSS* (Howitt & Cramer, 2020). It is also discussed in Box 9.3 below. So long as the correlation is substantial and significant, there is no problem. If it is not, then the test of the difference between the two means may well be not very powerful.

In a within-subjects design, the different conditions should not be run in the same order every time in case there is an effect of a particular order. In a design consisting of only two conditions, these order effects are dealt with (controlled) by counterbalancing the two orders so that both orders occur equally frequently. This counterbalancing is important, since the data may be affected by any of a number of effects of order. The main ones are as follows:

● *Fatigue or boredom*   Participants may become progressively more tired or bored with the task they are performing. So the number of mistakes they make may be greater in the second than in the first condition, regardless of which condition, because they are more tired. An example of a fatigue effect is illustrated in the bar chart in Figure 9.7

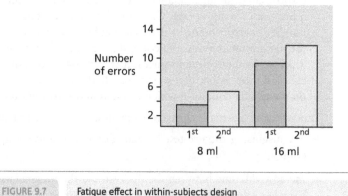

FIGURE 9.7   Fatigue effect in within-subjects design

for the effect of two different amounts of alcohol on the number of mistakes made. The vertical axis shows the number of errors made. The horizontal axis shows the two conditions of 8 ml and 16 ml of alcohol. Within each condition, the order in which the conditions were run is indicated. So '1st' means that that condition was run first and '2nd' that that condition was run second. We can see that there is a similar fatigue effect for both conditions. More errors are made when the condition is run second than when it is run first. In the 8 ml condition, six errors are made when it is run second compared with four when it is run first. The same difference holds for the 16 ml condition where 12 errors are made when it is run second compared with 10 when it is run first.

- *Practice* Participants may become better at the task they are carrying out. So the number of mistakes they make may be less in the second than in the first condition, regardless of which condition, because they have learnt to respond more accurately. Sometimes the term 'practice effect' is used to cover both learning as described here and fatigue or boredom.

- *Carryover, asymmetrical transfer or differential transfer* Here the effect of an earlier condition affects a subsequent one but not equally for all orders. (Technically this is an interaction between the conditions and the order of the conditions.) For example, if the interval between the two alcohol conditions is small, the carryover effect of drinking 16 ml of alcohol first on the effect of drinking 8 ml of alcohol second may be greater than the carryover effect of drinking 8 ml of alcohol first on the effect of drinking 16 ml of alcohol second. This pattern of results is illustrated in Figure 9.8. When the 8 ml condition is run second, the number of mistakes made is much greater (12) than when it is run first (4) and is almost the same as the number of mistakes made when the 16 ml condition is run first (10). When the 16 ml condition is run second, the number of mistakes made (13) is not much different from when it is run first. This asymmetrical transfer effect reduces the overall difference between the 8 and 16 ml conditions. If one finds such an asymmetrical transfer effect, then it may be possible to make adjustments to the research design to get rid of them. In the alcohol example, one could increase the amount of time between the two conditions. In this way, the alcohol consumed in the first condition may have worked its way out of the blood system. Of course, this has disadvantages. It might involve participants returning to the laboratory at a later time rather than the entire study being run at the same time. This increases the risk that participants may not return. Worse still, you may find that participants in one of the conditions may fail to return more frequently than participants in the other condition. Of course, this implies that counterbalanced designs are not always effective at balancing any effects of order. They clearly do balance out order effects in circumstances in which there is no significant interaction between the conditions and the order in

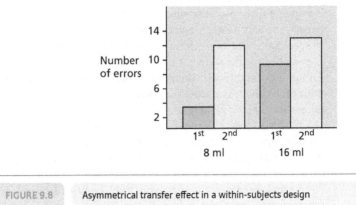

FIGURE 9.8   Asymmetrical transfer effect in a within-subjects design

Table 9.4	Fictitious scores for a within-subjects design with two conditions	
	Condition 1	Condition 2
Condition 1 first	$P_{1,1} = 3$	$P_{1,2} = 11$
	$P_{2,1} = 4$	$P_{2,2} = 10$
	$P_{3,1} = 5$	$P_{3,2} = 9$
Sum	12	30
Mean	$12/3 = 4$	$30/3 = 10$
Condition 1 second	$P_{4,1} = 11$	$P_{4,2} = 13$
	$P_{5,1} = 12$	$P_{5,2} = 12$
	$P_{6,1} = 13$	$P_{6,2} = 14$
Sum	36	39
Mean	$36/3 = 12$	$39/3 = 13$

which the conditions are run. If there is a significant interaction between the conditions and the order in which they are run, we need to describe what this interaction is. We can illustrate the interaction summarised in Figure 9.8 with the fictitious raw data in Table 9.4 where there are three participants who carry out the two different orders in which the two conditions are run. Each participant is signified by the letter P with a subscript consisting of two whole numbers. The first number refers to a particular participant and varies from 1 to 6 as there are six participants. The second number represents the two conditions. We could analyse these data with a mixed analysis of variance. This statistical procedure is described in some introductory statistics texts such as the companion text *Understanding statistics in psychology with SPSS* (Howitt & Cramer, 2020).

With counterbalancing, it is obviously important that equal numbers of participants are included in each condition. The random assignment of participants to different orders in a within-subjects design is necessary to ensure that the orders are exactly the same apart from the order in which the conditions are run. For example, in our study of the effects of alcohol on the number of errors made, it is important that the proportion of people who are inclined to make more errors is the same in the two different orders. If the proportion is not the same, there may be a difference between the two orders, which may result in a significant interaction effect.

If there is a significant interaction effect in a counterbalanced design, the analysis becomes a little cumbersome. Essentially, one regards the study as having two different parts – one part for each different order. The data from each part (order) are then analysed to see what is the apparent effect of the experimental treatment. If the same conclusions are reached for the different orders, then all is well as far as one's findings are concerned. Things become difficult when the conclusions from the different orders are not compatible with each other. Also note that this effectively reduces the maximum sample size and so takes away the main advantage of a within-subjects design.

Of course, researchers using their intelligence would have anticipated the problem for a study such as this in which the effects of alcohol are being studied. To the extent that one can anticipate problems due to the order of running through conditions, one would be less inclined to use a within-subjects design. This is a case where noting problems with counterbalanced designs that have been identified by researchers investigating similar topics to one's own may help decide whether a within-subjects design should be avoided.

Stable individual differences between people are controlled in a within-subjects design by requiring the same participants take part in all conditions. Nevertheless, it remains a requirement that assignment to different orders is done randomly. Of course, this does not mean that the process of randomisation has not left differences between the orders. This may be checked by pre-testing participants prior to the different first conditions to be run. One would check whether the pre-test means were the same for those who took condition 1 first as for those who took condition 2 first. In other words, it is possible to have a pre-test–post-test within-subjects design. It would also be possible to extend the Solomon four-group design to investigate not only the effects of pre-testing but also the effects of having participants undertake more than one condition.

Box 9.3   Key Ideas

Statistical significance

Statistical significance is something that many students have difficulty with. So in this book we have returned to it from time to time in order to reinforce the main ideas. Here we will discuss the concept of statistical significance using the example of the experiment on the effects of alcohol on errors. Suppose that we found in our study that the participants who drink less alcohol make fewer errors than those who drink more alcohol. We may find that we obtain the results shown in Table 9.5. All the participants who drink less alcohol make fewer errors than those who drink more alcohol.

The mean number of errors made by the participants who drink less alcohol is 2, compared with a mean of 5 for those who drink more alcohol. The absolute difference (which ignores the sign of the difference) between these two means is 3 ($2 - 5 = 3$). (To be precise, this should be written as ($|2 - 5| = 3$) which indicates that the absolute value of the difference should be taken.) Can we conclude from these results that drinking more alcohol causes us to make more mistakes? No, we cannot draw this conclusion without determining the extent to which this difference could be found simply by chance when in reality alcohol has no effect. If this difference has a probability of occurring by chance of 5 per cent or .05 or less, we can conclude that this difference is quite unusual and unlikely to be due to chance. It represents a real difference between the two conditions. If this difference has a probability of occurring by chance of more than 5 per cent or .05, we would conclude that this difference could be due to chance and so does not represent a real difference between the two conditions. It needs to be stressed that the 5 per cent or .05 significance level is just

Table 9.5	Fictitious data for a two-group between-subjects post-test-only design	
		Post-test
Condition 1		$P_{1,1} = 1$
		$P_{2,1} = 2$
		$P_{3,1} = 3$
Sum		6
Mean		$6/3 = 2$
Condition 2		$P_{4,2} = 4$
		$P_{5,2} = 5$
		$P_{6,2} = 6$
Sum		15
Mean		$15/3 = 5$

→

a conventional and generally accepted figure. It indicates a fairly uncommon outcome if differences between groups were simply due to chance factors resulting from sampling.

The probability of this difference occurring by chance can be demonstrated in the following way. Suppose that it is only possible to make between 1 and 6 mistakes on this task. (We are using this for convenience; it would be more accurate in terms of real statistical analysis to use the same figures but arranged in a bell-shaped or normal distribution in which scores of 3 and 4 are the most common and scores of 1 and 6 were the least common.) If we have only three participants in each condition and the results were determined simply by chance, then the mean for any group would be the mean of the three numbers selected by chance. We could randomly select these three numbers in several ways. We could toss a die three times. We could write the six numbers on six separate index cards or slips of paper, shuffle them, select a card or slip, note down the number, put the card or slip back, shuffle them again and repeat this procedure three times. We could use a statistical package such as SPSS. When using SPSS, we would enter the numbers 1 to 6 in one of the columns. We would then select *Data, Select Cases . . . , Random sample of cases, Sample . . . Exactly*, and then enter one case from the first six cases. We would note down the number of the case selected and repeat this procedure twice.

As we have two groups, we would have to do this once for each group, calculate the mean of the three numbers for each group and then subtract the mean of one group from the mean of the other group. We would then repeat this procedure 19 or more times. The results of our doing this 20 times are shown in Table 9.6.

The mean for both the first two groups is 2.00, so the difference between them is zero. As the six numbers are equally probable, the mean of three of these numbers selected at random is likely to be 3.5. This value is close to the mean for the 40 groups, which is 3.52. However, the means can vary from a minimum of $1\,[(1 + 1 + 1)/3 = 1]$ to a maximum of $6\,[(6 + 6 + 6)/3 = 6]$.

The distribution of the frequency of an infinite number of means will take the shape of an inverted U or bell, as shown by what is called the normal curve in Figure 9.9, which has been

| Table 9.6 | Differences between the means of three randomly selected numbers varying between 1 and 6 |

	Condition 1				Condition 2				
	P11	P21	P31	Mean	P42	P52	P62	Mean	Difference
1	1	3	2	2.00	2	3	1	2.00	0.00
2	5	1	2	2.67	5	5	4	4.67	− 2.00
3	6	1	4	3.67	6	1	6	4.33	− 0.66
4	6	3	6	5.00	5	6	6	5.67	− 0.67
5	1	5	3	3.00	6	3	1	3.33	− 0.33
6	1	2	4	2.33	1	3	6	3.33	− 1.00
7	3	6	2	3.67	6	3	5	4.67	− 1.00
8	1	2	5	2.67	5	5	4	4.67	− 2.00
9	6	2	3	3.67	2	4	4	3.33	0.34
10	6	1	1	2.67	6	3	3	4.00	− 1.33
11	4	4	6	4.67	2	3	1	2.00	2.67
12	1	6	2	3.00	2	5	2	3.00	0.00
13	2	5	5	4.00	5	3	6	4.67	− 0.67
14	2	1	2	1.67	6	5	1	4.00	− 2.33
15	4	6	3	4.33	6	5	6	5.67	− 1.34
16	2	4	5	3.67	6	1	3	3.33	0.34
17	2	5	4	3.67	5	1	5	3.67	0.00
18	2	2	2	2.00	1	6	6	4.33	− 2.33
19	2	1	2	1.67	3	1	5	3.00	− 1.33
20	6	3	6	5.00	2	2	2	2.00	3.00

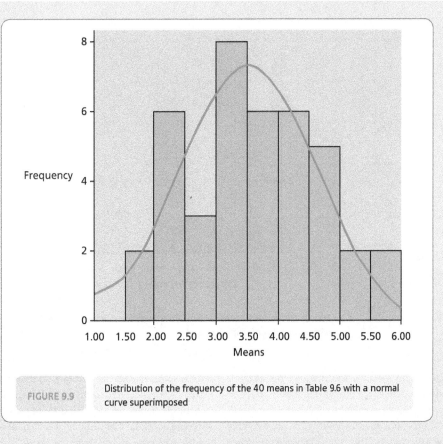

8

6

Frequency 4

2

0
1.00 1.50 2.00 2.50 3.00 3.50 4.00 4.50 5.00 5.50 6.00
Means

FIGURE 9.9   Distribution of the frequency of the 40 means in Table 9.6 with a normal curve superimposed

superimposed onto the histogram of the means in Table 9.6. Of these means, the smallest is 1.67 and the largest is 5.67. The distribution of these means approximates the shape of an inverted U or bell as shown in the histogram in Figure 9.9. The more samples of three scores we select at random, the more likely it is that the distribution of the means of those samples will resemble a normal curve. The horizontal width of each rectangle in the histogram is 0.50. The first rectangle, which is on the left, ranges from 1.50 to 2.00 and contains two means of 1.67. The last rectangle, which is on the right, varies from 5.50 to 6.00 and includes two means of 5.67.

If the means of the two groups tend to be 3.5, then the difference between them is likely to be zero. They will vary from a difference of $-5(1 - 6 = -5)$ to a difference of $5 (6 - 1) = 5$, with most of them close to zero as shown by the normal curve superimposed on the histogram in Figure 9.10. Of the 20 differences in means in Table 9.6, the lowest is −2.33 and the highest is 3.00. If we plot the frequency of these differences in means in terms of the histogram in Figure 9.10, we can see that its shape approximates that of the bell-shaped normal curve. If we plotted a very large number of such differences, the distribution would resemble a normal curve. The horizontal width of

each rectangle in this histogram is 1.00. The first rectangle, which is on the left, ranges from −3.00 to −2.00 and contains two differences in means of −2.33. The last rectangle, which is on the right, varies from 2.00 to 3.00 and includes two differences in means of 2.67 and 3.00.

We can see that the probability of obtaining by chance a difference as large as −3.00 is quite small. One test for determining this probability is the unrelated t-test. This test is described in most introductory statistics texts, including our companion volume *Understanding statistics in psychology with SPSS* (Howitt & Cramer, 2020). If the variances in the scores for the two groups are equal or similar, the probability obtained from the unrelated t-test will be the same as that obtained from a one-way analysis of variance with two groups. If we had strong grounds for thinking that the mean number of errors would be smaller for those who drank less rather than more alcohol, then we could confine our 5 per cent or .05 probability to the left tail or side of the distribution which covers this possibility. This is usually called the *one-tailed level* of probability. If we did not have good reasons for predicting the direction of the results, then we are saying that the number of errors made by the participants drinking less alcohol could be either less or more

→

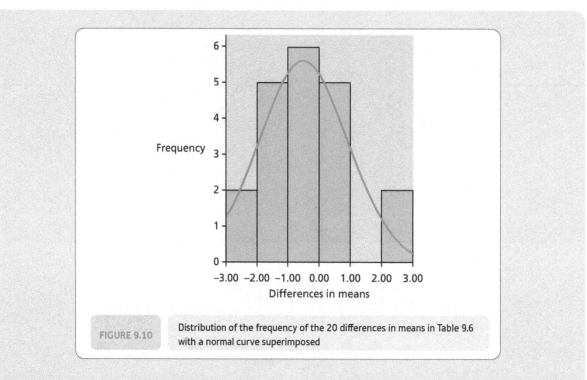

FIGURE 9.10   Distribution of the frequency of the 20 differences in means in Table 9.6 with a normal curve superimposed

than those made by the participants drinking more alcohol. In other words, the difference between the means could be either negative or positive in sign. If this was the case, the 5 per cent or .05 probability level would cover the two tails or sides of the distribution. This is normally referred to as the *two-tailed level* of probability. To be significant at the two-tailed rather than the one-tailed level, the difference in the means would have to be bigger, as the 5 per cent or .05

level is split between the two tails so that it covers a more extreme difference. If the difference between the two means is statistically significant, which it is for the scores in Table 9.5, we could conclude that drinking less alcohol results in making fewer errors.

Our companion statistics text, *Understanding statistics in psychology with SPSS* (Howitt & Cramer, 2020), presents a more extended version of this explanation of the *t*-test.

Box 9.4   Research Example

Mixed-design true experiment on the effects of alcohol and sleep deprivation on various measures, including performance

Peeke, S. C., Callaway, E., Jones, R. T., Stone, G. C., & Doyle, J. (1980). Combined effects of alcohol and sleep deprivation in normal young adults. *Psychopharmacology, 67,* 279–287.

The laboratory experiment, the true experiment, the randomised trial or call it what you will is part of the DNA of psychologists. As such, whether or not you are convinced that such experiments are the best way to do research, you really need to understand just how much experiments have influenced the thinking of researchers for much of the modern history of psychology. While the laboratory experiment no longer dominates psychological research in the way that it once did, no matter what field of research attracts you, it will almost certainly have adherents of the experimental method. Besides that, to be able to use the logic of experimental designs effectively is almost a mental exercise in many aspects of psychological research. We are not suggesting for one moment that one research method is superior to the others – they each have their strengths and their limitations of which all researchers need to be aware – but merely that understanding the experimental method well is good preparation for understanding many of the characteristics of psychological research in general, including hypotheses, cause and effect, variables and the like. These are matters which feature much less strongly in the research writings of members of closely related disciplines such as sociology.

Background

Shirley Peeke and her colleagues (1980) were interested in looking at the effects of alcohol and sleep deprivation on various physiological and psychological variables, as there appeared to have been few studies that had done this.

Hypotheses

There were no specific hypotheses as such, as it was thought that whether alcohol had a stimulating or depressing effect depended on the dose of alcohol as well as the particular behaviour that was being measured.

Method

There were two independent variables. One independent variable was alcohol dose. There were three levels of this, measured in terms of millilitres of 95 per cent ethanol per kilogram of body weight: 0 ml/kg (placebo), 0.45 ml/kg (low dose) and 0.90 ml/kg (moderate dose). The ethanol was mixed with fruit juice and diluted to a total volume of 400 ml. Two drops of mint extract were added to disguise the taste and smell of the drink. The other independent variable was sleep deprivation, which consisted of normal sleep or 26 hours of sleep deprivation. In the sleep-deprived condition, participants arrived at the laboratory at 10 p.m. and spent the night playing cards or reading with a research assistant present. Figure 9.11 shows the research design.

Each of 24 male adults was assigned to one of the three alcohol conditions although it is not stated whether this was done randomly. This was a between-subjects condition. There were two sessions separated by four to nine days. Half of the men did the normal sleep condition first, followed by the sleep-deprived condition, whereas the other half did the two conditions in the reverse order to control for order effects. The two sleep conditions were a within-subjects condition, whereas the two orders were a between-subjects condition. In the Abstract, the experiment is described as being

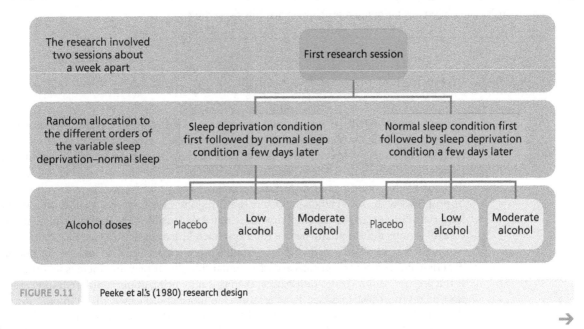

FIGURE 9.11   Peeke et al.'s (1980) research design

double-blind, which means that neither the participants nor the experimenters running the study knew which dose of alcohol was given at the time.

It is common for researchers to use a number of dependent measures, and this study was no exception. So in this case the researchers measured, among others, the percentage of errors made and the reaction time taken to carry out a categorisation task. Only this task and its results are presented here. Participants were shown a visual stimulus which varied in terms of colour and form. They were then shown another visual stimulus. They had to say whether the colour and form of this second stimulus were the same as or different from the colour and form of the first one. In other words, there were four possible responses: (1) same colour, same form; (2) same colour, different form; 3) different colour, same form and (4) different colour, different form. This was done a number of times. There were six blocks of 20 trials each. Each block was separated by a one-minute interval and each trial within a block was separated by an 11-second interval. It is not clear to what response the reaction time was measured. For example, was it to the first response made, regardless of whether it was correct, or to the first correct response made?

Results

Analysis of variance was carried out separately on the percentage of errors made and the reaction time to conduct the task. Analysis of variance is a common statistical procedure to apply in experimental designs, as it can detect patterns of differences between the means of groups on one or more independent variables at the same time. Alcohol dose and order of sleep conditions were the between-subjects conditions. Sleep condition and blocks of trials were the within-subjects conditions. An interaction or moderating effect was found if the interaction effect between dose and sleep conditions was significant. The effect of dose alone was assessed by comparing the placebo with the two alcohol conditions in the normal sleep condition. The effect of sleep deprivation was evaluated by comparing the two sleep conditions in the placebo condition.

The dose by sleep interaction was statistically significant for these two measures. The nature of the interaction differed for the two measures. There appeared to be little difference in the percentage of errors in the placebo condition between the normal and the sleep-deprived condition. The percentage of errors increased as the dosage of alcohol increased, and this increase was greater in the sleep-deprived than in the normal sleep group. There did not appear to be a significant effect for alcohol dose or sleep deprivation on its own.

Reaction time was significantly slower for the normal than for the sleep-deprived condition for the moderate dose of alcohol. The other conditions were not reported as differing significantly at the conventional .05 level.

Authors' suggestions for future research

In this journal article, no suggestions for future research were made by the authors.

9.4 Conclusion

The basics of the true or randomised experiment are simple. The major advantage of such a design is that it is easier to draw conclusions about causality, since care is taken to exclude other variables as far as possible. That is, the different experimental conditions bring about differences on the dependent variable. This is achieved by randomly allocating participants to conditions or orders and standardising procedures. There are a number of problems with this. The major one is that randomisation equates groups only in the long run. For any particular experiment, it remains possible that the experimental and control groups differ initially before the experimental manipulation has been employed. The main way of dealing with this is to employ a pre-test to establish whether or not the experimental and control groups are very similar initially. If they are, there is no problem. If the pre-test demonstrates differences, then this may bring about a different interpretation of any post-test findings. Furthermore, the more complicated the manipulation is, the more likely it is that variables other than the intended one will be manipulated. Consequently, the less easy it is to conclude that the independent variable is responsible for the differences. The less controlled the setting in which the experiment is conducted, the more likely it is that the conditions under which the experiment is run will not be the same and that other factors than the manipulation may be responsible for any observed effect.

Key points

- The laboratory experiment has the potential to reveal causal relationships with a certainty that is not true of many other styles of research. This is achieved by random allocation of participants and the manipulation of the independent variable while standardising procedures as much as possible to control other sources of variability.

- The between-subjects and within-subjects designs differ in that in the former participants take part in only one condition of the experiment whereas in the latter participants take part in all conditions (or sometimes just two or more of the conditions). These two different types of design are analysed using rather different statistical techniques. Within-subjects designs use related or correlated tests. This enables statistical significance to be achieved with fewer participants.

- The manipulated or independent variable consists of only two levels or conditions in the most basic laboratory experiment. The level of the manipulated variable is higher in one of the conditions. This condition is sometimes referred to as the experimental condition, as opposed to the control condition where the level of the manipulated variable is lower.

- Within-subjects (related) designs have problems associated with the sensitisation effects of serving in more than one of the conditions of the study. There are designs that allow the researcher to detect sensitisation effects. One advantage of the between-subjects design is that participants will not be affected by the other conditions, as they will not have taken part in them.

- Pre-testing to establish that random allocation has worked, in the sense of equating participants on the dependent variable prior to the experimental treatment, sometimes works. Nevertheless, pre-testing may cause problems due to the sensitising effect of the pre-test. Complex designs are available which test for these sensitising effects.

- The extent to which random assignment has resulted in participants being similar across either conditions or orders can be determined by a pre-test in which participants are assessed on the dependent variable before the manipulation is carried out.

- Any statistical differences between the conditions in the dependent variable at post-test are very likely to be due to the manipulated variable if the dependent variable does not differ significantly between the conditions at pre-test and if the only other difference between the conditions is the manipulated variable.

ACTIVITY

1. Design a basic randomised experiment to test the hypothesis that unemployment leads to crime. After thinking about this, you may find it useful to see whether and how other researchers have tried to study this issue using randomised designs. How are you going to operationalise these two variables? Is it possible to manipulate unemployment and how can you do so? If you are going to carry out a laboratory experiment, you may have to operationalise unemployment in a more contrived way than if you carry out an experiment in a more natural or field setting. How can you reduce the ethical problems that may arise in the operationalisation of these variables? How many participants will you have in each condition? How will you select these participants? Will you pre-test your participants? Will you use a between-subjects or a within-subjects design? How will you analyse the results? What will you say to participants about the study before and after they take part?

CHAPTER 10

Advanced experimental designs

Overview

- Laboratory experiments consisting of just an experimental group and a control group are a rarity in published research. The information obtained from such a study would be very limited for the time, money and effort expended. So a simple experimental group – control group study is often extended to include perhaps as many as four or five different conditions. Every condition of an experiment should be justifiable. Collecting data for its own sake is not the way to do research.

- Most behaviours are multiply affected by a range of factors (i.e. variables). Consequently, it can be advantageous to study several factors at the same time and to compare their relative effects. The number of manipulated variables in a study should be manageable and typically, no more than two or three. With more the interpretation of the statistical findings can become extremely complex and, possibly, misleading.

- A study may include variables which by their nature cannot be randomised (or manipulated) such as gender, age and intelligence. These are sometimes referred to as subject variables.

- Multiple dependent variables are often employed in a study since independent variables may have a variety of effects. Where there are several dependent variables, controlling for any order effects by varying their measurement order may be beneficial. This can be done systematically using a Latin square.

- Latin squares are also used to systematically vary the order of running the various conditions in a within-subjects (i.e. related) design.

- Comparisons planned in advance of data collection have distinct advantages, for example, in terms of the ease of making multiple comparisons. Statistical analyses of planned and unplanned comparisons in factorial designs are rather different.

● Quite distinct from any of the above, advance designs may include additional methods of controlling for potential nuisances, such as (a) the use of placebos and (b) double-blind procedures. Quasi-controls to investigate the experience of participants in the research might be regarded as good practice since, in part, they involve discussions after the study between participant and researcher in order to jointly develop an understanding of the research findings. They are essentially a variant of the post-experimental debriefing interviews discussed earlier (Chapter 9) but with a more focused and less exploratory objective.

10.1 Introduction

This chapter will extend our understanding of experimental design in four ways:

● Increasing the number of levels of the independent variable so that there are three or more groups.

● The use of two or more independent variables. This substantially increases the amount of information which can be obtained from a single study.

● Using more than one dependent variable.

● Aspects of experiments which create problems in the interpretation of research findings. Some of these are usually termed experimenter effects and are researched under the rubric of the social psychology of the laboratory experiment.

The simple two-groups design – an experimental group and a control group – provides relatively little information for the considerable resources involved. The basic experimental design may be extended by using a greater variety of conditions or levels of the independent variable. More likely, perhaps, two or three or more independent variables will be used instead of just one:

● Just having two conditions or levels of an independent variable, such as the amount of alcohol consumed (as in the example used in Chapter 9), is not very informative about the relationship between the independent and dependent variables. Is the relationship linear or curvilinear? If the latter, what kind of curvilinear relationship is it? Having several levels of the dependent variable helps identify the nature of the trends because of the extra information they supply.

● If we have several independent variables, then whether the independent variable interacts with other independent or subject variables can be addressed. For example, is the effect of alcohol on errors similar for both males and females or different?

● Does the independent variable affect more than one dependent variable? For example, does alcohol affect the number of speech errors made as well as typing errors?

These three main ways of extending the basic two-group design are discussed below and highlighted in Figure 10.1.

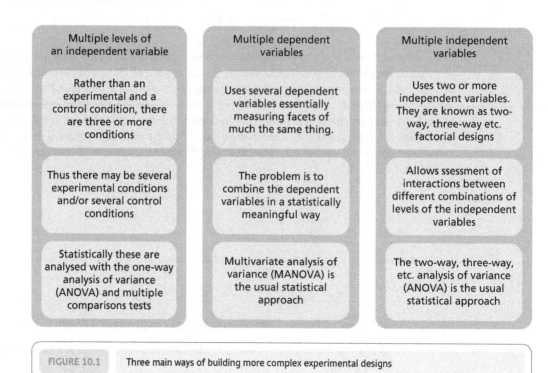

Multiple levels of an independent variable	Multiple dependent variables	Multiple independent variables
Rather than an experimental and a control condition, there are three or more conditions	Uses several dependent variables essentially measuring facets of much the same thing.	Uses two or more independent variables. They are known as two-way, three-way etc. factorial designs
Thus there may be several experimental conditions and/or several control conditions	The problem is to combine the dependent variables in a statistically meaningful way	Allows ssessment of interactions between different combinations of levels of the independent variables
Statistically these are analysed with the one-way analysis of variance (ANOVA) and multiple comparisons tests	Multivariate analysis of variance (MANOVA) is the usual statistical approach	The two-way, three-way, etc. analysis of variance (ANOVA) is the usual statistical approach

FIGURE 10.1   Three main ways of building more complex experimental designs

10.2   Multiple levels of the independent variable

Multiple levels of the independent variable mean that it has three or more different levels. Sometimes this is described as having several levels of the treatment. Figure 10.2 gives an example. The independent variable may vary either quantitatively or qualitatively:

- *Quantitative* would be, for example, when the amount of alcohol consumed in the different conditions can be arranged in order of numerical size. In general, the order is

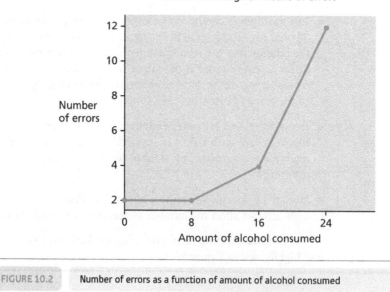

FIGURE 10.2   Number of errors as a function of amount of alcohol consumed

from smaller quantities to larger ones ordered either across or down a table or across a graph such as Figure 10.2.

- *Qualitative* would be, for example, when we study the effects of the kind of music being played in the different conditions. There is generally no one way in which the levels or categories can be ordered in terms of amount. The categories will reflect a number of different characteristics, such as whether the music is popular or classical or fusion and whether the music is predominantly a band or a soloist. In other words, qualitative is the equivalent of a nominal, category or categorical variable. When studying the effect of a qualitative variable which varies in numerous ways, it is not possible to know which particular features of the qualitative variable produce any differences found.

Multiple comparisons

The analysis of designs with more than two conditions is more complicated than for a design with only two conditions. One reason is that the more conditions there are, the more comparisons have to be made between conditions. In the case of three conditions, there are three possible different comparisons to be made:

- condition 1 with condition 2,
- condition 1 with condition 3, *and*
- condition 2 with condition 3.

That is, a total of up to three different comparisons. With four conditions, there are six different comparisons. With five conditions there are 10, and so on. (The number of comparisons is obtained from the sum of numbers from 1 to the number of conditions minus 1. That is, for four conditions, one less than the number of conditions is $4 - 1$ or 3. So we add $1 + 2 + 3$ which gives us six comparisons.) Whether or not one wishes to make all of the possible comparisons depends on the purpose of one's research. The temptation is, of course, to do them all. For example, you may have a study in which there are two experimental groups and two control groups. You may, for this particular study, only be interested in the differences between the experimental groups and the control groups. You may not be interested in whether the control groups differ from each other or even whether the experimental groups differ from each other. If a comparison does not matter for your purposes, then it does not have to be included in your analysis. In your report, of course, you would justify the number of comparisons that you choose to make. Psychologists have a tendency to over-analyse their data, in the eyes of some statisticians.

The more comparisons we make, the greater the likelihood of finding ones which are statistically significant by chance. If these comparisons are completely independent of each other, the probability of finding one or more of these comparisons to be statistically significant can be calculated with the following formula:

$$\text{Probability of statistically significant comparison} = 1 - (1 - .05)^{\text{number of comparisons}}$$

where .05 represents the 5 per cent or .05 significance level. With three comparisons, this probability or significance level is about 14 per cent or .14 $[1 - (1 - .05)^3 = .14]$. With four comparisons, it is 19 per cent or .19 $[1 - (1 - .05)^4 = .19]$. With five comparisons, it is 23 per cent or .23 $[1 - (1 - .05)^5 = .23]$, and so forth. This probability is known as the *family-wise* or *experiment-wise* error rate, because we are making a number, or family, of comparisons from the same study or experiment. By making a lot of comparisons we increase the risk that some of our seemingly significant findings are in fact due to chance. Leaving out purposeless comparisons means that there is less chance of making this sort of 'error' in the interpretation of our findings. Box 10.1 discusses this sort of interpretation 'error' and related issues.

Risks in interpreting trends in our data

Since research data in psychology are based on samples of data rather than *all* of the data, there is always a risk that the characteristics of our particular sample of data do not represent reality accurately. Some outcomes of sampling are very likely and some are very unlikely to occur in any particular study. Most randomly drawn samples will show similar characteristics to the population from which they were drawn. In statistical analysis, the working assumption is usually the null hypothesis, which is that there is no difference between the various conditions of the dependent variable, or that there is no relationship between two variables. In other words, the null hypothesis says that there is no trend in reality. Essentially, in statistical analysis we assess the probability that the null hypothesis is true. A statistically significant statistical analysis means that it is unlikely that the trend would have occurred by chance if the null hypothesis of no trend in reality was true. The criterion which we usually impose to make the decision is that a trend which is likely to occur in 95 per cent of random samples drawn from a population is not statistically significant. This is assuming that there is no trend in

the population. However, trends which are so strong that they fall into the 5 per cent of outcomes are said to be statistically significant, and we accept the hypothesis that there is in reality a trend between two variables – a difference or a relationship. The upshot of all of this, though, is that no matter what we decide, there is a risk that we will be wrong.

Type I error refers to the situation in which we decide on the basis of our data that there is a trend but in actuality there is really no trend (see Figure 10.3). We have set the risk of this at 5 per cent. It is a small risk but nevertheless there is a risk. Psychologists tend to be very concerned about Type I errors.

Type II error refers to a different situation. This is the situation in which in reality there is a trend involving two variables but our statistical analysis fails to detect this trend at the required 5 per cent level of significance. Psychologists seem to be less worried about this in general. However, what it could mean is that really important trends are overlooked. Researchers who studied a treatment for dementia but whose findings did not reach

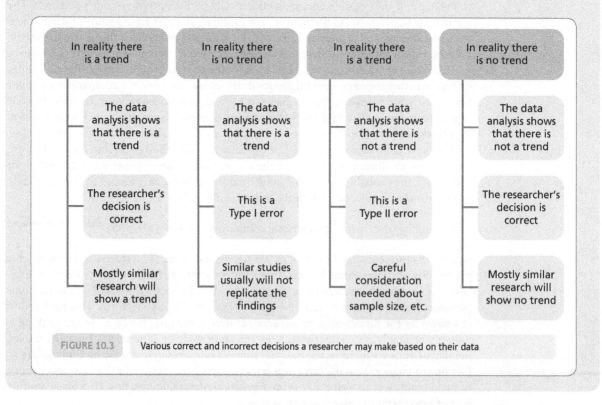

In reality there is a trend	In reality there is no trend	In reality there is a trend	In reality there is no trend
The data analysis shows that there is a trend	The data analysis shows that there is a trend	The data analysis shows that there is not a trend	The data analysis shows that there is not a trend
The researcher's decision is correct	This is a Type I error	This is a Type II error	The researcher's decision is correct
Mostly similar research will show a trend	Similar studies usually will not replicate the findings	Careful consideration needed about sample size, etc.	Mostly similar research will show no trend

FIGURE 10.3   Various correct and incorrect decisions a researcher may make based on their data

statistical significance – maybe because the sample size was too small – would be making a Type II error. Furthermore, by other criteria, this error would be a serious one if as a result this treatment were abandoned. This stresses the importance of using other criteria relevant to decision-making in psychological research. Statistical significance is one criterion, but it is most certainly not the only criterion when reaching conclusions based on research. Many professional researchers go to quite considerable lengths to avoid Type II errors by considering carefully such factors as the level of statistical significance to be used, the size of the effect (or trend) which would minimally be of interest to the researchers, and the sample size required to achieve these ends. This is known as power analysis. It is covered in detail in our companion book *Understanding statistics in psychology with SPSS* (Howitt & Cramer, 2020). Figure 10.3 gives some of the possible decision outcomes from a statistical analysis.

Experimental designs which consist of more than two conditions or more than two independent variables would normally be analysed by one of a group of tests of significance known collectively as the analysis of variance (ANOVA; Fisher, 1925, 1935). Although statisticians recognise that there may not always be a need to use analysis of variance in these circumstances, most psychologists probably would. If we had good grounds for predicting which conditions would be expected to differ from each other and the direction of those differences, then an overall or omnibus test such as an analysis of variance may be unnecessary (e.g. Howell, 2013; Keppel & Wickens, 2004). An omnibus test simply tells us whether the independent variable has a significant effect overall, but it does not tell us which conditions are actually different from each other. Regardless of whether we carry out an omnibus test, the conditions we expect to differ still have to be compared. These comparisons have been called planned or *a priori* comparisons. (*A priori* is Latin for 'from what is before'.) We could use a simple test such as a *t*-test to determine which conditions differ from each other, provided that we test a limited number of comparisons (e.g. Howell, 2013; Keppel & Wickens, 2004). If we make a large number of comparisons, then we should make an adjustment for the family-wise error rate. The point is that if we plan a few comparisons, we have effectively pinpointed key features of the situation. The more comparisons we make, the less precision is involved in our planning. Hence the need to make adjustments when we are making a high proportion of the possible comparisons. Very little student research, in our experience, involves this degree of pre-planning of the analysis. It is hard enough coming up with research questions, hypotheses and research designs without having to add to the burden by meticulously planning in advance on a theoretical, empirical or conceptual basis just what comparisons we will make during the actual data analysis.

The more common situation, however, is when we lack good reasons for expecting a particular difference or for predicting the direction of a difference. The procedure in these circumstances is to employ an omnibus statistical test such as an analysis of variance. If this analysis is significant overall, unplanned, *post hoc* or *a posteriori* comparisons can be carried out. These comparisons determine which conditions differ significantly from each other. (*Post hoc* is Latin for 'after this' and *a posteriori* is Latin for 'from what comes after'.) With the *post hoc* test, it is necessary to adjust the significance of the statistical test to take into account the number of comparisons being made.

The simplest way to do this is to divide the .05 level of statistical significance by the number of comparisons to be made. This is known as a Bonferroni adjustment or test. So with three comparisons, the adjusted level is about .0167 (.05 ÷ 3 = .0167). With four comparisons, it is .0125 (.05/4 = .0125), and so on. Be careful! What this means is that a comparison has to be statistically significant at this adjusted level to be reported as being statistically significant at the .05 level of significance. So, if we make four comparisons, only differences which are statistically significant at the .0125 level can be reported as being significant at the .05 level. It is easier to do this with SPSS output, since the exact probability found for a comparison simply has to be multiplied by the number of comparisons to give the appropriate significance level. The finding is significant only if the *multiplied* exact significance is below .05. This is discussed in the companion text *Understanding statistics in psychology with SPSS* (Howitt & Cramer, 2020).

The Bonferroni test is a conservative test if we are comparing all the conditions, because at least one of the comparisons will not be independent of the others. Conservative basically means less likely to give statistically significant results. Suppose we wanted to compare the mean scores for three conditions, which are 2, 4 and 8, respectively. If we work out the differences for any two of the comparisons, then we can derive the difference for the third comparison by subtracting the other two differences from each other. For instance, the differences between conditions 1 and 2 ($4 - 2 = 2$) and between conditions 1 and 3 ($8 - 2 = 6$) are 2 and 6, respectively. If we subtract these two differences from each other ($6 - 2 = 4$), we obtain the difference between conditions 2 and 3 ($8 - 4 = 4$), which is 4. In other words, if we know the differences for two of the comparisons, we can work out the difference for the third comparison. Thus the third value is not independent of the other two.

So, in this situation, the Bonferroni test is a conservative test in the sense that the test assumes that three rather than two independent comparisons are being made. The probability level is lower for three comparisons ($.05/3 = .017$) than for two comparisons ($.05/2 = .025$) and so is less likely to occur.

There is some disagreement between authors about whether particular multiple comparison tests such as the Bonferroni test should be used for *a priori* or *post hoc* comparisons. For example, Howell (2013) suggests that the Bonferroni test should be used for making planned or *a priori* comparisons, while Keppel and Wickens (2004) recommend that this test be used for making a small number of unplanned or *post hoc* comparisons! The widely used statistical package SPSS also lists the Bonferroni test as a *post hoc* test. There are also tests for determining the shape of the relationship between the levels of a quantitative independent variable and the dependent variable, which are known as trend tests (e.g. Kirk, 1995).

In many instances such disagreements in the advice of experts will make little or no difference to the interpretation of the statistical analysis – that is, the findings will be unaffected – even though the numbers in the statistical analyses differ to a degree. Since multiple comparison tests are quickly computed using SPSS and other statistical packages, it is easy to try out a number of multiple comparison tests. Only in circumstances in which they lead to radically different conclusions do you really have a problem. These circumstances are probably rare. It is more likely that some comparisons which are significant with one test might be marginally non-significant with another. In these circumstances, it would be appropriate to highlight the problem in your report.

10.3   Multiple dependent variables

As we saw earlier (Chapter 9), sometimes researchers use a number of different measures of the dependent variable within a single study. For example, we can assess the effects of alcohol on task performance for both the number of errors made and the speed of doing the task. Performance on a number of tasks such as simple reaction time, complex reaction time, attention span and distance estimation could be studied. One could, of course, carry out separate studies for each of these different measures of performance. However, it would be more efficient to examine them in the same study. In these circumstances, randomising the order of presentation of the various measurements of the dependent variables is potentially worthwhile to control order effects. Univariate analysis of variance (ANOVA) is not appropriate for analysing these data, since it deals with only one dependent variable. Multivariate analysis of variance (abbreviated to MANOVA; Hotelling, 1931; Fisher, 1925; Wilks, 1932) is used instead, since it handles multiple dependent variables. Essentially, the multiple dependent variables are combined statistically into smaller numbers of 'variables' (known as latent roots). A description of MANOVA can be found in Chapter 29 of the companion text *Understanding statistics in psychology with SPSS* (Howitt & Cramer, 2020) together with instructions for doing one.

MANOVA may sometimes be superfluous. For example, a researcher may measure a variable such as reaction times several times in order to give a sample of the participant's performance on this task. Such data are better analysed by simply averaging their scores over several trials of what is the same task. Nothing is gained by treating these several measures of the same thing as multiple dependent variables.

10.4 Factorial designs

A factorial design is a study which investigates two or more independent variables (Crutchfield, 1938; Fisher, 1935), see Table 10.1. Variables like gender may be referred to as subject variables. They involve characteristics of the participants impossible to be independently manipulated (and randomly assigned). Gender, age and intelligence are good examples of subject variables. They are also independent variables if they are seen as potential causes of variations in the dependent variable.

Terms such as two-way, three-way and four-way are frequently mentioned in connection with factorial research designs. The word 'way' really means factor or independent variable. Thus a one-way design means one independent variable, a two-way design means two independent variables, a three-way design means three independent variables and so forth. The phrase is also used in connection with the analysis of variance. So a two-way analysis of variance is an appropriate way of analysing a two-way research design. The number of factors and the number of levels within the factors may be indicated by stating the number of levels in each factor and by separating each of these numbers by a multiplication sign, $\times$, which is referred to as 'by'. So a design having two factors with two levels and a third factor with three levels may be called a $2 \times 2 \times 3$ factorial design. ANOVA is the usual statistical analysis for factorial designs since it has versions which cope with virtually any variant. For example, it is possible to have related variables and unrelated variables as independent variables in the same design (i.e. a mixed ANOVA).

When quantitative subject variables such as age, intelligence or anxiety are used in a factorial design and analysed using ANOVA, they can be categorised into ranges or groups of scores. Age, for example, could be categorised as from 18 to 22 years, from 23 to 30 years, from 31 to 40 years and so forth. The choice of ranges used depends on the nature of the study. The use of ranges is particularly helpful if there is a non-linear

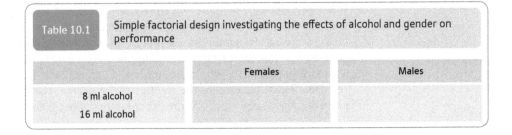

Table 10.1	Simple factorial design investigating the effects of alcohol and gender on performance		
		Females	Males
8 ml alcohol			
16 ml alcohol			

relationship between the subject variable and the dependent variable. This would be assessed by drawing a scatterplot of the relationship between the subject variable and the dependent variable. If the relationship between the two seems to be a curved line, then there is a non-linear relationship between them. Some researchers prefer to use a subject variable as a covariate in an analysis of covariance design (ANCOVA). This essentially adjusts the data for subject differences, before carrying out a more or less standard ANOVA analysis.

Using subject variables in factorial designs can result in the different conditions (cells) in the analysis containing very different numbers of participants. This can happen in all sorts of circumstances but, for example, it may be easier to recruit female participants than male participants. The computer program will calculate statistics for an analysis of variance which has different numbers of participants in each condition. Unfortunately, the way in which it makes allowance for these differences is less than ideal. However, having equal numbers of participants in each condition ensures the most powerful statistical analysis. Not using subject variables makes having equal cell numbers much easier. But if there is no choice, then stick with the unequal cell sizes.

An alternative way to analyse complex factorial designs is to use multiple regression. This statistical technique identifies the pattern of independent variables which best account for the variation in a dependent variable. This readily translates to an experimental design which also has independent and dependent variables. If there are any subject variables in the form of scores, then they may be left as scores. (However, this requires that the relationship between the subject variable and the dependent variable is linear.) Qualitative variables (i.e. nominal, category or categorical variables) may also be included as predictors. They may need to be converted into *dummy variables* if the qualitative variable has more than two categories.

Basically, a dummy variable involves taking each category of a nominal variable and making it into a new variable. Participants are simply coded as either having or not having the characteristic to which the category refers. For example, in answer to the question, 'What is the participant's favourite animal?', if the category variable has the categories of cat, dog and other, this can be turned into two dummy variables such as cat and dog. Participants are coded as choosing cat *or not* and choosing dog *or not*. There is always one fewer dummy variable than the number of categories, because the third category only contains information which has already been incorporated in the first two dummy variables. Participants choosing 'other' will be those who have not chosen cat or dog. A good description of dummy variables is provided by Cohen, Cohen, West and Aiken (2003), and they are explained also in the companion text *Understanding statistics in psychology with SPSS* (Howitt & Cramer, 2020).

The advantages of using multiple regression to analyse multifactorial designs include the following:

- The subject variables are not placed into fairly arbitrary categories.

- The variation (and information) contained in the subject variable is not reduced by turning the subject variable into a small number of categories or ranges of scores.

There are three main advantages to using a factorial design:

- It is more efficient, or economical, in that it requires fewer cases or observations for approximately the same degree of precision or power. For example, a two-factor factorial design might use just 30 participants. To achieve the same power running the two-factor factorial design as two separate one-factor designs, twice as many participants would be needed. That is, each one-factor design would require 30 participants. In the multifactorial design, the values of one factor are averaged across the values of the other factors. That is to say, the factorial design essentially can be considered as several non-factorial designs – hence, the economy of numbers.

- Factorial designs enable greater generalisability of the results in that a factor is investigated over a wider range of conditions. So, for example, we can look at the effects of alcohol under two levels of noise rather than, say, a single one, and in females and males rather than in just one of these two groups.

- A third advantage is that a factorial design allows us to determine whether there is an interaction between two or more factors in that the effect of one factor depends on the effect of one or more other factors. Box 10.2 deals with interactions.

Box 10.2 Key Ideas

Nature of interactions

One of the consequences of employing multifactorial designs is that the combined influences of the variables on the dependent variable may be identified. An interaction is basically a combination of levels of two or more variables which produces effects on the dependent variable that cannot be accounted for by the separate effects of the variables in question. Interactions must be distinguished from main effects. A main effect is the influence of a variable acting on its own – not in combination with any other variable. Interactions can only occur when there are two or more independent variables.

Interactions may be most easily grasped in terms of a graph such as Figures 9.4 and 9.5 in the previous chapter where the vertical axis represents the dependent variable, the horizontal axis represents one of the independent variables, and the lines connecting the points in the graph represent one or more other independent variables. Thus the vertical axis shows the number of errors made, the horizontal axis represents the time of testing (pre-test and post-test) and the two lines represent the two alcohol conditions, 8 and 16 ml. An interaction effect occurs if the lines in the graph are substantially out of parallel, such as when the lines diverge or converge (or both). We saw earlier (in Figures 9.4 and 9.5) that the effect of differing amounts of alcohol appears to depend on the time of testing. In other words, there seems to be an interaction between the amount of alcohol consumed and the time of testing. In both figures the difference in errors between the two amounts of alcohol is greater at the pre-test than the post-test. Of course, in terms of a true or randomised

pre-test–post-test experimental design, we would hope that the pre-test scores were similar, as illustrated in Figure 10.4, as the main purpose of randomisation is to equate groups at the pre-test. But randomisation is randomisation, and what the researcher hopes for does not always happen.

In Figure 10.4, there still appears to be an interaction, but the difference between the two amounts of alcohol is greater at post-test than at pre-test. Drinking 16 ml of alcohol has a greater effect on the number of errors made than drinking 8 ml of alcohol, which is what we would anticipate. In pre-test–post-test experimental designs, this is the kind of interaction effect we would expect if our independent variable had an effect.

The absence of an interaction between time of testing and alcohol is illustrated in Figure 10.5, as the two lines representing the two alcohol conditions are more or less parallel. There also appears to be a main effect for the time of testing in that the number of errors made at post-test seem to be greater than the number made at pre-test, but there does not seem to be a difference between the two alcohol conditions.

Figure 10.6 shows an apparent interaction effect for a between-subjects factorial design, which consists of the two factors of amount of alcohol and level of noise. The difference in the number of errors made between the two alcohol conditions is greater for the 60 dB condition than for the 30 dB condition. Figure 10.7 illustrates the lack of an interaction effect for these two factors. The difference in performance between the two alcohol conditions

→

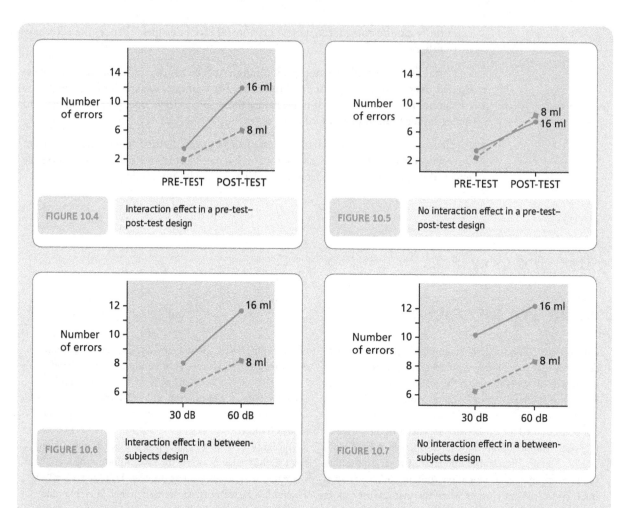

FIGURE 10.4   Interaction effect in a pre-test–post-test design

FIGURE 10.5   No interaction effect in a pre-test–post-test design

FIGURE 10.6   Interaction effect in a between-subjects design

FIGURE 10.7   No interaction effect in a between-subjects design

appears to be similar for the two noise conditions. There are circumstances in which one should be very careful in interpreting the results of a study. These are circumstances such as those illustrated in Figure 10.6. In this diagram, we can see that the only difference between the conditions is the 16 ml 60 dB condition. All other three conditions actually have a similar mean on the numbers of errors. This is clearly purely an interaction with no main effects at all. The problem is that the way the analysis of variance works means that it will tend to identify main effects

which simply do not exist. That is because to get the main effects, two groups will be combined, such as the two 30 dB groups and the two 60 dB groups. In other words, at least part of the interaction will be subsumed under the main effects.

It is not possible to determine whether there is an interaction between two or more factors simply by looking at the plot of the scores on a graph. It is necessary to establish that this is a statistically significant interaction by carrying out a test such as an analysis of variance.

There are special problems facing a researcher designing a related-design study. If participants are to be studied in every possible condition of the study, then the order ought to be counterbalanced such that no order is more common than any other order. These designs are known as Latin square designs (Fisher, 1935, p. 87) and are discussed in Box 10.3.

Box 10.3   Key Ideas

Latin squares to control order effects

In a within-subjects design, you need to control for order effects by running the levels or conditions in different orders. The more conditions you have, the more orders there are for running those conditions. With three conditions called A, B and C, there are six different orders: ABC, ACB, BAC, BCA, CAB and CBA. With four conditions there are 24 possible orders. With five conditions there are 120 possible orders, and so on. We can work out the number of potential orders by multiplying the number of conditions by each of the numbers that fall below that number. For three conditions this is $3 \times 2 \times 1$ which gives 6. For five conditions it is $5 \times 4 \times 3 \times 2 \times 1$ which gives 120. Often there are more possible orders than actual participants. Suppose, for example, you required only 12 participants in a within-subjects design which has four conditions. In this situation, it is not possible to run all 24 possible orders. To determine which orders to run, one could randomly select 12 out of the 24 possible orders. However, if you do this, you could not guarantee that each condition would be run in the same ordinal position (e.g. the first position) the same number of times and that each condition precedes and follows each other condition once. In other words, you could not control for these order effects. The way to control for these order effects is to construct a Latin square.

A Latin square has as many orders as conditions. So a Latin square with four conditions will have four orders. To make a Latin square, perform the following steps:

- Create a random order of the conditions. This random order will be used to generate the other orders in the Latin square. There are several ways to create this initial random order. Suppose there are four conditions

labelled A, B, C and D. One way is to write each letter on a separate slip of paper or index card, thoroughly shuffle the papers or cards and choose a sequence. (Randomisation is dealt with in Section 9.2.)

- Suppose the starting random order from step 1 is BACD. Sequentially number the conditions in this random order starting with 1. For this example, B = 1, A = 2, C = 3 and D = 4.

- To create the first order in the Latin square, put the last number or condition (N) in the third position as follows:

$$1, 2, 3, 4$$

which corresponds to the conditions as initially lettered B, A, D, C. If we had more than four conditions, then every subsequent unevenly numbered position (e.g. 5, 7 and so on) would have one less than the previous unevenly numbered position, as shown in Table 10.2.

- To create the second order in the Latin square, add 1 to each number apart from the last number N, which now becomes 1. So, in terms of our example with four conditions, the order is:

$$2 \, (1 + 1), 3 \, (2 + 1), 1 \, (N), 4 \, (3 + 1)$$

which corresponds to the conditions as first lettered A, C, B, D.

- To create further orders, we simply proceed in the same way by adding 1 to the previous numbers except that the last number (4) becomes the first number (1). So, the order of the third row in our example becomes:

Table 10.2	Position of unevenly numbered conditions in the first order of a Latin square									
Order number	1	2	3	4	5	6	7	8	9	10
Condition number	1	2	N	3	N − 1	4	N − 2	5	N − 3	6

$\rightarrow$

3 (2 + 1), 4 (3 + 1), 2 (1 + 1), 1

which corresponds to the conditions as originally lettered C, D, A, B.

Our Latin square will look as follows:

B, A, D, C
A, C, B, D
C, D, A, B
D, B, C, A

We can see that each of the four letters occurs only once in each of the four orders or four columns of the square. Each letter is preceded and followed once by every other letter. For example, B is preceded once by C, A and D in the second, third and fourth rows, respectively. It is also followed once by A, D and C in the first, second and last rows, respectively.

- If there is an odd number of conditions, then two Latin squares are constructed. The first square is created as just described. The second square is produced by reversing the order of each of the rows in the first square, so that the first condition becomes the last, the second condition becomes the second to last and so on. So, if we have five conditions and the first row of our initial Latin square is

C, A, D, E, B

the first row of our reversed Latin square becomes

B, E, D, A, C

With five conditions we would have 10 rows or orders.

- Participants are randomly assigned to each order. The number of participants for each order should be the same.

The Latin square could be used for controlling the order in which we measure the dependent variable when there are several of these being measured in a particular study.

10.5 Psychology and social psychology of the laboratory experiment

There is no doubt that the design of effective experiments is problematic. Some of the most troublesome issues in psychology experiments are not about the detail of design or the statistical analysis, but a consequence of the psychology laboratory being a social setting in which people interact and, it has to be said, in far from normal circumstances. Generically, this can be referred to as the psychology and social psychology of the laboratory experiment. These issues are largely about the interaction between the participants and the experimenter, and the experimental procedures. Their consequence is to somewhat muddy the interpretation and validity of laboratory experiments. These are not recent ideas. Some stretch back into the history of psychology and most can be traced back 50 years. Critics regard these features as rendering experimentation untenable as psychology's fundamental research method, while others regard them as relatively trivial, but interesting, aspects of experimental research.

■ Placebo effect

Placebo effects have long been recognised in the evaluation of drugs and clinical treatments (Diehl, 1933; Rivers, 1908; Rivers & Webber, 1908; Tyler, 1946). Careful attempts are made to control placebo effects in clinical trials, though somewhat similar effects in other fields of psychological research may be left uncontrolled (Orne, 1959, 1969). A drug has two aspects: what the medication looks like and the active ingredients that it contains. Long ago, the medical researcher Beecher (1955) noted that participants who believed they were receiving the active medication but were in fact receiving bogus medication (which lacked the active ingredient) nevertheless showed similar improvement (treatment effects) to those who received the active ingredient. Possibly their expectations about the effectiveness of the drug brought about the apparent therapeutic change. The treatment that does not contain the active ingredient is called a placebo or placebo treatment. *Placebo* is Latin for 'I shall be pleasing or acceptable'. The treatment may be called a placebo because it is given to patients to please them into thinking that they are being treated.

In clinical trials of the effectiveness of drugs or clinical treatments, participants are told that either (a) they are being given the treatment (even though they are not) or (b) they may receive either the placebo or the treatment and they are either told (open-label) or not told (closed-label) which they are getting. In other words, they may not be aware of (i.e. 'blind' to) which condition they are in. Furthermore, the administrator of the study should, ideally, be ignorant of what is actually happening to the participant just in case they unconsciously or inadvertently reveal which treatment the participant will receive. If the administrator does not know what treatment is being given, then no subtle cues may be communicated about whether or not the placebo was given, for example. This is known as a 'double-blind' – which means both the participants and the administrator of the research are ignorant of whether the active or the placebo treatment has been given.

Sheldrake (1998) surveyed experimental papers that were published in important journals in a number of fields. Blind experimental procedures were infrequently used. Such procedures were by far the most common in the field of parapsychology, where over four out of five studies used blind procedures. This is important, since parapsychological research (i.e. research into supernatural phenomena) is one type of research about which there is a great deal of scepticism. Hence parapsychological researchers need to employ the most exacting research methods, since critics are almost certain to identify methodological faults. Equally clearly, some fields of research do not equally fear similar criticisms – or blind procedures would be rather more common. So there may be an important lesson: that the more likely one's findings are to be controversial, the greater the need for methodological rigour in order to avoid public criticism.

Experimenter effects

In all of the concern about experimental design and statistical analysis, it is easy to overlook some important parameters of the experimental situation. If we concentrate on what participants do in an experiment, we may overlook the effect the researcher is having. There is some evidence that the role of the researcher is not that of a neutral and unbiased collector of scientific data. Instead, different characteristics of the experimenter such as race and gender may affect the outcome of the research. But there are other features of experimenters which are shared by experimenters in general, an important one being that experimenters generally have a commitment to their research and its outcomes.

Rosnow (2002) indicates something of the extent to which the experimenter can influence the accuracy of the observations they record. For example, in an overview of a sizeable number of studies involving the observations of several hundred researchers, something like one in every 100 observations was incorrect when measured against objective standards. Some of the inaccuracy appears to be just that, but about two-thirds of the errors tended to support the experimenters' hypotheses. Seemingly then there is a small trend for researchers to make errors favouring their position on a topic (Rosenthal, 1978). Whether or not these 'consistent' errors are sufficient to determine the findings of studies overall is difficult to assess. However, even if they are insufficient acting alone, there is a range of other influences of the researcher which may be compounded with recording errors.

Of course, here we are talking about non-intentional errors of which the researchers would probably be unaware. Furthermore, we should not assume that biases exist solely at the level of data collection. There are clearly possibilities that the literature review or the conclusions include some form of systematic bias. One of the best ways of dealing with these is to be always sceptical of the claims of other researchers and to check out key elements of their arguments, including those of Rosenthal. That is the essence of the notion of the scientific method, anyway.

Experimenter expectancy effect

Rosenthal (1963, 1969) raised another potential problem in experimental studies. The idea is that experimenters may unintentionally influence participants into behaving in the way that the experimenter wants or desires. Barber (1973, 1976) described this as the experimenter unintentional expectancy effect. A typical way of investigating this effect involves using a number of student experimenters. Participants in the study are asked to rate the degree of success shown in photographs of several different people (Rosenthal & Rubin, 1978). Actually the photographs had been chosen because previous research had shown them to be rated at the neutral midpoint of the success scale. In this study, the student experimenters were deceived into believing that previous research had shown the photographs to be rated as either showing success or showing failure. However, of the 119 studies using this experimental paradigm (procedure), only 27 per cent found that student experimenters were affected by their expectations based on the putative previous research. So in most cases there was no evidence for expectancy effects. Nevertheless, if over a quarter of studies found evidence of an effect, then it should always be considered a possibility when designing research. Very few studies have included control conditions to determine to what extent expectancy effects may occur when the focus of the study is not the examination of expectancy effects.

Demand characteristics

Orne (1962, 1969) proposed that certain features or cues of the experimental situation, including the way the experimenter behaves, may lead the participant to behave in certain ways. These cues are called the demand characteristics of the experiment. The demand characteristics approach takes account of the totality of cues in the situation – it is not specifically about the experimenter's behaviour. This effect is thought to be largely unconscious in that participants are not aware of being affected in this way. Of course, some might question this, as the cognitive processes involved seem quite complex. In many ways, the concept of demand characteristics cannot be separated from the notion of helpful and cooperative participants. Orne, for example, had noticed that participants in research when interviewed afterwards make statements indicating that they are aware that there is some sort of experimental hypothesis and that they, if acting reasonably, should seek to support the researcher in the endeavour. So, for example, a participant might say 'I hope that was the sort of thing you wanted' or 'I hope that I didn't mess up your study'.

Orne gives only a few examples of studies where demand characteristics may be operating, and these examples do not seem to quite clinch the matter. One study examined sensory deprivation effects. The question was whether the apparent effects that researchers had found of the deprivation of sensory stimulation for several hours could be the result of something else. Could it be that sensory deprivation effects were simply the result of the participants' *expectations* that they should be adversely affected (Orne & Scheibe, 1964)? To test this, a study was designed. In one condition, participants underwent various procedures which indicated that they may be taking part in a study which had deleterious effects. For example, they were given a physical examination and were told that, if they could not stand being in the sensory deprivation condition any longer, they could press a red 'panic' button and they would be released from the situation. In the other condition, participants were put in exactly the same physical situation but were simply told that they were acting as the controls in a sensory deprivation study. The effects of these two conditions were examined in terms of 14 different measures (an example of a study using multiple dependent variables). However, there were significant differences in only three of the 13 measures where this difference was in the predicted direction.

It has to be stressed that Orne did not regard demand characteristics as just another nuisance source of variation for the experimenter to control. Indeed, the demand characteristics could not be controlled for, for example, by using sophisticated control conditions. Instead, the demand characteristics needed to be understood using one major resource – the participants in the study themselves. Rosnow (2002) likens the role of demand characteristics to the greengrocer whose thumb is always on the scale. The bias may be small but it is consistent and in no sense random.

Orne's solution was to seek out information which would put the researcher on a better track to understanding the meaning of their data. Quasi-control strategies were offered which essentially change the status of the participants in the research from that of the 'subject' to a role which might be described as co-investigators. In the post-experiment interview, once the participant has been effectively convinced that the experiment is over, the experimenter and the participant are free to discuss all aspects of the study. Matters like the meaning of the study as experienced by the participant could be explored. Of course, the participant needs to understand that the experimenter has concerns about the possibility that demand characteristics influenced behaviour in the experiment.

An alternative to this is to carry out a pre-inquiry. This is a mind game really, in which the participants are asked to imagine that they are participating in the actual study. The experimental procedures are described to the participants in the mind experiment in a great deal of detail. The participant is then asked to describe how they believe they would behave in these circumstances. Eventually, the experimenter is in a position to compare the conjectures about behaviour in the study with what actually happens in the study. An assessment may be made of the extent to which demand characteristics may explain the participants' actual behaviours. The problem is, of course, that the behaviours cannot be decisively identified as the consequence of demand characteristics.

Imagine an experiment (disregarding everything you learnt in the ethics chapter) in which the experimental group has a lighted cigarette placed against their skin, whereas the control group has an unlighted cigarette placed against their skin. In a quasi-control pre-inquiry, participants will probably anticipate that the real participants will show some sort of pain reaction. Would we contemplate explaining such responses in the real experiment as the result of demand characteristics? Probably not. But what, for example, if in the actual experiment the participants in the lighted cigarette condition actually showed no signs of pain? In these circumstances, the demand characteristics explanation simply is untenable. What, though, if the pre-inquiry study found that participants expected that they would remain stoical and stifle the expression of pain? Would we not accept the demand characteristics explanation in this case?

There are a number of demonstrations by Orne and others that participants in experiments tend to play the role of good participants. That is, they seem especially willing to carry out tasks which, ordinarily away from the laboratory, they would refuse to do or question. So it has been shown that participants in a laboratory will do endless body press-ups simply at the request of the experimenter. This situation of 'good faith' in which the participant is keen to serve the needs of the experiment may not always exist, and it is a very different world now from when these studies were originally carried out in the middle of the twentieth century. But this too could be accommodated by the notion of demand characteristics.

Not surprisingly, researchers have investigated demand characteristics experimentally, sometimes using aspects of Orne's ideas. Demand characteristics have been most commonly investigated in studies manipulating feelings of elation and depression (Westermann, Spies, Stahl, & Hesse, 1996).

In an early study Velten (1968) examined the effect of demand characteristics by having participants in the control conditions read various information about the corresponding experimental condition – for example, by describing the procedure used in this condition, by asking participants to behave in the way they think participants in that condition would behave, and by asking them to act as if they were in the same mood as that condition was designed to produce. These are known as quasi-control studies. Participants in an elation condition rated their mood as significantly less depressed than those in the elation demand characteristics condition, and participants in the depression condition rated their mood as significantly more depressed than those in the depression demand characteristics condition. These findings suggest that the demand characteristics conditions were less effective in producing the expected emotions than the real conditions.

The debate over demand characteristics has, at times, been somewhat robust with some experimentalists dismissing the arguments of Orne and others on various grounds. Probably more important has been the generally limited impact that demand characteristics have made on experimentation in psychology. Sharpe and Whelton (2016) document the way in which psychologists' interest in demand characteristics has waxed and waned over the 60 or so years since the idea was first proposed by Orne. They describe the current state of psychology as being one of a crisis in psychology largely because of the focus on notorious failures to replicate important research findings (see Chapter 20). Such crises, they suggest, encourage the resurgence of interest in demand characteristics. However, Klein et al. (2012) found that words and ideas related to demand characteristics are less likely to appear in relevant databases in recent times than fifty or so years ago. A detailed study of articles in two important psychology journals by Klein et al. suggested that information about the social context of the studies described was somewhat sparse. Even information about whether or not the researcher was actually present in the laboratory was largely missing. It was also not possible to find information about whether any assessment had been made about the possible impact of demand characteristics.

What to conclude? Orne-style quasi-control studies of the sort described above have one feature that would be valuable in any study, that participants and researcher get together as equals to try to understand the experience of participants in the research. Out of such interviews, information may emerge which can help the researcher understand their data. Not to talk to research participants is a bit like burying one's head in the sand to avoid exposure to problems. Researchers should want to know about every aspect of their research – whether or not this knowledge is comfortable. On the other hand, studies into the effects of demand characteristics often produce at best only partial evidence of their effects, as we saw above. That is, quasi-participants who simply experience descriptions of the experimental procedures rarely if ever seem to reproduce the research findings in full. Whether such 'partial replications' of the findings of the original study are sufficient to either accept or reject the notion of demand characteristics is difficult to arbitrate on. Furthermore, it is not clear to what extent interviews with participants may themselves be subject to demand characteristics where participants tend to give experimenters the kinds of answers they think the experimenter wants to hear.

The important lesson learnt from the studies of the social psychology of the laboratory experiment is the futility of regarding participants in research as passive recipients of stimuli which affect their behaviour (Sharpe & Whelton, 2016). The old-fashioned term 'subject' seems to encapsulate this view better than anything. The modern term 'participants' describes the situation more accurately.

> ## Box 10.4   Research Example
>
> # True experiment on the effect of alcohol and expectations on performance
>
> Vuchinich, R. E., & Sobell, M. B. (1978). Empirical separation of physiologic and expected effects of alcohol on complex perceptual motor performance. *Psychopharmacology, 60,* 81–85.
>
> The levels of complexity and sophistication which can be achieved by extending the basic two-group laboratory experimental design are truly remarkable. It is questionable, however, whether it is wise to emulate the most complicated designs in your own work – certainly until you gain more knowledge and experience. The complexity involved can arise from the number of independent variables you have, the number of dependent variables you have and the use of both related and unrelated groups within the same design. By all means use more complex experimental designs, but do not be over-ambitious too soon. For example, it is easy to add more and more independent variables and covariates into your research design. Indeed, you may have so many levels of complexity that you impress even yourself. The trouble is that with these greater levels of complexity the problems of interpreting your data become more difficult. This involves both the statistical analysis (some form of analysis of variance) and understanding the meaning of this analysis. Easy, you might think: SPSS or some other computer program will do this at the blink of an eye. Unfortunately, this is not the case. For one thing, interpreting the output of an ANOVA analysis involves a lot more judgement than most psychologists allow. You really need to understand how the analysis works, or you are likely to be tripped up if you try to apply SPSS too mechanically. The example which follows is relatively simple but allows you to understand some of the problems.
>
> ### Background
>
> Studies which have varied whether alcohol was or was not given and whether participants were told whether or not they had been given alcohol have found that being told whether alcohol had been given had a stronger effect on various social behaviours than whether alcohol had actually been given. In other words, it seemed that the participants' expectations about alcohol had a greater effect than the alcohol itself. Rudy Vuchinich and Mark Sobell (1978) wanted to see whether this was also the case for behaviour such as perceptual motor performance, which may be expected to be less affected by the social context in which it occurs.
>
> ### Hypotheses
>
> There were no specific hypotheses as such.
>
> ### Method
>
> There were two independent variables. One independent variable was whether the participants were given alcohol and tonic water or tonic water only. The other independent variable was whether they were told they had been given alcohol or tonic water. In other words, this was a 2 × 2 factorial design with two levels of two conditions. This design (Figure 10.8) resulted in the following four conditions: (1) given alcohol, told alcohol; (2) given tonic, told alcohol; (3) given alcohol, told tonic and (4) given tonic, told tonic.
>
> Forty male introductory psychology students were randomly assigned to one of these four conditions. Participants receiving alcohol were given a mixture of one part 80-proof vodka and five parts tonic water, as it has been noted that this mixture does not enable alcohol to be reliably detected. Each participant received one ounce (29.57 ml) of liquid per 10 pounds (4.53 kg) of body weight. This meant that participants in the alcohol condition received 0.414 grams of
>
> →

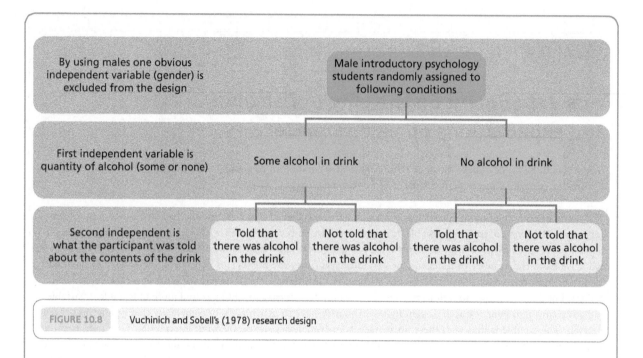

FIGURE 10.8   Vuchinich and Sobell's (1978) research design

ethanol per kilogram of body weight. This, of course, reduces the possibility that the different groups received different amounts of alcohol relative to body weight.

Being told which drink they were given was manipulated by having participants think that they had been randomly selected to be in the alcohol or the tonic condition. Where they were told they were being given alcohol, part of the drink was in a vodka bottle and part in a tonic water bottle. Where they were told they were being given tonic water, all the drink was in the tonic bottle.

There were four dependent measures which were derived from a divided-attention task where the participant had to follow with a stylus in their dominant hand a dot on a rotating disk. At the same time, they had to carry out a choice reaction time test with their non-dominant hand by pressing one of three appropriately coloured buttons to one of three correspondingly coloured lights. The four dependent measures were as follows:

- The time on target in the pursuit rotor task
- The time taken to initially press the correct response in the choice reaction test
- The time taken to initially press the wrong response in this test
- The number of errors made on this test.

Participants carried out five one-minute trials on the pursuit rotor task before receiving the manipulated variables.

Some results

There was a significant alcohol effect on the time of target in the pursuit motor task when the pre-manipulation performances on the last three one-minute trials were statistically controlled in an analysis of covariance. Participants receiving alcohol performed significantly better than those receiving tonic water only. There was no effect for what participants were told and no significant interaction between what they were told and alcohol.

There was a significant effect on the number of errors made for the alcohol condition, for the being-told condition and for the interaction between these two conditions. As the interaction was significant and seemed to account for the main effects, only the interaction effect will be described here. Participants who were given tonic and told they were given tonic made the smallest number of errors ($M = 1.25$) and made significantly fewer errors than those who were given alcohol and told they were given tonic ($M = 3.05$). Participants who were told they were given alcohol and were given alcohol ($M = 3.40$) did not make significantly more errors than those who were told they were given alcohol but were given tonic ($M = 3.35$). This last finding suggested that being told one is given alcohol when one has not been given alcohol may adversely affect one's performance on another task.

There were no significant effects for the two reaction time measures.

Authors' suggestions for future research

Vuchinich and Sobell (1978) briefly concluded that the effects of expectancy on behaviour which is affected by alcohol need to be investigated as well as the way in which expectancy effects may occur.

10.6   Conclusion

Most true or randomised experimental designs include more than two conditions and measure more than one dependent variable, which are more often than not treated separately. Where the design consists of a single factor, the number of conditions is limited and may generally consist of no more than four or five conditions. The number of factors that are manipulated in a true or randomised design should also be restricted and may usually consist of no more than two or three manipulated variables. The reason for this advice partly rests on the difficulty of carrying out studies with many independent variables – planning them introduces many technical difficulties. Furthermore, the statistical analysis of very complex factorial designs is not easy and may stretch the statistical understanding of many researchers to the limit. For example, numerous complex interactions may emerge which are fraught with difficulties of interpretation. A computer program may do the number-crunching for you but there its responsibility ends. It is for the researcher to make the best possible sense of the numbers, which is difficult when there are too many layers of complexity.

Hypotheses often omit consideration of effects due to basic demographic factors such as gender and age. Nevertheless, factorial designs can easily and usefully include such factors when numbers of participants permit. Of course, where the participants are, for example, students, age variation may be too small to be worthy of inclusion. Alternatively, where the numbers of females and males are very disproportionate, it may also be difficult to justify looking for gender differences.

It is wise to make adequate provision in terms of participant numbers for trends to be statistically significant, otherwise a great deal of effort is wasted. A simple but good way of doing this is to examine similar studies to inform yourself about what may be the minimum appropriate sample size. Alternatively, by running a pilot study a more direct estimate of the likely size of the experimental effect can be made and a sample size chosen which gives that size of effect the chance of being statistically significant. The more sophisticated way of doing this is to use power analysis. This is discussed in the companion book *Understanding statistics in psychology with SPSS* (Howitt & Cramer, 2020). The way in which the results of factorial randomised designs are analysed can also be applied to the analysis of qualitative variables in non-randomised designs such as surveys, as we shall see in the next chapter.

A pilot study is also an opportunity to explore the social psychological characteristics of the experiment being planned. In particular, it can be regarded as an opportunity to interview participants about their experience of the study. What they have to say may confirm the appropriateness of your chosen method, but, equally, it may provide food for thought and a stimulus to reconsider some of the detail of the planned experiment.

Key points

- Advanced experimental designs extend the basic experimental group-control group paradigm in a number of ways. Several experimental and control groups may be used. More than one independent variable and several measures of the dependent variable may be employed.

- Because considerable resources may be required to conduct a study, the number of conditions run must be limited to those which are considered important. It is not advisable simply to extend the number of independent variables, since this can lead to problems in interpreting the complexity of the output. Further studies may be needed when the interpretation of the data is hampered by a lack of sufficient information.

- Multifactorial designs are important, since not only are they efficient in terms of the numbers of participants needed, but they also can help identify interactions between the independent variables in the study. Furthermore, the relative influences of the various factors are revealed in a factorial design.

- Research which has insufficient cases to detect the effect under investigation is a waste of effort. The numbers in the cells of an experimental design need to be sufficient to determine that an effect is statistically significant. Previous similar studies may provide indications of appropriate sample sizes, or a pilot study may be required to estimate the likely size of the effect of the factors. From this, the minimum sample size to achieve statistical significance may be assessed.

- As with most designs, it is advantageous if the cells of a design have the same number of cases. For factorial designs, this ensures that the effects of the factors are independent of one another. The extent to which factors are not independent can be determined by multiple regression. Many statistical tests work optimally with equal group sizes.

- Placebos and double-blind procedural controls should be routinely used in the evaluation of the effects of drugs to control for the expectations that participants and experimenters may have about the effects of the drugs being tested. Some of these procedures are appropriate in a variety of psychological studies.

- In general, it would seem that few researchers incorporate checks on demand characteristics and other social psychological aspects of the laboratory experiment. This may partly be explained by the relative lack of research into such effects in many areas of psychological research. However, since it is beneficial to interview participants about their experiences of the experimental situation, it is possible to discuss factors such as demand characteristics and expectancy effects with participants as part of the joint evaluation of the research by experimenter and participants.

ACTIVITIES

1. Answer the following questions in terms of the basic design that you produced for the exercise in Chapter 9 to investigate the effect of unemployment on crime. Can you think of reasons for breaking down the independent variable of unemployment into more than two conditions? If you can, what would these other conditions be? Are there ways in

which you think participants may be affected by the manipulation of unemployment which are not part of unemployment itself? In other words, are there demand-type characteristics which may affect how participants behave? If there are, how would you test or control these? Which conditions would you compare and what would your predictions be about the differences between them? Is there more than one way in which you can operationalise crime? If there is, would you want to include these as additional measures of crime? Are there any subject or other independent variables that you think are worth including? If there are, would you expect any of these to interact with the independent variable of unemployment?

2. What is your nomination for the worst experiment of all time for this year's Psycho Awards? Explain your choice. Who would you nominate for the experimenter's Hall of Fame and why?

CHAPTER 11

Cross-sectional or correlational research

Non-manipulation studies

Overview

- Various terms describe research that, unlike the true or randomised experiment, does not involve the deliberate manipulation of variables. These include 'correlational study', 'survey study', 'observational study' and 'non-experiment'. A more general term is 'non-manipulation study'.

- Experimental or laboratory research cannot address every research need in psychology. Sometimes important variables simply cannot be manipulated. Laboratory experiments can handle effectively only a small number of variables at any one time, sometimes making comparing the relative influence of variables difficult. Experiments cannot investigate patterns or relationships among a large number of variables.

- Cross-sectional designs are typical of most non-experimental psychological research. In cross-sectional designs, the same variable is measured only once for each participant.

- Causality cannot be tested definitively in cross-sectional designs, though the relationships obtained are often used to support potential causal interpretations. These designs, however, help determine the direction and the strength of the association between two or more variables. Furthermore, the extent to which this association is affected by controlling other variables can also be assessed.

11.1   Introduction

Various terms describe the most common alternative form of psychological research to the true or randomised experiment – the non-experimental, correlational, passive observational, survey or observational study. Each of these terms has its own inadequacies. An experiment has the implication of some sort of intervention in a situation in order to assess the consequences. This was more or less its meaning in the early years of psychological research. Gradually, the experiment in psychology took on the more formal characteristics of randomisation, experimental and control groups, and control of potentially confounding sources of variation. However, in more general terms, an experiment can be defined along the lines of being a test or trial (Allen, 1992), which in itself does not necessarily involve all of the formal expectations of the randomised psychology experiment. Using Allen's definition, we could be interested in testing whether one variable is related to another variable, such as academic achievement at school and parental income. Unfortunately, this would be a very loose use of language since the key defining feature of experiments in psychology is the manipulation of a variable. This is clear, for example, when Campbell and Stanley (1963, p. 1) state that an experiment is taken to refer to 'research in which variables are manipulated and their effects upon other variables observed'. This indicates that a non-experiment in psychology refers to any research not involving the manipulation of a variable. So it might be better to state this directly by referring to a non-manipulation rather than a non-experimental study. We could adopt the phrase 'field work' or 'field study' for research outside the laboratory although some randomised experiments do take place in the field.

Campbell and Stanley (1963, p. 64) used the term 'correlational' to describe designs not involving the manipulation of variables. Today this is a very common term to describe this sort of research. Later, however, Cook and Campbell (1979, p. 295) argued that 'correlational' is a misnomer because it describes a statistical technique, not a research design. So statistical correlational methods can be used to analyse the data from an experiment just as they can be used in many other sorts of quantitative research. A particular set of statistical tests have traditionally been applied to the data from experiments (e.g. t-tests, analyses of variance). However, it is perfectly possible to analyse the same experiment with a correlation coefficient or multiple regression or other correlational techniques.

Although it is common even in textbooks, the distinction between statistics to show relationships (e.g. the correlation coefficient) and those to show differences between means is more apparent than real (see Box 11.1). Data from non-experimental studies can often be analysed using the statistical techniques common in reports of experiments – t-tests and analyses of variance, for example. We would most probably apply a two-way analysis of variance to determine whether the scores on a measure of depression varied according to the gender and the marital status of participants. Although researchers would not normally do this, the same data could be analysed using multiple regression techniques (see Field, 2013, for an extended discussion of this). In other words, analysis of variance and multiple regression are closely linked. This is quite a sophisticated matter and it requires a degree of experience with statistics to understand it fully.

Although it never gained popularity, Cook and Campbell (1979, p. 296) suggested the term *passive observational* to describe a non-manipulation study. The adjective 'passive' implies here that the study does not involve a manipulation. Most research procedures are anything but passive. For instance, observation is often thought of as active rather than passive since there is a degree of selectivity in terms of what is being observed (Pedhazur & Schmelkin, 1991, p. 142). Furthermore, the term 'observational' even does not work

---

Box 11.1 Key Ideas

Tests of correlation versus tests of difference

Although at first there may seem to be a confusing mass of different statistical techniques, many of them are very closely related, as they are based on the same general statistical model. For example, both a Pearson's product moment correlation (*r*) and an unrelated *t*-test can be used to determine the relationship between a dichotomous variable such as gender and a continuous variable such as scores on a measure of depression. Both these tests will give you the same significance level when applied to the same data, though, of course, the statistic itself is *t* in one case and *r* in the other. This implies that the Pearson correlation coefficient and the *t*-test are related. The relationship is fairly simple and is as follows:

$$r = \sqrt{\frac{t^2}{t^2 + df}}$$

where *df* stands for the degrees of freedom. The degrees of freedom are two fewer than the total number of cases (participants).

The dichotomous variable could equally be the experimental condition versus the control condition, hence the applicability of both tests to simple experiments. The dichotomous variable is coded 1 and 2 for the two different values, whether the variable being considered is gender or the independent variable of an experiment (this is an arbitrary coding and could be reversed if one wished).

The term 'survey' is not particularly appropriate, either. It too refers to a particular method of data collection which typically involves asking people questions. It also has the connotation of drawing a precise sample from a population, such as in stratified random sampling (see Section 13.2). Many studies in psychology have neither of these features and yet are not randomised experiments.

---

in this context since it applies to data collected from randomised experiments as well as non-experimental research. Cook and Campbell (1979, p. 296) themselves objected to using the term 'observational study', because it would apply to what they called quasi-experiments which did not involve randomisation.

In view of the lack of a satisfactory term, we have given in to the temptation to use 'non-manipulation study' to refer to this kind of research. This term is less general than non-experimental, refers to the essential characteristic of an experiment and does not describe a method of data collection. However, we realise we are even less likely than Cook and Campbell (1979, p. 295) 'to change well-established usage'. In the majority of the social sciences, the distinction would be unimportant. It matters in psychology for the simple reason that psychology alone among the social sciences is strongly committed to laboratory experiments. Of course, medicine and biology do have a tradition of strict experimentation and may have similar problems over terminology. In this context, it is useful to remember that psychology has a foot in both the social and biological sciences.

11.2 Cross-sectional designs

The most basic design for a cross-sectional study involves just two variables. These variables may both be scores, or may both be nominal categories, or there may be a mixture of nominal and score variables. For example, we could examine the relationship between gender and a diagnosis of depression. In this case, both variables would consist of two binary values – male versus female, diagnosed as depressed versus not diagnosed as depressed. Such basic designs provide very limited information, which restricts their appeal to researchers and consequently their use in professional research. They are resource hungry for the small amount of findings they provide and for a little extra effort a wider variety of data could be collected. So professional researchers use more complex research designs – a trend which more advanced students should emulate.

So, ideally, think in terms of a minimum of three variables for a cross-sectional study, but substantially more may have advantages. Three variables mean that controls can be included for potentially confounding variables or investigating possible intervening variables. Also consider having more than one measure of the same variable. Extending the amount of data collected by introducing more variables allows more sophisticated forms of analysis. This is *not* an invitation to throw into your study every variable that you can think of and have a means of measuring. Each additional variable measured needs to be justifiable in terms of their potential to clarify the meaning of the relationship between your primary variables of interest. Care and thoughtfulness are needed so that the researcher anticipates the possible outcomes of the research and adds only variables which potentially help clarify the interpretation of the key relationships. Merely throwing in everything can only lead to more confusion rather than clarification, so don't do it. You should be able to make a rational case for every variable you decide to include.

The cross-sectional design is as difficult to execute as any other form of study, including the laboratory experiment. The skills required to effectively carry out field work are not always the same as those for doing experiments, but they are in no sense less demanding. Indeed, when it comes to the effective statistical analysis of cross-sectional data, this may be more complex than that required for some laboratory experiments. The reason for this is that non-manipulation studies employ statistical controls for unwanted influences, whereas experimental studies employ procedural controls to a similar end. Furthermore, the cross-sectional study may be more demanding in terms of numbers of participants, simply because the relationship between the variables of interest is generally smaller than would be expected in a laboratory experiment. In the laboratory, it is possible to maximise the obtained relationships by controlling for the 'noise' of other variables, that is, by standardising and controlling as much as possible. In a cross-sectional design, we would expect the relationships between variables to be small, and a correlation of about .30 would be considered quite a promising trend by many researchers, though, bear in mind that for a correlation of this size to be statistically significant at the two-tailed 5 per cent or .05 level would require a minimum sample size of over 40.

The need for statistical controls for the influence of third variables in cross-sectional and all non-manipulation studies makes considerable demands on the statistical knowledge of the researcher. Many of the appropriate statistics are not discussed in many introductory statistics texts in psychology. One exception to this is *Understanding statistics in psychology with SPSS* (Howitt & Cramer, 2020). The complexity of some of the statistical techniques together with the substantial numbers of variables that can be involved means that statistical computer packages are essential. The companion computing text *Introduction to SPSS in psychology* (Howitt & Cramer, 2017) will help you make light work of this task.

Many of the variables of interest will tend to be correlated with each other. One consequence of this is that samples have to be larger when the relationships between three or more variables are investigated. It is difficult to specify exactly what the minimum sample size should be, because this depends on the expected sizes of the associations. In the absence of any better estimate, consider the minimum sample size to be 60 or more. This is merely a suggestion based on a reasonable expectation of the likely size of correlations in a cross-sectional study. A really strong relationship can be statistically significant with a smaller sample. If previous research suggests that relationships are likely to be small, then a larger sample size would be needed.

11.3   The case for non-manipulation studies

There are a number of circumstances which encourage the use of non-manipulation studies just as there are other circumstances in which the randomised laboratory experiment may be employed to better effect (see Figure 11.1):

● *Naturalistic research settings*   Generally speaking, randomised experiments have a degree of artificiality which varies but is almost inescapable. Although there have been some successful attempts to employ randomised experiments 'in the field' (in natural settings), these have been relatively few and risk losing advantages of the laboratory experiment such as standardisation. Given that research involves choices, many psychologists prefer to avoid randomised experiments entirely. There are arguments on all sides, but research is a matter of balancing a variety of considerations, and different researchers will make different decisions according to circumstances. Non-manipulation studies seem more naturalistic and so more attractive to some researchers.

● *Manipulation not possible*   Sometimes it is impossible, impractical or unethical to manipulate the variable of interest. This would be the case, for example, if you were investigating the effects of divorce on children. Divorce cannot be assigned at random

Non-manipulative studies can be much more naturalistic

In much research it is not possible to manipulate variables

To establish that there is an association before carrying out an experiment to further examine this

You may wish to understand just what the strength of the real-life relationship is between two variables

To determine what variables might be potentially the most important influences on other variables

You might wish to predict values of one variable from another, for example when making selection choices

Developing explanatory models in real life prior to testing aspects of the model in the laboratory

You might wish to understand the structural features of things such as intelligence

You may wish to study how something changes over time

You may wish to understand the temporal direction of associations – what changes come before other changes

FIGURE 11.1   Summary of the various uses of non-manipulative studies

by the researcher. In this situation, you could compare children from parents who were together with children from parents who were divorced.

● *Establishing an association*   You may wish to see whether there is a relationship between two or more variables before committing resources to complex experiments designed to identify causal relationships between those variables. For example, you may wish to determine whether there is an association between how much conflict there is in a relationship and how satisfied each partner is with that relationship before studying whether reducing conflict increases satisfaction with the relationship. Finding an association does not mean that there is a causal relationship between two variables. This could be an example of where a third variable is confusing things. For example, low income may make for stressful circumstances in which couples are (1) in conflict more often and (2) less satisfied with their relationship because shortage of cash makes them less positive about life in general. In this example, this confounding factor of income makes it appear that conflict is causally related to dissatisfaction when it is not. Conversely, the failure to find an association between two variables does not necessarily mean that those variables are not related. The link between the variables may be suppressed by other variables. For instance, there may be an association between conflict and dissatisfaction, but this association may be suppressed by the presence of children. Having children may create more conflict between partners but may also cause them to be more fulfilled as a couple.

● *Natural variation*   In experiments, every effort is made to control for variables which may influence the association between the independent and dependent variables. In a sense, by getting rid of nuisance sources of variation, the key relationship will be revealed at its strongest. But what if your desire is to understand what the relationship is when these other factors are present, as they normally would be in real life? For example, when manipulating a variable, you may find that there is a very strong association between the dependent variable and the independent variable, but this association may be weaker when it is examined in a natural setting.

● *Comparing the sizes of associations*   You may want to find out which of a number of variables are most strongly associated with a particular variable. This may help decide which ones would be the most promising to investigate further or which need controlling in a true experiment. For example, if you wanted to develop a programme for improving academic achievement at school, it would be best to look at those variables which were most strongly related to academic achievement rather than those which were weakly related to it.

● *Prediction and selection*   You may be interested in determining which variables best predict an outcome. These variables may then be used to select the most promising candidates. For example, you may be interested in finding out which criteria best predict which prospective students are likely to be awarded the highest degree marks in psychology and use these criteria to select applicants.

● *Explanatory models*   You may want to develop an explanatory model for some behaviour and examine whether your data fit that model. This could be followed by detailed research into whether your assumptions about causes are correct. For example, you may think that children with wealthier parents perform better academically than children with less well-off parents due to differences in the parents' interest in how well their children do academically. Maybe the wealthier parents demonstrate more interest in their children's academic progress than less well-off ones. Consequently, children of wealthier parents may try harder and so do better. In this case, parental interest is a mediating or intervening variable which links parental wealth with academic achievement.

- *Structure*   You may be interested in determining what the structure is of some characteristic such as intelligence, personality, political attitudes or love. For example, you may be interested in seeing whether there is a general factor (i.e. dimension) of intelligence, or whether there are separate factors of intelligence such as memory, verbal ability, spatial ability and so on.

- *Developing or refining measures*   You may want to develop or refine a measure which you will validate against some criterion. For instance, you may want to refine a measure of social support. More social support has been found to be related to less depression, so you may wish to see whether your refined measure of social support correlates more strongly with depression than the original measure.

- *Temporal change*   You may wish to see whether a particular behaviour changes over time and to what variables is change related. For example, has the incidence of divorce increased over the last 50 years and with what factors is any increase associated?

- *Temporal direction of associations*   You may want to know what the temporal direction is of the association between two variables. Does parental interest in their child's academic achievement affect the child's achievement, or is it that a child who achieves well academically influences their parent's interest? Both temporal sequences could be correct, of course. An association where both variables affect each other is variously known as a bidirectional, bilateral, non-recursive, reciprocal or two-way association.

Chapter 12 discusses methods of researching changes over time.

11.4   Key concepts in the analysis of cross-sectional studies

There are a number of conceptual issues in the analysis of cross-sectional studies which need to be understood as a prelude to the more purely statistical matters (see Figure 11.2).

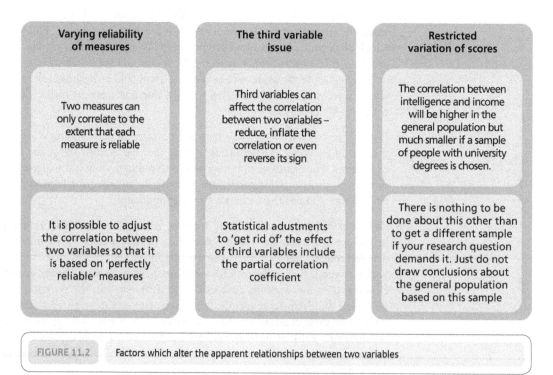

Varying reliability of measures	The third variable issue	Restricted variation of scores
Two measures can only correlate to the extent that each measure is reliable	Third variables can affect the correlation between two variables – reduce, inflate the correlation or even reverse its sign	The correlation between intelligence and income will be higher in the general population but much smaller if a sample of people with university degrees is chosen.
It is possible to adjust the correlation between two variables so that it is based on 'perfectly reliable' measures	Statistical adustments to 'get rid of' the effect of third variables include the partial correlation coefficient	There is nothing to be done about this other than to get a different sample if your research question demands it. Just do not draw conclusions about the general population based on this sample

FIGURE 11.2   Factors which alter the apparent relationships between two variables

■ Varying reliability of measures

The concept of reliability is quite complex and is dealt with in detail in Chapter 16. There are two broad types. The first type is the internal consistency of a psychological scale or measure (i.e. how well the items correlate with the other items ostensibly measuring the same thing). This may be measured as the split-half reliability which, as the name implies, is based on calculating the correlation between two halves of a scale or measure. However, internal consistency is most often measured using Cronbach's alpha (Cronbach, 1951), which is a more comprehensive index than split-half reliability. (It calculates the average reliability based on all possible ways of splitting the scale or measure into two halves.) Generally speaking, a reliability of about .70 would be regarded as satisfactory (Nunnally, 1978). The other type of reliability is the stability of the measure over time. This is commonly measured using test–retest reliability. All of these measures vary from 0 to 1.00 just like a correlation coefficient.

The crucial fact about reliability is that it limits the maximum correlation a variable may have with another variable. The *maximum* value of the correlation of a variable with a reliability of .80 with any other variable is .80, that is, the figure for reliability. The *maximum* value that the correlation between two variables may have is the square root of the product of the two reliabilities. That is, if one reliability is .80 and the reliability of the other measure is .50, then the maximum correlation between these two variables is:

$$.63 [\sqrt{(.80 \times .50)} = \sqrt{.40} = .632].$$

Remember that is the maximum, and also remember that we suggested that quite a good correlation between two variables in a cross-sectional study might be .30. So that correlation might be stronger than it appears if it were not for the lack of reliability of one or both of the variables. This is a fundamental but frequently overlooked problem. Unless the measures used in your research are highly reliable, it is easy to confuse problems due to low reliability with a genuine lack of a relationship between variables.

If one knows the reliabilities (or even one reliability), then it is quite easy to correct the obtained correlation for the unreliability of the measures. One simply divides the correlation coefficient by the square root of the product of the two variables. So in our example, the correlation is .30 divided by the square root of (.80 × .50). This gives:

$$.30 / \sqrt{.40} = .30/.63 = .48.$$

This is clearly a stronger relationship than originally found, as might be expected.

While such statistical adjustments are a possibility if one knows the reliabilities of one's measures, they are not always available but are easily calculated. For this reason, the other way of dealing with reliability is to ensure that one's measures have the best chance of being reliable. This might be achieved, for example, by standardising one's procedures to eliminate unnecessary sources of variability. So, for example, if different interviewers ask about a participant's age in different ways, this will be a source of unnecessary variation (and consequently unreliability). For example, 'What age are you now?', 'About what age are you?' and 'Do you mind telling me your age?' might produce a variety of answers simply because of the variation in wording of the question. For example, 'Do you mind telling me your age?' might encourage the participant to claim to be younger than they are, simply because the question implies the possibility that the participant might be embarrassed to reveal their age.

Another problem for student researchers is the ever-increasing sophistication of the statistics used by professional researchers when reporting their findings. For example, the statistical technique of structural equation modelling is quite commonly used to correct for reliability. Structural equation modelling is also known as analysis of covariance structures, causal modelling, path analysis and simultaneous equation modelling. In their survey of statistical tests reported in a random sample of papers published in the *Journal of Personality and Social Psychology,* Sherman and his colleagues (1999) found that 14 per cent of the papers used this technique in 1996 compared with 4 per cent in 1988 and 3 per cent in 1978. A brief introduction to structural equation modelling may be found in the fifth edition of our companion book, *Introduction to SPSS in psychology* (Howitt & Cramer, 2017). For the example above, structural equation modelling gives a standardised coefficient which has the same value as the correlation corrected for unreliability. We cannot imagine that undergraduate students would use this technique except when closely supervised by an academic, but postgraduate students may well be expected to use it.

▪ Third-variable issue

The confounding variable problem is the classic stumbling block to claiming causal relationships in non-experimental research. The problem is really twofold. Firstly, it is impossible to be sure that the relationship between two variables cannot be explained by the fact that both of them are to a degree correlated with a third variable; these relationships may bring about the original correlation. Remember that we want to establish whether variable A is the *cause* of variable B. Secondly, it is very difficult to anticipate quite what the effect of a third variable will be – it actually can increase correlations as well as decrease them. Either way it confuses the meaning of the correlation between variables A and B.

Suppose we find that the amount of support in a relationship positively correlates with how satisfied partners are. The correlation is .50 as shown in Figure 11.3. Further, suppose that the couple's income is also positively related to both how supportive the partners are and how satisfied they are. Income is correlated .60 with support and .40 with satisfaction. Because income is also positively related to both support and satisfaction, is it possible that part or all of the association between support and satisfaction is accounted for by income? To determine whether this is the case, we can 'partial out' or remove the influence of income. One way of doing this is to use partial correlation. This is the statistical terminology for what psychologists would normally call controlling for a third variable, that is, partialling = controlling.

Partialling is quite straightforward computationally and so relatively easy to calculate. Partialling is discussed in detail in the companion book *Understanding statistics in psychology with SPSS* (Howitt & Cramer, 2020). However, we recommend using SPSS or some other package, since this considerably eases the burden of calculation and risk of error when controlling for several variables at the same time. It is also infinitely less tedious.

The (partial or first-order) correlation between support and satisfaction is .35 once income has been partialled out. This is a smaller value than the original (zero-order) correlation of .50. Consequently, income explains part of the association between support and satisfaction. How is this calculated?

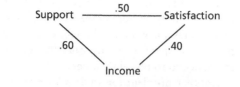

FIGURE 11.3　Factors which alter the apparent relationships between two variables

The following formula is used to partial out one variable, where A refers to the first variable of support, B to the second variable of satisfaction and C to the third or confounding variable of income:

$$r_{\text{AB.C}} = \frac{r_{\text{AB}} - (r_{\text{AC}} \times r_{\text{BC}})}{\sqrt{(1 - r_{\text{AC}}^2) \times (1 - r_{\text{BC}}^2)}}$$

The subscripts indicate what variables the correlations are between. So $r_{\text{AB.C}}$ is the correlation between variables A and B controlling for variable C.

We can substitute the correlations in Figure 11.3 in this formula:

$$r_{\text{AB.C}} = \frac{.50 - (.60 \times .40)}{\sqrt{(1 - .60^2) \times (1 - .40^2)}} = \frac{.260}{.733} = .35$$

So sometimes the influence of the third variable is to make the association between the two main variables bigger than it actually is. This kind of variable is known as a *suppressor* variable. The sign of the partial correlation can also be opposite to that of the original correlation (Cramer, 2003). This radical change occurs when the correlation has the same sign as, and is smaller than, the product of the other two correlations. An example of this is shown in Figure 11.4. The correlation between support and satisfaction is .30. The signs of all three correlations are positive. The product of the other two correlations is .48 (.60 × .80 = .48), which is larger than the correlation of .30 between support and satisfaction. When income is partialled out, the correlation between support and satisfaction becomes − .38. In other words, when income is removed, more support is associated with less rather than greater satisfaction.

Rosenberg (1968) refers to variables which, when partialled out, change the direction of the sign between two other variables as *distorter* variables. He discusses these in terms of contingency tables of frequencies rather than correlation as is done here. Cohen and Cohen (1983), on the other hand, describe change of sign as a suppressor effect. Different types of third variables are discussed in detail in Chapter 12.

Restricted variation of scores

This is probably the most technical of the considerations which lower the correlation between two variables. Equally, it is probably the least well recognised by researchers. A good example of a reduced correlation involves the relationship between intelligence and creativity in university students. University students have a smaller range of intelligence than the general population because they have been selected for university, as they are more intelligent. The correlation between intelligence and creativity is greater in samples where the range of intelligence is less restricted.

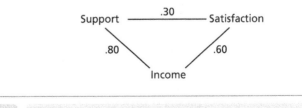

FIGURE 11.4   Partialling leading to a change in sign of the association between support and satisfaction

To be formal about this, the size of the correlation between two variables is reduced when:

- the range or variation of scores on one variable is restricted, *and*

- the scatter of the scores of two variables about the correlation line is fairly constant over the entire length of that line (e.g. Pedhazur & Schmelkin, 1991, pp. 44–45).

A correlation line is the straight line which we would draw through the points of a scattergram (i.e. it is a regression line), but the scores on the two variables have been turned into *z*-scores or standard scores. This is simply done by subtracting the mean of the scores and then dividing it by the standard deviation. This straight line best describes the linear relationship between these two variables (see, e.g. Figure 11.5). If the scatter of scores around the correlation line is not consistent, then it is not possible to know what the size of the correlation is, as this will vary according to the scatter of the scores.

The effects of restricting range can be demonstrated quite easily with the small set of 10 scores shown in Table 11.1. The two variables are called, respectively, A and B. The scores of these two variables are plotted in the scattergram in Figure 11.5 which also shows the correlation line through them. Although the set of scores is small, we can see that they are scattered in a consistent way around the correlation line. The correlation for the 10 scores is about .74. If we reduce the variation of scores on B by selecting the five cases with scores either above or below 5, the correlation is smaller at about .45. The correlation is the same in these two smaller groups because the scatter of scores around the correlation line is the same in both of them.

Of course, you need to know whether you have a potential problem due to the restricted range of scores. You can gain some idea of this if you know what the mean or the standard deviation of the unrestricted scores is:

- If the mean score is much higher (or lower) than the mean score of unrestricted scores, then the variation in scores is more likely to be restricted, as the range for scores to be higher (or lower) than the mean is reduced. For example, the mean score for the two variables in Table 11.1 is 5.00. The mean score for the five cases scoring higher than 5 on variable B is 7.20 $[(6 + 8 + 6 + 7 + 9)/5 = 36/5 = 7.20]$. As the mean of these five scores is higher than the mean of 5.00 for the 10 cases, the potential range for these five scores to be higher is less than that for the 10 scores.

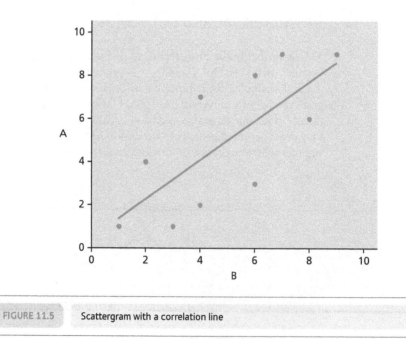

FIGURE 11.5   Scattergram with a correlation line

Table 11.1	Scores on two variables for 10 cases				
Case number	**A**	**B**	**Case number**	**A**	**B**
1	1	1	6	6	8
2	1	3	7	7	4
3	2	4	8	8	6
4	3	6	9	9	7
5	4	2	10	9	9

- The standard deviation (or variance) is a direct measure of variance. If the standard deviation of a set of scores is less than that for the unrestricted scores, then the variance is reduced. The standard deviation for variable B for the 10 scores is about 2.63, whereas it is about 1.30 for the five scores both above and below the mean score of 5.

It is important to understand that generally the effects of the range of scores may be of no consequence. For example, if one is interested in the relationship between creativity and intelligence in university students, then there is no problem. However, it would be a problem if one were interested in the general relationship between intelligence and creativity but only used university students in the study. In this case, the restriction on the range of intelligence in the university sample might be so great that no significant relationship emerges. It is misleading to conclude from this that creativity is not related to intelligence, since it may well be so in the general population. Equally, you may see that studies, ostensibly on the same topic, may appear to yield seemingly incompatible findings simply because of the differences in the samples employed.

Another implication, of course, is of the undesirability of using restricted samples when exploring general psychological processes. The study of university students as the primary source of psychological data is bad not only simply because of the restrictions of the sampling but also because of the restrictions likely on the distributions of the key variables.

There is more information on statistics appropriate to the analysis of cross-sectional designs later (Chapter 12). Multiple regression and path analysis are discussed there and can help the researcher take full advantage of the richness of the data which cross-sectional and other non-manipulation designs can provide.

Box 11.2   Research Example

Cross-sectional study of moderators and mediators on the relation between work–home conflict and domestic violence

VanBuren Trachtenberg, J., Anderson, S. A., & Sabatelli, R. M. (2009). Work–home conflict and domestic violence: A test of a conceptual model. *Journal of Family Violence*, 24, 471–483.

Many researchers eschew the tight discipline of the laboratory experiment for more situationally relevant field research. Our example is a good one in terms of showing the complexity of field work as well as the distinction between moderator

→

and mediator variables. Picking one's way among the myriad of variables which are inherently measurable in field research is not easy, but it is aided by a whole range of analytical and statistical techniques which help the researcher explore the possibilities. The proper analysis of field-based research is probably a little more tricky than for experimental research but only for the reason that experimental designs imply the appropriate statistical analysis. That is, the planning work for experiments helps make the analysis process clearer. In the case of field work, usually more analytical possibilities are available, so it is difficult to know precisely where an analysis will lead before one begins to explore the data.

Background

Jennifer VanBuren Trachtenberg and her colleagues (2009) suggested that conflict between work and one's home life may spill over into domestic violence between partners. Work–home conflict involves the problems created by the nature of one's work and the nature of one's home life. So a long-distance lorry driver might experience a high level of work–home conflict because their partner wants them to be at home at regular times to help with childcare. In this study, the authors were initially interested in two questions: (1) which of various predictor variables such as job satisfaction were related to work–home conflict and (2) which of various moderating variables such as witnessing or experiencing domestic violence as a child may moderate the relation between work–home conflict and domestic violence. In the absence of finding expected moderating effects for variables such as negative communication skills, they subsequently sought whether these variables may act as mediating variables instead.

Hypotheses

There were three hypotheses:

- The first hypothesis was that the various predictors of their conceptual model would be related to domestic violence. For example, those with less job satisfaction will experience more work–home conflict than those with more job satisfaction. This is a directional, non-causal hypothesis.

- The second hypothesis was that work–home conflict will be related to domestic violence. Although this hypothesis is stated in a non-directional way, earlier on the direction of this relation was specified: greater work–home conflict will be related to greater domestic violence.

- The third hypothesis was that the relationship between work–home conflict and domestic violence will be moderated by various variables of the conceptual model. For example, those with higher work–home conflict and having experienced or witnessed domestic violence as a child will report more domestic violence. This hypothesis is also stated in a non-causal directional way.

Method

Participants

Participants had to be in a relationship for at least one year and to be in full-time work. They were recruited in various ways. The sample consisted of 230 women and 64 men, ranging in age from 18 to 62 years. As the smaller sample of men did not differ from women on many of the variables, women and men were analysed together as a single sample.

Measures

There were various measures which were briefly described. Further details of these measures such as the items and answer format used need to be looked up in the references provided. For example, looking up the reference for the measure of work–home conflict (Eagle, Miles, & Icenogle, 1997), we see that this scale combines three previous scales and consists of 24 items altogether. Two items on this scale are 'I'm often too tired at work because of the things I have to do at home' and 'My family or personal life interferes with my job'.

Domestic violence was assessed with the Revised Conflict Tactics Scale (Straus, Harmby, Boney-McCoy, & Sugarman, 1996) which comprised six subscales. One of these, injury to partner, was not used as it had a low Cronbach's alpha reliability of only .26 in this study. A low value of Cronbach's alpha reliability means that the internal consistency of the items being used to measure the subscale is poor – that is, the various items intercorrelate at very low levels. It also means that we should have low expectations about the correlation of this scale with other variables. Fortunately, in this case, the sample size is quite substantial.

Results

Only some of the results can be presented here.

Predicting work–home conflict

A backward stepwise multiple regression revealed that the only variable that predicted work–home conflict when the other variables were controlled was job satisfaction. In the Discussion, it is noted that this relationship was negative. In other words, greater work–home conflict was associated with less job satisfaction. Multiple regression is a statistical technique for working out which set of variables are the best for predicting levels of a particular variable – in this case work–home conflict. Backward stepwise multiple regression is just one of several different methods of doing multiple regression.

Work–home conflict and domestic violence

Work–home conflict was significantly positively but lowly related to three of the domestic violence subscales, with the highest correlation being .19 for the psychological aggression to partner subscale.

Moderated relationships

Moderating relationships were investigated by first entering work–home conflict and the moderating variables into a (hierarchical) multiple regression, followed by the interaction between work–home conflict and each moderating variable. This was done for each of the five outcome domestic violence subscales. The only significant moderated relationships were for the domestic violence subscales of physical assault to self and injury to self for the two moderator variables of witnessing domestic violence in parents and experiencing domestic violence as a child. The nature of the interactions was similar for the moderating variable of experiencing domestic violence as a child and the outcome measures of physical assault and injury to self. Both of these forms of violence were higher in those who experienced more domestic violence as a child and varied little according to work–home conflict. Work–home conflict was most strongly related to these two types of domestic violence in those who experienced less domestic violence as a child.

Mediated relationships

Mediating relationships were also tested with a hierarchical multiple regression. Details of hierarchical multiple regression may be found in Howitt and Cramer (2020). Multiple regression proceeds usually as a number of steps. In the first step, the two moderator variables of experiencing and witnessing domestic violence as a child were entered to control for them. In the second step, work–home conflict was entered to see whether it was related to domestic violence. It was only found to be significantly but weakly related to psychological aggression to and from the partner. In the third step, various mediating variables were entered together with work–home conflict. If the relation between work–home conflict and these two outcome measures became less positive and if the relation between one or more of the mediators and the two outcome measures of domestic violence were significant, these results suggest that these statistically significant mediators may mediate the relation between work–home conflict and these two forms of domestic violence. This pattern of results occurred for the mediating variable of a negative form of communicating style. This finding suggests that greater work–home conflict may lead to a more negative way of communicating with one's partner, which in turn leads to psychological aggression within the relationship.

Authors' suggestions for future research

VanBuren Trachtenberg and her colleagues (2009) briefly mention that future research could make a greater attempt to include more men, examine the type of violence shown, and measure variables at more than one time point.

11.5   Conclusion

One can find numerous examples of research which do not meet the requirements of the randomised controlled experiment. Indeed, psychology is somewhat unusual in its emphasis on laboratory experiments compared with other social science disciplines. We have used the term non-manipulation design for this sort of study, though we acknowledge the awkwardness of this and the many other terms for this type of design. Non-manipulation designs are also used to determine the size of the association between variables as they occur naturally. Studies using these designs generally involve testing more cases than true or randomised experiments, because the sizes of the associations or effects are expected to be weaker. Most of these studies use a cross-sectional design in which cases are measured on only one occasion (Sherman, Buddie, Dragan, End, & Finney, 1999). Although the causal order of variables cannot generally be determined from cross-sectional designs, these studies often seek to explain one variable in terms of other variables. In other words, they assume that one variable is the criterion or dependent variable while the other variables are predictor or independent variables.

Key points

- The main alternative to controlled and randomised experiments is the cross-sectional or non-manipulation study. There are numerous problems with the available terminology. We have used the term non-manipulation study.

- Non-manipulation studies enable a large number of variables to be measured relatively easily under more natural conditions than a true or randomised study. This allows the relationships between these variables to be investigated. The cost is that these studies can be complex to analyse, especially when questions of causality need to be raised.

- The more unreliable measures are, the lower the association will be between those measures. Adjustments are possible to allow for this.

- Partial correlation coefficients which control for third-variable effects are easily computed, though a computer is probably essential if one wishes to control for several third variables.

- Restricting the range of scores on one of the variables will reduce the correlation between two variables.

ACTIVITIES

1. Design a non-manipulation study that investigates the hypothesis that unemployment may lead to crime. How would you measure these two variables? What other variables would you investigate? How would you measure these other variables? How would you select your participants and how many would you have? What would you tell participants the study was about? How would you analyse the results?

2. What would be the difficulties of studying in the psychology laboratory the hypothesis that unemployment may lead to crime?

Longitudinal studies

Overview

- Longitudinal studies examine variables at different points in time.

- A panel or prospective study involves looking at the same group of participants on two or more distinct occasions.

- Ideally, exactly the same variables are measured on all occasions, although you will find studies where this is not achieved.

- Longitudinal studies may be used to explore the temporal ordering or sequence of variables (i.e. patterns of variation over time). This helps to determine whether the association is two-way rather than one-way, that is, both variables mutually affecting each other, although possibly to different degrees.

- The concepts of internal and external validity apply particularly to longitudinal studies. The researcher needs to understand how various factors such as history and changes in instrumentation may threaten the value of a study.

- Cross-lagged correlations are the correlations between variable X and variable Y when these variables are measured at different points in time. A lagged correlation is the correlation between variable X measured at time 1 and variable X measured at time 2.

- Multiple regression and path analysis are important statistical techniques in the analysis of complex non-manipulation studies. The extra information from a longitudinal study adds considerably to their power.

12.1 | Introduction

Variables are measured only once in the majority of studies. These are referred to as cross-sectional studies, as the variables are measured across a section of time (Chapter 11). Studies in which variables are measured several times at distinct intervals are called longitudinal, panel or prospective studies. However, each of these terms applies to somewhat different types of study (see Figure 12.1). For example, a panel study involves a group of participants (a panel) which is studied at several points in time. In contrast, longitudinal studies merely require data to be collected at different points in time. Studying patterns of change over time has important advantages. A far fuller interpretation of data is possible with longitudinal designs compared to cross-sectional designs. Of course, the study of change in any psychological variable over time, such as at different stages of the life cycle, is important in its own right. For example, changes in human memory at different stages in life are clearly important. Numerous studies examine such changes over time. Nevertheless, one distinct rationale for studying change over time has little to do with life cycle and other developmental changes.

Cause-and-effect sequences require that the cause must precede the effect and the effect must follow the cause. If these do not apply, then we do not have a causal sequence. Longitudinal studies allow us to assess the relationship between two variables over time. Consequently, longitudinal studies are attractive to researchers because they can help to sort out issues of causality. Many longitudinal studies focus on the issue of causality rather than studying change over time for their intrinsic value. Box 12.1 looks at threats to internal and external validity in more detail.

So there are various kinds of longitudinal designs depending on the purpose of the study. Designs where the same group of people are tested on two or more occasions are referred to as *prospective studies* (Engstrom, Geijerstam, Holmberg, & Uhrus, 1963) or *panel studies* (Lazarsfeld, 1948). This type of design was initially developed to study American presidential elections. Because American elections take place over several months every four years, voters are subject to intense media and other pressures. Some change their minds about the candidates; some change their minds about the parties they were intending to vote for. Some change their minds again later still. Enormous

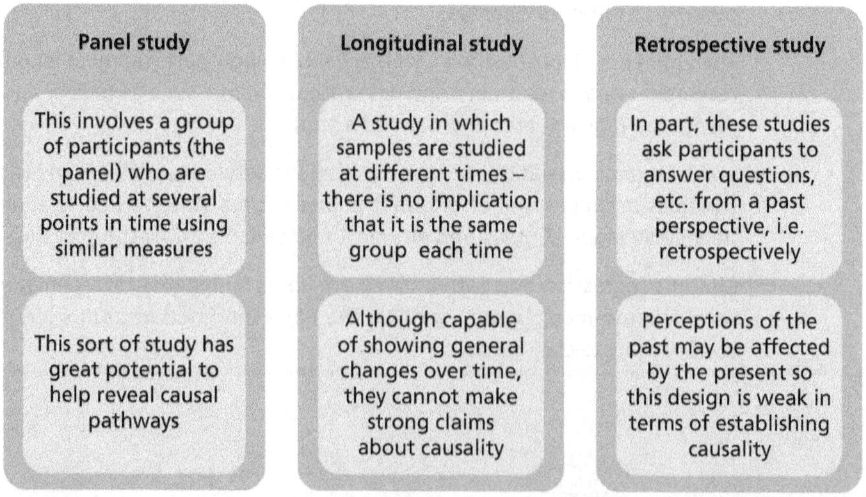

Panel study	Longitudinal study	Retrospective study
This involves a group of participants (the panel) who are studied at several points in time using similar measures	A study in which samples are studied at different times – there is no implication that it is the same group each time	In part, these studies ask participants to answer questions, etc. from a past perspective, i.e. retrospectively
This sort of study has great potential to help reveal causal pathways	Although capable of showing general changes over time, they cannot make strong claims about causality	Perceptions of the past may be affected by the present so this design is weak in terms of establishing causality

FIGURE 12.1   Types of study to investigate changes over time and the causal sequences involved

> ## Box 12.1   Key Ideas
>
> # Threats to internal and external validity
>
> Like many ideas to do with the design of experiments, the concepts of internal and external validity originated in the work of Campbell and Stanley (1963). Both are particularly important and salient to longitudinal studies.
>
> Internal validity concerns the question of whether the relationship between two variables is causal. That is, does the study help to identify the cause-and-effect sequence between two variables? But it applies where there is no apparent empirical relationship between them. In this case, does this mean that there is no causal relationship or is there possibly a relationship which is being hidden due to the masking influence of other variables? Cook and Campbell (1979) list a whole range of what they refer to as 'threats to internal validity'. Some of these are described briefly below:
>
> - *History*   Changes may occur between a pre-test and a post-test which are nothing to do with the effect of the researcher's variable of interest. In laboratory experiments, participants are usually protected from these factors. Greene (1990) was investigating the influence of eyewitness evidence on 'juries' under laboratory conditions. She found that a spate of news coverage of a notorious trial in which the accused was shown to be unjustly convicted on the basis of eyewitness evidence affected what happened in her laboratory. Her 'juries' were, for a period of time, much less likely to convict on the basis of eyewitness testimony.
>
> - *Instrumentation*   A change over time may be due to difference in the measuring instrument used. In the simplest cases, it is not unknown for researchers to use alternative or different versions of their measuring instrument over time. But instrumentation may change for other reasons. For example, a question asking how 'gay' someone felt would have meant something very different 50 years ago.
>
> - *Maturation*   During the course of a longitudinal study a variety of maturation changes may occur. Participants become more experienced, more knowledgeable, less energetic and so forth.
>
> - *Mortality*   People may drop out of a study. This may be systematically related to the experimental condition or some other characteristics. This will not be at random and may result in apparent changes when none has truly occurred.
>
> - *Statistical regression*   If groups of people are selected to be, say, extremely high and extremely low on aggression at point 1 in time, then their scores on aggression at point 2 in time will tend to converge. That is, the high scorers get lower scores than before and the low scorers get higher scores than before. This is purely a statistical artefact known as regression to the mean.
>
> - *Testing*   People who are tested on a measure may perform differently when they are retested later simply because of increased familiarity or practice.
>
> External validity is closely related to the issue of generalisation discussed in detail earlier (Chapter 4). It has to do with generalising findings to other groups of individuals, other geographic settings and other periods of time.

advantages follow from interviewing and re-interviewing the same group of participants at different points during the election. The alternative would be to study the electorate at several different points during the election but using different samples of the electorate each time. This causes difficulties, since although it is possible to see what changes over time, it is not possible to relate these changes to what went before easily. So such a design might fail to provide the researcher with information about what sort of person changed their minds due to the media and their peers.

Similarly, enormous benefits follow from studying criminals over the long term. For example, Farrington (1996) studied the same delinquent children from early childhood through adulthood. The logistical difficulties are enormous. Others have studied criminals who begin their criminal careers late in life. This is even more problematic logistically and is, as a consequence, little investigated. To study the criminal careers of late-onset criminals ideally requires an enormous sample of children. Some may turn out to be late-onset criminals but the vast majority would not. It is obviously easier to start with a sample of delinquents and study their progress than to try to obtain a sample of children, some of whom will turn criminal late in life. Hence the rarity of such studies.

Retrospective studies seek from participants information about events occurring prior to when they were questioned. Usually information about their current situation is collected at the same time. Of course, combining the retrospective and prospective designs together is perfectly feasible. Nevertheless, the logistical requirements of longitudinal studies should not be underestimated: following a sample of toddlers from childhood into middle age is full of practical challenges. Furthermore, the timescale is very long – possibly as long as a typical academic career. Consequently alternative research designs may have to be contemplated, such as using retrospective studies which truncate timescales in real time. The children could be interviewed as an adult about things which happened in their childhood. These adults can then be studied into middle age within a more practical timescale. However, one disadvantage is the fallibility of memory. Not surprisingly, longitudinal research is uncommon because it is so demanding, though good examples exist.

12.2   Panel designs

We can look at panel studies in a little more detail. Panel or prospective studies are used to determine the changes that take place in the same group of people over time. For example, in the late 1920s in the United States there were a number of growth or developmental studies of children such as the Berkeley Growth Study (Jones, Bayley, MacFarlane, & Honzik, 1971). This study was started in 1928 and was designed to investigate the mental, motor and physical development in the first 15 months of life of 61 children. It was gradually expanded to monitor changes up to 54 years of age. In the UK, the National Child Development Study was begun in 1958 when data were collected on 17 000 children born in the week of 3–9 March (Ferri, 1993). This cohort has been surveyed on six subsequent occasions at ages 7, 11, 16, 23, 33, 42, 46 and 50. Most panel studies are of much shorter duration for practical reasons such as resources.

Figure 12.2 gives a simple example of a panel design with three types of correlation. Data are collected at two different points in time on the same sample of individuals. One variable is the supportiveness of one's partner and the other is relationship satisfaction. The question is: does supportiveness lead to relationship satisfaction? In Figure 12.3

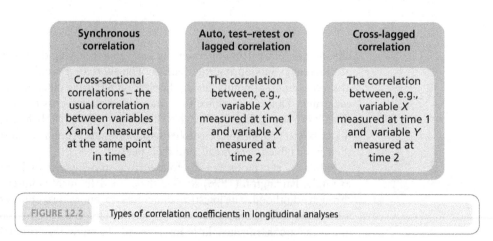

Synchronous correlation	Auto, test–retest or lagged correlation	Cross-lagged correlation
Cross-sectional correlations – the usual correlation between variables X and Y measured at the same point in time	The correlation between, e.g., variable X measured at time 1 and variable X measured at time 2	The correlation between, e.g., variable X measured at time 1 and variable Y measured at time 2

FIGURE 12.2   Types of correlation coefficients in longitudinal analyses

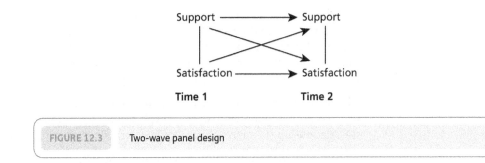

FIGURE 12.3   Two-wave panel design

essentially *two* measures of that relationship are made, but at different points in time. That is, there is a relationship between supportiveness and satisfaction measured at Time 1 and another measured at Time 2. These relationships assessed at the same time are known as *cross-sectional* or *synchronous correlations*. Generally speaking, they are just as problematic as any other cross-sectional correlations to interpret and there is no real advantage in itself to having the two synchronous correlations available.

There is another sort of relationship to be found in Figure 12.3. This is known as a *cross-lagged* relationship. A lag is, of course, a delay. The cross-lagged relationships in this case are a) the correlation of supportiveness at Time 1 with satisfaction at Time 2, and b) the correlation of satisfaction at Time 1 with supportiveness at Time 2.

Assume that we find supportiveness$_{Time1}$ correlates with satisfaction$_{Time2}$. Does this correlation establish that supportiveness causes satisfaction? It is congruent with this idea, but something quite simple would lend the idea stronger support. That is, we can partial out (control for) satisfaction$_{Time1}$. If by doing so, the correlation between supportiveness$_{Time1}$ and satisfaction$_{Time2}$ reduces to zero then we have an interesting outcome. That is, satisfaction$_{Time1}$ is sufficient to account for satisfaction$_{Time2}$.

Of course, another remaining possibility is that there is a different causal sequence in which satisfaction may be the cause of supportiveness. Initially this seems less plausible, but if we are satisfied with our partner then there may be a halo effect resulting in them being seen as more perfect in many respects. Anyway, this relationship could also be tested using cross-lagged correlations. A correlation between satisfaction$_{Time1}$ and supportiveness$_{Time2}$ would support the plausibility of this causal link. However, if we control for supportiveness$_{Time1}$ and find that the correlation declines markedly or becomes zero, then this undermines the causal explanation in that supportiveness at Time 1 is related to supportiveness at Time 2.

The cross-lagged correlations should generally be weaker than the cross-sectional or synchronous correlations at the two times of measurement, because things may change during the intervening period. The longer this period, the more possibility of change there is and so the weaker the association should be. This also occurs when the same variable is measured on two or more occasions. The longer the interval is, the lower the test–retest or auto-correlation is likely to be. If both cross-lagged correlations have the same sign (in terms of being positive or negative) but one is significantly stronger than the other, then the stronger correlation indicates the temporal direction of the association. For example, if the association between support at Time 1 and satisfaction at Time 2 is more positive than the association between satisfaction at Time 1 and support at Time 2, this difference implies that support leads to satisfaction.

There are several problems with this sort of analysis:

- The size of a correlation is affected by the reliability of the measures. Less reliable measures produce weaker correlations as we saw earlier (Chapter 11). Consequently, the reliability of the measures needs to be taken into account statistically when comparing correlations.

- The difference between the two cross-lagged correlations does not give an indication of the size of the possible causal association between the two variables. For example, the cross-lagged correlation between support at Time 1 and satisfaction at Time 2 will most probably be affected by satisfaction at Time 1 and support at Time 2. To determine the size of the cross-lagged association between support at Time 1 and satisfaction at Time 2, controlling for satisfaction at Time 1 and support at Time 2, we would have to partial out satisfaction at Time 1 and support at Time 2.

- This method does not indicate whether both cross-lagged associations are necessary in order to provide a more satisfactory explanation of the relationship. It is possible that the relationship is reciprocal but that one variable is more influential than the other.

One solution to the above problems involves using *structural equation modelling* which is generally the preferred method for this kind of analysis. It takes into account the unreliability of the measures. Structural equation modelling provides an indication of the strength of a pathway taking into account its association with other variables. In addition, it offers an index of the extent to which the model fits the data and is a better fit than models which are simpler subsets of it. There are various examples of such studies (e.g. Cramer, Henderson, & Scott, 1996; Jang, 2018; Rousseau & Eggermont, 2018). However, one problem with structural equation modelling is that once the test–retest correlations are taken into account, the size of the cross-lagged coefficients may become non-significant. In other words, the variable measured at the later point in time seems to be completely explained by the same variable measured at the earlier point in time (e.g. Cramer, 1994, 1995).

12.3   Different types of third variable

The general third-variable issue was discussed in the previous chapter. Conceptually there is a range of different types of third variable (see Figure 12.4). They are distinguishable only in terms of their effect and, even then, this is not sufficient. These different types may

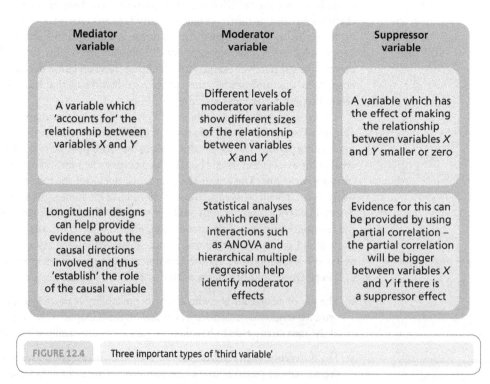

Mediator variable	Moderator variable	Suppressor variable
A variable which 'accounts for' the relationship between variables *X* and *Y*	Different levels of moderator variable show different sizes of the relationship between variables *X* and *Y*	A variable which has the effect of making the relationship between variables *X* and *Y* smaller or zero
Longitudinal designs can help provide evidence about the causal directions involved and thus 'establish' the role of the causal variable	Statistical analyses which reveal interactions such as ANOVA and hierarchical multiple regression help identify moderator effects	Evidence for this can be provided by using partial correlation – the partial correlation will be bigger between variables *X* and *Y* if there is a suppressor effect

FIGURE 12.4   Three important types of 'third variable'

be illustrated by reference to the example of whether the supportiveness of one's partner in relationships leads to greater satisfaction with that partner.

Mediator (or intervening or mediating) variables

A variable which reduces the size of the correlation between two other variables may serve to explain the link between the other two variables. In these circumstances, it is described as a mediating or intervening variable. According to Baron and Kenny (1986, p. 1176): 'In general, a given variable may be said to function as a mediator to the extent that it accounts for the relation between the predictor and the criterion'. Imagine that there is a correlation between the variable *supportiveness of partner* and the variable *relationship satisfaction*. Why should this be the case? Imagine, further, that controlling for another variable *income* reduces the correlation between *supportiveness of partner* and *relationship satisfaction* to zero. It could be that income is a *mediating* variable. That is to say, having a supportive partner helps progress at work and so leads to greater income which means fewer money worries and quarrels about money resulting in greater relationship satisfaction.

Of course, in this case, there are other ways of conceiving the relationship between the three variables. This is because with cross-sectional data it is not possible to establish the causal or the temporal direction between two variables. Nonetheless, researchers may suggest a direction even though they cannot determine this with cross-sectional data. For example, they may suggest that having a supportive relationship may lead to greater satisfaction with that relationship when it is equally plausible that the reverse is true or that it is a bidirectional relationship.

Making the distinction between a confounding and an intervening variable is usually not easy to do theoretically. Suppose that we think that the direction of the association between supportiveness and satisfaction goes from support to satisfaction. With a variable which can change, like income, it is possible to argue that it may act as an intervening variable as we did earlier. If instead of *income*, the third variable was one which cannot be changed such as age or gender at birth, then this cannot be a mediator variable. It is easier to argue that this variable is a confounding variable because it cannot be changed by supportiveness or relationship satisfaction. However, many variables in psychology can change and so are potential intervening variables.

Moderator (moderating) variables

The size or the sign of the association between two variables may vary according to the values of a third variable, in which case this third variable is known as a moderator or moderating variable. For example, the size of the association between support and satisfaction may vary according to the gender of the partner. It may be stronger in men than in women. For example, the correlation between support and satisfaction may be .50 in men and .30 in women. If this difference in the size of the correlations is statistically significant, we would say that gender moderates the association between support and satisfaction.

If we treated one of these variables, say, support, as a dichotomous variable and the other as a continuous variable, we could display these relationships in the form of a graph, as shown in Figure 12.5. Satisfaction is represented by the vertical axis, support by the horizontal axis and gender by the two lines. The difference in satisfaction between women and men is greater for those with more support than for those with less support. In other words, we have an interaction between support and gender like the interactions described for experimental designs. A moderating effect is an interaction effect.

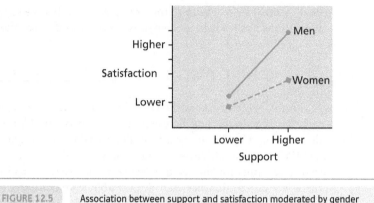

FIGURE 12.5   Association between support and satisfaction moderated by gender

If the moderating variable is a continuous rather than a dichotomous one, then the cut-off point used for dividing the sample into two groups may be arbitrary. Ideally the two groups should be of a similar size, and so the median score which does this can be used. However, the natural variation in the scores of a continuous variable is lost when it is converted into a dichotomous variable. Consequently, it is better to treat a continuous variable as such rather than to change it into a dichotomous variable.

The recommended method for determining the statistical significance of an interaction is to conduct a hierarchical multiple regression (Baron & Kenny, 1986). The two main variables or predictors, which in this example are support and gender, are standardised and entered in the first step of the regression to control for any effects they may have. The interaction is entered in the second step. The interaction is created by multiplying the two standardised predictors together, provided that neither of these is a categorical variable with more than two categories. If this interaction is significant, there is a moderating effect as this means that the interaction accounts for a significant proportion of the variance in the criterion (satisfaction). The nature of the interaction effect needs to be examined. One way of doing this is to divide the sample into two, based on the median of the moderating variable, produce a scatterplot of the other two variables for the two samples separately, and examine the direction of the relationship in the scatter of the two variables. If you need them, the calculation steps to assess for moderator variables can be found in the companion statistics text, *Understanding statistics in psychology with SPSS* (Howitt & Cramer, 2020).

Suppressor variables

Another kind of confounding variable is one that appears to suppress or hide the association between two variables so that the two variables seem to be unrelated. This type of variable is known as a suppressor variable. When its effect is partialled out, the two variables are found to be related. This occurs when the partial correlation is of the opposite sign to the product of the other two correlations and the other two correlations are moderately large. When one of the other correlations is large, the partial correlation is large (Cramer, 2003). Typically, the highest correlations are those where the same variable is tested on two occasions with little delay between them. When both the other correlations are large, the partial correlation is greater than 1.00! These results are due to the formula for partialling out variables and arise when correlations are large, which is unusual.

There appear to be relatively few reported examples of suppressor effects. We will make up an example to illustrate one in which we suppose that support is not correlated with satisfaction with the relationship (i.e. $r = .00$.) Both support and satisfaction are

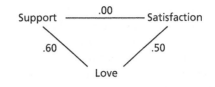

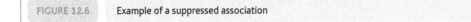

| FIGURE 12.6 | Example of a suppressed association |

positively related to how loving the relationship is, as shown in Figure 12.6. If we partial out love, the partial correlation between support and satisfaction changes to $-.43$. In other words, we now have a moderately large correlation between support and satisfaction whereas the original or zero-order correlation was zero. This partial correlation is negative because the product of the other two correlations is positive.

12.4   Analysis of non-experimental designs

It should be clear by now that the analysis of non-experimental designs is far from simple both conceptually and statistically. Furthermore, the range and scope of studies are much wider than we have covered so far. Subsumed under this heading is every study which does not meet the requirements of a randomised experimental design. Quite clearly, it is unlikely that any single chapter can cover every contingency. So you will find in many of the remaining chapters of this book a whole range of different styles of non-experimental data collection and analysis methods. To the extent that they are quantitative studies, they share a number of characteristics in terms of analysis strategies. In this section, we will briefly review two of these as examples. They are both dealt with in detail in the companion statistics text, *Understanding statistics in psychology with SPSS* (Howitt & Cramer, 2020). Although some such designs may be analysed using the related *t*-test and the related analysis of variance, for example, the variety of measures usually included in such studies generally necessitates the use of more complex statistics designed to handle the multiplicity of measures.

Multiple regression

Multiple regression refers to a variety of methods which identify the best pattern of variables to distinguish between higher and lower scorers on a key variable of interest. For example, multiple regression would help us identify the pattern of variables which differentiates between different levels of relationship satisfaction. Using this optimum pattern of variables, it is possible to estimate with a degree of precision just how much satisfaction a person would feel given their precise pattern on the other variables. This could be referred to as a model of relationship satisfaction. (A model is a set of variables or concepts which account for another variable or concept.)

Another way of looking at it is to regard it as being somewhat like partial correlation. The difference is that multiple regression aims to understand the components which go to make up the scores on the key variable – the criterion or dependent variable. In this case, the key variable is relationship satisfaction. There is a sense in which multiple regression proceeds simply by partialling out variables one at a time from the scores on relationship satisfaction. For example, how much effect on the scores does removing income, then social class, then supportiveness have? If we know the sizes of these effects, we can evaluate the possible importance of different variables on relationship satisfaction.

Technically, rather than use the partial correlation coefficient, multiple regression uses the part correlation coefficient or semi-partial correlation coefficient. The proportion of variance attributable to or explained by income or supportiveness is easily calculated. The proportion is simply the square of the part or semi-partial correlation. (This relationship is true for many correlation coefficients too.) We use the part or semi-partial correlation because it is only one variable that we are adjusting (relationship satisfaction). Partial correlation actually adjusts two or more variables, which is not what we need.

The part correlation between support and satisfaction partialling out income for the correlations shown in Figure 11.3 is .33, which squared is about .11. What this means is that support explains an additional 11 per cent of the variance in satisfaction to the 16 per cent already explained by income. The following formula is used to calculate the part correlation in which one variable is partialled out, where B refers to satisfaction, A to support and C to income:

$$r_{(BA.C)} = \frac{(r_{BA} - (r_{BC} \times r_{AC}))}{\sqrt{1 - r_{AC}^2}}$$

If we insert the correlations of Figure 11.3 into this formula, we find that the part correlation is .33:

$$\frac{.50 - (.40 \times .60)}{\sqrt{(1 - .60^2)}} = \frac{.26}{.80} = .33$$

Multiple regression has three main uses:

- To predict what the likely outcome is for a particular case or group of cases. For example, we may be interested in predicting whether a convicted prisoner is likely to re-offend on the basis of information that we have about them.

- To determine what the size, sign and significance of particular associations or paths are in a model which has been put forward to explain some aspect of behaviour. For example, we may wish to test a particular model which seeks to explain how people become involved in criminal activity. This use is being increasingly taken over by the more sophisticated statistical technique of structural equation modelling.

- To find out which predictors explain a significant proportion of the variance in the criterion variable such as criminal activity. This third use differs from the second in that generally a model is not being tested.

There are three main types of multiple regression for determining which predictors explain a significant proportion of the variance in a criterion:

- *Standard or simultaneous multiple regression*   All of the predictors are entered at the same time in a single step or block. This enables one to determine what the proportion of variance is that is uniquely explained by each predictor in the sense that it is not explained by any other predictor.

- *Hierarchical or sequential multiple regression*   In this, the group of predictors is entered in a particular sequence. We may wish to control for particular predictors or sets of predictors by putting them in a certain order. For example, we can control for basic socio-demographic variables such as age, gender and socio-economic status before examining the influence of other variables such as personality or attitudinal factors.

- *Stepwise multiple regression*   In this, statistical criteria are used to select the order of the predictors. The predictor that is entered first is the one which has a significant and the largest correlation with the key variable (the criterion or dependent variable). This variable explains the biggest proportion of the variation of the criterion variable because it has the largest correlation. The predictor that is entered second is the one which has a significant and the largest part correlation with the criterion. This, therefore, explains the next biggest proportion of the variance in the criterion. This part correlation partials out the influence of the first predictor on the criterion. In this way, the predictors are made to contribute independently to the prediction. The predictor that is entered next is the one that has a significant and the next highest part correlation with the criterion. This predictor partials out the first two predictors. If a predictor that was previously entered no longer explains a significant proportion of the variance, it is dropped from the analysis. This process continues until there is no predictor that explains a further significant proportion of the variance in the criterion.

One important feature of multiple regression needs to be understood, otherwise we may fail to appreciate quite what the outcome of an analysis means. Two or more predictors may have very similar correlations or part correlations with the criterion, but the one which has the highest correlation will be entered even though the difference in the size of the correlations is tiny. If the predictors themselves are highly related, then those with the slightly smaller correlation may not be entered into the analysis at all. Their absence may give the impression that these variables do not predict the criterion when in fact they do. Their correlation with the criterion may have been slightly weaker because the measures of these predictors may have been slightly less reliable. Consequently, when interpreting the results of a stepwise multiple regression, it is important to look at the size of the correlation between the predictors and the criterion. If two or more predictors are similarly correlated with the criterion, it is necessary to check whether these predictors are measuring the same rather than different characteristics.

An understanding of multiple regression is very useful as it is commonly and increasingly used. Sherman and his colleagues (1999) found that 41 per cent of the papers they randomly sampled in the *Journal of Personality and Social Psychology* used it in 1996 compared with 21 per cent in 1988 and 9 per cent in 1978.

Path analysis

A path is little more than a route between two variables. It may be direct but it can be indirect. It can also be reciprocal in that two variables mutually affect each other. For a set of variables, there may be a complex structure of paths, of course. Figure 12.7 has examples of such paths and various degrees of directness. Multiple regression can be used to estimate the correlations between the paths (these are known as path coefficients). However, structural equation modelling is increasingly used instead. This has three main advantages over multiple regression:

- The reliabilities of measures are not taken into account in multiple regression but they can be in structural equation modelling if available. As explained earlier, reliability places a strict upper limit on the maximum correlation between any two variables.

- Structural equation modelling gives an index of the extent to which the model provides a satisfactory fit to the data. This allows the fit of a simpler subset (version) of the model to be compared with the original model to examine whether the simpler model fits the data just as well. Simpler models are generally preferred to more complicated ones, as they are easier to understand and use.

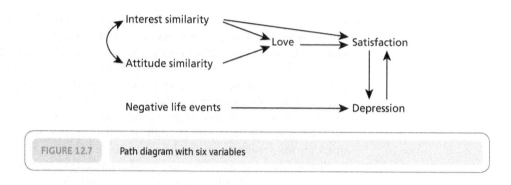

FIGURE 12.7 Path diagram with six variables

- Structural equation modelling can explain more than one outcome variable at the same time, like the two presented in the path diagram of Figure 12.7.

The path diagram or model in Figure 12.7 seeks to explain the association between depression and satisfaction with a romantic relationship in terms of the four variables of attitude similarity, interest similarity, love and negative life events. The path diagram shows the assumed relationship between these six variables. The temporal or causal sequence moves from left to right. The direction of the sequence is indicated by the arrow on the line. So interest similarity leads to love which in turn leads to satisfaction. There is a direct association between interest similarity and satisfaction, and an indirect association which is mediated through love. In other words, interest similarity has, or is assumed to have, both a direct and an indirect effect. The association between satisfaction and depression is a reciprocal or bidirectional one, as the arrows go in both directions. Being satisfied results in less depression and being less depressed brings about greater satisfaction. The lack of a line between two variables indicates that they are not related. So attitude similarity is not related to negative life events, depression or satisfaction. The curved line with arrows at either end shows that interest similarity and attitude similarity are related but that they are not thought to affect each other. Ideally, we should always try to develop a model to explain the relationships between the variables measured in our study.

Box 12.2   Research Example

Panel study of the relation of marital satisfaction to depression

Fincham, F. D., Beach, S. R. H., Harold, G. T., & Osborne, L. N. (1997). Marital satisfaction and depression: Different causal relationships for men and women? *Psychological Science, 8*, 351–357.

Longitudinal research is among the most difficult research to administer. Most researchers have the frustrating experience that participants do not exactly flock to take part in their research or that, if they do agree to participate, they fail to turn up for the appointment. This is clearly compounded in longitudinal research where the problems of re-recruiting the same participants provide additional difficulties. Originally, the 'panels' of participants were a regular broadcasting research audience panel, so repeated measurement was relatively easily achieved simply because this is what the panel members expected to do. In psychological research, such ready-made panels are not available routinely. One has simply to imagine the changes in membership of the audience for a series of psychology lectures to begin to understand the problems. Panel studies are relatively uncommon in psychological research for this very reason and others. There are exceptions, such as the work of David Farrington (1996) who followed a group of children from early childhood until middle age in order to study criminality. Things are not made easier by data protection legislation. In this, a researcher who recruits a sample of participants at Time A must explicitly ask their permission at this time to contact them again in the future at Time B, or they are not allowed to do so. In other words, you cannot simply decide to do a follow-up study unless you have specifically made provision for doing so when planning your research. All of this puts into context the percentages of couples who survived in the research from the first assessment to the second.

Background

Marital dissatisfaction has been found to be similarly positively related to depressive symptoms in both women and men when measured at the same point in time. Cross-sectional correlations like these do not enable the causal direction of their relationship to be determined. It is possible that marital dissatisfaction leads to depression, is brought about by depression, both leads to and is brought about by depression, or is not related to depression but is the result of both marital dissatisfaction and depression being related to some other factor such as social class. Frank Fincham and his colleagues (1997) wanted to examine the possible causal relationship between marital dissatisfaction and depression by looking at the way these two variables were related at two points in time. One of the ways they did this was to see whether the relation between marital dissatisfaction at time 1 and depression at time 2 is more positive than the relation between depression at time 1 and marital dissatisfaction at time 2. This pattern of results would imply that marital dissatisfaction may lead to depression. These relationships are known as cross-lagged ones because they are between two different variables crossed over a period or lag of time. Fincham and his colleagues wanted to examine these relationships in women and men separately, because they thought that marital dissatisfaction may be more likely to lead to depression in women than men. They wanted to do this in a sample of people who had been married for a similar period of time, so they chose a group of people who had been married for 3–8 months.

Hypotheses

The objectives of this study were not described in specific hypotheses but in terms of more general aims such as examining the 'possible causal relations between depressive symptoms and marital discord over time' (Fincham et al., 1997, p. 352) (Figure 12.8).

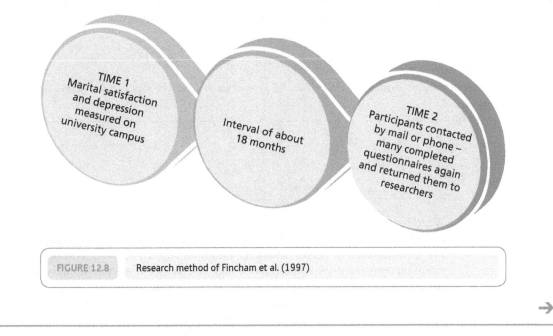

| FIGURE 12.8 | Research method of Fincham et al. (1997) |

Method

Participants

The sample consisted of 150 couples who had been married from 3 to 8 months and who came from small towns. They were identified from marriage licence records.

Measures

Marriage satisfaction was measured with the Marital Adjustment Test. Depressive symptoms were assessed with the Beck Depression Inventory. No details of the nature or the number of items were given and these sorts of details need to be sought from the references provided.

Procedure

Couples came to the university where they individually completed the questionnaires. About 18 months later an attempt was made to contact them again by post or phone. Seven couples could not be contacted, six declined to take part, eight had either separated or divorced and one husband had died, leaving 128 couples. These couples were sent two copies of the questionnaire together with two postage-paid return envelopes. Nine couples failed to return the questionnaires despite repeated phone calls, and three provided incomplete data, leaving 116 couples altogether.

Results

Only the results of the cross-lagged analysis will be reported here. This analysis was carried out using structural equation modelling, which enables more than one variable to be predicted at the same time, unlike multiple regression analysis which only allows one such variable. This form of modelling also permits the unreliability of measures to be taken into account, but this was not done.

At each of the two time points, marital satisfaction was significantly negatively related to depression for both women and men, showing that more satisfied individuals were less depressed. Across the two points of time, earlier marital satisfaction was significantly positively related to later marital satisfaction, and earlier depression was significantly positively related to later depression. This means that individuals who were maritally satisfied or depressed initially tended to be maritally satisfied or depressed 18 months later. The cross-lagged relation between these two variables differed for wives and husbands. For wives, only marital satisfaction at time 1 was significantly negatively related to depression at time 2. Depression at time 1 was not significantly related to marital satisfaction at time 2. This pattern of results suggests that marital dissatisfaction may precede depression in wives. For husbands, both cross-lagged relationships were significantly negative. These results imply that there may be a two-way relationship between marital satisfaction and depression for husbands with each affecting the other.

Authors' suggestions for future research

One of the suggestions made for further research is that this type of study should be repeated for individuals who are clinically depressed.

12.5   Conclusion

Where the primary aim is to determine the temporal ordering of variables, a panel or prospective study is required. In these, the same participants are studied on two or more occasions. The main variables of interest should be measured on each of these occasions, so that the size of the temporal associations can be compared. Statistical analysis for non-manipulation studies is generally more complicated than for true or randomised studies. This is especially the case when causal or explanatory models are being tested. Familiarity with statistical techniques such as multiple regression is advantageous for a researcher working in this field.

Key points

- Panel or prospective designs measure the same variables in the same cases on two or more occasions. It is possible to assess whether variables may be mutually related.

- Longitudinal studies may be especially influenced by a number of threats to their internal and external validity. For example, because of the time dimension involved, the participants may change simply because they have become a little older.

- There are a number of types of variable which may play a role in the relationship between two variables. These include intervening variables and suppressor variables. Conceptually, it is important to distinguish between these different sorts of third variables, although they are very similar in practice.

- The complexity of these designs encourages the use of complex statistical techniques such as multiple regression and path analysis.

ACTIVITIES

1. Draw a path diagram for the following:

   - Couples who are similar fall in love more intensely.

   - They marry but tend to grow apart and stop loving each other.

2. Couples who love each other tend to have better sexual relationships with each other. It is found that once couples have a baby, the physical side of their relationship declines. What sort of variable is the baby?

CHAPTER 13

Sampling and population surveys

Overview

- When making inferences about finite populations such as the people of Britain, ideally a representative sample should be used in order to estimate the characteristics of the population precisely.

- The ideal sample size depends on various factors. The bigger the characteristic's variation, the bigger the required sample. The smaller we want the sampling error or margin of error, the larger the sample has to be. It is usual to set the confidence interval at the 95 per cent or .95 level or higher. The confidence interval is that range of results within which we can be confident that the population figure is likely to be found with repeated sampling.

- In probability sampling, every unit or element in the population has an equal and a known probability of being selected.

- Where the population is spread widely geographically, multi-stage sampling may be used, in which the first stage is to select a limited number of areas from which further selections will be made.

- Computer programs are available to help conduct Internet surveys.

13.1   Introduction

As we have seen, psychologists test their generalisations or hypotheses on a limited sample of people – usually those who are convenient to recruit. Students are no longer the main source of recruits for these samples (Bodner, 2006a). Certainly they cannot be regarded as a representative or random sample of people. The time, effort and expense of recruiting representative samples are deterrents. Time and money are often in short supply in research. Research psychologists are usually under various pressures to conduct their research quickly and economically. To the extent that one believes that the idea being tested applies widely, then a representative sample might not seem necessary. You would choose a more representative sample if you believe that different types of people were likely to produce rather different responses in the study. However, even in these circumstances a sample with very different characteristics from those already studied might be just as informative as a more representative sample.

The assumption that findings apply widely (i.e. are generalisable) ought to be more controversial than it is in psychology. Just to indicate something of the problem, there have been very carefully controlled laboratory studies which have produced diametrically opposite findings from each other. For example, using more sophisticated students from the later years of their degree has on occasion produced findings very different from using first-year students (Page & Scheidt, 1971). So what is true of one type of participant is not necessarily true for another type. Although partly the consequence of sampling variation, differences between the findings of similar studies may also be due to other sources of variability such as the characteristics of the samples used. So possibly the question of whether to use convenience samples rather than representative samples is best addressed by considering what is already known. Past research on a particular topic, for example, may indicate little or no evidence that different samples produce very disparate findings. This may bolster the researcher's confidence in a convenience sample for their research.

Researchers should know how to go about representative sampling – if only as a possible ideal sampling method for quantitative research. When a study aims to make statements about a representative sample of people then such knowledge is essential. Researchers who are interested in how people in general behave may be disinclined to give much attention to a student-based study. Sociologists, for example, have lampooned psychology, sometimes unfairly, for its dependence on university students. Studies which have found similar results in a more representative sample lend extra credibility to their findings and allow generalisation. Figure 13.1 shows different types of sampling.

Research on the Internet has obvious attractions given how much time and effort may be involved in collecting a sample of data by conventional means. The Internet involves a seemingly endless number of people who surf it for a wide variety of reasons though generally not to take part in research. Of course, it may be possible to target people for research using the convenience of email assuming that ethically acceptable procedures are available within the limits of data protection legislation. Unfortunately, you will not have everything under control should you use the Internet for surveys. For example, you may have no idea about how many people decide not to respond, you may find a disproportionate number of mischievous or joking respondents, and so forth. Most of the issues discussed in this chapter have serious implications for Internet research.

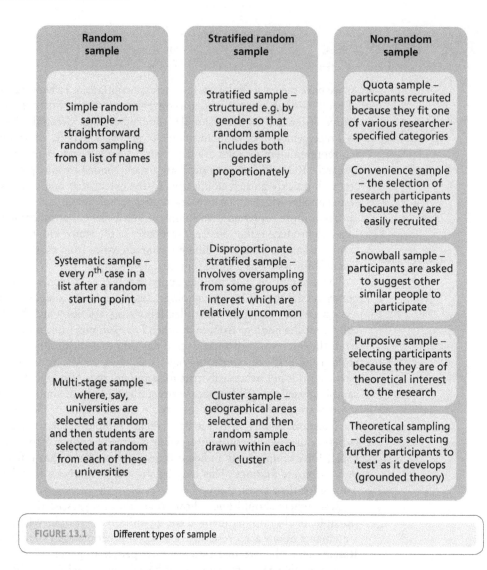

FIGURE 13.1   Different types of sample

13.2   Types of probability sampling

The characteristics of very large populations can be estimated from fairly small samples as is argued towards the end of this chapter. In this context, an important distinction is made between two types of sampling – *probability* and *non-probability sampling*:

- Probability sampling is typically used when we have a clearly defined and accessible population which we want to make inferences about or when we want to know how characteristic a behaviour is of a particular population, such as the people of Britain.

- Non-probability sampling is normally used in psychological research. This is because we are generally not interested in getting precise population estimates of a particular feature or characteristic in psychology. In psychology, the emphasis in research tends to be on relationships between variables and whether or not this relationship differs significantly from a zero relationship.

The main advantage of probability sampling is that every person or element in the population has an equal and known probability of being selected. Suppose we want to use probability sampling to select 10 per cent or 100 people out of a total population of 1000 people. In accordance with the concept of random sampling, everyone in that sample should have an equal probability of .10 of being selected $(100 \div 1000 = .10)$. The simplest procedure is to give each member of the population a number from 1 to 1000 and draw 100 of these numbers at random.

There are various ways of drawing a sample of 100 numbers representing the 100 people we need for the probability sampling:

● We could use a statistical package such as SPSS. We would enter the numbers 1 to 1000 in one of the columns. We would then select *Data, Select case. . . , Random sample of cases, Sample. . . , Exactly,* and then enter 100 cases from the first 1000 cases. The 100 numbers that were selected would be the 100 people in the sample. Alternatively, you will find applets on the web which will generate a random sample of cases for you.

● We could write the numbers 1 to 1000 on 1000 index cards or slips of paper, shuffle them and then select 100 cards or slips of paper. These 100 numbers would represent the people in our sample.

● We could use a table of random numbers which was once a common method used in psychology. It is quicker and simpler to use a computer to generate the random numbers so random number tables are obsolete.

This form of probability sampling is called *simple random sampling.* An alternative procedure is to select every 10th person on the list. We have to decide what our starting point is going to be, which can be any number from 1 to 10 and which we can choose using a random procedure. Let us suppose it is 7. This would be the first person we select. We then select every 10th person after it, such as 7, 17, 27 and so on. This procedure is known as *systematic sampling.* The advantage of systematic sampling is that it is simpler to use with a printed list such as a register of electors. It is quicker than random sampling and has the advantage that people close together on the list (e.g. couples) will not be selected. Its disadvantage is that it is not completely random. For instance, the list may not be arranged in what is effectively a random order, for some reason. Generally speaking, though, so long as the complete list is sampled from (as the above method will ensure), there are unlikely to be problems with systematic sampling. If the entire list is not sampled, then this method may introduce biases. For example, if the researcher simply took every, say, 5th case, then those at the end of the list would not be included in the sample.

Neither simple random sampling nor systematic sampling ensures that the sample will be representative of the population from which the sample was taken. For example, if the population contained equal numbers of females and males, say, 500 of each, it is possible that the sample will contain either all, or a disproportionate number of, females or males. It may be important that the sample is representative of the population in respect of one or more characteristics such as gender. This is achieved by dividing the population into groups or strata representing that characteristic, such as females and males. Then the random sampling is essentially done separately for each of these two groups. In terms of our example of selecting a sample of 100 people, we would select 50 from the 500 females and 50 from the 500 males. This form of sampling is known as *stratified random sampling* or just *stratified sampling.*

As the proportion of females in the sample (.50) is roughly the same as the proportion of females in the population (approximately .50), this kind of stratified sampling may be called proportionate stratified sampling. It may be distinguished from *disproportionate stratified sampling* in which the sampling is not proportionate to the size of the group in the population. Disproportionate stratified sampling is used when we want to ensure that a sufficient number of people are sampled of whom there are relatively few in the population. For example, we may be keen to determine the behaviour of unemployed people in our population of 1000 people. Suppose there are only 50 unemployed people in our population. If we used proportionate stratified sampling to select 10 per cent or 100 people from our population, then our sample of unemployed people is $5(10/100 \times 50 = 5)$, which is too few to base any generalisations on. Consequently, we may use disproportionate stratified sampling to obtain a bigger sample of unemployed people. Because the number of unemployed people is small, we may wish to have a sample of 25 of them, in which case the proportion of unemployed people is .50 $(25/50 = .50)$ instead of .10 $(5/50 = .10)$. As our overall sample may still be limited to 100 people, the number of people in our sample who are not unemployed is now 75 instead of 95. So, the proportion of people who are not unemployed is smaller than .10 $(95/950 = .10)$ and is about .08 $(75/950 = .0789)$.

One of the problems with stratified sampling is that relevant information about the characteristic in question is needed. For a characteristic such as gender, this is easily obtained from a person's title (Mr, Miss, Ms or Mrs), but this is the exception rather than the rule. If a person's title is Dr then this does not indicate gender, for example. Otherwise, more work is involved in obtaining information about that characteristic prior to sampling.

If our population is dispersed over a wide geographical area, we may use what is called *cluster sampling* in order to restrict the amount of time taken to draw up the sampling list or for interviewers to contact individuals. For example, if we wanted to carry out a probability survey of all British university students, it would be difficult and time-consuming to draw up a list of all students from which to select a sample. What we might do instead is to select a few universities from around the country and sample all the students within those universities. The universities would be the group or cluster of students which we would sample. The clusters need not be already existing ones. They may be created artificially. For example, we may impose a grid over an area and select a number of squares or cells within that area. The advantage of cluster sampling is that it saves time and money. Its disadvantage is that it is likely to be less representative of the population, because the people within a cluster are likely to be more similar to one another. For example, students at one university may be more inclined to come from fee-paying rather than state schools or to be female rather than male.

Another form of probability sampling is called *multi-stage sampling* in which sampling is done in a number of stages. For example, we could have a two-stage sample of university students in which the first stage consists of sampling universities and the second stage of sampling students within those universities.

The *representativeness of a sample* can be evaluated against other information about the population from which it was drawn. For example, in trying to determine whether our sample is representative of the British population, we can compare it with census or other national data on characteristics such as gender, age, marital status and employment status. It should be noted that these other sources of information will not be perfectly accurate and will contain some degree of error themselves.

Sampling, no matter how carefully planned, involves considerable practical considerations in its final implementation. Quite simply, a researcher will often need a great deal of cooperation from others – not simply the eventual participants but others such as those who might provide access to lists from which to sample, for example. Not everyone will be keen to provide researchers with what they need. In other words, the researcher's sampling plan may be compromised by circumstances. The sampling plan may also need to be tailored to the researcher's available resources. This is one of the reasons why the details of the sampling should be supplied in any report in order that readers can understand what was actually done.

13.3   Non-probability sampling

The cost, effort and time involved in drawing up a representative or probability sample are clearly great. A researcher without these resources may decide to use a *quota sample* instead. In a quota sample, an attempt is made to ensure that different groups are represented in the proportion in which they occur within that society. So, for example, if we know that 5 per cent of the population are unemployed, then we may endeavour to ensure that 5 per cent of the sample are unemployed. If our sample consists of 100 people, we will look for five people who are unemployed. Because we have not used probability sampling, we may have a systematically biased sample of the unemployed. The numbers of people in the different groups making up our sample do not have to be proportionate to their numbers in society. For example, if we were interested in looking at how age is related to social attitudes, we may choose to use equal numbers of each age group regardless of their actual frequencies in the population.

Where we need to collect a sample of very specific types of people, we may use *snowball sampling*. For example, this would be an appropriate way of collecting a sample of drug addicts, banjo players or social workers experienced in highly publicised child abuse cases. Once we have found an individual with the necessary characteristic, we ask them whether they know of anyone else with that characteristic who may be willing to take part in our research. If that person names two other people and those two people name two further individuals, then our sample has 'snowballed' from one individual to seven.

There are a number of other versions of non-probability sampling:

- *Quota sampling* is used in marketing research, etc., and requires that the interviewer approaches people who are likely to fill various categories of respondent required by the researcher (e.g. females in professional careers, males in manual jobs).

- *Convenience sampling* is used in much quantitative research in psychology and simply uses any group of participants readily accessible to the researcher.

- *Purposive sampling* is recruiting specified types of people because they have characteristics of interest to the theoretical concerns of the researcher.

- *Theoretical sampling* comes from grounded theory (see Chapter 22) and occurs after some data are collected and an analysis is formulated such that further recruits to the study inform or may challenge the developing theory in some way.

In general, psychologists would assume a sample to be a non-random one unless it is specifically indicated. If it is a random sample, then it is necessary to describe in some detail the particular random procedure used to generate that sample. In much psychological research, the sample will be a convenience one and it may be sufficient to refer to it as such. This leads to an interesting issue concerning random sampling discussed in Box 13.1.

Box 13.1 Key Ideas

Is a random sample needed for statistical significance testing?

This chapter discusses random sampling but rarely is random sampling used in psychological research studies and usually convenience samples are used instead. These are, literally, just that – groups of participants whom the researcher can recruit to their study easily such as when a university professor uses their students for a research project. Of course, randomisation is used in experiments but this takes the form of random allocation to an experimental and control group, for instance. It does not involve the random selection of the participants in the first place. A simple random sample is where every unit in a population of units has an equal and known probability of occurring. So, for example, our unit is a student and our population might consist of a 100 female and male students. Imagine that we wish to draw a sample of 10 students from that population, then every student has an equal and known probability of being selected. In random sampling, we assume that a selected individual is returned to the population so, in theory, they can be selected again. This ensures that each individual has an equal chance of being selected on every occasion. (In practice, however, we do not return the selected individual to the population for possible reselection for practical reasons. With a large population, this introduces very little error and the maths are simpler this way.) Random sampling has the advantage that our selection will not be biased in terms of selecting certain kinds of students in preference to other kinds and that each student will be chosen independently of each other. The sample that we obtain is free from systematic biases and, in the long run, samples will reflect the population.

This is useful if we want to know any characteristic of that population or to compare two or more groups from that population. We could, for example, calculate their mean age, mean simple reaction time or mean number of romantic partners had. Suppose we wanted to know whether the females in our population had faster reaction times than the males. We would select a simple random sample of those students and compare the mean reaction time of the females and males. If we had chosen what might be called a convenience sample, we might have

inadvertently selected females who had had faster times and males who had slower times, thereby biasing our results and our conclusions about those results.

Of course simple random sampling does not guarantee that we have selected a representative sample on any particular occasion and it could be that we selected by chance the biased samples we just described. That is to say, it is possible that the difference in reaction times between the females and males is merely due to the contingencies of random selection. After all if we toss a coin six times, we will not always obtain three heads and three tails but this outcome will be most likely if we toss the coin a large number of times. So what we do next is to see how likely our result will have happened by chance. The null hypothesis is that there will be no difference between females and males in mean reaction time. If we find that there is a difference, then we want to know how likely it is that difference will have arisen by chance. If that difference has a probability of 5 per cent or .05 or less, then we reject the null hypothesis and accept the alternative hypothesis that such a difference is unlikely to be due to chance. If we had not chosen our sample at random, then we would not be able to work out what the likelihood was of obtaining our result by chance.

Some researchers have introduced arguments which they believe undermine standard practice in psychology, It is unlikely that we would just be interested in whether females had faster reaction times than males for the particular group of individuals studied using a convenience sample. That would be of very limited importance. What we most probably want to know is whether females have faster reaction times than males in general. But how general do we want this statement to be? Are we talking about all the females and males in the world? If so, obtaining a simple random sample from that population would be an impossible task. It would be difficult enough obtaining a simple random sample of people from the UK population. So what we do is to take a non-random sample and assume that it is a random sample although we have no means of knowing what sort of sample it actually is (e.g. Reichardt & Gollob, 1999). But it might be of some comfort to us and to others to know that the difference we have obtained would be statistically significant if it had been a random sample (Falk & Greenbaum, 1995). Most studies in psychology do not select their samples at random (e.g. Grichting, 2011; West, Newsom, & Fenaughty, 1992) as is the case with other disciplines such as education (e.g. Shaver & Norton, 1980a), medicine (e.g. Ludbrook & Dudley, 1998), social studies (e.g. Shaver & Norton, 1980b) and sociology (e.g. Grichting, 2011).

This problem with statistical significance testing does not seem to be mentioned in many statistics books, as noted by some scholars (Hunter, & May, 1993; Shaver & Norton, 1980a), perhaps because authors are not aware of it, assume it to be taken for granted, think it does not matter, consider it to be incorrect or believe it will undermine the aim of their book. But there are some exceptions. For example, Hays (1994) wrote:

All the techniques and theory that we discuss apply to random samples and do not necessarily hold for any old data collected in any old way. In practical situations, you, as the investigator, may be hard put to show that a given sample is truly random, but you must realize that you are acting as *if* this were a random sample from some well-defined population when you apply ordinary methods of statistical inference. Unless the assumption of random sampling is at least reasonable, the probability results of inferential methods mean very little, and these methods might as well be omitted. . . This is a most serious problem in the development of the social sciences and has not been given the attention that it deserves.

(p. 227)

Similarly Glass and Hopkins (1984) also noted 'Inferential statistics is based on the assumption of random sampling from populations' (p. 177). The person who is usually credited with developing statistical significance tests, Sir Ronald Aylmer Fisher (1936b), considered it a serious problem. He stated: 'If the two groups have been chosen from their respective populations in such a way as not to be random samples of the populations they represent, then an examination of the samples will clearly not enable us to compare these populations' (p. 58). However, he did not ensure that the plots of land or the seed varieties that were employed for agricultural research at Rothamsted Experimental Station were randomly sampled but used what was available – that is, a convenience sample. What researchers typically do to determine whether a finding seems to be generally true is to try to replicate it (e.g. Shaver & Norton, 1980a; Simons, 2014; Smith, 1970), ideally partially or conceptually. If we cannot replicate a finding, we will assume that it is not general.

13.4   National surveys

Most of us are familiar with the national opinion polls frequently reported in the media. National studies are rare in psychological research. Using them would be an advantage but not always a big one. Generally, psychologists see little need to collect data from a region or country unless they have a specific interest in the psychology of people in that region or country. Researchers from other social sciences, medical science and similar disciplines are more likely to carry out national surveys than psychologists. This is partly because these researchers are more interested in trends at the national and regional levels. Nonetheless, the results of these surveys are often of relevance to psychologists.

It is not uncommon for survey data to be archived for access by other researchers. For example, in Britain many social science surveys are archived at the Economic and Social Research Council (ESRC) funded UK Data Service. The datasets that are available there for further or secondary analysis are listed at http://www.data-archive.ac.uk. The ESRC requires data sets from studies it funds to be lodged with the UK Data Service, which also accepts data sets from other sources. International datasets are also available.

Major surveys include the Crime Survey for England and Wales (called the British Crime Survey prior to 2012), British Social Attitudes and the National Child Development Study. Students are not allowed direct access to these datasets, but they may be obtained via a lecturer who has an interest in them and the expertise to analyse them. This expertise includes an ability to use a statistical computer package such as SPSS Statistics which is widely used and taught to students. There are books which show you how to use SPSS, such as the companion computing text, *Introduction to SPSS in psychology* (Howitt & Cramer, 2017).

Box 13.2   Research Example

National representative survey

2017 British Social Attitudes Survey. http://www.natcen.ac.uk/series/british-social-attitudes

The British Social Attitudes Survey is a good example of the use of a representative sample in research which may be of relevance to psychologists. The detail is less important to absorb than the overall picture of the meticulous nature of the process and the need for the researcher to make a number of fairly arbitrary decisions. This survey has been carried out more or less annually since 1983. The target sample for the 2017 survey was 9386 adults aged 18 or over living in private households (http://www.bsa.natcen.ac.uk/media/39284/bsa35_full-report.pdf). The *sampling list* or *frame* was the Postcode Address File. This is a list of addresses (or postal delivery points) which is compiled by, and which can be bought from, the Post Office. The multi-stage sampling design consisted of three stages of selection:

- Selection of postcode sectors

- Selection of addresses within those postcode sectors

- Selection of an adult living at an address.

The postcode sector is identified by the first part of the postcode. It is LE11 3 for Loughborough, for example. Any sector with fewer than 500 addresses was combined with an adjacent sector. Sectors north of the Caledonian Canal in Scotland were excluded, due to the high cost of interviewing there. The sectors were stratified into:

- 37 sub-regions;

- three equal-sized groups within each sub-region varying in population density; and

- ranking by the percentage of homes that were owner-occupied.

The sampling frame may look something like that shown in Table 13.1 (Hoinville & Jowell, 1978, p. 74).

The total number of postcode sectors as from 2017 in the UK was 12 381 (https://www.ons.gov.uk/methodology/geography/ukgeographies/postalgeography, n.d.) from which 361 were selected. Probability-to-size sampling was used, in which the probability of selection was made proportional to the number of addresses in each sector. The reason for using this procedure is that the number of addresses varies considerably among postcode sectors. If postcode sectors have an equal probability of being selected, the more addresses a postcode sector has, the smaller is the chance or probability that an address within that sector will be chosen. So not every address has an equal probability of being selected for the national sample.

To ensure probability-to-size sampling in which an address within a sector has an equal probability of being chosen, the following procedure was used (Hoinville & Jowell, 1978, p. 67). Suppose we have six postcode sectors and we have to select three of these sectors. The number of addresses in each sector is shown in Table 13.2. Altogether we have 21 000 addresses. If we use systematic sampling to select these three sectors, then we need to choose the random starting point or address from this number. We could do this using a five-digit sequence in a table of random numbers. Suppose this number was 09334. If we add the number of addresses cumulatively as shown in the third column of Table 13.2, then the random starting point is in the second postcode sector. So this would be the first postcode sector chosen randomly.

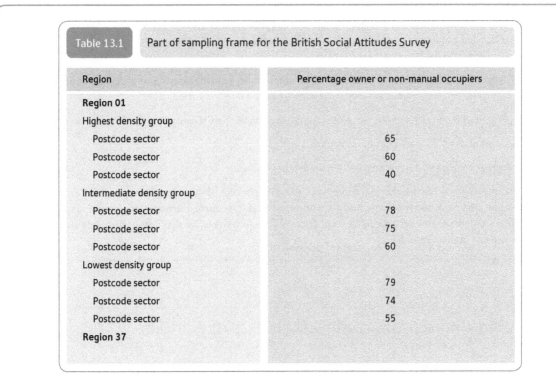

Table 13.1 Part of sampling frame for the British Social Attitudes Survey

Region	Percentage owner or non-manual occupiers
Region 01	
Highest density group	
Postcode sector	65
Postcode sector	60
Postcode sector	40
Intermediate density group	
Postcode sector	78
Postcode sector	75
Postcode sector	60
Lowest density group	
Postcode sector	79
Postcode sector	74
Postcode sector	55
Region 37	

Source: Adapted from Hoinville & Jowell (1978)

Table 13.2 Example of sampling sectors with probability proportional to size

Sector	Size	Cumulative size	Points
1	4000	0–4000	2334 (second point)
2	6000	4001–10 000	9334 (random start)
3	5000	10 001–15 000	
4	2000	15 001–17 000	16 334 (third point)
5	3000	17 001–20 000	
6	1000	20 001–21 000	

Source: Adapted from Hoinville & Jowell (1978)

In systematic sampling we need to know the sampling interval between the addresses on the list. This is simply the total number of addresses divided by the number of samples $(21\,000/3 = 7000)$. As the random starting point is greater than 7000, a second point is 7000 below 9334, which is 2334 $(9334 - 7000 = 2334)$. This point falls within the first postcode sector, which is the second postcode sector to be selected. A third point is 7000 above 9334, which is 16 334 $(9334 + 7000 = 16\,334)$. This point falls within the fourth postcode sector, which is the third postcode sector to be chosen. So these would be our three sectors.

Twenty-six addresses were systematically selected in each of the 361 postcode sectors chosen. This gives a total of 9386 addresses $(26 \times 361 = 9386)$. A random starting point was chosen in each sector and 26 addresses were selected

→

at equal fixed intervals from that starting point. The number of adults aged 18 and over varies at the different addresses. A person was selected at random at each address using a computerised random selection procedure.

Response rates were affected by a number of factors:

- About 9 per cent of the addresses were outside the scope of the survey (e.g. they were empty, derelict or otherwise not suitable).

- About 40 per cent of the available 8781 or so selected refused to take part when approached by the interviewer.

- About 8 per cent of the 8781 could not be contacted.

- About 5 per cent of the 8781 did not respond for some other reason.

This means that the response rate for the final survey was about 41 per cent of the original sample of 9672. This is quite a respectable figure and many surveys obtain much lower return rates. Of course, the non-participation rate may have a considerable impact on the value of the data obtained. There is no reason to believe that non-participants are necessarily similar to participants in their attitudes.

13.5   Socio-demographic characteristics of samples

National samples usually gather socio-demographic information about the sample studied. Which characteristics are described depends on the kind of participants and the purpose of the study. If the participants are university students, then it may suffice to describe the number of female and male students and the mean and standard deviation of their age either together or separately. If the participants are not students, then it is generally necessary to provide further socio-demographic information on them, such as their educational, employment, and social status. Socio-demographic categories are subject to change over time and according to the nature of the sample. For example, categories of sexuality have shown marked change in recent years as have those concerning race or ethnicity. It is wise to consult widely or refer to recent research reports in order to avoid using inappropriate or outmoded categories or terminology.

In the UK, one measure of social status is the current or the last job or occupation of the participant (visit https://www.bsa.natcen.ac.uk/. Choose 'Read the key findings' and then Download the full report). The latest government scheme for *coding* occupations is the Standard Occupational Classification 2010. The previous version was the Standard Occupational Classification 2000 (visit https://www.ons.gov.uk and use the search facility to find 'occupational classification information' including the 2010 and the 2000 classification documents). The main socio-economic grouping based on the latest scheme is the National Statistics Socio-Economic Classification, which consists of the following eight categories:

- Employers in large organisations and higher managerial and professional occupations

- Lower professional and managerial and higher technical and supervisory occupations

- Intermediate occupations

- Employers in small organisations and own account workers

- Lower supervisory and technical occupations

- Semi-routine occupations

- Routine occupations

- Never worked and long-term unemployed.

Previous schemes include the Registrar General's Social Class, the Socio-Economic Group and the Goldthorpe (1987) schema. There is a computer program for coding occupations based on the Standard Occupational Classification 2010 (https://warwick.ac.uk/fac/soc/ier/software/cascot/) called Computer-Assisted Structured COding Tool (CASCOT). It is freely available to you if your institution subscribes to it.

A measure of race may be included to determine how inclusive the sample is and whether the matter of interest differs with race. Since 2010, the British Social Attitudes Survey measured race with the question and response options below (http://www.bsa.natcen.ac.uk/media/39284/bsa35_full-report.pdf). From 1996 to 2009, the 'White: of any origin' response consisted of the two options 'White: of any European origin' and 'White: of other origin (please state)'. The percentage of people choosing these categories in the 2016 survey is shown below after each option.

To which one of these groups do you consider you belong?	
Group	%
Black: of African origin	1.4
Black: of Caribbean origin	0.8
Black: of other origin (please state)	0.0
Asian: of Indian origin	1.7
Asian: of Pakistani origin	0.8
Asian: of Bangladeshi origin	0.2
Asian: of Chinese origin	0.6
Asian: of other origin (please state)	0.9
White: of any origin	91.4
Mixed origin (please state)	1.1
Other (please state)	0.9

About 0.1 per cent or 2 of the 2942 people in the sample did not know which category they fell in, and only 0.1 per cent or 4 people did not answer this question.

13.6 Sample size and population surveys

When carrying out research, an important consideration is to estimate how big a sample is required. For surveys, this depends on a number of factors:

- How big the population is

- How many people you will be able to contact and what proportion of them are likely to agree to participate

- How variable their responses are

- How confident you want to be about the results

- How accurate you want your estimate to be compared with the actual population figure.

Not everyone who is sampled will take part. Usually in national sampling some sort of list of members of the population is used. This is known as the *sampling frame*. Lists of the electorate and telephone directories are examples of such lists, though both have obvious inadequacies. Some of the sample will have moved from their address to an unknown location. Others may not be in when the interviewer calls, even if they are visited on a number of occasions. Others refuse to take part. It is useful to make a note of why there was no response from those chosen to be part of the sample. The *response rate* will differ depending on various factors, such as the method of contact and the topic of the research (Groves et al., 2006; Groves & Peytcheva, 2008). The response rate is likely to be higher if the interviewer visits the potential participant than if questionnaires are mailed out. The most probable response rate may be estimated from similar studies or from a pilot or exploratory study.

How variable the responses of participants are likely to be can be obtained in similar ways. It is usually expressed in terms of the *standard* deviation of values, which is similar to the average extent to which the values deviate from the mean of the sample.

Confidence interval

When one reads about the findings of national polls in the newspapers, statements like this appear: 'The poll found that 55 per cent of the population trust the government. The margin of error was plus or minus 2 per cent'. Of course, since the finding is based on a sample, we can never be completely confident in the figure obtained. Usually the confidence level is set at 95 per cent or .95. The interval is an estimate based on the value obtained in the survey (55 per cent of the population) and the variability in the data. The variability is used to estimate the range of the 95 per cent of samples that are most likely to be obtained if our data were precisely the same as the values in the entire population. The single figure of 55 per cent trusting the government is known as a *point estimate,* since it gives a single value. Clearly, the confidence interval approach is more useful, since it gives some indication of the imprecision we expect in our data. This is expressed as the margin of error in survey research. Twice the margin of error is the confidence interval.

One could think of the confidence interval as being the range of the most common sample values we are likely to obtain if we repeated our survey many times, that is, the 95 most common sample values if we repeated the study 100 times. If this helps you to appreciate the meaning of confidence intervals, then all well and good. Actually it is not quite accurate, since it is true only if our original sample data are totally representative of the population. This is not likely to be the case, of course, but statistics operates with best guesses, not certainties. If the confidence interval is set at 95 per cent or .95, this means that the population value is likely to be within the confidence interval for 95 per cent of samples.

The confidence level is related to the notion of statistical significance that was introduced in Chapter 4. A detailed discussion of confidence intervals may be found in Chapter 38 of the companion text *Understanding statistics in psychology with SPSS* (Howitt & Cramer, 2020). Confidence intervals apply to any estimate based on a sample. Hence, there are confidence intervals for virtually all statistics based on samples. Both statistical significance and the confidence level are concerned with how likely it is that a result will occur by chance. Statistical significance is normally fixed at 5 per cent or .05. This means that the result will be obtained by chance five (or fewer) times out of 100. If we find that a result is statistically significant, this means that the result is so extreme that it is unlikely to occur by chance. A statistically significant finding is one which is outside the middle 95 per cent of samples defined by the confidence interval.

■ Sampling error (margin of error) and sample size

How accurately one's data reflect the true population value is dependent on something known as sampling error. Samples taken at random from a population vary in terms of their characteristics. The difference between the mean of your sample and the mean of the population of the sample is known as the *sampling error*. If several samples are taken from the same population, their means will vary by different amounts from the value in the population. Some samples will have means that are identical to that of the population. Other samples will have means that differ by a certain amount from the population value. The variability in the means of samples taken from a population is expressed in terms of a statistical index known as the *standard error*. This is really a theoretical exercise, as we never actually know what the population mean is – unless we do research on the entire population. Instead, we estimate the mean of the population as being the same as the mean for our sample of data. This estimate may differ from the population mean, of course, but it is the best estimate we have. It is possible to calculate how likely the sample mean is to differ from the population mean by taking into account the variability within the sample (the measure of variability used is the standard deviation of the sample). The variability within the sample is used to estimate the variability in the population, which is then used to estimate the variability of sample means taken from that population.

If we want to be 95 per cent or .95 confident of the population mean, then we can work out what the sampling error is using the following formula, where *t* is the value for this confidence level taking into account the size of the sample used (Cramer, 1998, pp. 107–108):

$$\text{sampling error} = t \times \frac{\text{standard deviation}}{\sqrt{\text{sample size}}}$$

The standard deviation is calculated using the data in our sample. The sample size we are considering either is known or can be decided upon. The appropriate *t* value can be found in the tables of some introductory statistics textbooks, such as the companion text *Understanding statistics in psychology with SPSS* (Howitt & Cramer, 2020).

If we substitute values for the standard deviation and the sample size, we can see that the sampling error becomes progressively smaller the larger the sample size. Say, for example, that the standard deviation is 3 for scores of how extraverted people are. For a sample size of 100 people, the *t* value for the 95 per cent confidence level is 1.984 and so the sampling error is about 0.60:

$$\text{sampling error} = 1.984 \times \frac{3}{\sqrt{100}} = 1.984 \times \frac{3}{10} = \frac{5.952}{10} = 0.5952 = 0.60$$

If the mean score for extraversion for the sample was about 16, then the sample mean would lie between plus or minus 0.60 on either side of 16 about 95 per cent of the time for samples of this size. So the mean would lie between 15.40 ($16 - 0.60 = 15.40$) and 16.60 ($16 + 0.60 = 16.60$). These values would be the 95 per cent or .95 confidence limits. The confidence interval is the range between these confidence limits, which is 1.20 ($16.60 - 15.40 = 1.20$). The confidence interval is simply twice the size of the sampling error ($0.60 \times 2 = 1.20$). It is usually expressed as the mean plus or minus the appropriate interval. So in this case the confidence interval is 16.00 ± 0.60.

If the sample size is 400 people instead of 100, the t value for the 95 per cent confidence level is slightly smaller and is 1.966. The sampling error for the same standard deviation is also slightly smaller and is about 0.29 instead of about 0.60:

$$1.966 \times \frac{3}{\sqrt{400}} = 1.966 \times \frac{3}{20} = \frac{5.898}{20} = 0.2949 = 0.29$$

In other words, the sampling error in this case is about half the size for a sample of 400 as for a sample of 100.

We can also see that if the variation or standard deviation of the variable is greater, then the sampling error will be greater. If the standard deviation was 6 instead of 3 with this sample and confidence level, then the sampling error would be about 0.59 instead of about 0.29:

$$1.966 \times \frac{6}{\sqrt{400}} = 1.966 \times \frac{6}{20} = \frac{11.796}{20} = 0.5898$$

The sampling error is sometimes known as the margin of error and may be expressed as a percentage of the mean. If the mean of the extraversion scores is 16 and the sampling error is about 0.60, then the sampling error expressed as a percentage of this mean is 3.75 per cent ($0.60/16 \times 100 = 3.75$). If the sampling error is about 0.29, then the sampling error given as a percentage of this mean is about 1.81 per cent ($0.29/16 \times 100 = 1.8125$). A margin of error of 2 per cent for extraversion means that the mean of the population will vary between 0.32 ($2/100 \times 16 = 0.32$) on either side of 16 at the 95 per cent confidence level. In other words, it will vary between 15.68 ($16 - 0.32 = 15.68$) and 16.32 ($16 + 0.32 = 16.32$).

Suppose that we want to estimate what sample size is needed to determine the population mean of extraversion for a population of infinite size at the 95 per cent confidence level with a margin of error of 2 per cent. We apply the following formula, where 1.96 is the z value for the 95 per cent confidence level for an infinite population:

$$\text{sample size} = \frac{1.96^2 \times \text{sample standard deviation}^2}{\text{sample error}^2}$$

If we substitute the appropriate figures in this formula, we can see that we need a sample of 346 to determine this:

$$\frac{1.96^2 \times 3^2}{0.32^2} \times \frac{3.84 \times 9}{0.10} = \frac{34.56}{0.10} = 345.60$$

If the margin of error was set at a higher level, then the sample size needed to estimate the population characteristic would be smaller. If we set the margin of error at, say, 5 per cent rather than 2 per cent, the sampling error would be 0.80 ($5/100 \times 16 = 0.80$) instead of 0.32 and the sample required would be 54 instead of 346:

$$\frac{1.96^2 \times 3^2}{0.80^2} \times \frac{3.84 \times 9}{0.64} = \frac{34.56}{0.64} = 54.00$$

Remember that the above formula only deals with a situation in which we have specified a particular margin of error. It has very little to do with the typical situation in psychology in which the researcher tests to see whether or not a relationship differs significantly from no relationship at all.

It should be noted that the formula for calculating sampling error for proportionate stratified sampling and cluster sampling differs somewhat from that given above, which was for simple random sampling (Moser & Kalton, 1971, pp. 87, 103). Compared with simple random sampling, the sampling error is likely to be smaller for proportionate stratified sampling and larger for cluster sampling. This means that the sample can be somewhat smaller for proportionate stratified sampling but somewhat larger for cluster sampling than for simple random sampling.

Sample size for a finite population

The previous formula assumes that we are dealing with an infinitely large population. When dealing with big populations, this formula is sufficient for calculating the size of the sample to be used. When the populations are fairly small, we do not need as many people as this formula indicates. The following formula is used for calculating the precise number of people needed for a finite rather than an infinite population, where n is the size of the sample and N is the size of the finite population (Berenson, Levine, & Krehbiel, 2009):

$$\text{adjusted } n = \frac{n \times N}{n + (N - 1)}$$

We can see this if we substitute increasingly large finite populations in this formula while the sample size remains at 346. This has been done in Table 13.3. The first column shows the size of the population and the second column the size of the sample needed to estimate a characteristic of this population. The sample size can be less than 346 with finite populations of less than about 250 000.

When carrying out a study, we also need to take account of the response rate or the number of people who will take part in the study. It is unlikely that we will be able to contact everyone or that everyone we contact will agree to participate. If the response rate is, say, 70 per cent, then 30 per cent will not take part in the study. Thus, we have to increase our sample size to 495 people ($346/.70 = 494.29$). A 70 per cent response rate for a sample of 495 is 346 ($.70 \times 495 = 346.50$). Often response rates are much lower than this.

Table 13.3	Sample size for various finite populations with 95 per cent confidence level, 2 per cent sampling error and standard deviation of 3	
Population size		**Sample size**
1000		257
5000		324
10 000		334
100 000		345
250 000		346
Infinite		346

Box 13.3   Research Example

Violence in teenage dating

Hamby, S., & Turner, H. (2013). Measuring teen dating violence in males and females: Insights from the National Survey of Children's Exposure to Violence. *Psychology of Violence, 3,* 323–339.

Psychologists working with professionals from other disciplines will note the lack of survey research in psychology compared to disciplines such as sociology, medicine and the like. There are probably many reasons for this, which can be found in the primacy of the laboratory experiment and questions of cause and effect which dominated much of psychology until recently. Survey research is diametrically opposite to laboratory experimentation in many ways – it is based in the field rather than the laboratory, it almost invariably involves verbal rather than behavioural measures, and matters such as causality are not a primary concern. Such surveys are often very pertinent to modern psychological practice and research, which makes a working knowledge of survey methods more important to psychologists now than it ever was in the past. Furthermore, working alongside researchers trained in other disciplines often means that psychologists are exposed to a wider variety of research methods as well as distinctly different intellectual traditions. Hence, survey research is increasingly familiar to psychologists in their work, despite the scarcity of psychological survey studies. One exception to this is research into survey methodology – for example, comparisons of different ways of doing survey research, such as the Internet versus face-to-face surveys. The research featured here also reflects some of the problems with using operational definitions of variables (see Chapter 3). In addition, our summary of the paper tries to bring out some of the practical matters which the survey researcher may have to address.

Background

In a US study, Sherry Hamby and Heather Turner (2013) were interested in teenage dating violence (TDV), which is essentially aggressive behaviour inflicted by a girlfriend or boyfriend in the context of an intimate relationship. Such behaviours are known to be associated with undesirable things such as poor achievement in the educational system. One of the issues, naturally, is the question of whether this is typically male behaviour. The answer is somewhat difficult because how aggression is defined has a bearing on which sex is most likely to be perpetrators. For example, if being a victim was limited to circumstances of a sexual assault, the use of a weapon, and where there is injury, then females are rather more likely to be victims of TDV. But there are other circumstances which leave females on a par with males in terms of perpetrating TDV. So Hamby and Turner decided to explore the way in which teenage dating violence is measured (operationalised) in order to understand better the gender implications of TDV.

Hypothesis

The researchers hypothesised 'that inclusion criteria that restrict TDV cases to more serious incidents will have significantly more female victims than male victims' (Hamby & Turner, 2013, p. 327).

Method

Procedure

Hamby and Turner's study was a secondary analysis of a survey which had already been conducted, so they were not responsible for the original data collection. It is not unusual for survey data to be made available to other researchers in this way, and it can be a requirement of research funding bodies that it is. They concentrated on the data from young people in the age range 12–17 years – this was about 1700 out of the total of about 4500 children up to the age of 17 years. The survey in question was the National Survey of Children's Exposure to Violence (NatSCEV). The survey was funded by the Office of Juvenile Justice and Delinquency Prevention and documented the frequency (incidence and prevalence) with which the children were exposed to violence, especially domestic, community and school violence. A professional research interviewing company carried out the interviews and obtained the sample using a random digit dialling procedure to create a sample of phone numbers to contact. The researchers deliberately oversampled children living in homes in areas particularly vulnerable to violence. Since many households had more than one child in the desired age range, the researchers chose a target child from the household on the basis of whichever child had had their birthday most recently.

A short interview was conducted with the child's caregiver to obtain some basic information. Then the main interview was conducted with the child if they were aged 10 or over or with an adult familiar with the child if the child were younger. So, for Hamby and Turner's analysis, all of the children in their subsample were interviewed. The response rate was maximised by repeatedly telephoning up to 13 times to make contact. When contact had been made, up to 25 calls were made in order to make sure that the interview was completed. Overall, about two-thirds of households approached completed the interviews. A university ethics committee supervised the research, and the research also followed the rules for research of the US Department of Justice. If evidence of abuse by the caregiver was revealed in the interviews with the child, the children were followed up by a clinically trained research team member skilled in telephone crisis counselling. The clinician stayed in touch with the child until either the situation was resolved or the relevant authorities were involved.

Some results

If the criterion of violence was based on physical force alone, the overall rate of violence in dating was 6.2 per cent and it was significantly more common for males to be victims of such physical violence than for females (chi squared was the statistical test used because the data consisted of frequencies). This pattern was reversed when the criterion for violence was sexual force alone. It was less common at 2 per cent overall, but for this definition it was found that females were more than twice as likely as males to be victims. For violence involving injury, it was found that female victims were twice as common as male victims but, this time, not statistically significantly so. Combining different criteria for violence together as well as taking them separately produced seven different 'operational definitions' of violence. Of these, just two suggested that males were more likely to be victims – physical force alone and physical and sexual force combined into one category. This was because physical force is much more frequent than sexual force and so dominated in the data. Fear of the different types of violence was much more common for females than for males.

Authors' suggestions for further research

Hamby and Turner suggest that one important unaddressed question was why female victims of teenage dating violence are more likely to seek help than male victims.

13.7   Conclusion

Most psychological research is based on convenience samples which are not selected randomly and which often consist of students. The aim of this type of research is often to determine whether the support for an observed relationship is statistically significant. It is generally not considered necessary to ascertain to what extent this finding is characteristic of a particular population. Nonetheless, where this is possible, it is useful to know the degree to which our findings may be typical of a particular population. Consequently, it is important to understand what the basis is for selecting a sample which is designed to be representative of a population. Furthermore, in some cases, the population will be limited in size, so that it is possible with relatively little effort to select a sample randomly. For example, if we are interested in examining the content of, say, recorded interactions or published articles, and we do not have the time or the resources to analyse the whole content, then it is usually appropriate to select a sample of that content using probability sampling. The great advantage of probability sampling is that the sample is likely to be more representative of the population and that the sampling will not be affected by any biases we have of which we may not even be aware.

Key points

- A random or probability sample is used to estimate the characteristics of a particular finite population. The probability of any unit or element being selected is equal and known.

- The population does not necessarily consist of people. It may comprise any unit or element, such as the population of articles in a particular journal for a certain year.

- The size of the sample to be chosen depends on various factors such as how confident we want to be that the results represent the population, how small we want the sampling error to be, how variable the behaviour or characteristic is, and how small the population is. Bigger samples are required for higher confidence levels, smaller sampling errors, more variable behaviour and bigger populations.

- Fairly small samples can be used to estimate the characteristics of very large populations. The sample size does not increase directly with the population size.

- Where the population is widely dispersed, cluster sampling and multi-stage sampling may be used. In the first stage of sampling, a number of clusters such as geographical areas (e.g. postcode sectors) may be chosen, from which further selections are subsequently made.

- Where possible, the representativeness of the sample needs to be checked against other available data about the population.

- Where the sample is a convenience one of undergraduate students, it may suffice to describe the number of females and males, and the mean and standard deviation of their ages. Where the sample consists of a more varied group of adults, it may be necessary to describe them in terms of other socio-demographic characteristics such as whether or not they are employed, the social standing of their occupation and their racial origin.

ACTIVITIES

1. How would you randomly select 10 programmes from the day's listing of a major TV channel to which you have ready access?

2. How would you randomly select three 3-minute segments from a 50-minute TV programme?

3. How would you randomly select 10 editions of a major Sunday newspaper from last year?

CHAPTER 14

Data analysis issues and scientific progress

Overview

- This chapter discusses some important arguments about the analysis of quantitative data.

- It has been suggested that the body of knowledge in psychology is distorted by the quest for statistical significance and the use of Null Hypothesis Significance Testing. Significance testing merely addresses the question of how likely it is to find a particular size of effect greater by chance in a study if the null hypothesis that there is a zero effect is true. It helps stop false positive errors where on the basis of a fluke of sampling, a researcher's data shows a difference, trend or relationship which is not true of the population from which the sample came.

- There is evidence that the meaning of statistical significance is poorly understood leading to mistaken comparisons between studies. Replication studies are not always encouraged by journals, leaving some uncertainty about progress in areas of research.

- There are many other important things to consider apart from statistical significance in a data analysis.

- Confidence intervals, effect sizes and statistical power analysis have been proposed as a way forward. Each of these provides additional information beyond what significance testing can achieve allowing for a fuller interpretation of a study's findings.

- Researchers use a range of practices which have been identified as being questionable in nature though apparently quite common. Generally these tend towards making statistical significance more likely and reducing obstacles in the way of supporting the researcher's hypothesis.

Data analysis does not have to be complex to be good. A basic rule-of-thumb is to keep to your limits in terms of design and method of analysis. The American Psychological Society's Task Force on Statistical Inference (Wilkinson, 1999) recommend that researchers choose a minimally sufficient analysis to address their research question:

> Although complex designs and state-of-the-art methods are sometimes necessary to address research questions effectively, simpler classical approaches often can provide elegant and sufficient answers to important questions. Do not choose an analytic method to impress your readers or to deflect criticism. If the assumptions and strength of a simpler method are reasonable for your data and research problem, use it.
>
> (p. 598)

Choosing all of the options on a statistics computer program does not ensure a good data analysis though it may give you a reassuring amount of numbers to include in your report. It is more important to ask whether your analysis actually addresses the things that your research design was intended to capture. Knowing what you want to get from your analysis is the first thing. You are the best person to understand this as usually you planned the study from the start. But equally important is understanding how your analysis relates to other studies and how best you can ensure that your study is part of the knowledge building process of psychology.

There is a seeming wonderland of quantitative research designs and ways to analyse them. We have covered the basics of research design in previous chapters. However, data analysis and the use of statistical methods warrant careful consideration. So in this chapter important issues in quantitative data analysis are discussed. It is not intended to explain the use of statistical techniques such as ANOVA, regression, and other rather more arcane statistical procedures but to present some of the arguments for a better approach to the use of statistics in psychology. There have been numerous critiques of quantitative data analysis over the years and a primary focus of criticism is the use of statistical methods in psychological research. The purpose of research is to build a body of psychological knowledge and it is somewhat unfortunate that many psychologists do statistics in ways which hamper the growth of sound, psychological knowledge. New areas of psychological research often appear chaotic as a consequence of these practices. One might see this chapter as a succession of parables to encourage you to do the right thing in your research. Nothing in this chapter is demanding mathematically.

What principles should guide the analysis of data? Over the decades, a degree of consensus has been reached by critics of statistics in psychology and forms the basis of this chapter. Many of the statistical procedures employed by psychologists have their roots in the late 1800s and the early 1900s and, to make a sweeping generalisation, psychologists have stuck to these early techniques. However, these time-honoured practices have come increasingly under fire and many argue that it is time to change. In particular, despite repeated criticisms, psychology as a whole has been reluctant to move away from the null hypothesis significance testing (NHST) approach to statistics which encourages the question 'Is it statistically significant?' to dominate statistical analyses. Controversy surrounds NHST together with a certain amount of confusion. Increasingly demands are being made for better strategies to be employed when reaching decisions in data analysis than simply addressing the issue of statistical significance/non-significance. The pressure to change comes from a number of sources including individual scholarly critiques of current practices, initiatives by psychology journal editors, and the pronouncements of the American Psychological Association.

A major move by the American Psychological Association came with the introduction of the sixth edition of its *Publication Manual of the American Psychological Association* (APA, 2010). The *Publication Manual* gives the nitty-gritty detail of how to prepare a journal article for publication in any of the APA journals. It is full of stuff about how, for example, to cite studies with six or more authors for the first time in your report and other matters! Most publications in psychology follow or are influenced by the APA style for doing things. Those hours that students spend typing out lists of references usually involve them employing APA style or something close. Because its standards are adopted widely by non-APA journals, something in excess of a thousand journals require the use of APA style worldwide. The *Publication Manual* dropped something of a bombshell when it finally became more prescriptive about reporting the data analysis:

> Historically, researchers in psychology have relied heavily on null hypothesis statistical significance testing (NHST) as a starting point for many (but not all) of its analytic approaches. APA (the American Psychological Association) stresses that NHST is but a starting point and that additional reporting elements such as effect sizes, confidence intervals and extensive description are needed to convey the most complete meaning of the results . . . However, complete reporting of all tested hypotheses and estimates of appropriate effect sizes and confidence intervals are the minimum expectations for all APA journals.

(p. 3)

And

> . . . routinely provide evidence that the study has sufficient power to detect effects of substantive interest.

(p. 30)

There is nothing new about effect size, confidence intervals and power. They are not the latest hot news in psychology and have been around for a good few decades though they are sometimes known as *the new statistics*. What is new, is that they are beginning to be insisted upon. Rather more dramatic and extreme was the announcement in *Basic and Applied Social Psychology* that its editors were banning NHST testing from the journal (Trafimow & Marks, 2015). Their argument is that NHST stultifies thinking and obstructs creativity. They describe *p* values (significance levels) as being a crutch for researchers who have weak data and who argue, in so many words, that so long as a study shows statistical significance somewhere then it can't be that bad as there is something there. The precedent set by the journal is intriguing though difficult to envisage it being widely adopted in the short term. Many a statistics phobic student might rejoice in the idea of no more stats but this was not Trafimow and Marks' intention. They say that instead they will expect larger sample sizes than typify psychological studies in general because larger sample sizes lead to stable descriptive statistics which reduces the impact of sampling error. What they term 'strong' descriptive statistics (including effect sizes) are required and detailed frequency/distribution data should be included whenever possible. The publicity given the ban in major journals like *Nature* (Woolston, 2015) brought the issues to the attention of many psychologists.

Significance testing was developed nearly 100 years ago by Ronald Fisher and is an index of the strength of the evidence against the null hypothesis. The idea that we reject a null hypothesis in favour of a hypothesis is taken from Neyman and Pearson's work in the 1930s. (The null hypothesis and the hypothesis are statistical concepts and are inherent in any significance test, even if not formally stated.) Null hypothesis significance testing, to borrow an analogy from Kraemer and Thiemann (1987), is rather like the Anglo-Saxon system of trial by jury. Perhaps the greatest similarity is between the decisions made – guilty or not guilty, significant or not significant. NHST focuses attention on the issue of statistical significance to the exclusion of the wider picture. Having to choose literally between the null hypothesis and the hypothesis leads to black and white (dichotomous) decision-making. There are no shades of grey but there should be. A poorly conducted experiment in which procedures are not standardised, the use of dependent variables which are lacking in terms of reliability or validity, the use of too few participants in the sample, weak measurement or manipulation of the independent variable, and the smallness of the actual effect being studied are the main reasons for non-significance. Many of these should make it difficult to reject a hypothesis even where the analysis is non-significant statistically.

The quest for statistical significance becomes too important and statistical significance can be confused with other forms of significance. All that statistical significance testing does is help the researcher avoid the embarrassment of interpreting a chance finding as being a real trend. Research is based on samples from the population, samples fluctuate to varying degrees from the population, and so there is always the possibility that a particular sample shows a trend which does not exist in reality. In NHST terms, you must try to avoid what is known as a Type 1 error – which is nothing other than a false positive (Neyman & Pearson, 1933b). Assuming the null hypothesis is true (and allowing for the amount of variability in our sample of data), statistical significance testing merely provides an answer to the question of how likely it is that the trend in our sample is just a random fluke. Reinhart (2015) puts things this way (with reference to a study of whether or not a medicine works): 'Remember, a p value is not a measure of how right you are or how important a difference is. Instead think of it as a measure of surprise' (p. 9). That is, if the null hypothesis that the medicine does not work is true, then it would be surprising to find a trend which has a less than one in twenty chance of occurring. Statistical significance protects us from the happenchance of sampling – that is, falsely claiming that we have found a trend or effect when it is merely a matter of chance when, in reality, there is no trend or effect.

Understanding the meaning of the significance or p level that we get in NHST testing appears to be poor among students and professionals. Overwhelmingly students go for the statement that 'p is the probability that the results are due to chance, the probability that the null hypothesis (H_0) is true' when faced with a number of correct and incorrect options (Field, 2005). Very few go for the correct answer which is that 'p is the probability of observing results as extreme (or more) as observed, if the null hypothesis (H_0) is true'. The significance levels we get in NHST are NOT the probability that the null hypothesis is untrue. However, assuming the null hypothesis is true, the significance levels give the probability of getting an effect in our data as big as we have or bigger. Small values for this probability (usually 5 per cent or .05 or less) are treated as evidence that the null hypothesis is false.

We should write about statistical non-significance if the null hypothesis cannot be rejected and statistical significance if the hypothesis is favoured. Statistical significance is dependent on both the size of the effect and the sample size. So absolutely uninteresting and trivial things psychologically can be statistically significant. Indeed, statisticians will tell you that if you have a big enough sample size, just about any trend, no matter how small, may be statistically significant. They also go so far as to say that few if any null hypotheses are actually true in the real world. So statistical significance is not a gold standard indicating the value of a study.

Avoiding the trap of making decisions solely on the basis of significance levels is a sign of a researcher's maturity in research and statistical analysis. The temptation to dwell on statistical significance at the expense of other perhaps more important aspects of your analysis is understandable from a practical perspective. We all like statistically significant findings. The joy of statistical significance for the professional researcher that their study becomes much more publishable. Since publications are a part of career progression, it is no small wonder that researchers can be short-sighted and focus on statistical significance. Students like statistically significant findings since they impress and make it easier to refute any suggestion that the research design is fundamentally flawed in some way.

More than 60 years ago Theodore Sterling (1959) noted that most papers (81 per cent of them) published in four randomly selected psychology journals had used statistical significance tests when reporting their findings. Moreover almost all of such papers using statistical tests (97 per cent of them) had rejected the null hypothesis, applying what may be considered as the rather arbitrary critical criterion of a probability level of .05 or less. As no replication studies were published in those particular journals and as we do not know how many such studies were carried out and not published, we have no idea as to what the probability is of preferring statistically significant results in general. Sterling seemed to suggest somewhat tentatively that negative studies (i.e. those accepting the null hypothesis) should be published as the probability of obtaining negative results is likely to be higher than that which appears in the published literature. Over 30 years later, he and some colleagues repeated his study with these same journals together with other ones and found similar results (Sterling, Rosenbaum, & Weinkam, 1995). In other words, the situation had not changed over that period.

Following Sterling's research, other researchers have documented something of the lack of null or negative findings in journals (Chan, Hróbjartsson, Haahr, Gøtzsche, & Altman, 2004; Coursol & Wagner, 1986; Easterbrook, Berlin, Gopalan, & Matthews, 1991; Reysen, 2006) which, of course, was known informally but which there had been no published evidence for. Moreover, these studies were found to be less likely to be submitted for publication (Coursol & Wagner, 1986), and once submitted were less likely to be accepted for publication (Chan et al., 2004; Coursol & Wagner, 1986; Dickersin, Min, & Meinert, 1992; Easterbrook et al., 1991). Now it is perfectly possible that null or negative findings are more likely to occur because these studies are less well-designed. Nevertheless research shows that editors are more likely to reject a paper finding statistically nonsignificant rather than statistically significant findings when the paper is otherwise identical (Atkinson, Furlong & Wampold, 1982). Thus the nonsignificance of the results can lead to a paper being rejected. Clearly, there is a case for publishing nonsignificant findings. Perhaps this should be done in an abbreviated form after the paper has been peer reviewed and evaluated as being sound. Such a procedure has been advocated (e.g. Atkinson et al., 1982; Dirnagl & Lauritzen, 2010; Smart, 1964).

14.2   Confidence intervals

Those who propose 'new' approaches to statistics in psychology promote the use of confidence intervals which have frequently been neglected in psychological research reports. Under the influence of the NHST approach, psychologists commonly use point estimates when describing their data. That is, they use a single number as their best estimate of the population parameter. So their estimate of the population mean will be given as 4.62, for example. Outsiders might find this a little odd. How can an estimate be so precise? Doesn't everyone know that samples vary from the population characteristics? Nevertheless, point estimates, in contrast, imply a high level of accuracy unrealistically and spuriously. Let us be clear, based on a sample, the point estimate is the best estimate but it is far from being the only viable estimate. The alternative would be to give a range such as 2.12 to 7.12 which reflects the amount of uncertainty we have about the actual population mean. So instead of the point estimate of 4.62 we would give a range. Cumming (2012) points out that there is nothing new about this to ordinary people. When the media claim based on a poll that support for the President is 42 per cent with a margin of error of 2 per cent, we understand that 42 per cent is the best estimate of the population's opinion within a margin of 2 per cent above and below.

In psychology, we do not normally speak in terms of margins of error but about confidence intervals instead. Confidence intervals contain twice the margin of error. In our example the margin of error is half of the difference between 7.12 and 2.12, that is, 2.5 above and below the midpoint of 4.62. The wider the confidence interval, the more uncertainty there is about the population value. The narrower the confidence interval is the less uncertainty there is. A confidence interval of 95 per cent is highly likely to include the population or true value. Many psychologists interpret this as meaning that there is a 95 per cent probability that the confidence interval includes the population or true value. This is not quite correct as we will see. Cumming (2016) describes values inside the confidence interval as the most plausible values for the true value. Confidence intervals are routinely displayed by statistics programs like SPSS in the analysis output so there is little excuse for omitting them. Of course, by including them, we reveal how big our confidence intervals are which may cause us a little embarrassment. A wide confidence interval should make us more modest in our claims.

If the spread of the confidence interval is wide, then the precision of the estimate is, of course, low. With confidence intervals it is easier to see that the findings from different studies overlap irrespective of issues of statistical significance. Confidence intervals give you a clear indication of what to expect in a replication study. That is, you have good reason to expect that the replication will produce outcomes in the range of the confidence interval from the first study. Confidence intervals make it harder to draw overly-simplistic conclusions. If we read that (based on a sample) the correlation between the number of hours of study a week and university grades at the end of the year was $r = .3$, then we might interpret this as suggesting that study is good for academic achievement. However, what if we were told that it is likely that the true correlation is somewhere between $r = -.2$ and $r = .5$? The possibility now is that the correlation could be zero and negative as well as positive. Of course, were we told that the confidence interval was between $r = .2$ and $r = .4$, then once again we would home in on the idea that study is good for academic achievement.

Can psychologists use confidence intervals effectively? Do confidence intervals improve decision-making over and above NHST? Coulson, Healey, Fidler & Cumming (2010) studied groups of experienced, published researchers. They were given information about the outcomes of one of two different studies which had similar outcomes in terms of the size of the trend in the data but in one case there was statistical significance and in the other there was not. The way this information was provided was varied. Some received NHST-oriented information which provided the size of the difference between the experimental and control group together with its statistical significance. The others received the information in the form of confidence intervals but no information about statistical significance. According to Coulson et al. (2010), interpretation overall was poor irrespective of whether NHST or confidence intervals were used. Despite the size of the effect in the studies being similar, the two studies were interpreted as having very different outcomes.

Null hypothesis testing focuses thinking on significance versus non-significance, hence the participants' belief that the studies had different outcomes. There was information about how each participant reached their conclusion from their explanations. So they could be sorted into NHST thinkers or confidence interval thinkers irrespective of which version of the information they had received. Sixty per cent of those using NHST thinking incorrectly concluded that the two fictitious studies differed. (Some participants given the confidence interval version actually explained their decision in NHST terms. If a confidence interval passes through zero, then the trend in the data is non-significant.) In contrast, 95 per cent of the researchers who explained their conclusion exclusively in terms of confidence intervals correctly concluded that the two studies did not differ. In other words, if NHST dominates one's thinking, then incorrect interpretations of studies are more likely.

But this sort of error is far from infrequent. There are other common misunderstandings (Belia, Fidler, Williams, & Cummings, 2005). In particular, researchers often fail to understand, for example, that even where two means differ significantly, then there can be considerable overlap between the confidence intervals around these means. If the confidence intervals are equally wide, an overlap of about a quarter of the size of the confidence intervals would indicate that the means differ at the .05 (5 per cent) level of statistical significance. When put to the test, researchers from a number of disciplines thought that more-or-less non-overlapping confidence intervals indicated statistical significance at the .05 or 5 per cent level (it actually reflects the 1 per cent or .01 level). Less than a fifth came up with the right answer. It is also not correct to assume that a 95 per cent confidence interval indicates that a replication has a 95 per cent probability of having its mean within the initial study's confidence interval (Cumming, Williams, & Fidler, 2004). For this to be true, then the initial study would have to have hit the population mean exactly which is not likely. (On average, the probability of the confidence interval including the mean of the next sample is about 83 per cent.) There is clearly room for improvement, as they say. Box 14.1 raises other concerns about psychologists' understanding of confidence intervals.

Box 14.1 Talking Point

Do psychologists understand the statistics they use?

Hoekstra, Morey, Rouder and Wagenmakers (2014) claimed that there is an alarming lack of understanding of confidence intervals. Psychology students and researchers were informed that the 95 per cent confidence interval for the mean was 0.1 to 0.4 for a particular fictitious study. They chose between the following options (though none are correct): (a) The probability that the true mean is greater than 0 is at least 95 per cent; (b) the probability that the true mean equals 0 is smaller than 5 per cent; (c) the null hypothesis that the true mean equals 0 is likely to be incorrect; (d) there is a 95 per cent probability that the true mean lies between 0.1 and 0.4; (e) we can be 95 per cent confident that the true mean lies between 0.1 and 0.4; and (f) if we were to repeat the experiment over and over, then 95 per cent of the time the true mean falls between 0.1 and 0.4. Only about 3 per cent of participants avoided choosing any wrong answers. Options (a), (b), (c) and (d) are incorrect because they infer that parameters and hypotheses can have probabilities.

Options (e) and (f) are incorrect because they mention the boundaries whereas confidence intervals evaluate the procedure and not a specific interval. Option (c) was the most popular choice. A correct definition is 'If you run 100 identical experiments, about 95 of the confidence intervals will include the true value you're trying to measure' (Reinhart, 2015, p. 13). In other words, for the pernickety statistician, the 95 per cent refers to the confidence interval and not to the population parameter. GraphPad (2015) wondered whether it really matters if you correctly say that 'there is a 95 per cent chance that the confidence interval you calculated contains the true population mean' rather than incorrectly say that 'there is a 95 per cent chance that the population mean lies within the interval' (home page). Whether Hoekstra et al.'s study was based on a too demanding technical criterion is an issue then. That total novice psychology students with no training in statistics did about as well as professional researchers may suggest this.

That there are questions about how well psychologists and psychology students understand confidence intervals may reflect that they are too dependent on NHST. Confidence intervals are informative in ways which significance testing was not designed to be and ought to be better employed in research. Even when the confidence interval includes zero (which means non-significance in NHST terms), the extent of the confidence interval can give you very useful additional information. So a narrow confidence interval around zero suggests that the mean, etc. has been more precisely estimated. Conversely, a wide confidence interval would imply the estimate was imprecise, thus making it hard to draw conclusions (Reinhart, 2015). Although it has been very common in the past, omitting to give confidence intervals is a disservice to everyone. There is no problem in calculating confidence intervals – they litter SPSS output, for example, so are hard to miss. Try to go beyond merely reporting them to discussing their implications for the interpretation of your research.

14.3   Effect sizes

Null hypothesis significance testing encourages the concentration on statistical significance rather than the size of the effect, difference or trend in one's data. However, surely the primary focus of the researcher should be on the question of how big the effect or trend in the data is. Blindingly obvious as this is, many research reports fail to give it the prominence it warrants. The *Publication Manual of the American Psychological Association* stresses the importance of including a measure of the *size* of the effect that has been found. If a salesperson promises you a discount on new windows for your house you naturally would want to know how big a discount in money. You wouldn't be satisfied with the assurance from the salesperson that their company offered significantly bigger discounts than other companies.

So why do psychologists often settle for statistical significance as being the only important thing? One would expect that the size of the effect would be central to any analysis and a feature of any discussion of the research findings. But discussing the implications of the effect size is rather more complex, as we shall see, than running a quick test of statistical significance and reporting the outcome. Statistical significance is drummed into the collective consciousness of psychologists to an extent to which issues like effect size are not. Quite the reason for this is not so clear – perhaps training in statistics is to blame. Whatever the reason, psychologists in the past have hyped-up the importance of NHST to the exclusion of other aspects of the analysis. Good researchers, nevertheless, take the issue of effect size seriously when reporting their research findings.

Effect size, quite simply, is the size of the difference or relationship that you find in your study, say, for example, the experimental and control group differ on average by 9.3. There are at least two meanings of effect size – one is simply a measure of the size of the effect such as the above figure of 9.3. Sometimes, effect sizes can be reported in easily understood ways and the units of measurement employed described precisely. It is easy to understand that there is a mean difference of 0.43 seconds between the experimental and control conditions because it refers to something concrete (if one can call time concrete). But writing that there is a mean difference of 2.4 on a measure of depression is not quite so instantly meaningful without knowing quite a lot about the scale and even then it can be tricky. Of course, one could add something like the mean difference of 2.4 was equivalent to a treatment group agreeing with two depression items more on the depression scale than the non-treated control group. Even this, though, remains somewhat abstract compared to being able to say something like treatment for depression reduced time off work by an average of 15 days compared to the control group.

Many of the measures used in psychology are difficult to make meaningful even within the profession because psychologists very often employ arbitrary scales which do not link directly to things in the real world (Ellis, 2010). So what would a 5-point difference between two groups on measures like the *Body Esteem Scale,* the *Current Thoughts Scale,* the *Driving Anger Scale* and the *Cognitive Failure Questionnaire* indicate? They may be reasonably valid predictors of things in real life but that only partially addresses the issue. Is it possible to convert scores on the *Driving Anger Scale* into road rage attacks, hostile and persistent horn blowing, or swearing unheard at other drivers? Difficult, isn't it? So one inhibition on discussing effect sizes rather than merely reporting them is knowing just what to write because of the arbitrariness of the measures used. Anything that can help contextualise effect sizes is welcome. For example, Ellis (2010) points out that jargon-free metrics are available including the common language effect size (McGraw & Wong, 1992) and the binomial effect size display (Rosenthal & Rubin, 1982).

The other meaning of effect size is more technical but can be easier to write about in a report. You may be aware that there are standardised ways of reporting effect sizes – maybe as many as 80. Cohen's *d* is a frequently mentioned example but another important one is the correlation coefficient which is more familiar. A standardised effect size is the size of the trend or difference adjusted for the variability in the data. Standardising measures make comparing outcomes of different studies possible even when, for example, they use different measures of the dependent variable. Standardised effect sizes now come with a built-in advantage for researchers. That is, there are generally accepted criteria for deciding whether the effect is large, medium or small. For example, Cohen (1988) suggested that for his *d* statistic (which could be used to give the effect size of a comparison between the means of two groups) a large effect would be .8, medium .5 and small .2. These labels are sort of comforting as they can be quoted when you wish to describe an effect size that you have obtained in a study. If Jacob Cohen says it's a small effect size, then it must be a small effect size! No argument. Nevertheless, things are not quite that simple as context can make a lot of difference to what we consider important, if not what we consider large. So if aspirin has only a small effect size for preventing heart attacks, then it may still be important and of practical value. We will return to this later. However, standardised versions of effect sizes are not required by the *Publication Manual* though it does point out that standardised measures are useful for meta-analyses that may be conducted at some stage by other researchers. Meta-analyses amalgamate statistically the findings of many studies on a topic. There is no excuse for omitting to discuss effect size.

14.4 Power

More than anything, statistical power addresses what is a fundamental question for any research study – what should the sample size be? A simple enough question but prone to inadequate answers such as the bigger the better. Guesstimates are not really good enough since you need to be able to justify your planned sample size on a rational basis. In this section, we will look at power especially in relation to sample size. A researcher needs to have a good idea of whether their study is capable of detecting the effects they hope to find. Is it likely that the study could find trends of substantial interest to the research community and others? Power assessment is the way of making sure that your research has the potential to substantiate your hypotheses if they are, indeed, true. Rosnow and

Rosenthal (1989) tell an amusing story of the sort of embarrassing situations than can arise if this issue is ignored:

> Consider the following example (the names have been changed to protect the guilty): Smith conducts an experiment (with $N = 80$) to show the effects of leadership style on productivity and finds that style A is better than B. Jones is skeptical (because he invented style B) and replicates (with $N = 20$). Jones reports a failure to replicate; his t was 1.06, $df = 18$, $p > .30$, whereas Smith's t had been 2.21, $df = 78$, $p < .05$. It is true that Jones did not replicate Smith's p value. However, the magnitude of the effect obtained by Jones ($r = .24$ or $d = .50$) was identical to the effect obtained by Smith. Jones had found exactly what Smith had found even though the p values of the two studies were not very close. Because of the smaller sample size of 20, Jones's power to reject the null hypothesis at .05 was .18, whereas Smith's power (N of 80) was .60 — more than three times greater.

(pp. 1277–1278)

The obvious way of avoiding such situations is to take seriously the question of what the minimum sample size should be to address your research question adequately. This is one of the important things that power analysis helps with. One could imagine Professor Jones's joy when he decided that because his replication was not significant that leadership style A was not better than style B. Unfortunately, as you will realise, this joy was misplaced and reflects a fundamental misunderstanding of null hypothesis statistical testing (NHST) as well as a failure to understand power. This is not to suggest that Professor Smith necessarily understood things any better – he merely had used a sample size big enough to detect the effect. So a non-significant test does not mean that the effect is zero. A sample may seem big enough to detect an effect but, in reality, may turn out to be way too small if a power calculation is done using a web applet, G*Power or similar.

When we first learn about inferential statistics, it should be explained to us that there are two sorts of fundamental errors. Type 1 error is a false positive in which the researcher incorrectly rejects the null hypothesis when it is in fact true. Null Hypothesis Statistical Testing is all about preventing this sort of error. It helps us avoid the situation in which we confuse random sampling contingencies for true effects. Type 2 errors are a false negative in which a hypothesis is rejected despite being true. Type 2 errors occur in the following circumstances:

- If the effect size in the population is too small.

- If the sample size is too small.

- If the level of statistical significance (alpha) is set at too small (stringent) a level.

Statistical power analysis reduces the risk of making Type 2 errors or false negatives. The most obvious way of preventing Type 2 errors is to make sure that the sample size you use is large enough to detect effects which are real most of the time. In this way, your (alternate) hypotheses have a better chance of being supported. There are no absolute safeguards against Type 2 errors but power analysis allows you to set the bar to determine what level of risk Type 2 error you are prepared to accept. This risk is called beta or β. (The risk set for Type 1 errors is known as alpha or α and is involved in Power Analysis as well as NHST.) Power is defined as $1 - \beta$.

Effect size, sample size, alpha and beta are all interrelated though not in ways which make life easy. The consequence is that power calculations are somewhat complex or impossible to be done by hand.

There are several forms of power analysis including *a priori* and *post hoc* power analysis. *A priori* implies before the data are collected. The purpose of this form of power analysis is to assess what sample size is needed to detect the likely effect size for the prospective study you are planning. This may initially seem impossible since how do you know the outcome of a study before the data are collected? The answer is that you estimate the likely effect size as best you can in a rational and justifiable way. If you can run a small pilot study, then this will give you an effect size whether or not the study is statistically significant, for example. Previous research on similar topics using, perhaps, similar measures may give you strong indications of what effect size to expect in your new study. In the absence of either of these, it is still possible to carry out a prospective power analysis. One could use standard small, medium and large effect sizes as laid down by Cohen.

The numerical values of these standard effect sizes depend on the effect size measure in question. We gave earlier the values of Cohen's *d* which are conventionally defined as large, medium and small effect sizes as being .8, .5 and .2. The corresponding figures for the correlation coefficient as a measure of effect size are .5, .3 and .2. But there are other measures of effect size which would have different values. This may help you decide whether you are prepared to devote your time and resources to the topic – you may not have the resources to do the study given the sample size involved and the importance you would otherwise place on your study.

Post hoc refers to the power actually achieved in a study. Because you have the data then what you need for the power calculation is available to you. This is less valuable than *a priori* power is. Nevertheless it might help you decide whether the study was overpowered, for instance. If you have statistically significant results, then automatically you will have sufficient power but you may find that you have been using substantially more participants than need be. One objection to *post hoc* power assessments is that it lulls one into a false sense of security. Effect sizes, like anything else, vary from sample to sample. By showing that a study has sufficient power you may be doing nothing other than capitalising on a chance finding in much the same way that NHST can produce significant results by chance. Clearly it is better to base any analysis more widely than a single study in order to understand what is going on in research.

One thing is certain, you won't want to do power analysis unaided. Fortunately, then, on the Internet you will find programs which do power calculations though some of them cost quite a lot of money. G*Power is a particularly well-established comprehensive power calculation program and benefits (us) from being free of charge. It is well documented with a substantial users' manual which can be download from the G*Power website. G*Power actually calculates five different types of power analysis if you want them all. It covers many statistical tests including correlation, regression, comparisons of pairs of means, and ANOVA. What the appropriate effect size measure is varies according to the statistical test in question but G*Power will calculate an appropriate one for you based on available statistical information. There may be other power analysis programs available where you are studying. Failing that, Cohen (1988) provided tables to help you.

So Beta (β) is the risk of falsely rejecting a hypothesis. We, of course, reject hypotheses because they are not statistically significant at the 5 per cent or .05 level of probability or smaller. Power, as we have seen, is simply $1 - \beta$. A value of .80 is widely regarded as a reasonable level of power. This means that you have an 80 per cent chance of detecting hypotheses (or trends) which are true. That is, you expect that proportion to be statistically significant. Power levels are not set in stone and you may vary them if you so wish. Lower them and you lessen the chances of obtaining statistically significant findings. So if you set the power level at .5, then you only have a fifty-fifty chance that your hypothesis will be supported if it is true. These seem unacceptably low odds given the resources that have to be put into any research study. (Of course, many studies are inadvertently unpowered because researchers use small samples without regard to power.) So why not raise your power criterion to .9 or even .95? The problem here is that by doing so you may bump up the required sample size more than you can afford or cope with. For example, if the correlation between two variables is .4 (which for a correlation coefficient is also the effect size), then with .8 as the power level and the significance level alpha set at .05 you need a minimum sample size of 47. Increase the power level to .95 and the required sample size leaps to 75.

You probably will have realised that power analysis involves matters of judgement and not just number crunching. This is because there are no rules of thumb to follow. What is the minimum size of effect that you are prepared to devote resources to? This depends probably on things like the practical and theoretical importance of the effect. How big a study is feasible given the limitations on you time-wise, economically and in other respects? A tiny effect in medical research, for example, may be worth pursuing because of the number of lives it saves. The effect size of aspirin on reducing heart attacks is very small at $r = .034$. To detect this effect requires a sample size of 6787 with .80 as the power level. One would rarely if ever see sample sizes of this order in psychology. Nevertheless, the study showed that, compared to placebo controls, taking aspirin reduced the risk of heart attack by 3 per cent (Rosnow & Rosenthal, 1989). In other words, a statistically tiny effect size may be of importance depending on context. That is, there are no absolute values which make an effect big or too small to be of interest.

Power analysis and effect sizes encourage a perspective on psychological knowledge which embraces the building of the discipline's knowledge base. They are not simply about taking individual studies in isolation and reaching a conclusion. In contrast, NHST tends to be focused on a single study. The null hypothesis is either supported or rejected. Effect sizes by their very nature encourage comparisons with other studies so that consistencies in outcomes can be identified whether or not findings are statistically significant. Building a coherent corpus of knowledge in psychology requires a broader perspective than significance testing alone stimulates. Researchers need to understand just why different studies of much the same thing produce apparently different findings.

It is a common complaint made by psychology students that research findings are inconsistent – one study says this and another study says the opposite or so it appears to them. Why should there be this sort of inconsistency? One reason is that paradoxically, psychologists persist in carrying out underpowered research (Rossi, 1997). As a result, they often fail to get statistical significance for their hypotheses, for example. Without statistical significance somewhere it is harder to get a study published in a learned journal. The data get filed away in a corner of the research office not to see the light of day again. From any perspective, this is not a good thing and it does nothing to promote understanding of a research topic. Since the studies which get published are essentially the accumulated knowledge in a field of study, it is important to understand the relationship between completed studies and what goes into professional journals. There are a number of possible ways of handling this. A researcher may choose to omit from their journal articles any discussion of hypotheses which failed. Often this is not too difficult because most studies by professional researchers involve a large number of tests of significance and so there are plenty of things to write-about anyway. As a consequence, failed tests of hypotheses do not enter the body of available knowledge.

Alternatively researchers may engage in what Kerr (1998) provocatively described as HARKing (Hypothesizing After the Results are Known) when their main hypotheses fail. That is, they look for significant relationships anywhere in the data. When they find any, the researcher generates new hypotheses to predict these outcomes chosen because they just happen to be statistically significant. These new hypotheses are written up as the focus of the study using a perspective which the researcher had not previously envisaged. Of course, these newly interpreted significant findings include those produced by sampling error. So the research literature is not just distorted, it is diluted by random 'findings'.

One study compared journal articles and postgraduate dissertations looking for evidence of this sort of distortion (Mazzola & Deuling, 2013). The idea was that postgraduate dissertations are closely supervised and students have to present their hypotheses prior to data collection, for example. Consequently, there is little opportunity for selectivity in terms of what is included in a dissertation in comparison to journal articles. The trends were very clear. There were proportionately 40 per cent more supported hypotheses in journal articles than in dissertations. Journal articles had 30 per cent fewer unsupported hypotheses. This is evidence in a process of publication selectivity favouring statistically supported hypotheses. Researchers may choose not to submit failed hypotheses for publication and journals may 'weed out' studies which report failed tests of hypotheses. One remedy for this problem is some form of pre-registration of research hypotheses by universities or journals, it has been suggested.

A reasonable assumption from the *publish or perish* research ethos is that psychologists try hard to ensure that their research has sufficient power to provide support for the hypothesis. A lack of power means that statistical significance is less likely which reduces the likelihood that a study will be published. Researchers generally believe that studies which are statistically significant are more publishable and some evidence supports this view (Atkinson et al., 1982; Coursol & Wagner, 1986; Smart, 1964; Wampold, Furlong, & Atkinson, 1983). Despite this, underpowered studies are common in psychology journals. Since the 1960s, a succession of authors have documented the paucity of statistical power in much psychological research (Bezeau & Graves, 2001; Clark-Carter, 1997; Cohen, 1962; Rossi, 1990; Sedlmeier & Gigerenzer, 1989). One exception to the rule is the field of health research possibly because funding bodies in that field require evidence of power as a condition of financing the research (Maddock & Rossi, 2001). Why is there this paradoxical lack of power in research when a sufficiently powered study is more likely to find support for a researcher's ideas?

Maxwell (2004) argued that underpowered research studies remain common because they do provide significant results – though not necessarily the ones the researcher originally thought important. Most studies in psychology involve tests of several hypotheses. In Cohen's (1962) classic study of the power of research studies, there was an average of almost 70 significance tests per study. Despite the low power to detect a particular effect, nearly all of the studies he reviewed reported significant effects. The power of a study to test a specific single effect is not the same as its power for a collection of several effects, according to Maxwell. So these things need to be considered separately. Power can be hopelessly inadequate for the study to test a specific effect of interest but the study can have a somewhat higher probability of getting a statistically significant result somewhere in the analysis. Maxwell gives the example of a 2×2 ANOVA design with a *medium* level of effect size with 10 cases per cell (a number which some have recommended for ANOVAs of this size). There are three effects, of course, which are two main effects and an interaction in Maxwell's example. For such a study, the power to demonstrate any single pre-specified effect is .35 which is unacceptably low power compared to the usual .80 power level. Despite the study being extremely underpowered in this way, the chance of having at least one significant effect is much higher at 71 per cent. Remember that the effect size for each effect was medium. Nevertheless, with 10 participants per cell the probability of all three effects being statistically significant is only 4 per cent. That is, there is a 96 per cent probability of making at least one Type 2 error (falsely rejecting the hypothesis) in this study. Satisfactory power to find all of the effects for this example would require 48 cases per cell – 192 cases in all.

If we forget the numbers for now, the bottom line is that underpowered studies can still produce statistically significant findings. Just which of the findings are statistically significant and which are not may be haphazard. Small samples are much more unstable than large samples so studies with small samples will be more prone to sampling error. This adds to the haphazard nature of the outcome of a study. Yet such studies have regularly contributed to the body of knowledge which is psychology. Hardly a situation to build confidence in the research literature.

Another consequence of underpowered studies is *magnitude error.* Imagine that in reality there is an effect, say, studying statistics makes you brainier. The research topic is novel so no previous research exists to help you judge the likely effect size. Since they vary more (i.e.

are less stable), small samples will show big effects from time to time. This is the case irrespective of the true effect size. Oblivious to the fact that your study lacks power, you carry out your research and by chance you just happen to have picked a sample which is extreme enough to reach statistical significance. You get excited and submit your study to one of the most prestigious journals who are equally excited and publish your research. People sit up and take notice, since after all studying statistics makes you brainier. The size of the effect has been inflated because of the lack of power built into your study. Intrigued by your findings and the sizeable effect found, other researchers try to replicate your published study. However, the effects they obtain are somewhat smaller and, consequently, less interesting than yours. Often the earliest research on a topic shows substantial effects but later replications much more modest ones. Magnitude error may partly explain this.

The Mozart Effect seems to be a good example of this sort of process. It was claimed that listening to Mozart's *Sonata for Two Pianos in D Major* for eight minutes increased scores on spatial reasoning subscales of the Stanford Binet Intelligence Scale by 8 to 9 IQ points compared to listening to nothing or a relaxation tape (Rauscher, Shaw & Ky, 1993; Rauscher, Shaw, Levine, Wright, Dennis, & Newcomb 1997). The dramatic findings of the study were first reported in the prestigious journal *Nature*. There was a rush to put the findings of the study into practice. The effect size of the original research was a Cohen's d of 0.72 which approaches the 'recommended' size of a large effect. Don't overlook the fact that effect sizes are subject to sampling fluctuations as is any statistic. Pietschnig, Voracek and Formann (2010) reviewed a total of 39 published and unpublished studies into the Mozart Effect. Overall, the effect size was quite small ($d = .37$) for comparisons with control conditions which is much smaller than for the original study and is even smaller if the studies by the original researcher Rauscher and her affiliates are omitted.

One obvious question is whether other forms of music are as effective as Mozart's sonata. The answer from Pietschnig et al.'s study was that studies which involved some other musical pieces produced similar effect sizes as Mozart (.38). However, comparing other forms of musical stimulus to control groups yielded a similar effect size (.38) implying that there is no specific Mozart Effect distinct from the effect of other forms of music. Publication bias was also evident in that published research showed larger effects than unpublished research. Pietschnig et al. (2010) concluded, 'The large effect demonstrated in the initial publication faded away as more research was done on this subject' (p. 323).

14.5 Replication Crisis

One of the bugbears of psychological research for any student is what they perceive as the inconsistency of research findings. Sometimes two studies of ostensibly much the same topic literally produce opposite findings, sometimes one of the studies will show statistical significance, whereas the other does not but sometimes both studies show similar trends. One might expect that the latter to be the most common but this may not be the case, as we shall see in a moment. A study which is essentially a repeat of an earlier study is known as a replication study. The question is whether the second study replicates the findings of the first study.

Leaving aside the issue of just what a replication consists of, it is worth noting that there are a number of reasons why replication studies fail. The two studies may differ in important respects which may account for the different findings. Reports of studies frequently lack the detail to make a precise replication possible. There is evidence, also, that there is selectivity in the publication system which means that studies with significant results are more likely to be published as are the studies with the more significant findings. An attempt to replicate a published study has a good chance of not demonstrating the same significance level. Furthermore, the findings of the original study may be a false positive or the findings of the replication study a false negative.

Many psychologists are aware of the replicability issue in their discipline (as are researchers in other fields). One good thing is that psychologists are beginning to address the issue of replicability seriously. The Open Science Collaboration (2015) reported the findings of 100 replication attempts in order to estimate the reproducibility (replicability) of the findings of psychological research. The replication studies were conducted by volunteer researchers though their work was monitored and reviewed by the original authors of the research and by staff members of the Open Science Collaboration. In this way, the fidelity of the replication study to the original study was maximised. The studies replicated were limited to the year 2008 and the following prestigious journals: *Psychological Science, Journal of Personality and Social Psychology,* and *Journal of Experimental Psychology: Learning, Memory and Cognition.*

Overall, the research provided a variety of evidence to suggest the relatively low levels of replicability of the findings of studies. For example, only 35 per cent of the replication studies achieved statistical significance at the .05 level though 97 per cent of the original studies had reached this level of significance. This constitutes one measure of replicability. Another is the extent to which the size of the effect (i.e. trend or difference or relationship) is the same for the original and the replication study. The average size of the effect in the original papers was .40 (expressed as a correlation coefficient r) whereas that of the replication studies was .20. This is a big difference in the size of the effects. The researchers also used subjective judgements to assess replicability. Only 39 per cent of the replication studies were subjectively judged to replicate the findings of the original study.

To suggest that replication studies are essential to the progress of a discipline like psychology is correct though somewhat mundane. One could argue that a replication study should be part of the analysis of any study before it is published. Despite recognising their importance, psychologists generally do not relish doing such studies – no kudos is to be had. Also replication studies have a reputation for being hard to get published. So there has been a disincentive to do replication work in general. This cannot be a satisfactory situation. Things may be changing following a number of high profile failures to replicate. Among the most informative case studies we could discuss is Daryl Bem's precognition study (Bem, 2011). Bem's credentials as a respected social psychologist are excellent yet he stirred up the psychology community with his research which provided evidence for the phenomenon of precognition. This is the idea that events which will take place in the future influence the past. If this is true, then psychic abilities transcend time and allow the future to change the past (Frazier, 2013).

One of Bem's studies concerned retroactive facilitation of recall. Participants saw a list of words presented serially which they had to type into a computer in an unexpected recall test. When this was over, Bem had the computer randomly select half of the words and show them back to the participants. This exposure to the random selection of words appeared to influence their recall on the earlier recall test – they remembered more of the words that they were shown randomly again in the future! Had Bem just carried out a single study then one might think that Type 1 error was the explanation. But he did nine studies which were published in the one article. Furthermore, the work was published by a prestigious American Psychological Association journal (the *Journal of Personality and Social Psychology*) and not in some fringe parapsychology journal. Unless you believe in parapsychology, Bem's findings are hard to swallow. As might be expected, psychologists lined up in depth to pooh-pooh Bem's findings and to criticise the methods that he had used (e.g. Alcock, 2011; LeBel & Peters, 2011; Yarkoni, 2011).

No matter how convincing these critiques were, the acid test of Bem's effects would be replication studies. What was needed was precise, as-close-as-possible replications which leave no wriggle room for claims that the replication was flawed somehow. A number of researchers attempted replications of this high profile study. The journal that published Bem's article refused to consider for publication failures to replicate Bem's findings thus stoking up more controversy. For example, in Britain, Ritchie, Wiseman and French (2012) carried out three separate replications in different laboratories of the retroactive facilitation of recall study but could not replicate the original findings. The journal would not publish their replications either and held fast no matter the arguments Ritchie et al.

made. They tried submitting to a British journal but the paper was rejected on the grounds that the findings merely reflected an experimenter effect – which, of course, misses the point of the replication. Finally in late 2012 the original journal had a change of heart and published replications of Bem's studies in an article by Galak, LeBoeuf, Nelson & Simmons (2012). They reported that the effect size of the 19 known replication studies yielded an overall effect size which was no different from zero.

Replication by the original research team is common practice in some areas of psychology such as cognitive psychology where the most prestigious journals expect the research team to have carried out a replication study themselves (Roediger, 2012). However, research is constrained by resources and so self-replication may not be feasible. Obviously, self-replication is insufficient in the longer term as evidence of the robustness of the effect. A major obstacle to replication studies is the rewards-cost ratio. Generally speaking, replicating the studies of others is not the most glamorous of research activities and not good for career progression given the publication bias against them. With something as controversial as the Bem studies or where the study is of major importance for other reasons, there is potentially some kudos in a replication study. But for more run-of-the-mill work replication is far less likely. More common is a constructive replication which introduces variations on the basic research procedure. These are much more likely to be published and are less likely to invoke impressions of a mediocre researcher with no good ideas of their own.

Replication is universally held to be important in quantitative research so what can be done to encourage better replication studies? It is fairly obvious that journals are a major part of the gatekeeping process so initiatives from them are essential. The solution adopted as an experiment by the *Journal of Research in Personality* (2015) was simply to actively encourage the submission of top quality replication studies of studies published in the previous five years in the journal. Replication studies add important information to cumulative knowledge in a field and consequently better generalisation. Of course, weak replications are of no interest to any journal. Good replications are those which exhibit high statistical power. We have already seen how low statistical power in a replication can lead to misleading claims of a failure to replicate. The journal's editors also warned that effect sizes for replications are likely to be smaller than those of the original study because of publication biases. So the replication may well need larger sample sizes than the original study. In addition, the journal stipulated that the confidence intervals for the effect size should be included and compared with those from the original study. All of this, of course, is good advice for any researcher planning a replication study. The journal editor indicated that the peer review process for replications would be based solely on whether the study had been competently carried out. Criteria such as originality are clearly inappropriate for exact replication studies.

14.6   Questionable research practices and truth inflation

Psychological research has shown that listening to Beatles records can make you younger (Simmons, Nelson, & Simonsohn, 2011). Not just feeling younger, but younger by over a year on average, in fact. You want the proof? Here is the relevant information from the original paper:

> . . . we asked 20 University of Pennsylvania undergraduates to listen to either 'When I'm Sixty-Four' by The Beatles or 'Kalimba' [a free tune on the Windows 7 operating system]. Then, in an ostensibly unrelated task, they indicated their birth date (mm/dd/yyyy) and their father's age. We used father's age to control for variation in baseline age across participants.

An ANCOVA revealed the predicted effect: According to their birth dates, people were nearly a year-and-a-half younger after listening to 'When I'm Sixty-Four' (adjusted

$M = 20.1$ years) rather than to 'Kalimba' (adjusted $M = 21.5$ years), $F(1,17) = 4.92$, $p = .040$.

(p. 1360)

It is not surprising if you read this with incredulity, but it is what the article in a highly respected journal stated. Of course, it is impossible to affect a person's age by playing them a Beatles record – even 'When I'm Sixty-Four'. You are quite right that, literally, there is more to things than meets the eye, but just how could the researchers obtain such findings? No, they did not fabricate their data as such and they did not simply capitalise on a chance research finding. We all know that it is possible to get some false positives by chance (the 5 per cent significance level means just that), but the explanation is not really quite that simple, either. What the researchers did was to employ what is termed 'researchers' degrees of freedom'. That is, they employed procedures which no research methods textbook would recommend or even suggest but which are fairly commonplace in psychology.

For example, take the question of just how many participants should there be in each condition of a research study. Often the researcher does not know, as it depends on so many factors such as the size of the effect in question – smaller effects require bigger sample sizes and vice versa. So sometimes, as a way around this problem, researchers analyse their data on a serial basis as new participants are run. They then stop running extra participants when statistical significance is reached or even ignore the data from additional participants. They do not regard this as cheating but as a way of optimising their work in trying to establish the truth of their hypothesis. They also do other things such as failing to mention other conditions of the study which unfortunately undermine support for their hypothesis. Furthermore, by controlling for some additional variables, they may find that some trends become significant and thus they feel it desirable to report these but ignore those which fail to produce significant trends.

The authors provide a more informative (perhaps honest is the word) version of the data analysis. This more complete version includes many of the aspects of the study which were omitted from the version reproduced above:

. . . we asked 34 University of Pennsylvania undergraduates to listen only to either 'When I'm Sixty-Four' by The Beatles or 'Kalimba' or 'Hot Potato' by the Wiggles. We conducted our analyses after every session of approximately 10 participants; we did not decide in advance when to terminate data collection. Then, in an ostensibly unrelated task, the participants indicated only their birth date (mm/dd/yyyy) and how old they felt, how much they would enjoy eating at a diner, the square root of 100, their agreement with 'computers are complicated machines', their father's age, their mother's age, whether they would take advantage of an early-bird special, their political orientation, which of four Canadian quarterbacks they believed won an award, how often they refer to the past as 'the good old days', and their gender. We used father's age to control for variation in baseline age across participants.

(p. 1364)

An ANCOVA revealed the predicted effect: According to their birth dates, people were nearly a year-and-a-half younger after listening to 'When I'm Sixty-Four' (adjusted) rather than to 'Kalimba' (adjusted $M = 21.5$ years), $F(1, 17) = 4.92, p = .040$. Without controlling for father's age, the age difference was smaller and did not reach significance ($M = 20.3$ and 21.2, respectively), $F(1, 18) = 1.01, p = .33$.

(p. 1364)

Most, if not all, is revealed in this more honest version. Even if things are not directly stated, this version is far more transparent to other researchers about what actually went on in the study and its analysis. Notice that the number of participants changes between the two accounts which is because the smaller number of participants generated the significant findings and not the larger one. One thing that is revealed is that the findings were not statistically significant unless father's age was controlled for. Another is that there were several other control variables which would have been controlled for in the analysis of covariance (ANCOVA) but were not reported in the paper because they did not help yield statistically significant findings. The 5 per cent level of significance is used in research precisely because it keeps false positive findings (i.e. finding a difference which does not exist in reality) to a reasonable minimum of 5 per cent. In the present context, however, the 5 per cent level cannot be claimed to represent the likelihood of a false positive, though its use is like a gold standard which helps enormously the acceptance of a study for publication in a journal.

Simmons and colleagues are not cheats but concocted their study to make an important point about false-positive research findings – that they are much more common than might be assumed. The researchers went on to conduct computer simulations to investigate just how far it would be possible to encourage false-positive findings using 'researchers' degrees of freedom'. These are procedures which researchers employ which can affect the apparent outcome of a study – we will discuss them in a moment. We won't go into detail here, but by combining a number of 'researchers' degrees of freedom' they achieved a false-positive rate of 61 per cent rather than the 5 per cent rate that would follow from proper adherence to sound statistical and methodological principles. And there is clear evidence, which they cite, that a substantial number of researchers deliberately or inadvertently use various 'researchers' degrees of freedom' procedures. The extent to which their use is responsible for the high percentage of studies which report positive findings in psychology is not known but the potential is there.

They are not cheating as such but there are questionable research practices which may systematically distort the research literature. They probably result in 'truth inflation' which results in published research showing something other than what is the ground truth reality. As we have seen, the journal system itself tends to favour significant findings of a larger magnitude. Evidence suggests that psychologists do things which no textbook or lecturer would dare recommend. John, Loewenstein and Prelec (2012) conducted a large e-mail-based survey into some of these practices. Examples of such questionable research practices (QRP) together with an estimate of the percentage admitting doing them include:

- Deciding whether to collect more data after looking to see whether the results were significant (56%).

- In a paper, selectively reporting studies that 'worked' (46%).

- Making the decision not to include some data after checking the effect of this on the results (32%).

- In a paper, reporting an unexpected finding as having been predicted from the start (27%).

- In a paper, 'rounding of' a p-value (e.g., reporting that a p-value of .054 is statistically significant (22%).

- Stopping collecting data earlier than planned because the result that one had been looking for had been found (16%).

- In a paper, failing to report all of a study's dependent measures (63%).

- In a paper, failing to report all of a study's conditions (28%).

Those admitting any of these things felt that their actions were defensible. There are grey areas, of course. For example, excluding some data after checking the effect of this on the outcome. Excluding outliers is generally accepted as legitimate – if carried out correctly and openly. Outliers are exceptionally large or small data points which are out of keeping with the general run of the data. A single outlier is capable of distorting trends considerably. So it is quite reasonable to be on the look-out for outliers. But this is not *carte blanche* to remove or exclude any of the data simply because it is inconvenient and obstructs achieving statistical significance. A good reason is needed for doing so. One way of addressing the outlier issue is to trim off the extreme 5 per cent, say, of the scores on the variables. Then see whether the analysis for the trimmed data differs from that of the full data. If it does, then you have evidence that outliers are having an effect. However, the criteria by which researchers remove outliers vary quite considerably – Simmons et al. (2011) noted that for reaction time experiments outliers have been defined variously as the extreme 2.5 per cent, more than two standard deviations from the mean, or faster than anything from 100 to 300 milliseconds in a selection of articles. These differences in definition may affect the outcome of the study.

Another conceivable defence of some of the dubious practices might be that by omitting to mention a dependent variable or condition in a study the researcher can write another publication based on the left-over material. In general, though, there is not too much that can be offered to justify these questionable practices. A common consequence of employing questionable research practices is that significance levels are bumped up in various ways. Sometimes this may happen because of the extra opportunities that the researcher gives for statistical significance to occur. In other cases, it may be that non-supportive-of-the-hypothesis findings are essentially suppressed. John et al. (2012) draw an interesting analogy for questionable research practices (QRPs):

> QRPs are the steroids of scientific competition, artificially enhancing performance and producing a kind of arms race in which researchers who strictly play by the rules are at a competitive disadvantage. QRPs, by nature of the very fact that they are often questionable as opposed to blatantly improper, also offer considerable latitude for rationalization and self-deception.

(p. 524)

Some questionable research practices seem almost normative within the research community and adopted because 'everyone uses them'. Unfortunately, the outcome is just the same – the psychology knowledge base becomes chaotic and incoherent as a consequence of the distortions which questionable research practices introduce. This is particularly relevant when considering Box 14.2 and recent developments in big data and data mining.

Box 14.2   Key Idea

Big data and data mining

The world is awash with data. Almost everywhere we turn somebody wants to collect data from us. Data is big business and the social media like Facebook and Twitter, for example, generate masses of new data provided by us. Similarly smartphones can provide data about us in huge amounts, including things like our daily number of steps, GPS position, and masses of text. The internet proclaims that 2,500,000,000,000,000,000 bytes of information are produced every day. A lot by anyone's standards! These bounteous quantities of data are described as 'big data'. The size of the data sets and the highly varied nature of the data available make statistical analysis somewhat difficult using the traditional statistics taught to psychology students. In order to handle the demands of big data, new statistical techniques

→

have been developed with fresh approaches to data analysis which are generally referred to as data mining. Put simply, data mining is about finding patterns in data which can be put to practical use. It is usually described as being led by the data without the researcher suggesting hypotheses, for example. One might ask in what way is this different from when psychologists try to identify patterns in their data? Things get a little vague at this point since it is possible to do data mining with traditional statistical techniques but, often, desirable to employ newer approaches which can achieve much more. So data mining can use techniques like those taught on psychology degrees though sometimes with useful modifications. Data mining was not a response to the needs of psychological researchers but more to do with the problems of handling big data. No precise definition demarcates what amount of data make it big data. But it can be so big that a typical workstation computer has insufficient processing power. It is not necessary to use a big data set in its entirety, sometimes much smaller data sets are extracted from big data. These may be much like the typical data set used in psychological research. Although psychology is not a primary driver of big data, Harlow and Oswald (2016) suggest that areas of psychological research such as mental health, workplace well-being, and substance abuse are ripe for big data research.

Now, most psychology students will be used to psychological data being collected in a very neat fashion which will fit readily into a spreadsheet like the SPSS Data View. That is, a single entry in each cell of a spreadsheet in which there are numerous columns (or rows) for separately measured variables and numerous rows (or columns) for each case or participant. Although these spreadsheets may look formidable, they are nothing compared to big data. Big data is being continuously produced so a spreadsheet would probably need a time dimension as well as variables and cases. Indeed, what big data appears to offer is large numbers of participants, large numbers of variables, and large numbers of data collection points in time which could transform how some psychological research is done (Adjerid & Kelley, 2018). In addition, big data offers many different types of variables.

The problem is threefold or worse: a) massive amounts of data cannot always be processed by a single computer, b) the data is far from neat and tidy and includes strings of texts and other things which mostly we would not recognise as data, and c) the data is hard to get one's hands on. As a consequence, a) big data analysis needs technical people knowledgeable about how to get numerous computers to work together on an analysis, b) you are going to spend an awful lot of time preparing the data for analysis, and c) you would need to negotiate to obtain access to these data sets which may prove to be rather difficult. You could resort to data scraping from websites.

Finding big data

Data scraping, or web scraping, is simply using a program which copies human readable or textual information from websites – for example, price comparison sites do this. It is possible to use Microsoft Excel for this but you would probably find a dedicated data scraping program advantageous in the long run. One notable thing about web scraping is that the data retrieved is people's actual behaviours – that is, they may have posted sexist material on Facebook, for example (Landers, Brusso, Cavanaugh, & Collmus, 2016). Landers et al. mention that web scraping can be directed by theoretical interests and that it does not have to involve the collection of massive data sets. There is also the possibility of running experiments on big data platforms though this requires cooperation from the platform owner and, inevitably, raises ethical and privacy issues (Adjerid & Kelley, 2018). An example of the sort of research for which data mining has proven valuable is the investigations of the impact of traumatic events such as campus shootings in the USA on people in the locality. A data scraping exercise on Twitter accounts, for example, has revealed an increase in the expression of negative emotions in Twitter postings (Jones, Wojcik, Sweeting, & Silver, 2016). HTML does not simply use codes but deals with meaning at a certain level. As a consequence, it is not necessary to have humans coding HTML as it is machine readable. Parsing in this context refers to the computer analysis of textual data into its component parts and their syntactical relationships. This can include semantic information. You will probably, by now, be beginning to get the impression that you would need quite a lot of expert help with each of these things. Actually you should be thinking of working as part of a team, members of which have different specialisms in the field. You should assume that quite a lot of your time involved with data mining would be spent on preliminaries like negotiating access to the data, cleaning up variables, and file transfers. How long is difficult to say. How long, for example, do you think that it would take to obtain data from a social media company? That is assuming that you have any luck in getting them to agree. Also, bear in mind that any expert help you seek is likely to be expensive. Data mining is frequently done for commercial decision-making reasons where expense may not be the top priority but a commercial return is.

What is different?

Perhaps the biggest difference between the familiar, traditional psychological data analysis and data mining is that the former is theory and hypothesis led and the latter is driven by the data. By data driven we mean that the analytic priorities are determined by what is happening in the data in question. So data mining prioritises the data rather than what the researcher hypothesises, hopes, predicts or expects might be shown by the data. The traditional approach is not really interested in patterns which it does not seek. Furthermore, it sets clear limits on the range of variables which it employs by demarcating a narrow range of variables believed to be relevant to the researcher's expectations. Data mining is not hidebound in this way. Given that data mining is used in some very different contexts from those of traditional research, it is perhaps not surprising that data mining eschews some very basic principles that psychology students learn. The commercial use of data mining by companies to help them target types of customers, for example, probably prioritises data mining's pragmatic agenda. So what works is what is important. This means that even where familiar statistics are used in data mining, there is sometimes little regard to the underlying classical statistical theory like the appropriateness of the data to the statistical method. The statistical technique either produces helpful outcomes or another one is tried. Some researchers claim that there are two distinct cultures in statistical analysis corresponding to the traditional and data mining ethoses (Cheung & Jak, 2018). Get one thing clear, data mining is not the same thing as data dredging which is all about taking advantage of chance findings and hiding the fact that you have done so (Norman, 2014). Such a strategy would be counterproductive in data mining as your findings, for example, would lead to hapless commercial decisions.

Another issue is frequently dealt with in a somewhat pragmatic way. That is, what confidence can be placed in the data mining analysis? This topic is often dealt with in regular psychological analyses by references to statistical significance and the like. Regrettably, the replication of the findings is left to other researchers. Data mining often takes advantage of the large amounts of data available to the analyst by splitting the data into parts to provide what is called a hold-out sample or having an alternative data set available. These alternative data sets then provide a means of testing the original findings. In a sense this is possibly superior to what typically happens in psychology. The sample on which the statistical model is developed is often called the training data and the sample on which the data is tested is the testing data.

There are a lot of data mining programs available. These include commercial packages but there are also free ones which may appeal to students and academics. A good example is R from the R Foundation which may be familiar to you. An important commercial offering is SPSS Modeller produced by IBM. Every psychologist and student will know

the SPSS statistical package. Modeller is separate but related. But these are just two of a wide variety of free and commercial packages. Brown (2014) lists a good few more. Ideally they should facilitate the use of large amounts of data, show flexibility in terms of manipulating the variables into a useful form for the analysis, allow high quality graphical representations of the analysis, allow a wide range of statistical techniques, and retain a 'map' of the steps taken by the analyst in the course of the analysis. The last thing is especially important given the exploratory nature of much of the analysis and the need to keep a record of what was done. A lot of time can be spent in data mining on optimising the variables for the analysis. For example, there is a good case for normalising each variable statistically. Also data mining involves routine procedures for spotting and removing 'outliers' (impossible or unique data points which risk distorting the analysis). The data mining program should also make light work of importing data files of all types.

The outcome of data mining is usually described in terms of models. This sounds rather grand but it is simply an equation linking two or more variables together. So height $\rightarrow$ weight is a model which suggests that height is related to weight. A better model for weight might be height + girth $\rightarrow$ weight. In other words, there is nothing complicated about the idea of a model though, of course, sometimes models may be very complex. The way in which models are expressed depends somewhat on the nature of the statistical analysis which generated the model.

What are the data analysis methods available for the analysis of big data? This is impossible to deal with comprehensively here but we can give a few indications. Truly big data really calls for computerised methods which are essentially automated. This is very different from the standard statistical methods familiar to most psychologists. However, big data methods may generate automated small data sets very much like the typical psychology data set in size. This means that regular statistical techniques for exploring data may be appropriate such as correlation matrices and multiple regression. Remember though that data mining is primarily about exploring data for relationships and not using data to test hypotheses. Chen and Wojcik (2016) describe many big data and data mining analytic techniques and list resources to help carry them out. There are good reasons why traditional statistical techniques are not always helpful with big data (Cheung & Jak, 2018). For example, traditional statistical analyses based on statistical significance may identify weak predictors as important when applied to big data. Newer statistical techniques may be required to permit the analysis of big data on the typical computer found at researchers' workstations. The textual nature of

→

many big data sets means that text analytic approaches may be essential. These are used in many disciplines where text is the focus. Such analyses may simply be counts of the frequencies with which words of interest occur. The researcher defines what these are. A rather different approach is to use programs which seek to identify key differences between, say, two different sorts of text. For example, do certain words differentiate the text produced by 'suicide attempters' from that of 'suicide threateners'? At another pole, data mining can employ machine learning methods in a number of ways. For example, multiple regression could be used to develop models predictive of a particular stipulated variable. One problem is that with the large number of variables inherent in much big data, a prohibitive amount of computer power and time is needed. Big data contains many variables, many of which may not be particularly helpful so techniques are employed to help manage these. There are various approaches to achieving this which go under the name of regularised regression. These tend to minimise the regression weights or sometimes make them zero. It can be done by squaring the regression weights then normalising the outcomes. The important thing is that this is efficient in terms of computing power and produces models with a few strong predictors. Clustering of variables using cluster analysis is another possibility but also finding clusters of people on the basis of their patterns across variables offers distinct advantages.

As yet, big data and data mining have only made a modest contribution to psychology and you will not find research based on them in textbooks. However, much big data is about things which are basically psychological in nature so we can expect its impact to expand. The problem is that both big data and data mining require computational and statistical expertise beyond most psychological training. The need for multidisciplinary teams capable of integrating psychology, computing and statistics at an advanced level is patently clear.

14.7 Conclusion

What most clearly emerges from this chapter is that there is rather more to research than working out an appropriate design, running the study and testing the data for statistical significance. There are seemingly small decisions to take which may substantially affect outcomes and findings. They include things like whether more data should be collected, what control variables should be involved, should measures be combined or transformed, and which conditions ought to be compared and which combined. Decisions like these are rarely made prior to data collection and often psychologists use the data in ways which lead to statistical significance. Outcomes of these processes which worked are written-up and those which did not work are conveniently neglected. These have been referred to as the researcher degrees of freedom and include things like simply deciding when enough data has been collected. Simply running a study until statistical significance is found increases the likelihood of publication but it merely capitalises on chance.

Much of what is discussed in this chapter involves taking a harder and more honest look at one's own study and data. Simple things like examining the confidence intervals and effect sizes can make a big difference to how data are interpreted. Getting the sample size right helps ensure that you get the statistically significant findings that you want rather than random ones. It is not a good strategy to cherry pick the best bits of the data in the hope that this convinces reviewers that the study should be published. Publication pressures on researchers are continuous and career-long. Universities and other institutions are rewarded for having productive researchers and have appraisal systems to make sure that quality research is produced in quantity. Not surprisingly, then, researchers do the things which get their work published. They are not fabricating data but 'encouraging' statistical significance and describing their research in the best possible light. Non-significant findings are much harder to get published and, consequently, statistical significance is in the forefront of researchers' minds. By avoiding the bad practices and misunderstandings highlighted in this chapter, researchers can contribute to the creation of a more coherent and, consequently, more meaningful body of psychological research findings.

Research Example

Is a statistically significant result seen as more publishable?

Atkinson, D. R., Furlong, M. J., & Wampold, B. E. (1982). Statistical significance, reviewer evaluations, and the scientific process: Is there a (statistically) significant relationship? *Journal of Counseling Psychology, 29*, 189–194.

Most journal articles report statistically significant findings. Maybe studies which do not find statistically significant results are less interesting both to the researcher and to others because we feel that they do not tell us anything useful. But that's not necessarily the case. We would most probably not carry out a study we were planning to do if we knew from previous published research that it had already been done and that it had not 'worked' in the sense of failing to show a significant result. If it had worked, it would have been more likely to have been published. But this would not necessarily be much more helpful to us if other researchers had carried out the same or similar study, found that it had not worked and either did not try to publish it or could not get it published. We would then be left with a misleading impression of how easy it would be to obtain that result. But yet some null or negative findings are of theoretical and/or practical interest and so do deserve to be published. For example, knowing that relaxation training has not been shown to be necessary for getting rid of phobias is practically helpful in that it suggests we do not have to spend time learning or teaching it. It is also theoretically helpful in that it casts doubt on the idea that relaxation can be used to inhibit anxiety, an idea known as reciprocal inhibition. So, knowing that there is no evidence for a particular idea is useful and the only way we can be aware of that is if that knowledge is made public.

While we realise that journals are less likely to publish null or negative findings, we do not know if this is because the findings are non-significant or because of some other reason such as the design being judged to be less sound or the writing to be less clear. The study described below was conducted to see whether if you hold all such factors constant, editors are more likely to recommend rejecting a paper having statistically nonsignificant findings than statistically significant ones. In other words, it was carried out to see if editors were biased against publishing studies with non-significant results. Holding everything else constant apart from statistical significance can only be done by carrying out a true or randomised experiment which this is. One cannot help wondering if this study would have been published had it not demonstrated an effect and how replicable this effect is.

Background

There is evidence to suggest that most papers in at least some psychology journals show statistically significant results and that papers reporting statistically significant findings are evaluated more positively than papers reporting non-significant results. However, it is not known whether papers which report non-significant findings are more likely to be recommended for rejection than papers which report significant findings because these papers will differ in numerous other ways. For instance, it is possible that papers reporting non-significant findings have less adequate designs and that this is why they are less likely to be accepted than papers reporting significant findings.

Hypotheses

There were two main hypotheses. One hypothesis was that a research design reporting a statistically significant result would be judged by journal editors as being more adequate than a research design reporting either a statistically non-significant finding or a finding approaching non-significance. The other hypothesis was that a paper reporting a statistically significant outcome would be judged by journal editors as being more publishable than a research design reporting either a statistically non-significant finding or a finding approaching non-significance.

→

Method

Participants

A sample of 101 consulting editors from one clinical and one counselling journal were asked to take part in a study of the manuscript reviewing process. After an initial and a follow-up letter, usable replies were obtained from 50 editors, giving a 49.5 per cent response rate.

Procedure

The cover letter and rating form were the same for both journals apart from the journal name being made appropriate to the journal. Also included was the same 10-page manuscript written according to APA requirements but without a Discussion section. The Discussion was omitted because it would have had to vary for the three conditions which may have confounded the manipulation of the report of statistical significance.

The main difference in the manuscript was the final part of the concluding sentence of the Results section which varied for the three conditions. The sentence was:

1. 'The ethnicity by distance interaction, however, was found to be significant at the .01 level ($F_{4,72} = 3.65, p < .01$)' for the statistically significant condition;

2. 'The ethnicity by distance interaction, however, was found to approach significance ($F_{4,72} = 2.17, p < .10$)' for the approaching statistically significant condition; and

3. 'The ethnicity by distance interaction was also found to be non-significant ($F_{4,72} = 1,41, p < .25$)' for the statistically non-significant condition.

Editors within each journal were randomly assigned to one of the three conditions.

Editors were asked to rate: (1) the rationale of the study; (2) the clarity of the presentation; (3) the quality of the design; and (4) the appropriateness of the analysis as being either (1) poor; (2) marginal; (3) adequate or (4) excellent. They also had to recommend accepting or rejecting the manuscript for publication.

Results

The number of returned forms for the non-significant, approaching significance and significant conditions was 14, 19 and 17, respectively although it was not stated how many of the three manuscripts were sent out. However, it would appear from the figures reported that the return rate was roughly comparable. The second hypothesis was tested with a 2 (accept/reject) $\times$ 3 (conditions) chi-square which was statistically significant ($p < .0146$). The percentage of editors recommending accepting the paper was 43, 37 and 82 for the non-significant, approach significance and significant conditions respectively. In other words, the manuscript reporting a non-significant or approaching significance finding was about three times (61 per cent) as likely to be rejected than the one reporting a significant finding (18 per cent).

The authors, however, actually wrote 'The manuscript was more than three times as likely to receive a rejection recommendation when it reported statistically significant findings' (p. 192). The last part of this sentence is clearly a mistake, which is easily made. They presumably meant to say something like 'The manuscript was more than three times as likely to receive a rejection recommendation when it *did not report* statistically significant findings'. Note that the size of the ratio of these two percentages depends on which way the results are reported. If we described this ratio in terms of recommending acceptance of the paper, then we would need to say something like 'The manuscript reporting a significant finding was about twice (82 per cent) as likely to be accepted than one reporting a non-significant or approaching significance finding (39 per cent)' which is a smaller ratio.

The hypothesised difference in the rating of quality of design was tested with two orthogonal (i.e. independent) planned contrasts using unrelated t tests. The mean rating of the statistically significant condition ($M = 3.06$, corresponding to the rating of 'adequate') was significantly higher than that of the combined mean rating for the non-significant condition ($M = 2.36$, corresponding more to the 'marginal' than the 'adequate' rating) and the approaching significance condition ($M = 2.33$, also closer to a 'marginal' than an 'adequate' rating), $t(44) = 2.94, p < .005$. The mean rating of the non-significant and of the approaching significance conditions did not differ significantly from each other, $t(44) = 0.09$, $p < .25$. The three other ratings, which were not predicted to differ significantly between the three conditions, did not differ significantly between them using one-way analysis of variance F tests.

Authors' suggestions for further research

The authors mentioned several limitations to their study such as the paper not containing a Discussion section and not necessarily being in the area of expertise of the editors. Limitations such as these could form the basis for further studies on this issue.

Key points

- Inadequacies in the way researchers approach their data can be summarised in terms of overemphasis on null hypothesis statistical testing, the failure to focus on effect size, the absence of confidence intervals and the lack of consideration of whether the study has sufficient power to support true hypotheses. Most of these are easily rectified by the researcher.

- Replication studies are a particularly problematic area for several reasons. Precise replications are rare for the vast majority of new research findings. The success or failure of a replication study should be judged in terms of the similarity of its effect size with that of the original study. That a replication is non-significant does not, in itself, indicate a failure to replicate as the replication study may not have sufficient power.

- There are a number of practices adopted by researchers from time-to-time which may contribute to inflating the apparent statistical significance of findings or to making them statistically significant when in reality there is no effect. These are possible because of researcher degrees of freedom which is a phrase to describe the ways in which the researcher is free to make choices in the data analysis which impinge on the outcome of the analysis although these choices are unlikely to be mentioned in the journal article.

ACTIVITIES

1. Select an individual study that interests you. If it has confidence intervals, see if you can understand what these mean. Do you think the study is underpowered? If the study reports an effect size, how big in words rather than in numbers would you describe it as being? Do a literature search to see if you can find other studies which are similar. Do they find similar results? If not, why do you think this is?

2. Think of a study you would like to carry out. How big an effect do you expect to find? How big a sample would you need to be reasonably confident that your finding is a statistically reliable one? What else would you have to do to increase the chances of it being a reliable one?

PART 3

Fundamentals of testing and measurement

CHAPTER 15

Psychological tests

Their use and construction

Overview

- Psychological tests and measures are commercially available, can sometimes be found in the research literature, or may be created by the researcher. The construction of a psychological measure is relatively easy using statistical packages.

- Tests used for clinical and other forms of assessment of individuals need to be well standardised and carefully administered. Measures used for research purposes only do not need the same degree of precision to be useful.

- Psychologists tend to prefer 'unidimensional' scales, which are single-dimensional 'pure' measures of the variable in question. However, multidimensional scales may be more useful for practical rather than research applications.

- Item analysis is the process of 'purifying' the measure. Item–total correlations simply correlate each individual item with the score based on the other items. Those items with high correlations with the total are retained. An alternative is to use factor analysis, which identifies clusters of items that measure the same thing.

15.1 Introduction

Standardised tests and measures are very commonly used in psychological research. They are, perhaps, even more frequently used in psychological assessment of clients such as in clinical, educational, and occupational psychology. The term *standardised* can mean several things:

- Consistency of results is achieved using prescribed administration and scoring procedures on identical tests so that inconsistency between different psychologists is minimised. Way back in 1904 when Alfred Binet and Theodore Simon (1904, 1916) presented the world's first psychological scale – one essentially measuring intelligence – they were adamant that their scale should be administered in settings with certain characteristics. They suggested an isolated, quiet room in which the child was alone with the test administrator and, ideally, an adult familiar to the child present to help reassure the child but should be 'passive and mute' and not intervene in any way.

- Consistency of interpretation is maximised by providing normative or standardisation data based on a large sample of participants. So it is possible to provide statistical data on the range and variability of scores between people. Consequently, the psychologist can compare the scores of their clients or research participants with those of this large sample. These statistical data are usually referred to as the norms (or normative data), but they are really just the standard against which individuals are evaluated. Often tables of *percentiles* are provided which indicate, for any given score on the test or measure, the percentage of individuals with that score or a lower score (see the companion book *Understanding statistics in psychology with SPSS,* Howitt & Cramer, 2020). Norms may be provided for different genders and/or age groups and so forth.

Standardised tests and measures are available to measure various characteristics, including attitudes, intelligence, aptitude, ability, self-esteem, musicality, personality and so forth. Publishers and suppliers of commercially available measures often issue catalogues of their offerings. These are frequently quite expensive, elaborate products which are only available to specialist professionals. Their commercial potential and practical application partly explain the cost. For example, a big market exists for recruitment measures used in employee selection, especially in the US, since selection interviews may be insufficient for assessing the abilities and potential of job applicants. By helping select the best potential employee, the costs of wasted training are minimised. Clinical work and education may be similarly enhanced by the availability of quality tests and measurements, such as for screening for dyslexia.

Although some commercially available tests and measures can be employed in research, they are often developed to meet the needs of practitioners. They may not always be the ideal choice for research, for several reasons:

- Expense which may prohibit their use for research using large samples.

- Administration costs can be high in time and money since they are often administered on a one-to-one basis by trained personnel. Some take two hours or more to administer which is a significant cost but a deterrent to potential research participants.

- They are often not intended for the general population but for specific populations. A test used by clinical psychologists, for example, may help identify schizoid thought tendencies in psychiatric settings but is of little worth with people in general.

- Restriction in availability, say, to qualified clinical psychologists only. Students may have no direct access to them though university departments may, perhaps, allow their use by students under the supervision of a member of staff.

It is not certain that a test or measure will be available for the variable(s) a researcher wants to measure so they must construct one for themselves. Many *research instruments* are available but not from commercial sources. Often these can be obtained from relevant journal articles, books and websites or directly from authors. They would usually be located as part of the literature review since, for example, journal articles often describe or use them. Among the advantages of using the same measures as other researchers is comparability and their recognition by the research community as useful. Care is needed, however, since your research's purpose may be different in some way or there may be other reasons why the measure is unsuitable (e.g. it is for use with children and you are studying adults or it is for a different culture). It may be possible to modify the test or measure but it may be so unsuitable that a new instrument needs to be created.

The mechanics of test construction are generally straightforward especially using computer packages such as SPSS. So bespoke measures are feasible even as part of student research. However, standardisation of the measure demands large, carefully selected samples which are too big to be considered for a student project. For research purposes, smaller samples can work and so the need for large samples is not normally a problem.

15.2   Concept of a scale

Scales are often discussed in relation to psychological measures. In general English dictionaries, the term 'scale' is defined as a graded classification system. In psychology, scales allow individuals to be numerically graded on the basis of their scores on a measure. There are two important ways of creating such graded scales:

- Providing a series of test or measurement items which span the range from lowest to highest. So, if a measure of intelligence is required, a whole series of questions is provided which vary in terms of their difficulty. The most difficult question that the participant can answer is an indicator of their level of intelligence. An item's difficulty can simply be the percentage of a relevant sample of participants who answer the question correctly. This approach was applied in modified form to attitude measurement using the Thurstone Scale. To measure racial attitudes, a pool of statements related to racism, including extremely racist and non-racist ones are used. A panel of judges rates each of the statements in terms of the extent it reflects racism. The most hostile item that a participant agrees with is an indicator of their level of racism. This is known as the 'method of equal-appearing intervals', because the test constructor endeavours to make the items cover all points of the possible range evenly.

- A much more common way of constructing psychological tests and measures operates on a quite distinct principle, although the two often produce substantially the same outcomes. In the method of summated scores, the researcher creates a pool of items believed to measure the variable. The final score is based on the sum of the items. Usually, an additional criterion is introduced, which is that the items should correlate with the total scores on the test or measure. We will return to this in the next section.

Psychological tests and measures are frequently described as unidimensional or multidimensional. A *unidimensional* scale is one in which the correlations of the items with each other are determined as a result of a single underlying dimension. This is analogous to measuring the weights of 30 people using 10 different sets of bathroom scales – there will be strong intercorrelations between the weights as assessed by different sets of bathroom scales. A *multidimensional* scale has two or more underlying dimensions which result in a pattern of intercorrelations between the items in which there are distinct clusters or groups of items that tend to intercorrelate with each other but not so well (or not at all) with other items. This is analogous to measuring the weights of 30 people using 10 different sets of bathroom scales and their heights using five different tape measures. In this case, we would expect for the sample of people:

● Strong intercorrelations of their weights as measured using the 10 different sets of bathroom scales.

● Strong intercorrelations of their heights as measured with the five different tape measures.

● Poor intercorrelations between the 10 sets of bathroom scale measurements and the five sets of tape measure measurements.

This is simply because our 15 different measures (analogous to 15 different items on a questionnaire) are measuring two different (but not entirely independent) things: weight and height.

Which of these is the best? For most purposes in *research* unidimensional scales are preferred since they imply that you have a relatively 'pure' measurement. That is, unidimensional scales seem to be good measures of a single concept. Multidimensional scales are sometimes the more useful for practical purposes. A multidimensional measure of intelligence is likely to predict university achievement better. University achievement involves a variety of factors (e.g. maths ability, comprehension, motivation, etc.), not just one. So multidimensional scales may be preferred when making real-life predictions.

A number of fundamental and generally unavoidable problems beset measurement in psychology. The weakness or imprecision of psychological measurements is a major difficulty. A centimetre is a standard, well-established and precisely measurable amount but psychological variables cannot be measured so precisely. Every psychological measurement will vary somewhat each time it is taken – apparently in an unsystematic or random fashion. If we measure age by asking participants their age, we might expect a degree of imprecision – some participants may deliberately lie, others will have forgotten their age, we may mishear what they say and so forth. If this can happen with something so easily defined as age, the problem will be much worse when measuring difficult to define, vague and unclear concepts like self-esteem, happiness or cognitive distortions. This is partly why psychologists tend to use several items in their measures rather than a single item. By using a number of imprecise measures of the concept in question, the aggregate of these measures is likely to be a better measure than any of the constituent individual items.

There is nothing wrong with using a single item to measure a psychological variable – one would not measure age by using a 20-item age scale, for example. However, we would use a long scale to measure a less clear variable such as happiness. So the use of scaling is really confined to circumstances in which you wish to get a decent measure of a variable that is difficult to measure. Thus, you would not use scaling if you wished to measure gender or age since a single question will generally produce high-quality, highly valid answers.

It's a bit like finding out the cost of the Tube fare to Oxford Street station in London by asking lots of friends. Probably none of your friends knows the precise fare, but several would have a rough idea. By combining several rough estimates together by averaging, the probable outcome is a reasonable estimate of the train fare. Obviously, it would be better to use a more accurate measure (e.g. by checking on the Internet), but if this is not possible, the rough estimates would do. In other words, there is an objective reality (the actual fare that you will pay) but you cannot find that out directly. This is much the same as psychological variables – there may be an objective reality of happiness, but we can only measure it satisfactorily by using an aggregate of imprecise measures.

15.3   Scale construction

It is important to stress that psychological tests and measures are not created simply on the back of statistical techniques. Ideally, psychologists constructing a measure should be familiar with the relevant theory and research concerning what is to be measured. Familiarity with related concepts, expert opinion, and feedback from focus groups etc. about how individuals understand and experience the thing to be measured can all help too. For example, how do people experience depression? Such information contributes to the development of insightful and pertinent ideas as a basis for the measure. The following points are especially important:

- Every effort should be made to specify the nature of the concept we wish to measure – just what do we mean by loneliness, depression or staff burnout, for example? Often by reflecting on this, we begin to realise that different features of the concept need to be incorporated into the *pool of items* forming the basis of the measure.

- Even after we have developed our understanding of the concept as well as we can, we may find it impossible to phrase a single question to assess it. Take loneliness: is a question such as 'How many friends do you have?' a good measure of loneliness? It depends on many things – what an individual classifies as a friend, whether loneliness is determined by the number rather than the quality of friendships, the age of the individual (since an elderly person may have fewer friends simply as a consequence of bereavements) and so forth. This does not mean that the question is useless as a measure of the concept, merely that it is not a particularly accurate measure.

- Variables do not exist in some sort of rarefied form in the real world. They are notions which psychologists and other researchers find extremely useful in trying to understand people. So sometimes it will appear appropriate to a researcher to measure a range of things which seem closely related. For example, loneliness might be considered to involve a range of aspects – few friendships, feelings of isolation, no social support, geographical isolation and so forth.

Once a pool of potential items has been developed, the next stage is administering the test's first draft to as substantial as possible a sample of people. Advice on how to formulate questions is to be found in Box 15.1. Assume we have gone through that process

Box 15.1   Practical Advice

Writing items for questionnaires

Writing questions or items for a psychological measure requires a focus on concocting unambiguous and clear items. They should also seem to measure a range of aspects of the topic. Once again the important lesson is to research and explore the topic in a variety of ways. Only in this way can you acquire the depth of knowledge to create a good measure. To be frank, anyone can throw together a list of questions, but it requires commitment and work to write a good questionnaire. Of course, it takes time to achieve satisfactory outcomes. One needs to understand the topic at as many levels as possible. What do you think the important things are likely to be? What do people you know regard as important aspects of the topic? What does a focus group or some other

→

group of research participants talk about when they are asked to discuss the topic? How have previous researchers attempted to measure a similar topic? What does the empirical evidence indicate about the major dimensions of the topic? What does theory say about the topic? Once you have drafted the questionnaire, there are a number of processes that you will need to go through to assess its adequacy. These include item analysis, reliability assessment and perhaps validity assessment.

Here are a few tips for writing questions:

- Use short and simple sentence structures.

- Short, everyday words are better than long, obscure ones.

- Avoid complex or problematic grammar, such as the use of double negatives, for example, 'You ain't seen nothing yet'.

- Leading questions which suggest the expected answer should be avoided, largely because of the limiting effect this will have on the variability of the answers. An example would be 'Most people think it essential to vote in elections. Do you agree?'

- Choose appropriate language for the likely participants – what is appropriate for high court judges may be inappropriate for nursery children.

- Tap as many resources for items and questions as feasible.

- Accept that you cannot rely on yourself alone as a satisfactory source of questions and ideas for questions.

- People similar to the likely participants in your research are a good starting point for ideas.

- Relax – expertise in question and item writing is a rare commodity. Most researchers mix trial and error with rigorous item analysis as a substitute.

You may wish to consult the chapter on coding data (Chapter 17) in order to appreciate the variety of ways in which the researcher can structure the answers further.

and have a list of such items. For illustrative purposes, we have 10 different items but the list would probably be more like 30 or 40 items. We have decided to attempt to measure *honesty*. Our 10 items are:

Item 1	I am an honest person.
Item 2	I have frequently told little lies so as not to offend people.
Item 3	If I found money in the street, I would hand it in to the police.
Item 4	I have never told even the slightest untruth.
Item 5	I would always return the money if I knew that I had been given too much change in a shop.
Item 6	I would never make private phone calls from work.
Item 7	I have shoplifted.
Item 8	It is always best to tell the truth even if it hurts.
Item 9	I usually tell the boss what I think they would like to hear even if it is not true.
Item 10	If I were to have an affair, I would never tell my partner.

Several things are readily apparent about this list:

- There is a wide range of items which seem to be measuring a variety of things. Probably all of the items are measuring something that may be regarded as honesty (or lack of it).

- Some of the items are positively worded in terms of honesty (e.g. items 1, 6 and 8). That is, agreeing with these items is indicative of honesty. Other items are negatively worded in that *disagreeing* with them is indicative of honesty (e.g. items

7, 9 and 10). Often, positively and negatively worded items are both included deliberately in order to help deal with 'response sets'. Briefly, some people tend to agree with items no matter the content of the item – the acquiescence response set. They tend to agree with an item but also *agree* with an item worded in the opposite direction. That is, they might agree with the statement that 'I am an honest person' and also agree with the statement that 'I am not an honest person'. One way of dealing with this is to use both positively and negatively worded items – mixing items for which agreement is indicative of the variable with those for which disagreement is indicative of the variable. There are many examples where this is not done, however.

- You must remember to reverse-score the negatively worded items. If they are scored in the same way as the positively worded items, then the positively worded items would be cancelled out by the negatively worded ones.

- Item 4, 'I have never told even the slightest untruth', seems unlikely to be true of any human. Items like this are sometimes included in order to assess faking 'good' or 'social desirability', that is, trying to give an impression of meeting social standards, even unobtainable ones. On the other hand, it is possible that the researcher has simply written a bad item. That is, if everyone disagrees with an item then it cannot discriminate between people in terms of, in this case, honesty. Useful items need to demonstrate variability (variance) between people.

Reading the items carefully suggests that there are at least two different sorts of honesty being measured – one is *verbal honesty* (not lying, basically) and the other is *not stealing*. That is, it is measuring two distinct things which makes it multidimensional. This can be assessed examining empirically whether verbally honest people also tend not to steal. Basically, this is a matter of correlating the different items one with another.

Scaling – or the process of developing a psychological scale – deals with the ways in which items are combined in order to get a better measure of a concept than could be achieved using a single item. The common methods of psychological scaling employed by most modern researchers involve one or other of two general principles:

- If we sum the scores on the individual items of a test or measure to give the *total score,* then each of the individual items should correlate with this total score if the items are measuring the same thing as each other. *Items which do not correlate with the total score are simply not measuring what the majority of the other items are measuring and may be eliminated from the scale.* This is also known as the *item–whole* (Cowen, Underberg, & Verrillo, 1958) or *item–total* (Gleser & Dubois, 1951) approach to scale construction.

- If items on the scale are measuring the same thing, then they should correlate substantially with each other (and with the total score as well, for that matter). Items which measure very different things will correlate with each other either very poorly or not at all. This is the basis of internal consistency approaches to scale construction as well as *factor analytic* methods. With a multidimensional scale, expect to find distinct groups of items which correlate well with each other but not with other groups of items. These procedures are discussed later in this chapter.

We will consider each of these approaches in turn. They are known as *item analysis* techniques: see Box 15.2 and Figure 15.1.

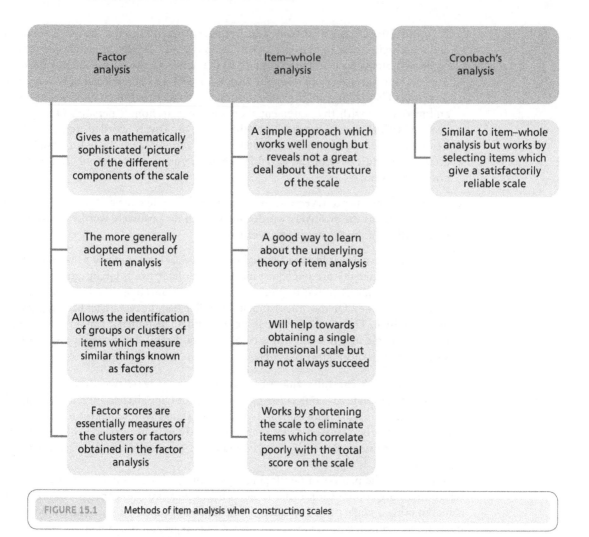

FIGURE 15.1   Methods of item analysis when constructing scales

Box 15.2   Key Ideas

Item analysis

Item analysis refers to the process of examining each item of the scale – its good and bad points. The main points are:

- Items showing little variation between people are omitted because they contribute little since they are not discriminating between people. Low variability may be assessed from statistics such as variance, standard error and standard deviation or by examining histograms of responses to each item.

- Ideally, all items should show similar, high levels of variation. If items do not have similar variability, then simply summing scores on individual scores for items

to give a total score on the scale can be problematic. If the items have dissimilar variabilities then one could use standard scores for each item instead (see the companion book *Understanding statistics in psychology with SPSS* (Howitt & Cramer, 2020, Chapter 6) and then sum these to give an individual's combined score on the scale. In some psychological tests and measures, you will find that certain items are given extra scoring weight. This is to take this very problem into account.

- Items which are commonly omitted (not responded to) and ones which participants frequently comment on adversely are also candidates for omission. They are signs that participants have difficulty understanding or addressing certain items. Rephrasing such items is an option, but ideally requires readministration of the revised scale using a new sample.

● The final stage of item analysis is to examine the consistency with which the individual items contribute to whatever is being measured by the total scale. Item–whole correlation and factor analytic approaches to doing this are discussed in the main body of the text.

■ Item–whole or item–total approach to scale construction

Item analysis helps to eliminate bad items that do not measure the same thing as the complete scale. So what would we expect our data to show if we had managed to produce a good measure of, say, honesty? Remember that we are doing little more than simply adding up the answers to a range of questions about honesty to give a total score:

● In item–whole item analysis we calculate a total score for honesty probably by simply adding the total of each individual's scores on all the items. (Don't forget to reverse-score items as appropriate.) This total score is also referred to as the *whole-scale* score.

● If all of the individual items on the scale are measuring the same thing then each of them should correlate with the total score on the scale. Items not correlating with the whole-scale score (total score) are clearly measuring something different from what the whole scale is measuring. It can safely be eliminated.

By dropping items, a shorter and probably more consistent scale will be obtained.

Another way of doing much the same thing is to take extreme groups on the whole or total test. That is, we could take the top 25 per cent of scores and the bottom 25 per cent of scores on the entire scale. Items answered very differently by high scorers on the whole scale compared with low scorers should be retained because they are good. Items which high scorers and low scorers answer similarly are not discriminating and may be dropped. There is no advantage of this method over using item–whole correlations.

Table 15.1 contains, among other things, item–total correlations for our honesty scale. What does it tell us? It is important to note that all but one of the relationships is positive and the exception has a correlation very close to zero. Substantial negative relationships suggest that an item probably has been scored the wrong way round. It might be a negatively worded item which has not been reverse-scored. The researcher

Table 15.1	Item–total correlation		
	Scale mean if item deleted	Scale variance if item deleted	Corrected item–total correlation
Honest	26.00	40.33	.38
Offend	25.38	37.76	.43
Street	25.77	37.36	.46
Untruth	25.69	35.23	.74
Change	26.00	37.00	.56
Phone	25.31	36.40	.55
Shoplift	25.85	36.97	.69
Hurts	25.23	44.86	−.04
Boss	25.38	37.76	.43
Affair	25.54	37.94	.36

needs to check whether this is indeed the case. Wrongly scored items should be rescored in the opposite direction. This necessitates that all of the correlations are recalculated since the total score will have changed – one good reason for using a computer. (This is easily done when using computer packages like SPSS using recoding procedures.)

Item–whole correlation coefficients indicate the extent to which individual items are contributing to whatever the total score measures. Looking at Table 15.1, it is clear that some of the items correlate rather better with the total score than others. If we wished to shorten the scale (though this one is short), then the obvious items to drop are the ones which relate poorly to the total score. The items which have good correlations with the total score are retained for inclusion in the final scale – by doing so we increase the likelihood that all of our remaining items are measuring much the same thing. This is a matter of judgement, of course, but is easily reversible if it seems that too many items have been omitted. Remember that since items have been dropped, the new total score and the item–total correlations need recalculating. Again, statistical computer software such as SPSS makes this a fairly minimal chore.

Item 8 on the honesty scale ('It is always best to tell the truth even if it hurts') is the obvious item to eliminate first, given its near-zero correlation with the total score.

So as a reminder, just what has leaving out items achieved?

- The scale has become a more refined measure of whatever it is that it measures. That is to say, the remaining items increasingly tend to measure the same thing.

- The scale becomes shorter – which may be more acceptable to participants. Be careful, though, since a short scale may not be as reliable as a longer scale (see Chapter 16 for a discussion of reliability), all other things being equal.

What constitutes a good item–whole correlation cannot be defined absolutely. Normally it is unwise to retain items not showing a significant relationship with the total. For measures exclusively for research, tests and measures with just a few items may be preferred simply because they are less demanding for participants. There is a trade-off between length of the test or measure and the number of participants in the study. The greater the number of participants, the shorter the scale may be.

Small refinement

Item–total correlation analysis may be refined, especially for short scales. This involves correlating the item with the total score *minus* the score on that particular item. That is, we correlate each item with the total of all of the *other* items. Unless this is done, the item–whole correlations include in part the correlation of the item with itself which systematically inflates the item-total correlations somewhat. The fewer items, the greater the impact of any one item. This inflation is probably negligible with a long scale. The adjustment is straightforward and is recommended as the preferred approach. Computer software such as SPSS will do both versions of the analysis, so there is virtually no additional effort required.

This form of item analysis is very much a process and not a single step. By reducing the number of items one at a time, the value and influence of each variable may be assessed. The researcher simply removes items from the scale in order of their item–whole correlations. The item with the lowest item–whole correlation at any stage is normally the next candidate for omission. Box 15.3 explains another approach – how the alpha coefficient of Cronbach (1951) may be used similarly to shorten scales and to increase measurement consistency.

Factoring approach

The item analysis approach described above is important since it is the basis of many common psychological tests and measures. There is an alternative – factor analysis – which is easily calculated thanks to computer packages. Factor analysis was developed early in

Box 15.3   Practical Advice

Using Cronbach's alpha to shorten scales and increase consistency of items

Poor items may be eliminated with a different procedure to that described in the main text. This is based on (Cronbach's) coefficient alpha reliability coefficient which is discussed in more detail in Chapter 16. Regard it for now as an index of the consistency with which all of the items on the scale measure whatever the total scale measures. Using computer software such as SPSS, it is possible to compute the alpha coefficients of the test. There is also an option which computes the alpha coefficients with each item omitted in turn. This gives as many alpha reliabilities as items in the test. Items which are not measuring the same thing as the other items may be dropped without reducing alpha

reliability, simply because they are adding nothing to the consistency of the test. (Obviously, if they added something to the consistency of the test, removing them would lower the reliability of the measure.)

The researcher simply looks through the list of alpha coefficients, and selects the item with the lowest alpha reliability. This item may be omitted from the scale, as this item is not a good measure of what the scale itself measures. This process is repeated for the 'new' scale and an item dropped. Eventually a shortened scale will emerge which may have a sufficiently high overall alpha coefficient. One of .70 or so is usually regarded as satisfactory (Nunnally, 1978).

the history of modern psychology as a means of studying the structure of intelligence (and consequently measures of intelligence). Its primary uses are in the context of psychological test and measure construction.

First, in factor analysis the computer calculates a matrix of correlations between all of the items on the test or measure (see Table 15.2). Often special versions of the correlation coefficient are used for this and these are discussed in Box 15.4. Then mathematical routines are calculated which detect patterns in the relationships between items on the psychological test. These patterns are presented in terms of factors. A factor is simply an empirically based hypothetical variable formed from items that are strongly associated with each other. Usually, several factors will emerge in a factor analysis. The precise number depends on the data and it can be that there is simply one significant or dominant factor. More practical details on factor analysis can be found in the two companion texts

Table 15.2   Correlation matrix for the 10-item honesty scale

	Honest	Offend	Street	Untruth	Change	Phone	Shoplift	Hurts	Boss	Affair
Honest	1	− .17	.54	.58	.55	.43	.48	.24	− .17	− .28
Offend	− .17	1	− .04	.20	− .03	.05	.30	.09	.99	.68
Street	.54	− .04	1	.55	.46	.58	.45	− .00	− .04	.08
Untruth	.58	.19	.55	1	.77	.72	.70	− .08	.19	.21
Change	.55	− .03	.46	.77	1	.55	.72	.04	− .03	.08
Phone	.43	.05	.58	.72	.55	1	.34	− .29	.05	.50
Shoplift	.48	.30	.45	.70	.72	.34	1	.14	.30	.16
Hurts	.24	.09	− .00	− .08	.04	− .29	.14	1	.09	− .31
Boss	− .17	.99	− .04	.19	− .03	.05	.30	.09	1	0.68
Affair	− .28	.68	.08	.21	.08	.50	.16	− .31	.68	1

> ## Box 15.4 | Key Ideas
>
> ## Phi and point–biserial correlation coefficients
>
> Before computers, psychological test construction required numerous, time-consuming calculations. The phi and point–biserial correlation coefficients were developed as ways of speeding up the calculations by using special formulae in special circumstances. These formulae are now essentially obsolete, because computers can do the calculations quickly and easily – see the companion text *Introduction to SPSS in psychology* (Howitt & Cramer, 2017).
>
> The phi coefficient is merely the Pearson correlation coefficient calculated between two binary (binomial or
>
> yes/no) variables. Many psychological tests have this form – one simply agrees or disagrees with the test item. So the phi coefficient provided a quicker way of calculating a correlation matrix between the items on a test.
>
> The point–biserial correlation is merely the Pearson correlation calculated between a binary (yes/no) test variable and a conventional score. Thus item–whole (item–total) correlations could be calculated using the point–biserial correlation. One variable is the binomial (yes/no) item and the other variable is the total score on the test.

Understanding statistics in psychology with SPSS (Howitt & Cramer, 2020) and *Introduction to SPSS in psychology* (Howitt & Cramer, 2017).

Each individual test item has some degree of association with each of the major patterns (i. e. the factors found through factor analysis). This degree of association ranges from a zero relationship through to a perfect relationship. In factor analysis, the relationship of a test item to the factor is expressed in terms of a correlation coefficient. These correlation coefficients are known as *factor loadings*. So a factor loading is the correlation coefficient between an item and a factor. Usually there will be more than one factor but not necessarily so. So each test item may have a loading on each of several factors. This is illustrated for our honesty scale in Table 15.3. This table is a factor-loading matrix – it gives the factor loadings of each of the test items on each of the factors. Since they are correlation coefficients, factor loadings can range from -1.0 through 0.0 to $+1.0$. They would be interpreted as follows:

Table 15.3	Factor loadings for the honesty scale		
	Factor 1	Factor 2	Factor 3
Honest	.64	$-.52$	.26
Offend	.28	.90	.28
Street	.70	$-.26$	.01
Untruth	.92	$-.01$	$-.00$
Change	.82	$-.26$	.01
Phone	.78	$-.00$	$-.49$
Shoplift	.80	.00	.33
Hurts	$-.00$	$-.12$	.87
Boss	.28	.90	.28
Affair	.35	.79	$-.37$

- A factor loading of 1.0 would indicate a perfect correlation of the item with the factor in question. It is unlikely that you will get such a factor loading.

- A factor loading of .8 would be a high value and you would often find such values in a factor analysis. It means that the item correlates well with the factor, though less than perfectly.

- A factor loading of .5 would be a moderate value for a factor loading. Such factor loadings are of interest, but you should bear in mind that a correlation of .5 actually means that only .25 of the variation of the item is accounted for by the factor. (See Chapter 4 of this book and Chapter 8 of the companion text *Understanding statistics in psychology with SPSS* (Howitt & Cramer, 2020).)

- A factor loading of .2 generally speaking should be regarded as very low and indicates that the item is poorly related to the factor.

- A factor loading of zero means that there is no relationship between that item and the factor. That is, none of the variation in the item is associated with that factor.

- Negative (−) signs in a factor loading should be interpreted just as a negative correlation coefficient would be. If the item were to be reverse-scored, then the sign of its factor loadings would be reversed. So a negative factor loading may simply indicate an item which has not been reverse-scored.

All of this may seem to be number-crunching rather than psychological analysis. However, the end point of factor analysis is to put a psychological interpretation on the factors. This is done in a fairly straightforward manner, though it does require a degree of creativity or imagination on the researcher's part. The factor loadings refer to items which are usually presented verbally. It is possible to take the items with high factor loadings and see what the pattern is that defines the factor. This merely entails listing the items which have high loadings with factor 1, first of all. If we take our cut-off point as .5, then the items which load highly on factor 1 in descending order of size are:

Item 4 (loading = .92) 'I have never told even the slightest untruth'.
Item 5 (loading = .82) 'I would always return the money if I knew that I had been given too much change in a shop'.
Item 7 (loading = .80) 'I have shoplifted'.
Item 6 (loading = .78) 'I would never make private phone calls from work'.
Item 3 (loading = .70) 'If I found money in the street, I would hand it in to the police'.

Remember that some of the items would have been reverse-scored, so that a high score is given to the honest end of the continuum.

The next step is to decide what is the common theme in these high-loading items. This simple step may be enough for you to say what the factor is. It can be helpful to compare the high loading items on a factor with the low loading items – they should be very different. The success of this process depends as much on the insight of the researcher about psychological processes as it does on their understanding of the mechanics of factor analysis.

Looking at the items which load highly on the first factor, most of them seem to relate to matters of theft or white-collar crime (e.g. abusing the phone at work). So we might wish to label this factor as 'financial honesty', but there may be better descriptions. Further research may cause us to revise our view, but in the interim this is probably as good as we can manage.

The process is repeated for each of the factors in turn. It is conventional to identify the factors with a brief title.

Just what can be achieved with factor analysis?

- It demonstrates your measure's underlying dimensions.

- It allows you to dispense with any items which do not load highly on the appropriate factors, that is, those which do not seem to be measuring what the test is designed to measure. In this way, it is possible to shorten the test.

- It is possible to compute factor scores. This is easy with SPSS-see the companion text *Introduction to SPSS in psychology* (Howitt & Cramer, 2017). A factor score is merely a score based on the participants' responses to the test items which load heavily on the various factors. So instead of being a score on the test, a factor score is a score on one of the factors. One advantage of using factor scores is that they are standardised scores unaffected by differences in the variance of each of the items. As an alternative, it is possible to take the items which load heavily on a factor and derive a score by totalling those items. This is not so accurate as the factor score method. A disadvantage of using factor scores is that they can vary somewhat from sample to sample.

Factor analysis generates variables (factors) which are pure in the sense that the items which load highly on a factor are all measuring the same underlying thing. This is not true of psychological measures created by other means.

15.4   Item analysis or factor analysis?

We have described item analysis and factor analysis. In many ways they seem to be doing rather similar jobs. Just what is the difference between the two in application?

- Factor analysis works using the intercorrelations of all of the items with one another. Item analysis works by correlating the individual items with the total score. Factor analysis is more subtle as a consequence, since the total score obtained by adding together items in item analysis might include two or more somewhat distinct sets of items (though they are treated as if they were just a single set).

- Factor analysis allows the researcher to refine their conceptualisation of what the items on the test measure. That is, the factors are fairly refined entities which may allow psychological insight into the scale. Item analysis merely provides a fairly rough way of ridding a scale of bad items which are measuring somewhat different things from those measured by the scale. In that sense it is much cruder.

It should be mentioned that extremely refined scales may not be as effective at measuring complex things as rather cruder measures. For example, we could hone our honesty scale down by factor analysis so that we have just one measure. The trouble is that honest behaviour, for example, may be multiply determined such that a refined measure does not predict honesty very well. In contrast, a cruder test that measures different aspects of honesty may do quite a good job at predicting honest behaviour simply because it is measuring more aspects. In other words, there may be a difference between a test that is useful for the development of psychological theory and one that is practically useful for the purpose of, say, clinical, educational or forensic practice. Of course, one of the bug-bears with questionnaires is that participants may deliberately choose to or accidentally omit giving answers to a question. This is known as missing data and ways of dealing with it are discussed in Box 15.5.

Box 15.5   Key Idea

Handling missing data

One aspect of quantitative research seldom reported in journal papers is how much data was missing from the original sample and how missing data was handled (Bodner, 2006b; Rousseau, Simon, Bertrand, & Hachey, 2012). What do we mean by missing data? An example would be when a participant does not report their age or it is not clear what they have written. We can only report descriptive statistics for age (such as the mean and standard deviation) for the part of the sample providing usable information. The size of this smaller sample should also be mentioned. If age was one of the main variables of interest in the study, individuals failing to give their age would have to be omitted from the research.

Other examples of missing data are when the responses of participants are incomplete for measures such as for a questionnaire scale or for the performance of some task such as simple reaction time. For simple reaction time, a response may be missing when the participant presses the key before the signal is presented, resulting in an anticipatory response which is unrealistically fast (e.g. under 100 msec.) and which therefore should be omitted. For these sorts of measures, we may calculate a mean score for the individual's valid data depending on what is usually done in these cases by other researchers.

Obviously, if only a couple of responses are missing for a participant, it is wasteful to exclude that person from the analysis. However, if a substantial number of responses are missing, we should most probably exclude them from the analysis as we may not have a sufficient number of responses to form a sufficiently reliable, valid score for that individual. We need to decide a criterion or cut-off point for what is a reasonable number of non-missing or valid responses still to be included. This criterion will depend on the number of possible responses for the measure. If the measure consists of only four responses, we may decide to permit one of those responses to be missing in order to provide an overall score for that measure. Of course, this procedure will create problems if we carry out a factor analysis or a Cronbach's alpha reliability test on this measure as these statistical tests will be computed for only those individuals who have complete data. This will be a smaller sample than the original one. If more than one response is missing from our four response measure, we may decide

to exclude the score for that measure for that person. If responses are missing for a large number of participants, we may conclude that there is something wrong with our measure which needs looking into.

If we decide to use participants who have supplied incomplete data, we need a system for adjusting the data to take their missing data into account. One way of doing this is to calculate each participant's mean scores for whatever valid data is supplied. We do this by calculating their mean score for that measure. So, for four responses, we divide their total score by four, for three responses we divide their total score by three, and so on. Where the cut-off point is three or more non-missing or valid responses, we would not work out the mean score for individuals with less than three non-missing or valid responses. If the measure is usually expressed as a total rather than a mean score, we need to multiply the mean score by the total number of responses for that measure. So for a four response measure, we would multiply the mean by four to obtain the total score. We would do this for measures such as the Eysenck personality scales and the Beck Depression Inventory which use total scores. Calculating these scores is relatively easily done with software such as SPSS when all the responses have been included in the database. How to do this is shown in the companion books to this one called *Understanding statistics in psychology with SPSS* (Howitt & Cramer, 2020) and *Introduction to SPSS in psychology* (Howitt & Cramer, 2017). There is a choice to be made about whether to omit a participant who has supplied some missing data from the entire study or just from analyses of the variables which have missing responses.

Ultimately, what a researcher does about missing values is a matter of judgement bearing in mind the specific characteristics of the research. There are no right or wrong decisions, in general. If you decide to omit any participant who fails to supply complete data you run the risk of excluding a particular type of person – after all, there may be good and systematic reasons why some people omit answers. They may have concentration deficits, for example. If you decide to substitute a value for the missing data then what this should be is not entirely obvious. You could decide to simply insert a random (but possible) value since this

→

can only have a random influence. Alternatively, using an estimate such as the mean of valid scores from the rest of the sample may have some systematic effect though you probably will never know what that is. There are various more sophisticated ways of handling missing data but some students and, even, researchers may find these too complicated (e.g. Graham, 2009). Whatever you decide should be made absolutely clear in your report. Of course, you might choose to explore the differential effects of different procedures.

15.5 Other considerations in test construction

Of course, this chapter can only outline the important aspects of psychological scale construction. Other considerations include:

- Participants should receive instructions about how to respond to the test. Similarly, the researcher/administrator needs instructions about the standard method of administering and scoring the test.

- Tests intended for administration to individuals as part of a psychological assessment of them may have great significance for their future. In these circumstances, the precision of the measure is greatly important. Often tables of norms, which are data on how the general (or some other) population scores on the test, are available for these measures. In this way, a particular clinical client may be compared with people in general. Norms, as they are called, are often presented as percentiles, which are the cut-off points for the bottom 10 per cent, bottom 20 per cent or bottom 50 per cent of scores in that population. Norms may be subdivided by features such as gender or age for greater precision in the comparison.

- Tests for research purposes do not require the same degree of precision or development as tests for practical purposes. This does not mean that the same high standards that are needed for clinical work are inappropriate, merely that, for research involving a substantial number of participants, sometimes circumstances may mean that a weaker or less precise test is used.

Box 15.6   Research Example

Psychometric properties of a personality test: reliability and construct validity

Arribas-Aguila, D. (2011). Psychometric properties of the TEA Personality Test: Evidence of reliability and construct validity. *European Journal of Psychological Assessment, 27*, 121–126.

When reading journal articles, it is important not to be too perplexed when the authors use unfamiliar measures. Although you may struggle to understand the detail, the broad thrust of what they involve may be worked out from what you already know. Typically, if an author employs an unusual procedure, they will go out of their way to explain why they used it and what it is in a reasonably clear fashion. Often understanding the gist of what a measure involves may be sufficient for you to follow the rest of the paper. The study reported here adopts very sophisticated statistical approaches because of limitations with the conventional statistics for test construction discussed in this chapter. So, for example, there is evidence that Cronbach's alpha coefficient (which assesses the internal consistency of a scale) tends to underestimate internal consistency when applied to data with just a small number of response alternatives. Other methods, based on factor analysis, may be more appropriate in these circumstances, as in the journal article.

Background

The TEA Personality Test (TPT) is the third most common personality questionnaire used by psychologists in Spain, where it was developed. Primarily it has been used for employment selection in the workplace, a common application of psychological tests and measures in many countries. It is a self-completion (i.e. self-administered) questionnaire. It consists of 160 items accompanied by response scales from 0 (which equates to almost never) to 3 (which equates to almost always). Fifteen personality traits are measured using the simple procedure of adding the 'scores' on the relevant items. The traits are as follows:

1 Emotional instability or maladjustment (Emotionally unstable, easily upset, and tending to misinterpret the reality of situations)

2 Anxiety (Tense, overexcited and worried)

3 Depression (Unhappy about self and negative about things generally)

4 Stress tolerance (Problems when required to cope with difficult situations)

5 Self-concept (Underestimates own capabilities and feels insecure)

6 Tolerance and flexibility (Over-cautious and inflexible)

7 Adaptation to change (Difficulty in coming to terms with new situations)

8 Interest in other cultures (Little or no interest in other cultures)

9 Approachability or availability (Unwilling to participate with others)

10 Social intelligence (Difficulties in developing normal relationships with other people)

11 Social integration (Standoffish and uncomfortable in new situations)

12 Teamwork (Individualistic, preferring not to work with others)

13 Professional motivation or professional self-demanding (Lacking ambition and not motivated to produce high standard of work)

14 Dynamism and activeness (Passive, demonstrating little energy)

15 Tenaciousness and constancy (Readily gives up when things are not going well)

The traits can be grouped together to form three personality dimensions (see Figure 15.2):

1. Emotional stability

2. Open-mindedness

3. Responsibility.

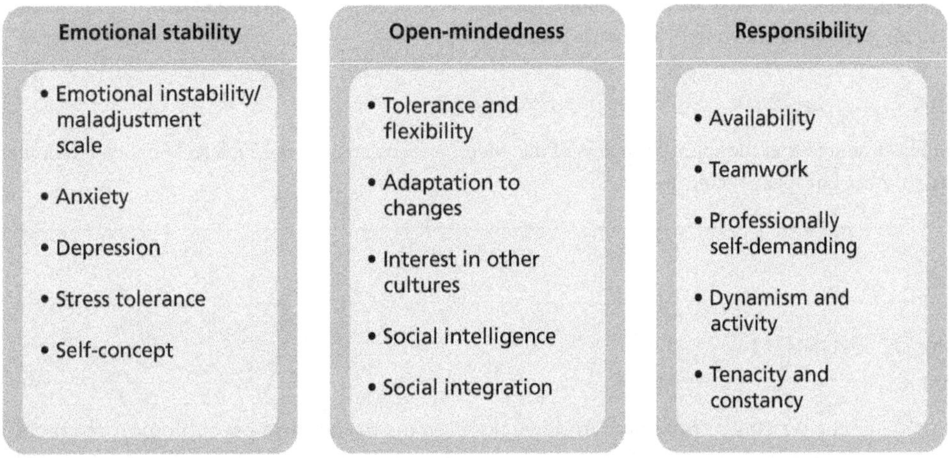

Emotional stability	Open-mindedness	Responsibility
• Emotional instability/ maladjustment scale	• Tolerance and flexibility	• Availability
• Anxiety	• Adaptation to changes	• Teamwork
• Depression	• Interest in other cultures	• Professionally self-demanding
• Stress tolerance	• Social intelligence	• Dynamism and activity
• Self-concept	• Social integration	• Tenacity and constancy

FIGURE 15.2   Underlying structure of the TEA Personality Test (TPT)

The questionnaire includes a social desirability measure, as is common in testing, and yields an overall measure of 'success at work' based on the entire scale. However, research into the psychometric properties of the measure was sparse or non-existent, except for the original research in the test's manual. Against this background, David Arribas-Aguila provides further systematic evidence on aspects of its psychometric properties.

Hypothesis

No specific hypothesis was suggested, but the author proposes that the 'present study is aimed at providing updated evidence on the psychometric properties of the TPT in terms of reliability and construct validity' (Arribas-Aguila, 2011, p. 122).

Method

The research was based on archival data from 23 000 Spanish adults who had completed the test, so this was a secondary analysis of available data. As such a large sample would be expensive to collect, it makes sense to use this to address pertinent research questions. The database consisted of the data that many examiners had entered in order to get information such as raw scores, standard scores, and so forth. Because Cronbach's alpha tends to underestimate internal consistency when the data are not continuously distributed, a different version of alpha is used. This is known as ordinal alpha and uses the statistical technique of factor analysis as the basis of the calculation. Also, because the factorial structure of the test had been established using (exploratory) factor analysis, the researcher sought to assess the adequacy of that structure using confirmatory factor analysis.

Some results

It was very clear that internal consistency was always higher using the ordinal alpha than using Cronbach's alpha for all 15 subscales of the measure. For example, the new analysis found that emotional instability or maladjustment had a Cronbach's alpha of only .50 according to the test's technical manual but an ordinal alpha of .77 in the reanalysis. This presents a much more promising picture of the reliability of the test. Cronbach's alpha is discussed in some detail in Chapter 16.

In this chapter, we discuss factor analysis extensively in relation to psychological test construction. This form of factor analysis explores the data and suggests a structure that may underlie the data. However, there was already evidence of the factorial structure of the TEA test (i.e. emotional stability, open-mindedness and responsibility), so Arribas-Aguila used a different form of factor analysis – confirmatory factor analysis. This is used when the researcher feels that there is a particular structure underlying the data (possibly based on exploratory factor analysis as discussed in this chapter) and tries to see how well this structure fits the data empirically. This is often referred to as testing a particular model. Actually, what Arribas-Aguila did was to test two models against each other – the one which suggests that there are three major dimensions (emotional stability, open-mindedness and responsibility) underlying the personality test against another which suggested that there is just one underlying dimension. The data showed clearly that the model assuming three underlying dimensions fitted the data much better.

Author's suggestions for further research

Arribas-Aguila suggested that the appropriateness of the underlying structure of the TEA Personality Test could profitably be explored in other European countries.

15.6 Conclusion

Writing appropriate and insightful items to measure psychological characteristics can be regarded as a skill involving a range of talents and abilities. In contrast, the creation of a worthwhile psychological scale based on these items is relatively simple once the basics are appreciated. The modern approach based on factor analysis using computers can be routinely applied to data requiring scaling. Factor analysis identifies the major dimensions underlying the intercorrelations of the items on the measure – this could be a single dimension (unidimensional) or two or more dimensions (multidimensional). It is up to the researcher to decide which of these to retain. Scaling basically works to make the items of the scale consistent with each other and to remove any which are not consistent with the others. However, at the end of the process we will have, hopefully, a scale high on internal consistency. This does not mean that the scale is anything other than internally consistent and the fitness of the measure for its purpose needs assessment separately. This is largely a question of its validity but to some extent also one of its reliability. These are dealt with in Chapter 16.

Key points

- Standardised tests are available for assessment purposes. They may be suitable for research purposes also but not necessarily so. They may be too long, too time-consuming or in some other way not fully appropriate to the purpose of the research. Hence a researcher may find it necessary to develop new measures.

- Many psychological characteristics are difficult to measure with precision using any single item or question. Consequently, it is common to combine several items in order to obtain a more satisfactory measure. This involves selecting sets of items which empirically appear to be measuring much the same thing. This process is known as item analysis.

- The most common methods of item analysis are item–whole (or item–total) correlations and factor analysis. The item–whole method simply selects items which correlate best with the sum of the items. That is, items which measure the same thing as the total of the items are good items. Factor analysis is a set of complex mathematical procedures which identifies groups of items which empirically are highly intercorrelated with each other. A factor, then, could be the basis of a single-dimensional scale.

- There are other skills required in scale construction such as the ability to write good items, though the processes of item analysis may well get rid of badly worded items because they do not empirically relate well to other items.

- Some items need to be reverse-scored if they are worded in the opposite direction to the majority of items.

- Internal consistency of items does not in itself guarantee that the scale can be vouchsafed as a useful measure of the thing it is intended to measure.

ACTIVITIES

1. We made up the data for the honesty scale. Why don't you actually collect the data in real life? Take our items, turn them into a questionnaire, get as many people as possible to fill it in, and once that is done, analyse them using SPSS. This is quite easy if you use the companion text *Introduction to SPSS in psychology* (Howitt & Cramer, 2017). Were our made-up data anything like your data?

2. Try extending our honesty scale by including items which measure extra facets of honesty that were not included in our original. How satisfactory empirically is your new scale? How could you assess its validity?

CHAPTER 16

Reliability and validity

Evaluating the value of tests and measures

Overview

- Reliability and validity are the principal means by which we judge the value of psychological tests and measures used in quantitative research.

- Objectivity is the extent to which different administrators of the test would obtain the same outcome when testing a particular participant or client.

- Reliability involves: (a) the consistency of items within the measure and (b) the consistency of the measure over time.

- Validity concerns the evidence that the measure actually measures what it is intended to measure.

- Both reliability and validity are multifaceted concepts and each involves a number of approaches. For example, validity ranges from a measure's correlation with similar measures through to a thorough empirical and theoretical assessment of how the measure performs in relation to other variables.

- Reliability and validity are not inherent characteristics of measures. They are affected by the context and purpose of the measurement. So, for example, a measure that is valid for one purpose may not be valid for another purpose.

Having created our measure using item analysis procedures described earlier (Chapter 15), what next? Assessment of its reliability and validity are the usual next steps. Several different sorts of reliability and validity should be differentiated. Reliability includes internal, test–retest and alternate-forms reliabilities. Validity includes face, content, concurrent and construct validity. Each of these assesses different aspects of reliability and validity. The appropriate uses of a measure depend partly on its reliability and validity. Many psychological measures, for example, consist of a list of questions which, at best, cannot fully reflect the characteristics of what they are intended to measure. Depression, for instance, cannot be fully captured by the words used to measure it. Inevitably, then, we need to ask just how well a test or measure captures the essence of a particular concept.

There are a number of criteria to consider which apply as much to measures being used for research purposes as those used for the psychological assessment of a client:

- *Objectivity*   The test or measure should yield similar outcomes, irrespective of who is administering the measure – though this is only true with trained personnel skilled in using it. The opposite of objectivity is subjectivity, that is, the outcome of the measure will depend on who is administering the test. Some measures (e.g. Hare's psychopathology scale) are more reliant than others on the judgement of the administrator. Training in the use of these is normally rather intensive.

- *Reliability*   This term actually has several, rather distinct meanings. One important meaning is reliability or consistency of the measure at different points in time or across different circumstances. If a psychological characteristic can be expected to be stable over time then a measure of this characteristic should also be stable over time. A measure of dyslexia which one month indicates that 10 children in a school class may be dyslexic but the next month picks out 10 totally different children would not be reliable. Since dyslexia is a stable characteristic, the test is patently useless. A reliable test would pick out more or less the same group of children as potentially dyslexic no matter when the test was administered. Some psychological characteristics can be expected to be relatively unstable over time – a person's mood such as happiness, for example. A good measure of an unstable characteristic like mood should not be expected to be stable. It may be stable over a short period of time such as Monday morning compared with Monday afternoon but unstable from week to week. There are relatively few measures that involve unstable characteristics, so generally reliability over time is regarded as important in psychology.

- *Validity*   Broadly speaking, this refers to the extent to which a measure assesses what it is intended to measure. Different aspects of validity are measurable. They range from whether the items in the measure appear to assess what they are intended to measure (face validity) to whether the measure of variable A is capable of distinguishing variable A from, say, variables C and D (discriminant or discriminative validity).

The different types of reliability and validity will be dealt with in detail in subsequent sections.

Reliability and validity are not inbuilt qualities of psychological measures. They vary with the context and purpose of the measurement, and between different samples of participants. Measurements intended purely for use in research may be useful despite having only modest reliability and validity. The inadequacies of measures for research purposes can be partially compensated for by having larger sample sizes, though this may itself be difficult to achieve. Measures for the assessment of individuals in, say, clinical, educational or forensic settings need much better levels of reliability and validity quite simply because it may have a major impact on a person's life. A child, wrongly assessed, may not receive the special educational provision it needs. In other words, there may be measuring instruments that are adequate for research purposes but unsatisfactory for assessing individuals and vice versa. The reasons for this include the following:

- Research is almost always based on a sample of individuals rather than a particular case. That means that a psychological test that discriminates between groups of people may be useful for research purposes, despite being hopelessly imprecise for the assessment of individuals. A forensic psychologist, for example, may need to assess the intelligence of an offender to determine whether their intellectual functioning is so low as to render them incapable of making a plea in court because they are incapable of understanding relevant concepts. A test used in this way needs to be precise.

- Much time and effort is involved in developing a measure with the best reliability and validity. Researchers frequently need measures of things which have not yet been developed. The researcher may have to choose between constructing a new measure or using a poorly documented measure simply because it is available.

- Even if there does appear to be a ready-made measure available already, don't assume that it is satisfactory for your purpose. For example, depression as a clinical syndrome may be different from depression as it is experienced by people in general. A measure of value for use with clinical samples may be hopeless when used with non-clinical samples.

- Measures useful for the assessment of individuals often take a lot of time to administer: perhaps more than two hours for a major test. This is almost certainly far too long for a researcher to use with large samples. Hence, a less good but short measure might be the pragmatic choice.

How can one find out about ready-made psychological tests? The following are the main information sources:

- The measure's instruction manual (if there is one). Students may find that their department has a collection of tests and measures for teaching and research purposes.

- Books or journal articles about the measure. Published research on a particular measure may be accessed through normal psychological databases (see Chapter 7). There is no guarantee that published information is anything other than sparse.

- Catalogues of published measures. These are distributed by psychological measures publishers. University psychology departments generally hold copies.

- The Internet is a useful source – some tests are published on it.

As always, exercise caution. A measure which worked for other researchers may be hopelessly flawed for your study.

16.2   Reliability of measures

The major types of reliability are reviewed in this section (see Figure 16.1). All reliability concerns the consistency of the measure, but the type of consistency varies. Broadly, the main types are internal consistency of the measure's items and consistency over different measurements such as differences over time. Internal consistency was discussed earlier (Chapter 15). There are several measures of internal consistency which can be readily computed using programs such as SPSS – Cronbach's (1951) coefficient alpha and split-half reliability are examples. Stability across measures involves the stability of the measure

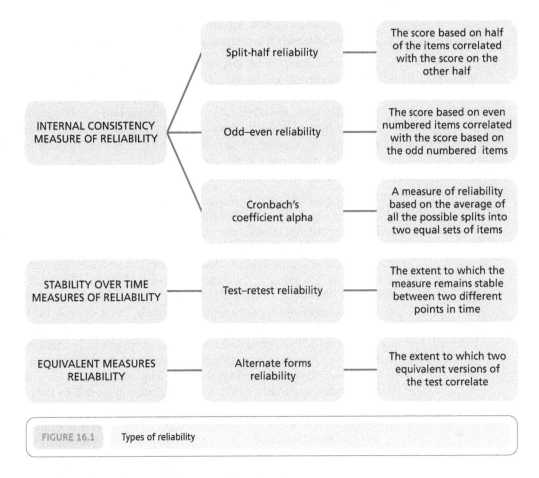

FIGURE 16.1   Types of reliability

between different versions or across different points in time. Consistency over time must be evaluated considering the size of the interval between administrations of the test. A measure's reliability over a one-week period will almost certainly be better than over a month. As with other forms of reliability and validity, variants of the correlation coefficient are used as a numerical index.

Internal reliability

Internal reliability indicates how consistently *all* of the items in a scale measure the concept in question. If a scale is perfectly internally reliable, any set of items from the scale could be selected and they will provide a measure that is more or less the same as any other group of items taken from that scale. Correlating the scores based on one half of the items with the scores based on the other half is a traditional approach used for several measures of internal reliability. Alpha reliability may be construed as just a variant on this theme:

- *Split-half reliability*   The first half of the items on the test are summed, then the second half of the items are summed (for each participant). The Pearson correlation between the two halves is calculated – this is referred to as the split-half reliability (though a correction for length of the scale is sometimes applied such that the reliability given is for the full-length scale).

- *Odd–even reliability*   The two halves are created differently for this. One half comprises the odd-numbered items (e.g. items 1, 3, 5, 7) and the other half the even-numbered items (e.g. items 2, 4, 6, 8). The correlation between these two sets of scores is the odd–even reliability. Once again, an adjustment for the length of the scale can be made.

- *Alpha reliability (Cronbach's alpha)* Split-half and odd–even reliability are dependent on the particular items included in the two halves. Alpha reliability improves on this by being an average of every possible half of the items correlated with every possible other half. Since alpha reliability takes all items into account and all possible ways of splitting them, it gives the best overall picture. Fortunately, the calculation of alpha reliability can be achieved more directly using a method based on the analysis of variance. This is described in the companion text *Understanding statistics in psychology with SPSS* (Howitt & Cramer, 2020).

The first two measures of internal reliability are based on halves of the items rather than of the entire scale. The Spearman-Brown formula allows us to estimate what the reliability of the full length scale would be. It can be used to estimate the reliability of the full scale, or to estimate what the reliability of an even shorter scale would be. (If one can achieve the desired level of reliability with a short scale, then this may be preferred.) The procedure is given in the companion book *Understanding statistics in psychology with SPSS* (Howitt & Cramer, 2020) – it is relatively simple to compute by hand. SPSS does not compute the Spearman–Brown formula, but it can give the Guttman reliability coefficient. This is much like the split-half reliability adjusted to the full-scale length using the Spearman–Brown formula and is actually more generally applicable. Why is internal consistency or reliability important? Quite simply because high internal consistency means that all items are measuring much the same thing which makes for a better measure. Also the higher the consistency within a measure, the higher will be the correlation between that measure and other variables. It is fairly intuitive that a bad measure of honesty, say, will correlate less well with, say, lying to get out of trouble than would a good measure of honesty. The correlation of any variable with another variable is limited by the internal reliability of the variables. So, when interpreting any correlation coefficient, information on the reliability of the variables involved is clearly desirable. The maximum possible size of the correlation between variables A and B is the square root of the product of the reliability of variable A (say .8) and that of variable B (say .9) which gives $\sqrt{.8 \times .9} = .85$. Without knowing this, the researcher who obtains a correlation of .61 between variable A and variable B might feel that the correlation is just a moderate one. So it is between the two measures, but actually the correlation between two variables could be only .85 at most. Hence the correlation of .61 is actually quite an impressive finding, given the unreliability of the measures. There is a simple correction which allows one to adjust a correlation by the reliabilities of one or both of the variables. This was described earlier (Chapter 4). Given the difference that this adjustment can make to the interpretation of the obtained relationships, it is probably too often neglected by researchers.

Finally, a note of caution is appropriate. Many textbooks stress that internal reliability is an important and essential feature of a good measure. This is true, but only up to a point. If one is trying to measure a carefully defined psychological construct (intelligence, extraversion and need for achievement), then internal reliability should be as high as can be practically achieved. On the other hand, the measurement of such refined psychological concepts may not be the main objective of the measure. Since much human behaviour is multiply determined (being the result of the influence of a number of variables, though not necessarily all of them), a measure that combines several different variables may actually predict better.

A good example of this is Hare's psychopathy checklist (Hare, 1991). Psychopaths are known to be especially common in criminal populations, for example. The checklist is scored by simply adding up the number of different characteristics of psychopathy that an individual demonstrates. These features include glibness, pathological lying, manipulativeness and grandiose estimates of self-worth. For a characteristic such as psychopathy which is a syndrome of diagnostic features, internal reliability is less crucial than including all possible diagnostic features of the syndrome.

Stability over time or between different measures

Psychologists also apply the consistency criterion to another aspect of measurement: how their tests and measures perform at a time interval or across similar versions of a test. There are several different types of this:

- *Test–retest reliability* This is simply the correlation between scores from a sample of participants on a test measured at one point in time with their scores on the same test administered at a later time. Remember that test–retest reliability is a correlation between scores so the mean scores may change between administrations of the test. The size of test–retest reliability is limited by the *internal reliability* of the test. Of course, the test–retest reliability is affected by any number of factors in addition. The longer the interval between the test and retest is the more opportunity there is for the characteristics of individuals to simply change, thus affecting the test–retest reliability adversely. However, test–retest reliability may be affected by carry-over from the first administration of the test to the second, that is, participants may simply remember their answers to the first test when they complete the retest.

- *Alternate-forms reliability* The relationship between two different versions of the same measure is known as alternate-forms reliability. Since repeated measurement may be affected by 'memory' contamination, some measures are available in two versions or forms. Since these contain different items, 'memory' contamination may be reduced in test–retest research – though possibly not entirely. Once again, the maximum value of alternate-forms reliability is the product of the two internal reliabilities. If the alternate-forms reliability is similar to this value, then it seems clear that the two forms of the test are assessing much the same things. If the alternate-forms reliability is much lower than the maximum possible, then the two forms are measuring rather different things. A correlation between two tests does not mean that they are measuring the same thing – it means that they are partially measuring the same thing. The bigger the correlation up to the maximum, given the reliabilities of the tests, the more they are measuring substantially the same things.

The reason for the close relationship between internal reliability and other forms of reliability has already been explained. To repeat, the lower the internal reliability of a test is, the lower the maximum correlation of that test will be with any other variable (including alternate forms of the test and retests on the same variable). The bigger the internal reliability value, all other things being equal, the bigger the correlation of the test with any other variable it correlates with. In other words, there is a close relationship between different forms of reliability despite their superficial differences.

Remember that a measure should be reliable over time if the concept to which it refers is chronologically stable. We do not expect a thermometer to give the same readings day after day but we do expect bathroom scales to give more or less stable readings of our weight over a short period of time. That is, we expect the temperature to vary but our weight should be largely constant. In the same way, reliability over time (especially test–retest reliability) should only be high for psychological characteristics which are themselves stable over time. Psychological characteristics which are not stable over time (attention, happiness, alertness, etc.) should *not* necessarily give good levels of test–retest reliability. Characteristics which we can assume to be stable over time (intelligence, honesty, religious beliefs) should show strong test–retest reliability. So reliability should be carefully assessed against how it is being measured and what is being measured. That accepted, psychologists generally seek to measure stable and enduring psychological characteristics, hence test–retest reliability is generally expected to be good for most psychological tests and measures.

<h2>16.3   Validity</h2>

Validity is usually defined as 'whether a test measures what it is intended to measure'. This fits well with the dictionary definition of the term *valid* as meaning well founded, sound or defensible. The following should be considered when examining the validity of a test:

- Validity is not a property of a test itself but a complex matter of the test, the sample on which a test is used, the social context of its use and other factors. A test which is good at measuring religious commitment in the general population may be woefully useless when applied to a sample of priests. A test which is a good measure in research may prove to be flawed as a part of job selection in which applicants will put their best face forward (i.e. maybe not tell the truth). Famously, this issue is often put as the question, 'Valid for what?'. The implication being that validity is not an inherent feature of a test or measure but should be expected to vary according to the purpose to which it is being put.

- Reliability and validity are, conceptually, distinct and there need not be any necessary relationship between the two. So be very wary about statements which imply that a valid test or measure has to be reliable. We have already seen that in psychology the emphasis in measurement is generally on relatively stable and enduring characteristics of people (e.g. their creativity). Such a measure should be consistent over time (reliable). It also ought to distinguish between inventors and the rest of us if it is a valid measure of creativity. A measure of a characteristic which varies quite rapidly over time will not be reliable over time – if it is, then we might doubt its validity. For example, a valid measure of suicide intention may not be particularly stable (reliable) over time, though it may be good at identifying those at imminent risk of suicide. How reliable it is will depend on the interval between the test and the retest.

- Since validity is often expressed as a correlation between the test or measure and some other criterion, the validity coefficient (as it is called) will be limited by the reliability of the test or measure. Once again, the maximum correlation of the test or measure with any other variable has an upper limit determined by its internal reliability.

<h2>16.4   Types of validity</h2>

There are a number of generally recognised types of validity – face, content, criterion; that is, concurrent and predictive validity, construct, known-group and convergent validity (see Figure 16.2). (Other types of validity such as internal validity and external validity concern research design rather than measurement as such. These were dealt with earlier – see Chapter 12.) Over the years, the distinction between these different types of validity has become a little blurred in textbooks. We will try to reinstate the distinctive features of each.

Face validity	• From the appearance of the items, does this scale measure what it claims to measure?
Content validity	• Do the items of the scale cover the important characteristics of the concept being measured?
Concurrent validity	• Does the scale correlate well with other measures of the same concept taken at the same time?
Known-groups validity	• Does the measure distinguish between groups that it should be expected to? e.g. do university students have higher IQs than those who do not go to university?
Predictive validity	• Does the measure predict accurately future behaviours, e.g. does IQ predict those who eventually go to university?
Construct validity	• This involves developing theoretical and conceptual understanding of the thing being measured. How well do we understand the construct?
Triangulation	• Using multiple types of measures to assess something – such as verbal measures and behavioural measures of a concept. Triangulation is more generally familiar in qualitative research.
Convergent validity	• Do different sorts of measures of the same concept tend to intercorrelate together?
Discriminant validity	• Do measures of apparently different concepts not correlate with each other?

FIGURE 16.2   Types of validity

Face validity

Face validity can only be judged informally. The test items are reviewed to assess whether on the face of things (i.e. in terms of the content of the items) the test measures the psychological concept concerned. The researcher inevitably applies this validity criterion while constructing the test, since the researcher will only include items they consider to be viable. The problems with face validity are obvious, especially bearing in mind the need for item analysis techniques. The fact that item analysis techniques identify poor items, clearly a measure which appears to have face validity cannot be guaranteed to meet more stringent validity requirements. Among the reasons for this is that items which appear valid to the researcher may be understood very differently by the participants.

Face validity is a very minimal assessment of validity and is subjective in that different researchers may perceive the face validity of the same test very differently. Some tests and measures are constructed to measure what they measure without the researcher being concerned about what the test might correlate with or predict. In these circumstances, face validity may be just about the only option. For example, if a researcher wished to measure opinions about the causes of crime, the content of the items would be important. Whether these opinions are associated with something else might not concern the researchers.

Content validity

In its classic formulation, good content validity follows from the careful creation of a broad range of items. These items are carefully collected together to reflect facets of the concept being assessed. Using diverse means of eliciting or creating potential items for inclusion helps enhance content validity. Such diversity would include the research literature, interviews with people similar to potential participants, and relevant established theory.

Some authors present a rather different version of what constitutes content validity. They suggest that content validity is achieved by reference to experts on the topic being measured. The task of the expert is to offer insight into whether the items cover the range needed or whether significant aspects of the construct being measured have been omitted. This is a very limited view of what content validity is, although it is one aspect of it.

Concurrent validity

This is simply how well the test correlates with appropriate criteria measured at the same time. One way of doing this is to correlate the test with another (possibly better established) test of the same thing applied to the same group of participants at the same time. So, if one proposed replacing examinations with multiple-choice tests, then the concurrent validity of the multiple-choice test would be assessed by correlating the multiple-choice test scores with marks from an examination taken at the same time. It stands to reason that a new test which purports to measure the same thing as the examination should correlate with examination marks. The better the correlation is, the more confidence can be placed in the new measure. Concurrent validity is assessed against a criterion, as we have seen. The next form of validity, predictive validity, is equally criterion-based.

Predictive validity

This is the ability of the measure to predict future events. For example, does our measure of honesty predict whether a person will be in prison in five years' time? Of course, the predictive validity depends on the future event's nature. Not all psychological tests are intended to predict future events so it is of little consequence if their predictive validity is poor. A measure intended to predict future events does not always have to be rich in psychological detail in order to be effective – and it need not show good internal consistency. For example, if we wished to predict future offending, then a measure consisting of variables such as number of previous convictions and gender may be the best way of predicting it. The important thing is that it does predict the future event. Predicting from psychological traits may be relatively ineffective in these circumstances.

Construct validity

For some researchers, life is not quite so simple as the criterion-based validity methods imply. Take a concept such as self-esteem, for example. If we develop what we see as being an effective measure of self-esteem, can we propose criteria against which to assess the concurrent and predictive validity? We might think that self-esteem is inversely related to future suicide attempts, though probably very weakly. Alternatively, we might think that the measure of self-esteem should correlate with other measures of self-esteem, as in concurrent validity. However, what if we developed a measure of self-esteem which utilised new theoretical conceptualisations of self-esteem? In these circumstances, relating our new measure of self-esteem to existing measures would not be sufficient. Since our new measure is regarded as an improvement, its lack of concurrent validity with older methods of measurement might be a good thing.

Construct validity is generally poorly understood and even more poorly explained in research methods textbooks. The reason is that it is presented as a technical measurement issue whereas, in its original conceptualisation, construct validity was more about theory development and general progress of knowledge. So it is much more concerned with being able to specify the nature of the psychological construct that underlies our measure than demonstrating that a test measures what it is supposed to measure. In one of the original classic papers on construct validity, Cronbach and Meehl (1955) put the essence of construct validity in the form of a graphic example very apposite for students:

> Suppose measure X correlates .50 with Y, the amount of palmar sweating induced when we tell a student that he has failed a Psychology I exam. Predictive validity of X for Y is adequately described by the coefficient, and a statement of the experimental and sampling conditions. If someone were to ask, 'Isn't there perhaps another way to interpret this correlation?' or 'What other kinds of evidence can you bring to support your interpretation?' we would hardly understand what he [sic] was asking because no interpretation has been made. These questions become relevant when the correlation is advanced as evidence that 'test X measures anxiety proneness'. Alternative interpretations are possible; for example, perhaps the test measures 'academic aspiration', in which case we will expect different results if we induce palmar sweating by economic threat. It is then reasonable to inquire about other kinds of evidence.

(p. 283)

Cronbach and Meehl then report a variety of 'findings' from other studies which help us understand the nature of test X better:

- Test X has a correlation of .45 with the ratings of the students' 'tenseness' made by other students.

- Test X correlates .55 with the amount of intellectual inefficiency which follows the administration of painful electric shocks.

- Test X correlates .68 with the Taylor anxiety scale.

- The order of means on test X is highest in those diagnosed as having an anxiety state, next highest in those diagnosed with reactive depression, next highest in 'normal' people, and lowest in those with a psychopathic personality.

- There is a correlation of .60 between palmar sweat when threatened with failure in psychology and when threatened with failure in mathematics.

- Test X does not correlate with social class, work aspirations and social values.

The reason why Cronbach and Meehl include all of this extra information is that it seems to confirm that academic aspiration is not the explanation of the relationship between test X and palmar sweating. The above pattern of findings better supports the original interpretation that the relationship between test X and palmar sweating is due to anxiety. Cronbach and Meehl go on to suggest that, if the best available theory of anxiety predicts that anxiety should show the pattern of relationships manifested by test X, the idea that test X measures anxiety is even more strongly supported.

So delving into the origins of the concept of construct validity clearly demonstrates it to be a complex process. Test X is assessed in relation to a variety of information about it, but also to other variables associated with it. Put another way, construct validity is a method of developing psychological understanding that seeks to inform the researcher about the underlying psychological construct. In this sense, it is about theory building, because we need constructs upon which to build theory. It should also be clear that construct validity is much more an attitude of mind on the part of the researcher than it is a technical methodological tool. If one likes, construct validity is a methodological approach in the original sense of the term 'methodological', that is, strategies for enhancing and developing knowledge. In modern usage, methodological simply refers to the means of collecting data. There is more to knowledge than just data. So it is possible for a construct to be refined and clarified during the progress of research in a field – the definition of a construct is not fixed for all time.

Construct validity may include a vast range of types of evidence, including some that we have already discussed – the correlations between items, the stability of the measure over time, concurrent and predictive validity findings and so forth. What constitutes support for the construct depends on what we assume to be the nature of the construct. Finding that a test tends to be stable over time undermines the validity of a test which measures transitory mood, as we have already indicated.

Anyone struggling to understand how construct validity fits in with their work should note the following: 'The investigation of a test's construct validity is not essentially different from the general scientific procedures for developing and confirming theories' (Cronbach & Meehl, 1955, p. 300). This does not particularly help one apply construct validity to one's own research – it merely explains why the task is rather difficult. Construct validity is so important (and difficult) because it basically involves many aspects of the research process.

The following types of validity can be considered to be additional ways of tackling the complex issue of construct validity.

Known-groups validity

If we can establish that scores on a measure differ in predictable ways between two specified groups of individuals, then this is evidence of the value of the test – and its known-groups validity. For example, a test of schizoid thought should give higher scores for a group of people with schizophrenia than for a group of individuals without schizophrenia. If it does, then the test can be deemed valid by this method. But we need to be careful. All that we have established is that the groups differ on this particular test. It does not, in itself, establish definitively that our test measures schizoid thought. Many factors may differentiate people with schizophrenia from others – our measure might be assessing one of these and not schizoid thought. For example, if people with schizophrenia are more likely to be men than women, then the variable gender will differentiate the two groups. Gender is simply not schizoid thought.

A measure which has good known-groups validity is clearly capable of more or less accurately differentiating people with schizophrenia from others. Being able to do this may add little to our scientific understanding of the construct of schizoid thought. It is only when it is part of a network of relationships that it is capable of adding to our confidence in the scientific worth of the construct – or not.

Triangulation

Triangulation uses multiple measures of a concept. If a relationship is established using several different types of tests or measures, then this is evidence of the validity of the relationship, according to Campbell and Fiske (1959). Ideally, the measures should be quite different, for example, using interviewer ratings of extraversion compared with using a paper and pencil measure of the same concept. In some ways, triangulation can be seen as a combination of concurrent and predictive validity. The basic assumption is that if two different measures of ostensibly the same construct both correlate with a variable which the construct might be expected to relate to, then this increases our confidence in the construct.

For triangulation to help establish the construct, all three components of the triangle ought to correlate with each other as in Figure 16.3. All of the arrows represent a relationship between the three aspects of the triangle. If test A and test B correlate, then this is the basic requirement of demonstrating concurrent validity. If test A correlates with variable X, and test B also correlates with variable X, then this is evidence of the predictive validity of tests A and B. Notice that in effect this approach is building up the network of associations which Cronbach and Meehl regard as the essence of construct validation. As such, it is much more powerful evidence in favour of the construct than the evidence of either concurrent validity or predictive validity taken separately. Imagine tests A and B both predict variable X but do not correlate. The implication of this is that tests A and B are measuring very different things, although they clearly predict different aspects of variable X.

Triangulation might be regarded as a rudimentary form of construct validation. It is clearly an important improvement over the crude empiricism of criterion validity (predictive and concurrent validity). Nevertheless, it is *not* quite the same as construct validity. Its concerns about patterns of relationships are minimal. Similarly, triangulation has only weak allegiances with theory.

Convergent validity

This introduces a further dimension to the concept of validity, that is, measures of, say, honesty should relate irrespective of the nature or mode of the measure. This means that:

- For example, a self-completion honesty scale should correlate with a behavioural measure of honesty (e.g. handing in to the police money found in the street) *and* assessments of lying on a polygraph (lie detector) test. All should correlate well with each other and be distinguishable from measures of different but partially related concepts such as religiousness.

- The *type* of measure should not unduly determine the relationships. If we find that our best correlations among measures of honesty and religiosity all use self-completion

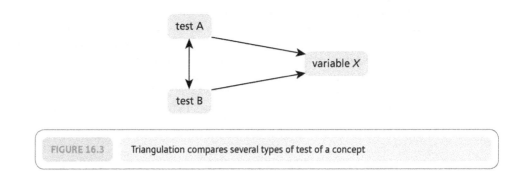

| FIGURE 16.3 | Triangulation compares several types of test of a concept |

questionnaires, then there may be a validity issue. The domain of measurement (self-completion) seems to be having a greater bearing on the relationships than the construct being measured. If self-completion measures of religiousness and honesty have higher correlations with each other than self-completion measures of honesty have with behavioural measures of honesty, there is clearly a validity problem. In other words, validity is enhanced by evidence that the concept may be measured by a multiplicity of measures from a wide variety of domain. While this is a reasonable validity criterion, some of its underlying assumptions are questionable. One of these assumptions is that there should be a strong relationship between different types of measure of a concept. This can sometimes be a debatable assumption. For example, would we expect a strong relationship between racial attitudes as assessed by a self-completion attitude questionnaire, and a behavioural measure of racial attitudes such as abusive racist behaviour in the street? Many people with racist attitudes are unlikely to express their attitudes in crude racist chants at a football match, simply because 'they do not do that sort of thing' or they fear arrest by the police.

Discriminant validity

Convergent validities indicate that measures which are measuring the same thing ought to correlate with each other substantially. Discriminant validity is just the opposite. If measures are apparently measuring different things then they should not correlate strongly with each other. It should be obvious, then, that convergent and discriminant validity should be considered together when assessing the validity of a measure.

It is fairly obvious that there is a degree of overlap in the different sorts of validity, though, broadly speaking, they are different.

Box 16.1   Research Example

Should you believe a smoker?

Ramo, D. E., Hall, S. M., & Prochaska, J. J. (2011). Reliability and validity of self-reported smoking in an anonymous online survey with young adults. *Health Psychology, 30*, 693–701.

There are obvious advantages in using the Internet for research purposes. People trawl the Internet for information in large numbers. If a research team is able to attract such people over the Internet, then the possibility of recruiting substantial samples for research at minimum cost seems obvious. But, of course, the problems of Internet research can undermine the value of any data obtained. In circumstances of anonymity, a person may deliberately submit entirely bogus data or, alternatively, they may be far more open and honest because of this anonymity. The user of the Internet may be somewhat different in characteristics from people who do not use the Internet, thus creating bias. At the same time, there may be advantages in that Internet research may recruit subpopulations of people who would rarely be included in a community survey, for example. The consequence of these and other considerations is that it is unwise for researchers to assume that research on the Internet and research in the community will generate similar data. All psychological variables are subject to the requirements of being reliable and valid. Even a simple variable may exhibit measurement problems. Gender and age are good examples in which reliability and validity are simply assumed, but we can all imagine circumstances in which the participant gives data which are not accurate – for example, providing incorrect information about one's age for reasons of vanity. So, do not assume that reliability and validity are only issues for psychological tests and measurements such as those discussed in Chapter 15, they apply to every psychological measure no matter how humble. The study by Ramo, Hall, and Prochaska (2011) employed quite a variety of measures of smoking behaviour and related variables and employed information on a variety of approaches to reliability and validity, not all of which can be dealt with here.

Background

Research on smoking has many potential health benefits. It is commonly the case that smoking behaviour is assessed using self-report measures. Like any measure in psychology, this is potentially flawed, since the researcher does not observe smoking behaviours directly but relies on the smoker's own reports which may not be accurate. The researcher might ask others to rate the smoking behaviour of, say, their partner or their children, but such measures are equally fraught. There is a lot of research on the reliability and validity of self-reported measures of smoking in community-based research, but the question of the reliability and validity of data collected from the Internet warrants special attention. The paper in question is densely packed with statistical analyses and variables. This is common in research papers but should cause even the novice reader few problems, as the basic elements of the analysis are relatively simple – however, their sheer volume makes life difficult. So below we present only a simplified version of the study and recommend that you download the original for comparison.

Hypothesis

According to the authors, 'The purpose of the current study was to examine the psychometric properties of established measures commonly administered in face-to-face interviews to determine whether they perform similarly when administered anonymously online to a national, representative sample of young adult tobacco users' (Ramo et al., 2011, p. 693). Also, 'Based on previous findings in the literature, in tests of convergent validity of smoking behavior, we hypothesized that cigarettes smoked per day would be associated with dependence symptoms and that both variables would be associated with years of smoking, making an attempt to quit in the past-year, abstinence duration, desire to quit, efficacy for quitting, abstinence goal, and smoking-related expectancies. In tests of divergent validity, we expected that cigarettes per day and nicotine dependence would be unrelated to subjective social status and motivations to abstain from alcohol and marijuana' (p. 694).

Method

Participants in the research were 248 younger-age adults between the ages of 18 and 25 years. It was a requirement of selection that they had smoked a minimum of one cigarette in the 30 days before they were recruited. The recruitment was online and involved a survey of tobacco and use of other substances. Recruitment involved Internet advertisements which offered the chance to win $25 or $400 in a prize draw. The advertisements ran for a period of six months. Each advertisement included a link to a consent form and a survey questionnaire. Security protection was provided in the form of data encryption and similar.

The analysis of the questionnaires was extensive, so we can only choose the highlights. Statistics involved in the study included the Pearson correlation coefficient as well as comparisons of means using the analysis of variance.

→

Table 16.1	Correlations between similar smoking measures on different questionnaires illustrating internal reliability of smoking measures			
Smoking questionnaire	**Timeline follow back smoking questionnaire**			
	No. of cigarettes smoked between today and yesterday	Number smoked in past 7 days	Average number smoked per day	Average number of smoking days per week
Number of cigarettes in past 24 hours	.8	.8	.8	.5
Number of cigarettes in past 7 days	.8	.9	.9	.5
Usual number of cigarettes a day	.9	.9	.9	.5
Average number of days smoked each week	.5	.5	.5	.8

Table 16.2	Construct validity correlations of number of cigarettes smoked per day	
	Those smoking every day	Those who do not smoke every day
Longer length of time smoking	.4	Not significant
Greater number of quit attempts in lifetime	.2	Not significant
Lower effectiveness of quit attempts	–.2	Not significant
Quitting perceived as difficult	.3	Not significant

Findings

There was a high level of internal consistency or internal reliability for smoking behaviours as assessed in terms of quantity and frequency of smoking as well as smoking-related expectancies of various sorts. The analysis for the smoking behaviours is given in Table 16.1. This involves two separate questionnaires to measure smoking which produced variables that could be compared. Table 16.1 shows that variables measuring ostensibly the same thing on the two different questionnaires were highly correlated, as one might expect. The correlations were generally high except for the participants' estimates of the number of days a week that they smoked.

There was evidence of validity using a concurrent criterion as well as divergent validity for smoking behaviour. That is, there were some moderate correlations between amount smoked and various variables which for theoretical reasons might be expected to correlate with smoking. Table 16.2 shows that for people who smoke every day, there were some positive correlations with the number of cigarettes smoked, though this was not always the case. For those who did not smoke every day, these same correlations were not statistically significant. So there is some evidence of convergent validity, though the data we have selected tended to be that which showed evidence of this.

Smoking quantity estimates were similar in the online survey to those from a household survey-based study, though smoking frequency did not follow this pattern.

Authors' suggestions for further research

The authors argued that the ease of access and anonymity offered by the Internet make that medium attractive to researchers. They recommend that 'Investigations should continue to evaluate the psychometric properties of health risk behaviors assessed online' (p. 700).

16.5 Conclusion

A crucial feature of the concepts of reliability and validity is that they are tools for thinking and questioning researchers. Employed to their fullest potential, they constitute a desire to fully engage with the subject matter of the research. They should not be regarded as kitemark standards which, if exceeded, equate to evidence of the quality of the test or measure. Properly conceived, they invite researchers to explore both the theoretical and the empirical relationships of their subject matter. The value of a measure cannot be assessed simply in terms of possessing both high validity and high reliability. What is reasonable by way of reliability and validity is dependent on the nature of what is being measured as well as on the ways available to measure it.

Key points

- All measures need to be assessed for objectivity, reliability and validity. There is no minimum criterion of acceptable standards of each of these, since the nature of what is being measured is also crucial.

- Information about the reliability and validity of some measures is readily available from standard databases, journal articles and the Internet. However, this is not always the case for every measure.

- Reliability is about consistency within the measure or over time.

- Cronbach's alpha, split-half reliability and odd–even reliability are all measures of internal reliability. Cronbach's alpha is readily computed and should probably be the measure of choice.

- Reliability is also assessed at correlating a measure given at different time points (test–retest reliability) and between different versions of the test (alternate-forms reliability).

- Reliability over time should be high for measures of stable psychological characteristics but low for unstable psychological characteristics.

→

- Validity is often described as assessing whether a test measures what it is supposed to measure. This implies different validities according to the purpose to which a measure is being put.

- Face validity is an examination of the items to see whether they appear to be measuring what the test is intended to measure.

- Content validity refers to the processes by which items are developed – sampling from a wide variety of sources, using a wide variety of informants and using a variety of styles of item may all contribute to content validity.

- Construct validity involves a thorough understanding of how the measure operates compared with other measures. Does the pattern of relationships between the measures appear meaningful for a variety of other constructs? Does the measure do what pertinent theory suggests that it should?

- Construct validity is an extensive and complex process which relates more to the process of the development of science than to a single index of validity.

- Known-groups validity, triangulation and convergent validity can all be seen as partial aspects of construct validity. After all, they each examine the complex patterns of relationships between the measure, similar measures, different measures and expectations of what types of person are differentiated by the measure.

ACTIVITY

You ask your partner if they love you. Their reply is 'yes, very much so'. How would you assess the reliability and validity of this measure using the concepts discussed in this chapter?

CHAPTER 17

Coding data

Overview

- Coding is the process of categorising the raw data, usually into descriptive categories.

- Coding is a basic process in both quantitative and qualitative research. Sometimes coding is a hidden process in quantitative research.

- In pre-coding, the participants are given a limited number of replies to choose from, much as in a multiple-choice test.

- Whenever data are collected qualitatively in an extensive, rich form, coding is essential. However, some researchers will choose to impose their own coding categories, whereas others will endeavour to develop categories which match the data as supplied by the participants and which would be meaningful from the participants' perspectives.

- Coding schedules may be subjected to measures of inter-coder reliability and agreement when quantified.

17.1 Introduction

Coding is the point of overlap between quantitative and qualitative methods and marks a dividing line between the two. The topic of coding allows us to discuss various issues at the heart of psychology and enables us to understand the fundamental differences between quantitative and qualitative psychology. Coding in some form or another is central to all psychological research irrespective of its style. Inevitably, when we research any complex aspect of human activity the richness of what we observe has to be simplified in order to describe and even explain it. No researcher simply videos people's activities and compiles these for publication, no matter how much they abhor quantification. Always some form of analysis is involved. In this way, all researchers impose structure on the world. Quintessentially, coding is about how we develop understanding of the nature of things we research. Nevertheless, radical differences exist between the ways quantitative and qualitative researchers go about categorisation. It is important to recognise these differences and to appreciate their relative strengths.

Crucially, Figure 17.1 distinguishes the data collection phase of research and data analysis. It shows four possible combinations of quantitative and qualitative data collection and analysis methods. Three of the combinations are fairly common approaches. Only the qualitative analysis of quantitative data is rare or non-existent, although some researchers have argued for its feasibility. Figure 17.1 implies that quantitative analysis may use much the same data collection methods as qualitative analysis. Thus, in-depth interviews, focus groups, biographies and so forth may be equally amenable to quantitative analysis as qualitative analysis.

Coding has two different meanings in research:

- The process by which observations, text, recordings and generally any sort of data are categorised according to a classificatory scheme. Indeed, categorisation is a better description of the process than is the word coding.

- The process by which items of data are given a number for the purposes of computer analysis. For example, a variable such as gender consists of the two categories male and female. It simplifies computer applications if these are entered with a numerical code in which, say, 1 represents male and 2 represents female. This seems closer to dictionary definitions of code which suggests that coding is to represent one thing by another.

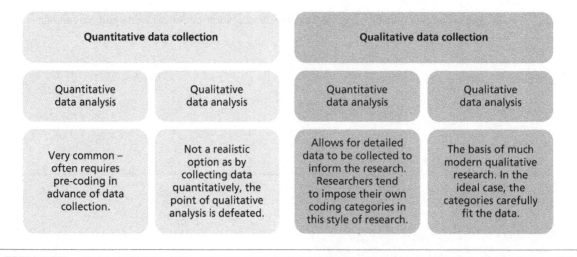

Quantitative data collection		Qualitative data collection	
Quantitative data analysis	Qualitative data analysis	Quantitative data analysis	Qualitative data analysis
Very common – often requires pre-coding in advance of data collection.	Not a realistic option as by collecting data quantitatively, the point of qualitative analysis is defeated.	Allows for detailed data to be collected to inform the research. Researchers tend to impose their own coding categories in this style of research.	The basis of much modern qualitative research. In the ideal case, the categories carefully fit the data.

FIGURE 17.1   Relation between quantitative and qualitative data collection, and quantitative and qualitative data analysis

Often both of these meanings of coding occur in the same research. In highly structured materials such as multiple-choice questionnaires, the categorisation is actually done by the participant, leaving only the computer coding to the researcher. Coding reflects a major step between data collection and the findings of the research. It is really the first stage of the process by which the data are given structure.

Content analysis is a common term referring to the coding of, especially, mass media content – books, television programmes, the Internet, and so forth. Each of these provide sources of 'rich', complex data. An important part of the work of many communications researchers is to systematically classify or categorise media content. Frequently, they provide rates or frequencies of occurrence of different sorts of content. For example, the researcher might study sexism in television programmes. This might involve counting the number of times women are portrayed in domestic settings as opposed to work settings, or how often women are used as authoritative voice-overs in advertising. Content analysis typifies the categorisation process needed as part of the analysis of a variety of data.

17.2 Types of coding

There are at least three types of coding (see Figure 17.2):

- Pre-coding

- Researcher-imposed coding

- Qualitative coding – coding emerging from the data.

The final form of coding is characteristic of qualitative data analysis. Aspects of it are covered in a later chapter (Chapter 22) on grounded theory, for example. The other two are rather more characteristic of quantification. Pre-coding is readily seen in highly structured measures such as self-completion questionnaires. Researcher-imposed coding is more typical of circumstances in which the data have been collected in a fairly rich or

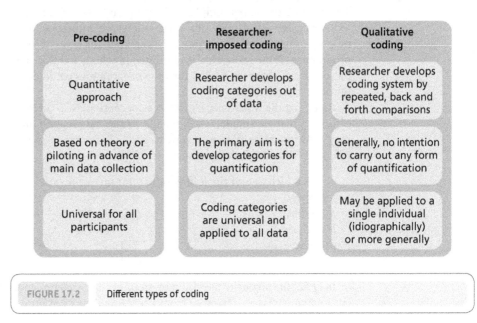

Pre-coding	Researcher-imposed coding	Qualitative coding
Quantitative approach	Researcher develops coding categories out of data	Researcher develops coding system by repeated, back and forth comparisons
Based on theory or piloting in advance of main data collection	The primary aim is to develop categories for quantification	Generally, no intention to carry out any form of quantification
Universal for all participants	Coding categories are universal and applied to all data	May be applied to a single individual (idiographically) or more generally

FIGURE 17.2 Different types of coding

qualitative form but the researcher's intention is to carry out a quantitative or statistical analysis. Coding emerging from the data is more typical of research not involving numerical or statistical analysis.

Pre-coding

This is very familiar, since it is the basis of much quantitative research in mainstream psychology. It is so common nowadays that it has a taken-for-granted quality. Not only that but it is also familiar from surveys in magazines and other forms of popular entertainment. Typical examples of pre-coding are found in attitude and personality questionnaires. In these the participant replies to a series of statements relevant to a particular area of interest. However, typically the respondent only has a very limited predetermined list of alternative replies. In the simplest of cases, for example, participants may be asked to do no more than *agree* or *disagree* with statements like 'Unemployment is the most important issue facing the country today'.

By definition, pre-coding occurs prior to data collection. That is, the coding categories are predetermined and are not amenable to change or re-coding (other than the possibility of combining several categories together for the purposes of data analysis). Furthermore, participants code their own 'responses' into one of the available coding categories. As a consequence, the researcher is oblivious to how the coding is actually done.

Let us examine the reasons for pre-coding by taking an example of a simple research study. A researcher asks a group of young people at a school to answer the following question:

Q 43: What is your favourite television programme? _____

A sample of 100 young people might write down as many as 100 different television programmes. There may be overlaps, so the actual total may be lower. What can one do with these data, which might include answers like football, *Game of Thrones*, *The Simpsons* and *X Factor*? Given that research should give structure to data, simply listing all of the named programmes is not in itself the solution. The researcher must categorise (or code) the replies of the participants in some way. There is no obvious, single way of doing this. The purpose of the research has a bearing on how the data are coded. If the research is to investigate violent television programmes, then the researcher could code the favourite programme as violent or not, or even code the level of violence characteristic of the programme. If the researcher is interested in whether children are watching programmes put on late at night for adults, then the programmes could be coded in terms of the time of their transmission.

Assuming the researcher has a clear conception as to their question's purpose, coding categories that are simple, relevant and obvious may suggest themselves. So circumstances may allow the researcher to choose to pre-code the range of answers that the respondent may give. Take the following question:

Q 52: Which one of the following is your favourite type of television programme?
(a) Sport
(b) Films
(c) Music
(d) Cartoons ❑
(e) Other   c.61

In Q 52, the favourite television programme has been pre-coded by asking the respondent to nominate their favourite from a few broad types of programme. Notice the box to the right of the question in which the researcher enters the computer code for the partici-pant's chosen answer. The variable in question is identified by a code, in this case 'c.61'. Apart from putting the respondent's replies into a computer-friendly form, the researcher's input is minimal (but nevertheless crucial) with pre-coded material. Notice that the pre-coding has restricted the information the participant can provide quite considerably. So in this example nothing at all is known about the specific programmes liked. In other words, pre-coding actually eliminates information which the qualitative researcher might find of value. In fact, it misses the point of qualitative data analysis entirely. Qualitative researchers often rail against pre-coded data.

Pre-coding is not exclusively a feature of the analysis of self-completion question-naires. It can be used as an approach to analysing interviews, for example. Or the research may involve observing behaviour. Those observations may involve detailed note-taking, but there is no reason why the observation categories cannot be pre-coded. Leyens, Camino, Parke, and Berkowitz (1975) used a pre-coded observational schedule in order to observe the aggressive behaviour of boys before and after they had seen violent or non-violent films. Such pre-coded observations greatly facilitate matters such as calculating the degree of agreement between different observers as in inter-observer or inter-rater reliability.

So pre-coding sets limitations on the information available to the researcher. Unless the participant writes something in the margin or qualifies their choice, no one would be the wiser. Research interviews in which the interviewer simply notes which pre-coded category applies means that a great deal of what the interviewee says is disregarded. Pre-coding reduces the richness of the data to a level manageable by the researcher and adequate to meet the research's purpose. Inevitably, pre-coding means that nuances and subtleties are filtered out. This is neither a good nor a bad thing in any absolute sense. For some purposes, the researcher-imposed broad-brush categories may be perfect; for other purposes, pre-coding is woefully inadequate.

So where do the pre-coded categories come from? There is a range of answers to this question, as a perusal of the research literature will demonstrate:

- *Conventional formats* Some pre-coding formats are conventional in the sense that they have been commonly used by researchers over several decades. For example, the yes–no, agree–disagree pre-coded response formats are so established that we tend to take them for granted. However, even using such a simple format raises questions, such as what if someone does not disagree and does not agree? In consideration of this, some response formats include a 'don't know' or '?' category. Similarly, the five-point Likert scale answer format (strongly agree, agree, ?, disagree and strongly disagree) is conven-tional and generally works well for its purpose. But there is no reason why seven- or nine-point scales cannot be used instead. Actually, there is no absolutely compelling reason why the middle, neutral or '?' point cannot be omitted leaving a four-, six- or eight-point scale. Some argue that the neutral point provides an easy option of not making a choice between one side of the scale and the other.

- *Piloting* Many researchers will try out or pilot their materials on a group of individu-als similar to the eventual sample. This is done in such a way as to encourage the par-ticipants to raise questions and problems causing difficulties filling in the questionnaire such as problems with the response format. The small number of gradations in this sort of answer format, inevitably makes difficulties in finally making a choice. Participants may feel frustrated if forced to make, to them, arbitrary and rather meaningless choices between limited answer categories. Consequently, they may feel alienated from the research, that the researcher is not really interested in their opinions, that the researcher is incompetent by not getting at what they really think or feel, or that there is little point in putting any effort into thinking about the issues. Some may be relieved that completing the questionnaire is so simple and straightforward.

- *Focus groups, etc.* By using focus groups or individual interviews (see Chapter 18), the researcher may develop an understanding of the main responses given to a question. Certain themes may be very common and others so rare that they apply to only a few individuals. Crucial themes to include may be apparent as well as the mundane. Some may seem irrelevant to the research. Knowing the dominant responses helps the researcher identify useful pre-coded answers.

In some cases, the pre-coded categories are entirely the researcher's invention. The pre-coded categories will be influenced by the research's priorities. The purpose of the research, the consumers of the research and the insightfulness of the researchers will all affect the choice of pre-coded categories. Pre-coding is not necessarily inferior to other forms of coding. The value of research can never be assessed against absolute standards. Fitness for purpose should be the main criterion. There is a risk, naturally, that the coding categories created in advance of data collection will match the actual data badly.

Researcher-imposed coding

Sometimes a researcher will collect data in qualitative form because pre-structuring of the response categories is impossible or undesirable. For example, anticipating the nature of their data may be difficult. As a consequence, the data are collected in a richer, fuller format which can then be used to develop a coding scheme. While this material may be 'ethnographically' coded (see Chapters 18–26 for some of the possibilities), the researcher may prefer to quantify the data. Quantification in this case involves imposing coding categories in the light of the qualitative data and then counting their frequencies.

Any number of factors which influence the nature of the coding categories developed include:

- The researcher is interested in a theory which strongly suggests a system of analysis.

- The research may be guided by matters of public policy or seeks to address a politically important topic. These issues need to reflect the coding categories used.

- The researcher is interested only in strong trends in the data, so simple, very broad categories may be appropriate.

- The research task may be so big that the researchers have to employ workers to do the coding. This tends to demand simpler coding categories.

- Many coding categories do not work (i.e. produce inconsistent or unreliable results across different coders) or are virtually unusable for other reasons.

The coding schedule is a very important document together with the coding manual. The coding schedule is the list of coding categories to be applied to the data in question. The coder would normally have this list of coding categories – usually one schedule per set of data from a participant – and the data would be coded using the schedule. Most probably the coding schedule will be in a computer-friendly form. Often numbered boxes corresponding to the various variables being coded are used. So the coding schedule is rather like a self-completion questionnaire but consisting of a list of implied questions (do the data fit this category?) about which categories best fit the data. Usually the coding schedule is a relatively brief document which lists very simple descriptions of each of the coding categories.

Whoever is doing the coding, the researcher or an assistant, needs details about the meaning of the various coding categories. To this end, the coding manual needs giving specific definitions of each coding category, examples of material which would fit into each category and examples of problematic material. There are no rules about how detailed the manual needs to be, and ultimately coders may have to consult together to resolve difficulties. The basic idea, though, is to develop a coding process which can be delegated to a variety of individuals to enable them to code identical material identically. Such an ideal may not be fully met.

One coder is simply not enough and each individual's data should be independently coded by at least *two* coders. In this way, patterns of agreement between coders can be assessed. This is generally known as inter-rater or inter-coder reliability. Very often two independent coders are used but only for a sample of the data. There are obvious time and expense savings in doing so. However, coders may become sloppy if they believe nobody is checking their work. Evidence of inter-coder reliability is often collected only in the initial stages of the research. Over the research period subtle changes can occur in the meanings of the coding categories as used by the coder. Ideally, then, inter-rater reliability should be assessed at various stages in the coding process. Bear in mind, though, that if checking is done early on, problems probably can be sorted out; problems identified later on in coding are harder to correct.

Inter-rater reliability is rarely perfect. This raises the question of how disagreements between coders should be handled. Possible solutions vary according to circumstances:

- If the second coding is intended just as a reliability check, then nothing needs to be done about disagreements. The codings supplied by the main coder may be used for the full analysis. Inter-rater reliability assessments should nevertheless be given.

- If coders disagree, then they could be required to reach agreement or a compromise whenever this arises. This might involve a revision of the coding manual in serious cases. In minor cases, it may simply be that one of the coders had made an error and the coding schedule or manual does not need amendment.

- Reaching a compromise is a social process in which one coder may be more influential than the other. Consequently, some researchers prefer to resolve disagreements by an equitable procedure. For example, coding disagreements may be resolved by a random process such as the toss of a coin. Randomisation was discussed earlier in this book (Chapters 9 and 13).

- If the coding category is a rating (that is, a score variable), then disagreements between raters may be dealt with by averaging. For example, the coders may be required to rate the overall anxiety level of an interviewee. Since the ratings would be scores, operations such as averaging are appropriate. If the data are simply named categories, averaging is impossible.

17.3   Reliability and validity when coding

Like any other form of measurement, the issues of reliability and validity apply to coding categories. Validity is a particularly problematic concept in relation to coding categories. Quite what does validity mean in this context? One could apply many of the conceptualisations of validity already discussed in Chapter 16. Face and content validity are probably the most frequent ways of assessing the validity of coding. It is more difficult to measure things such as concurrent and predictive validity, since it is often hard to think of appropriate validation criteria. Qualitative researchers, however, have a particular problem, since the development of categories is often the nub of their research. In response, a wide range of suggestions about tackling validity in qualitative research have been put forward. These are dealt with in some detail later in this book (Chapter 26) and more extensively in Howitt (2019).

Coding reliability is far more commonly assessed than its validity. Reliability of coding is actually much more straightforward for scales and measurements than for coding categories. The following goes some way to explaining why this is the case:

- Where ratings (scores) are involved, the reliability of the coding is easily calculated using the correlation coefficient between the two sets of ratings. However, it is harder to establish the degree of agreement between raters on their ratings, since the correlation coefficient simply shows that the two sets of ratings correlate, not that they are identical. They may correlate perfectly but each coder's ratings are entirely different. Correlation only establishes covariance, not overlap or exact agreement.

- The percentage agreement between the two coders in terms of which coding category they use might be considered. However, there is a difficulty in that agreement will tend to be high for codings which are very common. The overlap between coders may largely be a consequence of the coders choosing a particular coding category frequently. Rarely used coding categories may appear to have low levels of agreement simply because they are rarely chosen. Suppose two raters, for example, code whether or not people arrested by the police are drunk. If they both always decide that those arrested were drunk, then the agreement between the coders is perfect. But this perfect agreement is not very impressive. Far more impressive are the circumstances in which both raters rate, say, half of those arrested as being drunk and the other half as sober. If the two raters agree perfectly, then this would be impressive evidence of inter-rater reliability or agreement between raters.

For this reason, numerical indices which are sensitive to the frequency with which a category is chosen are more appropriate. Coefficient kappa (see the companion statistics book, *Understanding statistics in psychology with SPSS* (Howitt & Cramer, 2020, Chapter 37) is one such reliability formula. Coefficient kappa is sensitive to when both raters are not varying the coding categories used much or using one coding to the exclusion of the others.

What are the requirements of a good coding schedule and manual? We have seen that a coding schedule can be construed as a questionnaire – albeit one which is addressed to the researcher or coder and not the participant. So all of the requirements of a good set of questions on a questionnaire would be desirable, such as clarity, which could be seen as the appropriateness of the category names and language for the coder, who may not be as familiar with the aims and objectives of the research as the researchers in charge of the research and so forth. Other considerations include:

- The number of potential coding categories may be large for any variable. If in doubt, err towards using too many categories. Computer analysis is practically universal nowadays and it is easy to amalgamate (collapse) categories as necessary using statistical programs.

- It is usual, and probably essential, to have an 'other' category for every variable. Even the best set of coding categories may not fit every participant's data completely. Unfortunately, if the 'other' category gets large, it may swamp the actual coding categories used. Warning bells should ring if the 'other' category becomes a dominant coding as it suggests that the coding categories need to be revised to give a better fit with the data. Notes should be made about the sort of data which is being put in the 'other' category as this may suggest new coding categories which could be used. Where the 'other' category consists of just a variety of very different material, nothing needs to be done.

- Serious consideration should be given to whether a variable may be multi-coded. That is, will the coder be confined to using just one of the coding categories for each case or will they be allowed to use more than one category? Generally speaking, we would recommend avoiding multi-coding wherever possible because of the complexity it adds to the statistical analysis. For example, multi-coding may well mean that dummy variables will have to be used. Their use is not too difficult, but is nevertheless probably best avoided by novices.

- Coding categories should be conceptually coherent in themselves. While it is possible to give examples of material which would be coded into a category, this does not, in itself, ensure the coherence of the category. This is because the examples may not be good examples of the category. Hence the coder may be coding into the category on the basis of a bad example rather than on the basis that the data actually fit the category.

- The process of developing a coding schedule and coding manual is often best regarded as a drafting and revision process rather than something achieved in a single stage – trial and error might be the best description. The reason is obvious: it is difficult to anticipate the richness of the data in advance of examining the data.

17.4   Qualitative coding

The final type of coding process is that adopted in qualitative data analysis. Characteristically, this form of coding seeks to develop coding categories on the basis of an intimate and detailed knowledge of the data. This is an ideal which some qualitative analyses fail to reach. For example, one finds qualitative analyses which do no more than identify a few major themes in the data.

The next part of the book contains a number of chapters on various aspects of qualitative data analysis. Anyone wishing to carry out a qualitative analysis needs to understand its historical roots as well as important practicalities. Qualitative analysis is *not* any analysis which does not include statistics. Qualitative analysis has its own theoretical orientations which are very different from mainstream research involving quantification, hypothesis testing, numbers and objectivity.

Box 17.1   Research Example

Romantic relationships coding scheme

Humbad, M. N., Donnellan, M. B., Klump, K. L., & Burt, S. A. (2011). Development of the Brief Romantic Relationship Interaction Coding Scheme (BRRICS). *Journal of Family Psychology, 25*, 759–769.

For psychologists, data coding has often seemed to be a somewhat subjective approach to data which lacks objectivity. In part, the reason for this is psychologists' preference for pre-coded data especially when self-completed by participants. Multiple-choice question and answer formats, for example, dominate in many areas of psychological research such as personality, intelligence, social psychology and so forth. Not surprisingly given this ethos, many students will seek so-called objective measures (tests and questionnaires) based on this approach when planning their data collection and analysis.

→

There are many reasons for this preference – pre-coding and self-completion are extremely time-efficient ways of collecting data. Indeed, many of the questionnaires need little work on the part of the researcher other than the distribution of the questionnaires to an appropriate sample. Some of them are even machine readable, so the researcher has little to do when inputting the data into a computer for analysis. Pre-coding involves limiting the replies to questions, etc., to those provided by the researcher. In other words, responses not included by the researcher cannot be chosen because they are not included. One consequence of this, of course, is that participants in the research may not be able to provide a response that they feel is truly appropriate. The alternative is simply to let the participant respond in whatever way they choose by, for example, allowing them to write down their own answers to a question. This may be empowering for the participant, but the variety of responses may be perplexing and provide problems for the researcher who has to prepare these in some way for analysis. Qualitative researchers rejoice in this opportunity (see later chapters), but quantitative researchers are constrained by the need to turn words into numbers. In other disciplines, the post-coding of data, once collected, is rather more usual than it is in psychology with its tradition of 'objectivity'.

Background

There are various positive and negative patterns in the relationship between couples (spouses) which are predictive of marital harmony or discord. Such problems or discord are associated with poor physical and psychological health in the couple and their children. Consequently, researchers from various disciplines, including psychologists, have turned their attention to these negative aspects of relationships. Not surprisingly, observational studies of interacting couples have been a frequent research technique. Research shows that there appears to be a general positive or negative filter which mediates the perceptions of the partner's behaviour – with a positive filter, the behaviour is seen in a good light, while a negative filter means that exactly the same behaviour will be interpreted negatively. So, a gift of flowers may be seen as a romantic gesture in one couple but as indicative that the partner is trying to cover up an affair in another couple. This is known as sentiment override (e.g. Cornelius, Alessi, & Shorey, 2007; Weiss, 1980) (Figure 17.3). Observational studies may, for example, involve the couple being observed in a naturalistic discussion task. These observational studies tend to reinforce the view that interaction patterns may be predictive of marital problems and even divorce. The events which happen in the interaction are observed by the researcher who must code them into categories. The interaction could be videoed and coded retrospectively by the researcher, who develops coding categories based on what they observe.

Hypothesis/objectives

The objective of the researchers was to introduce a method of coding observational data on interacting couples which was efficient in terms of resources.

Method

In their paper, Mikhila Humbad, Brent Donnellan, Kelly Klump, and Alexandra Burt (2011) describe a coding scheme known as the BRRICS (the Brief Romantic Relationship Interaction Coding Scheme), which they claim is quick and efficient. This

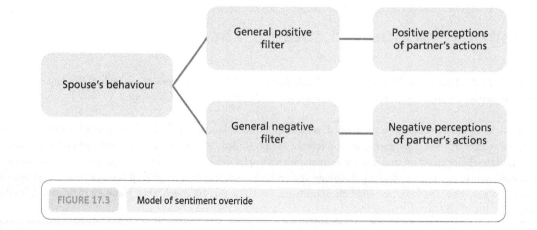

FIGURE 17.3   Model of sentiment override

coding scheme is summarised in Figure 17.4. It is offered as a quick, 'global' coding scheme for the behaviour of couples. The study involved the interactions of 118 couples. These couples were taking part in a wider study and were all parents of twins. The average age was 40 years for both males and females and the couples averaged 15 years of marriage. They were asked to identify the areas of conflict in their relationship (e.g. finances, childcare, sex and so forth). Those identified by both husband and wife formed the basis of the discussion task upon which the ratings were based. Undergraduate students were asked to code each of the videoed interactions using the coding scheme in Figure 17.4. Of course, the agreement levels of raters need to be calculated and this was done using Cohen's coefficient kappa statistic (Howitt & Cramer, 2017, 2020). Other measures such as the Dyadic Adjustment Scale were taken against which to validate the ratings by the student observers.

Findings

- The previously untrained undergraduate raters were able to reach an adequate level of reliability in their codings compared with each other with relatively little training. Reliability for codings reached a high level of .85 after training.

- In terms of the validity of the observational measures, correlations and other statistics were computed between these and a scale measuring the children's perceptions of interparental conflict. These include measures of conflict severity

Husband shows positive affect	• Smiles, laughs or says humorous things (e.g. one-line jokes) • Says things encouraging a feeling of being understood /worth
Wife shows positive affect	• Same criteria as the above
Husband shows negative affect	• Harsh tone/facial expression. • Negative statements including criticism/shows hostility
Wife shows negative affect	• Same criteria as above
Reciprocity – positive	• Overall couple positive towards each other • Including joking, etc. but positive not negative
Reciprocity – negative	• Overall couple negative towards each other • Joking, etc. hostile
Demand-withdrawal pattern	• One partner nags the other whose response is to clam up or go silent
Overall satisfaction	• Researcher's overall rating of how happy/satisfied partners are with each other

FIGURE 17.4   BRRICS coding scheme

and conflict frequency as perceived by the children. There were generally modest correlations between the observational measures and the measures obtained from the children (about .20 was the typical correlation – it could be positive or negative according to the nature of the observation measure).

Authors' suggestions for further research

The authors suggested that more diverse samples might be chosen. The couples, for example, had typically been married for quite a long time. Greater relationship conflict might be expected in samples with shorter histories together.

17.5   Conclusion

The process of turning real life into research involves a number of different stages. Among the most important of these is that of coding or categorisation. All research codes reality in some way or another, but the ways in which the coding is achieved vary radically. For some research, the development of the coding categories is the main purpose of the research endeavour. In other research, coding is much more routine and standardised, as in self-completion questionnaires with a closed answer format. Not only are there differences in the extent and degree of elaboration of the coding process, but also there are differences in terms of who does the coding. The participant does the coding in self-completion questionnaires using codes (multiple choices, etc.) developed by the researcher.

Key points

- Through coding, in quantitative research, data are structured into categories which may be quantified in the sense that frequencies of occurrence of categories and the co-occurrence of categories may be studied. In qualitative research, often the end point is the creation of categories which fit the detail of the data.

- Coding is a time-consuming activity which is sometimes economised by pre-coding the data, that is, the participants in the research are required to choose from a list of response categories. In this way, the data collection and coding phases of research are combined. This is essentially a form of quantitative data collection.

- Coding of data collected qualitatively (i.e. through in-depth interviews and focus groups) may be subject to researcher-imposed coding categories which have as their main objective quantification of characteristics judged important by the researcher for pragmatic or theoretical reasons, or because they recognise that certain themes emerge commonly in their data.

- Coding requires a coding schedule, which is a sort of questionnaire with which the researcher interrogates the data in order to decide in what categories the data fit. A coding manual details how coding decisions are to be made – what the categories are, how the categories are defined and perhaps examples of the sorts of data that fit into each category.

- Such coding, which is almost always intended for quantitative and statistical analysis, may be subjected to reliability tests by comparing the codings of two or more independent coders. This may involve the use of coefficient kappa if exact correspondence of codings needs to be assessed.

- If the analysis is intended to remain qualitative, then the qualitative analysis procedures discussed in the chapters on Jefferson coding, discourse analysis and conversation analysis, for example, should be consulted (Chapters 20, 23 and 24). The general principles of qualitative research are that the coding or categorisation process is central and that the fit of the categories to the data and additional data is paramount.

ACTIVITIES

1. Create a list of the characteristics that people say make other people sexually attractive to them. You could interview a sample to get a list of ideas. Formulate a smaller number of coding categories which effectively categorise these characteristics. Try half the number of categories as characteristics first, then halve this number, until you have two or three overriding categories. What problems did you have and how did you resolve them? Is there a gender difference in the categories into which the characteristics fall?

2. Obtain a pre-coded questionnaire and work through it yourself (or use a volunteer). What were the major problems in completing the questionnaire using the pre-coded categories? What sorts of things did you feel needed to be communicated but were not because of the format?

Qualitative research methods

CHAPTER 18

Why qualitative research?

Overview

- This chapter presents essential conceptual and other background to qualitative research. The broad underlying theoretical stance common to much qualitative research needs to be understood prior to examining in detail methods of data collection, recording and analysis.

- Qualitative research describes and categorises the qualities of data. In contrast, quantitative research concentrates on quantifying (giving numbers to) variables.

- Quantitative research is often described as positivist, which is regarded as the basis of the 'hard' sciences such as physics and chemistry.

- The search for general or universal 'laws' of psychology (universalism) is held to stem from positivism and is generally regarded as futile from the qualitative point of view.

- Qualitative researchers attempt to avoid some of the characteristics of positivism by concentrating on data obtained using much more natural methods.

18.1 Introduction

Qualitative and quantitative research are often portrayed as complete opposites. *Qualitative* research focuses on the description of the qualities (or characteristics) of data. It has been suggested that in the history of psychology case studies of individuals were the most common qualitative research. Case studies, however, share little with modern qualitative studies. Individual case studies involve the detailed description of the psychological characteristics of a person (or perhaps a single organisation). Sigmund Freud's psychoanalyses of individual patients are early examples. Other classic examples include *The man who mistook his wife for a hat* by Oliver W. Sacks (1985). This book details how a man with neurological problems dealt with his memory and perceptual problems. However, it is doubtful that most case studies are examples of qualitative research, since the method's origins were in medicine and they were used to illustrate knowledge obtained using quantitative methods. Modern qualitative research generally involves a detailed study of text, speech and conversation (which generically may be termed text) and other symbolic material. They do *not* concern specific characteristics of psychologically interesting individuals. Text is a very general concept in qualitative methods and refers to anything which may be given meaning.

Qualitative research often concentrates on real-life conversations, interviews, the media, counselling and so forth. It is rarely concerned with analysis at the level of individual words or phrases. It analyses broad units of text, though the minimum unit of analysis depends on the theoretical orientation of the research.

One problem facing would-be qualitative researchers is the relatively recent emergence of qualitative studies in psychology. For example, there remain fields of psychology which are yet to involve qualitative approaches though this will likely change. In contrast, *quantitative* research is undeniably at psychology's centre. Indeed, quantification characterises most psychology more effectively than the subject matter of the discipline. Introductory psychology textbooks are likely to be based on material almost exclusively based on quantitative research methods. References to personality tests of many sorts, intelligence quotients, ability and aptitude measures, attitude scales and similar feature heavily, as do physiological measures such as blood pressure, brain rhythms, PET (positron emission tomography) scans and so forth. While all of these measure qualities ascribed to the data (usually called variables in the quantitative context), they are quantified with numerical values or scores. The numerical values indicate the extent to which each individual possesses the characteristic or quality.

Probably the most famous quantitative measure in psychology is the IQ (intelligence quotient) score, which assigns a (usually) single number to represent such a complex thing as a person's mental abilities. Comparisons between individuals and groups of individuals are relatively straightforward. Sometimes quantitative data are gathered directly in the form of numbers (such as when age is measured by asking a participant's age in years). Sometimes the quantification is made easy by collecting data in a form which is rapidly and easily transformed into numbers. A good example of this is the Likert attitude scale in which participants are asked to rate their agreement with a statement such as 'University fees should be abolished'. They are asked to indicate their agreement on a scale of strongly agree, agree, neutral, disagree and strongly disagree. These different indicators are assigned the numbers 1–5. So common are self-completion questionnaires and scales in psychological research that there is a danger of assuming that such methods are synonymous with quantitative methods and not merely examples of them.

The growth of psychology into a major academic discipline and field of practice was almost certainly possible because of increased quantification. Psychology adopted quantification from scientific disciplines like biology, physics, and medicine in the hope of emulating their success. It was successful. Historically, many of psychology's decisive moments were associated with developing ways of quantifying the previously unquantifiable:

- Psychophysics was an early such development that found ways of quantifying subjective perceptual experiences.

- The intelligence test developed in France by Alfred Binet at the start of the twentieth century provided a means of integrating a wide variety of nineteenth-century ideas concerning the many qualities of intellectual functioning.

- Louis Thurstone's methods of measuring attitudes in social psychology and the more familiar methods today of Likert were methodological breakthroughs which allowed the development of empirical social psychology.

The invention of good quantitative techniques encourages fields of research to develop by facilitating them. Examples of research fields spurred on by quantification include authoritarianism, psychopathy, suggestibility and many other psychological concepts. All of this documents a great, collective achievement. Nevertheless, quantification squeezed out other, less quantifiable, subject matter. Perhaps in response, the history of psychology is dotted with critiques of this focus on quantification (e.g. Hepburn, 2003). Often these critiques are portrayed as 'crises', though probably this term is more self-serving than an accurate assessment of the views of the majority of researchers and practitioners.

There is a danger of presenting quantitative and qualitative research as antagonistic since it neglects numerous examples of quantitative research which include qualitative components. Examples of this are quite common in the history of psychology. Even archetypal, classic laboratory studies sometimes collected significant amounts of qualitative material, for example, Milgram (1974) in his studies of obedience to authority – the famous electric shock studies. It has to be said, though, that recent developments in qualitative methods in psychology would probably eschew this sort of combined approach. Whatever, it is evidence of an underlying view of many psychologists that quantification alone provides only partial answers.

18.2   What is qualitative research?

So, is qualitative research that which is concerned with the nature or characteristics of things? One obvious problem with this is that one could ask, does not *all* research, qualitative or quantitative, seek to understand the nature and characteristics of its subject matter? Possibly this indicates that the dichotomy between qualitative and quantitative research is more apparent than real. If the distinction between qualitative and quantitative is of value, then it should be apparent in the relationship between qualitative and quantitative research. Immediately we explore this question, we find that several different claims are made about the interrelationship:

- Qualitative methods are a preliminary stage in the research process which contributes to the eventual development of adequate quantification. Quantification is, in this formulation, the ultimate goal of research. There is a parallel with the physical sciences. In many disciplines, such as physics, biology and chemistry, an early stage involves observation and classification. For example, botanists collected, described and organised plants into 'families' – groups of plants. Members of a 'family' tended to be similar to each other in terms of their characteristics and features. In chemistry, exploration of the characteristics of different elements led to them being organised into an important analysis tool – the periodic table – which allowed their characteristics to be predicted and undiscovered elements to be characterised. This was done on the basis of features such as the chemical reactivity and the electrical conductivity of elements. In many disciplines, qualitative methods (which largely involve categorisation) have led to attempts to quantify the qualities so identified. The model for this is:

Qualitative analysis → Quantitative analysis

This sequence is not entirely uncommon in psychology. Returning to the example of intelligence testing, we can illustrate this sequence. During the nineteenth century under the influence of an Austrian, Franz Joseph Gall, it began to be thought that the brain's different parts had specific mental functions. Unfortunately, the immediate consequence of this was the emergence of phrenology as a 'science'. Phrenology holds that each brain part is effectively a different organ of the mind. Furthermore, the degree of development of each brain part (assessed by the size of the 'bumps' on the skull at specific locations) indicates the degree of development of that mental faculty (or mental ability). Gall believed that the degree of development was innate in individuals. His proposed mental faculties included firmness, cautiousness, spirituality and veneration, which are difficult to define, and others such as constructiveness, self-esteem and destructiveness, which have their counterparts in current psychology. The point is that these mental faculties could only be suggested as a result of attempts to describe the characteristics of the mind, that is, a process of categorising what was observed. Phrenology's approach to quantification was immensely crude, based on the size of different bumps. But the idea that the mind is organised into various faculties was a powerful one, and attempts to identify them led to a conceptualisation of intelligence, which was so influential on Alfred Binet who developed the seminal measure of intelligence. For Binet, intelligence was a variety of abilities, none of which in themselves defined the broader concept of intelligence but all of which were aspects of it. The view that qualitative research is a first step to quantification is valuable but overlooks that the process is not entirely one way. There are many quantitative techniques (e.g. factor analysis and cluster analysis) which identify empirical patterns of interrelationships which may help develop theoretical categorisation or classification systems.

● Qualitative methods provide a more complete understanding of the subject matter of the research. Some qualitative researchers argue that quantification fails to come to terms with or misses crucial aspects of what is being studied, because it encourages premature abstraction from the subject matter of research and a concentration on numbers and statistics rather than concepts. Because quantification ignores a great deal of the richness of the data, the research instruments often appear to be crude and, possibly, alienating. That is, participants in quantitative research feel that the research is not about them and may even think that the questions being asked of them or tasks being set are simply stupid. Some research is frustrating since, try as the participant may, the questionnaires or other materials cannot be responded to accurately enough. They simply are not convinced that they have provided anything of value to the researcher. Of course, the phrase 'richness of data' might be regarded as a euphemism for unfocused, unstructured, unsystematic, anecdotal twaddle by the critical quantitative researcher. We will return to the issue of richness of data in subsequent chapters.

● A more humanistic view of qualitative data is that human experience and interaction are far too complex to be reduced to a few variables as is typical in quantitative research. This sometimes is clearly the case, especially when the research involves the study of topics involving interactive processes. A good example of this is when one wishes to study the detailed processes involved in conversation; there are simply no available methods for turning many of the complex processes of conversation into numbers or scores. To be sure, one could time the pauses in conversation and use similar measures, but selecting a variable simply because it is easy to quantify is unsatisfactory. Choosing a measure just because it is easy and available merely results in the researcher addressing questions other than the one they want to address. What, for example, if the researcher wants to identify the rules which govern turn-taking in conversation? The subtlety of the measurements needed may mean that the researcher has no choice but to choose a qualitative approach. Figure 18.1 gives some of the typical characteristics of the qualitative researcher.

It should be stressed that qualitative and quantitative methods are not necessarily stark alternatives. The choice between the two is not simple, nor is it always the case that one is clearly to be preferred over the other. Often much the same topic may be tackled

They reject positivism

They adopt relativist position of no fixed 'reality'

They use relatively unstructured data collection methods

They are concerned to captue the individual's perspective

They use highly detailed data analysis methods

They use richly descriptive data

They take the postmodernist perspective in general

They incorporate the constraints of everyday life in studies

They believe that reality is constructed socially/individually

They choose rich and deep data rather than 'hard' data

They tend to be 'closer' to their research participants

They often see themselves as 'insiders' to what is studied

They are concerned with interpretation not causal sequences

They largely reject hypothesis testing

They take the postmodernist perspective in general

Their theory emerges from close analysis of the data

Their approach, often ideographic, concentrates on the individual

FIGURE 18.1   Some of the characteristics of the typical qualitative researcher

qualitatively or quantitatively but with rather different objectives and consequently out-comes. Some research successfully mixes the two. Surprisingly, this was sometimes the case with classic studies in some fields of psychology that took the mixed approach, though this is usually disregarded and omitted in modern texts when they describe these studies. In these cases, the two approaches were intended to be complementary and sup-plementary. But some researchers are ideologically committed to one of the two and so invariably choose quantification irrespective of their research question, or qualification even where quantification might also be relevant. There are a number of reasons for this diversity:

● Quantification requires a degree of understanding of the subject matter. That is, it is unwise to prematurely quantify something which one cannot describe with any accuracy.

● Quantification may make the collection of naturalistic data difficult or impossible. Quantification (such as the use of questionnaires or the use of laboratory apparatus) by definition implies that the data are 'unnatural'. Quantified data are collected in ways which the researcher has highly structured.

● Some researchers see flaws in either quantification or qualitative research and so are attracted to the other approach. This can happen by virtue of their training and the influence of their teachers, or it can arise from frustration with the inadequacy of their data to address the important questions they want answered.

● Some research areas have had a long tradition of quantification, which encourages its further use. Research in new areas often encourages qualitative methods because measurement techniques have not been developed or because too little is known about the topic.

Apart from career quantifiers and career non-quantifiers who will not or cannot employ the other method, many researchers tailor their choice of methods to the situa-tion and, in particular, the research question involved. Research is normally construed as involving addressing chosen research questions as effectively as possible – it is not usually seen as an opportunity to employ preferred methods. All researchers need some appre-ciation of the strengths and limitations of each approach, though traditionally this has not been the case in psychology. Probably the healthiest situation is where researchers from both perspectives address similar research questions or where researchers employ either according to circumstances. Of course, you will find psychologists who advocate one and dismiss the worth of the other, but this is a very partisan strategy which is not generally helpful.

18.3 History of the qualitative/quantitative divide in psychology

By now we hardly need to repeat this, but laboratory experiments and statistical analyses dominate the contents of most introductory textbooks in psychology. One short explana-tion of this is that skills in experimentation and quantitative analysis are very marketable commodities in and out of academia. Few other disciplines adopted such an approach, though it has the advantage of creating psychology's aura of detachment and objectivity. These characteristics also tended to position psychology close to the physical sciences. The setting-up of the psychology laboratory at Leipzig University by Wilhelm Wundt in 1879 was a crucial moment for psychologists, according to psychology's historians

(Howitt, 1992a). A number of famous American psychologists trained at that laboratory. Wundt, however, did not believe that the laboratory was the place for all psychological research. Laboratories he believed were hapless contexts for the study of cultural matters, for example. Nevertheless, the psychological laboratory was regarded as the dominant emblem of psychology.

The term *positivism* dominates the quantitative–qualitative debate. Some use it as a pejorative term, though it is a word which, seemingly, is often misunderstood. For example, some writers imply that positivism equals statistics. It does not – positivism is a particular epistemological position. Epistemology is the study of, or theory of, knowledge. It is concerned with the methodology of knowledge (how we go about knowing things) and the validation of knowledge (the value of what we learn). Prior to the emergence of positivism during the nineteenth century, two methods of obtaining knowledge dominated:

- *Theism,* which held that knowledge was grounded in religion which enabled us to know because truth and knowledge were revealed spiritually. Most religious texts contain explanations and descriptions of the nature of the universe, morality and social order. While these are matters studied by psychologists, there is little in modern psychology which could be conceived as being based on theism.

- *Metaphysics,* which held that knowledge was about the nature of our being in the world and was revealed through theoretical philosophising. Relatively little psychology is based on this, either.

Neither theism nor metaphysics retained their historical importance. Religious knowledge was central and dominant throughout the history of civilisation. Only recently in terms of the human timescale has its pre-eminence faltered. Metaphysics had only a brief period of ascendancy during the period of the Enlightenment (in the eighteenth century) when reason and individualism were emphasised. Positivism is the third major method of epistemology and directly confronts theism and metaphysics as methods of achieving knowledge. Positivism was first articulated in the philosophy of Auguste Comte in nineteenth-century France. He stressed the importance of observable (and observed) facts in the accumulation of valid knowledge. It is a small step from this to appreciating how positivism is the basis of the scientific method in general. More importantly in this context, positivism is at the root of the so-called scientific psychology.

Positivism applies equally to quantitative methods and to qualitative research methods. It is *not* the province of quantitative psychology alone. There is very little work in either quantitative or qualitative psychology which does not rely on the collection of observed information in some way. Possibly just as a fish probably does not realise that it is swimming in water, qualitative researchers often fail to recognise positivism as the epistemological basis of their work. Silverman (1997) makes a number of points which contradict the orthodox qualitative research view of positivism:

> Unfortunately, 'positivism' is a very slippery and emotive term. Not only is it difficult to define but also there are very few quantitative researchers who would accept the label. . . . Instead, most quantitative researchers would argue that they do not aim to produce a science of laws (like physics) but simply to produce a set of cumulative, theoretically defined generalizations deriving from the critical sifting of data. So, it became increasingly clear that 'positivists' were made of straw since very few researchers could be found who equated the social and natural worlds or who believed that research was properly theory-free. (pp. 12–13)

The final sentence is very important. It highlights the difficulty, which is that, although positivism stresses the crucial nature of observation, it is the end-point or purpose of the observation which is contentious. The real complaint about positivism is that it operates as if there were permanent, unchanging truths to be found. That is, underlying our experiences of the world are consistent, lawful and unchanging principles. The phrase 'the laws of psychology' reflects this universality. The equivalent phrases in the natural sciences are ones like 'the laws of planetary motion', 'the laws of thermodynamics', 'the inverse square law of light', that $E = mc^2$ and so forth. These physical laws are believed to be universally applicable and apply no matter where in the universe. The trouble is that universalism encourages psychologists to seek principles of human nature in, say, New York which they would then apply unchanged in Addis Ababa, Beijing or Cairo and, equally, in 1850 as in 2050.

Some psychologists, very important ones in their time, operated more or less according to positivist maxims and the quest for universal psychological laws. These were members of the Behaviourist School of Psychology, which dominated much psychology between the 1920s and the 1960s and beyond. Everything they did reeked of a quest for general psychological laws. First of all, they argued the basic positivist position that knowledge comes from observation. So they believed that psychologists should study the links between incoming stimuli and outgoing responses. Nothing which could not be tested directly through observation should be considered. Primarily they were experimentalists since universal principles of psychology should apply in the laboratory as much as elsewhere. Since the laboratory had other advantages, then why not study human psychology exclusively in such laboratories? They went so far as to wear white coats in their laboratories to emulate their image of physical scientists, thereby enhancing their own stature. Famous names in behavioural psychology are B. F. Skinner (1904–1990), Clark Hull (1884–1952) and John Watson (1878–1958), the founder of behaviourism.

The term *realism* would apply to positivism of this sort (i.e. there is a reality which research is trying to tap into). *Subjectivism* is the view that there is no reality to be grasped and, in Trochim's (2006) phrase, 'we're each making this all up'. Since many psychologists nowadays reject the view that universal laws of human psychology are possible or desirable, it can be argued the current psychology is in a *post-positivist* stage. Postmodernist has virtually the same meaning in this context. Psychology's allegiance is still to the importance of observation. However, its aspirations of what knowledge is possible have changed. Probably the failure of the out-and-out positivists to find anything which constitutes a worthwhile general law of psychology led to the present situation. Silverman (1997), in the above quotation, characterises the quest of many modern researchers as being for 'cumulative, theoretically defined generalisations deriving from the critical sifting of data'. Perhaps psychologists, more than some other disciplines, remain inclined towards gross, decontextualised generalisations. They write as if their statements concerning their research findings apply beyond the context in which they were studied. Owusu-Bempah and Howitt (2000) are among a number of writers who point out that such a tendency makes psychology practically unworkable beyond limited Western populations and incapable of working with the cultural diversity to be found within modern Western communities.

Qualitative researchers tend to regard the search for the nature of reality as futile. *Critical realism* is the philosophy that accepts that there is a 'reality' out there but at best we view it through an infinite regress of windows. That is, there is always yet another window that we are looking through, and each window distorts reality in some way. While this implies that there will always be different views of reality depending on which particular window we are looking through, the major problem is the degree of distortion involved. Some qualitative analysts will point to the fact that much research in psychology and the social sciences relies on data in the form of language. Language, however, they say, is not reality but just a window on reality. Furthermore, different speakers will give a different view of reality. They conclude that the search for reality is a hopeless task and, to push the metaphor beyond the bounds of endurance, that we should just study the diversity of what is seen through the different windows. Well, that is one approach, but not the only one based on critical realism (which only demands that researchers try to get close to reality while realising that they can never achieve that goal). 'Every method of measuring reality is fallible, but if we use many different measures and they concur, then maybe we are getting towards our goal' might be the typical response of a mainstream psychologist. One of the reasons why our data are problematic is that our observations are theory laden. That is, the observer comes to the observation with baggage and expectations. That baggage will include our culture, our vested interests and our general perspective on life, for example. Psychologists are not born with the ability to see the world without these windows. One strategy to overcome our preconceptions is to throw our observations before others for their critical response as part of the process of analysing our observations.

We have seen that there is no justification for some of the characteristics attributed to positivism. As discussed, some critiques of mainstream psychology labour under the impression that positivism equates to statistical analysis. Yet some of the most important figures in positivistic psychology such as Skinner had little or no time for inferential statistics and did not use them in their work. The use, or not, of statistics does not make for positivism. Similarly, a theoretical empiricism – virtually the collection and analysis of data for their own sake – has nothing to do with positivism, which is about knowing the world rather than accumulating data as such.

18.4   Quantification–qualitative methods continuum

The conventional rigid dichotomy of quantitative–qualitative methodologies is inadequate to differentiate different types of research. It implies that research inevitably falls into one or other of these apparently neat boxes. This is not necessarily the case. There is some research which is purely quantitative and other research which is purely qualitative. However, this is to neglect much research that draws on both. Conceptually, research may be differentiated into two major stages:

- Data collection

- Data analysis.

Of course, there are other stages, but these are the important ones for now.

At the *data collection stage,* there is a range of possibilities. The degree of quantification (assigning of numbers or scores) and qualification (collecting data in terms of rich detail) may vary:

- *Pure quantitative*   The data are collected using highly structured materials (such as multiple-choice questionnaires or physiological indexes such as blood pressure levels) in relatively highly structured settings such as the psychological laboratory. A good example of such a study would be one in which the levels of psychoticism measured using a self-completion questionnaire were compared in sex offenders against those found in violent offenders (as assessed by their current conviction).

- *Pure qualitative*   The data are collected to give as full and complete a picture as the researcher can possibly make. This is done, for example, by video- or audio-recording extensive amounts of conversation (say, between a counsellor and a client). There may be little or no structuring to the data gathered other than that involved in obtaining the video or sound recording. However, there may be more structure imposed, such as when the researcher chooses to interview participants in an open-ended manner or to use focus group methods. Many qualitative researchers try to use as much naturalistic material as possible.

- *Mixed data collection* Between these extremes of quantification and qualitative data gathering are many intermediate possibilities. Some researchers choose to collect data in a quantitative form where there are good means of quantifying variables and concepts but use open-ended and less-structured material where the concepts and variables cannot be measured satisfactorily for some reason. Sometimes the researcher will use a mixture of multiple-choice type questions with open-ended questions which may help paint a fuller picture of the data. See Box 18.1 for a discussion of mixed-methods research.

Box 18.1 Key Ideas

Mixed-methods research

The following two terms superficially seem much the same but are not: *mixed-methods* and *multi-methods* research. They both refer to the use of two or more different methods in a study. The difference is that multi-method research is when two or more quantitative methods or two or more qualitative methods are used (Tashakkori & Creswell, 2007). However, mixed-methods research generally refers to a study employing both qualitative and quantitative methods (Anguera, Blanco-Villaseñor, Losada, Sánchez-Algarra & Onwuegbuzie, 2018). For example, if an experiment and a self-completion questionnaire are both used in a study then this is multi-method research since both are quantitative methods. If a narrative analysis and a thematic analysis are both used in a study then this is mixed-method research. Although mixed-method research is a simple enough idea, in practice it is more of a can of worms. It is one thing doing separate qualitative and quantitative studies on a topic such that the findings from both exist in sort of parallel universes. It is when we add in the requirement that the findings from the two studies should be integrated that the most intractable problems become apparent. There is no suggestion intended here that multi-methods research is straightforward as it may prove just as difficult to integrate two different types of qualitative research as it is a qualitative and quantitative combination. It should be noted that research suggests that overwhelmingly cross-sectional designs form the majority of studies in mixed methods research (Bryman, 2006). Experiments are rarely used in mixed methods research. Nevertheless, Bartholomew and Lockard (2018), in their survey of mixed-method psychotherapy

research, found good examples of the use of experimental or intervention designs.

Numerous justifications for using mixed-methods have been put forward (Bryman, 2006; Creswell & Plano Clark, 2007; Doyle & Brady, 2009; Greene, Caracelli & Graham, 1989). They include:

- *Obtaining a fuller picture* This is built on the assumption that neither qualitative nor quantitative data provide the full picture. Utilising both approaches is seen as providing a more complete view. A not dissimilar way of putting this is to suggest that mixed methods compensates for the inadequacies of a single method qualitative or quantitative study (Kelle, 2006).

- *Cross-validation of findings* If the two types of study generate findings which are mutually compatible, then this adds strength to the conclusions drawn. This has been termed triangulation by some researchers. Unfortunately, there are many types of triangulation (triangulation of data, researchers, method, and theory (Denzin, 1978) so the use of the term may be confusing. Respondent validation has also been considered a form of triangulation (Torrance, 2012). Of course, there may be a disparity between what emerges from the qualitative aspects of a study and that from the quantitative. Reconciling the two may be a productive process (Lund, 2012).

- *Uncovering hidden heterogeneity* Quantitative research may fail to reveal the heterogeneity in people's responses on a research topic. Qualitative elaboration of a quantitative study may show that diverse positions may underlie what seems to be the same response to the quantitative research.

- *Validation of quantitative measures*   Questions may be asked about the validity of quantitative scales and measures when explored using qualitative methods.

- *Case studies illustrating quantitative data*   The 'dry' findings from some qualitative studies are difficult to present to anything but a specialist audience. By supplementing the quantitative data with qualitative material from, say, in-depth interviews the material may be made more appealing to a more general audience. This is much the same as any case study or, even, some debriefing sessions in what is primarily a quantitative study.

- *Development of hypotheses for quantitative research*   Faced with the need for new research on a largely under-researched topic, the quantitative research may resort to focus groups, interviews, and similar approaches to get leverage on the topic.

- *Clarification of findings*   The usual way of seeking clarification of a study's findings in psychological research is to argue that further research is needed of a similar sort. This can create something of an impasse and one alternative is to employ a very different study using a very different methodology in the hope that it will add clarity. One could use additional research of a quantitative nature to help explicate findings from a qualitative study or vice versa. Impenetrable quantitative statistical findings may be clarified by appropriate qualitative research.

- *Dealing with complex topics*   It is notable that disciplines like nursing have been at the forefront of acceptance of mixed methods. Some have suggested that mixed-methods research is particularly suited to the needs of such disciplines as they incorporate a range of perspectives suited to dealing with complexity. Some practitioner-based areas of psychology such as educational psychology, forensic psychology, clinical psychology, and so forth share quite a lot in common with nursing research so might be improved using mixed-methods.

- *Focusing down on specific cases for qualitative analysis*   In circumstances in which, say, a qualitative survey is carried out first, the findings from this may help the researcher to focus down on the best selection of cases

for detailed investigation by, say, qualitative in-depth interviews (Kelle, 2006).

This list can be elaborated upon in a variety of ways. One of these is to look at the features of research designs to carry out mixed-method research on a particular topic. This has been done systematically by Cresswell and Plano Clark (2011). For example, the temporal order of the qualitative and quantitative parts of the study is important. There are three basic temporal orders possible using single qualitative and quantitative sub-studies. So the order may be a) qualitative $\rightarrow$ quantification, b) quantification $\rightarrow$ qualification, and c) quantification $\updownarrow$ qualification. Where qualification precedes quantification one of the purposes of the qualification phase is to explore the research topic in depth prior to confirmation using quantitative methods. This might include the development of hypotheses. Bartholomew and Lockard (2018) describe this as an exploratory sequential design. On the basis of their review of psychotherapy research they express regret that this design is somewhat rarely used. Where the qualitative component follows the quantitative then this provides an opportunity for the explication of the quantitative findings using qualitative methods. The reverse temporal order of the quantitative followed by the qualitative allows the explication of quantitative findings using qualitative techniques such as in-depth interviews. The third possible temporal sequence in which the qualitative and quantitative components are carried out at the same time does not permit exploration or responsive explication. It does, however, offer the possibility of cross-validating findings. Creswell and Plano Clark (2011) go into detail about potential mixed-method designs.

As yet, mixed-methods research does not seem to be accepted as a third tier of research, somewhere between qualitative and quantitative, as generally in psychology as in some other disciplines. Povee and Roberts (2015) suggest that this is partly because of the difficulty of obtaining the required level of in-depth training inside the discipline. Their interviews with psychology students and teachers also revealed that the time and other resources required to carry out a mixed methods study is a deterrent in circumstances in which a quick turnaround of research has career implications. One argument against using mixed-methods research designs is that one is attempting to shoe-horn together two very different approaches to research which, in the history of psychology, have been regarded as antagonistic or incompatible. It has to be said that both qualitative and quantitative protagonists have

$\rightarrow$

been dismissive of their non-preferred approach such as when qualitative research is described as soft or unscientific and quantitative research is seen as ignoring the person. Some qualitative methods are particularly hostile to mainstream psychology – forms of discourse analysis in particular. Other qualitative methods are more welcoming of findings from quantitative research such as Interpretative Phenomenological Analysis and Grounded Theory. One solution to the problem of disparate epistemologies for qualitative and quantitative research has been to offer a philosophical basis for mixed-methods research (Doyle, Brady & Byrne, 2016). According to Feilzer (2010), this should be pragmatism. As a basis for mixed-method research pragmatism does provide a framework upon which mixed-methods researchers may promote their cause. It largely originates in the writings of Charles Sanders Peirce (1839–1914) and concerns ways of thinking about problems – of which research is an example. Mainstream psychology and qualitative psychology share an interest in identifying what is the truth whether this is a single universal truth as in positivism or a multitude of truths as in qualitative research. At this level, qualitative and quantitative share something. The pragmatic perspective is that the search for truths should not be the purpose of research. Instead the issue should be whether research is useful or utilitarian in some way.

However, we ought also to consider the *data analysis stage* of research in terms of the qualitative–quantitative distinction. The same options are available to us:

- *Pure quantification*   If data have been collected solely in quantitative form, then there is little option but to analyse the data quantitatively. However, data may have been collected in qualitative form but the researcher wishes to quantify a number of variables or create scores based on the qualitative data. The commonest method of doing this is through a process known as coding (see Chapter 17). In this, the researcher develops a categorisation (coding) scheme either based on pre-existing theoretical and conceptual considerations or based on examining the data. This can involve the researcher rating the material on certain characteristics. For example, a global assessment of a participant's hostility to global environmental issues may be obtained by the researcher rating each participant on a scale. Usually, another rater also independently rates the participant on the same rating scale and the correspondence between the ratings is assessed (inter-rater reliability).

- *Pure qualitative*   This option is generally available only if the data have been collected in qualitative form (quantitative data are rarely suitable for qualitative analysis, for obvious reasons). Quite what the qualitative analysis should be depends to a degree on the purpose of the research. As conversation (interviews or otherwise) is a common source of qualitative data, discourse analysis and/or conversation analysis may be helpful. But this is a complex issue, which may best be left until qualitative methods have been studied in a little more depth.

- *Mixed data analysis*   This may follow from mixed data collection but equally may be the result of applying qualitative and quantitative methods to qualitative data. This is quite a common approach, though it is often fairly informally applied. That is, the researcher often has a primarily quantitative approach which is extended, illustrated or explicated using simple qualitative methods. For example, the researcher may give illustrative quotations from the open-ended material that is collected in addition to the more quantitative main body of the data. Such approaches are unlikely to satisfy the more demanding qualitative researcher.

The main points to emerge out of this are that we should distinguish data collection from data analysis and appreciate that quantitative and qualitative methods may be applied at either stage. This is summarised in Figure 18.2.

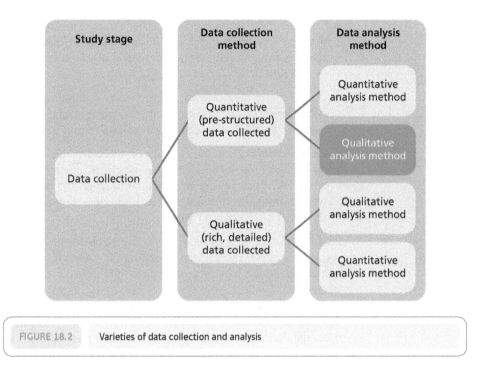

FIGURE 18.2   Varieties of data collection and analysis

18.5 Evaluation of qualitative versus quantitative methods

Denzin and Lincoln (2000) claim that there are five major features distinguishing quantitative from qualitative research *styles*. Some of these have already been touched on in this chapter but they are worth reiterating systematically:

● *Use of positivism and post-positivism*   Quantitative and qualitative methods are both based on positivism and many qualitative researchers have applied 'positivist ideals' to messy data. However, qualitative researchers are much more willing to accept the *post-positivist* position that whatever reality there is that might be studied, our knowledge of it can only ever be approximate and never exact. In their actions, quantitative researchers tend to reflect the view that there is a reality that can be captured, despite all the problems. Language data would be regarded by them as reflecting reality, whereas the qualitative researcher would take the view that language is incapable of representing reality. Quantitative researchers often treat reality as a system of causes and effects and often appear to regard the quest of research as being generalisable knowledge.

● *Qualitative researchers accept other features of the postmodern sensibility*   This really refers to a whole range of matters which the traditional quantitative researcher largely eschews. Examples of this include verisimilitude, in that the researcher studies things which appear to be real rather than the synthetic product of psychology laboratories, for example. The qualitative researcher is represented as having an ethic of caring as well as political action and dialogue with participants in the research. The qualitative researcher has a sense of personal responsibility for their actions and activities.

- *Capturing the individual's point of view*   Through the use of in-depth observation and interviewing, the qualitative researcher believes that the remoteness of the research from its subject matter (people) as found in some quantitative research may be overcome.

- *Concern with the richness of description*   Quite simply, qualitative researchers value rich description almost for its own sake, whereas quantitative researchers find that such a level of detail actually makes generalisation much more difficult.

- *Examination of the constraints of everyday life*   It is argued that quantitative researchers may fail to appreciate the characteristics of the day-to-day social world, which then become irrelevant to their findings. On the other hand, being much more wedded in society through their style of research, qualitative researchers tend to have their 'feet on the ground' more.

Probably the majority of these claims would be disputed by most quantitative researchers. For example, the belief that qualitative research is subjective and impressionistic would suggest the lack of grounding of qualitative research in psychology, not higher levels of it.

The choice between quantitative and qualitative methods when carrying out psychological research is not an easy one to make. The range of considerations is enormous. Sometimes the decision will depend as much on the particular circumstances of the research, such as the resources available, as on profound philosophical debates about the nature of psychological research.

When to use quantification

The circumstances in which quantification is most appropriate include the following:

- When addressing very clearly specified research questions.

- When there is a substantial body of good-quality theory from which hypotheses can be derived and tested.

- In addressing research questions for which there is high-quality research that has typically employed quantification.

- When it can be shown that there are very satisfactory means of collecting information using measures.

- When the researcher has a good understanding of quantitative methods combined with a lack of interest or knowledge concerning qualitative methods.

When to use qualitative research methods

A researcher might consider using qualitative research methods in the following circumstances:

- When the researcher wishes to study the complexity of something in its natural setting.

- When there is a lack of clarity about what research questions should be asked and what the key theoretical issues are.

- When there is generally little or no research into the topic.

- When the research question relates to the complex use of language, such as in extended conversation or other textual material.

- When the researcher has read qualitative research in some depth.

- Where the use of structured materials, such as multiple-choice questionnaires, may discourage individuals from participating in the research.

18.6 Conclusion

The divide between quantitative and qualitative research is not easily crossed in recent psychology. Whether or not this is desirable is questionable. It might be construed that there are two distinct cultures in psychology, though they may seek answers to radically different sorts of questions. However, there is more to it than that, since if there were simply two camps of psychologists – quantitative and qualitative – who just do totally different things, then that would be fine. After all, specialisms within psychology are very common and the demands of research make this inevitably the case. It is virtually unknown to come across psychologists who are well-versed in more than a couple of sub-disciplines of psychology. Where the situation of having quantitative and qualitative camps seems unsatisfactory is in so far as psychologists should be interested in the topic of research and not be straitjacketed within methods. So our preference is for *all* psychologists to have the choice of approaches from which to select when planning their research. This is a convoluted way of saying that the research problem should have primacy. The best possible answer to the question that the researcher is raising cannot lie in any particular method. The sooner that all psychologists are competent in the full range of qualitative and quantitative methods, the better for psychology.

This and the next few chapters are our modest answer to uniting the quantitative and qualitative camps in a joint enterprise, not a battle.

Key points

- Qualitative research, especially in the form of case studies, has been a significant but relatively minor aspect in the history of psychological methods. Nowadays, interest in qualitative methods has increased, especially in terms of the analysis of language-based data such as conversations, media content and interviews.

- Advances in quantification, nevertheless, have often been significant foci of new psychological research.

- Qualitative research can be regarded as a prior stage to quantitative research. However, there are research questions which are difficult to quantify, especially with complex processes such as conversation.

- Positivism is a philosophical position on how knowledge can be obtained, which is different from theism (religious basis of knowledge) and metaphysics (knowledge comes from reflecting on issues). Positivism required an empiricist (observational) grounding for knowledge. However, it became equated with relatively crude and quantified methods. Qualitative researchers often overlook their allegiance to positivism.

- Quantification may be applied to data collection or data analysis. Research data collected through the 'rich' methods may be quantified for analysis purposes. Whether or not this is appropriate depends on circumstances.

ACTIVITY

Many psychology students are unfamiliar with examples of qualitative research. Qualitative research needs a positive orientation and a great deal of reading. So now is the time to start. Spend half an hour in the library looking through likely psychology journals, for examples, to study. Failing that, the following paper is an excellent example which crosses a range of issues relevant to the work of many psychologists:

MacMartin, C., & Yarmey, A. D. (1998). Repression, dissociation, and the recovered memory debate: Constructing scientific evidence and expertise. *Expert Evidence, 6,* 203–226.

CHAPTER 19

Qualitative data collection

Overview

- The in-depth interview, participant observation and focus group are among the most common qualitative data collection methods. Their applicability to qualitative data analyses is considered.

- Most qualitative data collection methods have equivalent quantitative approaches. For example, structured ways of doing observations and interviews have qualitative alternatives.

- Qualitative data may be analysed either quantitatively or qualitatively, depending on the researcher's objectives and the detail of the data. Qualitative data collection should not be confused with qualitative data analysis.

- Details of observation, focus groups and interviews as qualitative data collection procedures are presented.

19.1 Introduction

Qualitative data collection is not necessarily followed by qualitative data analysis. Qualitatively collected data may sometimes be analysed quantitatively. Qualitative data collection methods seek to provide extensive, detailed and 'rich' data for later analysis. The researcher must decide whether qualitative or quantitative analysis best suits their purposes. If the analysis is to be quantitative, then the primary purpose of the analysis is to turn the complexity of the data into a relatively structured numerical analysis. At first sight, this may seem a little pointless. Why bother with qualitative data collection if the analysis is to be quantitative? However, there are circumstances in which it is simply impossible, or undesirable, to collect data quantitatively prior to quantitative analysis:

- Some data are intrinsically difficult to anticipate prior to being collected. It is difficult to design, for example, a self-completion questionnaire which effectively collects a biographical record of an individual or captures the detail of a complex sequence of events.

- Not everyone can be expected to supply data in a structured quantitative form. There may be factors that militate against some individuals supplying quantitative data. For example, a researcher wishing to collect accounts of the experience of depression from seriously depressed individuals may find greater success by employing a sensitive, in-depth interview technique than by mailing a structured questionnaire. Furthermore, some individuals may be challenged intellectually or in terms of literacy to respond to a self-completion questionnaire. It would be silly, for example, to carry out research into illiteracy through a structured questionnaire.

- Researchers may have problems in pre-structuring data collection on some topics and so feel more comfortable using a data collection method which allows a degree of exploration. The researchers may not have sufficient familiarity with the research topic to enable effective structuring of quantitative materials. They may have chosen an entirely novel area of research, for example, so they cannot draw ideas from previous research. Some researchers will collect data qualitatively, since this allows a degree of exploration of the topic with the participants. Interviews and similar techniques may be part of an exploration process.

A wide variety of methods allow appropriate data for a qualitative analysis to be gathered. Indeed, any data that are 'rich and detailed' rather than 'abstracted and highly structured' may be candidates for qualitative analysis. Some familiar data collection methods for qualitative analysis include:

- Observation: relatively unstructured observation and participation would be typical examples. Observation that involves just a few restricted ratings would probably not be appropriate.

- Focus groups

- In-depth interviews

- Recordings of conversations, including research interviews and recordings made for other purposes

- Biographies (or narratives), which are accounts of people's lives or aspects of their lives

- Documentary and historical records

- Mass media output

- Internet sources.

It is not unknown for researchers to use a variety of qualitative data collection methods in a single study.

All of these sources are, overwhelmingly, textual though photographs, pictures, and material artefacts can provide a source of data. Nevertheless, the dominance of words or text is obvious. (Text has a wider meaning in qualitative research than in everyday usage – it refers to anything imbued with meaning so it is not restricted to language.) However, the method of data collection used in itself does not determine its suitability for qualitative analysis. For example, interviews may be used to collect quantitative data only, or they may be used to collect qualitative data. It is the detail, expansiveness and richness of the data that determine their suitability for qualitative analysis. Imagine that researchers wish to study violence in television programmes. They might consider two options:

- They could count the number of acts of violence which occur in a sample of television programmes. The relative frequency of such violence in different types of television programme (e.g. children's programmes or imported programmes) could be assessed as part of this.

- Episodes of violence on television could be videoed, transcribed and described in prolific detail.

The first version of the research is clearly quantitative, as all that has happened is that a total amount of a certain category of content has been obtained. The second version of the research appears to be much more amenable to qualitative analysis strategies since it clearly involves a richness of the detail. The researchers may be studying exactly the same television programmes in both cases, but the nature of the data obtained is radically different. The qualitative research approach might allow the researcher to say much more about the context of the violence.

Before moving on, it is important to stress that the methods of data collection discussed in this chapter may not be the preferred options for all qualitative researchers. Many are happy to use these methods, but others stress the need for more naturalistic language such as that characterised by everyday conversation. Conversation analysis, in particular, takes this view, as does discourse analysis, especially where it is influenced by conversation analysis. But the reasons for using natural conversation simply do not apply to all qualitative analysis methods. Put another way, it is hardly surprising that those researchers interested in how conversation works should prefer natural, everyday conversation on which to base their analyses. However, it would be difficult, for example, to obtain a person's biographical account of their lives simply by recording them in interaction with their friends and family. The biographical information needed is unlikely to emerge in this context. An interview focused on their life would generate this information.

19.2   Major qualitative data collection approaches

So the key feature of qualitative data is encapsulated in the phrase 'richness of data'. This is the core feature, but many other characteristics are associated with qualitative data, such as unstructured data collection, extensive and interactive textual material such as that collected in some interviews, the speeches of politicians and so forth. Richness should not be confused with things such as how interesting or important the data are, for example. Some qualitative researchers actually like somewhat dull, mundane material, as this challenges their analytical skills greatly. It also means that the data are likely to concern the ordinary lives of ordinary people. Because of the very nature of qualitative data, the variety of sources and the range of collection methods are remarkable. Consequently, only a few examples of the main approaches involved are possible. Participant observation, focus groups and interviews are used as typical and common examples of qualitative data collection methods.

Method 1: Participant observation

Participant observation would seem to offer the opportunity to gather the richly detailed data that qualitative researchers seek. Ethnography is the more modern term especially in disciplines such as sociology, in which participant observation is seen as part of a wider complex of methods for collecting data in the field. Of course, cultural anthropology played an important role in the history of participant observation, although many early anthropologists collected their data not by immersion in a culture but from secondary sources such as the accounts of travellers. The origins of ethnography and participant observation in more modern times are usually attributed to the work of the so-called Chicago School of Sociology, starting in the 1920s which applied anthropological methods to Western communities. The key aim of participant observation is to describe and explain the social world primarily from the point of view of the actors or participants in that world. By being a participant and not just an observer, access to the point of view of the participant is assured. According to Bryman (2015), the major characteristics of participant observation are as follows:

- The researcher is 'immersed in a social setting' (p. 163) for a considerable period of time. The social setting could be, for example, an informal social group, an organisation or a community.

- The researcher observes the behaviours of members in that social setting.

- The researcher attempts to accurately record activity within that setting.

- The researcher seeks to identify the 'meanings' that members of that setting give to the social environment within which they operate and the behaviour of people within that setting.

In some disciplines, participant observation has been a central research tool. For example, observational research into human social activity is the most evident feature of several centuries of cultural or social anthropology. Stereotypically, the cultural anthropologist is a committed researcher who spends years living and working among an aboriginal group isolated from Western culture. The researcher is, therefore, most definitely an alien to the aboriginal culture – a fact which is regarded as part of the strength of the method. After all, it is hard to recognise the distinctive characteristics of routine parts of our own lives. This anthropological approach has occasionally found some resonance with psychology. For example, Margaret Mead's *Coming of age in Samoa* (1944) argued that adolescence is not always a period of upset, rebellion and conflict as characterised in Western cultures. It would appear that societies which do not have the West's rigid demarcation of childhood to adulthood may avoid the typical Western pattern of the adolescent in turmoil, though the adequacy of Mead's study has been questioned.

The term *participant observation* is a blanket term for a variety of related approaches. There are a number of important dimensions which identify the different forms of participant observation (Dereshiwsky, 1999 web pages, also Patton, 1986):

- *The observer's role in the setting*   Some observers are best described as outsiders with little involvement in the group dynamics, whereas others are full members of the group (see Figure 19.1).

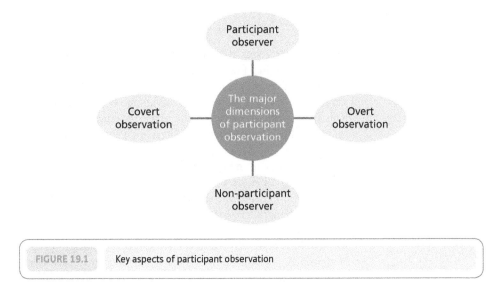

FIGURE 19.1   Key aspects of participant observation

- *The group's knowledge of the observation process*   Overt observation is when the participants know that they are being observed and by whom. Covert observation is when the participants in the study do *not* know that they are being observed and, obviously, cannot know by whom they are being observed (see Figure 19.1).

- *Explication of the study's purpose*   This is more than a single dimension and may fall into at least one of the following categories:

  - There is a full explanation given as to the purpose of the research prior to starting the research.

  - Partial explanation means that the participants have some idea of the purpose of the study, but this is less than complete for some reason.

  - There is no explanation of the study's purpose, because the observation is covert.

  - There is a misleading or false explanation as to the purpose of the study.

- *Length*   The observation may be a single session of a very limited length (e.g. a single session of one hour) or there may be multiple observation sessions of considerable length which may continue for weeks or years.

- *Focus*   The researcher may focus very narrowly on a single aspect of the situation; there may be an 'expanded' focus on a lengthy but nevertheless predetermined list of variables; there may be a holistic or 'rich data' approach which involves the observation of a wide variety of aspects in depth.

It is very difficult to set out the minimum requirements for a participant observation study. For example, what is required to justify the observation being described as a *participant* observation? Participant observation is uncommon in psychological research though more frequently a topic for research methods modules – and textbooks. One of its major difficulties in psychological research lies in its frequent dependency on the observations of just one researcher. That is, participant observation may be accused of subjectivity because it is dependent on uncorroborated observations. Traditionally, psychologists have abhorred subjectivity, though it is a bedrock of much qualitative research. Participant observation might be regarded as more objective by mainstream psychologists if the extent of agreement between different participant observers could be established, which is rarely the case.

■ Method 2: Focus groups

In some respects, focus groups are like the daytime television discussion shows in which the presenter throws in a few issues and questions, and the audience in the studio debates them among themselves. It is the dynamic quality of the focus group situation which differentiates it from interviews and is the main advantage of the method. Focus groups generate data which are patently the product of a group situation and so may, to some extent, generate different findings from individual interviews. Focus groups originated in the work of the famous sociologist Robert Merton when he researched the effectiveness of propaganda using a method he termed *focused interviewing* (Merton & Kendall, 1946). In subsequent decades, it was taken up by advertising and market researchers until eventually it became more accepted in academic research. Focus groups allowed researchers to concentrate on matters which market research interviews fail to assess adequately. In recent years, researchers have increasingly regarded focus groups as a means of generating ideas and ways of understanding, especially for new research topics, perhaps prior to another more quantitative approach. In effect, the members of the focus group are given the task of making sense of the issue – a duty which usually is assigned to the researcher in other forms of research. This is achieved through the group dynamics, that is, through the relatively normal processes of discussion and debate among ordinary people. Conventional interviewing techniques involving a single interviewee cannot do this effectively because of their very nature.

Focus groups may be used in at least three different ways:

- As an early stage of research in order to explore and identify what the significant issues are.

- To generate broadly conversational data on a topic to be analysed in its own right. This is a controversial area and lately qualitative researchers have preferred more naturalistic conversation sources in some areas of qualitative research, as mentioned earlier.

- To evaluate the findings of research in the eyes of the people that the research is about, that is, to discuss the research conclusions. This is sometimes known as respondent validation.

For the researcher, the focus group has other advantages in that most of the resources come from the participants. The researcher generally 'facilitates' the group processes in order to ensure that a pre-planned range of issues is covered while also allowing unexpected topics to enter the discussion. So, ideally, the researcher avoids dominating the proceedings. If necessary, the researcher steers the discussion along more productive lines when the group seems 'run out of steam'. The researcher conducting a focus group is usually called the moderator or facilitator.

In order to organise focus group research effectively, the following deserve consideration:

- Allow up to about two hours running time for a focus group. Short running times may indicate an unsatisfactory methodology.

- A single focus group is rarely, if ever, sufficient, even if the group seems very productive of ideas and discussion. The researcher will need several groups in order to ensure that a wide range of viewpoints is covered. It is difficult to say just how many groups are needed without some knowledge of the research's purpose and other factors. Indeed, the researcher may consider running groups until it appears that nothing new is emerging. In a sense this is subjective, but it is also practical within the ethos of qualitative methodology.

- The size of a focus group is important. If there are too many participants, some will be inhibited from talking or unable to find the opportunity to participate; too few and the limited range of viewpoints will risk stultifying the proceedings. Generally, the ideal is 6–10 individuals, though this may be ignored should circumstances demand something different.

- Participants in focus groups are not intended to be representative of anything other than variety. They should be chosen in order to maximise the productivity of the discussion. This is, of course, a judgement call which will get better with experience in focus group methodology.

- The moderator should avoid appearing judgmental and keep their personal opinions to themselves.

Gibbs (1997) offers practical advice which may be summarised as follows:

- Don't tell focus group members too much in advance of the meeting. If you do, there is a risk that they will figure out their own particular thoughts and attitudes on the topic and so may be unresponsive to the input of other group members.

- Unless there is a very good reason for doing otherwise, ensure that focus group members are strangers to each other prior to the meeting.

- Focus group members should generally be varied (heterogeneous) in terms of obvious factors. That is, they should vary in educational level, race and ethnicity, gender and social economic status. However, it should be appreciated that some of these factors in some circumstances may be inhibitory. For example, a discussion of race may be affected by having different races present.

The tasks of the focus group moderator include the following (Gibbs, 1997):

- Explaining the purpose and objectives of the focus group session

- Creating a positive experience for the group members and making them feel comfortable

- Posing questions that may open up the debate or focus on an issue

- Enabling participation by all group members

- Highlighting differences in perspective between people in order to encourage discussion of these differences

- Stopping conversational drifts from the point of the topic of the focus group.

It is nonsensical to evaluate a focus group in the same terms as, say, an individual interview. A focus group is not intended to be a convenient substitute for the individual interview and cannot compete with it in all respects. In particular, focus groups cannot be used to estimate population characteristics such as the percentage of people having a particular opinion. Focus groups do not involve, say, random sampling from the population, so cannot be indicative of population characteristics.

Focus groups have a number of disadvantages, which mean that they should not be undertaken without clear reasons:

- They take a great deal of time and effort to organise, run and transcribe. For example, bringing a group of strangers together is not always straightforward logistically.

- The focus group takes away power from the researcher to direct the research process and the kind of data collected. Consequently, it is difficult to imagine a profitable use of the focus group as a method of collecting data for the typical laboratory experiment.

Among the advantages of the focus group is the motivation aroused in the participants simply through being in a group situation. The participant is not a somewhat alienated individual filling in a rather tedious questionnaire in isolation. Instead, the participant is a member of a group being stimulated by other members of the group. So the experience is social, interesting and to a degree fun. Furthermore, membership of a focus group can be, in itself, empowering. Members of a focus group are given a voice to, perhaps, communicate to the management of their organisation via the focus group and the researcher.

The analysis of focus group data may follow a number of routes. The route chosen will largely be dependent on why the focus group approach was selected for data collection. If the focus group is largely to generate ideas for further research or as a preliminary to more structured research, the researcher may be satisfied simply by listing the major and significant themes emerging in the focus group discussions. On the other hand, the focus group may have served as a means of generating verbal data for detailed textual analysis. Detailed data analysis of this sort requires transcriptions to be made of the group discussion from the audio- or video-recording. The Jefferson transcription system (Chapter 20), for example, may be appropriate in many cases. However, the level of detail recorded in Jefferson transcription may be too much for some research purposes. Appropriately transcribed data may be analysed using the broad principles of grounded theory, discourse analysis or conversation analysis in particular (see Chapters 22, 23 and 24). Of these, grounded theory analysis may suit more researchers than the other, more specific approaches. In other words, the analysis, as ever, needs to be tailored to the purpose of the research.

■ Method 3: Interviews

The interview is a very diverse social situation with no universally accepted standard strategy. Interviews can be highly structured (little different in many ways from a self-completion questionnaire). These are known as structured interviews. Alternatively, interviews may be unstructured such that emerging issues can be explored rather than questions being answered in a fixed format. These are qualitative or in-depth interviews.

Structured interviews

Market research interviewers are commonplace and everywhere – in the streets, on our phones, etc. Characteristically, the questions they ask are precisely focused and the answers are selected from a set of alternative pre-coded possibilities. The interviewer mostly sticks to the 'script' of the questionnaire. Such interviews have a number of advantages for researchers:

- They are easily administered by relatively inexperienced interviewers.

- Because the replies are pre-coded in multiple-choice format, they may be quickly prepared for computer analysis thus economizing on time and money.

- The process is quick and it is perfectly feasible to plan research and have some sort of report ready for clients in a very short period of time – even just a few days.

- Since the interviewers have quotas of persons to interview, it is easy to ensure that satisfactory numbers of completed questionnaires are obtained. There is usually little or nothing in the interview that could not have been achieved by the questionnaire being completed by the interviewee alone.

- The interviewers recruit participants on the spot. Mailing questionnaires to a sample of people is likely to result in derisory return rates and sample sizes as a consequence.

Variants on structured interviewing are employed by academic researchers, and the strengths and weaknesses remain much the same. The drawbacks include the sparseness of the information obtained, possible difficulties for the interviewee to express what they would really like to say, the somewhat alienating processes involved, and so forth. Nevertheless, if the structured approach is adequate for your research, then consider using it if only for reasons of economy.

In-depth interviews

The in-depth or qualitative interview is imbued with the qualitative ethos. It reverses many of the quantitative principles of the structured interview. Some qualitative researchers have been attracted to in-depth interviews because they are conversational. Nevertheless, it is a mistake to regard them as normal or natural conversation. They are conversations determined by the rules of research, not those of everyday life. As such they are a highly specialised form of conversation with its own rules and special context. For one thing, they are very asymmetrical in their structure. For example, one unspoken rule is that the interviewee talks about themselves, whereas the interviewer does not. Most conversations tax neither of the participants. In-depth interviews can be very emotionally demanding for both interviewee and interviewer. The interviewee will be pressed for detail about matters beyond what is normal in everyday conversation. The interviewer will have prepared extensively for the interview and in addition must necessarily absorb a lot of information during the course of the interview in order to question and probe effectively. Using a digital or video-recorder does not do away with this demand, since the recording cannot be consulted during the course of the interview. In other words, one should expect in-depth interviews to be taxing in a number of ways. Table 19.1 extends the comparison of structured interviewing and qualitative interviewing including ideas influenced by Bryman and Bell (2015).

Table 19.1	Structured and qualitative interviewing contrasted

Structured interview	Qualitative interview
Based on a highly structured strategy which renders the structured interview inflexible.	Based on a flexible, interactive strategy.
There is a high degree of uniformity or consistency.	Interviews vary substantially across the sample interviewed.
Easily and quickly analysed because of pre-structuring.	Difficult and time-consuming to analyse because of their varied content.
The researcher has specific, precisely-formulated questions.	The agenda for the interview is not absolutely clear or fixed. Different interviews may not always use the same questions.
Questions have a largely closed and fixed list of answers to choose from.	Questions are intended to stimulate extensive, individual, and detailed replies.
Reliability is readily assessed though the validity of the method is often questioned.	There is a sense in which validity is intrinsically better for qualitative interviews. Reliability is somewhat difficult to ascertain.
The content of the interview is entirely within parameters determined by the researcher.	The content of the interview is a joint product of the researcher and interviewer within the overarching topic.
Participants are 'forced' to stick to the point and there is little or no scope for them to express idiosyncratic points of view. Sometimes token questions such as 'Is there anything that you think should be mentioned but has not been?' are appended.	According to some, rambling accounts are to be encouraged in qualitative interviewing, as this pushes the data far wider than the researcher may have anticipated.
Structured interviews allow little or no departure of the interviewer from the questionnaire in the interests of standardisation.	Qualitative interviewers expect to rephrase questions appropriately, formulate new questions and probes in response to what occurs in the interview, and generally engage in a relatively relaxed approach to standardisation.
Structured interviews are inflexible.	Qualitative interviews are flexible.
Answers generated are supposed to be readily and quickly coded with the minimum of labour.	The researcher is looking for rich and detailed answers which result in extensive and labour-intensive coding processes (for example, see Chapter 21 on grounded theory).
Repeat interviewing is rare, except in longitudinal studies in which participants may be interviewed on a number of separate occasions.	Repeat interviewing is not uncommon, since it allows the researcher to 'regroup' – to reformulate their ideas during the course of the research. Checking and gathering data that had previously been omitted from the first interview, etc., are among these characteristics.

At a minimum, the qualitative interviewer should have a basic skeleton of the interview structure in the form of a list of topics or questions to be covered. This is known as the *interview guide*. It is often little more than a memory aid giving the basics of what the researcher intends to cover and probably is a poor reflection of the contents of the interviews themselves. This is only to be expected if the ideals of qualitative research are met by the researcher. That is, the topics are partially formulated by the participant, the enterprise is very exploratory, and rich detail (which by definition is not routine) is the aim. The guide may be added to as the researcher interviews more participants and becomes aware of unanticipated issues at the start of the research. Experienced researchers will probably refer very little to the interview guide – perhaps only using it as a check at the end of the interview in order to ensure that the major issues have been covered.

Certain considerations need to be addressed in preparing the interview guide:

- The researcher may wish to record some routine, basic information in a simple structured form. Matters such as the participant's age, gender, qualifications, job title and so forth may involve a standardised list of answer categories, for example, the highest level of academic qualification obtained.

- The formulation of questions and topics needs to be more than a list of obvious questions. Questions should not be included because the replies *just might* be interesting. The requirements of the research plan should determine the questions selected. Just what sorts of information would help the researcher address the important things about the research topic? The interview guide may need modifying part-way through the research to take account of things learnt or overlooked during the earlier interviews.

- The questions or topics should be structured in a sensible and helpful order. This makes the interview easier for both the interviewer and interviewee. There is a lot of memory work and other thinking for both participants, so a logical structure is important.

- Frame the interview schedule using language appropriate for the participant group. Children will require different language from adults, for example. What is appropriate may not be known to the researcher without talking to members of the group in question or more systematically piloting the methodology.

If in-depth interviewing sounds easy, then the point has been missed. This is probably best illustrated by asking what the researcher is actually doing when conducting the interview. We can begin by suggesting what they do *not* do:

- The researcher is *not* taking detailed notes. A high-quality audio- or video-recording of the interview is the main record. Some researchers may make simple notes, but this is not a requisite of the sort that the recording is. These notes are more useful as a memory aid during the course of the interview rather than as data for future analysis. It is very easy to be overawed by the interview situation and to forget one's place in the schedule or forget what has been said.

So what *is* the interviewer doing? The following are the ideals from the perspective of qualitative methods, though they are difficult to achieve:

- The interviewer is actively building as best they can an understanding of what they are being told. In contrast, it hardly matters in a structured interview whether the interviewer gets an overview of this sort, since they merely write down the answers to individual questions. However, without concentrating intensely on the content of the interview, the qualitative researcher simply cannot function properly or effectively.

- The interviewer formulates questions and probes in a way which clarifies and extends the detail of the account being provided by the participant. Why did they say this? Who is the person being described by the participant? Does what is being said make sense in terms of what has been said before? Is what is being communicated unclear? The list of questions is, of course, virtually endless. But this aspect of the task is very demanding on the cognitive and memory resources of the interviewer, as it may also be for the participant.

- The interviewer is cognisant of other interviews which they (and possibly co-workers) have conducted with other participants. Issues may have emerged in those which appear missing in the current interview. Why is that? How does the participant respond when specifically asked about these issues?

- The objective of the interviewer's activity is to expand the detail and to interrogate the information as it is being collected. This is very much in keeping with the view that qualitative data analysis *starts* at the stage of data collection. It also reflects the qualitative ideal that progress in research depends on the early and repeated processing of the data.

In addition to all of this, there are practical issues which are too easily overlooked by the researcher but may have a significant impact on the quality of the research generated by the in-depth interview:

- Just how many different researchers will be conducting the interviews? Using two or more different interviewers produces problems in terms of ensuring similarity and evenness of coverage across interviews.

- How are developments communicated between the interviewers? It is probably worth considering the use of semi-structured interviews if the logistics of using several interviewers become too complex.

- The data are usually no more than whatever is on the recording. As a consequence, it is important to obtain the best possible recording, as this greatly facilitates the speed and quality of the final transcription (e.g. see Chapter 20). Beginners tend to assume that a recorder that functions well enough when spoken into by the researcher will be adequate to pick up an interview between two people, physically set apart, in perhaps a noisy environment. Consider the best equipment available as an investment in terms of the quality of recording commensurate with the saving in transcription time. A recorder which allows the recording to be monitored through an earphone as it is being made will help ensure that the recording quality is optimised.

- The physical setting of the interview needs to be considered. Sometimes privacy will be regarded as essential for the material in question. In other circumstances, privacy may not be so important (i.e. if the topic is in no way sensitive). Taking the research to the home or workplace of the participants may be the preferred option over inviting the participants along to the researcher's office, for example. Interviews at home may unexpectedly turn into family interviews if one does not take care to ensure that it is understood that this is an individual interview. Many homes will have just a couple of places in which the interview may take place, so be prepared to improvise.

Much of the available advice to assist planning an interview is somewhat over-general. What is appropriate in one sort of interview may be inappropriate in another. What may be appropriate with adults may not work with youngsters with learning difficulties. If one gets the impression that good interviewing requires social skills, quickness of thought or a great deal of concentration, and resourcefulness, then that is just about right. For example, *Child abuse errors* (Howitt, 1992b) contains psychological research based on in-depth qualitative interview methods. The research essentially addresses the question of the processes by which parents become falsely accused of child abuse. This was partly stimulated by the cases in Cleveland in England in which a number of parents were accused of child sexual abuse against their own children. The children were given a simple medical test which was erroneously believed by some doctors to be indicative of anal abuse. But these are not the only circumstances in which parents are accused, apparently falsely, of child abuse. The problems of this research in many ways are the ones that stimulate in-depth interviewing in general. That is, at the time there was virtually no research on the topic, indeed there was virtually nothing known about such cases. So inevitably the task was to collect a wide variety of accounts of the parents' experiences from a wide variety of circumstances. The initial interviews were, consequently, 'stabs in the dark'. The parents taking part in the study were participants with much, in general, to say about their experiences. Consequently, there was a complex account to absorb very quickly as the participants spoke. Furthermore, these were, of course, emotional matters for the parents who essentially had their identity as good parents and their role of parent removed. The complex and demanding nature of the in-depth interviewer's task in such circumstances is obvious.

19.3 Conclusion

The main criterion for an effective qualitative data collection method is the richness of the data it provides. Richness is difficult to define but refers to the lack of constraint on the data which would come from a highly structured data collection method. Part of the richness of data is a consequence of qualitative data collection methods being suitable for exploring unknown or previously unresearched research topics. In these circumstances, the researcher needs to explore a wide variety of aspects of the topic, not selected features. Some of the qualitative data collected by researchers using methods like those described in this chapter will be analysed in a traditional positivist way, with the participants' contributions being used as something akin to representing reality. Other data collected using these self-same methods might be subjected to discourse analysis, for example, which would eschew the representational nature of the material in favour of the language acts that are to be seen in the text.

Key points

- Qualitative data analysis is *not* the same thing as qualitative data collection. Qualitative data collection may in some cases become a quantitative analysis if quantifiable coding techniques are developed for the data.

- All qualitative data collection methods vary in terms of their degrees of structuring across different research studies. That is, there is no agreed standard of structuring which is applied in every case.

- Participant observation essentially has the researcher immersed as a member of a social environment. It has its origins in anthropology as a means of studying cultures. There is no strong research tradition of its use in psychology.

- Focus groups are increasingly popular in psychology and other disciplines as a means of collecting rich, textual material. This is a rather social research method in which the participants actively interact with others, under the gentle steering of the researcher. Because the method highlights similarities and differences between group members, it is very useful for generating ideas about the topic under research as part of the pilot work, though it is equally suitable for addressing more developed research questions.

- Interviewing may be structured or unstructured. Generally, somewhat unstructured interviews are most likely to be the foundation of qualitative research, simply because the lack of structure provides 'richer' unconstrained textual data. In-depth interviewing places a lot of responsibility on the interviewer in terms of the questioning process, coping with the emotions of the interviewee and ensuring that the issues have been covered exhaustively.

ACTIVITIES

1. Write a schedule for a structured interview on text messaging. Interview a volunteer using the schedule. Re-interview them using the schedule as a guide for a qualitative interview. What additional useful information did the structured interview uncover?

2. Get a group of volunteers together for a focus group on text messaging. What did you learn from the focus group compared with the interviews above?

CHAPTER 20

Transcribing language data

Jefferson system

Overview

- The transcription of auditory and visual recordings is a vital stage in analysing much qualitative data.

- Transcription is the process by which recordings are transformed into written text

- Transcription inevitably loses information from the original.

- Methods and transcribers differ in the extent to which they can deal with the nuances of the material on the original recording.

- The detail required in the transcription depends on the purposes of the research and the resources available. The purpose of the analysis will in part determine what transcription method is best. No single transcription method exists which is ideal for all purposes.

- The Jefferson transcription method places some emphasis on pauses, errors of speech and people talking over each other or at the same time. It is probably by far the most common transcription method in psychology, but this does not make it the automatic choice in every case.

- It is evident from research that 'errors' are not uncommon in transcriptions.

20.1 Introduction

Research imposes structure on its subject matter. The structuring occurs at all stages of the research process. For example, the way the researcher decides to collect research data affects the nature of the research's outcome. If the researcher takes notes during an interview, what is recorded depends on a complex process of questioning, listening, interpreting and summarising. It could not be otherwise. Research is the activity of humans, *not* super-humans. If a researcher audio-records conversation, then all that is available on permanent record is the recording. Visual information such as body posture and facial expression are lost forever. Once the recording is transcribed as text, further aspects of the original events are lost. The intonation of the speaker, errors of speech and other features cannot be retained if the recording is merely transcribed from the spoken word to the written word. This does not make the transcription bad; it just means that it may be useless for certain purposes while at the same time being perfectly useful for others. If the researcher wishes to obtain 'factual' accounts of a typical day in the life of a police officer, the literal transcription may be adequate. (i.e. the researcher is using language as a representation of reality and would have no problems with such a transcription. Qualitative researchers who argue that this view is wrong would regard such a transcription as useless or, at best, incomplete.)

Research may have a vast range of valid purposes, not all of which share identical transcription needs. Take, for example, the needs of a researcher interested in the process of conversation. The literal words used are insufficient to understand the nuances of conversation. On the other hand, a speech therapist might well be interested in transcribing particular features of speech which are most pertinent to a speech therapist's professional activities. Thus pronunciation of words may be critical, as may be recording speech impediments such as stuttering. In other words, the speech therapist may be disinclined to record information which helps to understand the structuring of conversation as opposed to the speech of a single individual (Potter, 1997). So there is a test of 'fitness or suitability for purpose' which should be applied when planning transcription.

An example may help. Take the following sentence as an example of 'literal' text:

Dave has gone on his holidays.

Strictly grammatically and literally, the meaning of this seems clear, but it is a sentence which may mean something quite different in the context of a real-life conversation. Perhaps the researcher has actually transcribed the sentence as:

Dave has gone on errrrr [pause] his holidays.

This second, more fully transcribed version could be understood to mean that Dave is in prison. The 'errrrr' and the pause are not words, but they may have meaning nevertheless. They are paralinguistic features which help us to revise the sentences' meaning. Given this, researchers studying language in its social context need to incorporate paralinguistic elements, since they provide evidence of how the words are interpreted by participants in conversation. The paralinguistic features of language often have subtle implications. For example, 'errrrr', which is a longer version of 'er', may often imply different things. 'Errrrr' implies a deliberate search for an appropriate meaning, whereas 'Er' may often simply signal that one has forgotten the word temporarily. The experts on the rules of subtle language use are ordinary, native speakers of a language – all of us understand language at this subtle level and respond to it appropriately in our day-to-day conversations. This is an ethnographic approach to social interaction, since it means that researchers need to understand conversation much as participants do. Of course, there is no *fixed* link between paralinguistic features of language and the meaning they add. So the presence of a particular feature should be regarded as informative rather than indicative. However, there are ways of understanding the meaning of these subtle features of language, as we shall see in later chapters (especially Chapters 22 and 23).

20.2 Jefferson transcription

One popular system for transcribing speech is the system developed by Gail Jefferson. This has its origins in her work with Harvey Sacks, the 'founding-parent' of conversation analysis (see Chapter 24). The Jefferson system can appear a little confusing to novices but it gets easier with practice.

Jefferson's system has *no* special characters, so it can be applied by anyone using a standard computer keyboard. Consequently, some familiar keystrokes have a distinctive meaning in Jefferson transcription. These keystrokes are used as symbols to indicate the way in which the words are delivered in the recording. The main Jefferson conventions are given in Table 20.1. There are symbols which are used to indicate pauses, elongations of word sounds, where two speakers are overlapping and so forth. Refer back to this table whenever necessary to understand what is happening in a transcript. You may also spot that there are slight differences between transcribers on certain matters of detail.

Jefferson transcription is not unproblematic in every instance. To illustrate this, take the following:

For:::get it

The ::: indicates that the 'For' should be extended in length. However, just what is the standard length of 'For' in 'Forget'? In some dialects, the 'For' will be longer than in others. And just what is the difference between 'For:::get' and 'For::get'?

■ Example of Jefferson transcription

The excerpt that follows is from a study of police interviews with paedophile suspects (Benneworth, 2004). The researcher had access to police recordings of such interviews. As a consequence, the data consist solely of audio-recorded text without any visual information. Of course, the researcher might have wanted to video-record the interviews in order to get evidence of facial expression, etc., but this was not an available option. Sound recordings are routine for British police interviews, so the transcription may be regarded as being of a naturally produced conversation (a recorded police interview), not an artefact of the research process. The people involved in the transcribed material below are a detective constable (DC) and the suspect being interviewed (Susp). The issue is the suspect's use of pornography in his dealings with a young girl. Transcripts can vary markedly in terms of how closely they adopt the Jefferson system and just what features are regarded as of significance in the recording. Furthermore, the Jefferson system has evolved over the years as Jefferson developed it. So transcriptions

Table 20.1	Main features of the Jefferson transcription system

Jefferson symbol	Meaning
CAPITALS	Word or words louder than the surrounding words.
Underlining	Emphasis, such as on a particular syllable.
Aster*isk	The speaker's voice becomes squeaky.
Numbers in brackets (1.2)	Placed in text to indicate the length of a pause between words.
A dot (.) in brackets	A micropause – a noticeable but very short pause in the speech.
[ ]	Square brackets are used when two (or more) speakers are talking together. The speakers are given different lines and the brackets should be in line where the speech overlaps.
//	Another way of indicating the start of the second overlapping speaker's utterance.
; or :	Used to separate the speaker's name from their utterances.
?;	The speaker is not recognisable to the analyst of the transcript.
?Janet;	Indicates a strong likelihood that Janet is the speaker.
…	A pause of untimed length.
??;	Two or more question marks indicate that this is a new unidentified speaker from the last unidentified speaker.
[…]	Material has been omitted at that point.
°I agree°	Words between ° signs are spoken more quietly by the speaker.
→	This is not part of the transcription. It is placed next to lines which the analyst wishes to bring to the reader's attention.
↑↓	Indicates substantial movements in pitch – out of the ordinary changes, not those characteristic of a particular dialect, for instance.
Hehheh	Laughter that is voiced almost as if it were a spoken word, rather than the uncontrolled noises that may constitute laughter in some circumstances.
I've wai::ted	The preceding sound is extended proportionate to the number of colons.
Hhh	Expiration – breathing-out sounds, such as when signalling annoyance.
(what about)	Words in brackets are the analyst's best guess as to somewhat inaudible passages.
((smiles))	Material in double brackets refers to non-linguistic aspects of the exchange.
(? ?)	Inaudible passage approximately the length between the brackets.
I don't accept your argument = and another thing I don't think you are talking sense	The = sign is placed between two utterances to indicate that there is no identifiable pause between the two. Also known as latching.
= signs placed vertically on successive lines by different speakers	In this context, the = sign is an indication that two (or more) speakers are overlapping on the text between the = signs.
[ ] placed vertically on successive lines by different speakers	As above, but instead the [ ] brackets are used to indicate that two (or more) speakers are overlapping on the text between the brackets.
> that's all I'm saying <	Talk between > and < signs is speeded up.
< that's it >	Talk between < and > signs is slowed down.

For more details of Jefferson coding, see Hutchby and Wooffitt (1998).

from different periods may show varying conventions and characteristics. Benneworth's transcription seems to us to be well balanced in that it is clear to read even by relative novices to transcription:

363 DC:	What made you feel okay about showing them to a
364	[11-year-old girl]
365 Susp:	[accidentally] she first saw them when
366	I opened my boot one day I forgot they were
367	there and then she (1.8) °expressed an interest
368	in them and like looking at them and that's how
369	it developed.°
370 DC:	So you felt confident about showing them to (.)
371	Lucy whereas you wouldn't have shown them to
372	[your wife].
373 Susp:	[yeah I was] I was (3.8) s::::exually (0.8) umm
374	(4.0) unconfident anymore about sex and Lucy
375	showing an interest in me and that was
376	flattering in itself and.hhhcos there was no
377	sexual relationships with my wife.
378 DC:	Was it easier to feel confident with Lucy
379	because she was so young? < And you were an
380	adult and [more in control. >]
381 Susp:	[no it's just that] > it was the first
382	.hhh first young lady that's ever expressed an
383	interest in me during my troubled (.) marriage
384	over the past three years < (.) °I said°.

Source: Benneworth (2004)

You will probably have noted a number of features of the transcript:

- Each line is numbered 363, 364, etc., so it is clear that this is just an excerpt from a much longer transcript. The numbering is arbitrary in the sense that another transcriber may have produced lines of a different length and hence different numbers would be applied in their transcriptions. Notice that the lines do not correspond to sentences or any other linguistic unit.

- Look at lines 364 and 365. The words enclosed in square brackets [ ] are parts of the conversation where the two participants overlap. It would not be possible to transcribe this if the system did not utilise arbitrary line lengths.

- Not only is the use of Jefferson notation time-consuming for the researcher, but it also makes it difficult for readers unskilled in the Jefferson system. Simply attempting to read the literal text, ignoring the transcription conventions, is not easy.

- Jefferson transcription cannot be carried out by untrained personnel such as secretaries.

- The researcher would almost certainly have used some sort of transcription device which allows rapid replays of short sections of the recording. In other words, transcription is a slow, detailed process that should only be undertaken if the aims and objectives of the research study require it.

It is also worth emphasising that Jefferson transcriptions of the identical recording will vary from researcher to researcher. It is probably fair to say that this transcription is at an intermediate level of transcription detail. In other words, by this stage the researcher has made a contribution to the nature of the data available for further analysis. Anyone carrying out Jefferson transcription will experience a degree of uncertainty as to whether they have achieved an appropriate level of transcription detail. It should be remembered that qualitative researchers tend to be very familiar with their texts before the transcription is complete. This familiarity will help them set the level of detail that is appropriate for their purposes.

An important question is what the Jefferson transcription enables which a secretary's word-by-word transcription might miss out. The following gives the above transcription with notation omitted. Often a secretary would fail to give the overlapping talk, so the dominant voice at the time of the overlap would be transcribed and the other voice perhaps noted as inaudible. This is possibly because a secretary would regard text as linear much as when taking dictation from the secretary's boss. The following is a guess as to what a typical secretary's transcription of the same type might be:

DC: What made you feel okay about showing them to an 11-year-old girl?

Susp: (inaudible) she first saw them when I opened my boot one day I forgot they were there and then she expressed an interest in them and like looking at them and that's how it developed.

DC: So you felt confident about showing them to Lucy whereas you wouldn't have shown them to your wife.

Susp: (inaudible) I was sexually unconfident anymore about sex and Lucy showing an interest in me and that was flattering in itself and cos there was no sexual relationships with my wife.

DC: Was it easier to feel confident with Lucy because she was so young? And you were an adult and more in control?

Susp: (inaudible) it was the first first young lady that's ever expressed an interest in me during my troubled marriage over the past three years I said.

Source: Benneworth (2004).

It has to be said that even in this version of the text there is a great deal that strikes one as important or anomalous, for example:

- The way in which the suspect presents the pornography as something that the girl happened on by chance and as a result of her actions. There is no indication that the suspect actively created a situation in which she was exposed to the pornography.

- The way in which the suspect excuses his behaviour by blaming his troubled marriage and his wife.

- The way in which the suspect represents his non-normative relationship (an adult man with an 11-year-old girl) as if two adults were involved. So the 11-year-old girl is represented as a 'young lady', indicating maturity, rather than a 'young girl' which represents an immature person.

Researchers and practitioners with knowledge and experience of paedophiles and other sex offenders have themselves noted such 'denial' and 'cognitive distortion' strategies (Howitt, 1995). Indeed, much of the therapy for sex offenders involves group therapy methods of modifying such cognitions. The above excerpt is perhaps not altogether typical of the sort of text used by qualitative researchers. For one thing, it is the sort of text which is unfamiliar to many and so is quite different from the everyday, routine conversation studied by many qualitative researchers. The implication is that unfamiliar subject matter is likely to reveal a lot because it contrasts markedly with more familiar sorts of conversation from everyday life. It is likely that at least some researchers would find in this simple transcription all that they require for their research purposes. For example, if a researcher was interested in the types of denial and cognitive distortions demonstrated by offenders, the transcription process may not need the Jefferson-style elaboration.

So what does the Jefferson transcription system add which a secretary's transcription omits? There are a few obvious things:

- The Jefferson transcription gives a lot more information about what happened in the conversation. The secretary's version gives the impression of a smooth, unproblematic conversational flow. The Jefferson transcription demonstrates a variety of turn-taking errors, quite lengthy pauses in utterances, and dynamic qualities of how the conversation is structured, for example, the very quiet passages.

- The time-consuming, painstaking work of producing a Jefferson transcription ensures that the researcher gains an intimate knowledge of their data. Inevitably this will provoke thought and stimulate possible analytic ideas, no matter how rudimentary. There is more than just this. Since the researcher is faced with a myriad of details in the recording, they may notice things which strike them as potentially important for the analysis. Had they left others to do the transcription, then significant features of the recording might be overlooked (Ochs, 1979). Considered seriously, the idea that transcription is an early stage of analysis is a powerful one. Transcription is not simply a matter of writing down what is in the recording, it involves deciding what is important in the recording (Bolden, 2015). This can only be achieved by thinking hard about the data which inevitably is the beginnings of analysis.

What else does the researcher gain by using the Jefferson transcription system? After all, some may regard the Jefferson system as merely providing irrelevant and obscuring detail. Suggestions include:

- If we look carefully for what the Jefferson transcription adds to the information available to the researcher, we find in lines 373–374 the following: 'Susp: [yeah I was] I was (3.8) s::::exually (0.8) umm (4.0) unconfident anymore about sex'. Not only is the word 'sexually' highlighted in speech by the elongation into 's::::exually', but it is also isolated by lengthy gaps of four or so seconds on each side. Benneworth (2004) refers to this as a 'conversational difficulty' which takes the form of 'hesitant speech' and 'prolonged pauses'. This may have led to her pointing out that the term 'sexually' is part of a particular language repertoire which the suspect only applies to relationships with an adult. When speaking of the child, he employs what Benneworth (2004) describes as 'relationship discourse and euphemism': '*Lucy showing an interest in me . . . that was flattering in itself*'. The suspect does not use the term 'victim' of the child, though it is a term that most of us would use. That is, the suspect is not using language repertoire which would indicate that the child has been abused sexually, as opposed to the language repertoire used to indicate a mutual relationship.

- The use of Jefferson transcription clearly encourages the researcher to concentrate closely on the text as a matter of a social exchange rather than information requested and supplied. For example, Benneworth notes how the detective constable constantly brings the youth of the girl into the conversation, which contrasts with the suspect's representation of the girl as if she were a mature female rather than a child. Furthermore, by taking this excerpt and contrasting it with other excerpts from other interviews, the researcher was able to explore different interview styles – one is more confrontational and challenging of the suspect, whereas the other almost colludes with the suspect's 'distorted' cognitions.

- Similarly, the use of the Jefferson transcription facilitates the linking of the text under consideration with established theory in the field. So Benneworth argues that the words 'I opened my boot one day' in line 366 grounds the suspect's account in common day-to-day experience rather than the more extraordinary abuse of a child. Such a device may be seen as a discursive device for creating a sense of ordinariness (Jefferson, 1984) and essentially creates a distance from the suspect's actions and the criminal consequences ensuing from them.

20.3   Advice for transcribers

It should be emphasised that the Jefferson system is just one of a number of systems of transcription. Indeed, there is no reason why a researcher should not contemplate developing their own system should circumstances require it. O'Connell and Kowal (1995) evaluated a number of text transcription systems employed by researchers, including that of Jefferson. They suggest that transcription is not and cannot be 'a genuine photograph of the spoken word' (p. 105). Generally, all transcription systems strive to record the exact words said. Nevertheless, transcription systems vary considerably in what other features of speech are included. So some systems include prosodic features such as how a word was spoken (loudly, softly, part emphasised, etc.), paralinguistic features (such as words said with a laugh or sigh) and extralinguistic features (facial expressions, gestures, etc.); some systems exclude some or all of them.

Potter (2004) suggested that technological advances have made transcription easier. Transcription is labour-intensive and 20 hours of transcription may be necessary for one hour of recording. Some generic suggestions have been offered to transcribers by O'Connell and Kowal though each of them is a little more controversial than at first appears:

- Parsimony: transcribe only those features of speech that are to be analysed. The argument is that it is pointless to include extralinguistic features such as gestures in the transcription that will not be analysed. Unfortunately, this means that other researchers will be unaware of aspects of the recording which they may consider important for the analysis. Typically, other researchers do not have access to the original recording, just the transcript.

- Similarly, the transcriptions provided in reports should only include whatever is necessary to make the analysis intelligible to the reader. While it may be desirable to de-clutter transcripts to aid readability, this actually stacks things in favour of the original researcher's analysis since only supportive information will tend to be included.

- Subjectively assessed aspects of conversation should not be included in the transcription as if they are objective measurements. For example, transcribers may subjectively estimate the lengths of short pauses (0.2) but enter them as if they are precise measures. O'Connell and Kowal report that transcribers omitted almost four out of five of such pauses in radio interviews. This begs the question why the other pauses were included. Transcribers using computer programs may have high levels of accuracy. Furthermore, there are digital editing programs (e.g. Cool Edit/Adobe Audition) which allow the transcription of recordings on screen. As the recording is held as a file on the computer, the system allows frequent checking against the original. Since the recording may be displayed as a visual waveform, it becomes easier to measure precisely gaps and pauses in conversation and speech despite this, simply because the silences are very apparent and measurable on graphs.

● Transcribers make frequent, uncorrected errors. For example, verbal additions, deletions, relocations and substitutions are commonly found when a transcript is compared with the original recording. Qualitative researchers often stress the importance of checking the transcription against the original source in order to minimise this problem. It is a valuable tip to always compare the transcript with the recording as the recording will provide the researcher with fuller information.

20.4 Conclusion

Although normally described as a *transcription* system, Jefferson's approach is also a low-level coding or categorisation system. If researchers want a perfect transcription of the recording, then what better than their original recording? Of course, what they want is a simplified or more manageable version of the recording. Inevitably this means coding or categorising the material and one can only capture what the system of coding can capture. Conversational difficulties, for example, are highlighted by the Jefferson system, so these are likely to receive analytical consideration. Facial expression is not usually included, so facial expressions (which may totally negate the impression created in a conversation) are overlooked.

Transcription is a very time-consuming process. The Jefferson system is more detailed than most and takes up even more time. So there is little point in using any system of transcription unless it adds something to achieving the sort of analysis the researcher requires. Transcription is generally regarded by qualitative researchers as a task for the researcher themselves. Ideally it is not something farmed out to junior assistants or clerical workers. Qualitative researchers need intimate familiarity with their material, and this is facilitated by doing one's own transcriptions.

Key points

● Transcription is the stage between the collection of data in verbal form and analysis. Usually it is producing a written version of audio-recordings, but video material may also be transcribed.

● In qualitative data analysis, transcription may take into account more than the words spoken by indicating how the words are spoken. That is, errors of speech are included, pauses are indexed and times when people are speaking at the same time are noted.

● Transcription is regarded not as a necessary chore but as one of the ways in which the researcher becomes increasingly familiar with their data. Transcription is not a task usually passed over to others.

● Inevitably, transcription omits aspects of the original and there is the risk that the transcription is inadequate. It is normally recommended that the researcher refers back to the original recording when the transcription appears complete or considers asking another researcher to assess the veracity of it.

● The most common form of transcription is the Jefferson method, which has its roots in conversation analysis. It is very commonly used by qualitative researchers but can be unnecessarily time-consuming if the analysis is only of the words.

ACTIVITIES

1. In pairs, act out the conversation which was subject to Jefferson transcription in the main body of the chapter between the police and the suspect. Record the conversation if you can and compare the product of the attempts of different pairs of actors.

2. Record a conversation, select an interesting part, transcribe it and annotate it with Jefferson transcription symbols. List the difficulties you experience for discussion.

CHAPTER 21

Thematic analysis

Overview

- Thematic analysis is among the most commonly used qualitative analysis methods. Despite this, accounts of how to do thematic analysis are scarce. Many researchers gloss over what they actually did when reporting a thematic analysis.

- Thematic analysis is not dependent on specialised theory as some other qualitative techniques are such as discourse analysis (Chapter 23) and conversation analysis (Chapter 24). Consequently, thematic analysis is more accessible to novices unfamiliar with the general theory underlying qualitative methods.

- In thematic analysis, researchers identify a limited number of themes which adequately reflect their textual data. Hard to do well, a few superficial themes are easily generated but they do not reflect the required level of analysis adequately.

- As with all qualitative analysis, the researcher needs to be extremely familiar with their data in order to expedite an insightful analysis. Data familiarisation is key to thematic analysis, as it is for other qualitative methods. Consequently, it is generally recommended that researchers collect and transcribe them personally.

- Following data familiarisation, the researcher will normally code their data. That is, they apply brief verbal descriptions to small chunks of data. The detail of this process will vary according to circumstances, including the researcher's expectations about the direction in which the analysis will proceed. Probably the analyst will be making codings every two or three lines of text, but there are no rules about this and some analyses may be more densely coded than others.

- At every stage of the analysis, the researcher will alter and modify the analysis in the light of experience and as ideas develop. Thus the researcher may adjust earlier codings in the light of the full picture of the data. The idea is really to get as close a fit of the codings to the data as possible without having a plethora of idiosyncratic codings.

- The researcher then tries to identify themes which integrate substantial sets of these codings. Again this is something of a trial-and-error process in which change and adjustment are to be expected. The researcher needs to define each theme sufficiently so that the nature of the theme is clear to others.

- The researcher needs to select examples of each theme to illustrate what the analysis has achieved.

- As in all report writing, writing up the analysis and its findings is part of the analysis process. New analytic ideas may be introduced even at this late stage.

- There is no reason why researchers cannot give numerical indications of the incidence and prevalence of each theme in their data. For example, what percentage of participants mention things which refer to a particular theme?

21.1   Introduction

Almost certainly, thematic analysis will be the first qualitative analysis method considered or used by newcomers to qualitative research. Thematic analysis needs little knowledge of the theoretical intricacies of the qualitative ethos compared to most other qualitative techniques. Compared with, say, discourse analysis or conversation analysis, thematic analysis can proceed without much recourse to theory and no theory is especially relevant to it. Hence, it is amenable to novices. It can be used with textual data of just about any sort including in-depth interviews, focus groups, and so forth.

Thematic analysis is flexible in terms of how and why it is carried out. So one will see thematic analyses by researchers with no particularly strong affinity to qualitative research. Thematic analysis does not demand the intensely closely detailed analysis which typifies conversation analysis, for example. Whether this is strong praise for thematic analysis or damning criticism depends on one's point of view. Like anything else in research, thematic analysis can be well done or poorly done. Until you understand the difference then do not expect to do good work. All in all, with a little care, thematic analysis can be recommended as a useful initiation for students into qualitative research.

There is a downside to all of this. Thematic analysis is not a single, identifiable approach to the analysis of qualitative data. Different researchers do thematic analysis differently and there is no universal standard approach to doing it. While this is typical of qualitative methods generally, it is clearly something of an obstacle. Fortunately, researchers have noted this problem and have begun to systematise the approach (Braun & Clarke, 2006). Nevertheless, thematic analysis studies vary substantially. This is generally the case with all forms of research. For example, the same quantitative data often may be analysed statistically using a wide variety of statistical methods. All of them legitimate.

Sometimes rather rudimentary and unsystematic approaches are used in studies described as thematic analysis. Seemingly, the researcher merely reads through their transcribed data looking to identify, say, half a dozen pervading themes. These are then written up in a report which laces together these themes with illustrative quotes from the transcript. So what is wrong with this? The problem is that the researcher is doing

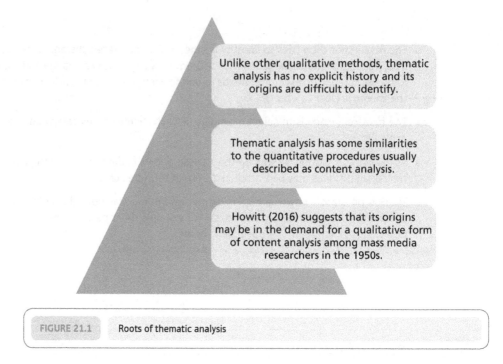

Unlike other qualitative methods, thematic analysis has no explicit history and its origins are difficult to identify.

Thematic analysis has some similarities to the quantitative procedures usually described as content analysis.

Howitt (2016) suggests that its origins may be in the demand for a qualitative form of content analysis among mass media researchers in the 1950s.

FIGURE 21.1   Roots of thematic analysis

minimal analytic work. The task is too easy in the sense that, so long as the researcher can suggest some themes and provide illustrative support for them, there is little intellectual demand on the researcher. Who is to say that the themes are 'wrong', since there is no criterion to establish that they are wrong? But think about it. The process involved in this analysis lacks a great deal in terms of transparency. It is unclear how the researcher processed their data when developing the themes; it is unclear the extent to which the themes encompass the data – do the themes exhaust the data or merely cover a small amount of the transcribed material?

Generally, such reports do not establish the amount of the data represented by the themes. Furthermore, the task need not be very onerous for the researcher who, once he or she has thought of a handful of themes, has little more work to do apart from writing up the report. Nothing requires them to develop themes which collectively describe the entirety of the data, which is far more demanding. The greater the demands made by the researcher on the analysis, the greater the likelihood that they will generate themes which cover the data at greater depth in original and subtle ways. 'The more work that goes into the analysis, the better the analytic outcome' would be one way of putting this. Figure 21.1 gives some indications of the roots of thematic analysis.

21.2 What is thematic analysis?

The phrase 'thematic analysis' first appeared in the psychological journals in 1943 and is a quite common research method nowadays. Nevertheless, thematic analysis is something of the poor relative in the qualitative methods family. It has few, if any, high-profile advocates and, possibly as a consequence, it has been slow to be formalised as a method. Very little is available by way of systematic instruction about conducting a thematic analysis. Reports of thematic analysis studies tend to pay scant attention to describing the method and how the researcher went about using it. Typically, instead of describing in detail how the analysis was done, thematic analysts simply write something like 'a thematic analysis was carried out on the data'. In other cases, reports which describe themes identified in qualitative data may make no reference at all to thematic analysis; for example, Gee, Ward, and Eccleston (2003) report 'A data-driven approach to model development (grounded theory) was undertaken to analyse the interview transcripts' (p. 44). Since the method tends to be glossed over in reports, it is difficult to use published papers as guides to how to do thematic analysis.

Thematic analysis seems like a poor relative of other qualitative methods, and often appears sloppily conducted and very subjective in comparison. The lack of detail about methodology in thematic analysis reports leaves the reader thinking that the researcher merely perused a few transcripts and then identified a number of themes suggested by the data. The only support provided for the analysis is the one or two illustrative quotes from the transcript used to clarify the meaning of each theme. Put this way, thematic analysis does not amount to much and there are plenty of published thematic analyses which do nothing to correct this impression. However, carried out properly, thematic analysis is quite an exacting process requiring a considerable investment of time and effort by the researchers.

Just as the label says, thematic analysis is the analysis of textual material (newspapers, interviews, and so forth) in order to indicate the major themes to be found in it. A theme, according to *The concise Oxford dictionary,* is 'a subject or topic on which a person speaks, writes or thinks'. This is not quite the sense of the word 'theme' used in thematic analysis. When a lecturer stands up and talks about, say, eyewitness testimony for an hour, the theme of the lecture would be eyewitness testimony, according to the dictionary definition. However, in thematic analysis the researcher does not identify the overall topic of the text. Instead, the researcher digs deeper into the text of the lecture to identify a variety of themes which describe significant aspects of the text. For example, the following themes may be present in the lecture: the unreliability of eyewitness testimony, the ways of improving the accuracy of testimony and methodological problems with the research into eyewitness testimony. This may not be the most scintillating thematic analysis ever carried out, but nevertheless it does give us some understanding of this particular lecture as an example of text.

Of course, a lecture is normally a highly organised piece of textual material which has been split up by the lecturer into several different components and given a structure so that everything is clear to the student. This is not the case with many texts such as in-depth interviews or transcripts of focus groups. People talking in these circumstances simply do not produce highly systematic and organised speech. Thus the analytical work is there for the researcher to organise the textual material by defining the main themes which seem to represent the text effectively. While it is possible to carry out thematic analysis on a single piece of text, more generally, researchers use material from a wider range of individuals or focus groups, for example.

There are other methods of qualitative research which seem to compete with thematic analysis in the sense that they take text and, often, identify themes. Grounded theory (Chapter 22) is a case in point. Indeed, if the basic processes involved in carrying out a grounded theory analysis are compared with those of thematic analysis, then differentiating between the two is difficult. But there is a crucial difference: grounded theory is intended as a way of generating theory which is closely tied to the data. Theory development is not the intention of thematic analysis. Of course, any process which leads to a better understanding of data may lead subsequently to the development of theories.

Thematic analysis is not aligned with any particular theory or method, though overwhelmingly it is presented from a qualitative perspective which is data-led. However, sometimes the approach taken is to develop predetermined themes based on theory and then test the themes against the actual data – though this violates basic assumptions from most qualitative perspectives. One also sees from time-to-time, thematic analyses quantified in the sense that the researcher counts the number of interviews, for example, in which each theme is to be found. Thematic analysis, used in this way, is difficult to distinguish from some forms of content analysis described earlier (Chapter 17). The lack of a clear theoretical basis to thematic analysis does not mean that theory is not appropriate to your research – it merely means that the researcher needs to identify the theoretical allegiance of his or her research. For example, is the research informed by feminist thinking, is it phenomenological in nature, or does it relate to some other theory? Purely empirical thematic analyses may be appropriate in some cases, but they may not be academically very satisfying as a consequence.

There seems to be a range of possibilities which can be referred to as thematic analysis (Crowe, Inder, & Porter, 2015) which, at one extreme, is little different from quantitative content analysis but highly distinct at the other. They suggest that the terms manifest, descriptive, and deductive typify the content analysis pole and latent, interpretive, and inductive the thematic analysis pole. In other words, thematic analysis can dig deeper than superficial for its themes into the realm of interpretation. Not surprisingly, then, is the lack of clarity in researchers' minds about thematic analysis since potential thematic analysis range from the atheoretical to the theoretically sophisticated, from the relatively casual to the procedurally exacting, and from the superficial to the sophisticated in terms of the themes suggested. At the most basic level, thematic analysis can be described as merely empirical, as the researcher creates the themes simply from what is in the text before him or her; this may be described as an inductive approach. On the other hand, the researcher may be informed by theory in terms of what aspects of the text to examine and in terms of the sorts of themes that should be identified and how they should be described and labelled. If there is a theoretical position that informs the analysis, then this should be discussed by the researcher in the report of their analysis; in this sense, the analysis may be theory driven.

21.3 Basic approach to thematic analysis

The basic essential components of a thematic analysis are shown in Figure 21.2. They are transcription, analytic effort and theme identification. It is important to note that the three aspects are only conceptually distinct: in practice, they overlap considerably. Briefly, the components of thematic analysis can be described as follows:

- *Transcribing textual material* The data may be from any qualitative data collection method, including in-depth interviews and focus groups. The level of transcription may vary from a straightforward literal transcript much as a secretary would produce to, for example, a Jefferson-transcribed version of the text which contains more information than the literal transcription (see Chapter 20). Generally speaking, there is no good reason for using Jefferson transcription with thematic analysis but, by the same token, if a researcher sees a place for it, then nothing prevents its use. No qualitative researcher should regard transcription as an unfortunate but necessary chore, since the work of transcribing increases the familiarity of the researcher with his or her material. In other words, transcription is part of the analytic process. In the best-case circumstances, the researcher would have conducted the interviews or focus groups themselves and then transcribed the data themselves. Thus the process of becoming familiar with the text starts early and probably continues throughout the analysis.

● *Analytic effort*   This refers to the amount of work or processing that the researcher applies to the text in order to generate the themes at the end-point of thematic analysis. There are several components to analytic effort: (a) the familiarisation process which ensures the best understanding of the data; (b) the detail with which the researcher studies his or her data, which may range from a line-by-line analysis to a much broader-brush approach that merely seeks to summarise the overall themes; (c) the extent to which the researcher is prepared to process and reprocess the data in order to achieve as close a fit of the analysis to the data as possible; (d) the extent to which the researcher is presented with difficulties during the course of the analysis which have to be resolved; and (e) the willingness of the researcher to check and recheck the fit of his or her analysis to the original data.

● *Identifying themes and sub-themes*   While this appears to be the end-point of a thematic analysis, researchers can differ considerably in terms of how carefully or fully they choose to refine the themes which they suggest. One researcher may be rapidly satisfied with the set of themes, since they seem to do a 'good enough' job of describing what they see as key features of the data. Another researcher may be dissatisfied with the same themes at this stage because they, for example, seem to only describe a part of the data and there is a lot of material which could not be coded under these themes. Hence the latter researcher may seek to refine the list of themes in some way, for example by adding themes and removing those which seem to do a particularly poor job of describing the data. Of course, by being demanding in terms of the analysis, the researcher may find that they need to refine all of the themes and may find that for some of the themes, substantial sub-themes emerge. Also, again as a consequence of being demanding, the researcher may find it harder to name and describe the new or refined themes accurately. All of this continues the analytic work through to the end of the total thematic analysis.

On the basis of this, the flow diagram of the process perhaps is as shown in Figure 21.2. In the next section, we go on to provide a more sophisticated version of thematic analysis. An example of thematic analysis is described in Box 21.1.

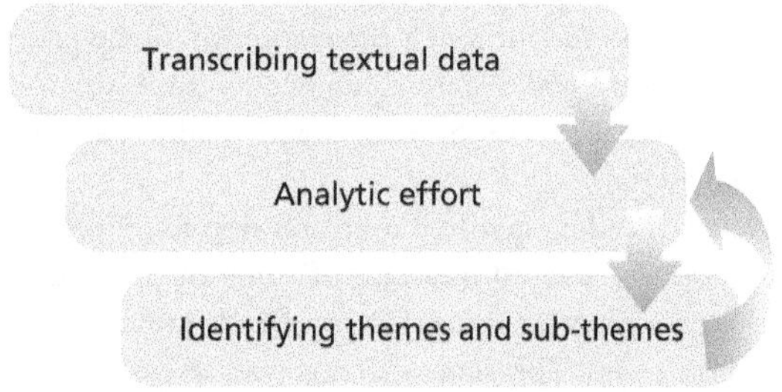

Transcribing textual data

Analytic effort

Identifying themes and sub-themes

FIGURE 21.2   Basic thematic analysis

Box 21.1 Research Example

Thematic analysis

Sheldon, K., & Howitt, D. (2007). *Sex offenders and the Internet*. Chichester, UK: Wiley.

Sheldon and Howitt (2007) compared offenders convicted of using the Internet for sexual offending purposes (e.g. downloading child pornography) with child molesters (the traditional paedophile). They were interested in: (a) the 'function(s)' of Internet child pornography for Internet sex offenders and (b) the concept of desistance from child molestation. Internet offenders have a strong sexual proclivity towards children (e.g. they are sexually aroused by children) but mainly do not go on to sexually molest children. Despite their close similarities to traditional paedophiles, Internet offenders were desisting from offending against children. How do Internet offenders explain why they do not express their paedophilic orientation towards children by directly assaulting children sexually? The researchers carried out a thematic analysis of what the offenders told them about the functions of Internet child pornography in their lives and their desistance from offending directly against children. The offenders provided detailed data on a topic which has not been extensively researched.

So, during the course of lengthy interviews, Internet offenders were asked why they did not contact-offend (i.e. physically offend) against children, and contact paedophiles were asked why they used child pornography on the Internet as a substitute for contact-offending. All of the fieldwork for this study was conducted by one researcher who therefore had (a) interviewed all of the participants in the study herself and (b) transcribed in full all of the interviews using direct literal (secretarial) methods. The transcriptions were not 'Jeffersoned' (see Chapter 20), since the researchers simply wanted to study broadly how offenders accounted for these aspects of their offending.

Of course, the interviews and transcripts contained much data irrelevant to the question of desistance (e.g. matters such as childhood experiences, details of the offending behaviour and their cognitive distortions). Hence, the researchers needed to identify relevant material for this aspect of the study which was confined to answers to specific questions (e.g. their reasons for not engaging in a particular sort of offending behaviour). This was done by copying and pasting the material from the computer files of the transcripts into a new file, but it could have been done by highlighting the relevant text with a highlighter pen or highlighting the material on the computer with a different font or font colour. Because of the sheer volume of data in this study, coming from over 50 offenders, it was best to put the pertinent material into a relatively compact computer file. In this way, the material can easily be perused for the coding process.

The phases of thematic analysis are very similar to those of other forms of qualitative analysis. The process began with a descriptive level of coding with minimal interpretation. The researchers applied codes to 'chunks' of data, that is, a word, a phrase, a sentence or even a paragraph. For example, one of the functions of child pornography according to offenders was to avoid negative feelings/moods encountered in their everyday lives and so was coded as 'negavoidance' each time this occurred in the transcripts. Coding was not a static process, so initial codes were revised as the researcher proceeded through the transcript. Some codes became subdivided or revised if the initial codes were not adequate; some codes were combined as there was too much overlap in meaning. Jotting down of ideas and codes was an integral part of this early stage. As the researcher had conducted the interviews, she was also very familiar with the material.

The next formal level of coding involved a greater degree of interpretation. More superordinate constructs were identified which captured the overall meaning of some of the initial descriptive codes used at the earlier stage. Throughout the entire process of analysis, the researcher moved constantly backwards and forwards between the interview extracts and the codes. This stage also involved an early search for themes. This process of moving towards identifying themes involved writing the codings onto different postcards (together with a brief description of them) and organising them into 'theme piles'. This allowed the researcher to check whether the themes worked in relation to the coded extracts.

In the final stage of this particular thematic analysis, psychological theories were drawn upon to aid interpretation of the codings and to identify the overarching themes. At the same time, it was essential that the analysis remained grounded in the actual data. Engaging with previous research and theory was very important in this particular study, as it helped in understanding the meaning and implications of the patterns in the codings or the themes identified. At the same time, the researcher was engaged in the process of generating clear definitions and names for each theme. Overall, this thematic analysis generated only a few themes, but these themes represented more general concepts within the analysis and subsumed the lower-level codes.

If themes are clearly defined, then it is possible within a qualitative analysis to add a quantitative component. Just how common are the themes in the data? There are different ways of determining this. It can be asked just how prevalent a theme is, meaning just how many of the participants mention a particular theme in their individual accounts. Alternatively, one might ask how many incidents of a particular theme occur in a particular account. In this study, following the thematic analysis, each interview was studied again and the percentage of each type of sex offender mentioning a particular theme at least once was assessed. Ideally, there should be several instances of a theme across the data, but more instances of a theme do not necessarily mean that the theme is any more crucial. Key themes capture something important in terms of the research question and this is not entirely dependent on their frequency of occurrence in the data.

Three strong themes were identified in what the offenders told the researchers about desistance: (a) focus on fantasy contact; (b) moral/ethical reasoning and (c) fear of consequences. These are very different themes and probably not entirely predictable. Certainly, the idea of moral/ethical reasoning in terms of child pornography and child molestation is not a common-sense notion. The themes identified by the study were illustrated by excerpts such as the following:

- *Focus on fantasy contact*   'I never got to the point where I would want to touch . . . looking at the images is enough, though a lot of people will disagree . . . I mean I've met people in prisons . . . who are in for the same thing and . . . their talk was never of actual sexual contact. Definitely. No. No. I would never'.

- *Moral/ethical reasoning*   'No . . . because as an adult you've got to be thinking for the child . . . they've got to live with it for the rest of their life'.

- *Fear of consequences*   'Partly because I wouldn't want the guy to go "Ahh! This man's trying to grope me!" . . . and I'd have his big brothers' mates coming with baseball bats'.

Notice that if one checks the excerpts against the name of the theme, then only the one theme seems to deal with the data in each case. Try to switch around the names of the themes with the different excerpts and they simply do not fit. This is an illustration of back-checking the themes against the data, though in the study proper the researchers were far more comprehensive in this checking process.

We are grateful to Kerry Sheldon for her help with this box.

21.4 More sophisticated version of thematic analysis

Braun and Clarke (2006) provide what is probably the most systematic introduction to doing thematic analysis to date. This is a fully-fledged account of thematic analysis which seeks to impose high standards on the analyst such that more exacting and sophisticated thematic analyses are developed. They write of the 'process' of doing a thematic analysis which they divide into six separate aspects that very roughly describe the sequence of the analysis, though there may be a lot of backtracking to the earlier aspects of the process in order to achieve the best possible fit. The simple approach as described previously includes some elements similar to the Braun–Clarke approach, but they are aiming for a somewhat more comprehensive and demanding kind of thematic analysis. Their six aspects or steps are:

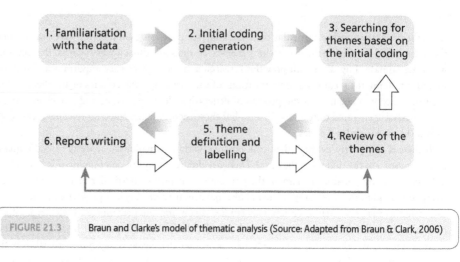

Braun and Clarke's model of thematic analysis (Source: Adapted from Braun & Clark, 2006)

- Familiarisation with the data

- Initial coding generation

- Searching for themes based on the initial coding

- Review of the themes

- Theme definition and labelling

- Report writing.

The entire process is summarised in Figure 21.3. Notice that the figure indicates a sort of flow from one aspect to the next, but there are many loops back to the earlier aspects of the analysis should circumstances demand it. In truth, at practically any stage of the process the analyst may go back to any of the earlier stages for purposes of refinement and clarification. Not only do the six steps in the analysis loop back to earlier stages, but also the stages are best regarded as conceptually distinct, since in practice there may be considerable overlap.

Step 1   Familiarisation with the data

This is the early stage, in which the researcher becomes actively involved with the data. The familiarisation process depends partly on the nature of the text to be analysed. If the text is interview data, for example, the researcher has probably been actively involved in interviewing the participants in the research. Inevitably, while interviewing the participants, the interviewer will gain familiarity with what is being said. Unless the interviewer is so overwhelmed by the interview situation that they fail to pay proper attention to what the participant is saying, features of what each interviewee is saying will become familiar to the researcher.

Equally, over a series of interviews, most interviewers will begin to formulate ideas about what is being said in the interview just as we get ideas about this in ordinary conversation. In the research context, the researcher will be well aware that they will eventually have to produce some sort of analysis of the interviews. Thus, more than in ordinary conversation, there is an imperative to absorb as much of what is being said as possible and to develop ideas for the analysis. Of course, the more interviews that have been carried out, the easier it is to begin to recognise some patterns. These may stimulate very preliminary ideas about how the data will be coded and, perhaps, ideas of the themes apparent in the data.

Furthermore, interview data have to be transcribed from the recording, partly because this facilitates more intense processing of the text by the researcher at the later stage when the text needs to be read and reread, but also because excerpts of text are usually included in the final report to illustrate the themes. Usually in thematic analysis, the transcription is a literal transcription of the text, much as a secretary would do. It is far less common to use Jefferson transcription (Chapter 20) with thematic analysis. Jefferson transcription is more laborious than literal transcription. The choice of how the transcribing is done depends partly on whether the thematic analysis can effectively utilise the additional information incorporated in the Jefferson transcription.

In thematic analysis, the researcher tends to have a realist perspective on the text, that is, the belief that the text represents a basic reality and so can largely be understood literally – hence there is little need for the Jefferson system. The process of transcription in qualitative analysis should be regarded as a positive thing, despite the tedium that may be involved. Ideally, doing the transcription will make the researcher even more familiar with their research data. With such a focused process, the risk is that the fuller picture is not seen.

Finally, the transcriptions will be read and reread a number of times to further familiarise the researcher with the material and as an *aide-mémoire*. Researchers who do not themselves actively collect and transcribe the text they intend to analyse will be at a disadvantage; they would need to spend much more time on reading the transcripts. There are no short cuts in this familiarisation process if a worthwhile analysis is to be performed. All other things being equal, a researcher who is well immersed in their data will have better ideas about later stages of the process and may, early on, have ideas about the direction in which the analysis will go. Writing notes to oneself about what one is reading is part of the process of increasing familiarity with the data but also constitutes an earlier stage in the coding process, which technically comes next.

> **Useful tip**   As a novice researcher, it is likely that you will have to do all of the data collection and transcriptions yourself. This is an advantage, not a hindrance.

Step 2   Initial coding generation

Initial coding is a step in the process by which themes are generated. The research suggests codings for the aspects of the data which seem interesting or important. The initial coding process involves the analyst working systematically through the entirety of the data, making suggestions as to what is happening in the data. Probably this is best done on a line-by-line basis, but sometimes this will be too small a unit of analysis. The decision about how frequently to make a coding depends partly on the particular data in question but also on the broader purpose of the analysis. As a rule-of-thumb, a coding should be made at fairly regular intervals – every line may be too frequent, every two or three lines would probably be acceptable.

The chunk of text being coded does not have to be exactly the same number of lines long each time a coding is made. We are analysing people's talk, which does not have precise regularity. The initial codings are intended to capture the essence of a segment of the text and, at this stage, the objective is *not* to develop broader themes. At first, the initial codings may seem like jottings or notes rather than a sophisticated analysis of the data. If so, all well and good, because this is precisely what you should be aiming for. Of course, the analyst will be pretty familiar with the text already, so the initial codings will be on the interviews that the researcher conducted and the transcripts that the researcher made of the interviews in the first stage of data familiarisation. As a consequence, they will already have an overview of the material, so they are not simply responding to a short piece of the text in isolation.

There may be two different approaches, depending on whether the data are data-led or theory-led, according to Braun and Clarke (2006):

- *The data-led approach*   This is dominated by the characteristics of the data and the codings are primarily guided by a careful analysis of what is in the data.

- *The theory-led approach*   The structure for the initial codings is suggested by the key elements of the theory being applied by the researcher. Feminist theory, for example, stresses that relationships between men and women are dominated by the power and dominance of the male gender over the female gender in a wide variety of aspects of the social world, including employment, domestic life and the law. Thus, a thematic analysis based on feminist theory would be oriented to the expression of power relationships in any textual material.

Of course, there is something of a dilemma here, since it is unclear how a researcher can avoid applying elements of a theoretical perspective during the analysis process. Just how would it be possible to differentiate between a theory-led coding and a data-led coding unless the researcher makes this explicit in their writings?

Usually in reports of thematic analyses, such initial codings are not included by the researcher for the obvious reason that there is rarely sufficient space to include all of the data, let alone the codings in addition. Consequently, those new to thematic analysis may assume that the initial codings are more sophisticated than they actually are. The following is a brief piece of transcript provided by Clarke, Burns, and Burgoyne (2006) which includes some initial codings for a few lines of text:

	Initial coding
it's too much like hard work I mean how much paper have you got to sign to change a flippin' name no I I mean no I no we we have thought about it ((inaudible)) half heartedly and thought no no I jus' – I can't be bothered, it's too much like hard work. (Kate F07a)	1. Talked about with partner 2. Too much hassle to change name

The initial codings can be seen to be little more than a fairly mundane summary of a few lines of text. Thus, the coding 'too much hassle to change name' is not very different from 'it's too much like hard work' and 'I can't be bothered, it's too much like hard work' which occur in the text at this point. So the initial coding stage is not really about generating substantial insights into the data but is merely a process of identifying and summarising the key things about what is going on in the text. Of course, this same piece of text could be coded in any number of different ways. For example, 'half heartedly' in the text might have been coded 'lack of commitment'. The researcher will normally have some ideas about the direction in which the analysis is going by this stage in the analysis. Consequently, the codings do not have to be exhaustive of all possibilities and, indeed, over-coding at this stage may make it difficult for the analyst to move on to the later phases of the analysis, because too much coding obscures what is going on; it is important to remember that the initial codings are brief summaries of a chunk of text and not the minutiae of the text expressed in a different way. The researcher is trying to simplify the text, not complicate it.

Also notice that, in the example, the same segment of the text is coded in more than one way. This is more likely where one is coding bigger chunks of text than if the coding is line by line.

At this stage, the analyst will typically wish to collate the data which have so far been given a particular initial code. In this way, the researcher is essentially linking a particular code with the parts of the text to which the code has been applied. So, for example, the researcher would bring together the different parts of the text which have been coded as 'Talked about with partner' in the same place. A simple way of doing this is to copy and paste the relevant text material under the title of that particular initial coding. It is possible at this stage that the analyst will feel it appropriate to change the initial coding's name to fit better with the pattern of textual material which has received that particular code. Furthermore, it is likely that the researcher will notice that two or more initial codings mean much the same thing despite being expressed in different words. For example, 'discussed matter with husband' may be the same as 'talked about with partner' so should not be regarded as a distinct coding.

Initial coding development (and the later development of themes) is an active process on the part of the researcher. Braun and Clarke (2006) are extremely dismissive of the idea that codings (and themes) 'emerge', that is, suddenly appear to the researcher as part of the analysis process. Codings and themes are synthesised actively from the data by the researcher; they are not located in the data as such but are created by the minds and imaginations of researchers.

| Useful tip | As a novice, it would be very daunting for you to write down codings without some practice, so why not select a page of transcript which you found particularly interesting and try to code that material first? |

Step 3   Searching for themes based on the initial coding

The relationship between text, codings and themes is illustrated in Figure 21.4. The initial codings, of course, are likely to be used quite frequently in the coding of the text, though we illustrate them as occurring only once. Then the themes are essentially obtained by joining together (or collapsing together) several of the codings in a meaningful way. Thus the process of initial coding has involved the researcher in formulating descriptive suggestions for the interesting aspects of their data. As we have seen, these codings are fairly close to the text itself. So, if you like, a theme can be seen as a coding of codings. Thus themes identify major patterns in the initial codings and so are a sort of second level of interpretation of the text, in which the analyst focuses on the relationships between the codings. In some instances, it is possible that a theme is based simply on one of the initial codings. Of course, it is difficult for the analyst to separate the coding phase from the theme-generation phase, so one might expect the occasional close correspondence between a single coding and a theme.

This begs the question of how an analyst suggests the themes which bring together the initial codings in a meaningful way. Of course, this may be instantly obvious, but it is not always clear. One way of identifying themes would be to write each of the different initial codings onto a separate piece of paper or card. Then the initial codings may be sorted into separate piles of codings which seem to be similar. The remaining task would be to put words to the ways in which the similar codings are, indeed, similar. Since the sorting process has an element of trial and error, this procedure will allow the analyst to change the groupings (piles) as their analytic ideas develop. Alternatively, one could place the slips of paper on a table top and physically move them around, so that

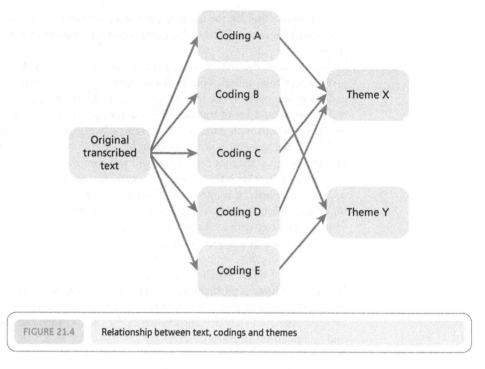

FIGURE 21.4   Relationship between text, codings and themes

initial codings which are similar are next to each other and those which are dissimilar are physically apart. In this way, the relationships between the codings may be made more apparent. It may be that it becomes clear that some apparently very different codings are merely the opposites of each other, so perhaps they should actually be part of the same theme.

The entire process is trying to understand just what are the overarching themes which bring together the individual codings in a meaningful way. Of course, the themes have to be related back to the original data, so the data associated with each theme need to be compiled/collated; in this way, the themes can be related back easily to the original textual data. Moreover, the more systematic the analysis is, the greater are the data management tasks involved in collating the themes with the original material. The use of computers – if only word-processing programs – should greatly facilitate the process of linking together the data for the themes that the researcher is developing. There are specialist computer programs which also do much the same job.

Useful tip

Unfortunately, developing themes will be easier the harder you work. Just sitting and staring at a computer screen or the coded transcript will waste time. So any of the active procedures we have suggested in this section are recommended. Spreading the themes on a table top and actively moving them together or apart, depending on how similar they are, is likely to lead to dividends.

Step 4   Review of the themes

By this stage you will have a set of tentative themes which help one understand what is in the transcriptions. However, these themes are probably not very refined at this stage and need to be tested against the original data once again. There are a number of possibilities:

- You may find that there is very little in the data to support a theme that you have identified, so the theme may have to be abandoned or modified in the light of this.

- You may find that a theme needs to be split up, since the data which are supposed to link together into the theme imply two different themes or sub-themes.

- You may feel that the theme works, by and large, but does not fit some of the data which initially you believed were part of that theme, so you may have to find a new theme to deal with the non-fitting data. You may need to check the applicability of your themes to selected extracts as well as to the entire dataset.

Step 5   Theme definition and labelling

All academic work aims at accuracy and precision. The definition and labelling of themes by the researcher are unlikely to meet these criteria without considerable refinement. In particular, just what is it about a particular theme which differentiates it from other themes? In other words, part of the definition of any theme includes the issue of what it is not, as well as the issue of what it is. In most instances, this is probably not so complicated as it sounds, and the less ambitious your analysis, the less likely it is to be a problem; where one is trying to provide themes for the entirety of the data, it is likely to be a more exacting and difficult process.

At this stage, the analyst may find it appropriate to identify sub-themes within a theme, which adds to the task of defining and labelling these accurately. Of course, defining themes and sub-themes precisely cannot take place in a vacuum but needs to be done in relation to the data too. So the researcher would have to go through the data once again to ensure that the themes (and sub-themes) which have been defined in this stage actually still effectively account for the data, since the definition imposes a structure and clarity that may not have been present in the initial coding process and the identification of themes. As you do this, you may well find that there are data that have not previously been coded which can be coded now using your refined themes and better level of understanding of the material.

Useful tip   At this stage, you might wish to go 'public' with your ideas. By this we mean that discussing your analysis with others may pay dividends, as you have to explain your themes clearly to what may be a sceptical friend or colleague. You have, in this way, a challenge to your theme definition and labelling which may stimulate further thought or revision.

Step 6   Report writing

All research reports tell a story that you want to tell about your data, and this applies equally to reports of thematic analysis. Of course, the story being told relates back to the research question which initiated your research – and the stronger the research question, all other things being equal, the more coherent a story you can tell. One should not regard report writing as merely telling a story about the steps in your research; the report-writing stage is a further opportunity for reflecting on one's data, one's analysis and the adequacy of both with respect to each other. So what emerges at the end of the report-writing process may be a somewhat different and probably more refined story than was possible before starting the report. In other words, report writing is another stage in the analysis and not just a chore to be completed to get one's work published or the grades one wants for a psychology degree.

The final report requires that you illustrate your analysis using extracts from your data. Of course, it is more than appropriate to choose the most apposite extracts to illustrate the outcome of your analysis. But, in addition, the selected extracts may be the most vivid of the instances that you have. The final report also provides the opportunity to discuss your analysis in the light of the previous research literature. This may be either (a) the literature that you choose to discuss in order to justify why you have chosen to research a particular research question in a particular way, or (b) relating your analyses to the findings and conceptualisations of other analysts. In what way does your analysis progress things beyond theirs? What distinguishes your analysis from theirs? Is it possible to resolve substantial differences?

Useful tip	Most reports of thematic analysis avoid describing in any detail just how the analysis was carried out. Do not emulate this but instead try to be as systematic as you possibly can be about just how the analysis was done. If there are problems defining a theme then identify these and do not simply sweep difficulties under the carpet.

Thematic analysis involves three crucial elements – the data, the coding of data and the identification of themes. The procedure described above essentially stresses the way in which the researcher constantly loops back to the earlier stages in the process to check and to refine the analysis. In other words, the researcher constantly juxtaposes the data and the analysis of the data to establish the adequacy of the analysis and to help refine the analysis. A good analysis requires a considerable investment of time and effort.

Braun and Clarke's (2006) approach to thematic analysis has been widely cited as the methodology researchers have employed in their thematic analyses. This is no bad thing as Braun and Clarke's instructions are steeped in the well-established traditions of other types of qualitative analysis such as grounded theory and discourse analysis. So by adopting Braun and Clarke's analytic principles students not only maximise their chances of success with thematic analysis but they substantially pave their way to skill in using other qualitative data analysis methods. However, does this not beg the question whether these better established analytic techniques should underpin the data analysis? That is, if the procedures used in thematic analysis are little different from those used in Interpretative Phenomenological Analysis or Grounded Theory, why not carry out one of these latter analyses?

21.5   Conclusion

Probably, thematic analysis can best be seen as a preferred introduction to qualitative data analysis. Its lack of bewildering amounts of theoretical baggage makes it relatively user-friendly to novices to qualitative analysis. Nevertheless, it is an approach which can fail to be convincing if not performed in sufficient depth. The simplicity of thematic analysis is superficial and disguises the considerable efforts that the analyst needs to make in order to produce something that goes beyond the mundane (or, perhaps, what merely states what the researcher 'knew' already). While the temptation may be to pick out a few themes which then become 'the analysis', the researcher must push further than this. Simple notions such as ensuring that the themes cover as much of the material in the data as possible help ensure that the analysis challenges the researcher. So thematic analysis is as demanding as any other form of analysis in psychology. The important thing is that the researcher does not stint on the analytical effort required to produce an outcome which is stimulating and moves our understanding of the topic on from the common-sense notions which sometimes pass as thematic analysis. But this is no different from the challenge facing most researchers, irrespective of the method they employ.

Key points

- The secret of a good thematic analysis lies in the amount of analytical work that the researcher contributes to the process. Researchers unwilling to spend the time and effort required in terms of familiarisation with the data, coding, recoding, theme development and so forth will tend to produce weaker and less convincing analyses. They have only superficially analysed their data, so they produce less insightful and comprehensive themes.

- It improves a report of a thematic analysis if detail of the method used by the researcher is included. It is insufficient (and perhaps misleading) to merely say that a thematic analysis was carried out and that certain themes 'emerged' during the course of the analysis. This gives no real indication of how the analysis was carried out or the degree to which the researcher was active in constructing the themes which their report describes.

- A good thematic analysis usually can be quantified in terms of the rates of prevalence and incidence of each of the themes. Prevalence is the number of participants who say things relevant to a particular theme, and incidence is the frequency of occurrence of the theme throughout the dataset or the average number of times it occurs in each participant's data.

ACTIVITY

Thematic analysis can be carried out on any text. For example, it could be tried out on two or three pages of a novel you are reading (or a magazine article, for that matter). Try to develop initial codes of each line of a few pages of a novel or some other text. What themes can these be sorted into? How good is the fit of the set of themes to the actual text? Do some lines of text fail to appear in at least one theme?

CHAPTER 22

Grounded theory

Overview

- Grounded theory involves various techniques enabling researchers to analyse 'rich' (detailed) qualitative data effectively.

- It reverses the classic hypothesis-testing approach to theory development (favoured by some quantitative researchers) by emphasising data collection as the primary stage and requiring theory to be closely linked to the entire data.

- The analyst keeps close to the data when developing theoretical analyses. In this way the analysis is 'grounded' in the data (rather than being based on speculative theory which is then tested using hypotheses derived from the theory).

- Grounded theory methodology involves the analyst in a constant process of comparison backwards and forwards between the different stages of the analysis and also within the data.

- In grounded theory, categories are developed and refined by the researcher in order to explain whatever the researcher regards as the significant features of the data.

22.1 Introduction

Sometimes qualitative data analysis is derided as an easy way to do research. After all, it does not involve writing questionnaire items, planning experimental designs or even doing statistics. All of these tasks are difficult and, if possible, they are best avoided. Or so the argument goes. Superficially, qualitative data analysis does seem to sidestep the problems of quantification and statistical analysis. Carry out an unstructured interview or conduct a focus group or get a politician's speech off the Internet or something of the sort. Record it using an audio-recorder or video-recorder, or just use the written text grabbed from the World Wide Web. Sounds like a piece of cake. You are probably familiar with the caricature of quantitative researchers as boffins dressed in white laboratory coats. The qualitative researcher may similarly be caricatured. The qualitative researcher is more like a manic newspaper or television reporter who asks a few questions or takes a bit of video and then writes an article about it. What is the difference between the qualitative researcher and the TV reporter with the audio-recorder or camera crew? The answer to this question will take most of this chapter.

We can begin with one of the most important and seminal publications in qualitative research. This book, *The discovery of grounded theory* (Glaser & Strauss, 1967), is regarded as a classic and remains a major source on the topic of grounded theory despite numerous developments since its publication. Historically, Glaser and Strauss's approach was as much a reaction to the dominant sociology of the time as it was radically innovative. Basically, the book objected to the largely abstract sociological theory of the time, seemingly divorced from any social or empirical reality. Indeed, at that time empirical research in sociology was as atheoretical as theory was unempirical. In its place, the book offered a new, data-based method of theory development. Grounded theory reversed many of the axioms of conventional research in an attempt to systematise qualitative research. As such, it should be of interest to quantitative researchers, since it highlights many of the fundamental characteristics of their methods.

You probably will not yet have read any research involving grounded theory methodology. So the characteristics of a grounded theory analysis need explaining. Ultimately the aim is to produce a set of categories into which the data fit closely and which amount to a theoretical description of the data. Since the data are almost certain to be textual or spoken language, some of its analytic strategies are very similar to those employed by other qualitative methods. A word of warning: to carry out a grounded theory analysis is a somewhat exacting task. Sometimes authors claim to have used grounded theory, though perusal of their work reveals no signs of the rigours of the method. Sometimes the categories developed fit the data because they are so broad that anything in the data is bound to fit into one or other of the coding categories. As in all forms of research, there are excellent grounded theory analyses but also inadequate or mundane ones.

Like properly done qualitative data analyses in general, grounded theory approaches are held to be time-consuming, arguably because of the need for great familiarity on the part of the analyst with the data, but also because the process of analysis can be quite exacting. Grounded theory employs a variety of techniques designed to ensure that researchers enter into the required intimate contact with their data as well as bringing into juxtaposition different aspects of the data.

Just to stress, grounded theory methods result in categories which encompass the data (text or speech, almost invariably) as completely and unproblematically as the researcher can achieve. In this context, theory and effective categorisation are virtually synonymous. Or, more precisely, theory is how the category system is conceptualised. This causes some confusion among those better versed in quantitative methods who tend to assume that theory means an elaborate conjectural system from which specific hypotheses are derived for testing. That is not what grounded theory provides – the categorisation system is basically the theory, though the method can involve attempts to generalise the theory beyond the immediate data. Furthermore, researchers seeking a theory that yields precise predictions will be disappointed. While grounded theory may generalise to new sets of data, it is normally *in*capable of making predictions of a more precise sort. Charmaz (2000, p. 509) explains:

> . . . grounded theory methods consist of systematic inductive guidelines for collecting and analyzing data to build middle-range theoretical frameworks that explain the collected data. Throughout the research process, grounded theorists develop analytic interpretations of their data to focus further data collection, which they use in turn to inform and refine their developing theoretical analyses.

Several elements of this description of grounded theory warrant highlighting:

- Grounded theory consists of *guidelines* for conducting data collection, data analysis and theory building, which may lead to research that is closely integrated to social reality as represented in the data.

- Grounded theory is *systematic*. In other words, the analysis of data to generate theory is not dependent on a stroke of genius or divine inspiration, but on perspiration and application of general principles or methods.

- Grounded theory involves *inductive* guidelines rather than deductive processes. This is very different from what is often regarded as conventional theory building, sometimes described as the 'hypothetico-deductive method', in which theory is developed from which hypotheses are derived. In turn, these hypotheses may be put to an empirical test.

Research is important, because it allows researchers to test these hypotheses and, consequently, the theory. The hypothetico-deductive method characterised psychology for much of its modern history. Without the link between theory building and hypothesis testing, quantitative research in psychology probably deserves the epithet of 'empiricism gone mad'. Particularly good illustrative examples of the hypothetico-deductive approach are to be found in the writings of psychologists such as Hans Eysenck (e.g. Eysenck, 1980), though his methodological stance increasingly seems out of date. However, grounded theory itself was not really a reaction against the hypothetico-deductive method but one against over-abstracted and untestable social theory.

- Grounded theory requires that theory should develop out of an understanding of the complexity of the subject matter. Theories (i.e. coding schemes) knit the complexity of the data into a coherent whole. Primarily, such theories may be tested effectively only in terms of the fit between the categories and the data, and by applying the categories to new data. In many ways, this contrasts markedly with mainstream quantitative psychology where there is no requirement that the analysis fits all of the data closely – merely that there are statistically significant trends, irrespective of magnitude, which confirm the hypothesis derived from the theory. The unfitting data are regarded as measurement error rather than a reason to explore the data further in order to produce a better analysis, as may be the case in qualitative research.

- The theory-building process is a continuous one rather than a sequence of critical tests of the theory through testing hypotheses. It is impossible to separate the different phases of the research into discrete and successive components, such as theory development, hypothesis testing, refining the theory and so on. The data collection phase, the transcription phase and the analysis phase all share the common intent of building theory by matching the analysis closely to the complexity of the topic of interest.

The idea of a middle-range theory is likely to prove a difficult one for many psychology students because of the way that they are trained to think of theory. This essentially is to regard a theory as an explanatory system which is empirically testable and capable of being refuted. Included in this is the idea that theories should be able to make predictions. This is to place high demands on theory which, by and large, grounded theories do not try to achieve but some aim to. So most of us are probably thinking high level theory when we hear the term theory. Classic examples include social comparison theory, cognitive dissonance, and attribution theory each of which has been tested on the basis of predictions made from the theory. Grounded theory does aim at less than this as, generally, such a level of theory is unrealistic. At the opposite pole, psychologists are familiar with references to theory when they are really only dealing with simple and somewhat speculative explications of relationships found empirically. There is no claim that the relationship is generalisable beyond the immediate circumstances of the study. So middle-range theory occupies the space between these two extremes. The testing of middle-range theories in grounded theory is built into the process of analysis and theory building. By demanding the cohesiveness of an integration of all aspects of the grounded theory using the method of constant comparison, grounded theory establishes its value. Should it be possible to push the theory towards other forms of testing then this is embraced in the classic formulation of grounded theory.

22.2   Development of grounded theory

Grounded theory is usually described as being a reaction against the dominant sociology of the twentieth century, specifically the Chicago School of Sociology. Some of the founders of this school specifically argued that human communities were made up of sub-populations, each of which operated almost on a natural science model – they were like ecological populations. For example, sub-populations showed a pattern whereby they began to invade a territory, eventually reaching dominance and finally receding as another sub-population became dominant. This was used to explain population changes in major and developing cities such as Chicago. Large-scale social processes, not the experiences of individuals, came to be the subject of study. The characteristics which are attributed to the Chicago School are redolent of a lot of psychology from the same period. In particular, the Chicago School sought to develop exact and standard instruments (scales, questionnaires and the like) to measure a small number of key variables that were readily quantified. In sociology, research in natural contexts began to be unimportant in the first half of the twentieth century; the corresponding change in psychology was the increased importance of the psychology laboratory as a research base. In sociology, researchers undertook field research mainly in order to develop their measuring instruments. Once developed, they became the focus of interest themselves. So social processes were ignored in favour of broad measures such as social class and alienation, which are abstractions. The theorist and the researcher were often different people, so much so that much research became alienated from theory, that is, atheoretical (Charmaz, 1995).

Grounded theory methodology basically mirror-imaged or reversed features of the dominant sociology of the 1960s in a number of ways:

- Qualitative research came to be seen as a legitimate domain in its own right. It was not a preliminary or preparatory stage for refining one's research instruments prior to quantitative research.

- The division between research and theory was undermined by requiring that theory comes after or as part of the data collection and is tied to the data collected.

- Furthermore, the collection and analysis of the data were reconstrued as being virtually inseparable. That is, analysis of the data was encouraged early in the collection process and this early analysis could be used to guide the later collection of data.

In order to achieve these ends, grounded theory had to demonstrate that qualitative research could be made rigorous, systematic and structured. The idea that qualitative data analysis is no more than a few superficial impressions of the researcher was to be no part of grounded theory.

Despite being the mirror image of mainstream research, grounded theory analysis does not share some features of other qualitative methods, such as discourse analysis and conversation analysis. In particular, there is no given set of theoretical as opposed to methodological ideas. Some exponents of grounded theory reject *realism* (the idea that out there somewhere is a social reality which researchers will eventually uncover), whereas others accept it. Similarly, some grounded theorists aim for objective measures and theory development that does not depend on the researcher's subjectivity. Others regard this as a futile and inappropriate aim. See Figure 22.1 for some of the key aspects of the development of grounded theory.

Grounded theory now has a long history and, not surprisingly, it now includes some variants partly as a result of a well-publicised intellectual split between Glaser and Strauss. Nevertheless, at the core is a single method which has features which distinguish it from other methods (Bertero, 2012). These include a distinctive approach to sampling which is designed to aid theory building rather than to enforce representativeness, the lack of a boundary between data collection and data analysis such that data collection may be

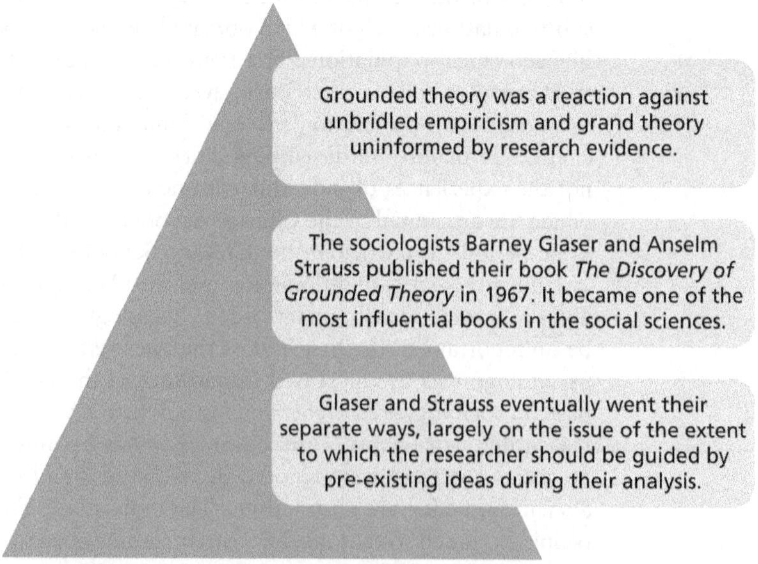

Grounded theory was a reaction against unbridled empiricism and grand theory uninformed by research evidence.

The sociologists Barney Glaser and Anselm Strauss published their book *The Discovery of Grounded Theory* in 1967. It became one of the most influential books in the social sciences.

Glaser and Strauss eventually went their separate ways, largely on the issue of the extent to which the researcher should be guided by pre-existing ideas during their analysis.

FIGURE 22.1   Roots of grounded theory

guided by data analysis, the use of constant comparison which loops the researcher's attention back and forth between all aspects of the data analysis, and carrying out the literature review retrospectively.

22.3   Data in grounded theory

Grounded theory is not primarily a way of collecting data but a means of data analysis leading to theory. However, grounded theory does have things to say about the way in which data should be collected in a manner guided by the needs of the developing grounded theory. Grounded theory does not require any particular type of data, although some types of data are better for it than others. The use of quantitative data is not debarred, especially in the early formulations of grounded theory. So, for example, grounded theory can be applied to interviews, biographical data, media content, observations, conversations and so forth, or anything else which can usefully inform the developing theory. The key thing is, of course, that the primary data should be as dense and richly detailed as possible, that is, not simple or simplified. Charmaz (1995, p. 33) suggested that richly detailed data involve 'full' or 'thick' written descriptions. So, by this criterion, much of the data collected by quantitative researchers would be unsuitable as the primary data for analysis. There is little that a grounded theory researcher could do with answers to a multiple-choice questionnaire or personality scale. Yes–no and similar response formats do not provide detailed data – though the findings of such studies may contribute more generally to theory building in grounded theory. The data for grounded theory analysis mostly consist of words, but this is typical of much data in psychology and related disciplines. As such, usually data are initially transcribed using a transcription system, though normally Jefferson's elaborate method (Chapter 20) would be unnecessary. However, it has been argued that recording of data may be counterproductive in that it takes up time which the researcher could use more productively. Instead, by taking field notes at the time of the interview in question, the analysis can be based on these rather than transcripts.

22.4   How to do grounded theory analysis

Potter (1998) likened grounded theory to a sophisticated filing system. This filing system does not merely put things under headings; there is also cross-referencing to a range of other categories. This is a bit like a library book that may be classified as a biography but may also be a political book. Keep this analogy in mind, as otherwise the temptation is to believe that the data are filed under only one category in grounded theory analysis. It is notorious that, academically speaking, Glaser and Strauss did not see eye-to-eye later in their careers, so rather different varieties of grounded theory evolved. The main difference between them was in the extent to which the researcher should come to the data with ideas and thoughts already developed or, as far as possible, with no preconceptions about the data. There seems to be a general acceptance that grounded theory analysis has a number of key components, and the following summarises some of the important analytic principles that can broadly be described as grounded theory. Much of the following uses Charmaz's (1995, 2000) recommendations about how to proceed. As such, they are updated from Glaser and Strauss's original ideas.

■ Constant comparison

A common criticism of quantitative research is that the researcher forces observations into ill-fitting categories for the purpose of analysis; in grounded theory this should not happen since the good fit of the categories to the data is all important. Partly to achieve this, the method of constant comparisons is employed. At each and every stage of a grounded theory study the researcher should go back and forwards within and between the different stages considering all aspects of the data and analysis with each other. This ensures that the integrity of the analysis and the data on which it is based is maintained. There are no rules about how to carry out the process of constant comparison; it essentially sets out the objective of offering constant challenges to the analysis at every stage. The following are some aspects of the comparison process:

- People may be compared in terms of what they have said or done or how they have accounted for their actions or events, for example.

- Comparisons are made of what a person does or says in one context with what they do and say in another context.

- Comparisons are made of what someone has said or done at a particular time with a similar situation at a different time.

- Comparisons of the data with the category suggested by the researcher may account for the data.

- Comparisons are made of categories used in the analysis with other categories used in the analysis.

■ Coding/naming

Grounded theory principles require that the researcher repeatedly examines the data closely in the process of theory development. To this end, the lines of the data transcription will be numbered to aid comparison and reference. In the initial stage of the analysis, the day-to-day work involves coding or describing the data line-by-line. It is as straightforward as that – and as difficult. (Actually, there is no requirement that a line be the unit of analysis, and a researcher may choose to operate at the level of the sentence or the paragraph.) The line is examined and a description (it could be more than one) is provided by the researcher to summarise what is happening or what is 'represented' by that line. In other words, a name is being given to each line of data. The descriptions or codings are different from codings used in quantitative research as they are stimulated by the data rather than the researcher's ideas or theories. Others describe the process in slightly different terms. For example, Potter (1997) suggests that the process is like giving labels to the key concepts that appear in the line or paragraph. The point of the coding is that it keeps the researcher's feet firmly in the grounds of the data. Without coding, the researcher may be tempted to over-interpret the data by inappropriately attributing 'motives, fears or unresolved personal issues' (Charmaz, 1995, p. 37) to the participants. At the end of this stage, we are left with numerous codings or descriptions of the contents of many lines of text. This is known as initial or open coding.

It is difficult to give a brief representative extract of grounded theory style codings. Table 22.1 reproduces a part of such codings from Charmaz (1995) which illustrates aspects of the process. Take care, though, since Table 22.1 contains a very short extract from just one out of nearly 200 interviews conducted by Charmaz. It can be seen that

Table 22.1	A modified extract of grounded theory coding	
Interview transcript		**Coding by researcher**
If you have lupus, I mean one day it's my liver		Shifting symptoms
One day it's in my joints; one day it's in my head, and		Inconsistent days
It's like people really think you're a hypochondriac if you keep		Interpreting images of self
... It's like you don't want to say anything because people are going to start thinking		Avoiding disclosure

Source: Adapted from Charmaz (1995)

the codings/categories are fairly close to the data in this example. It should be noted that these are not the only codings which would work with the data.

Categorisation

Quite clearly, the analyst has to try to organise these codings. Remember that codings are part of the analysis process and the first tentative steps in developing theory. These are the smallest formal units in the grounded theory analysis. While they may describe the data more or less adequately, by organising them we may increase the likelihood that we will be able to effectively revise them. This is a sort of reverse filtering process: we are starting with the smallest units of analysis and working back to the larger theoretical descriptions. So the next stage is to build the codings or namings of lines of data into categories. By categorising codings one is essentially coding those codings into similar groups. This is a basic strategy in many sorts of research. In quantitative research, there are statistical methods that are commonly used in categorising variables into groupings of variables, for example, factor analysis and cluster analysis. These statistical methods are not generally available to the grounded theorist, so the categorisation process relies on other methods. Once again, of course, the process of constant comparison is crucial. The analyst essentially has to compare as many of the codings as possible with the other codings. That is, is the coding for line 62 really the same as that for line 30, since both lines are described in very similar words? Is it possible to justify coding lines 88 and 109 in identical fashion, since these data lines appear to be very different when they are examined?

The constant comparing goes beyond this. For example, does there seem to be a different pattern of codings for Mr X than for Mrs Y? That is, does the way they talk about things seem to be different? We might not be surprised to find different patterns for Mr X and Mrs Y when we know that this is a couple attending relationship counselling or that one is the boss of a company and the other an employee. The data from a person at a particular point in time or in a particular context may be compared with data from the same person at a later point in time or in different contexts.

It need not stop there. Since the process is one of generating categories for the codings of the data which fit the data well and are coherent, one must also compare the categories with each other as they emerge or are developed. After all, it may become evident, for example, that two of the categories cannot be differentiated – or you may have given identical titles to categories which actually are radically different. The process of categorisation may be facilitated by putting the data or codings or both onto index cards which can be physically moved around on a desk or table in order to place similar items close together and dissimilar items further apart. In this way, relationships can begin to be identified in a more active visual way.

In grounded theory, it is common to speak of three different levels of coding or categorisation:

- Initial coding is the process by which the researcher summarises the lines of text in a few words.

- Axial coding is the process of indicating the relationships between categories of codings.

- Selective coding is deciding what the overall theme of the analysis is.

Selective coding basically is the stage when it becomes clear to the researcher what the dominant, significant, most important, and central category of codings is. That is, the idea which holds the data and theory together. Once this has been decided, then it becomes the focus of further analysis and theory development.

Memo writing

The stages in grounded theory analysis are not distinct. The process of analysis is not sequential, although explaining grounded theory analysis makes it appear so. Analysis is integral with data collection and reference back and forth through the data, data analysis, and theory development stages is continual. Memo writing describes the aspect of the research in which the data are explored rather than described and categorised. The memo may be just as one imagines – a notebook – in which the researcher notes suggestions as to how the categories may be linked together in the sense that they have relationships and interdependencies. But the memo does not have to be a purely textual thing. A diagram – perhaps a flow diagram – could be used, in which the key concepts are placed in boxes and the links between them identified by annotated arrows. What do we mean by relationships and interdependencies? Imagine the case of male and female. They are conceptually distinct categories but they have interdependencies and relationships. One cannot understand the concept of male without the concept of female.

The memo should not be totally separated from the data. Within the memo one should include the most crucial and significant examples from the data that are indicative and typical of the more general examples. So the memo should be replete with illustrative instances as well as potentially ill-fitting or problematic instances of ideas, conceptualisations and relationships that are under development as part of the eventual grounded theory. As Charmaz (1995) says:

> If you are at a loss about what to write about, look for the codes that you have used repeatedly in your data collection. Then start elaborating on these codes. Keep collecting data, keep coding and keep refining your ideas through writing more and further developed memos. (p. 43)

In a sense, this advice should not be necessary with grounded theory, since the processes of data collection, coding and categorisation of the codes are designed to make the researcher so familiar with their data that it is very obvious what the frequently occurring and pervasive codings are. However, it is inevitable that those unaccustomed to qualitative analysis will have writing and thinking blocks, in much the same way as a quantitative researcher may have problems writing questionnaire items or formulating hypotheses.

Sometimes the memo is regarded as an intermediate step between the data and the final written report. As ever in grounded theory, however, in practice the distinction between the different stages is not rigid. Often the advice is to start memo writing just as soon as anything strikes one as interesting in the data, the coding or categorisation. The sooner the better would seem to be the general consensus. This is very different from the approach taken by quantitative researchers. Also bear in mind that the process of theory development in grounded theory is not conventional in that the use of a small number of parsimonious concepts is not a major aim. (This is essentially Occam's razor, which is the logical principle that no more than the minimum number of concepts or assumptions is necessary. This is also referred to as the principle of parsimony.) Strauss and Corbin (1999) write of conceptual density, which they describe as a richness of concept development and relationship identification. This is clearly intended to be very different from reducing the analysis to the very minimum number of concepts, as is characteristic of much quantitative research.

Theoretical sampling

Theoretical sampling is about how to validate the ideas developed within the memo. If the ideas in the memo have validity, then they should apply to some samples of data but not to others. The task of the researcher is partly to suggest which samples the categories apply to and which they should not apply to. This will help the researcher identify new sources of data which may be used to validate the analysis to that point. As a consequence of the analysis of such additional data, subsequent memo writing may be more closely grounded in the data which it is intended to explain.

Literature review

In conventional methodological terms, the literature review is largely carried out in advance of planning the detailed research. That is, the new research builds on the accumulated previous knowledge. In grounded theory, especially in its original formulation, the literature review should be carried out after the memo-writing process is over – signed, sealed and delivered. In this way, the grounded theory has its origins in the data collected, *not* the previous research and theoretical studies. So why bother with the literature review? The best answer is that the literature review should be seen as part of the process of assessing the adequacy of the grounded theory analysis. If the new analysis fails to deal adequately with the older research, then a reformulation may be necessary. On the other hand, it is feasible that the new analysis helps integrate past grounded theory analyses. In some respects, this can be regarded as an extension of the grounded theory to other domains of applicability.

That is what some grounded theorists claim. In contrast, Strauss and Corbin (1999) added that the grounded theory methodology may begin in existing grounded theories so long as they 'seem appropriate to the area of investigation' and then these grounded theories 'may be elaborated and modified as incoming data are meticulously played against them' (pp. 72–73).

An overall picture of the stages of grounded theory is shown in Figure 22.2. This includes an additional stage of theory development which does not characterise all grounded theory studies in practice.

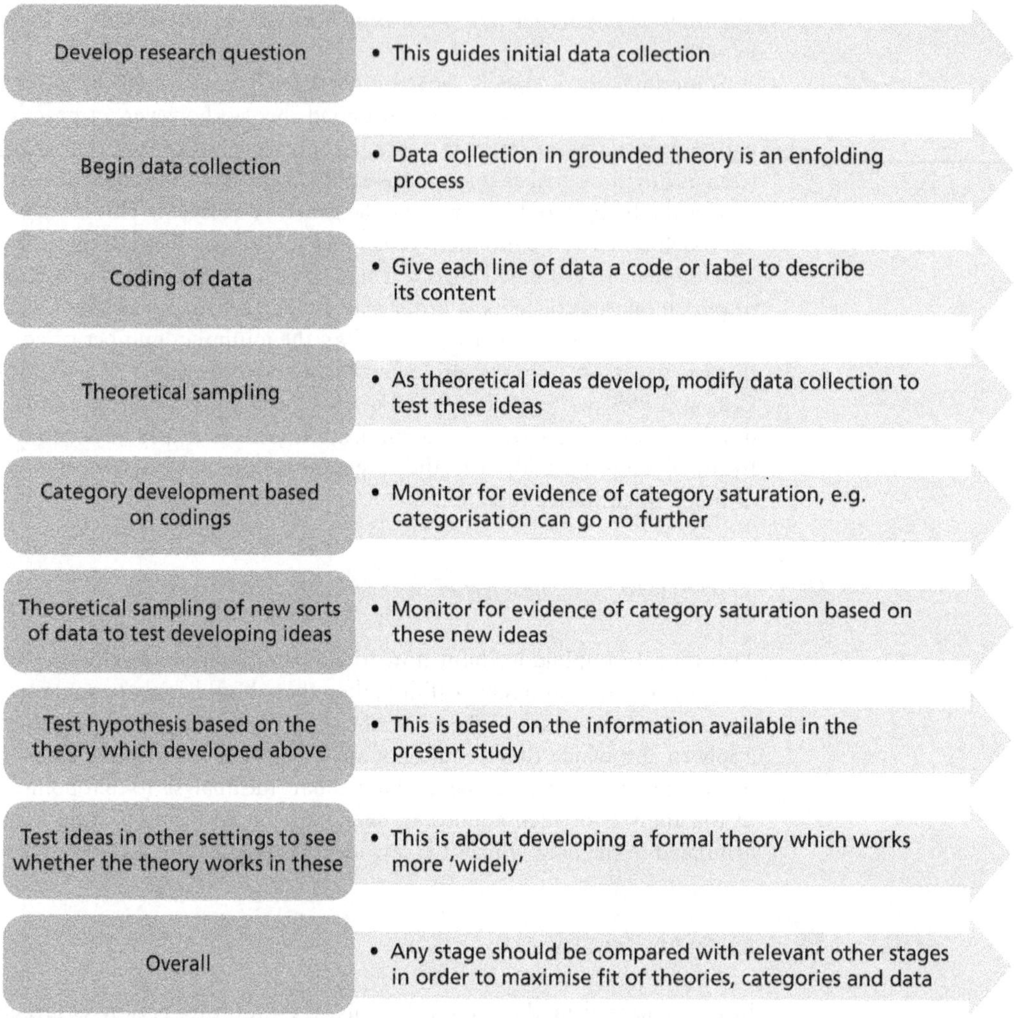

Develop research question	• This guides initial data collection
Begin data collection	• Data collection in grounded theory is an enfolding process
Coding of data	• Give each line of data a code or label to describe its content
Theoretical sampling	• As theoretical ideas develop, modify data collection to test these ideas
Category development based on codings	• Monitor for evidence of category saturation, e.g. categorisation can go no further
Theoretical sampling of new sorts of data to test developing ideas	• Monitor for evidence of category saturation based on these new ideas
Test hypothesis based on the theory which developed above	• This is based on the information available in the present study
Test ideas in other settings to see whether the theory works in these	• This is about developing a formal theory which works more 'widely'
Overall	• Any stage should be compared with relevant other stages in order to maximise fit of theories, categories and data

FIGURE 22.2   Some of the analytic stages in grounded theory

22.5 Computer grounded theory analysis

A number of commercially available grounded theory analysis programs are available. Generically, they are known as CAQDAS (Computer-Assisted Qualitative Data Analysis Software). NVivo is the current market leader but there are others. These programs may help with the following aspects of a grounded theory analysis:

● There is a lot of paperwork with grounded theory analysis as currently conceptualised. Line-numbered transcripts are produced, coding categories are developed, and there is much copying and pasting of parts of the analysis in order to finely tune the categories to the data. There is almost inevitably a large amount of textual material to deal with – a single focus group, for example, might generate 10 or 20 transcribed pages. Computers, as everyone knows, are excellent for cutting down on paper when drafting and shifting text around. That is, the computer may act as a sort of electronic office for grounded analyses.

- One key method in grounded theory is searching for linkages between different aspects of the data. A computer program is eminently suitable for making, maintaining and changing linkages between parts of a document and between different documents.

- Coding categories are developed but frequently need regular change, refinement and redefinition in order for them to fit the data better and to fit further data that may be introduced, perhaps to test the categories. Using computer programs, it is possible to recode the data more quickly, combine categories and the like.

Box 22.1 discusses computer-based support for grounded theory analysis.

Box 22.1　Practical Advice

Computers and qualitative data analysis: computer-assisted qualitative data analysis software (CAQDAS)

Using computer programs for the analysis of qualitative data is something of a mixed blessing for students new to this form of analysis. The major drawback is the investment of time needed to learn the software. This is made more of a problem because no qualitative analysis program does all of the tasks that a qualitative analyst might require. Thus it is not like doing a quantitative analysis on a computer program such as SPSS, where you can do something useful with just a few minutes of training or just by following a text. Furthermore, qualitative analysis software is much more of a tool to help the researcher, whereas SPSS, certainly for simple analyses, does virtually all of the analysis. So think carefully before seeking computer programs to help with your qualitative analysis, especially if time is short, as it usually is for student projects. There is little or nothing that can as yet be done by computers which cannot be done by a researcher using more mundane resources such as scissors, glue, index cards and the like. The only major drawback to such basic methods is that they become unwieldy with very substantial amounts of data. In these circumstances, a computer may be a major boon in that it keeps everything neat and tidy and much more readily accessible on future occasions.

There are two main stages for which computer programs may prove helpful: data entry and data analysis.

Data entry

All students will have some word-processing skills which may prove helpful for a qualitative analysis. The first major task after data have been collected is transcription. This is probably best done by a word processing program such as Microsoft's Word which is by far the most commonly used of all such programs. Not only is such a program the best way of getting a legible transcript of the data, but it is also useful as a resource of text to be used in illustrating aspects of the analysis in the final research report. Word-processing programs can be used for different sorts of transcription, including Jefferson transcription (see Chapter 20) which utilises keyboard symbols that are universally available. Of course, the other big advantage of word-processing programs is that they allow for easy text manipulation. For example, one can usually search for (find) strings of text quickly. More importantly, perhaps, one can copy and paste any amount of text into new locations or folders. In other words, key bits of text can be brought together to aid the analysis process simply by having the key aspects of the text next to each other.

Computers can aid data entry in another way. If the data to be entered are already in text form (e.g. magazine articles or newspaper reports), then it may be possible to use a scanner to read the text into a computer. Alternatively, some may find it helpful to use voice recognition software to dictate such text into a computer as an alternative to typing. Of course, such programs are still error-prone, but then so is transcribing words from the recording by hand. All transcripts require checking for accuracy, no matter how they are produced.

In the case of discourse analysis or conversation analysis (see Chapters 23 and 24), features of the data such as pauses, voice inflections and so forth need to be recorded. Editing software such as Adobe Audition are useful for these specialised transcription purposes. This program, for example, has the big advantage that it shows features of the sound in a sort of continuous graphical form which allows for the careful measurement of times of silences and so forth. There

→

is a free-to-download computer program to help transcribe sound files. It is known as SoundScriber and can be obtained at http://www-personal.umich.edu/~ebreck/sscriber.html.

The downside is that by saving the researcher time, the computer program reduces their familiarity with their data. This undermines one of the main strategies of qualitative analysis, which is to encourage the researcher to repeatedly work through the analysis in ways that encourage greater familiarity.

Data analysis

There are many different forms of analysis of qualitative data, so no single program is available to cope with all of these. For example, some analyses simply involve counts of how frequently particular words or phrases (or types of words or phrases) occur in the data or how commonly they occur in close physical proximity. Such an analysis is not typical of what is done in psychology and, of course, is really a type of quantitative analysis of qualitative data rather than a qualitative data analysis as such. The most common forms of qualitative analysis tend to involve the researcher labelling the textual data in some way (coding) and then linking the codings together to form broader categories which constitute the bedrock of the analysis. The most famous of the computer programs helping the researcher handle grounded theory analyses are NUD*IST, which was developed in the 1980s, and NVivo, which was developed a decade or so later but is closely related. The researcher transcribes their data (usually these will be interviews) and enters the transcription into one of these programs, usually using RTF (rich text format) files which Word can produce. The programs then allow you to take the text and code or label small pieces of it. Once this is complete, the codes or labels can be grouped into categories (analogous to themes in thematic analysis – Chapter 21). The software company which owns NVivo suggests that it is useful for researchers to deal with rich-text data at a deep level of analysis. They identify some of the qualitative methods discussed in this book as being aided by NVivo, such as grounded theory, conversation analysis, discourse analysis and phenomenology. The software package is available in a student version at a moderate price, but you may find that a trial download is sufficient for your purposes. At the time of writing, this was available at http://www.qsrinternational.com/products_free-trial-software.aspx.

The system allows the user to go through the data, coding the material a small amount at a time (the unit of analysis can be flexible), or one can develop some coding categories in a structured form before beginning to apply them to the data. In NVivo there is the concept of *nodes*, which it defines as 'places where you store ideas and categories'. There are two important types of nodes in the program that are worth mentioning here:

- *Free nodes* These can most simply be seen as codings or brief verbal descriptions or distillations of a chunk of text. They are probably best used at the start of the analysis before the researcher has developed clear ideas about the data and the way the analysis is going.

- *Tree nodes* These are much more organised than the free nodes (and may be the consequence of joining together free nodes). They are in the form of a hierarchy, with the parent node leading to the children nodes, which may lead to the grandchildren nodes. The hierarchy is given a numerical sequence such as 4 2 3, where the parent node is here given the address 4, one of the child nodes is given the address 2 and the grandchild node is given the address 3. Thus 4 2 3 uniquely identifies a particular location within the tree node. So, for example, a researcher may have as the parent node problems at work, one of the child nodes may be interpersonal relationships (another child node might be redundancy, e.g.), and one of the grandchild nodes might be sexual harassment.

These nodes are not fixed until the researcher is finally satisfied but can be changed, merged together or even removed should the researcher see fit. This is the typical process of checking and reviewing that makes qualitative research both flexible and time-consuming.

NVivo has other useful features, such as a 'modeller' which allows the researcher to link the ideas/concepts developed in the analysis together using connectors that the researcher labels. There is also a search tool which allows the researcher to isolate text with particular contents or text that has been coded in a particular way.

An alternative to NUD*IST/NVivo is to use CDC EZ-Text, which is free to download from https://www.cdc.gov/hiv/library/software/index.html

If you want to access a qualitative analysis program without the expense of the commercial alternatives, EZ-Text is available for researchers to create and manage databases for semi-structured qualitative interviews and then analyse the data. The user acts interactively with the computer during the process of developing a list of codes to be applied to the data (i.e. creating a codebook) which can then be used to give specific codes to passages in the material. The researcher can also search the data for passages which meet the researcher's own preset requirements. In many respects, this is similar to NVivo.

There is no quick fix for learning any of these systems. There are training courses for NVivo, for example, lasting several days, which suggests that the systems cannot be mastered quickly.

22.6 Evaluation of grounded theory

Potter (1998) points out that central to its virtues is that grounded theory:

> . . . encourages a slow-motion reading of texts and transcripts that should avoid the common qualitative research trap of trawling a set of transcripts for quotes to illustrate preconceived ideas. (p. 127)

This is probably as much a weakness as a strength, since the size of the task may well defeat the resources of novices and others. Certainly it is not always possible to be convinced that preconceived ideas do not dominate the analysis rather than the data leading the analysis. There are a number of criticisms which seem to apply to grounded theory:

● It encourages a pointless collection of data, that is, virtually anything textual or spoken could be subject to a grounded theory analysis. There are no clear criteria for deciding, in advance, what topics to research on the basis of their theoretical or practical relevance. Indeed, the procedures tend to encourage the delay of theoretical and other considerations until after the research has been initiated.

● Potter (1998) suggests that 'The method is at its best where there is an issue that is tractable from a relatively common-sense actor's perspective . . . the theoretical notions developed are close to the everyday notions of the participants' (p. 127). This means that common-sense explanations are at a premium – explanations which go beyond common sense may be squeezed out. Potter puts it another way elsewhere on page 127: 'how far is the grounding derived not from theorising but from reproducing common-sense theories as if they were analytic conclusions?'. This may be fair criticism. The difficulty is that it applies to any form of research which gives voice to its participants. Ultimately, this tendency means that grounded theory may simply codify how ordinary people ordinarily understand the activities in which they engage.

● There is a risk that grounded theory, which is generally founded on admirable research ideals, is used to excuse inadequate qualitative analyses. It is a matter of faith that grounded theory will generate anything of significant value, yet at the same time, done properly, a grounded theory analysis may have involved a great deal of labour. Consequently, it is hard to put aside a research endeavour which may have generated little but cost a lot of time and effort. There are similar risks that grounded theory methods will be employed simply because the researcher has failed to focus on appropriate research questions, so leaving few available analysis options. These risks are particularly high for student work.

● Since talk and text are normally analysed line by line (and these are arbitrarily divided – they are not sentences), the researcher may be encouraged to focus on small units rather than the larger units of conversation as, for example favoured by discourse analysts (Potter, 1998). Nevertheless, grounded theory is often mentioned by such analysts as part of their strategy or orientation.

So it is likely that grounded theory works best when dealing with issues that are amenable to common-sense insights from participants. Medical illness and interpersonal relationships are such topics, where the theoretical ideas that grounded theory may develop are close to the ways in which the participants think about these issues. This may enhance the practicality of grounded theory in terms of policy implementation. The categories used and the theoretical contribution are likely to be in terms which are relatively easy for the practitioner or policymaker to access.

Box 22.2   Research Example

Grounded theory on the football ground

Groom, R., Cushion, C., & Nelson, L. (2011). Delivery of video-based performance analysis by England youth soccer coaches: Towards a grounded theory. *Journal of Applied Sport Psychology, 23*, 16–23.

Sports psychology is one of the areas of psychology in which the use of qualitative methods is expanding. The study in this case concerns the ways in which video-based performance analysis is used by youth soccer coaches. Ryan Groom, Christopher Cushion and Lee Nelson (2011) specifically sought to build a theory in order to understand this area of sports coaching. One of the cornerstones of understanding sporting performance is the role of performance analysis in the work of sports coaches. This involves factors such as the assessment of performance, the diagnosis of problems, and the provision of information to the sportsperson to help correct the problems. Video and digital technologies have increased the range of opportunities for performance analysis. In elite soccer, the use of such methods is practically universal nowadays. Despite this, the delivery of this analysis is somewhat haphazard and certainly not based on established pedagogic principles from research. Evidence-based theories of performance analysis are clearly needed, according to the authors of the paper.

Groom, Cushion, and Nelson's research was with 14 England youth soccer coaches (11 male and 3 female). This was nearly all of the population of such coaches. They were selected using purposive sampling, and the researchers noted that after 12 interviews there were no new concepts or categories. This was the point of theoretical saturation, though a close reading of the paper indicates that two additional coaches were interviewed. All of the coaches had a minimum of three years' experience using video-based analysis in their work with young footballers. The interviews used a combination of open-ended and semi-structured approaches.

The researchers chose Strauss and Corbin's (1998) approach to grounded theory. The decision to use this approach and the details of the method are carefully presented. An interview guide was used based on the authors' preliminary fieldwork. Each interview began with opening questions, including 'How do you use video analysis in your practice?' and 'What kind of things do you like to show the players?'. More questions followed, which included themes that were developing in the analysis such as 'Why do you use the analysis with the players like that?'. Things which emerged in the interviews were followed up until the researcher felt that the coach in question had reached a stage of repetition in their replies. The interviews were conducted by one of the authors who received feedback on their technique from another of the authors.

The data analysis process employed by Groom and colleagues is summarised in Figure 22.3. Most of it can be readily understood as conventional grounded theory methodology. The researchers used the literature review as a retrospective tool in terms of the analysis, though not in the prospective way that quantitative researchers employ to identify research questions and hypotheses. But this is a typical grounded theory approach. Member checking, which involved re-contacting two participants to check their practitioner views of the categories developed, is quite frequently employed by qualitative researchers in order to maximise the relevance of their analysis and data collection to the experience of their participants.

The results of the analysis are a little complex. The researchers present their analysis in various stages in order to help the reader understand the outcome of their grounded theory analysis. That is, in particular, they concentrate on describing the main conceptual areas and their subcategories that they identify. Taken collectively, these findings form the basis of the grounded theory which emerges from the grounded analysis. Theory in grounded theory research consists mainly of the interrelationships between categories and subcategories in the data. This produces a theory which is somewhat different from the causal theories that are familiar in quantitative research. The grounded theory is much more like a framework in which to place the different elements which are involved in the situation. As it is a framework for the data, it encompasses all elements of the data as far as possible. It does not focus on a small part of the data to the exclusion of the rest, as is common in quantitative research. In Figure 22.4, we present a simplified version of Groom et al.'s grounded theory of presentational analysis in soccer coaching. Their model differs from that in Figure 22.4 mainly in that they include numerous double-headed arrows, and so forth to indicate the interrelations between the subcategories, the categories and all elements of the model. Assume the interconnectedness of the elements and you have Groom et al.'s theory in a nutshell.

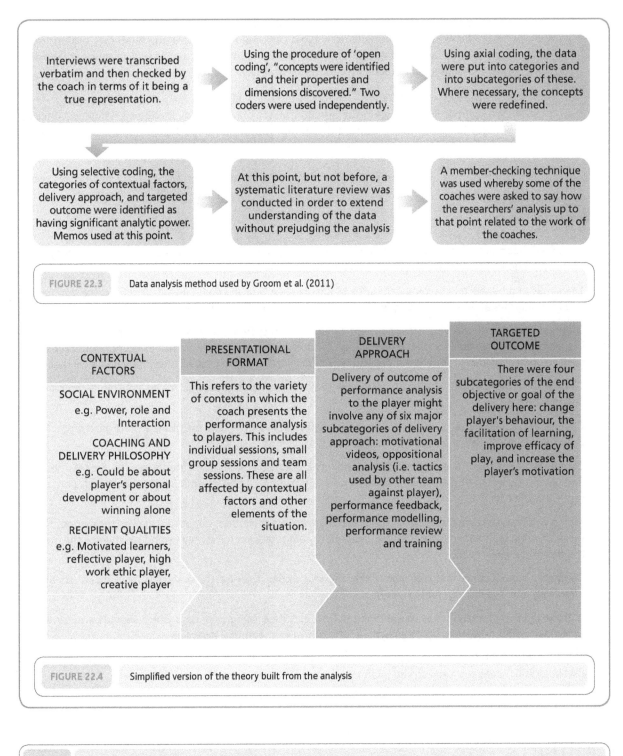

FIGURE 22.3   Data analysis method used by Groom et al. (2011)

FIGURE 22.4   Simplified version of the theory built from the analysis

22.7   Conclusion

Especially pertinent to psychologists is the question of whether grounded theory is really a sort of Trojan horse which has been cunningly brought into psychology, but is really the enemy of advancement in psychology. Particularly troubling is the following from Strauss and Corbin (1999):

. . . grounded theory researchers are interested in patterns of action and interaction between and among various types of social units (i.e., 'actors'). So they are not especially interested in creating theory about individual actors as such (unless perhaps they are psychologists or psychiatrists). (p. 81)

Researchers such as Strauss and Corbin are willing to allow a place for quantitative data in grounded theory. So the question may be one of how closely psychological concepts could ever fit with grounded theory analysis, which is much more about the social (interactive) than the psychological.

Key points

- Grounded theory is an approach to analysing (usually textual) data designed to maximise the fit of emerging theory (categories) to the data and additional data of relevance.

- The aim is to produce 'middle-range' theories which are closely fitting qualitative descriptions (categories) and their interpretation rather than, say, cause-and-effect or predictive theories.

- Grounded theory is 'inductive' (that is, does not deduce outcomes from theoretical postulates). It is systematic in that an analysis of some sort will almost always result from adopting the system. It is a continuous process of development of ideas – it does not depend on a critical test as in the case of classic psychological theory.

- Comparison is the key to the approach – all elements of the research and the analysis are constantly compared and contrasted.

- Coding (or naming or describing) is the process by which lines of the data are given a short description (or descriptions) to identify the nature of their content.

- Categorisation is the process by which the codings are amalgamated into categories. The process helps find categories which fit the codings in their entirety, not simply a few pragmatic ideas which only partially represent the codings.

- Memo writing is the process by which the researcher records their ideas about the analysis throughout the research process. The memo may include ideas about categorisation but it may extend to embrace the main themes of the final report.

- Computer programs are available which help the researcher organise the materials for the analysis and effectively alter the codings and categories.

- A grounded theory analysis may be extended to further critical samples of data which should be pertinent to the categories developed in the analysis. This is known as theoretical sampling.

- The theoretical product of grounded theory analysis is not intended to be the same as conventional psychological theorisation and so should not be judged on those terms.

ACTIVITY

Grounded theory involves the bringing of elements together to try to forge categories which unite them. So choose a favourite poem, song or any textual material, and write each sentence on a separate sheet of paper. Choose two at random. What unites these two sentences? Then choose another sentence. Can this be united with the previous two sentences? Continue the exercise until you cease coming up with new ideas. Then start again.

CHAPTER 23

Discourse analysis

Overview

- There are two main forms of discourse analysis in psychology. One is the social construction-ist approach of Potter and Wetherell (1995), which we concentrate on because it is the more student-friendly. The other approach is Foucauldian discourse analysis, which is not accessible so readily. Discourse analysis refers to a variety of ways of studying and understanding talk (or text) as social action.

- The intellectual roots of social constructionist discourse analysis are largely in the linguistic philosophy of the 1960s. The central idea to come from this is that discourse is designed by people to do things linguistically and that the role of the discourse analyst is to understand what is being done and how it is done through speech and text.

- At one level, discourse analysis may be regarded as a body of ideas about the nature of talk and text which can be applied to psychological data collected in the form of language.

- A number of themes are common in discourse analysis. These include rhetoric, voice, footing, discursive repertoires and the dialogical nature of talk.

- The practice of discourse analysis involves a variety of procedures designed to encourage the researcher to process and reprocess their material. These include transcription, coding and re-coding.

There are two major types of discourse analysis in psychology. They are equally important, but one is initially somewhat daunting for newcomers to qualitative research, whereas the other has numerous applications to student work throughout psychology. We shall, of course, devote more of this chapter to the latter than to the former. The first sort of discourse analysis originates in the work of Michel Foucault (1926–1984), the French academic. Foucault was trained in psychology at one stage, though he is better described as a philosopher and historian. His work focused on critical studies of social institutions such as psychiatry, prisons, human sciences and medicine. Foucault saw in language the way in which institutions enforce their power. So, for example, he argued that the nineteenth-century medical treatment of mentally ill people was not a real advance on the crudity and brutality which characterised the treatment of 'mad' people before this time. Mental illness had become a method of controlling those who challenged the morality of bourgeois society. Madness is not a permanently fixed social category but something that is created through discourse to achieve social objectives. Foucauldian discourse analysis made its first significant appearance in psychology in the book *Changing the subject: Psychology, social regulation and subjectivity* (1984) by Henriques, Hollway, Urwin, Venn, and Walkerdine. Other examples of the influence of Foucauldian ideas on psychology can be found in the work of Ian Parker, particularly in the field of mental health, in the books *Deconstructing psychopathology* (Parker, Georgaca, Harper, McLaughlin, & Stowell-Smith, 1995) and *Deconstructing psychotherapy* (Parker, 1999). This branch of discourse analysis is most closely linked to critical discourse analysis (see Box 23.1).

The other approach to discourse analysis also has its roots outside psychology. It can be described as a social constructionist approach to discourse analysis and came into psychology through the work of Jonathan Potter and Margaret Wetherell (1987). It is this form of discourse analysis that will be our focus. According to *The Oxford companion to the English language* (McArthur, 1992), discourse analysis's origins lie in work which pushed linguistics towards being the study of language beyond the individual sentence. Perhaps the earliest of these was Zellig Harris, who developed his ideas in the USA in the 1950s on issues such as how text is related to the social situation within which it was created. A little later, a linguistic anthropologist, Dell Hymes, investigated forms of address between people – that is, speech as it relates to the social setting. In the 1960s, a group of British linguistic philosophers (J. L. Austin, J. R. Searle & H. P. Grice) reconstrued language as social *action* – a key idea in discourse analysis. Potter (2001) takes the roots back earlier to the first half of the twentieth century by adding the philosopher Ludwig Wittgenstein into the melting pot of influences on discourse analysis theory. Particularly important is Wittgenstein's idea that language is a toolkit for *doing* things rather than a means of merely representing things (see Figure 23.1).

Searching for publications on discourse analysis by psychologists before the 1980s is a somewhat hapless task. The term first appeared in a psychology journal in 1954 but applied to ideas very different from its current meaning. However, despite its late appearance in psychology, the study of discourse began to grow rapidly in the 1960s in other disciplines. Consequently, early psychological discourse analysis drew on a variety of disciplines, each with a different take or perspective on what discourse analysis is. Because of the pan-disciplinary base for discourse analysis, a psychologist, no matter how well versed in other aspects of psychology, may feel overawed when first exploring the approach. Not all psychologists have, say, the detailed knowledge of linguistics, sociology and other disciplines which have contributed to discourse analysis.

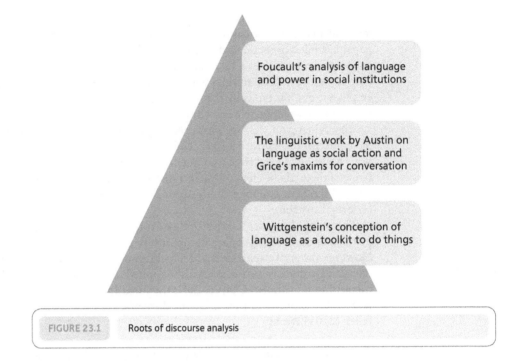

FIGURE 23.1   Roots of discourse analysis

Furthermore, the distinctive contribution made by psychologists to discourse analysis is not always clear.

So discourse analysis conceptualises language in ways very different from traditional linguistics which was largely concerned with word sounds (phonetics and phonology), units which make up words (morphology), meaning (semantics), and word order within sentences (syntax). Beaugrande (1996) refers to this traditional style of linguistics, in a somewhat derogatory fashion, as 'language science'. For him, traditional linguistics was at fault for profoundly disconnecting language from real-life communications – to study just sounds, words and sentences. In discourse analysis, language is regarded as being much more complex. Discourse is how language operates in real-life communicative events. Discourse analysis involves the analysis of speech, text and conversation, so its concerns are with analyses beyond the level of the sentence. (All of these three can be termed 'text'.) Hence, Stubbs (1983, p. 1) defines discourse analysis as being about the way in which language is used at the broader level than the sentence and other immediate utterances. A good illustration of this (Tannen, 2007) are the two signs at a swimming pool:

Please use the toilet, not the pool.
Pool for members only.

Considered separately, just as sentences, the signs convey clear messages. However, if they are read as a unit of two sentences, then they constitute either a request for non-members to swim in the toilet or an indication that members have exclusive rights to urinate in the swimming pool! Analysing just two sentences at a time as in this example causes us to rewrite the meaning of both sentences.

Discourse analysis emphasises the ways in which language interacts with society, especially in the nature of dialogue in ordinary conversation. Above all, then, discourse analysis is a perspective on the nature of language. Discourse analysis does *not* treat language as if it were essentially representational – language is not simply the means of articulating internal mental reality. Quite the reverse: discourse analysis is built on the idea that truth and reality are *not* identifiable or reachable through language.

Language for the discourse analyst is socially situated and it matters little whether the text under consideration is natural conversation or written text in the form, say, of newspaper headlines or social media. Each of these provides suitable material for analysis. Discourse analysis involves a shift in the way language is conceptualised: what language does becomes more important than what it represents. Researchers in this field have different emphases, but it is typically the case that language is regarded as doing things, especially in relation to other people in a conversation. As such, discourse analysis employs 'speech act theory' (Austin, 1975), which regards language as part of a social performance. In the course of this performance, social identities are formed and maintained, power relations are created, exercised and maintained, and generally a lot of social work is done. None of these can be effectively construed as language simply and directly communicating internal thought. Language in this context becomes a practice, not a matter of informal or formal structures.

The term 'discourse analysis' may arouse images of a well-established empirical method of analysing people talking, interviews and so forth. In a sense it is in part. However, discourse analysis is *not* merely a number of relatively simple analytical skills that can be quickly learnt and easily applied. Some aspects are relatively simple like transcription methods (Chapter 20). Discourse analysts themselves have frequently presented the definition and practice of discourse analysis as problematic. For example, Edley (2001) wrote:

> . . . there is no simple way of defining discourse analysis. It has become an ever broadening church, an umbrella term for a wide variety of different analytic principles and practices. (p. 189)

Potter (2004) added to the sense of incoherence:

> . . . in the mid 80s it was possible to find different books called Discourse Analysis with almost no overlap in subject matter; the situation at the start of the 00s is, if anything, even more fragmented. (p. 189)

and Taylor (2001) reinforces the view that discourse analysis should not be regarded as merely another variant or sub-discipline of methods:

> . . . to understand what kind of research discourse analysis is, it is not enough to study what the researcher does (like following a recipe!). We also need to refer back to these epistemological debates and their wider implications. (p. 12)

Even discourse analysts with backgrounds in psychology do not offer a united front on its nature. Different viewpoints exist partly because they draw on different intellectual roots. Consequently, there is no consensus position which can be identified as the core of discourse analysis. If there were, then this would focus and facilitate the theoretical debate. The lack of consensus should not be considered a criticism.

23.2   Basic discourse analysis theory

Discourse analysis is built on a variety of ideas, observations and concepts which suggest features of language which the discourse analyst should concentrate on. These are theoretical notions which suggest some of the ways in which language and text can be analysed. They include the following:

■ Speech acts

Of particular importance to psychologists working in discourse analysis is the theory of *speech acts*. This originated in the work of Austin (1975). 'Performatives' was his term for utterances which have a particular social effect. For Austin, all words perform social acts:

- *Locution*   This is simply the act of speaking.

- *Illocution*   This is what is done by saying these words.

- *Perlocution*   This is the effect or consequence of the words on the hearer who hears the words.

To speak the words is essentially to do the act (speech act). For the words to have an effect, certain conditions have to be met. These were illustrated in Searle (1969) using the following utterances:

> Sam smokes habitually
> Does Sam smoke habitually?
> Sam. Smoke habitually!
> Would that Sam smoked habitually.

Saying the words constitutes an *utterance act* or *locutory act*. They constitute the act of uttering something. At the same time, they are also propositional acts because they refer to something and predicate something. Try introducing any of them into a conversation with a friend. It is unlikely that the sentence could be said without some sort of response from the other person on the topic of Sam, smoking or both. Each of the sentences also constitutes an *illocutory act* because they do things like state, question, command, promise, warn, etc.

For example, in some contexts each of these sentences may contain an unstated indication that the speaker wishes to do something about Sam's smoking. 'Would that Sam smoked habitually' may be a slightly sardonic way of suggesting that it would be great if Sam could be persuaded to smoke as infrequently as habitually! Equally, if they were uttered by a shopkeeper about his customer, Sam, who spends large amounts on chocolates for his wife every time he calls in for a packet of cigarettes, the same words would constitute a different *illocutory act*. The sentences are also *perlocutionary* acts in that they have an effect or consequence on the hearer, though what this effect is depends on circumstances. For example, the locution 'Sam smokes habitually', if said by Sam's landlord to Sam's wife, might be taken as a warning that the landlord is unhappy about Sam smoking in violation of his tenancy contract. In speech act theory, the indirect nature of speech is inevitably emphasised, since the interaction between language and the social context is partially responsible for meaning.

■ Grice's maxims of cooperative speech

Another contribution which comes from the philosophy of language is Grice's (1975) maxims. These indicate something of the rule-based nature of exchanges between people. The overriding principle is conversational cooperativeness over what is being communicated at the time. Cooperativeness is achieved by obeying four maxims:

- Quality, which involves making truthful and sincere contributions

- Quantity, which involves the provision of sufficient information

- Manner, which involves making one's contributions brief, clear and orderly

- Relation, which involves making relevant contributions.

These maxims contribute to effective communications. They are not the only principles underlying social exchanges. For example, unrestrained truthfulness may offend when it breaches politeness standards in conversation.

■ Face

Similarly, language often includes strategies for protecting the status of the various participants in the exchange. The notion of 'face' is taken from the work of Goffman (1959) to indicate the valued persona that individuals have. We speak of saving face in everyday conversation. Saving face is a collective phenomenon in which all members of the conversation may contribute, not simply the person at risk of losing face.

■ Register

The concept of register highlights the fact that when we speak, the language style that we use varies according to the activity being carried out. The language used in a lecture is not the same as that used in a sermon. This may be considered a matter of style, but it is described as register. Register has a number of components, including:

- Field of activity (e.g. police interview, radio interview)

- Medium used (e.g. spoken language, written language, dictated language)

- Tenor of the role relationship in a particular situation (e.g. parent–child, police officer–witness).

23.3   The agenda of discourse analysis

It should be clear by now that discourse analysis is not a simple to learn, readily applied technique. Discourse analysis is a body of theory and knowledge accumulated over a period of 60 years or more. It is far from being a single, integrated theory. Instead it provides an analytical focus for a range of theories contributed by a variety of disciplines such as philosophy, linguistics, sociology and anthropology. Psychology, as somewhat a latecomer to the field, has set about the process of imposing its own distinctive stamp on discourse analysis. To re-stress the point, there are no short cuts to successful discourse analysis. Various intellectual and theoretical roots are more apparent in the writings of discourse analysts than in practically any other field of psychology. In other words, the most important *practical* step in using discourse analysis is to immerse oneself in its theoretical and research literature. One cannot just get on with doing discourse analysis. Without understanding in some depth the constituent parts of the discourse analytic tradition, the objectives of discourse analysis cannot be appreciated fully. This would be equally true of designing an experiment – we need to understand what it does, how it does it, why it does it, and when it is inappropriate.

The disparate nature of discourse analysis and the varied origins of its theoretical base begin to raise questions about what is distinctive, if anything, in psychological discourse analysis. The agenda of psychological discourse analysis, according to Potter and Wetherell (1995), includes the following:

- *Practices and resources*   Discourse analysis is not simply an approach to the social use of language. It focuses on discourse practices – the things that people do in talk and writings. But it also focuses on the resources that people employ when achieving these ends, for example, the strategies employed in their discourse, the systems of categorisation they use, and the interpretative repertoires that are used. Interpretative repertoires are the 'broadly discernible clusters of terms, descriptions, and figures of speech often assembled around metaphors or vivid images' (Potter & Wetherell, 1995, p. 89). So, for example, when newspapers and politicians write and talk about drugs, they often use the language repertoire of war and battle, hence the 'war on drugs', 'the enemy drugs' and so forth. Discourse analysis seeks also to provide greater understanding of traditional (socio-)psychological topics such as the nature of individual and collective identity, how to conceive social action and interaction, the nature of the human mind, and constructions of the self, others and the world.

- *Construction and description*   During conversation and other forms of text, people create and construct 'versions' of the world. Discourse analysis attempts to understand and describe this constructive process.

- *Content*   Talk and other forms of discourse are regarded as the important site of psychological phenomena. No attempt is made to postulate 'underlying' psychological mechanisms to explain that talk. So racist talk is regarded as the means by which discrimination is put into practice. There is no interest in 'psychological mechanisms' such as authoritarian personalities or racist attitudes.

Box 23.1   Key Ideas

Critical discourse analysis

The term 'critical discourse analysis' can be rather confusing since it is applied to a variety of different approaches to the analysis of text. Searching PsycINFO using critical discourse analysis produces predominantly hits on studies influenced by the work of the linguist Norman Fairclough (1989, 1992, 1995). While this is essentially compatible with other forms of discourse analysis, it is a distinct tradition. In its various manifestations, critical discourse analysis focuses on the ways in which language is used to construct power, maintain power, and resist power. Critical does *not* mean crucial in this context or that discourse analysis is generally radical. Critical discourse analysis, then, concentrates on the relationship of discourse with *power and social inequality*. It studies the way in which power is attained and maintained through language. According to van Dijk (2001), *dominance* is the exercise of social power by elites, institutions and social groups. Consequences of the exercise of power include varieties of social inequality – ethnic, racial and gender inequality, for example. Equally, language has the potential to serve the interests of disadvantaged groups in order to redress and change the situation. The phrase 'black is beautiful', for example, was used to counter the destructive effects of racism on the self-image of black children of themselves.

Dominance is achieved using language in a variety of ways, for example, the way a group is represented in language, how language is used to reinforce dominance, and the means by which language is used to deny and conceal dominance:

> . . . critical discourse analysts want to know what structures, strategies or other properties of text, talk, verbal interaction or communicative events play a role in these modes of reproduction.
>
> (van Dijk, 2001, p. 300)

→

Brute force is generally regarded as an unacceptable means of achieving power in modern society. Persuasion and manipulation through language provide a substitute for violence, and so power is achieved and maintained through language.

Others extend the notion of 'critical' to include a wider set of concerns than van Dijk's. Hepburn (2003) suggests that it also includes issues of politics, morality and social change. These are all components or facets of van Dijk's notion of power. Concerns such as these link to a long tradition of concerned psychology in which power, politics, morality and social change are staple ingredients (e.g. Howitt, 1992a).

- *Rhetoric*   Discourse analysis is concerned with how talk can be organised so as to be argumentatively successful or persuasive.

- *Stake and accountability*   People regard others as having a vested interest (stake) in what they do. Hence they impute motives to the actions of others which may justify dismissing what these others say. Discourse analysis studies these processes.

- *Cognition in action*   Discourse analysis actively rejects the use of psychology's cognitive concepts such as traits, motives, attitudes and memory stores. Instead it concentrates on the text by focusing on, for example, how memory is socially constructed between people, such as when reminiscing over old photographs.

This agenda constitutes the broad framework for social constructionist psychological discourse analysis. It points to aspects of text which the analyst may take into account. At the same time, the reaction of discourse analysis against traditional forms of psychology is apparent.

23.4   Doing discourse analysis

Be aware that the objectives of discourse analysis are limited in a number of ways – especially the focus on socially interactive uses of language. There is little point in doing a discourse analysis to achieve ends not shared by discourse analysis. Potter (2004) put the issue as follows:

> To attempt to ask a question formulated in more traditional terms ('what are the factors that lead to condom use among HIV + gay males') and then use discourse analytic methods to answer it is a recipe for incoherence. (p. 607)

Only when the researcher is interested in language as social action is discourse analysis appropriate. Some discourse analysts have contributed to the confusion by offering it as a radical and new way of understanding psychological phenomena, for example, when they suggest that discourse analysis is anti-cognitive psychology. This, taken superficially, may imply that discourse analysis supersedes other forms of psychology. It is more accurate to suggest that discourse analysis performs a different task. Discourse analysis would be useless for biological research on genetic engineering but an excellent choice to look at the ways in which the moral and ethical issues associated with genetic engineering are dealt with in speech and conversation.

Although a total novice can easily learn some of the skills of discourse analysis (e.g. Jefferson transcription), conducting good discourse analyses is far harder. Reading is crucial but experience and practice also play their parts. The best way to understand what discourse analysis involves is to read the work of the best discourse analysts, as would be the case for all forms of research. Reports of discourse analytic studies make frequent reference to research and theory in the field. Some of this we have outlined, but ideas are developing continually.

There is a degree of smog surrounding the process of discourse analysis. It is not like calculating a *t*-test or chi-square in a step-by-step fashion. No set of procedures exists which, if applied, guarantee a successful discourse analysis. Potter (2004) puts it as follows:

> There is no single recipe for doing discourse analysis. Different kinds of studies involve different procedures, sometimes working intensively with a single transcript, other times drawing on a large corpus. Analysis is a craft that can be developed with different degrees of skill. It can be thought of as the development of sensitivity to the occasioned and action-oriented, situated and constructed nature of discourse. Nevertheless, there are a number of ingredients which, when combined together are likely to produce something satisfying. (p. 611)

The use of the word 'craft' suggests the carpenter's workshop in which nothing of worth can be produced until the novice has learnt to sharpen tools, select wood, mark out joints, saw straight and so forth. Likewise in discourse analysis, the tools are slowly mastered. Actually, Potter (1997) put it even more graphically when he wrote that for the most part:

> . . . doing discourse analysis is a craft skill, more like bike riding or chicken sexing than following the recipe for a mild chicken rogan josh. (p. 95)

Publications which seek to explain the process of discourse analysis often resort to a simple strategy: students are encouraged to apply the concepts developed by major contributors to discourse theory. In other words, tacitly the approach encourages the novice discourse analyst to find instances in their data of key discourse analytic concepts. For example, they are encouraged to identify which register is being employed, what awkwardness is shown in the conversation, which rhetorical devices are being used, which discourse repertoires are being employed and so forth. Some of this is redolent of the work of expert discourse analysts. If one initially attempts to understand the text under consideration using standard discourse analytic concepts, the later refinement and extension of these concepts will be facilitated. Areas which are problematic in terms of the application of standard concepts will encourage the revision of those concepts. At this stage, the analysis may begin to take a novel turn.

Some features of language which need to be examined in a discourse analysis can be listed. This may be described as an itinerary for discourse analysis (Wetherell & Taylor, 2001). Where to go and what to look for, as well as the dead-ends that should be ignored, are part of this. So one may interrogate one's data to find out which of the following are recognisable or applicable to the particular text in question:

- Language is an inappropriate way of accessing reality. Instead, language should be regarded as constructive or constitutive of social life. Through discourse, individuals and groups of individuals build social relations, objects and worlds.

- Since discourse constructs versions of social reality, important questions of any text are why is a particular version of reality being constructed through language and what does this particular version accomplish?

- Meaning is produced in the context of speech and does not solely reside in a cultural storehouse of agreed definitions. Discourse analysts refer to the co-production of meaning. The analysis partly seeks to understand the processes by which meaning is created. Meaning, for example, is a 'joint production' of two or more individuals in conversation.

- Discursive practice refers to the things which happen in language to achieve particular outcomes.

- Discursive genres are the types of language extract under consideration. So the discourse analyst may study the particular features of news and how it differs from other types of language. There are cues in news speech which provide indicators that it is news speech rather than, say, a sermon (contextualisation cues).

- Footing (a concept taken from the sociologist Goffman) refers to whether the speaker talks as if they are the author of what is being said, they are the subject of the words that are being said, or they are presenting or animating the words of someone else. These different footings are not mutually exclusive and all may be present in any text.

- Speech is dialogical. That is, when we talk, we combine or incorporate things from other conversations. Sometimes this is in the form of reporting what 'he said' or what 'she replied'. More often, however, the dialogical elements are indirect and not highlighted directly as such. For example, children who say something like 'I mustn't go out on my own' reflect previous conversations with their parents and teachers.

Taylor (2001) characterises discourse analysis as an 'open-ended' and circular (or iterative) process. The task of the researcher is to find patterns without a clear idea of what the patterns will be like. She writes of the 'blind faith' that there must be something there worthy of the considerable effort of analysis. The researcher will need to go through the data repeatedly, 'working up' the analysis on the basis of what fits and does not fit tentative patterns. 'Data analysis is not accomplished in one or two sessions' (Taylor, 2001, pp. 38–39). The process of examination and re-examination may not fit comfortably with conventional research timescales. The direction or end-point of the analysis is also difficult to anticipate. She feels that qualitative data are so 'rich' (that is, detailed) that there may be more worth studying in the data even when the possibilities seem to be exhausted.

The process of carrying out a discourse analysis can be summarised in the five steps illustrated in Figure 23.2. The steps are superficially straightforward, but this belies the need for a level of intensity in examining and re-examining the data. What the analyst is looking for are features which stand out on reading and rereading the transcript. These are then marked (coded) systematically throughout the transcript to be collected together later – simply by copying and pasting the excerpts from the transcript into one file, perhaps. It is this collection that is subject to the analytic scrutiny of the researcher, concentrating on things like deviant cases which do not seem to fit the general pattern. When the analysis is complete, the issue of validity may be addressed by, for example, getting the participants in the research to comment on the analysis from their perspective.

Gathering materials for analysis including making recordings

Transcription of any recordings using the Jefferson system

Generating hypotheses based on one's familiarity with the material

Coding – that is, building up a collection of the instances of the aspects that interest you

The analysis including: (1) identifying patterns; (2) deviant cases and (3) what happens next in discourse

FIGURE 23.2   Steps involved in a typical discourse analysis

Box 23.2   Research Example

Discourse analysis

Lovering, K. M. (1995). The bleeding body: Adolescents talk about menstruation. In S. Wilkinson & C. Kitzinger (Eds), *Feminism and discourse: Psychological perspectives* (pp. 10–31). London: Sage.

In research on menstruation, Lovering (1995) talked with 11- and 12-year-old boys and girls in discussion groups. Among a range of topics included in her guide for conducting the discussions were issues to do with menstruation. These included questions such as 'Have you heard of menstruation?'; 'What have you been told about it?'; 'What do you think happens when a woman menstruates?'; 'Why does it happen?'; and 'Who has told you?' (Lovering, 1995, p. 17). In this way, relatively systematic material could be gathered in ways closer to ordinary conversation than would be generated by one-on-one interviews. She took detailed notes of her experiences as soon as possible after the discussion groups using a number of headings (p. 17):

- How she (Lovering) felt
- General emotional tone and reactions
- Non-verbal behaviour
- Content recalled
- Implications and thoughts.

→

This is a form of diary writing of the sort discussed already in relation to grounded theory. Lovering transcribed the tape-recording herself – eventually using the Jefferson system (Chapter 20). She also employed a computer-based analysis program (of the kind that NVivo is the modern equivalent). Such a program does not do the analysis for you; it allows you to store and work with a lot of text, highlight or mark particular parts of the text, sort the text and print it out. All of these things can be achieved just using pencil and paper, but a computer is more convenient.

The next stage was to sort the text into a number of categories – initially, she had more than 50. She developed an analysis of the transcribed material partly based on her awareness of a debate about the ways in which male and female bodies are socially construed quite differently. Boys' physical development is regarded as a gradual and unproblematic process, whereas in girls the process is much more problematic. The following excerpts from a transcript illustrate this:

> A: They [school teachers] don't talk about the boys very much only the girls $=$ yes $=$ yes.
>
> A: It doesn't seem fair. They are laughing at us. Not much seems to happen to boys.
>
> A: Girl all go funny shapes $=$ yes $=$ like that $=$ yes.
>
> A: Because the boys, they don't really . . . change very much. They just get a little bit bigger.
>
> A: It feels like the girls go through all the changes because we are not taught anything about the boys REALLY.
>
> (Lovering, 1995, pp. 23–24)

Menstruation was learnt about from other people – predominantly female teachers or mothers. Embarrassment dominated, and the impression created was that menstruation was not to be discussed or even mentioned as a consequence. Talk of female bodies and bodily functions by the youngsters features a great deal of sniggering. In contrast, when discussing male bodies things become more ordinary and more matter of fact. Furthermore, boys are also likely to use menstruation as a psychological weapon against girls. That is, menstruation is used to make jokes about and ridicule girls. In Lovering's analysis, this is part of male oppression of females: even in sex education lessons learning about menstruation are associated in girls' minds as being 'laughing at girls'.

Of course, many more findings emerged in this study. Perhaps what is important is the complexity of the process by which the analysis proceeds. It is not possible to say that if the researcher does this and then does that, a good analysis will follow. Nevertheless, it is easy to see how the researcher's ideas relate to key aspects of discourse analytic thinking. For example, the idea that menstruation is used as a weapon of oppression of females clearly has its roots in feminist sexual politics, which suggests that males attempt to control females in many ways from domestic violence through rape to, in this example, sex education lessons. One could equally construe this as part of Edwards and Potter's (1993) discursive action model. This suggests, among other things, that in talk, conversation or text, one can see social action unfolding before one's eyes. One does not have to regard talk, text or conversation as the external manifestation or symptom of an underlying mental state such as an attitude. A topic such as menstruation may be seen not merely to generate hostility in the form of laughter towards the female body, but also as a means of accessing concepts of femininity in which the female body is construed as mysterious, to be embarrassed about, and sniggered over by both sexes. Horton-Salway (2001) uses the same sort of model to analyse how the medical profession went about presenting the medical condition ME in a variety of ways through language.

Discourse analysis, like other forms of qualitative analysis, is not amenable to short summaries. This might be expected, given that a discourse analysis seeks to provide appropriate analytic categories for a wide range of texts. The consequence is that anyone wishing to understand discourse analytic approaches will need to read the original analyses in detail.

23.5   Conclusion

One of the significant achievements of discourse analysis is that of bringing to psychology a theoretically fairly coherent set of procedures for the analysis of the very significant amounts of textual material which form the basis of much psychological data. It has to be understood that discourse analysis has a limited perspective on the nature of this data. In particular, discourse analysts reject the idea that language is representational, that is, that in language there is a representation of, say, the individual's internal psychological state. Instead, they replace it with the idea that language is action and is designed to do something, not represent something. As a consequence, discourse analysis is primarily of use to researchers who wish to study language as an active thing. In this way, discourse analysis may contribute a different perspective on many psychological processes, but it does not replace or supersede the more traditional viewpoints within psychology.

Key points

- Discourse analysis is based on early work carried out by linguists, especially during the 1950s and 1960s, which reconstrued language much as a working set of resources to allow things to be done rather than regarding language as merely being a representation of something else.

- The analysis uses larger units of speech than words or sentences, such as a sequence of conversational exchanges.

- Precisely how discourse analysis is defined is somewhat uncertain, as it encompasses a wide range of practices as well as theoretical orientations.

- Central to most discourse analysis is the idea of speech as doing things – such as constructing and construing meaning.

- Discourse analysis has its own roadmap which should be considered when planning an analysis. Discourse practices and resources, for example, are the things that people do in constructing conversations, texts and writings. Rhetoric is about the wider organisation of language in ways that facilitate its effectiveness. Content is regarded for what it is rather than what underlying psychological states it represents.

- Critical discourse analysis has as its central focus the concept of power. It primarily concerns how social power is created, reaffirmed and challenged through language.

ACTIVITIES

1. When having a coffee with friends, note occasions when the conversation might be better seen as speech acts rather than taken literally. Better still, if you can record such a conversation, transcribe a few minutes' worth and highlight in red where literal interpretations would be appropriate and in yellow where the concept of speech act might be more appropriate.

2. Study day-to-day conversations of which you are part. Is there any evidence that participants spare other participants in the conversation embarrassment over errors? That is, to what extent does face-saving occur in your day-to-day experience?

3. Choose a chapter of your favourite novel: does discourse analysis have more implications for its contents than more traditional psychology?

CHAPTER 24

Conversation analysis

Overview

- Conversation analysis studies the structure of conversation by the detailed examination of successive turns or contributions to a conversation.

- It is based on ethnomethodological approaches derived from sociology that stress the importance of participants' understandings of the nature of the world.

- Many of the conventions of psychological research are turned on their head in conversation analysis. The primacy of theory in developing research questions and hypotheses is replaced by an emphasis on the importance of the data in generating explanations.

- Because of its reversal of conventional psychological research methodology, conversation analysis warrants the careful attention of all psychologists, since it helps define the nature of psychological research.

24.1   Introduction

Conversation analysis has its intellectual roots in ethnomethodology, championed in the 1960s by the American sociologist Harold Garfinkel (1967). He wanted to study ordinary aspects of society in order to understand the way in which interactions in everyday life are conducted. In particular, ethnomethodologists were concerned with ordinary everyday conversation. The term 'ethnomethodology' signifies Garfinkel's method of studying the common-sense 'methodology' used by ordinary conversationalists to conduct social interactions. Just how is interaction constructed and managed into largely unproblematic sequences?

One of Garfinkel's major contributions was to show that everyday interaction between people involves a *search for meaning*. Care is needed, because this is *not* saying that everyday interaction is meaningful as such – only that participants in that interaction regard it as meaningful. To demonstrate this, he relied on a form of experimental research. In one example, students attended a 'counselling' session in a university's psychiatry department (McHugh, 1968). The situation was such that participants communicated only indirectly with the 'counsellor' who, totally at random, replied to the client with either 'yes' or 'no'. In this instance, essentially the real world was chaotic and meaningless (unless, of course, one is aware of the random process and the purpose of the study). Nevertheless, the participants in the research dealt with this chaotic situation of random responses by imposing a meaningful and organised view of the situation. The concern of ethnomethodologists such as Garfinkel and Aaron Cicourel with the fine detail of this sense-making process influenced others, the most important of whom was Harvey Sacks, who is regarded as the founder of conversation analysis. Also influential on Sacks was the work of Erving Goffman, who stressed the nature of social interaction as a social institution which imposed norms and obligations on members (see Figure 24.1).

In the 1960s, Harvey Sacks became interested in the telephone calls made to hospital emergency departments (Sacks, 1992). While some researchers might have sought to

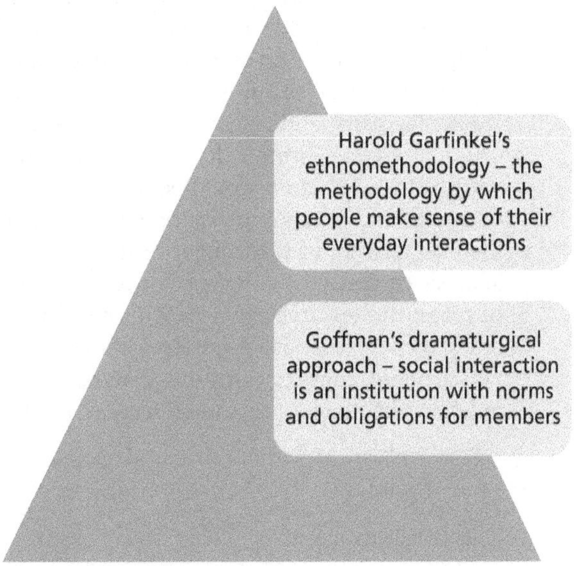

Harold Garfinkel's ethnomethodology – the methodology by which people make sense of their everyday interactions

Goffman's dramaturgical approach – social interaction is an institution with norms and obligations for members

FIGURE 24.1   Roots of conversation analysis

classify the types of call made, for example, Sacks had a much more profound approach to his chosen subject matter. Substantial numbers of callers to the emergency department would wind up not providing their name. Obviously, this limited the possible response of the hospital once the conversation ceased – in those days, without a name it would be virtually impossible to track down the caller. Sacks wanted to know by what point in a telephone conversation one could know that the caller would be unlikely to give their name. That is, what features of the telephone conversation were associated with withheld names?

His research strategy involved an intense and meticulous examination of the detail of such conversations. In conversation analysis, emphasis is placed on the analysis of turn-taking – members of conversations take turns to speak and these turns provide the basic unit for study in a conversation. Look at the following opening turns in a telephone conversation:

> *Member of staff*: Hello, this is Mr Smith. May I help you?
> *Caller*: Yes this is Mr Brown.

The first turn is the member of staff's 'Hello, this is Mr Smith. May I help you?'. In this case, by the second turn in the conversation (the contribution of the caller), the caller's name is known. However, if the *second* turn in the conversation was something like:

> *Caller*: Speak up please – I can't hear you.

Or

> *Caller*: Spell your name please.

there would be the greatest difficulty in getting the caller's name. Often the name would not be obtained at all. One reason for this is that the phrase 'May I help you?' may be interpreted by the caller as indicative of a member of staff who is just following the procedures laid down by the training scheme for staff at the hospital. In other words, if the caller believes that they have unusual needs or that their circumstances are special, 'May I help you?' merely serves to indicate that they are being treated as another routine case.

Two conversation turns (such as in the above examples) in sequence are known as 'adjacency pairs' and essentially constitute one of the major analytic features in conversation analysis. Without the emphasis on adjacency pairs, the structured, turn-taking nature of conversation would be obscured. A prime objective of conversation analysis is to understand how an utterance is 'designed' to fit in with the previous utterances and the likely nature of subsequent turns in the conversation. In other words, conversation analysis explores the coherence of patterns in turns. By concentrating on adjacent pairs of turns, the researcher works with much the same building blocks as the participants in the conversation use themselves in their task of giving coherence to the conversation.

Telephone conversations illustrate conversation analysis principles well in that they indicate something of the organised nature of even the simplest of conversational acts:

> *a*: Hello
>
> *b*: Hello it's me
>
> *a*: Hi Jenny
>
> *b*: You took a long time to answer the phone

It is quite easy to see in this the use of greetings such as *Hello* to allow for the voice identification of the speaker. There is also an assumption that the hearer should be able to recognise the voice. Finally, there is an expectation that the ring of a telephone should initiate the response fairly rapidly in normal circumstances. It does not take a great deal to figure out that this is likely to be a call between close friends rather than, say, a business call. This interpretation may not be sophisticated in terms of the principles of conversation analysis, but it does say a good deal about the nature of turn-taking in general and especially in telephone calls.

It is one of the assumptions of conversation that the speaker will either indicate to another speaker that it is their turn to speak or provide the opportunity for another to take their turn. So it is incumbent on the speaker to include a 'transition relevance space' which provides the opportunity for another speaker to take over speaking. The approach in conversation analysis is to study the various things which can occur next and not the most likely thing to occur next, as probably would be the objective of a mainstream quantitative psychologist. Figure 24.2 illustrates the basic situation and the possible broad outcomes. Although there is a conversationally presented opportunity for another person to take over the conversation, there is no requirement that they do. Hence, there are two possible things that can happen next – one is that the conversation shifts to another speaker, and the other is that the original speaker carries on speaking. There is a third option which is that nobody speaks so there is a lapse in the conversation. The question is just how all of this happens and the consequences for the later conversation of its happening.

For anyone grounded in the mainstream methods of psychology, there is a major 'culture shock' when confronted with a research paper on conversation analysis. It is almost as if one is faced with a research paper stripped bare. The typical features of a psychology report may well be missing. For example, the literature review may be absent or minimal, details of sampling, or of participant or interaction selection, are often sparse, and generally details of the social context in which the conversation took place are largely missing. Some of the reasons for this are the traditions and precepts of conversation analysis. More important, though, is the realisation that the way in which the conversation is understood structurally by the participants is crucial to understanding conversation. As such, academic theoretical discussions would obstruct ethnomethodological understanding, since the theory is not being used by the participants in the conversation. Similarly, details of the social context of the conversation, while important from some perspectives, miss the point for a conversation analyst. The key idea is that in conversation analysis, the principles of conversation are regarded as directly governing the conversation. The consideration of factors extraneous to the conversation merely diverts attention away from this.

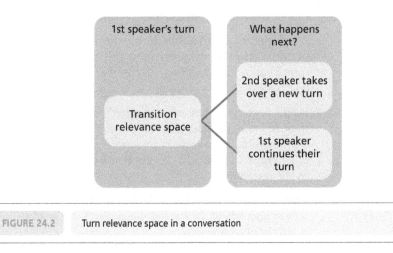

FIGURE 24.2   Turn relevance space in a conversation

In conversation analysis, the study of how ordinary life conversation is conducted involves the following stages:

- The *recording* stage, in which conversation is put on video or audio-only recording equipment.

- *Transcription,* in which the recording or parts of the recording are transcribed using the minutely detailed methods of Gail Jefferson's transcription system (see Chapter 20). This system includes not merely *what* has been said but, crucially, a great deal of information about the *way* in which it has been said.

- *Analysis* consists of the researcher identifying aspects of the transcription of note for some reason, then offering suggestions as to the nature of the conversational devices, etc., which may be responsible for the significant features. But things do not come quite as easily as this implies.

Conversation analysis essentially eschews the postulate that there are key psychological mechanisms which underlie conversation. Interaction through talk is not regarded as the external manifestation of inner cognitive processes. Whether or not participants in conversation have intentions, motives or interests, personality and character is irrelevant. The domain of interest in conversation analysis is the structure of conversation (Wooffitt, 2001). We are referring to the researcher's theorising, the participants in the conversation may well incorporate psychological factors into their understanding of the conversation and, more importantly, refer to them in the conversation.

24.2   Precepts of conversation analysis

So conversation analysis's objective involves identifying repeated patterns in conversation that arise from the joint endeavour of the speakers in the production of conversation. One such pattern would be the preference of people to allow self-correction of conversational errors (as opposed to being corrected by other participants). The next person to speak after the error may offer some device to prompt or initiate the 'repair' without actually making the repair. For example, a brief silence may provide the opportunity for the person who has said the wrong thing to correct themselves.

Drew (1995) listed methodological precepts or principles for doing a conversation analysis:

- The principal objective of conversational analysis is to identify the sequential organisation or patterns in conversation.

- A participant's contribution (turn) is regarded as the product of the preceding sequence of turn. Turns are basically required to fit appropriately and coherently with the prior turn. That is, adjacency pairs gel together effectively and meaningfully. Of course, there will be deviant cases when this does not happen.

- People develop analyses of each other's verbal conduct. The nature of these analyses is to be found in the detail of each participant's utterances. Contributors to a conversation interpret one another's intentions and attribute intention and meaning to each other's turns in their talk. (Notice that intentions and meanings are *not* being provided by the researcher.)

- Conversation analysts study the design of each turn in the conversation. That is, they seek to understand the activity that a turn is designed to perform in terms of the details of its verbal construction.

- The recurrence and systematic nature of patterns in conversation are demonstrated and tested by the researcher. This is done by reference to collections of cases of the conversational feature under examination.

- Data extracts are presented in such a way as to enable others to assess or challenge the researcher's analysis. That is, detailed transcriptions are made available in a conventional transcription format (Jefferson transcription).

To make things more concrete, conversation analysts have a special interest in the following:

- How turn-taking is achieved in conversation

- How the utterances within a person's turn in the conversation are constructed

- How difficulties in the flow of a conversation are identified and sorted out.

Having addressed these basic matters, conversation analysts then attempt to apply them to other domains of conversation. So they might study what happens in hearings in courts of law, in telephone conversations, when playing games or during interviews. In this way, the structure of conversation can be explored more deeply and more comparatively.

24.3 Stages in conversation analysis

Unlike most other approaches to research, conversation analysis rejects prior theoretical speculation about the significant aspects of conversation. A conversation analysis should *not* start with theory which is explored or tested against conversation. Instead it seeks to understand the rules that ordinary people are using in conversation. So the ethnomethodological orientation of conversation analysis can be seen in its stress on peoples' interpretations of their interaction as revealed in their conversation. The participants' interpretations manifested in their verbal exchanges are assumed to be much more salient than any arbitrary, theory-led speculative set of priorities established by researchers (Wooffitt, 2001). That is, conversation analysis does *not* involve hypothesis testing based on cumulative and all-embracing theory.

The conversation analyst fundamentally works through fragments of conversation, making notes of anything which seems interesting or significant. There is no limit to the number of observations that may be written down as part of the analysis process. However, it is crucial that the conversation analyst confines themselves solely to the data before them. They should not move beyond the data to speculate whether, for example, someone has made a revealing Freudian slip or that in reality they meant to say something quite different. If you like, this is the conversation analysis mindset – a single-minded focus on seemingly irrelevant, trivial detail. Nothing in the interaction being studied can be discarded or disregarded as inconsequential. Consequently, the transcripts used in conversation analysis are messy in that they contain many non-linguistic features. In order to ensure the transcript's fidelity to the original recording, Jefferson transcripts contain such things as false starts to words and the gaps between words and participants' turns. In conversation analysis, tidying up transcripts is something of a cardinal sin.

Paul ten Have (2004) provided a seven-step model of conversation analysis research practices. Practice implies the way things are done rather than some idealised concept of a research method. Conversation analysts frequently claim that there are no set ways of proceeding. Nevertheless, analysis is confined by fairly strict parameters, knowledge

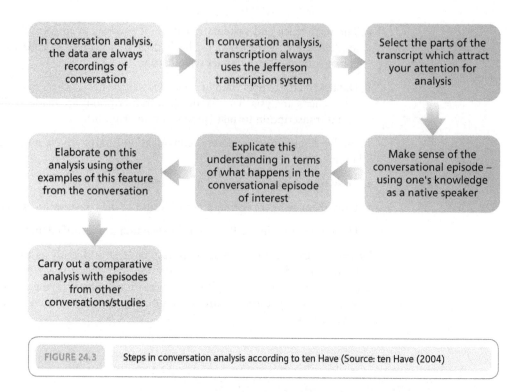

FIGURE 24.3 Steps in conversation analysis according to ten Have (Source: ten Have (2004)

of which should help the novice to avoid straying too far beyond the purview of conversation analysis. Ten Have's steps are best regarded as an ideal for researchers in the field. They are not necessarily characteristic of any particular analyst's work in their entirety (see also Figure 24.3).

Step 1 Digital production of the primary database (materials to be analysed)

Data recording is done by a digital recorder. A human decides what and when to record, but the recording is basically unselective, so that what is recorded is not filtered through human thinking systems, tidied up and the like. This original recording may be returned to at any point. For that reason, the recording remains available continually throughout the analysis for checking purposes by the researcher or even by others (Drew, 1995).

Step 2 Transcription

The production of the transcript should ideally be free from the researcher's expectations and biases. It is all too easy for a transcriber to make systematic errors, some of which fall into line with their expectations (Chapter 20). To this end, the transcript may be checked against the original recording by the transcriber or other researchers. There are, of course, several possible 'hearings' for any recording. Each transcriber needs to be alert to this possibility. Many regard it as essential that the researcher themselves transcribes the recording. This ensures the close familiarity that is needed for effective analysis. However, no matter how good the transcription is, it cannot be complete and something must be lost in the process compared with the original recording. Nevertheless, the transcription enables the researcher both to confront but also to cope with the rich detail of the conversation. The presence of the transcript in the research report means that the analyst and others must be precise in their analysis of the detail of the conversation. This direct link with the data is not possible in some other styles of research. The summary tables of statistics, for example, found in much psychological research cannot be related directly back to the data that were collected by the researcher. The links are too deeply buried in the analysis process for this to happen. Few researchers present their data in such a relatively raw form as is conventional in conversational analysis.

Step 3 Selection of aspects of the transcript to be analysed

There are no formal rules for this and it can simply be a case of the analyst being intrigued by certain aspects of the conversation. Others may be interested in particular aspects of an interaction – as Sacks was when he investigated name-giving in telephone conversations to emergency units. Others may wish to concentrate on the contributions of particularly skilled contributors to a conversation, such as where a major shift in the conversation is achieved. Just one adjacency pair (the minimum unit that makes up a conversation) may be sufficient to proceed.

Step 4 Making sense of or interpreting the conversational episode

Researchers are part of the culture that produced the conversational episode. Hence, they can use their own common-sense knowledge of language to make sense of the episode. This is appropriate, since it reflects exactly what participants in the interaction do when producing and responding in the conversation (constructing adjacency pairs). Typically, the analyst may ask what aspects of the conversation do or achieve during specific conversational exchanges. The relation between different aspects of conversation can then be assessed.

Step 5 Explication of the interpretation

Because the conversation analyst is a member of the broad community whose conversations they study, the researcher's native or common-sense understanding of what happens in an episode is clearly a useful resource, as we have seen. Nevertheless, this is insufficient as an explication without bringing the links between this resource and the detail of the conversational episode together. That is, the analyst may feel they know what is happening in the conversation, but they need to demonstrate how their understanding links to the detail of the conversation. Just what is it that happens in each turn of the conversation which leads to what follows, and why?

Step 6 Elaboration of the analysis

Once a particular episode has been analysed, the rest of the transcription can be used to elaborate on it. Later sequences in the conversation may in some way, directly or indirectly, relate back to the analyst's central conversational episode. For example, the conversationalists may hark back to the earlier episode and reveal ways in which they understood it. As a consequence, the analyst may need to reformulate the analysis in some way or even substitute a substantially different one.

Step 7 Comparison with episodes from other conversations

The analysis process does not end with a particular transcription and its analysis. It continues to other instances of conversation which are apparently similar. This is vital, because a particular conversational episode is *not* considered to be unique, since the devices or means by which a conversational episode is both recognised and produced by the conversationalists are the same for other conversationalists and conversations. Some studies specifically aim to collect together different 'samples' of conversation in order that these different samples may be compared one with the other. In this way, similarities and dissimilarities may encourage or demand the analysis's refinement.

Steps 4 to 7 may seem less distinct in the analysis process itself than is warranted by describing them as separate steps. Ten Have's steps are schematic. They do not always constitute a precise and invariant sequence of steps which analysts must follow rigidly. Ultimately, the aim of most conversational analysts is not the interpretation of any particular episode of conversation. Conversation analysis delves into its subject matter thoroughly and deeply, which means that a psychologist more familiar with mainstream psychological research may find the attention to detail somewhat daunting. Instead of establishing broad trends, conversation analysis seeks to provide a full account of the phenomena in conversation that are studied. So the ill-fitting case may be given as much emphasis as common occurrences.

Box 24.1　Research Example

Conversation analysis

There are a number of good examples of conversation analysis in the work of psychologists – even though it is difficult to specify how the work of a sociologist, for example, analysing the same conversation would be different. The following are particularly useful in that they clearly adopt some of the sensibilities of mainstream psychology.

Cold reading

Wooffitt, R. (2001). Researching psychic practitioners: Conversation analysis. In M. Wetherell, S. Taylor, & S. J. E. Yates (Eds), *Discourse as data: A guide for analysis* (pp. 49–92). London: Sage.

Psychic phenomena are controversial. Wooffitt (2001) studied 'cold reading', which is the situation when, on the basis of very little conversation with a client, the medium seems to have gathered a great deal of information from beyond the grave. Some commentators suggest that the medium simply uses the limited interaction with the client to gather information about the client. This information is then fed back to the client as evidence of the medium's psychic powers.

Conversation analysts might be expected to have something to say about these 'conversations' between a medium and a client. The following excerpt from such a conversation is typical of what goes on between a psychic (P) and a client (S) (Wooffitt, 2001):

Extract 31

P:　h Ty'ever though(t) o(f).h did you want to go into a caring profession early *on*, when you were choosing which way you were gonna go.

(.)

S:　yeah I wanted to: go into child care actually when I

P:　MMMmmm….

S:　 = when I left school

P:　That's right yeah > well < h (.) 'm being shown that > but (t)–< h it's (0.2) it's not your way ye(t) actually but i(t) y'y may be caring for (t-)ch- children or whatever later on okay?

Although this excerpt is written using Jefferson transcription methods (Chapter 20 will help you decode this), in this case the importance of the excerpt can be understood simply on the basis of the sequence of words.

What happens? Well, first of all the psychic asks a question about caring professions. Then the client replies, but the reply is fairly extended as the client explains that they wanted to go into child care. The psychic then interrupts with 'MMMmmm'. The client carries on talking, but quickly at the first appropriate stage the psychic takes over the conversation again with 'That's right yeah'. The information is then characterised by the psychic as emanating from the spiritual world. In terms of the conventional explanation of cold reading phenomena, this is a little surprising. One would expect that the psychic would allow the client to reveal more about themselves if the purpose of the conversation is to extract information that is then fed back to the client as if coming from the spiritual world.

In contrast, what appears to be happening is that the psychic rapidly moves to close down the turn by the client. Wooffitt (2001) argues that the first turn in the sequence (when the medium asks the question) is constructed so as to elicit a relatively short turn by the client (otherwise the psychic might just as well have asked the client to tell the story of their life). So ideally the client will simply agree with what the psychic says in the second turn of the sequence. This does not happen in the above example. If it had, then the floor (turn to speak) would have returned quickly to the psychic. As it happens, the psychic has to interrupt the client's turn as quickly as possible.

By analysing many such excerpts from psychic–client conversations, it was possible to show that if the client gives more than a minimal acceptance of what the psychic says, then the psychic will begin to overlap the client's turn, eventually forcing the client's turn to come to an end. Once this is done, the psychic can attribute their first statement (question) to paranormal sources. Wooffitt describes this as a three-turn series of utterances: a proposal is made about the sitter, this is accepted by the sitter, and then it is portrayed in terms of being supernatural in origin. Without the emphasis on the structure of turns which comes from conversation analysis, Wooffitt may well have overlooked this significant pattern.

Date rape

Kitzinger, C., & Frith, H. (2001). Just say no? The use of conversation analysis in developing a feminist perspective on sexual refusal. In M. Wetherell, S. Taylor, & S. J. E. Yates (Eds), *Discourse theory and practice: A reader* (pp. 167–185). London: Sage.

One notable feature of conversation analysis is that it dwells on the everyday and mundane. Much of the data for conversation analysis lacks any lustre or intrinsic interest. This is another way of saying that conversation analysis has explored ordinary conversation as a legitimate research goal. However, it is intriguing to find that the principles originating out of everyday conversation can find resonance in the context of more extraordinary situations – date rape, for example. Training courses to help young women prevent date rape often include sessions teaching participants how to say 'no', that is, refusal skills, in this case for unwanted sexual intercourse (Kitzinger & Frith, 2001).

Research by conversation analysts about refusals following invitations has revealed the problematic nature of saying 'no' irrespective of the type of invitation. That is, saying 'yes' to an invitation tends to be an extremely smooth sequence without gaps or any other indication of conversational hiccups. Refusing an invitation, on the other hand, produces problems in the conversation. For example, there is likely to be a measurable delay of half a second between invitation and refusal. Similarly, 'umm' or 'well' is likely to come before the refusal. Palliative phrases such as 'That's really kind of you but . . . ' may be used. Finally, refusal is likely to be followed by justifications or excuses for the refusal, whereas acceptance requires no justification. Kitzinger and Frith (2001) argue that date rape prevention programmes fail by not recognising the everyday difficulties inherent in refusing an invitation. That it is problematic (even when refusing sexual intercourse) can be seen in the following exchange between two young women:

Liz: It just doesn't seem right to say no when you're up there in the situation.

Sara: It's not rude, it's not rude – just sounds awful to say this, doesn't it.

Liz: I know.

Sara: It's not rude, but it's the same sort of feeling. It's like, 'oh my god, I can't say no now, can I?'

(Kitzinger & Frith, 2001, p. 175)

Using a focus group methodology, Kitzinger and Frith (2001) found that young women who participated in these groups deal with the problem of refusing sexual intercourse on dates by 'softening the blow' with a 'more acceptable excuse':

> . . . young women talk about good excuses as being those which assert their inability (rather than their unwillingness) to comply with the demand that they engage in sexual intercourse: from the vague (and perhaps, for that reason, irrefutable) statement that they are 'not ready', through to sickness and menstruation.

(Kitzinger & Frith, 2001, p. 176)

24.4 Conclusion

Conversation analysis provides psychology with an array of analytical tools and methods that may benefit a range of fields of application. Nevertheless, essentially conversation analysis springs from rather different intellectual roots from those of the bulk of mainstream psychology and specifically excludes from consideration many quintessential psychological approaches. Furthermore, in terms of detailed methodological considerations, conversation analysis reverses many of the conventional principles of mainstream research methods. For example, the context of the conversation studied is not a particular concern of conversation analysts, so detail about sampling and so forth may appear inadequate. This reversal of many of the assumptions of conventional psychological research methods warrants the attention of all researchers, as it helps define the assumptions of conventional research. That is, to understand something about conversation analysis is to understand more about the characteristics of mainstream psychology.

As in other areas of qualitative research, some practitioners are gradually beginning to advocate the use of quantification in the analysis of data. This is obviously not popular with all qualitative researchers. However, if a conversation analyst makes claims which imply that there are certain relationships between one feature of conversation and another, it might seem perverse to a mainstream psychologist not to examine the likelihood that one feature of conversation will follow another.

Conversation analysis and discourse analysis have moved closer together in recent years and it is difficult to separate one from the other.

Key points

- Conversation analysis emerged in the 1960s in the context of developments in sociological theory.

- Ethnomethodology was developed by Garfinkel almost as the reversal of the grand-scale sociological theories of the time. Ethnomethodology concerned itself with everyday understanding of ordinary events constructed by ordinary people.

- Harvey Sacks is considered to be the founder of conversation analysis. His interest was in the way conversation is structured around turns and how each turn melds with the earlier and later turns.

- Conversation analysis requires a detailed analysis and comparison of the minutiae of conversation as conversation. It draws little on resources outside the conversation (such as the social context, psychological characteristics of the individuals and so forth).

- Superficially, some of the features characteristic of conversation analysis may seem extremely sloppy. For example, the downplaying of the established research literature in the field prior to the study of data, the lack of contextual material on the conversation and the apparent lack of concern over such matters as sampling are reversals of the usual standards of psychological research.

- Carrying out conversation analysis involves the researcher in close analysis of the data in a number of ways. In particular, the Jefferson conversation transcription system encourages the researcher to examine the detail rather than the broad thrust of conversation. The transcription is interpreted, reinterpreted, checked and compared with other transcriptions of similar material in the belief that there is something 'there' for the analyst.

- Conversation analysis is commonly applied to the most mundane of material. Its primary concern, after all, is understanding the structure of ordinary or routine conversation. However, the insights concerning ordinary conversation highlight issues for researchers attempting to understand less ordinary situations.

ACTIVITIES

1. Collect samples of conversation by recording 'natural' conversations. Does turn-taking differ between genders? Does turn-taking differ cross-gender? Is there any evidence that 'repairs' to 'errors' in the conversation tend to be left to the 'error-maker'?

2. Make a list of points which explain what is going on in an episode of conversation. Which of your points would be acceptable to a conversation analyst? Which of your points involve considerations beyond the episode, such as psychological motives or intentions, or sociological factors such as social class?

3. Charles Antaki has a conversation analysis tutorial at http://ca-tutorials.lboro.ac.uk/sitemenu.htm. Go to this site and click on the link to 'Introductory tutorial on Conversation Analysis' to work through the exercises there to get an interesting, practical, hands-on insight into this form of analysis, which includes the source material in the form of a video.

CHAPTER 25

Interpretative phenomenological analysis

Overview

- Phenomenology has been part of psychology's rich legacy for many years following its introduction early in the twentieth century, through the philosopher Edmund Husserl's work. The writings of Amedeo Giorgi have had a modest impact on psychology since the 1960s.

- Interpretative phenomenological analysis (IPA) has roots in phenomenology and close links with hermeneutics and symbolic interactionism. Originating in the 1990s with the writings of Jonathan Smith, IPA is a modern, psychology-based qualitative method widely adopted by researchers in health studies, social psychology, clinical psychology etc.

- IPA's primary concern is in systematically obtaining and describing personal experiences of significant life events such as illness. Additionally, it seeks to interpret the psychological processes underlying these experiences. So it aims to explain people's accounts of their experiences in psychological terms. IPA assumes that people try to make sense of their experiences, and the method describes how they do this and the possible underlying meaning of their experiences.

- IPA researchers generally use semi-structured interviews in which people freely recall their experiences in order to obtain their data. However, IPA is not restricted to this, and other sources of accounts can be used. The questioning style used ideally encourages participants to talk about their experiences at length.

- Interview recordings are transcribed in a literal, secretarial style, though other information may be included if appropriate.

- The account is read several times to enable the researcher to become familiar with the material. Any impressions may be noted in the left-hand margin of the account as it is being read. There is no set way of doing this and no rules that must be followed.

- After familiarising themselves with the account, the researcher looks for themes in the material. Although themes are clearly related to what was said, they are usually expressed at a slightly more abstract or theoretical level than the original words. Themes are usually described in terms of short phrases of only a few words which are written in the right-hand margin of the account.

- Once the main themes have been identified, the researcher tries to group them together in broader and more encompassing superordinate themes. These superordinate themes and their subordinate components may be listed in a table in order of their assumed importance, starting with the most important. Next to each theme may be a short verbatim example which illustrates it, together with a note of its location in the account.

- The themes that have been identified are discussed in terms of the existing literature on that topic in the report.

- IPA, unlike some other forms of qualitative analysis, deals with internal psychological processes and does not eschew the use of psychology in general as part of the understanding of people's experiences.

25.1   Introduction

Interpretative phenomenological analysis (IPA) is a modern qualitative method which has rapidly grown in influence since Jonathan Smith first outlined it in the mid-1990s (Smith, 1996). It has formed the basis of numerous research studies and articles in peer-reviewed journals and books since then. While originally the application of IPA was in the fields of health and clinical psychology, it has increasingly been applied more widely. Smith and Eatough (2019) claim that over the last 25 years or so it has established itself internationally as an experiential qualitative method throughout the world. Its influence has spread into the humanities, organisation studies, and sports science. As its name implies, its primary concern is with providing a detailed description and interpretation of the accounts of particular experiences or phenomena as told by an individual or a small number of individuals.

A basic assumption of IPA is that people try to make sense of their experiences and understanding how they do that is part of an IPA study's aims. So the IPA researcher needs to (a) describe people's experiences effectively and (b) try to give meaning to these experiences. In other words, in part, the researcher attempts to interpret the interpretations of the individual. IPA acknowledges, however, that the researcher's own conceptions form the basis of the understanding of the phenomenological world of the person who is being studied. This means that the researcher can never entirely know this personal world but can only approach somewhere towards accessing it.

Interpretative phenomenological analysis has been used to address a wide variety of research questions. These include the experience of chronic back pain, transition to a non-smoker identity, the role of alcohol in unprotected sex, the return to normal life following spinal cord injury, and the experience of paranoia. Notice that these are fairly open and general research questions, and specific hypotheses are not involved. Smith (2019) argues that although IPA can be applied to a wide range of research topics, it is especially powerful when applied to topics which encourage people to personally seek an understanding of what they are going through. These are described as emotionally 'hot' for obvious reasons but result in possibly long-term attempts to imbue meaning to their experiences. This can involve the implications of the experience for their identity or a search for the meaning to life, for example.

25.2 Philosophical foundations of interpretative phenomenological analysis

It is important when trying to understand a research method to appreciate precisely what set of ideas one is 'buying into' if that particular method is to be adopted. This can be difficult, since the underlying assumptions of the major psychological methods are rarely directly spelt out by their advocates. This is particularly the case for much of the psychology which dominates introductory psychology textbooks and lectures. Earlier (Chapter 18), we explained the assumptions of logical positivism, which is at the root of much of what is written and taught as psychology. Its assumptions are not shared by all psychological methods, as was explained. Qualitative methods, in particular, generally reject most if not all of the assumptions of logical positivism and of positivism more generally. So a mature and proper understanding of research methods such as interpretative phenomenological analysis requires that their philosophical basis is clear to the researcher.

So just like all other forms of qualitative analysis, IPA has its own philosophical and theoretical roots. It may share some of the assumptions of other forms of qualitative analysis but does not necessarily give the same weight to each as other qualitative approaches. Shinebourne (2011) provides probably the most thorough account of the philosophical basis of IPA. Not surprisingly, phenomenology contributes a great deal, as do symbolic interactionism and hermeneutics (see Figure 25.1):

- *Phenomenology* is the study of conscious experiences. Its origins lie in the work of the Austrian-born German philosopher Edmund Husserl in *Logische Untersuchungen* (1900), translated as *Logical investigations* (1970), though he first used the term in a later book published in 1913, *Ideen zu einer reinen Phänomenologie und phänomenologischen Philosophie,* translated as *Ideas: A general introduction to pure phenomenology* (1962). Phenomenology is a philosophical movement which actively rejected the influential idea of the philosopher René Descartes that there is an objective physical world which exists independently of the mind – this is known as Cartesian Dualism or the body–mind problem. Dualism and the body–mind problem are fundamental

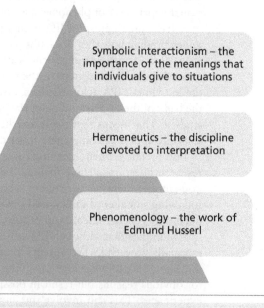

FIGURE 25.1 Roots of interpretative phenomenological analysis

philosophical problems in psychology. Just how can the mind (which is not physical) interact with the physical world? Husserl's argument was that we cannot know the physical world (or even whether it exists) except in terms of how it is experienced through human consciousness. In other words, Husserl's phenomenology eschews the idea of an objective reality independent of human experience. For Husserl, the task of phenomenology was to study things as experienced through consciousness. In order to do this, it is important to isolate the conscious experience from our thoughts about that experience. Reality can only be 'known' through how it is experienced by consciousness. So in phenomenology, the method of bracketing is used in an attempt to know what the pure experience is. The pure experience is not a matter of language, but the difficulty is that we speak of the pure experience through language. The phenomena studied from a phenomenological perspective include some familiar and some less familiar psychological concepts such as thought, memory, social action, desire and volition.

● While Husserl is usually described as a philosopher, the distinction between philosophy and psychology was not so strong when he was writing as it is now. So, important early psychologists such as Franz Brentano were particularly influential on Husserl. It was from Brentano that Husserl took the idea that consciousness involves intentionality – that is, consciousness is always of something and there is no consciousness without it being consciousness of something. The main thing that interpretative phenomenological analysis takes from phenomenology is its focus on conscious experience – how things like pain are experienced. Phenomenology in different guises had major influences on twentieth-century academic thinking, including the existentialism of such people as Jean-Paul Sartre and, in American sociology, major developments such as ethnomethodology (Chapter 24). See Figure 25.2 for a summary of the major figures in the development of phenomenology and Box 25.1 for more on phenomenology and psychology.

Rene Descartes 1596–1650	• Phenomenology rejected the ideas that Descartes had struggled to promote. In particular, the idea that the physical world (or the body) can meaningfully be distinguished from the mind which is non-physical. This is known as Cartesian Dualism. The term 'the body–mind problem' is used to refer to the essential problem of just how the non-physical mind can communicate with the physical body (and hence physical reality)
Edmund Husserl 1889–1938	• Husserl is a major figure in phenomenology. His primary task was to establish what could be known about 'reality' – and he concluded that the direct experience of phenomena through our conciousness was the only valid source of such knowledge • His important concepts include epoche and bracketing – the exclusion of all cognitions but for the direct experiences of consciousness • The idea of the life world or the lived world is central and refers to the focus of phenomenology on things as they are experienced.
Martin Heidegger 1889–1976	• Heidegger is held to be important in phenomenology since he emphasised the importance of meaning in phenomenology. • Hermeneutics provides a prerequisite for phenomenology since it is the method by which the meaning of texts may be uncovered. • There is always a prior historical, cultural and social context for the experienced phenomenon. Because of this, phenomenology should be seen as a profoundly social and cultural discipline – it is not primarily about a world constructed within the mind of the individual.
Amedeo Giorgi 1931–	• More than any other psychologist, Giorgi took Husserl's philosophical ideas and turned them into a systematic and practical psychological phenomenological method. • His work was the major focus for phenomenology in psychology prior to the development of Interpretative Phenomenological Analysis by Jonathan Smith.

FIGURE 25.2   Major figures in the development of phenomenology

- *Symbolic interactionism* assumes that the mind and the self emerge out of social interactions involving significant communications. It is a *sociological approach* to small-scale social phenomena rather than major social structures and so has had a substantial influence on social psychological thinking. Probably the best example of this influence is the work of Erving Goffman. Goffman's highly influential book *Asylums,* published in 1961, examined institutionalisation – a term which describes patients' reactions to the structures of total institutions such as mental hospitals. In order to understand interaction in these contexts, Goffman adopted the basic phenomenological perspective. George Herbert Mead was the major influence in the development of symbolic interactionism, though the term is actually that of Herbert Blumer.

- Symbolic interactionism regards mind and self as developing through social interaction, which constitutes the dominant aspect of the individual's experiences of the world. Of course, these social processes and social communication exist prior to any individual, so, in this sense, the social is the explanation of the psychology of the individual. The conversation of gestures is an early stage in which the baby communicates with others in that they respond to the baby's gestures although the child is unaware of this. This is communication without conscious intent. However, out of this the baby and child progresses towards the more advanced forms of social communication whereby they can communicate through the use of significant symbols. Significant symbols are those in which the sender of the communication has the same understanding of the communication as those who receive the communication. Language consists of communication using such significant symbols. Communication is not an individual act but one involving two individuals at a minimum. It provides the basic unit through which meaning is learnt and established, and meaning is dependent on interactions between individuals. The process is one in which there is a sender, a receiver *and* a consequence of the communication. In this way, the mind and understanding of self begin to arise. Of course, there develops an intentionality in communication, because the child learns to anticipate the responses of other individuals to the communication and can use them to achieve the desired response from others. So the self is purposive. It is in the context of communication or social interaction that the meaning of the social world comes about.

- *Hermeneutics* is, according to its Greek roots, the analysis of messages. It is about how we study and understand texts in particular. As a consequence of the influential Algerian/French philosopher Jacques Derrida, a text in this context is not merely something written down but can include anything that people interpret in their day-to-day lives, which includes their experiences. It is relevant to interpretative phenomenological analysis because of its emphasis on understanding things from the point of view of others. Meaning is a social and a cultural product and hermeneutics applies this basic conceptualisation to anything which has meaning. So it can be applied to many aspects of human activity which seem far removed from the biblical texts to which the term 'hermeneutics' originally applied. But the wider usage of the term 'hermeneutics' gives a primacy to matters to which tradition makes an important contribution.

- Hermeneutics, therefore, studies the meaning and importance of a wide range of human activity primarily from the first-person perspective. Looking at parts of the text in relation to the entirety of the text in a sort of looping process leads to understanding the meaning of the text. Hermeneutics is also responsible for originating the term 'deconstruction'. This was introduced by the German philosopher Martin Heidegger but with a different emphasis from its modern usage. Basically, he realised that the interpretation of texts tended to be influenced by the person interpreting the text. In other words, the interpreter was constructing a meaning of the text which may be different in some respects from the original meaning of the text. So, in order to understand the influence of these interpretations, one needs to deconstruct the interpretations to reveal the contributing constructions of the interpreters. Religious texts are clearly examples where constructions by interpreters essentially alter the meanings of texts. Thus there are various constructions of Islam, though the original texts on which each is based are the same. However, deconstruction under the influence of Derrida has come to mean a form of criticism of the interpreter's influence on the meaning of the text, whereas it was originally merely the identification of traditions of the understanding of text.

It is easy to see aspects of interpretative phenomenological analysis in phenomenology, symbolic interactionism and hermeneutics. However, analysts using the method do not simply take what the studied individual has to say as their interpretation. The analyst adds to the interpretation and does not act with straightforward empathy to the individual being studied. The approach includes what Smith and Osborn (2003) describe as a questioning hermeneutics (see later). To illustrate this they offer the following comment:

> . . . IPA is concerned with trying to understand what it is like, from the point of view of the participants, to take their side. At the same time, a detailed IPA analysis can also involve asking critical questions of the texts from participants, such as the following: What is the person trying to achieve here? Is something leaking out here that wasn't intended? Do I have a sense of something going on here that maybe the participants themselves are less aware of? (p. 51)

In this, the need for the use of the word 'interpretative' in interpretative phenomenological analysis becomes apparent, since the researcher is being encouraged not simply to take the interpretative side of the participant in the research but to question that interpretation in various ways. These are tantamount to critical deconstructions.

Box 25.1   Key Ideas

Giorgi's phenomenological method

Phenomenological research has been part of psychology from as early as the 1930s, though much of the early work can be traced to a few geographically and intellectually isolated psychologists (Giorgi, 2010). The phenomenological psychology of Amedeo Giorgi was different in that it encouraged the development of phenomenological psychology worldwide.

Giorgi had trained in conventional mainstream psychology in the 1950s but, importantly, in the 1960s he moved to Duquesne University in the USA. This university was unusual, since there was already an interest in Husserl's phenomenology among the psychologists there as well as in the sociology department. This context stimulated Giorgi to explore alternatives to the mainstream psychology that he had received his training in. So he read widely, including the works of Edmund Husserl as well as Husserl's 'followers', Martin Heidegger and Maurice Merleau-Ponty – the major founders of phenomenology – and many others. Giorgi led the search with co-workers at Duquesne to

develop a workable system, based on psychology, for doing phenomenological research. Giorgi modelled his work closely on the ideas of Husserl and, not surprisingly, one can regard Giorgi's work as Husserlian phenomenological psychology. One of the dominant ideas taken from Husserl was the emphasis on describing the phenomenon as experienced in the conscious mind by people. That is to say, Giorgi was primarily concerned not with understanding the meaning of the conscious experience (this was left to those following Heidegger and Merleau-Ponty) but with describing, with as much fidelity to the experience as possible, just how people experienced things like love, bereavement, envy and so forth.

As this implies, Giorgi's methods are primarily concerned with describing phenomena as experienced by individuals in detail and accurately. As with Husserl, the emphasis of Giorgi was on describing the phenomenon rather than an individual's experience of the phenomenon. So Giorgi uses the experiences of a number of individuals in an attempt

→

to see what the general experience of the phenomenon is. He writes about identifying the structure of the phenomenon. As a consequence, some find Giorgi's work rather like a catalogue of descriptions of phenomena. Unlike in IPA, there is no emphasis on understanding the individual for its own sake. So it is important in Giorgi's method that the researcher obtains descriptions of experiences which are as accurate as possible to the original experience itself. In a very real sense, the pure experience is pre-linguistic, though, of course, it has to be expressed linguistically. There is a problem with this, of course, as Husserl pointed out – that is, although the aim is to obtain detail of how the phenomenon is experienced when it is experienced, it is difficult to separate these experiences from thoughts such as reflections, evaluations and beliefs about the experience of the phenomenon. An experience may readily be confused with our thoughts about it, which means that the pure experience is hidden or lost. Husserl uses the term 'bracketing' to refer to the process by which these extraneous factors added to the pure experience are 'ignored', leaving the pure experience. Although this concept is controversial among phenomenological researchers because of the impossibility of achieving such a state, it is nevertheless the ideal towards which most researchers aim, despite knowing the limitations on doing so. This also extends to the activities of the researcher who should avoid presuppositions about the meaning of what their research participants tell them. This suspension of one's own presuppositions is essential if the analysis is to understand the participant's conscious experience (lived experience) rather than the researcher's own ideas.

Any source of descriptions of experience can be used, such as poetry, but the use of interviews is much more common. In Giorgi's method, the aim is to understand the structure of experience (or lived experience, as it is referred to) rather than to understand a single individual. So the experiences of a number of participants of a particular phenomenon are essentially combined in order to understand this more general structure. The phenomenological interview usually starts with the researcher asking the participant to describe a concrete example of the phenomenon that the research is concerned with (e.g. an instance of jealousy or an instance of grief). During the interview, the researcher may ask for more detail, clarification, examples and so forth in order to maximise the clarity of the description as well as its completeness.

There is no standard way of doing phenomenological research and different researchers will vary the procedure somewhat. Giorgi (1985) uses a four-stage approach:

- Stage 1: This involves an intensive reading of the material in detail over and over again.

- Stage 2: Following this, the researcher should be able to identify the 'meaning units' in the participant's descriptions. A meaning unit consists of a few words or a few sentences, usually, which express a clear idea about the experience of the phenomenon. The meaning unit is complete in itself and would lose its meaning if some part of the unit were omitted or were not there. By underlining or otherwise marking each of these 'units', the researcher's attention becomes more focused on the different things that the participant is saying about their experiences.

- Stage 3: The analysis then takes what the participant has said in each of these meaning units and re-expresses them in more psychological or abstract language.

- Stage 4: The final stage is to produce a list of descriptive dimensions of the phenomenon which account for the ways in which the various participants in the research experience the phenomenon in question. These are primarily dimensions or aspects used to describe the phenomenon; they are not the ways in which the participants differ in their experiences of the phenomenon. In other words, they are the characteristic features of the phenomenon. The researcher may wish to draw attention to unusual or idiosyncratic cases, but this is not the main focus of the analysis which is on the phenomenon as experienced by the participants.

This rather abstract discussion can be made more concrete by describing a study by Robbins and Parlavecchio (2006) into the experience of embarrassment. There are numerous situations in which embarrassment is experienced. These include things such as tripping in public and other physical pratfalls, errors of memory, public displays of emotion and lapses in privacy. There is, however, very little consensus in the research literature on just what embarrassment is and just how it differs from shame, for example. Robbins and Parlavecchio proposed that, at its core, embarrassment occurs in situations (accidental or deliberate) where the core of the self has been exposed by being brought to unwanted attention in a social setting. This model can be referred to as the unwanted exposure model. This is different from other models such as the personal standards model of Babcock (1988), which holds that embarrassment is the result of a failure to live up to one's personal standards. In Babcock's model, it is the evaluation of oneself rather than that of others which results in the embarrassment. The unwanted exposure model therefore suggests that embarrassment occurs when events conspire to reveal something to others or themselves which the person prefers to keep hidden. In itself, becoming the centre of attention does not necessarily result in the individual becoming embarrassed, but it does do so where the event leads to something that the individual wants to keep hidden being revealed in public. So, for example, a modest and unassuming person who receives recognition for a brave act may be embarrassed, because this reveals that their modest persona belies an exceptional individual. Another example would be an individual asking for the return of a loan – the embarrassment may be because asking for one's money back may reveal that one is short of cash oneself.

The research by Robbins and Parlavecchio involved three male and three female college students who were asked to write independently a reply to the following as concretely as possible: 'a situation in which you experienced embarrassment. Include as much detail as you can, including what led up to the situation, how the experience showed itself, and any resolutions that may have occurred'. These written reports were used as part of interviews with the students to gather more information. That is, the researcher read the student's report to them aloud and paused from time to time when the student was to provide additional information. The narrative and the interview were transcribed for analytic purposes.

The analysis followed broadly the phenomenological method of Giorgi (1985) described above, but each researcher carried out their analysis independently of the other. Their analyses were given to a class of students studying qualitative research who provided feedback to the researchers. The differences between the researchers were resolved through discussion between the class and the researchers. The stages of the analysis are given in Figure 25.3. This is a slightly extended version of the essential analytic steps as provided by Giorgi, discussed above, but gives a good idea about the process involved in Robbins and Parlavecchio's study. In generating the more general themes, the researchers used a process known as imaginative variation. This involves the researcher asking themselves whether any of the elements of the general themes could be modified, changed or omitted without changing the nature of the phenomenon being described. In other words, what in the general themes could be different for the phenomenon to no longer be embarrassment? In this way, the nature of the phenomenon is clarified. Imaginative variation is a method used in the classic formulations of phenomenology.

Among the instances of embarrassing situations was the example of a student who was going to a meal at the hall of residence. Being Sunday, the student was wearing his pyjama trousers and a pair of flip flops which were worn and slippery. The student put his meal on the tray but, not noticing a wet patch on the floor, he slipped on the wet floor and ended up on his backside on the floor:

> As I was falling everything felt like it was moving in slow motion, but it came so quick and unexpected. It's hard to explain, it was one of those moments – you could feel yourself physically falling but you couldn't do anything else to stop it and you knew you were gonna end up on the ground, but it came so quick, it was before you realized what had happened. So, it was like an instant, but dragged out. It totally caught me by surprise but I knew it was happening when it had started. I was taken by surprise when I found myself on the ground. My tray of food came crashing to the ground, I could see myself the way other people could see me, and oh my God I can't believe that just happened. There was a sense of being looked at and all the attention was on me and pretty much made me want to disappear . . . I wanted to crawl inside myself to avoid the stares of the crowded dining room onlookers . . . Before I made any more of a fool of myself in front of all those people, I stood up and walked straight to the back of the dining hall, sat with my friends and acted as if nothing happened. I did not even want to think about what had just happened let alone talk about it. After something really embarrassing happens you don't want to relive it, you don't want to tell people about what just happened because it just happened.

(Robbins & Parlavecchio, 2006, pp. 335–336)

A number of general themes were identified from this example and the others studied. There is not enough space here to give the full details of the examples, but the following themes were common to them all:

1. Embarrassment occurred in an interpersonal situation such as the dining hall or some other similar context.

2. The behaviour which led to the embarrassment was unintended and much to the surprise of the individual (e.g. as in the case of double entendre) or else it was really out of the ordinary for that individual.

3. There was a point of realisation of just what had happened which preceded the feeling of embarrassment.

4. The focus of the evaluation of the event as being in some way unacceptable was through the eyes of those witnessing the event rather than the person who had experienced the event.

→

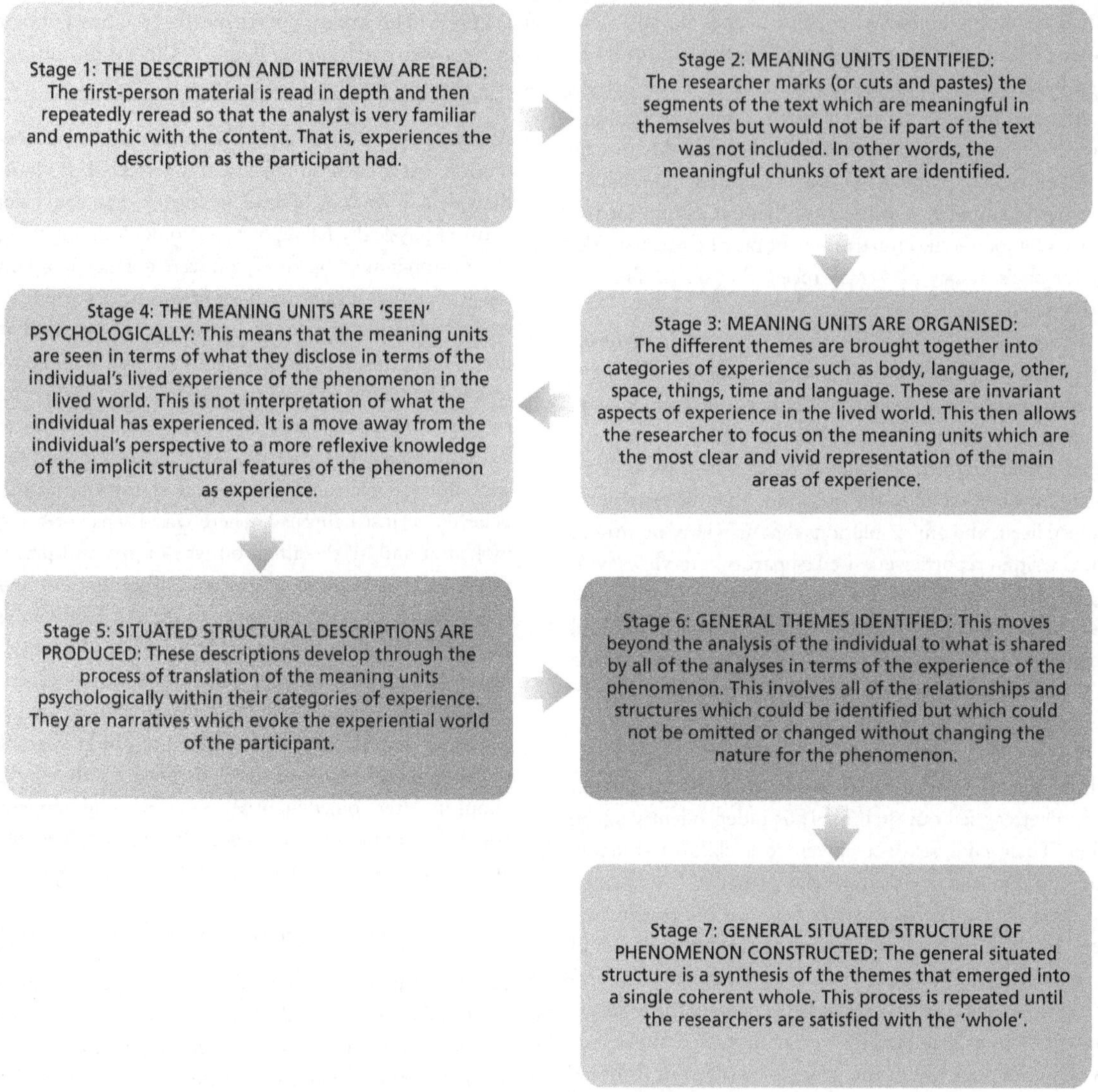

Stage 1: THE DESCRIPTION AND INTERVIEW ARE READ: The first-person material is read in depth and then repeatedly reread so that the analyst is very familiar and empathic with the content. That is, experiences the description as the participant had.

Stage 2: MEANING UNITS IDENTIFIED: The researcher marks (or cuts and pastes) the segments of the text which are meaningful in themselves but would not be if part of the text was not included. In other words, the meaningful chunks of text are identified.

Stage 4: THE MEANING UNITS ARE 'SEEN' PSYCHOLOGICALLY: This means that the meaning units are seen in terms of what they disclose in terms of the individual's lived experience of the phenomenon in the lived world. This is not interpretation of what the individual has experienced. It is a move away from the individual's perspective to a more reflexive knowledge of the implicit structural features of the phenomenon as experience.

Stage 3: MEANING UNITS ARE ORGANISED: The different themes are brought together into categories of experience such as body, language, other, space, things, time and language. These are invariant aspects of experience in the lived world. This then allows the researcher to focus on the meaning units which are the most clear and vivid representation of the main areas of experience.

Stage 5: SITUATED STRUCTURAL DESCRIPTIONS ARE PRODUCED: These descriptions develop through the process of translation of the meaning units psychologically within their categories of experience. They are narratives which evoke the experiential world of the participant.

Stage 6: GENERAL THEMES IDENTIFIED: This moves beyond the analysis of the individual to what is shared by all of the analyses in terms of the experience of the phenomenon. This involves all of the relationships and structures which could be identified but which could not be omitted or changed without changing the nature for the phenomenon.

Stage 7: GENERAL SITUATED STRUCTURE OF PHENOMENON CONSTRUCTED: The general situated structure is a synthesis of the themes that emerged into a single coherent whole. This process is repeated until the researchers are satisfied with the 'whole'.

FIGURE 25.3 Stages of the phenomenological analysis

5. The person who had been subject to the events saw what they had done negatively in terms of how those witnessing the event would construe it.

6. The individual in some way thought of getting out of the situation into one where they were not the object of the evaluative gaze of others.

7. The 'self' exposed in the incident was experienced by the individual as being an alienated, corporeal body

which often experienced the bodily expression of embarrassment such as blushing.

The phenomenological analysis seems to support Robbins and Parlavecchio's unwanted exposure model of embarrassment much better than, say, Babcock's (1988) personal standards model. It is fairly obvious that the structure of embarrassment identified in this study goes far beyond Babcock's approach and firmly calls for the sort of model that Robbins and Parlavecchio proposed.

25.3 Stages in interpretative phenomenological analysis

The key to interpretative phenomenological analysis lies in the nature of the data which IPA deals with – that is, the detail of people's experiences of significant happenings in their lives. This is quite different from other forms of qualitative analysis in which a particular domain of content may not be so important. Whatever the textual material used for IPA, it needs to involve detailed accounts of experiences. Not all textual material does this. Of course, the obvious way of obtaining rich textual material is to interview people about important things which happened in their lives. So long as the researcher takes care to maximise the richness of the description obtained by using carefully thought out and relevant questions, a semi-structured interview will generally be the appropriate form of data collection, though not exclusively so.

Smith and his colleagues have described how an IPA study is carried out (Smith & Eatough, 2006; Smith, Flowers, & Larkin, 2009; Smith & Osborn, 2003). They acknowledge that other researchers may adapt the method to suit their own particular interests, that is, the method is not highly prescriptive and is generally flexible in terms of implementation. For example, there has been a substantial growth in the use of longitudinal designs in IPA research. This was probably inevitable given that significant life experiences are usually transitional in nature. Farr and Nizza (2019) document this growth and find that predominantly health-related topics are involved and interviews employed.

Usually a great deal depends on the semi-structured interviews employed. The IPA interview consists of a series of open questions designed to enable participants to provide lengthy and detailed answers in their own words to the questions asked by the researcher. As with any other study, piloting of the research instruments is advisable, so the IPA researcher should try out their questions on a few participants. In this way, the researcher can check to make sure that the questions are suitable for their purpose, that is, the participants answer freely in terms of their experiences and views.

There are two major aspects of interpretative phenomenological analysis:

● Data collection

● Data analysis.

We will deal with each of these in turn (see Figure 25.4).

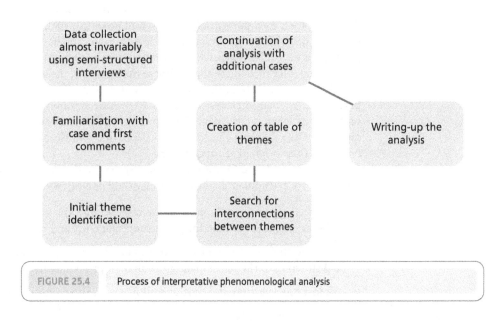

FIGURE 25.4   Process of interpretative phenomenological analysis

▦ Data collection

Smith and Osborn (2003) go into detail about the formulation of research questions in interpretative phenomenological analysis. There is no specific hypothesis as such, since the approach is exploratory of the area of experience that the researcher is concerned with. However, generally the IPA research question is to find out the perceptions that the individual has concerning a given situation they experience and how they make sense of these experiences.

Although IPA uses semi-structured interviews to provide data, any suitable rich textual data may also be used. Other forms of personal account such as diaries or autobiographical material may be appropriate depending on their content. IPA interviews are intended to be applied flexibly. So the questions are not read to the participant in a fixed order, since the intention is that the interviewer should be free to probe matters of interest which arise during the course of the interview. In particular, the interview can be led by the participant's particular issues rather than simply being imposed by the researcher. To some extent, the researcher can pre-plan the sorts of additional probes which are asked of participants in order to get them to supply more information on a particular topic. Consequently, these probes can be included in the interview schedule. Smith and Osborn (2003, pp. 61–62) provide advice on how to construct the interview questions:

- Questions should be neutral rather than value-laden or leading.

- Avoid jargon or assumptions of technical proficiency.

- Use open, not closed, questions.

Generally, this is the sort of advice appropriate for framing questions for any in-depth interviewing strategy aimed at eliciting rich data (see Chapter 19).

The semi-structured interview usually opens with a general question which is normally followed by more specific questions. For example, in a study on back pain, the researcher may begin by asking a participant to describe their pain before asking how it started and whether or not anything affects it (Smith & Osborn, 2007). The researcher should memorise the interview schedule so that the interview can flow more smoothly and naturally. The order in which the questions are asked and the nature of the questions asked may vary according to what the participant says. So, if the participant has already provided information to a question that has yet to be asked, there is no need to obtain that information again by asking that question. For example, if in answer to the first question on describing their pain the participant also said how it started, it would not be appropriate to ask the question on how it had started, as this question has already been answered. The participant may raise issues which the researcher had not anticipated and which seem of interest and relevance to the topic. Where this happens, the researcher may wish to question the participant about these matters, even though questions on these issues were not part of the original interview schedule. The researcher may decide to include questions on this issue when interviewing subsequent cases. In other words, researchers should be sensitive to the material that participants provide and should not necessarily be totally bound by their original set of questions.

However, Smith and Osborn (2003, p. 63) suggest that good interviewing technique in interpretative phenomenological analysis would comply with the following:

- Avoid rushing to the main area of interest too quickly, as this may be quite personal and sensitive. It takes time for the appropriate trust and rapport to build up.

- While the effective use of probes ensures good-quality data, the overuse of probes can be distracting to the participant and can disrupt the quality of the narrative.

- Ask just one question at a time and allow the participant time to answer it properly.

- Be aware of the effect that the interview is having on the participant. Adjustments may need to be made to the style of questioning, etc., should there appear to be problems or difficulties.

The interview is usually sound-recorded, providing a full record of what has been said. Recording also has the advantage of allowing the researcher to pay closer attention to what is being said as the participant is speaking, since the interviewer is not preoccupied with the task of taking detailed notes as the interview progresses. Generally, the advice is to transcribe the interviews prior to analysis, since the resulting transcript is quicker to read and check than it is to locate and replay parts of the interview. Furthermore, a transcript makes it easier for the researcher to see the relation between the material and the analysis which is to be carried out. With interpretative phenomenological analysis, the transcription may be the literal secretarial-style transcription, which simply consists of a record of what was said. There is no need for the Jefferson-style transcription (Chapter 19), which includes other features of the interview such as voice inflections and pauses, though it is not debarred. However, in some circumstances, it may be worth noting some of these additional features such as expressions of emotions if these help convey better just what the participant in the interview has said. It would be usual to have wide margins on either side of the pages of the transcript where one can put one's comments as the transcribed material is being analysed. While making the transcription, the researcher should make a note of any thoughts or impressions they have about what the interviewee is saying, since otherwise these may be forgotten or overlooked subsequently. These comments may be put in the left-hand margin of the transcription next to the text to which they refer (the right-hand margin is used for identifying themes). This sort of transcription of the recording can take up to about eight times the time taken to play the recorded material; it cannot be rushed if the material is to be transcribed accurately.

Smith and his co-workers suggest, as do many other qualitative researchers, that because the process of data collection, transcription and analysis is time-consuming, it is possible to interview only a small number of participants. Published studies include one with as many participants as 64 (Coleman & Cater, 2005) though studies with a single participant are to be found also (e.g. Eatough & Smith, 2006). The size of sample thought suitable for a study will vary according to its aims and the resources the researcher has. So, for student projects, there may be time and resources available to deal with, maybe, only three to six cases. It is recommended by Smith and Osborn (2003) that the sample should consist of relatively similar (homogeneous) cases rather than extremely different ones. Interpretative phenomenological analysis is at its roots ideographic and primarily focused on the individual as someone to be understood. This is one reason why single-case studies are common and acceptable in this sort of analysis. Of course, research may move from what has been learnt of the one individual to others, but it focuses primarily on individuals to be understood in their own right. The distinction between ideographic and nomothetic approaches to knowledge was introduced into psychology in the 1930s by Gordon Allport, though the concepts were originally those of the German philosopher Wilhelm Windelband. Ideographic understanding concerns the individual as an individual in his or her own right and emphasises the ways in which that individual is different from other individuals. Nomothetic understanding is based on the study of groups of individuals who are seen as representing all individuals in that class. Hence it is possible in nomothetic approaches to formulate abstract laws or generalisations about people in general.

Data analysis

The analysis of the data is seen as consisting of four to six main stages, depending on the number and duration of interviews carried out. Many of these steps are very similar to those of other forms of qualitative analysis.

Step 1   Initial familiarisation with a case and initial comments

The researcher should become as familiar as possible with what a particular participant has said by reading and rereading the account or transcript a number of times. The researcher may use the left-hand margin of the document containing the account to write down anything of interest about the account that occurs to them. There are no rules about how this should be done. For example, the account does not have to be broken down into units of a specified size and there is no need to comment on all parts of the account. Some of the comments may be attempts at summarising or interpreting what was said. Later on, the comments may refer to confirmation, changes or inconsistencies in what was said.

There is some discussion in the IPA literature of the role of the 'gem' in an IPA analysis. This is a particular aspect of the data which strikes the researcher as intriguing, incongruous, or in some other way special. The gem can constitute both a focus for the analysis and a stimulus to analytic effort. This idea was first discussed by Smith (2011) and discussed in detail by Clifford, Craig and McCourt (2019). Not all data will stimulate the researcher in this way.

Step 2   Initial identification of themes

The researcher needs to reread the transcript to make a note of the major themes that are identified in the words of the participant. Each theme is summarised in as few words as necessary and this brief phrase may be written down in the right-hand margin of the transcription. The theme should be clearly related to what the participant has said but should express this material at a somewhat more abstract or theoretical level.

Step 3   Looking for connections between themes

The researcher needs to consider how the themes that have been identified can be grouped together in clusters to form broader or superordinate themes by looking at the connections between the original themes. So themes which seem to be similar may be listed together and given a more inclusive title. This process may be carried out electronically by 'copying and pasting' the names of the themes into a separate document. Alternatively, the names of the themes may be printed or written down on cards or slips of paper, placed on a large flat surface such as a table or floor and moved around to illustrate spatially the connections between them. It is important to make sure that the themes relate to what participants have said. This may be done by selecting a short phrase the participant used which exemplifies the original theme and noting the page and line number in the document where this is recorded. Other themes may be omitted because they do not readily fit into these larger clusters or there is little evidence for them.

Step 4   Producing a table of themes

This involves listing the groups of themes together with their subordinate component themes in a table. They are ordered in terms of their overall importance to what the participant was seen to have said, starting off with the most important superordinate theme. This listing may include a short phrase from a participant's account to illustrate the theme, with information about where this phrase is to be found, as was done in the previous stage. This is illustrated in Table 25.1 in Box 25.2.

Step 5   Continuing with further cases

Where there is more than one case, the analysis proceeds with the other cases in a similar way. Themes from the first case may be used to look for similar themes in the ensuing cases, or each case can be looked at anew. It is important for the analyst to be aware of themes that are similar between participants as well as those that differ between participants, as these may give an indication of the variation in the analysis. Once all the accounts have been analysed, one or more final tables containing all the themes need to be produced.

| Step 6 | Writing up the analysis |

The final stage is to write up the results of the analysis. The themes seen as being important to the analysis need to be described and illustrated with verbatim extracts which provide a clear and sufficient example of these themes. The researcher tries in the analysis write-up to interpret or make sense of what a participant has said. It should be made clear where interpretation is being provided and the basis on which it has been done. There are two ways of presenting the results in a report. One way is to divide the report into separate 'Results' and 'Discussion' sections. The 'Results' section should describe and illustrate the themes, while the 'Discussion' section should relate the themes to the existing literature on the topic. The other way is to have a single 'Results and discussion' section where the presentation of each theme is followed by a discussion of the literature that is relevant to that theme.

Before attempting to carry out an interpretative phenomenological analysis, it is important to familiarise yourself with the method by reading reports of other studies that have used this approach. There are many suitable studies to draw which can be accessed through PsycINFO. Choose those that seem most relevant to your research interests. As you are unlikely to anticipate the themes that emerge in your study, there is scope to look for research relevant to the themes that you identify.

IPA researchers have provided relatively detailed and clear explanations of their methods, including examples of the questions used to collect data and the stages in the analysis of the data, giving examples of codings and theme developments (Smith & Eatough, 2006; Smith & Osborn, 2003). These can be consulted in order to develop a finer-tuned understanding of the method.

Box 25.2   Research Example

Interpretative phenomenological analysis

Campbell, M. L. C., & Morrison, A. P. (2007). The subjective experience of paranoia: Comparing the experiences of patients with psychosis and individuals with no psychiatric history. *Clinical Psychology and Psychotherapy*, *14*, 63–77.

Campbell and Morrison (2007) studied how people experience paranoia. They point out that it has recently been established that the sort of persecutory ideas that characterise paranoia are exaggerations of normal psychological processes. For example, individuals who show non-clinical levels of paranoia also tend to demonstrate self-consciousness in both public and private situations. One possible consequence of this sort of self-examination process is that self-recognised shortcomings may be projected onto other people who are then seen as threatening in situations which are themselves in some way threatening. Negative beliefs that sufferers have about the condition of paranoia, the world in general, and the self are responsible for the distress caused by psychoses such as paranoia. Campbell and Morrison point out that there have been no previous studies that have investigated the subjective experience of paranoia.

→

Based on these considerations, Campbell and Morrison designed a study to explore subjective experiences of paranoia by comparing patients and non-patients. They had a group of six clinical patients and a group of six other individuals who had no clinical history, although they had endorsed two questions on the Peters Delusions Inventory. One of these asked whether they ever feel that they are being persecuted in some way, and the other asked whether they ever feel that there is a conspiracy against them.

The participants were interviewed using a semi-structured method. Questions were asked about a number of issues, including the following (Campbell & Morrison, 2007, p. 77):

- *Content of paranoia* For example, 'Can you tell me what sort of things you have been paranoid about?'

- *Beliefs about paranoia* For example, 'What are your thoughts about your paranoid ideas?'

- *Functions of paranoia* For example, 'Do you think that your paranoid ideas have any purpose?'

- *Traumatic life experiences* For example, 'Have you ever experienced anything very upsetting or distressing?'

- *Trauma and paranoia* For example, 'Do you think that your paranoid ideas relate to any of your past experiences?'

Through a process of reading and rereading each of the transcripts, initial thoughts and ideas about the data were noted in the left-hand margin of the transcripts and these led to the identification of themes which were noted in the right-hand margin of the transcripts. Following this, the researchers compiled a list of the themes which had been identified. Superordinate themes were then identified which brought together a number of themes. These superordinate themes may have been themes already identified but sometimes they were new concepts. Interestingly, the researchers checked their analysis with the participants in the research as a form of validity assessment, which led to some updating and revision of the themes where the analysis was not accepted by the participants.

The researchers suggested that there were four superordinate themes of note which emerged in the analysis and which they defined as:

1. The phenomenon of paranoia

2. Beliefs about paranoia

3. Factors that influence paranoia

4. The consequences of paranoia.

They produced tables which illustrate these superordinate themes, the 'master' themes which are grouped together under this heading, and the subcategories of each 'master' theme. So, by way of illustration, we can take the first superordinate theme, described as the phenomenon of paranoia. This includes three master themes: (A) the content of paranoia; (B) the nature of paranoia; and (C) insight into paranoia. Again by way of illustration, we can take the first of these master themes, the content of paranoia, which breaks down into the following subcategories: (a) perception of harm; (b) type of harm; (c) intention of harm; and (d) acceptability of the belief. In their discussion, Campbell and Morrison illustrate each of the subcategories by a representative quotation taken from the transcripts of the data. This is done in the form of tables – there is one for each of the superordinate themes. Each master theme is presented and each subcategory listed under that heading. It is the subcategories which are illustrated by a quotation. Although this is a simple procedure, it is highly effective, because the reader has each subcategory illustrated but by looking at the material for all of the subcategories the 'master' theme is also illustrated. The general format of this is illustrated in Table 25.1. We have only partially given detail in the table to keep it as simple as possible in appearance and we have used fictitious quotes. Of course, this tabular presentation limits the lengths of quotations used and, inevitably, results in numerous tables in some cases. Thus it is only suitable when the number of superordinate themes is relatively small, since this determines the number of tables. Nevertheless, the systematic nature of the tabular presentations adds clarity to the presentation of the analysis.

A further feature of the analysis, not entirely typical of qualitative analyses in general, was the comparison between the clinical group and the normal group in terms of paranoia. For example, in terms of 'intention of harm' it was found that there was a difference between the two groups. For the normal group, the harm tended to be social harm, whereas for the patient group it tended to be physical or psychological harm.

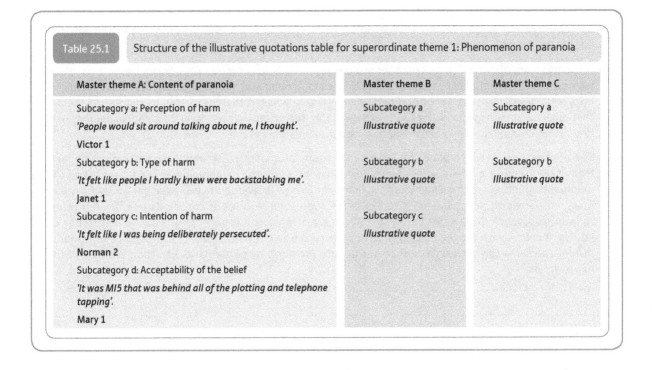

Table 25.1   Structure of the illustrative quotations table for superordinate theme 1: Phenomenon of paranoia

Master theme A: Content of paranoia	Master theme B	Master theme C
Subcategory a: Perception of harm	Subcategory a	Subcategory a
'People would sit around talking about me, I thought'.	*Illustrative quote*	*Illustrative quote*
Victor 1		
Subcategory b: Type of harm	Subcategory b	Subcategory b
'It felt like people I hardly knew were backstabbing me'.	*Illustrative quote*	*Illustrative quote*
Janet 1		
Subcategory c: Intention of harm	Subcategory c	
'It felt like I was being deliberately persecuted'.	*Illustrative quote*	
Norman 2		
Subcategory d: Acceptability of the belief		
'It was MI5 that was behind all of the plotting and telephone tapping'.		
Mary 1		

25.4   Conclusion

Interpretative phenomenological analysis (IPA) can be seen as a much more specific approach to qualitative research than, say, thematic analysis or grounded theory and discourse analysis or conversation analysis. Discourse analysis is really a theory of language-as-action and so can be seen as part of a theory of language use and its application. It focuses on how we talk about things. Conversation analysis is a very fine-grained approach to the study of how conversation proceeds and is organised. In contrast, IPA is not about how we talk about our experiences but, instead, it concentrates on what our experiences are. It is not particularly interested in how language is used, but it is interested in what people can tell us about their experiences through language. Indeed, in great contrast to discourse analysis, in particular, IPA is about internal psychological states, since it is about the conscious experience of events. There seems to be a clarity and transparency about data presentation in IPA which is not always emulated in other forms of qualitative research. The use of tables of data in IPA is in many ways redolent of the use of tables in quantitative analysis. The tables are systematic in IPA, but they are different from quantitative tables in that they only provide illustrations of the themes by illustrative quotations from the transcriptions.

Key points

- Interpretative phenomenological analysis (IPA) was first introduced as an analytical technique in the 1990s. It draws heavily on some of the more important developments in philosophy, psychology and sociology, *inter alia*, in the twentieth century. These have been identified as phenomenology, hermeneutics and symbolic interactionism.

- IPA is a variant of phenomenological analysis, though, to date, it has been second-party research in which a researcher guides the data collection and analysis, though phenomenological analysis can be solely first-party research in its original form. The aims of IPA research are to describe people's experiences in a particular aspect of life and to draw together explanations of these experiences. Much of the research to date has been in the field of health psychology.

● IPA shares many of the techniques of other qualitative methods. In particular, the primary aim of the analysis is to identify themes in what participants have to say about their experiences. The main processes of analysis involve the literal transcription of pertinent interview data which is then processed by suggesting themes that draw together aspects of the data. Further to this, the researcher may seek to identify superordinate themes which embrace a number of the major themes emerging in the analysis.

● The precise ways in which IPA differ from other forms of qualitative analysis are complex. It departs from, say, discourse analysis, for example, in having little interest in language as such, other than the medium through which the researcher can learn about how individuals experience particular phenomena. In other words, language helps to reveal the subjective realities of consciousness. Thus, it refers to internal psychological states of the sort which are often eschewed by the qualitative researcher. Of course, it shares with these other approaches the rejection of physical reality as the focus of research but, at the same time, it assumes that in the data provided by participants lies their reality of their experiences.

ACTIVITIES

1. Although interpretative phenomenological analysis has not been used in this way, phenomenological research can involve the researcher investigating his or her own experiences. Write a narrative account in the first person about your experiences of exams. Then explore your narrative using IPA. What are the major themes you can identify? What are the superordinate themes and what are the subordinate themes?

2. Plan a semi-structured interview on a topic such as childbirth, going to a doctor for a consultation or a turn on a fairground ride. Carry out and record an interview on this topic. Draw a table of superordinate themes, subordinate themes and illustrative quotes.

CHAPTER 26

Evaluating qualitative research

Overview

- Qualitative research is primarily evaluated in terms of the analysis process – typically, the coding and theory-building process involved.

- Suggestions are made as to how a newcomer to qualitative research should self-evaluate their work.

- Evaluating qualitative research requires a clear understanding of its roots and origins in psychology. Hence you need to study the previous chapters in this part of the book (Chapters 18–25) carefully to get the most out of this chapter.

- Many evaluation criteria are similar for qualitative and quantitative analyses. However, adherence to qualitative ideals is also emphasised.

26.1   Introduction

One of the big differences between quantitative and qualitative research is the way in which the credibility of the research is established. In quantitative research the onus on the researcher is to demonstrate that their measurement methods are sufficiently reliable and valid for their purposes. Generally speaking, the quality of the researcher themselves is not an issue, presumably because the methods and procedures of quantitative research are sufficiently robust that the researcher's impact is minimal. This is questioned, however, by the research on experimenter effects (see Chapter 10). In marked contrast is the situation in qualitative research where the influence of the researcher warrants serious attention. After all, the argument would go, qualitative research is dominated by the methodological procedures adopted by the researcher so the adequacy of these ought to be established (Levitt, 2019). Since the researcher is a key aspect of all aspects of qualitative research, this means that the qualitative researcher needs to be subject to this. Rather than speak of reliability and validity, the qualitative researcher will focus more on their study's trustworthiness and methodological integrity. A related concept is that of transparency which is essentially how available for inspection the data collection and analysis procedures are to the reader. Ways of establishing these things include evidence of the groundedness of the analysis in the data and the coherence of the study's findings. Qualitative research is evaluated in more idiosyncratic ways determined by the particular approach employed than quantitative research. While there is no gold standard for evaluating qualitative research, the variety of ways available is illuminating. Some of the criteria are quite close to the positivistic position (reliability and validity) but, as we saw in Chapter 18, these are eschewed by at least some qualitative researchers.

There is a preference for evaluation criteria based on qualitative research's distinctive philosophical underpinnings. For example, quantitative researchers take it for granted that observations should be reliable, which means that different researchers' observations of the same events should be similar. That is, different observers should observe the same thing if the data are of value. For qualitative researchers, this is an inappropriate criterion since different researchers will have different interpretations (readings) of events. The diversity of analytic interpretations, they argue, is right and proper given that there is no single fixed reality. Different 'readings' of the data should not be regarded as methodological flaws. The underlying difference between quantitative and qualitative researchers is not a matter of numbers and statistics. It is much more fundamental than that. Putting things as simply as possible, quantitative and qualitative research are alternative ways of seeing the world, not just different ways of carrying out research. The difference is that between the modern (scientific) approach with its emphasis on cause and the postmodern approach with its emphasis on interpretation.

26.2   Criteria for novices

Newcomers to qualitative research may feel insecure about their ability to conduct a qualitative study. Qualitative research is so very different from the technical approach characteristic of much mainstream psychology. Consequently, there may seem too little or no transfer of skills from quantitative research to qualitative. Significance testing, reliability estimates, validity coefficients and so forth are minimum quality indicators in mainstream psychology; those for qualitative research are not so easily fathomed. This section will present a few straightforward ideas of ways in which the novice qualitative researcher can self-evaluate their progress (see also Figure 26.1):

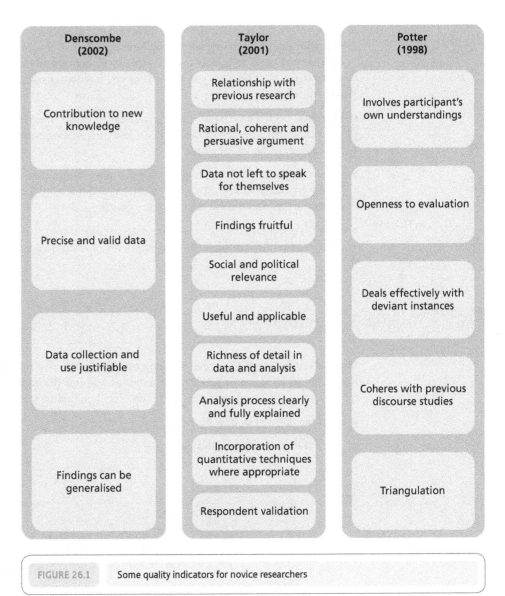

FIGURE 26.1   Some quality indicators for novice researchers

- Have you immersed yourself in the qualitative research literature or undergone training in qualitative research? Analytic success is a long journey and you need to understand where you are heading.

- Why are you not doing a quantitative analysis? Have you really done a quantitative analysis badly and called it qualitative research?

- Can you identify the specific qualitative method that you are using and why? Qualitative research is not an amorphous mass but a set of, only sometimes, interlinking approaches. Clarity about your chosen methodology and its special characteristics is essential.

- What resources are you devoting to your data collection and analysis? Qualitative data analysis probably requires more personal research skills than much quantitative data analysis. It requires a good interviewing technique, for example, to obtain the richness of data required. Qualitative data require transcription (or quantitative coding), which is time-consuming and exacting. If you do not understand the point of this, then your research is almost certainly of dubious quality.

● Have you coded or categorised *all* of your data? If not, why not? How do you know that your categories work unless you have tested them thoroughly against the entirety of what you want to understand? If you can only point to instances of categories you wish to use, then how do you know that you have a satisfactory fit of your categories with the data?

● Has there been a process of refining your categories? Or have you merely used categories from other research or thought of a few categories without these being worked up through revisions of the data?

● Can you say precisely what parts of your data fit your categories? Phrases such as 'Many participants . . . ', 'Frequently . . . ' and 'Some . . . ' should not be used to cover up woolliness about how your data are coded.

● How deeply engaged were you in the analysis? Did it come easily? If so, have you taken advantage of the special gains which may result from qualitative research?

26.3   Evaluating qualitative research

There is a substantial literature focusing on how qualitative research can be evaluated. According to Denscombe (2002), a number of features distinguish good research of all types from not so good research (see Figure 26.2), including the following:

● The contribution of new knowledge

● The use of precise and valid data

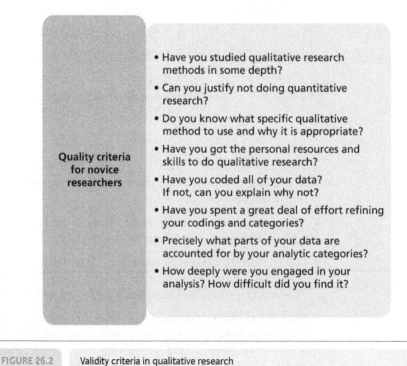

Quality criteria for novice researchers

- Have you studied qualitative research methods in some depth?
- Can you justify not doing quantitative research?
- Do you know what specific qualitative method to use and why it is appropriate?
- Have you got the personal resources and skills to do qualitative research?
- Have you coded all of your data? If not, can you explain why not?
- Have you spent a great deal of effort refining your codings and categories?
- Precisely what parts of your data are accounted for by your analytic categories?
- How deeply were you engaged in your analysis? How difficult did you find it?

FIGURE 26.2   Validity criteria in qualitative research

- The data being collected and used in a justifiable way

- The production of findings from which generalisations can be made.

These are tantalisingly simple criteria which are superficially difficult to question but they should be. They are fundamentally biased towards quantitative approaches. Perhaps the problem is that they are so readily unquestioningly accepted. Perhaps we are so imbued with positivist ideas that we no longer recognise them as such? Phrases such as 'new knowledge', 'precise/valid data', 'justifiable' and 'generalisation' may be more problematic than at first appears. What is new knowledge, for example? By what criteria do we decide that research has contributed new knowledge? What are precise and valid data? How precise need data be to make them acceptable in research? For what purposes do the data need to be valid to make them worthwhile? Why should worthwhile knowledge be generalisable? Should knowledge that works for New York City be generalisable to a village in Mali?

So evaluation criteria to be applied to quantitative research are problematic. One way of looking at this is to accept that much qualitative research has its intellectual roots in postmodernist ideas which, in themselves, are a reaction against modernist ideas in traditional science and positivism. This encourages the view that the evaluation criteria of qualitative and quantitative research need to be different no matter how tempting it is to seek universal criteria. Possible universal criteria for high quality scholarship include careful analysis, detachment, accuracy, a questioning stance and insight. But there is nothing in such criteria which clarifies what is good psychology and what is bad. Why is detachment a useful criterion, for example? It hints that the researcher ideally is an almost alienated figure. Indeed, criteria such as detachment have been criticised for encouraging research to be anodyne (Howitt, 1992a). As we saw earlier (Chapter 18), the intellectual roots of most qualitative analysis are outside psychology, where different priorities exist. The search for universal criteria for good psychology may be futile and possibly undesirable. It fails to acknowledge that the epistemological bases of qualitative and quantitative research can be incompatible. It is fair to say that qualitative researchers do not speak with one voice about what the evaluative criteria should be. Qualitative research is an umbrella term covering a multitude of viewpoints, just as quantitative research is. Many of the precepts of quantitative research are systematically reversed in some types of qualitative research. For example, when qualitative researchers reject psychological states as explanatory principles, they reject much psychology. Discourse analysts do this. The alternative to finding universal evaluation criteria is to evaluate qualitative and quantitative methods by their own criteria, that is, in many respects differently. The assumption that all qualitative methods should be evaluated against the same criteria should be avoided. The distinction between qualitative data collection and qualitative data analysis is paramount (Chapter 19). If the researcher seeks to quantify 'rich' data collected through in-depth methods such as open-ended interviewing, then criteria appropriate to qualitative analyses may not always apply.

Taylor (2001) discussed a number of evaluation criteria for qualitative research. Some of them apply to research in general, but often they take on a special significance in relation to qualitative research. The following are some of Taylor's more general criteria for evaluating qualitative research. They may or may not apply to quantitative research. We will discuss her more specific criteria and those of others later:

- *How the research is located in the light of previously published research*   Traditionally in psychological research, knowledge grows cumulatively through a process which begins with a literature search, through development of an idea based on that search and data collection, to finally reporting one's findings and conclusions. This is not the case in all forms of qualitative research. Some qualitative researchers begin with textual material that they wish to analyse, and delay referring back to previous research until after their analysis is completed. The idea is that the previous literature is an additional resource, more text if one likes, with which to explore the adequacy of the current analysis and its fit with other circumstances. The delay also means that the researcher is not so tempted to take categories 'off the peg' and apply them to their data. In some forms of qualitative analysis – especially conversation analysis – reference to the published research can be notably sparse. So the research literature in qualitative research can be used very differently from its role in quantitative research. In quantitative research, knowledge is regarded as building out of previous knowledge, so one reviews the state of one's chosen research and uses it as a base from which to develop further research. Traditionally, quantitative research demands the support of previous research in order to demonstrate the robustness and replicability of findings across samples and circumstances. Often, in the quantitative tradition, researchers resort to methodological considerations as an explanation of the variability in past and current findings. In the qualitative tradition, any disparity between studies is regarded much more positively and as less of a problem. Disparity is seen as a stimulus to refining the analytic categories used, which is the central activity of qualitative research anyway.

● *How coherent and persuasive the argument is, rather than emotional*   Argumentation and conclusion-drawing in psychology are typically regarded as dependent on precise logical sequences. It is generally not considered appropriate to express oneself emotionally or to engage in rhetorical devices in psychological report writing. This is quite a different matter from being dispassionate or uninvolved in one's subject matter. Sometimes qualitative reports seem to stray over this line. A great deal of fine psychological writing has been built on the commitment of the researcher to the outcomes of the research. Nevertheless, the expectation is that the researcher is restrained by the data and logic. In this way, the researcher is less likely to be dismissed as merely expressing personal opinions. This is the case no matter what research tradition is being considered.

● *Data should not be 'left to speak for themselves' and the analysis should involve systematic investigation*   The meaning of data does not reside entirely in the data themselves. Data need to be interpreted in the light of a variety of methodological and theoretical considerations. Few if any data have intrinsic, indisputable and unambiguous meanings. Hence the role of the researcher as interpreter of the data has to be part of the process. This interpretation has to be done with subtlety. There is a temptation among newcomers to qualitative analysis to feel that the set of data should speak 'for itself', so large amounts of text are reproduced and little by way of analysis or interpretation is offered. To do this, however, is to ignore a central requirement of research, which is to draw together the data to tell a story in detail. In qualitative research, this is through the development of closely fitting coding categories in which the data fit precisely but in a way which synthesises aspects of the data. Qualitative research may cause problems for novice researchers because they substitute the data for analysis of the data. Of course, ethnographically meaningful data should carry its meaning for all members of that community. Unfortunately, to push this version of the ethnographic viewpoint too far leaves no scope for the input of the psychologist. If total fidelity to the data is more important than the analysis of the data, then researchers may just as well publish recordings or videos of their interviews, for example. Indeed, there would be no role for the researcher, as anyone could generate a psychological analysis. But, of course, this is not true. It takes training to be capable of quality analyses.

● *Fruitfulness of findings*   Assessing the fruitfulness of any research is not easy. There are so many ways in which research may be fruitful, and little research is fruitful in every respect. Most research, however, can be judged only in the short term, and longer term matters such as impact on the public or other researchers may simply be inappropriate. Fruitfulness is probably best judged in terms of the immediate pay-off from the research in terms of the number of new ideas and insights it generates. Now it is very difficult to catalogue just what are new ideas and insights but rather easier to recognise work which lacks these qualities.

- *Relevance to social issues/political events*   Qualitative research in psychology often claims an interest in social issues and politics. There are a number of well-known studies which deal with social and political issues. The question needs to be asked, however, just how social and political issues need to be addressed in psychology, and from what perspective? Mainstream psychology has a long tradition of interest in much the same issue. Institutionally, the Society for the Study of Social Issues in the USA has actively related psychology to social problems (Howitt, 1992a), for example, for most of psychology's modern history. There is a distinct tradition of socially relevant quantitative research. Given the insistence of many qualitative researchers that their data are grounded in the mundane texts of the social world, one might expect that qualitative research is firmly socially grounded. One criticism of qualitative research, though, is that it has a tendency to regard the political and social as simply being more text that can be subjected to qualitative analysis. As such, the social and political text has no special status other than as an interesting topic for textual analysis. Some qualitative researchers have been very critical of the failure of much qualitative research to deal effectively with the social and political – concepts such as power, for instance (Parker, 1989). Since power is exercised through social institutions, one can question the extent to which analysis of text in isolation is sufficient analysis.

- *Usefulness and applicability*   The relevance of psychological research of any sort is a vexed question. Part of the difficulty is that many researchers regard their work as one aspect of an attempt to understand its subject matter for its own sake without the constraints of application. Indeed, applied research in psychology has often been seen as a separate entity from academic research and often somewhat derided as ordinary or pedestrian. Nevertheless, this point of view seems to have diminished in recent years, and it is increasingly acceptable to consider the application of research findings as an indication of the value of at least some research. It is fairly easy to point to examples from mainstream psychology of the direct application of psychological research – clinical, forensic and educational psychology all demonstrate this in abundance. Part of the success of psychology in these areas is in finding ways of dealing with the practical problems of institutions such as prisons, schools and the mental health system. Success in the application of psychology stems partly from the power of research findings to support practical activities. Qualitative researchers have begun to overlap some of these traditional fields of the application of psychology. Unfortunately, the claim that qualitative research is subjective tends to undermine its impact from the point of view of mainstream psychology. Nevertheless, topics such as counselling/psychotherapy sessions and medical interviews are to be found in the qualitative psychology literature. The attractiveness of qualitative research to government and other users of research though may be a consideration in relation to applicability.

26.4   Validity

The concept of validity is difficult to apply to qualitative research. Traditionally, validity in psychology refers to an assessment of whether a measure actually measures what it is intended to measure. This implies that there is something fixed which can be measured.

The emphasis is really on the validity of the measures employed as indicators of corresponding variables in the actual world. So the validity of a measure of schizophrenia is the extent to which it corresponds with schizophrenia in the actual world beyond that measure. This is not usually an assumption of qualitative research. In qualitative research, the emphasis of validity assessment is in terms of the question of how well the analysis fits the data. A good analysis fits the data very well. In quantitative research, often a very modest fit of the hypothesis to the data is acceptable – so long as the minimum criterion of statistical significance is met.

As we saw earlier (Chapter 16), there are a number of ways of assessing validity in quantitative research. They all imply that there is something in actuality that can be measured by our techniques. This is unlikely to be the case with qualitative research for a number of reasons. One is the insistence by some qualitative researchers that text has a multiplicity of readings, and that extends to the readings by researchers. In other words, given the postmodernist emphasis on the impossibility of observing 'reality' other than through a looking glass of subjectivity, validity cannot truly be assessed as a general aspect of measurement.

Discussions of validity by qualitative researchers take two forms:

- It is very common to question the validity of quantitative research, that is, to encourage the view that qualitative research is the better means to obtaining understanding of the social and psychological world.

- The tendency among qualitative researchers to treat any text (written or spoken) as worthwhile data means that the validity of the data is not questioned. The validity of the transcription is sometimes considered, but emphasis is placed on ways in which the fidelity of the transcription, say to the original audio-recording, may be maximised. The greatest emphasis is placed on ways in which the validity of the qualitative analysis as a qualitative analysis may be maximised. This really is the primary meaning of validity in qualitative research. So many of the criteria listed by qualitative researchers are ones which are only meaningful if we understand the epistemological origins of qualitative research. That is, there are some considerations about the worth of qualitative data which do not normally apply to quantitative research.

Potter (1998) uses the phrase 'justification of analytic claims' alongside using the word validity. The phrase 'justification of analytic claims' emphasises the value of the analysis rather than the nature of the data. He suggests four considerations which form the 'repertoire' with which to judge qualitative research. Different researchers may emphasise different combinations of these:

- *Participant's own understandings* When the qualitative material is conversation or similar text, we need to remember that speakers actually interpret the previous contributions by previous speakers. So the new speaker's understanding of what went before is often built into what they say in their turn. For example, a long pause and a change of subject may indicate that the speaker disagrees with what went before but does not wish to express that disagreement directly. Potter argues that by very carefully paying attention to such details in the analysis, the analyst can more precisely analyse the conversation in ways which are relevant to the participant's understandings. It is a way of checking the researcher's analysis.

- *Openness to evaluation* Sometimes it is argued that the readers of a qualitative analysis are more in contact with the data than typically is the case in quantitative research in which tables and descriptive statistics are presented but none of the original data directly. Qualitative analyses often incorporate substantial amounts of textual material in support of the analytic interpretation. Because of this, the qualitative analysis may be more open to challenge and questioning by the reader than other forms of research.

Relatively little qualitative research is open in this way, however. Potter suggests that for much reported grounded theory and ethnographic research, very little is presented in a challengeable form and a great deal has to be taken on trust, just as with quantitative research. Even where detailed transcripts are provided, however, Potter's ideal may not be met. For example, what checking can be done if the researcher does not report the full transcript but rather selected highlights? Furthermore, what avenues are open to the reader who disagrees with an analysis to challenge the analysis?

- *Deviant instances*   In quantitative research, deviant cases are largely treated as irrelevant. The participant who bucks the trend of the data is largely ignored – as 'noise' or randomness. Sometimes this is known as 'experimental error', but it is really an indicator of how much of the data is actually being ignored in terms of explanation. Often no attempt is made to explain why some participants are not representative of the trend. In qualitative research, partly because of the insistence on detailed analysis of sequences, the deviant case may be much more evident. Consequently the analysis needs to be modified to include what is truly deviant about it. It may be discovered that the seemingly deviant case is not really deviant – or it may become apparent why it 'breaks the rules'. It may also prove a decisive reason for abandoning a cherished analytic interpretation.

- *Coherence with previous studies*   Basically, the idea here is that qualitative studies which cohere with previous studies are more convincing than ones which are in some way at odds with previous research. There is a sense in which this is a replicability issue, since not only does coherence add conviction to the new study but it also adds conviction to the older studies. This is also the case with quantitative studies. But there are difficulties with this form of validity indicator. Qualitative research varies in terms of its fidelity to previous research when a replication is carried out. Some research will be close to the original and some may be substantially different. In this context, if a qualitative study is merely designed to apply the theoretical concepts derived from an earlier study, then the findings are more likely to cohere with the earlier studies. Studies not conceived in this way will be a more effective challenge to what has gone before – and potentially provide greater support if they confirm what went before.

Additional criteria for the evaluation of qualitative research are numerous (Taylor, 2001). These are not matters of validity, but they do offer means of evaluating the relative worth of different qualitative studies:

- *Richness of detail in the data and analysis*   The whole point of qualitative analysis is to develop descriptive categories which fit the data well. So one criterion of the quality of a study is the amount of detail in the treatment of the data and its analysis. Qualitative research requires endless processing of the material to meet its aims. Consequently, if the researcher just presents a few broad categories and a few broad indications of what sorts of material fit that category, then one will be less convinced of the quality of the analysis. Of course, richness of detail is not a concept which is readily tallied, so it begs the question of how much detail is richness. Should it be assessed in terms of numbers of words, the range of different sources of text, the verbal complexity of the data, or how? Similar questions may be applied to the issue of the richness of detail in the analysis. Just what does this mean? Is it a matter of the complexity of the analysis, and why should a complex analysis be regarded as a virtue in its own right? In quantitative research, in contrast, the simplicity of the analysis is regarded as a virtue if it accounts for the detail of the data well. It is the easiest thing in the world to produce coding categories which fit the data well – if one has a lot of coding categories, then all data are easily fitted. The fact that each of these categories fits only a very small part of the data means that the categories may not be very useful.

- *Explication of the process of analysis*   If judged by the claims of qualitative analysts alone, the process of producing an adequate qualitative analysis is time-consuming, meticulous and demanding. As a consequence of all of this effort, the product is both subtle and true to the data. The only way in which the reader can fully appreciate the quality of the effort is through the researcher giving details of the stages of the analysis process. This does not amount to evidence of validity in the traditional sense, but is a quality assurance indicator of the processes that went into developing the analysis. Another way of describing this is in terms of the transparency of the analysis.

- *Using selected quantitative techniques*   Some qualitative researchers are not against using some of the techniques of quantitative analysis. There is no reason in their view why qualitative research should not use systematic sampling to ensure that the data are representative. Others would stress the role of the deviant or inconsistent case in that it presents the greatest challenge to the categorisation process. The failure of more traditional quantitative methods to deal with deviant cases other than as 'noise', error or simply irrelevant should be stressed again in this context.

- *Respondent validation*   Given the origins of much qualitative research in ethnomethodology, the congruence of the interpretations of the researcher with those of the members of the group being studied may be seen as a form of validity check. This is almost a matter of definition – the meanings arrived at through research are intended to be close to those of the people being studied in ethnomethodology. Sometimes it is suggested that there is a premium in the researcher having 'insider status'. That is, a researcher who is actually a member of the group being studied is at an advantage. This is another reflection of the tenets of ethnomethodology. There is always the counter-argument to this that such closeness actually stands in the way of insightful research. However, there is no way of deciding which is correct. Owusu-Bempah and Howitt (2000) give examples from cross-cultural research of such insider perspectives. Of course, the importance of these criteria is largely the consequence of allegiance to a particular theoretical stance. It is difficult to argue for universality of this criterion.

- *Triangulation*   This concerns the validity of findings. When researchers use very different methods of collecting data yet reach the same findings on a group of participants, this is evidence of the validity of the findings or, in other words, their robustness across different methods of data collection or analysis. The replication of the findings occurs within settings and not across settings. This is then very different from triangulation when it is applied to quantitative data. In that case, the replication is carried out in widely different studies from those of the original study. The underlying assumption is that of positivist universality, an anathema to qualitative researchers. Triangulation in qualitative research is rather complex since it can involve different aspects of the research. So the data collection method could be different, there could be two or more studies, and so forth.

26.5   Conclusion

Very few of the traditional criteria which applied to quantitative research apply to qualitative research directly. They simply do not have the same intellectual roots and, to some extent, they are in conflict. There are a number of criteria for evaluating qualitative research, but these largely concentrate on evaluating the quality of the coding or categorisation process (the qualitative analysis). These criteria can be applied but, as yet, there is no way of deciding whether the study is of sufficient quality. They are merely indicators.

This contrasts markedly with quantitative and statistical research where there are rules-of-thumb which may be applied to decide on the worth of the research. Significance testing is one obvious example of this when we apply a test of whether the data are likely to have been obtained simply by sampling fluctuations. Internal consistency measures of reliability such as alpha also have such cut-off rules. This leaves it a little uncertain how inexperienced qualitative researchers can evaluate their research. It is clearly the case that qualitative researchers need to reflect on the value of their analysis as much as any other researcher.

Key points

- The criteria that novice researchers use to evaluate their own research may be a little more routine. Considerations include factors related to the amount of effort devoted to developing the analysis, the degree to which the analysis embraces the totality of the data, and even questioning whether a quantitative study would have been more appropriate anyway.

- Since qualitative research is a reaction to positivism and its influence on research, qualitative research needs to be evaluated in part on its own terms.

- Some criteria apply to both quantitative and qualitative research. The criteria include how the research is located in relation to previously published research, the coherence and persuasiveness of the argument, the strength of the analysis to impose structure on the data, the potential of the research to stimulate further research or the originality and quantity of new insights arising from the research, and the usefulness of applicability of the research.

- Yet other criteria which may be applied are much more specific to qualitative research. These include the correspondence of the analysis with the participant's own understandings, the openness of the report to evaluation, the ability of the analysis to deal with otherwise deviant instances in the data, the richness of detail in the analysis, which is dependent on the richness of the data in part, and how clearly the process of developing the analysis is presented.

ACTIVITIES

1. Could a qualitative researcher simply make up their analysis and get away with it? List the factors that stop this happening.

2. Develop a set of principles by which all research could be evaluated.

CHAPTER 27

Improving your qualitative write-up

Overview

- The core strategy for writing a qualitative research report is to ensure that it reflects the qualitative ethos.

- Avoid ideas taken from positivistic psychology in a qualitative research report. References to variable, cause and effect, and the like should be avoided.

- Your skills for writing quantitative reports (Chapter 5) generally transfer to qualitative research reports which usually use a similar structure.

- Read professional researchers' qualitative reports.

- A qualitative research report is provided in this chapter for critical evaluation.

27.1   Introduction

You cannot do too much reading of published research reports when seeking to write up your research at a high level of quality. Can you imagine a great novelist who had never read a novel? Such authors do not exist. The same is true of research. One researcher put things this way:

> As a beginning qualitative writer, I found imitating others to be essential in the learning process. By mimicking how other authors constructed qualitative papers, I began to pick up practices that helped me do it successfully. Eventually, I was able to develop my own voice.
>
> (Pratt, 2009, p. 861)

There is more to it than just reading, of course. It is easier to write a good qualitative research report if the research itself is of a high quality. Research report writing involves a degree of creativity, technical knowledge, application and determination. You need to know the basic stuff as well as details of report writing. Time and study are essential. Intellectual involvement in things like social change, the news, society, technology and anything else which may feed into the research process are important. Flawed research is exposed during the writing-up process and papering over the flaws is a challenging, possibly impossible, task. Inadequacies will almost certainly show through no matter how skilfully you write. So the quality of the design and execution of your research place limits on the quality of your research report. Of course, you can write up an excellent piece of research extremely badly thereby undermining your own achievements.

So in this chapter we will provide ideas about what goes into (or not) qualitative reports. Being aware of certain things will almost certainly improve your writings. Some suggestions are scattered throughout this book. We have already discussed structuring a quantitative report (Chapter 5) which largely generalises to qualitative reports. Technical things such as citations and reference lists are the same whichever sort of research is involved. The literature search proceeds in much the same way irrespective of the qualitative-quantitative distinction with only minor exceptions. Remember that the quality criteria for qualitative research (Chapter 26) apply for the most part to evaluating research reports. They give strong hints as to the general 'feel' of the qualitative report. Yes, it all demands effort and shortcuts are few.

Students are generally less familiar with qualitative than quantitative research because most substantive areas of psychological research remain primarily quantitative. So you need to prepare to ensure that you understand the particular epistemological roots of qualitative methods. Similarly, data collection in qualitative research is fundamentally different and these methods need to be understood. This book provides you with this basic understanding. The research question you employ should be one which requires a qualitative rather than a quantitative analysis. Do not ask a quantitative research question and try to address it qualitatively.

The chapters on the main qualitative methods (e.g. discourse analysis, interpretative phenomenological analysis, conversation analysis) provide much information about the sorts of research question the method addresses. In short, you cannot skimp on your preparation for qualitative research and writing it up. Although we provide many examples of qualitative research in earlier chapters, it is always wise to download and read a few qualitative reports in the field of research that you are engaged. In this way, you get a fuller picture of the qualitative style. That is, look at discourse analysis reports if you are planning a discourse analysis, look at grounded theory reports if you are planning to do a grounded theory analysis, and so forth. Of course, these are likely to be initially quite demanding but they are indicative of what you are aiming to achieve.

The following is a list which addresses some distinctive features of qualitative research. They should start you thinking about the general tone and style of your qualitative report:

- Qualitative research involves understanding and interpreting social life.

- In qualitative research, data is explored in order to generate new theory.

- Testing hypotheses and making predictions have little or nothing to do with qualitative research.

- The qualitative researcher is assumed to have biases and not the detached impersonal persona attributed to the quantitative researcher.

- Qualitative research assumes that there are multiple realities.

- Qualitative research looks for patterns and themes. Statistical relationships are of no interest.

- Subjectivity is generally accepted or assumed in qualitative research.

- Qualitative researchers do not rigorously control research conditions.

- Qualitative research studies the individual in their natural environment.

- In qualitative research, the entirety is studied rather than variables in isolation.

- The concept of variable is avoided in qualitative research.

To the extent that these things represent the qualitative ethos and epistemology, they should be apparent in qualitative reports. They should help you avoid straying into quantitative domains while writing a qualitative report. So if you spot yourself writing about 'variables' or if you find yourself being apologetic about the subjective nature of your data and analysis, then take action. Qualitative psychology critiques mainstream quantitative psychology so rejects many of its assumptions. Here are some substantive things to bear in mind which will help you write up a qualitative report:

- *Local arrangements for qualitative reports*   Check what the local 'rules' are for a qualitative report. These may not always be good news but failure to adhere to them may cost you marks. One of the rules may concern how qualitative data is counted in your allowed word count. Qualitative data is usually 'wordy' and so if the data you include in your report is counted as part of the word count, then the write-up becomes harder. Similarly, appendices can be a way of including extensive qualitative data including transcripts without affecting the word count. Ask for clarification if issues like these are unclear in local documentation such as that distributed by the teacher in charge of the module. Make sure that you understand just what additional rules apply. Is there a maximum length for the abstract, for instance? With any luck, the word length limits for a qualitative report may not include examples from the data.

- *Avoid positivist assumptions*   Meticulously avoid anything which implies positivistic assumptions in your qualitative write-up. Concepts like variable and reliability either have no meaning in qualitative research or have such a special meaning that they should be routinely avoided or discussed in a great deal of detail. Writing about independent variable, dependent variables, cause and effect, stimulus and response, intervening variables and the like is equally undesirable. None of this is to say that quantitative knowledge is entirely to be excluded from qualitative reports. Some qualitative methods such as grounded theory may involve past quantitative work as part of theory development.

- *The conventional structure of the quantitative report is usually used for qualitative write-ups* Always remember that the conventional structure used for quantitative report (Chapter 5) is much the same as that for qualitative research though there can be some flexibility if appropriate. It involves a title, abstract, introduction, methodology, results and discussion followed by the reference list and appendices. By modifying the basic structure, many of its advantages are retained in terms of structural clarity and reader-friendliness resulting from its basic familiarity. So you should write up qualitative research studies using the traditional laboratory report structure modified by adding additional headings or leaving some out as necessary. Consult journal articles which employ similar methods to your own for ideas about how to structure your report. These can, if chosen wisely and used intelligently, provide an excellent model for your report and are an easy way of accessing ideas about how to modify the conventional laboratory report structure for your purposes. Occasionally, you will come across a qualitative journal article which is somewhat 'off the wall' in terms of what you are used to, but we would not recommend that you adopt such extreme styles. It would take a lot of confidence, if not bravado, for a student to do so. You are writing a qualitative report in the context of the psychological tradition of academic work and you will do best by respecting this academic pedigree.

- *Advantages of the conventional structure* By adopting but adapting the conventional laboratory report structure, you are doing yourself a favour. Quantitative report writing is likely to be familiar to you, and you will very probably have had some opportunity to develop your skills in this regard. Everyone has difficulties writing quantitative reports, but this partly reflects the academic rigour that writing such reports demands. The reader of your report will benefit from the fact that they are reading something which has a more or less familiar structure where most of the material is where it is expected to be in the report. There will be differences, of course. In particular, it is unlikely (but possible) that you would include hypotheses in a qualitative report just as it is fairly unlikely that you would include any statistical analysis (though you might when using thematic analysis and similar methods).

- *Explicate your qualitative method* You will probably need to write more about the basic principles of your chosen qualitative method than one normally would when writing a quantitative report. One reason for this is that some readers may not be fully familiar with your chosen method. So you need to present some background. Just how long into the future this situation will prevail is difficult to say but, for now, you probably need to make space for a description of your methodology. This could include an explanation of why you chose one qualitative methodology rather than another. The other reason is to do with procedural 'oddities' in qualitative methods in the eyes of those who are more quantitatively oriented. For example, sampling really needs careful explanation in qualitative write-ups because sampling can mean something very different from its use in quantitative research. Rarely in qualitative research is 'representative' sampling employed. Sampling is more likely to be about the variety of positions than the mean on some sort of measure. Sampling is generally purposive in qualitative research and the purpose of the sampling needs explaining. Sample size is also differently applied in qualitative research compared to quantitative. For example, the idea of 'theoretical saturation' tells the qualitative researcher when to stop collecting data. It is when no new ideas or further clarification are being achieved in the additional data. Sample size is not a matter of statistical estimation in qualitative research – which should come as no surprise. Your description of your qualitative sample should be as precise as possible and may include pocket descriptions of each of the individuals taking part in your study.

● *Adopt the qualitative ethos in your writing*   You need to remember the general ethos of qualitative research and your specific qualitative method in particular. All qualitative methods are not the same! Some may be closely related but others far apart. So basically you need to understand the epistemological basis of your chosen analytic method. For example, just how accepting is your qualitative methods of inputs from quantitative research? Methods such as interpretative phenomenological analysis, thematic analysis and grounded theory are particularly open to quantitative research. Others such as discourse analysis and conversation analysis manifest more suspicion about such imports. But there are other matters such as when the literature review is carried out. There are no hard and fast rules but not all methods assume that research ideas are generated by the research review and tested in the research. In grounded theory and conversation analysis, for example, there are researchers who suggest that the literature review should be carried out after the data analysis is completed. Primarily this guards against the new analysis being guided by previous research.

● *Conceptual issues in your method*   The introduction is likely to discuss in some length conceptual issues concerning the type of analysis that you are performing. This is most likely to be the case when conducting a discourse analysis which is highly interdependent with certain theories of language. You will probably spend little time discussing conceptual issues like these when conducting a thematic analysis that is not based particularly on any theory.

● *Special role of the literature review*   The literature review is generally as important in qualitative write-ups as in quantitative ones. Indeed, especially when using qualitative methods in relation to applied topics, you may find that you need to refer to research and theory based on quantitative methods as well as qualitative research. While it is not common for quantitative methods to be looking at much the same issues as qualitative studies, there are circumstances in which each can inform the other. Although professional publications using conversation analysis often have very few references (as conversation analysis sees itself as data-driven and not theory-driven in terms of analysis), we would not recommend that students emulate this. As in any other writing you do as a student, we would recommend that you demonstrate the depth and extent of your reading of the relevant literature in your writings. You cannot expect credit for something that you have not shown you have done.

● *Clarity about the purpose of your research*   Although preliminary hypotheses are inappropriate for most qualitative analyses (since hypotheses come from a different tradition in psychological research), you should be very clear about the aims of your research in your report. This helps to focus the reader in terms of your data collection and analysis as well as demonstrating the purposive nature of your research. In other words, clearly stated aims are a helpful part of telling the 'story' of your research.

● *Method section*   This should be comparable in a qualitative report to the method section for a quantitative report in scope and level of detail. There are numerous methods of data collection in qualitative research, so it is impossible to give detailed suggestions that apply to each of these. Nevertheless, there is a temptation to give too little detail when reporting qualitative methods, since often the methods are superficially quite simple compared with the procedures adopted in some laboratory studies, for example. Avoid just saying that in-depth interviews or focus groups were used without giving substantial information about what was done. So it is best to be precise about the procedures used, even though these may at times appear to be relatively simple and straightforward compared with other forms of research.

● *Always explicate the process of analysis*   Too frequently, qualitative analysts fail to give sufficient detail about how they carried out their analysis. Writing things like 'a grounded theory analysis was performed' or 'thematic analysis was employed' says far too little. There is more to qualitative analysis than this and great variation in how analyses are carried out. To the reader, such brief statements may read more like an attempt to mystify the analysis process than to elucidate important detail. It is especially important for students to explain in some detail how they went about their analysis since, by doing so, not only does the reader get a clearer idea about the analytic procedures employed but the student demonstrates their understanding and mastery of the method. As ever in report writing, it is very difficult to stipulate just how much detail should be given – judgement is involved in this rather than rules, as well as constraints on the length of the report – but we would suggest that it is best to err on the side of too much detail.

- *How much data to supply*   Deciding just how much data to include in a qualitative report is difficult. A few in-depth interviews can add up to substantial numbers of words. However, in terms of self-presentation, such transcripts especially Jefferson's testify to how careful and thorough the researcher is. Not to include them as an appendix hides the amount of effort given to the analysis and denies others the opportunity to check your analysis or simply to get a fuller picture of the interview. Normally, transcriptions do not count towards word limits, though you might wish to check this locally with your lecturers.

- *Balance between presenting the data and its analysis*   Reaching a proper balance between presenting data and presenting your analysis is difficult. In particular, providing excerpts illustrating features of the analysis in sufficient quantity to allow the reader to evaluate the relationship between data and analysis is demanding. Illustrating a particular analytic feature with just one data excerpt may seem woefully inadequate to the reader. One device is to present several examples embedded in tables which may save space. Nevertheless, include at least one excerpt in the text so that the reader is not constantly refocusing between the main text and the tables (Pratt, 2009).

- *Make sure that the report includes a qualitative analysis*   One way in which this may not happen is when the student merely strings together quotations (illustrative excerpts) from their data with a commentary. This results in a low level description of some interesting points that the researcher finds in their data. This amounts to a commentary on the excerpts – sometimes more or less repeating what is in the excerpt in other words. A commentary on a few quotations is not what is meant by qualitative analysis.

- *Ensure that your data actually supports your analytic claims*   Your data should match your analytic claims. So you need to check that your interpretation of your data is actually reflected in the excerpts that you use.

- *Consider using tables of themes and quotes in your qualitative report*   The presentation of your analysis of qualitative data can be systematic. A good example of this is the way in which IPA analysts (see Chapter 25) produce tables to illustrate the themes which they identify. In this way, themes can be linked hierarchically and illustrative excerpts from the data included for each theme in a systematic manner.

- *Quantification is possible in a qualitative study sometimes*   With thematic analysis especially, it can be very helpful to give some basic statistical information about the number of interviews, for example, in which the theme was to be found, or some other indication of their rates of occurrence.

- *Use the quality criteria for qualitative research described in Chapter 26*   When it comes to discussing the findings from your qualitative research, you will find numerous criteria in this book by which the adequacy of a qualitative study can be assessed. Why not incorporate some of these criteria when evaluating your research findings?

This is an example of what a student might submit when asked to write up a qualitative report. There are quite a few problems with the report and your task is to identify what these problems are. We have provided some comments at various points in the write-up which you can check. The problems are identified with numerical superscripts in the text and our comments are supplied in the critical evaluation at the end. You may well find additional weaknesses which we have not commented on. This does not mean that you are wrong, of course, only that we have made no comment.

Box 27.1   Practical Report

Breaking-up is hard[1]: an IPA study of the experience of being dumped in dating relationships[2]

Becky Robertson

Abstract

This Interpretative Phenomenological Analysis study was based on the methods of Smith (Smith, Flowers, & Larkin, 2009). It seeks to understand the lived experiences of those going through significant life experiences. In depth interviews were conducted with three volunteers about being 'dumped' in a dating relationship[3]. It is considered important to differentiate between the partner who initiates the break-up and the partner who does not initiate the break-up as their experiences are somewhat different.[4] Relationship break-up has seldom been studied qualitatively and quantitative research involving dating relationships is not plentiful and is somewhat contradictory. Four themes revealed themselves[5] in the IPA: (1) negative emotions, (2) positive emotions, (3) seeing the way forward and (4) the benefits of being 'dumped'. Excerpts from the interviews are provided to illustrate each of these themes. The evidence in support of each theme from quantitative research is also discussed.

Introduction

There is an extensive research literature on divorce (Fine & Harvey, 2006), some of it qualitative. Divorce is a complex matter, of course, because issues such as the care of children and the economic consequences of divorce are at the forefront. This paper, however, concentrates on early dating relationships which, for the most part, do not involve children or finance. The decision to focus on first-time dating relationships can be justified in a number of ways. This is an area of research which has received proportionately little attention compared to topics such as marriage and adult intimate relationships. Yet these relationships are early examples of intimate relationships and so, potentially, may have implications for our understanding of later intimate relationships including marriage.[6] There is research to suggest that the better the quality of these early relationships then the better the individual's well-being as measured by various indicators (Viejo, Ortega-Ruiz, & Sánchez, 2015).[7] There appear to be no studies taking a developmental perspective on dating relations. It is notable that the research on dating relationships in young people has tended to concentrate on quantitative studies of 'dating violence'. The focus of this paper is on the break-up of these early relationships and, more particularly, the experience of being 'dumped'. This focus was the consequence of resource limitations. A qualitative methodology was adopted in order to provide rich data about the experience of being 'dumped' to fill the void in our knowledge.[8]

Because of the nature of the research, Interpretative Phenomenological Analysis (IPA) seemed[9] to be an appropriate choice of research method. IPA was developed by Jonathan Smith and first presented in a paper published in 1996. Among the main features of IPA are:

● IPA seeks to understand the 'lived experiences' of a person and takes an idiographic viewpoint.

● IPA regards the way a person goes about making sense of their experiences as central. Thus an IPA analysis focuses on the meanings of the person's experiences.

● IPA has its roots in Husserl's phenomenology and attempts to understand a person's perceptions of and accounts of events. IPA analysis is not seen as the quest for objective truth.

● In IPA, the level of analysis is the individual person though the analysis often is extended to involve additional cases which are subjected to detailed analyses in the same way. A single case may be sufficient for an IPA study.

● Drawing on hermeneutics, IPA stresses the importance of interpretation by the researcher and accepts the impossibility of the researcher directly sharing the individual's experience without this being mediated through the researcher's own conceptions. Interpretation stretches to drawing upon psychological research and theory if it is pertinent.[10]

IPA has gained popularity amongst researchers in fields such as nursing research and, especially, psychology in which it originated. The popularity of IPA may partly be a consequence of it being open to the use of quantitative research and theory and its unwillingness to be dismissive of mainstream psychology. The usual data collection technique employed in IPA is semi-structured interviews which are analysed to find themes which pervade what the participant has to say.

In sum, the research literature on intimate relationships has been dominated by studies of marriage and other long-term relationships with rather less emphasis on early dating relationships. Furthermore, this is an area in which qualitative research from a psychological perspective is needed. The purpose of the research is to identify the variables which predict the negative consequences of 'being dumped' and recovery from this.[11]

Method

Participants

The three cases involved were drawn from a population of university students. They were volunteers from the undergraduate psychology practical class of which the author is a member.[12] Members of the class were asked to volunteer to be interviewed about their experiences of being 'dumped' from their first relationship. It was stressed that by 'dumped' was meant that the other person without mutual consent ended their romantic relationship unexpectedly. Some of the class were still in their first relationship, some had not had a relationship, and some were not dumped but had terminated the relationship themselves. It was felt that these experiences would be sufficiently recent that the participant would still be able to recollect them in detail. There were five volunteers but only three could be interviewed, all of whom were female aged 18–19 years.[13]

Data collection

The three participants were interviewed, separately, in student accommodation – in one case that of the researcher and in the other two cases their respective student accommodation. No other persons were present at the time of the interviews. The interviews were conducted in a warm, friendly manner by the researcher whose first experience this was of interviewing.[14] The interviews were based on the first dating relationship which the participant had which lasted more than four weeks. Shorter relationships were excluded. The semi-structured interviews used a schedule which focused on the participant's experiences and feelings on being 'dumped'.[15] The recordings were transcribed using the Jefferson method.[16]

Analysis

Interpretative Phenomenological Analysis was employed (Smith, 2004, 2007; Smith & Osborn, 2008). This involved repeated in-depth reading of the transcripts while at the same time taking detailed notes about the content. In this way, it is intended to identify the themes contained in the text. The process of reading and note-taking is repeated many times

→

until the themes represent the transcript well and the way that the themes are structured is understood. This was done for each of the cases in turn.[17]

Results

The analysis revealed that the participants used four different themes while describing their experiences of being 'dumped' from an early relationship.[18] Subthemes were also found for each of these themes. The themes were: (a) negative emotion; (b) positive emotion; (c) seeing the way forward and (d) the benefits of being 'dumped'. These themes are discussed and illustrated in the next few paragraphs.[19]

a) Negative emotions: All three participants described negative emotions associated with being 'dumped'. The negative emotions intimated were not always the same or even similar between cases. Anger, humiliation, depression, suicidal feelings, revenge and embarrassment were all to be seen described in the transcripts. Having such negative feelings did not mean that they did not see positive aspects in the situation. One of the participants said:

"I know now it was only puppy love but I thought that it was the real thing. I couldn't believe it when he stood me up on our last date and didn't ring to apologise. He blocked my number on his phone so I knew that there hadn't been a misunderstanding. Obviously he didn't want to know anymore. I was angry as much at this treatment as anything else and, I must admit, I did plot revenge for weeks afterwards. But most of all I felt humiliated and embarrassed in the eyes of people who know me. Like it had destroyed my self-confidence. In fact, I stayed at home and avoided my friends when I should have been on the town. It took me a long time to get over."[20]

In this case, it can be seen that the participant identifies the manner of the dumping as being responsible for her anger rather than the fact of being dumped. Nevertheless, being dumped had substantial effects on her. She seems to have punished herself for being dumped when she describes how she felt humiliated and it destroyed her confidence.[21] This interpretation is supported by her feelings of being humiliated and embarrassed which led her to avoid her friends – a prime source of social support. This contrasts with the following excerpt from another of the participants:

"Well . . . I mean . . . I suppose I was peeved rather than angry. I was getting bored with him anyway but he was the one who dumped me. That's probably what hurt the most. Guess I felt sorry for him but I was more interested in another boy by that time. So it peed me off quite a bit. Disappointed in myself, I guess. Suppose I'm a bit soft really. He dumped me quite nicely if there is such a thing. I think that it had some effect on me as I have always been the one to do the dumping ever since then. My friends rallied around and someone was on the phone every minute of the day it seemed but it weren't necessary 'cos I started going out with the other lad almost immediately."

In common with the other two participants, this case manifested negative emotions but at the level of a relatively minor irritation with herself for letting things drift on despite knowing that she should have struck first and dumped the boy. In this case, however, the participant did not punish herself deeply or extensively but simply regretted not having struck first. She seems to have engaged straight away in a new dating relationship. The lack of intense negative emotion may simply be a reflection of the diminished commitment to the relationship that she demonstrated. Two out of the three described a period of sadness which followed the other negative feelings chronologically whereas the participant in the above comment did not in keeping with her feelings about the relationship at the time of being dumped.

b) Positive emotions: Although negative emotion seems to be the obvious and possibly natural response to being 'dumped', we have already seen that there is a variety of negative emotions some more superficial than others. It is less expected to find positive emotions as a consequence of being dumped. One participant reflected as follows:

"Looking back at it now, I think that being dumped was the best thing that happened to me. It wouldn't have worked out anyway and, if it had, we would probably be boring each other to death as we were so different. Although it is not all good, there were positive things apart from this. For one thing, I found my friends more rewarding and this made me happy. Also I finally made up my mind to go to university and I am so glad that I did. I really have loved my time here. Oh and I got to like myself so much better. I could have gone to pieces but I didn't."

This participant explains how, seemingly retrospectively, she regarded her 'dumping' as involving positive affective states such as happiness and as a consequence of which she began to regard herself more positively. The general implications of what she had to say seem to be that as a consequence of not succumbing to negative feelings such as anger or depression she saw herself as more resilient and capable than perhaps she had previously.[22] She is mindful of the role of friends in difficult times but does not indicate that her friends provided the social support but, instead, merely states that she found her friends more rewarding. The reasons for this were not given by her and this was an area which was not probed in the interview. One possible reason may be that freed from the demands of a relationship she was free to concentrate her attention on her friends, spend more time with them, and get more out of her friendships as a consequence.

c) Seeing the way forward: Being dumped might be conceived as a process rather than an event. Although the participants generally described negative emotional states following being dumped, it is difficult to understand the experience of being dumped solely in terms of the immediate consequence. These negative emotions do not last forever and eventually, sooner or later, the individual re-establishes themselves and becomes involved in new relationships. As part of their descriptions of the process of being dumped, the individuals described a stage where they begin to see their way forward with a positive viewpoint and confidence in the future. It would seem that reaching this stage of 'seeing the way forward' could occur quite quickly but sometimes this is quite delayed:

"Losing him hit me pretty hard. I was really low and my life felt like I was swimming in a pool of darkness dragging me down. The doctor gave me depression tablets. I couldn't eat or study properly. Seriously I couldn't imagine life without him. I pestered him with texts asking 'why' he had broken up with me. It took a couple of months but one day I just decided that I had had enough. I had to put it all behind me. Well at first I decided that he had been a waste of space but then it became important to appreciate the good things in the relationship – and about him. I started to believe that there was a future and started making plans. I flunked my exams but did resits and here I am at university having a whale of a time."

The way this participant experienced things paints a picture of a phase of depression in reaction to being dumped which went on for some time. Then, at some point, she seems to have come to the realisation that she needed to do something. This was essentially to reappraise what had happened to her in a more positive way and, while doing so, move on to a new stage in her life – university. The other participants showed a similar sort of pattern but not necessarily to the same depth. One participant, as we have already seen, was more peeved than depressed by being dumped and quickly found a new boyfriend and, seemingly, decided that she would be the dumper rather than the dumped in relationships. This participant seems to have suffered the least yet show signs of creating a way forward that was almost seamless. The third participant experienced being dumped negatively and blamed herself for the break-up due to her lack of commitment to the relationship. However, her self-recriminations were relatively short as she decided that her studies were the most important thing for her so she immersed herself in her work. The outcome was a perfect set of examination results.

d) The benefits of being dumped: The final theme highlights the benefits of being 'dumped'. Although in general the experience of being dumped was regarded by the participants as being negative because of the bad feelings, sense of isolation and disruption to other aspects of one's life, nevertheless all of the participants expressed benefits, at least in the long run. Among the things mentioned were:

"I honestly think that being dumped was good for me in a funny sort of way. It made me tougher and more self-assertive in relationships. In the first one I was a bit of a doormat but now things are completely different."

"Somehow I got by though it was tough."[23]

"Sometimes I think that it was one big favour that he did me. He wasn't interested in uni so I might not have gone to uni if he hadn't dropped me. But I did and here I am to prove it."

→

Discussion

This study shows that there are four themes related to experiences of being dumped in relationships. The four themes were negative emotions, positive emotions, seeing the way forward and the benefits of being dumped. The experience of a relationship break-up that was initiated by the other partner had negative aspects in all three cases but there were differences in the extent of the negative response. The termination of a romantic relationship is experienced as a form of rejection usually and is accompanied by negative emotions such as anger, humiliation and depression.[24] Sometimes it can be experienced as nothing more than an irritation or annoyance. However, the process of recovering from the relationship break-up involves considerable rumination about the relationship and the breakthrough of being able to see a way forward outside of the relationship as well as sometimes seeing good things emerge out of the process. The primary response is of negative emotion but in the process of recovery there may be positive emotions. Some participants mentioned some benefits of being dumped and there is considerable thought given to the future and recovery from the negative feelings.

The research concentrated on partners who had been dumped and excluded those who brought the relationship to an end. It is important to distinguish between the initiator of the break-up and the non-initiator. This is not done in all research and there is good reason to make this distinction. For example, there is evidence from quantitative research that such non-initiators suffer the greatest distress from the break-up (Perilloux & Buss, 2008). Helgeson (1994) provided evidence that men suffered less in a break-up if they initiated it though initiator status had no effect on the distress experienced by women.[25] She also found that women adjusted better than men to break-ups in general. This supports the findings of Hill, Rubin and Peplau (1976) in which non-initiators spent more time thinking and wondering about the break-up and making attempts to find out why the relationship had come to an end than did partners who initiated the break-up (Horwitz & Wakefield, 2007).[26]

Of course, it would be expected that in many cases finding a new relationship would be of benefit. This was apparent from the interviews especially the case in which the participant quickly formed a new relationship with a young man who she was already interested in.[27] From quantitative research, it is known that a new romantic relationship tends to reduce the distress following a break-up (Tashiro & Frazier, 2003). Those with a new romantic partner claim higher levels of self-rediscovery (Lewandowski & Bizzoco, 2007) and felt less lonely and less preoccupied with the previous relationship (Saffrey & Ehrenberg, 2007). Those who had not found a new relationship were not so well adjusted to the break-up. However, despite making intuitive sense, exactly why a new relationship should have such benefits is not quite so obvious despite the strong empirical evidence. The dependence model of break-ups might explain this (Kelley & Thibaut, 1978; Thibaut & Kelley, 1959). The basic idea of this is that dependence on a relationship makes it harder to leave a relationship. A person will show dependence on a relationship where there is no alternative way of satisfying the needs met by that relationship. This is illustrated by the participant who clearly showed signs of lacking dependence on her relationship since she had turned her attention to a new boy who she started dating very quickly after she was 'dumped'. She also seems to have been the least affected negatively by the 'dumping'. Although the dependence model of break-ups attempts to explain why individuals seek to end a relationship or stay in it, the model may explain differences in response to relationship break-ups. When satisfaction of needs is no longer possible because of the break-up, the individual may react with sadness or depression. If the needs are satisfied in a new relationship, then the broken relationship may not have the same negative influence because the new partner satisfies the same needs.

In support of this, Locker, McIntosh, Hackney, Wilson, and Wiegand (2010) also showed that finding a new partner quickly was associated with speedier recovery. Furthermore, they found that a break-up from a short relationship led to speedier recovery than a break-up from a longer relationship. Whether this can be explained by the dependence model is a difficult question. A short relationship may more easily break-up because the dependencies are not strong or, possibly, because the dependencies have not had time to build up. But equally, the depth of emotions may be less for the shorter relationship. Or the level of commitment may be less in a short relationship. Unfortunately, the questioning in the interviews in the present study was not based on an awareness of these possibilities.

This discussion in constrained by two main factors: (1) the lack of significant qualitative studies of dating relationships and relationship break-ups[27] and (2) the limited scope of the present study.[28] The lack of relevant qualitative studies is not easy to explain. One possibility is perhaps the complexity of dating relationships in terms of things such as the age of the partners, the past experiences of the partners, the fact that there are two partners to be considered, the gender of individuals and many personal and situational factors which may be involved. This variety perhaps hints at why a small sample of three participants seems to fail to lead to a coherent set of findings rich in theoretical potential.[29] One might suggest that the sampling strategy could have been more demanding. In particular, the number and range of the interviews could have been expanded and, perhaps, the theoretical saturation criterion applied rather than the somewhat arbitrary sampling criterion of the availability of resources.

Theoretical saturation would have almost certainly required a substantially larger sample size. It is worth mentioning the recent study by Hsueh, Morrison, and Doss (2009) which argues for a qualitative approach to marital, cohabiting and dating relationships. Their reason for this is that the use of closed-ended questionnaires and the like severely limits the richness of the questions which can be used. Unfortunately, their solution was to use open-ended questioning the answers to which were coded using a closed-ended schedule. The size of their sample was 1252 which is large by quantitative standards and unknown in qualitative research. None of the qualitative data analysis methods were employed apart from coding using a prepared coding schedule and so this does not meet the requirements of, say, interpretative phenomenological analysis.[30]

References

Fine, M. A., & Harvey, J. H. (Ed.). (2006). *Handbook of divorce and relationship dissolution*. Mahwah, NJ: Lawrence Erlbaum Associates.

Helgeson, V. S. (1994). Long-distance romantic relationships: Sex differences in adjustment and breakup. *Personality and Social Psychology Bulletin, 20*, 254–265.

Hill, C. T., Rubin, Z., & Peplau, L. A. (1976). Breakups before marriage: The end of 103 affairs. *Journal of Social Issues, 32*, 147–168.

Horwitz, A. V., & Wakefield, J. C. (2007). *The loss of sadness: How psychiatry transformed normal sorrow into depressive disorder*. New York, NY: Oxford University Press.

Hsueh, A. C., Morrison, K. R., & Doss, B. D. (2009). Qualitative reports of problems in cohabiting relationships: Comparisons to married and dating relationships. *Journal of Family Psychology, 23*, 236–246.

Kelley, H. H., & Thibaut, J. W. (1978). *Interpersonal relations: A theory of interdependence*. New York: Wiley.

Lewandowski, G. W., & Bizzoco, N. M. (2007). Addition through subtraction: Growth following the dissolution of a low quality relationship. *Journal of Positive Psychology, 2*, 40–54.

Locker, L., McIntosh, W. D., Hackney, A. A., Wilson, J. H., & Wiegand, K. E. (2010). The breakup of romantic relationships: Situational predictors of perception of recovery. *North American Journal of Psychology, 12*, 565–578.

Perilloux, C., & Buss, D. M. (2008). Breaking up romantic relationships: Cost experienced and coping strategies deployed. *Evolutionary Psychology, 6*, 164–181.

Saffrey, C., & Ehrenberg, M. (2007). When thinking hurts: Attachment, rumination, and postrelationship adjustment. *Personal Relationships, 14*, 351–368.

Smith, J. A. (1996). Beyond the divide between cognition and discourse: Using interpretative phenomenological analysis in health psychology. *Psychology and Health, 11*, 261–271.

Smith, J. A. (2004). Reflecting on the development of interpretative phenomenological analysis and its contribution to qualitative research in psychology. *Qualitative Research in Psychology, 1*, 39–54.

Smith, J. A. (2007). Hermeneutics, human sciences, and health: Linking theory and practice. *International Journal of Qualitative Studies on Health and Well-Being, 2*, 3–11.

Smith, J. A., & Osborn, M. (2008). Interpretative phenomenological analysis. In J. A. Smith (Ed.), *Qualitative psychology: A practical guide to methods* (2nd ed.). London: Sage.

Tashiro, T., & Frazier, P. (2003). "I'll never be in a relationship like that again": Personal growth following romantic relationship breakups. *Personal Relationships, 10*, 113–128.

Thibaut, J. W., & Kelley, H. H. (1959). *The social psychology of groups*. New York: Wiley.

Viejo, C., Ortega-Ruiz, R., & Sánchez, V. (2015) Adolescent love and well-being: The role of dating relationships for psychological adjustment, *Journal of Youth Studies, 18*, 1219–1236.

27.3 Critical evaluation

■ Title

1 Striking and amusing elements are common in qualitative research titles though often taken from the transcripts of interviews unlike here.

2 This is a perfectly satisfactory title though it might be better to write Interpretative Phenomenological Analysis rather than IPA which may be a little obscure to some readers.

■ Abstract

3 There is little by way of detail about the participants in the research. They were female volunteers from a university psychology practical class.

4 The abstract does nothing to explain to the reader why the study was considered worthwhile conducting – that is, no case is made for doing the research.

5 To write about themes 'revealing themselves' is to ignore the fact that the themes are constructed by the researcher rather than existing in some sort of reality. The themes are not something found by the researcher but actively constructed by the researcher in the analysis.

■ Introduction

6 There are a number of arguments being made which largely suggest that there is a need for research on dating relationships. However, the case for studying 'being dumped' especially is not really apparent other than unexplained resource limitations which hardly explains the particular choice made.

7 There is little by way of a literature review on 'being dumped'. The Viejo et al. study merely establishes that early dating relations are important for the individual's well-being which has nothing to do with 'being dumped'.

8 The case for using qualitative approaches to 'being dumped' could be made stronger. This might include a discussion of the limitations of the quantitative research on the topic and how a qualitative approach overcomes these limitations. The argument given is based on the claim that qualitative research would add a 'richness' to our understanding of the topic. One argument which might be used is that the experience of being 'dumped' is a process which involves recovery from the negative effects of being 'dumped' and that qualitative research is better at studying processes than are quantitative methods.

9 The choice of IPA could be explained more precisely since there are several qualitative data analysis methods which could have been employed including discourse analysis, narrative analysis, grounded theory and thematic analysis.

10 These bullet points are a reasonable summary of what IPA is. In themselves, they do not explain why it is the appropriate method.

11 The paper loses track here and gives as the research question ideas which stem from quantitative approaches. The use of words like 'variable' and 'prediction' come from quantitative research and do not fit in with qualitative data analysis methods.

■ Participants

12 There is a shortage of information about the sample used. With only three participants, it should be easily possible to provide a fairly detailed pen-picture of each of the participants in order to contextualise the interview material with some demographic, biographic and other details. Information on these things is sparse in the write-up.

13 It is unclear the extent to which the sampling method was tuned to the needs of a qualitative study. The sample seems to have been a convenience sample where a qualitative approach might have demanded a more directed or purposive selection. There are no details about the numbers not volunteering or about just why only three out of five volunteers were interviewed. A qualitative study demands as much or more detail as a quantitative one about sampling although the detail may be different.

14 The report could contain fuller details of the interviews. For example: How long did they last? Were probes used at any stage? What preliminary instructions were given? Whether the interviewee was encouraged to ask questions. What the debriefing session consisted of.

15 The interview schedule is not included in the report yet it is vital to the reader's understanding of the procedures employed. The schedule gives an indication of how open ended the questioning is, what the participants were questioned about and the sequencing of the questions. The reader might find, for example, that the themes identified in the analysis are signalled in the interview as areas for discussion thus opening up the possibility that the themes are directly consequent on the questions asked.

16 The transcription method was not Jefferson-style judging from the excerpts presented which include no Jefferson features. So how was the transcription done?

■ Analysis

17 This is the sort of account that you might find in a textbook. Unfortunately, having read the procedure for the analysis, the reader is little wiser about how the themes were actually generated in practice. It is worthwhile considering extending the description to give more detail based on exactly what was done. One suggestion is to include part of the annotated transcript to give some idea of the sort of notes that were made. Then it can be shown how the notes became combined into themes. This could be done in an appendix. As it stands, the relationship between the data and the analysis is unclear. It is likely that the transcripts of the interviews are quite short and so they might be included in their entirety together with the notes.

■ Results

18 The themes are categories generated by the analyst and not resources that the participants use. This sentence requires rewriting in a way which stresses that the themes are analytic categories in keeping with the qualitative ethos.

19 There are no subthemes discussed anywhere in this report despite the claim to have generated them.

20 There is no way of knowing in this report which excerpts belong to which of the three interviewees. It would have been a simple matter to give each participant a fictitious name and identify each excerpt with this name.

21 To write that this interviewee punished herself for being dumped seems to go beyond anything that she says. She describes being angry at the way she was treated and felt embarrassed and humiliated by it. But nothing points to the interpretation that she was punishing herself.

22 It is difficult to see the evidence that the interviewee had not succumbed to negative emotions in this excerpt. It is important to make sure that what appears in the excerpt corresponds with what is said about the excerpt.

23 This quotation simply does not match the title of the theme. The interviewee says nothing which implies a benefit of being dumped. If the excerpts chosen do not seem to fit with the theme then the analysis is undermined.

■ Discussion

24 Where is the evidence that the termination of a relationship is seen as a form of rejection? Rejection does not form a feature of the excerpts.

25 Since women respond in the same way whether or not they initiate the break-up but men are more badly affected if they were not the initiator, then this implies that the researcher should have sampled men rather than women. Had this research guided the sampling, the interviews should have been with men.

26 The discussion is not of the findings of the qualitative research but it is largely a discussion of some quantitative research in the field. By and large, where the findings of the qualitative study are discussed they merely are used to illustrate or add some support to the quantitative findings rather than the other way around.

27 It is questionable whether the shortage of qualitative material in this field is the limitation. The limitation seems to lie in the absence of a satisfactory analysis of the interviews. We do not have the transcripts available as, say, an appendix to the report which might indicate whether the interviews lacked richness. Furthermore, were the transcripts available, then judgements could be made about the adequacy of the themes developed during the analysis. As things stand, we do not know the extent to which the themes fit the interviews well or whether additional or different themes could be used.

28 It is not altogether clear what is meant by the scope of the study. Perhaps it is that the analysis is based on just three interviews. This is not the problem as there are many fine qualitative studies which are based on such a small number of interviews or even a single interview. The problem lies more in the analysis and the themes developed. One might suggest that the data were under-analysed or superficially analysed with little effort to engage with the material in depth.

29 The writer perhaps at this stage should be critical of the strategy of sampling rather than the sample size. If resources permitted just three interviews, the interviewees could have been more strategically chosen to make the data more demanding.

30 This is a curious way to finish a report and, once again, seems like material for the introduction. In the introduction, it could be used as justification for the qualitative study.

> ### Box 27.2   Research Example
>
> ## Layout and summary of an IPA paper on break-ups in British South Asian gay men
>
> Jaspal, R. (2015). The experience of relationship dissolution among British South Asian gay men: Identity threat and protection. *Sexuality Research and Social Policy, 12,* 34–46.
>
> We have chosen as a research example the same qualitative method on a similar topic to the fictitious one we previously used in this chapter to illustrate some of the problems students may have in writing up such reports. This study was carried out by Rusi Jaspal who is obviously an experienced researcher as he has cited five of his journal articles in this area, on all of which he is first author and which are published in reputable journals. The 54 references in the Reference section are formatted according to the 2010 APA style which authors are instructed to follow but the references cited in the text of the report do not fully reflect that style. Namely, the last names of three and up to six authors are not listed the first time they are mentioned, 'and' is used instead of the ampersand '&' symbol where there are only two authors and there is no comma separating the year of publication from the authors. Of course, these are trivial matters which do not reflect adversely on the quality of the paper and this format is presumably the journal's or publisher's publication style. To check whether it was the journal's house style, we looked at some other papers and the instructions for potential authors of this journal. These instructions state 'The style and punctuation of the references should conform to strict APA style' and 'In general, the journal follows the recommendations of the 2009 Publication Manual of the American Psychological Association (6th ed.)'. This aspect of the journal's style appears then to be an exception to the APA recommendation and we advise you not to follow it. Should you adopt it, your lecturer may pick you up on it. We have commented at some length on this relatively trivial matter simply to avoid any confusion should you read this paper and notice that the format of the references in the text are not as we have reported the APA as stipulating. After all, this chapter is about how to write a qualitative report appropriately.
>
> The journal's instructions for authors also say that the manuscript length 'should generally be no longer than 40 double-spaced pages', a requirement this paper meets as it consists of 30 typed pages of about 10,700 words. The instructions go on to state that 'Empirical articles should include standard sections, such as Introduction, Methods, Results, Discussion, and Conclusions' which this paper has. Its four main sections are Introduction, Method, Analysis and Discussion. Analysis is a more appropriate title in a qualitative paper for what is called Results in a quantitative paper. These four sections make up about 22, 6, 39 and 18 per cent respectively of the overall length of the article. Clearly the Analysis section forms the bulk of the paper as you might expect for a qualitative paper analysing text which is wordy. This main section is divided into three subsections of roughly similar length. Each subsection has about six relatively brief excerpts of what participants said. Each excerpt ends with what is presumably a fictitious name and the nationality of the participant's background. These are placed in parentheses as illustrated in the example below.
>
> ### Aim
>
> As stated in the Abstract and the Introduction, the aim of this study was to explore how British South Asian gay men experienced and coped with the unwanted break-up of a romantic-type relationship and how this break-up affected their identity as there did not seem to have been any published research on this topic. The study aimed to examine this by using thematic analysis and identity process theory. In other words, the analysis of the data was informed by a particular theoretical approach, namely Glynis Breakwell's identity process theory.
>
> →

Method

Participants

A snowball sampling strategy was used to recruit 16 self-defined British South Asian gay men in West London, nine of whom were from a Pakistani and Muslim background while the remaining seven were from an Indian and Sikh background. All of the men described themselves as being 'moderately religious'. They were aged between 23 and 31 years and all had a college or university education. The average or mean period that had elapsed since their relationship broke up was about three years.

Procedure with analytic approach

A semi-structured interview was conducted consisting of 10 open-ended questions. The interview began with questions about how they saw themselves, followed by how the relationship developed and broke up, how they felt about this, how it affected how they viewed themselves and how they coped. The interviews lasted between one and two hours, were digitally recorded and were transcribed verbatim.

The author used Jonathan Smith's interpretative phenomenological analysis to analyse the transcripts. Firstly, he noted preliminary interpretations of the transcripts in the left margin of the page followed by noting initial codes for identifying themes in the right margin of the page. Once this was done, specific extracts were selected for this paper which were 'vivid, compelling and representative of the themes' (p. 38). Finally, super- or higher-ordinate themes comprising these lower order themes were developed to form 'a logical and coherent narrative structure' (p. 38).

A taste of the analysis

There seemed to be three superordinate themes which were called '(i) constructing identity around the relationship; (ii) relationship breakdown and threats to identity; and (iii) repairing identity in silence' (p. 34). Below is one of the brief extracts used to illustrate the first theme of relationships helping participants to construct their identity:

'This just became the story of my life. The relationship did. I look back and I didn't really have a life. It was just him and my small little world with him. That's what it was. (Sukhy, Indian)' (p. 39)

Author's suggestions for future research

The author suggested two future lines of research on this topic. The first line was to look at the relation between relationship formation or satisfaction and willingness to disclose one's sexual identity. The second line was to explore the impact of relationship break-up on sexual identity. It is not stated whether these issues should be studied qualitatively, quantitatively or both but obviously this could be done quantitatively.

27.4 Conclusion

This chapter has encouraged you to develop your critical skills when reading psychological reports. University education encourages this. But one consequence of this is that a conclusions section to this chapter is not too easy. Writing your own conclusion about your thoughts on the material you read is an obvious next step. So long as your head is buzzing with ideas the chapter has achieved its objective. The main lesson is that research reports will have imperfections but they are compromises which have to fit in the word limit available.

Key points

- Quantitative and qualitative reports have a similar structure consisting of the Introduction, Method, Analysis/Results and Discussion. In qualitative reports, it is more common and appropriate to call the Results section the Analysis. Each part is important. Because illustrative excerpts are included, the qualitative report itself may be longer than a quantitative report, so do check the set word limit.

- There is no single qualitative approach, so justify the approach you are using. This contrasts with quantitative reports where the rationale for the method used is well established.

- We usually learn complex skills by observing others. Writing a qualitative report is a complex skill. Find and carefully read good examples of papers on your chosen research topic. Look at several papers by different authors in order to see how they can vary. There is not just one way of doing things.

- As with quantitative research, ensure that you make as strong and as clear a case as you can for the contribution your study seeks to make towards furthering understanding of the topic.

- While qualitative scholars differ about this, it is generally a good idea to do a thorough review of the literature as far as possible before you collect your data. Discuss aspects of this literature thoroughly in your report so the quality of your literature review will be apparent to the reader.

- Although the Abstract is the last part of the report you write, it is usually the first part of the paper that is read and may be the only part if it is poorly written. Be as clear and as detailed as you can be within its restricted word limit. Readers may refer back to the Abstract if they forget or lose the thread of what you are trying to say so it may continue to perform a vitally important function in understanding what you have done.

- While you may be delighted and relieved at having 'finished' your report, make sure you leave yourself time to read, reread and revise it as often as it takes to write the best possible report you can.

- Give yourself time away from the finished report so that you can reread it with a fresh perspective before submitting it.

ACTIVITIES

1. Select a qualitative paper that interests you and read it carefully. What would you have liked the paper to have described in more detail? Did the interpretation of the excerpts help your understanding of the topic? How did it succeed or fail in doing so? What do you think was original about the contribution of the paper to knowledge on this topic? Can you think of any ways in which this knowledge could be increased by a further qualitative study? What would this study entail?

2. Offer to read and to give constructive comments on a report written by one of your fellow students. Where appropriate, ask them to make clearer or better support what they have written or suggest to them another way of expressing it.

PART 5

Research for projects, dissertations and theses

CHAPTER 28

Developing ideas for research

- Students can experience difficulties when faced with generating ideas for a research project or dissertation. Don't worry too much if you are one of these. Having good ideas comes with practice, and is part of the learning processes involved in becoming a researcher.

- Planning research ideally should be firmly based on knowledge of psychology in general and the pertinent research literature in particular. Generally speaking, we find it personally unsatisfactory to simply reproduce (replicate) other researchers' work. However, using their work creatively and intelligently in a valuable variation or extension of previous research is more enjoyable. This is what most researchers do and it is an approach which your lecturers will appreciate.

- Initially, research ideas are rudimentary. They are 'knocked into shape' by a process of reading, discussion with a supervisor or peers and exploring the possibilities in a systematic, disciplined fashion.

- Try drawing up a list of ideas to be honed down to a few manageable and feasible research ideas. Practical limits of time and other resources mean that sometimes very good ideas have to be set aside. Do not spread your resources too thinly by retaining too many ideas since the time involved in reading pertinent material can be considerable.

- The research idea you ultimately focus upon ought to be satisfying to you in different ways. It should be of interest to you, it should be capable of making a contribution to the research field in question, and it should be feasible within your time and resource limits. Student research is confined by a fixed time schedule and the most brilliant student research project ever is a waste if essential deadlines are missed.

- After a number of years at university and having lived for a while, there will be some topics that you have studied or some life experiences that you have had that have interested you. You probably are even clearer about the sorts of thing which you find boring and which will not motivate you. Our best advice is to avoid these even if they could otherwise make good studies.

→

- At some stage, and the sooner the better, every researcher has to start reading the recently published literature on their topic of interest. This may be simply to 'keep up with the field' but it is more likely to be to survey an area that one is, or is becoming, interested in. This is demanding and time consuming – one has to try to understand the what, how and why of the materials you are choosing to read. Some papers would be difficult for any researcher to understand.

- Bear in mind just what you are trying to emulate. Think of what you believe a professor of psychology should be. Are they not expected to adopt a curious, questioning and critical attitude? Furthermore, they are very cautious people, unwilling to take things for granted and demanding evidence for everything – even things which seem self-evident to regular people. Reading like a professor should help you come up with a number of ideas about what needs to be done further.

- The more you read, the more ideas will come to you. It is a bit like writing music. Most of us would struggle to write a tune, whereas a skilled musician who has listened to and studied innumerable melodies can do so easily. Having heard and played thousands of tunes will make it easier, not harder, to write a new tune.

- Substantial student research projects are largely modelled on the style of academic publications – final-year dissertations, for example. Consequently, some of the better student projects may be worthy of publication even though this is not their prime purpose. While there is no guarantee that the results of your study will be publishable, it is a goal worth aiming at.

28.1 Introduction

It is almost universal that psychology students have to carry out a research project as part of their training – at the undergraduate level, the postgraduate level or both. Ability to do research is regarded as one of the primary skills of a psychologist. The main purpose of student research is to demonstrate what skill level they have achieved. Does their work demonstrate the necessary skills needed to design, plan, analyse and report research? This is the basic requirement. To this is added the hope that their work manifests extra finesse indicative of the quality of their research ideas and their execution.

Naturally, students vary considerably in their ability to use their own ideas as the basis of their work. Psychology departments vary in the extent to which they expect this of student research, as do members of staff within a department. Some departments require students to carry out research on topics already outlined by members of staff in a sort of apprenticeship system. Other departments will positively encourage students to come up with their own research ideas. Both of these are reasonable options and have their own pedagogic advantages and disadvantages. This situation is very much like academic research in general. For example, many junior research staff are employed simply to carry out the research plans of more senior staff – such as when they are employed as research assistants. In other situations you may be offered a rough idea of what to do, which you need to develop into a project yourself. Whatever the case where you study, remember that the quality of the outcome may have an important bearing on your future, so you should satisfy yourself that what you choose to do is worthwhile and capable of demonstrating that you have achieved high standards in terms of the skills most pertinent to research.

There are three main broad considerations to reflect upon when planning to carry out a research project (see Figure 28.1):

- *Motivation* We all differ to some extent in terms of what motivates us best. Some students work best in fields which are especially relevant to their experiences. For example, many students draw on their personal experiences as a basis for planning research – they want psychology to be relevant to their everyday life. Research into the experience of cancer, alcoholism, dyslexia and relationships may be firmly wedded to things which have happened in their lives. While it is often argued that academic researchers should be dispassionate, it does not follow that this excludes topics for research which are of personal relevance. Other students may be attracted to topics which are solely of intellectual interest to them – they may not expect or require the grounding of their research in real life. Given that a research project is a long-term investment of time and energy, it is a mistake to adopt a topic for research that cannot sustain one over a period of months. Many students find research projects and dissertations a major trial of stamina and character.

- *Practicality* There is little point in risking failure with a student research project. So be very cautious about planning research with unknown or unpredictable contingencies for completion. For example, it might be a wonderful idea to study cognitive processes in a group of serial killers and, if properly done, the research might make a major contribution and even save a few lives. But what are the practicalities of something like this for a student research project? Fortunately, most of us do not know any serial killers and probably would need to resort to getting the cooperation of the prison service in order to obtain a sample. The likelihood of the prison service cooperating ought to be assessed seriously, alongside the seriousness of the consequences should the prison service say no – as it is likely to in this case. Be very cautious of vague or even seemingly firm and well-intentioned promises of cooperation – we have seen cases where cooperation has been withdrawn at a late stage, leaving the student having to revamp their plans completely. This is obviously distressing and results in research which is very much a compromise and unlikely to show the student's true ability.

- *Academic value* Student research is most likely to be judged using conventional academic criteria. Research can be valuable for many other reasons, but this does not necessarily mean that its weight in academic content is strong. For example, it may be

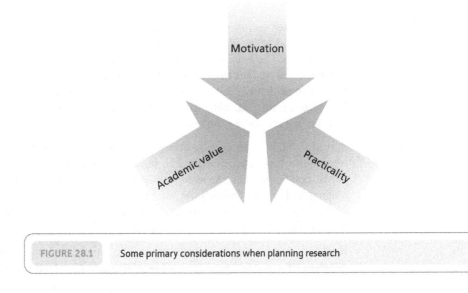

FIGURE 28.1   Some primary considerations when planning research

very important for practitioners to know young people's attitudes to safe sex and AIDS (acquired immunodeficiency syndrome). The information gathered in a survey of young people may be highly valued by such practitioners. On the other hand, in terms of academic weight, such a survey may meet few of the requirements of academics. The research might be seen by them as being atheoretical and merely a simple data-gathering task. Many academics would prefer research which helps develop new theories, validates theories, or is simply very smart or clever. So a student should try to ensure that their research is operating in the right playing field. Usually, the issue is one of ensuring that the theoretical concerns of the dissertation are made sufficiently strong – that is, there should be evidence that the research has an orientation towards theory.

28.2   Why not a replication study?

Research projects such as final-year projects and dissertations are in part judged in terms of their technical competence. They are also judged in the same terms as any other research work, for example on the extent to which the research potentially makes a useful or interesting contribution. One must be realistic about what any single research study can contribute, of course. Many published papers make only a small contribution, though, it should be stressed, there will probably be some disagreement as to the actual worth of any particular study. Excellence is often in the eye of the beholder. We have already seen that even experts can disagree widely as to whether a particular paper is of publishable quality in psychology (Cicchetti, 1991; Munley, Sharkin, & Gelso, 1988) as well as other disciplines such as medicine (Callaham, Baxt, Waeckerle, & Wears, 1998). Major theoretical or conceptual breakthroughs are *not* expected from student research, nor from the run-of-the-mill professional research paper, for that matter. However, it is not unknown for student projects, if they are of top quality, to be published in academic journals. For example, the undergraduate projects of a number of our students have been published (e.g. Cramer & Buckland, 1995; Cramer & Fong, 1991; Medway & Howitt, 2003; Murphy, Cramer, & Lillie, 1984). This is excellent, especially where the student has ambitions towards a career in research.

Not all research projects stand an even chance of being regarded as of good or high quality. Some projects are likely to find less favour than others simply because they reflect a low level of aspiration and fail to appreciate the qualities of good research. Here are two examples with comments:

- A study which examines the relationship between a commercial (ready-made) test of creativity and another commercially available test measuring intelligence. This study, even if it could be related to the theoretical literature on creativity and intelligence, does not allow the student to demonstrate any special skill in terms of method or analysis. It has also probably been carried out many times before. The value of the study might be improved if the variables measured were assessed using newly developed measuring instruments created by the researcher.

- A study which looks at, say, gender or age differences on a variable. Some research questions are mundane in research terms, although they may be important by other yardsticks. Sometimes, the technicalities of demonstrating a gender difference are challenging and would compensate for the lack of complexity of the research question. Unfortunately, a student's strengths are not indicated by simply showing that males and females differ on an easily measured variable.

Replication studies are an interesting case in point. It is important to understand why some replication studies would be highly valued, whereas others would be routine and pedestrian. A replication that simply replicates accurately a published study shows technical and organisational proficiency at best. Evidence of the student's conceptual ability, creativity and originality – that extra little spark – is missing. Regrettably, replications are not accorded the high status that they warrant, even in professional psychological research. Replication studies do have an important part to play in research – they are crucial to the question of the replicability of the findings. For example, if it were found that eating lettuce is associated with reductions in the risk of cancer then replicating this finding would be a priority. No matter how important replication should be to research work, it cannot effectively demonstrate the entire range of researcher skills. This does not mean that a straightforward replication is easy – the information in a journal article, for example, may well be insufficient and the researcher doing the replication may have to contribute a great many ideas of their own. Even simple things such as the sorts of participants are difficult to replicate precisely in replication research.

Professional psychological researchers can find it difficult to get replication studies published, despite the great emphasis placed on replicability in the physical sciences. One reasonable rule-of-thumb suggests that direct replication is valued only to the extent that the original study was especially important or controversial – and that in some way additional value has been added by the inclusion of additional manipulations, checks or measures. For example, you might consider the circumstances in which the original findings are likely to apply and those where they do not. Additional data could be collected to assess this possibility.

However, as soon as you begin to think of a replication study in this way, you are doing something very different from a simple, direct or straight replication. That is, you are including variations which were not part of the original study. To introduce meaningful variations means that you are also thinking psychologically and conceptually. This embellished form of replication we refer to as a part or partial replication. Some researchers have suggested that there are more types of replication than merely two (e.g. Darley, 2000; Gómez, Juristo, & Vegas, 2010; Lykken, 1968). However, these have not been widely adopted and would only obscure what we are trying to say. A straight replication study can only confirm the original findings completely or disconfirm them to some extent. In contrast, a partial replication offers the possibility that something new will be learnt over and above this. Partial replications have extra value as a consequence: they inform the researcher about the circumstances in which the original findings hold true as well as indicating the extent to which the original findings are replicable.

Examples of straight replication and partial replication may help:

- *Straight replication*   Suppose a study found that women were more accurate at recognising emotions than men. We need not be concerned with the exact details of the methodology. One approach would be to video people acting various emotions, play these videos to women and men and ask them to report what emotions were expressed. The outcome of the replication would simply establish the extent to which the original findings were reliable in the sense of being replicable.

- *Partial replication*   What if we noticed that the people acting out the emotions were all women? We may then be inclined to think that the results simply showed that women were more accurate than men at judging the emotions of women; we would not assume that women were generally more accurate at judging emotion than men. In order to extend our understanding, we may want to know whether women are also more accurate than men at recognising the emotions of men. This could be achieved simply by ensuring that the video material included both women acting out emotions (as in the original study) as well as men acting out the same emotions (unlike in the original study). This new research design is a partial replication, since it actually accurately reproduces the original study when using videos of women acting emotionally but extends it to cover men acting emotionally. Why is this more worthwhile? Simply because it allows us to answer more questions, such as:

- Are women better at recognising emotions in general?

- Are women better at recognising emotions exhibited only by members of their own gender?

Now, knowing this may not seem to be a huge amount of progress, but theoretical and other issues about emotion recognition between and within the genders are opened up. Just what would account for the research findings? Has something important been established which warrants careful future research? (It is one of the curiosities about research in psychology that the study that answers a research question definitively seems to have a lower status than one that stimulates a plethora of further studies to sort out a satisfactory answer to the original research question.)

So although a straight replication increases confidence in the original findings, it does nothing to further our understanding of the topic. It is of interest if the replication does not reflect the original findings, but it does nothing in itself to account for this discrepancy. We could speculate as to the reasons but we have no evidence to support this. Always, there is more to be gained from investigating the new questions generated by the original study than from merely replicating it. So, with care, a creative replication has a lot to commend it as a basis for student research.

When carrying out a replication study, you will almost certainly find that the published original study fails to include all the necessary detail to enable you to reproduce what the original researchers did precisely. The published paper may simply omit the necessary detail or may report it with less than due clarity. This leaves you with something of a dilemma – that is, should you fill in the gaps in the detail yourself? You might prefer to contact the authors of the original papers for the missing detail. It is relatively easy to track down academic authors using the Internet. You will know their name and likely academic location from the paper itself. They may have moved jobs, so some creative Googling may be necessary. Also, PsycINFO usually provides the e-mail address of the senior author of the paper, so this might be your first step. Remember, though, that language that might be fine when e-mailing your friends may be inappropriate when contacting an academic of an older generation.

Box 28.1 contains a discussion of the problematic nature of replication in psychology.

Box 28.1   Talking Point

The confusing role of replication in psychological research

At first sight, this is a simple matter: doesn't research develop through a process of discovery and replication? Is not replication the cornerstone of scientific progress? This basic principle is shared by psychology and is hard to dispute. Doesn't a replication of an important study make almost as big a contribution as the original study? Although in theory the answers to these questions ought to be 'yes', in practice this simply is not the case. Replication has a paradoxical position in psychology – although replication is lauded as the means of scientific progress,

obstacles are placed in the way of the researcher who seeks to replicate the work of another researcher. There are a number of aspects of this:

- Journals are very reluctant in many cases to publish papers that are straightforward replications of others as we saw in Chapter 14.

- Replication may be seen as a mundane, uncreative process done by researchers lacking in originality. So doing replications can be seen as a bad career move.

- Failures to replicate the original findings are often blamed on methodological shortcomings of the replication rather than the original study.

- Researchers can be proprietorial towards their own work and criticise failures to replicate their findings with some vigour.

The reluctance of journals to publish negative results is well known in psychology (Ritchie, Wiseman, & French, 2012). Doing research which is unlikely to get published is a poor choice in an environment of 'publish or perish'.

There is clear evidence also that researchers and journal editors are biased in favour of significant results. Researchers whose results are non-significant may avoid submitting a study for publication simply because they know that they risk wasting time or money. But they may also select for publication aspects of their research which show significant trends and omit or otherwise minimise aspects of the same study which failed to show significant trends. There may be many reasons for justifying this and these may appear in the published paper, but it is a bias towards positive findings nevertheless (Chapter 14). In terms of replication studies, this implies that a study obtaining non-significant findings is unlikely to be published even though it contradicts the original study. Psychologists regularly accepted the findings of a study despite there being little evidence of their replicability. Much of what is written in psychology textbooks now could not be published if replication of the findings were a requirement for inclusion.

So the forces encouraging replication studies are somewhat weak. However, there is a far more welcoming environment for what is known as the constructive replication which adds something to the original study – that is, it varies it in some way, such as by carrying it out in another context or location, or adding additional manipulations to the study in order to clarify some uncertainty about the implications of the original study. The problem is that if a constructive replication fails to reproduce findings similar to those of the original study, confusion is added to a complicated situation. If things are not being replicated precisely, just what differences caused the lack of replication?

There are other problems too. Tversky and Kahneman (1971) argued that researchers tend to have an unrealistic expectation that a replication will be successful in demonstrating the original effect. They told psychologists that a study with 20 participants had achieved significance at the 5 per cent level (two-tailed). Then they were asked what the likelihood is that a replication using 10 participants would reach statistical significance at the same 5 per cent level but

using a one-tailed test. These were not just any psychologists but were those attending sessions of the Mathematics Group of the American Psychological Association, so we might expect them to be accurate. Most of the researchers surveyed thought that there was a high likelihood of a successful replication. Generally their estimate of the probability was way out. The correct answer is less than .5, but less than one in ten of them estimated anywhere near that. Of course, the correct answer depends on the size of the trend in the original study as well as on the sample size for the replication. The general point is not that these mathematically oriented psychologists should have known better but that even they thought that the chance of a successful replication was far higher than it actually was. The statistical theory relevant to this is known as statistical power analysis (Howitt & Cramer, 2020) but many psychologists would be unaware of this approach. Clearly, the lesson is to make sure that your replication study is large enough for replication to be likely, based on the size of the trend in the original study. Probably the simplest way of doing this is to replicate as exactly as possible using at least the sample size used in the original study.

These are not just opinions: research over a number of decades has demonstrated that there is a dearth of published replication studies in psychology and that journal policy often excludes the straightforward replication study. Indeed, this is true for many disciplines and few studies failing to obtain statistically significant findings are published (Fanelli, 2012). Researchers could, of course, not attempt to publish research until they have completed a successful replication. The original researcher, after all, should be in the best position to replicate a study precisely. There are problems with this. Some sorts of research are extremely expensive and a researcher may think that their resources could be better used. However, if they do replicate their own study this may avoid the embarrassment of a failure to replicate in a study by another researcher. Self-replication could be made mandatory but is it such a good idea in research areas that are very costly? Furthermore, what if the replication fails to confirm the original findings – what does one conclude then and, more to the point, what does one do? Put the research into the file drawer and move on, or try to publish the research nevertheless? Or should self-replication always take the form of a constructive replication? There is a case for this, because if a study is replicable using different contexts or procedures then surely this is better evidence that the original findings are not simply reliable but also robust. If findings survive differences between studies then the findings are not easily negated by variations in methodology.

→

Part of the problem with replication is that it is generally understood within the content of scientific theory building where, in general, failures to support the hypothesis are somewhat uninteresting, as only positive support for the hypothesis is substantially informative. But not all research corresponds to this model. Take, for example, research into the effectiveness of psychological therapies. Therapies are sometimes suggested without there being any, or any significant, evidence of their effectiveness. Clients may pay substantial sums of money for such treatments and almost certainly will not undertake other treatments at the same time that might be more effective. In other words, a poor therapy may delay effective treatment. In these circumstances, evidence of the effectiveness of the treatment, or equally its lack of effectiveness, is important. Biases against publishing negative findings may prevent the timely abandonment of the ineffective treatment. A carefully designed study, whatever its outcomes, is informative in this practical context. In the more academic environment of theory building, there is always a feasible excuse to explain why a replication study failed to achieve the significant findings

of the original study. And we are well aware of the lack of robustness of many psychological effects, so replications may be seen as vulnerable to this.

It is difficult to discuss replication in abstract terms without losing track of one key aspect of research – that it is a complex, decision-making process. This is often overlooked in the environment of hypothesis testing, which offers a very simple approach to decision making: significant = accept, not significant = do not accept. In the more complex decision-making environment of modern psychological research, decisions about what to do next are built on much more complex considerations, although these are frequently omitted from reports. For example, the decision to carry on with the research may be down to the needs of the funder of the research as much as to the logic of hypothesis testing. Research may terminate because the funding body has moved on in its thinking and no longer needs the input of the research. In qualitative research, failures to replicate would be seen as a challenge for better synthesis rather than an indication that the original paper was simply wrong.

28.3 Choosing a research topic

Most researchers are, at times, stuck for ideas. They may be extremely well known and expert in their fields, yet research ideas do not flow simply because of this. Generating good research ideas is hard work, no matter what one's level of expertise. Convincing others that you have a good idea is even harder! Even when you have a promising idea, much intellectual sweat and labour is involved in turning it into a feasible, detailed research plan. Consequently, do not expect to wake up one morning with a fully-formed research question and plan in your mind. At first, there is a vague idea that one would like to do research on a particular topic or research question and, perhaps, a glimmering recognition that the idea is researchable. Then will follow steps such as discussing one's tentative ideas with anyone willing to listen and chip in thoughts, reading a lot around the topic and discarding what ideas do not seem to be working well. Usually some ideas with potential will establish themselves as worthy of development. Sometimes one's ideas are too big and consequently not practicable, so it is necessary to limit them in some way.

A good starting point is deciding which styles of research appeal to you most. These impact on what research is possible. For example, if you are interested in in-depth interviewing as a means of data collection, ask yourself what is possible on the topic using this method. If you think that a well-designed laboratory experiment is your preference then ask yourself what limitations this places on your research question.

Towards the end of their degree course, most students find some topics from their lecture modules are of particular interest. The research project provides an opportunity to tackle your interests in depth. Hopefully you will be spoilt for choice since many things intrigue you. There are several ways in which you may try to narrow down this choice:

- Try focusing on the topic that first aroused your interest in psychology. Does it still interest you? Have you been unable to satisfy your interest in the topic, perhaps because it was not covered in depth in your modules?

- Consider choosing a topic relevant to the kind of profession you intend to enter after graduating. For example, if you intend to go into teaching, it may be useful to look at some aspect of teaching, such as what makes it effective. This sort of interest may be advantageous when you apply for teacher training, for instance.

- Choose a topic that interests you which is part of a lecture module which is concurrent with your research project. In this way, the research and your studies will complement each. You are likely to have a greater in-depth knowledge to bring to the lecture module as a consequence.

- Try brainstorming a range of topics in which you have some interest. Try reading in depth some of these, possibly starting with what you see as your best bet. Does one of them emerge as a front-runner for your research? Does your reading on one topic have anything that might be transferred to another topic?

- If all else fails, try spending a couple of hours on a computer simply skimming through the latest research abstracts irrespective of topic. Out of what you read, does anything stand out as especially interesting? You should quickly get an idea of the range of topics psychologists study and how they study them.

Start thinking about the research possibilities that a topic offers as soon as possible. Make note of any ideas which you can link to your topic which you may have when you listen to lectures or read the literature. The best source of ideas, however, is likely to come from reading and thinking about other people's research. This is as true for professional researchers as for students. You will begin to see how professional researchers have conceived the topic you are interested in. This reading explains how researchers have conceived the topic of interest. Ignore the published literature at your peril since it amounts to a repository of hard thinking, good analysis and ways of conceptualising the important issues. In the Discussion section of their papers, authors may offer specific suggestions about further research work on the topic. The basic formula is that reading should lead to research ideas that work (see Figure 28.2).

There are surprisingly big gaps in psychological knowledge, and many potential research areas have simply received little or no previous attention. On the other hand, sometimes students feel disconcerted when they find published research they think similar to their own. So long as you have searched the literature diligently, this is just a matter of chance and could happen to any researcher. Actually the two pieces of research are likely to be different in any number of ways. You will want to discuss the other research in your project and it is commendable if you make a point of evaluating the two studies and describing their similarities and differences.

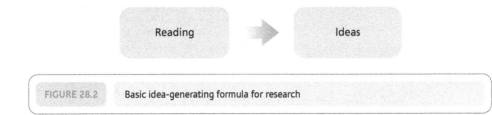

| FIGURE 28.2 | Basic idea-generating formula for research |

28.4 Sources of research ideas

Research into how psychologists get their research ideas seems conspicuously absent – a good research topic for a dissertation?! So there is little to be written based on this. Nevertheless, McGuire (1997) suggested 49 different ways or heuristics of generating hypotheses, which is one less than the number of ways to leave your lover! Our suggestions about sources of research ideas is a more modest list. Several different items on our list might be adopted in order to come up with ideas. Ours is not an exhaustive list, either. Others will have other ideas and if they work for you then they have done their job. We will illustrate our suggestions with brief examples of the sort of research ideas they might generate wherever possible (see Figure 28.3).

● *Detailed description of a phenomenon*   It is often important to obtain a thorough and accurate description of what occurs before trying to understand why it occurs. Possibly previous studies have done this in part but they may omit what appear to you to be critical aspects of the phenomenon. For example, we do not know why psychotherapy works. One way of trying to understand what makes it effective is to ask patients in detail how it has helped them cope with or overcome their problem.

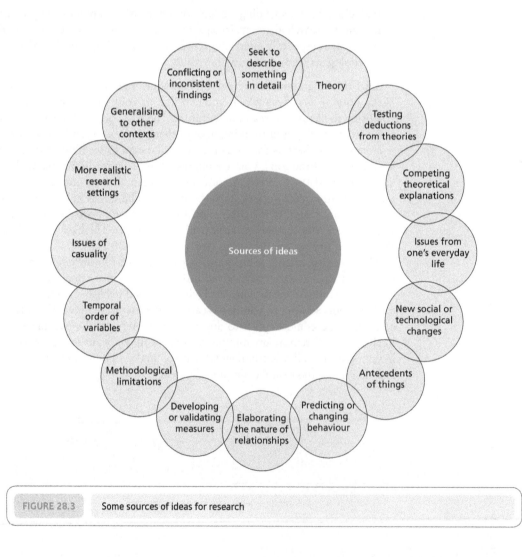

FIGURE 28.3   Some sources of ideas for research

- *Theory*   No matter what your chosen field of research, attention to relevant theories is invaluable. Remember that research is not primarily to produce more data but to extend our conceptual understanding of our chosen subject matter. Researchers are well advised to emphasise pertinent theory as a consequence. After all, the purpose of theory is to present a conceptual scheme to describe and understand a phenomenon. An absence of theory makes the conceptualisation of relevant issues much harder so you might explore the possibility of using theory from other, perhaps related, fields? The integration of theory with empirical work is the best approach. We are not referring to theory testing necessarily since many theories are too imprecise for such a test. If theory has potential for integrating various aspects of your analysis and discussion then it is advantageous to use it. Consider it a useful minimum requirement for your project that you introduce applicable theory. If you manage to integrate theory into your report to a substantial extent then you are doing very well indeed. The big limitation is that theory in psychology tends to generalise only to a modest extent which can make it difficult to apply in new contexts. Deductions from theories are discussed later. Box 28.2 shows that psychologists who make the biggest impact on the discipline are overwhelmingly those with a lot to say concerning theory.

- *Deductions from theories*   Much of psychology is about developing theories to explain behaviour. Theories involving a wider variety of behaviours are generally more useful than those with a narrower focus, for that very reason. While these theories may have been extensively tested in some applications, other interesting aspects may be under researched.

- *Competing theoretical explanations*   In the classic view of scientific progress, competing theories used to describe a phenomenon may be put to a critical decisive test. While many psychologists believe that few psychological theories are so precise that this is possible, nevertheless attempts to do so are well regarded. For example, there are a number of theories for explaining the occurrence of depression. It would be an intellectually satisfying challenge to take the main theories of depression and examine how they might be put to some sort of crucial test. So consider evaluating competing theoretical explanations of your chosen topic. While it is unlikely that a death blow will be struck against one of the competing theories, your contribution would be part of a longer term process of evaluating the tenability of the theories.

- *Everyday issues*   Frequently, there are a number of different ways in which something can be done in our everyday lives. There may be no research to help choose which is the most effective procedure to adopt or what the consequences might generally be of using a particular approach. We could carry out some research to help answer these questions. For example, if we concentrate on research itself for the moment, are potential participants less likely to agree to complete a longer than a shorter questionnaire? If they do fill in the longer questionnaire, are their answers likely to be less reliable or accurate than if they complete a shorter questionnaire? Does the order of the questions affect how accurate they are when disclosing more sensitive or personal information about themselves?

- *New or potential social, technological or biological developments*   We live in changing times when new biological, technological and social developments are being introduced, the significance of which we are not sure. Their effects, or what people perceive as being their potential effects, may be a topic of great public concern. What is the influence of the Internet or text messaging on our social behaviour? Has the development and spread of the human immunodeficiency virus (HIV) affected our sexual behaviour in any way? Do student fees influence the occupational aspirations of students?

Box 28.2   Talking Point

Top of the citations

It is intriguing to find that many of the most cited psychologists are very familiar names to psychology students. The majority have made highly influential theoretical contributions. Freud, for example, was a major theorist but a minor contributor of research. Remember that the theories referred to in journals are those which are usually influential on research. Haggbloom and his colleagues (2002) generated a list which ranked the 100 psychologists most frequently cited in journals. The first 25 of these are shown in Table 28.1. (Beside the name of each psychologist is one major contribution for which they are known,

although this may not be the reason for their citation.) Not everyone on this list has put forward a major theory. For example, Ben Winer, ranked fourth, is most probably cited for writings on statistical analysis. There are, of course, many other theories which are not listed that may be of greater interest to you. In this book, we have mentioned Hans Eysenck, Donald Campbell, Lee Cronbach, Donn Byrne and Robert Rosenthal. You can check the citations of any particular author by downloading *Publish or Perish* (http://www.harzing.com/pop.htm) and type their name in the box "Authors".

Table 28.1	25 psychologists cited most often in journals		
Rank	**Psychologist**	**Citations**	**Contribution**
1	Sigmund Freud	13 890	Psychoanalytic theory
2	Jean Piaget	8821	Developmental theory
3	Hans J. Eysenck	6212	Personality theory; behaviour therapy
4	Ben J. Winer	6206	Statistics
5	Albert Bandura	5831	Social learning theory
6	Sidney Siegel	4861	Statistics
7	Raymond B. Cattell	4828	Personality theory
8	Burrhus F. Skinner	4339	Operant conditioning theory
9	Charles E. Osgood	4061	Semantic differential scale
10	Joy P. Guilford	4006	Intelligence and personality models
11	Donald T. Campbell	3969	Methodology
12	Leon Festinger	3536	Cognitive dissonance theory
13	George A. Miller	3394	Memory
14	Jerome Bruner	3279	Cognitive theory
15	Lee J. Cronbach	3253	Reliability and validity
16	Erik H. Erikson	3060	Psychosocial developmental theory
17	Allen L. Edwards	3007	Social desirability
18	Julian B. Rotter	3001	Social learning theory
19	Donn Byrne	2904	Reinforcement-affect theory
20	Jerome Kagan	2901	Children's temperaments
21	Joseph Wolpe	2879	Behaviour therapy
22	Robert Rosenthal	2739	Experimenter expectancy effect
23	Benton J. Underwood	2686	Verbal learning
24	Allan Paivio	2678	Verbal learning
25	Milton Rokeach	2676	Values

Source: Adapted from Haggbloom, S. J., Warnick, R., Warnick, J. E., Jones, V. K., Yarbrough, G. L., Russell, T. M., et al. (2002), The 100 most eminent psychologists of the 20th century, *Review of General Psychology, 6,* 139–152, American Psychological Association.

- *The antecedent–behaviour–consequences (A–B–C) model*   Remember that any behaviour (B) usually has both antecedents (A) and consequences (C). For example, the antecedents of depressive behaviour may include unsatisfactory childhood relationships and negative experiences. The consequences may be unsatisfactory personal relationships and poor school or work attendance. Deciding whether we are more interested in the antecedents than in the consequences of a particular behaviour may also help us focus our minds when developing a research question. Once this decision has been made, we might try to investigate neglected antecedents of depression.

- *Predicting or changing behaviour*   How could you go about changing a particular behaviour? Do you think you could predict when that behaviour is likely to occur? Addressing these questions requires choosing the variables most likely to be, or have been found to be, most strongly associated with the behaviour. These variables form part of an explanation for this behaviour. You could investigate whether these variables are in fact related to the behaviour in question. This approach may encourage you to think of how your knowledge of psychology could be applied to practical problems.

- *Elaborating relationships*   There may be considerable research showing that a relationship exists between two variables. For example, there is probably a substantial amount of research which demonstrates a gender difference, such as females being less aggressive than males. Once this has been established, the next step would be to try to understand why this gender difference exists – what factors are responsible for this difference. If you believe that the factors are likely to be biological, you look for biological differences that might explain the differences in aggression. If you think that the factors are probably psychological or social, you investigate these kinds of factors. If you are interested in simply finding out whether there are gender differences in some behaviour, then it is more useful and interesting to include one or more factors which you think may explain this difference. In other words, it is important to test for explanations of differences or relationships rather than merely establish empirically that a difference exists.

- *Developing and validating measures*   Where there is no measure for assessing a variable that you are interested in studying, it is not too difficult to develop your own. This will almost certainly involve collecting evidence of the measure's reliability and, probably, its validity. For some variables, there may be a number of different measures that already exist for assessing them, but it may be unclear which is the most appropriate in particular circumstances or for a particular purpose. Alternatively, is it possible to develop a more satisfactory measure than those currently available? Your new measure may include more relevant aspects of the variable that you want to assess. Would a shorter or more convenient measure be as good a measure as a longer or less convenient one? Do measures which seem to assess different variables actually assess the same variable? For example, is a measure of loneliness distinguishable from a measure of depression in practice?

- *Alternative explanations of findings*   A researcher may favour a particular explanation for their findings, but there may be others which have not been considered or tested. Have you come across a research publication which has intrigued you, but you are not absolutely convinced that the researcher has come up with the best explanation? Do you have alternative ideas which would account for the findings? If so, why not try to plan research which might be decisive in helping you choose between the original researcher's explanation and yours? This is not quite as easy as it sounds. One of the reasons is that you need to read journal articles in a questioning way rather than as being information which should be accepted and digested. For much of your education, you have probably read uncritically merely to gain information. To be a researcher, you need a rather different mindset, which says 'convince me' to the author of a research paper rather than 'you're the expert, so I accept what you say'.

- *Methodological limitations*   Any study may suffer from a variety of methodological limitations. An obvious one for much research is the issue of high internal validity but low external validity. Basically, this is a consequence of using contrived laboratory experiments to investigate psychological processes. These experiments may be extremely well designed in their own terms, but have little relevance to what happens in the real world. For example, there are numerous laboratory studies of jury decision-making, but would one be willing to accept their findings as relevant in the world beyond the psychology laboratory? A study which explores in naturalistic settings phenomena which have been extensively studied in the psychology laboratory would be a welcome addition in many fields of research. Any variable may be operationalised in a number of different ways. How sound are the measures used in the research? For example, there are numerous studies of aggression which rely on the (apparent) delivery of a noxious electrical shock as a measure of aggressiveness. As you probably know from the famous Stanley Milgram studies of obedience, this same measure would be used by some researchers as an indicator of obedience rather than a measure of aggressiveness. Yet these are identical measures but are claimed to measure different things. Clearly there is the opportunity to question many measures, including those used in classic research studies.

- *Temporal precedence or order of variables*   Studies that involve change over a period of time are relatively uncommon in psychology, despite having many advocates. They are even rarer in student research. Obviously time constraints apply, which partially account for this. Longitudinal or panel designs, such as those outlined earlier in this book (Chapter 12) measure the same variables on the same individuals at two or more points in time. This enables temporal relationships between variables to be examined and compared. Often longitudinal research can take advantage of less contrived settings than a laboratory study. Consider the possibility of using a longitudinal design since it is challenging but may also generate new research possibilities in fields which are otherwise heavily researched.

- *Causality*   Student researchers can often benefit from conducting a well-designed experimental study. Despite their limitations for some purposes, experiments remain the quintessential research method in psychology. Remember that the main purpose of student research is for the student to demonstrate that they have mastered the crucial skills of research. Well planned and executed, an experimental design will garner favour.

- *More realistic settings*   One common criticism of psychology as taught at university is its undervaluing of research carried out in more naturalistic settings. Is it possible to take a somewhat contrived laboratory experiment and recast it in a more naturalistic and less contrived fashion? Often research is contrived because we try to control for variables which may affect our findings. But this is not the only reason. For example, take the example once again of Stanley Milgram's famous study of obedience in which participants ostensibly gave massive electric shocks to another person in the context of a study of learning. One might ask about obedience in real-life settings, for example. Just what are the determinants of obedience to authority in real-life settings such as a sports team? What determines whether the captain's instructions are adhered to? It is useful to find out whether similar findings can be obtained using less contrived methods than the original study, which helps show just how robust the original findings are.

- *Generalising to other contexts*   Theories or findings in one area may be applicable to those in other areas. For example, theories which have been developed to explain personal relationships may also apply to work relationships and may be tested in these contexts.

- *Conflicting or inconsistent findings*   It is a common comment that psychology is full of research on the same topic where some studies find one outcome and other studies find the precise opposite. That is, the findings of studies on a particular topic are less than consistent with each other. For example, some studies may find no difference between females and males for a particular characteristic, others may find females show more of this characteristic, while others may find females show less of this characteristic. Why might this be the case? If the majority of studies obtain a similar kind of finding, the findings of the inconsistent remaining studies may be due to sampling error, and many psychologists will ignore the inconsistent studies as a consequence. However, it is often better to regard the inconsistency as something to be explained and taken into account. Is it possible to speculate about the differences between the studies that might account for the difference in outcomes? In this situation, it is not very fruitful to repeat the study to see what the results will be, because we already know what the possible outcomes are. While it may not be easy to do this, it is better to think of explanations of these inconsistent findings and plan research to test your explanation. Consider carrying out a meta-analysis of the studies to explore a number of differences which possibly account for the variation in outcomes. Meta-analysis can be carried out using quite simple procedures. The technique is described in detail in the companion statistics text, *Understanding statistics in psychology with SPSS* (Howitt & Cramer, 2020) at a level which is within the capabilities of most students.

Box 28.3   Research Example

Study of differing predictions from consistency theory and enhancement theory

Swann, W. B., Jr, Griffin, J. J., Predmore, S. C., & Gaines, B. (1987). The cognitive–affective crossfire: When self-consistency confronts self-enhancement. *Journal of Personality and Social Psychology, 52,* 881–889.

One source of ideas for research is to find theories which seem to make different or competing predictions about a situation. One theory predicts one outcome, another theory predicts a different outcome. Finding out which outcome actually emerges provides evidence of the value of the different theories and might even suggest which theory is the best. This example is of one such study. As in this case, there may be research which has already tested these two theories but resulted in conflicting findings. Some studies find support for one theory and other studies support for the other. Where there are conflicting findings, can introducing new variables reconcile the conflict? The main purpose of this study was to see if conflicting findings are accounted for by introducing another variable.

Background

Some theorists have suggested that we seek to confirm our own views of ourselves, while other theorists have proposed that we try to enhance our views of ourselves. These two theoretical positions make the same prediction for people who like themselves. If we like ourselves, both positions hold that we will prefer favourable to unfavourable feedback, as this is both consistent with and enhances our views of ourselves. For people who dislike themselves, the two positions make

→

differing predictions. In this case, what has been called self-consistency theory predicts that we will prefer feedback that confirms our view of ourselves. In other words, we will prefer unfavourable to favourable feedback. In contrast, what has been referred to as self-enhancement theory predicts that we will prefer favourable to unfavourable feedback. Indeed, this difference in preference should be greater for people who dislike themselves than for those who like themselves.

A number of studies have tested these predictions and found mixed results. William Swann and his colleagues (1987) sought to reconcile these conflicting findings by testing the suggestion that self-consistency theory would apply to cognitive aspects of the situation, such as how accurate and competent the other person was seen as being. Conversely, self-enhancement theory would apply to the affective aspects of the situation such as mood. They also looked at how much the other person was liked, which they thought would be a reflection of both the cognitive and affective aspects of the situation.

Hypotheses

Swann and his colleagues appeared to make three major predictions.

- The first prediction was that the cognitive responses would be relatively independent of the affective responses.

- The second prediction was that 'cognitive reactions would be based on the degree to which the feedback confirmed participant's self-views, with confirmatory feedback regarded as more accurate, diagnostic, and so on' (Swann et al., 1987, p. 883).

- The third prediction was that 'affective reactions would be based on the favorability of the feedback, with favorable feedback producing more positive mood states than unfavorable feedback' (p. 883).

All three predictions are stated in a directional way. The second and third predictions may be interpreted as being expressed in a causal way in that the nature of the feedback has a causal effect on the response.

Method
Participants

A group of 58 female and 48 male introductory psychology undergraduates were selected from a larger group of students in terms of having either high or low scores on a questionnaire which primarily measured their social esteem or confidence.

Procedure

Participants were asked to deliver a short speech which they were told was being evaluated by someone behind a sound-proof one-way mirror. This person would evaluate them and then participants would have to assess the accuracy of this evaluation. Some of the participants received a written favourable evaluation which stated they were socially skilled, while others received an unfavourable one which said they were not socially skilled. It is not stated whether participants were randomly assigned to these two conditions.

Measures

Various questions were devised to assess cognitive aspects of the situation such as the accuracy and competence of the evaluator. Two questions were used to measure the attraction to the evaluator. All these questions were described verbatim in an appendix. An established mood questionnaire was employed to ascertain depression, anxiety and hostility.

Results
First prediction

The first prediction was tested with a form of factor analysis called principal components analysis. The components or factors were rotated so they could be related to one another (oblique rotation). Two factors were found. All five of the cognitive measures loaded or correlated highly on the first factor and all three mood measures on the second factor. The attraction measure loaded on both factors but was higher on the cognitive than on the affective one. These results confirmed that the cognitive measures were relatively independent of the affective ones, with attraction reflecting both of them.

Second prediction

The second prediction implied that there would be a significant interaction between self-esteem and feedback, which was found for all five cognitive measures. For example, participants who were self-confident thought that the favourable feedback was more accurate than the unfavourable feedback. Conversely, participants who were not self-confident thought that the unfavourable feedback was more accurate than the favourable feedback. These results confirmed the self-consistency theory prediction.

Third prediction

The third prediction implied that there would be a simple main effect for feedback in that both confident and unconfident participants would feel better after favourable than after unfavourable feedback. This was found for all three mood measures as well as for the attraction measure. These findings supported the self-enhancement theory prediction. The second and third predictions were tested with analysis of variance.

Authors' suggestions for future research

There were no suggestions for future research as such.

28.5   Conclusion

Research projects are intended to enhance a student's intellectual development and, at the same time, to assess this. While psychology students do research throughout their education and training, early on they usually complete research training exercises given to them by academic staff. Individual research projects are scheduled in students' final year because they need to have mastered many skills to enable them to plan and execute their own independent research well. For example, unless you have read examples of how researchers formulate and justify their research ideas, you will find it next to impossible to formulate your own psychological research questions. Even then, generating your own ideas is far from easy. It is something that cannot be done in a hurry so adequate time needs to be set aside to develop ideas. Usually students who have had a positive approach to reading and studying experience fewer problems since, after all, they have begun the groundwork.

Start thinking about possible research projects as early as possible. A year ahead of time is not too soon. If you have given yourself plenty of thinking time, keep a shortlist of possible research topics for consideration. This will help minimise the damage should you find that your preferred research topic does not generate workable research. One learns to think psychologically through a fairly lengthy process of reading and active study, and the same applies to thinking like a researcher.

You can get to understand how psychologists actually do research by reading a variety of research papers in any field that interests you. When you are planning research, however, you need to focus on and familiarise yourself with the established research literature on the topic – especially recent research. By reading in this way, you will learn something about what are sensible research questions to pose. You will gain insight into how researchers interested in the same issue as yourself have construed their study. You will know about what sorts of measures are typically taken and what procedures for doing research seem to work well in this field.

However, do not stop yourself from asking what might seem to be obvious questions about the topic which you cannot find addressed. These may not have been priorities for researchers but in need of research nevertheless. Think also of situations where previous findings might not apply. Humans have a tendency to seek instances which confirm what they know rather than ones disconfirming their preconceptions. Thinking of situations where previous findings may not apply should increase our awareness of the limitations of generalisation.

Practicalities may prevent you from doing your first choice of project. Try to be prepared for this and consider more modest possibilities. For example, you are unlikely to carry out an evaluation of a substantial therapeutic intervention, but you might be able to investigate people's preference for, attitudes towards, or experience of that intervention.

Key points

- Developing good research ideas is not easy. Even when you have developed the necessary academic skills, it takes time to choose a topic and become familiar with the relevant research. Start thinking about your research ideas as soon as possible.

- Be realistic about what you can achieve with your limited resources especially time. Most published research has probably taken much more time to conceive and execute than you have available for your project. Nonetheless, students at all levels can and have carried out research of value – some of which has been published.

- Simply replicating a published study is unlikely to advance our understanding of that topic. It probably won't impress those assessing your work too much either. While knowing that research findings are replicable is important, usually more is expected of a student project than just replicating a published study. While carrying out a replication, it is often possible to address new questions which emerge from the original research report. It is better to distinguish this kind of replication by calling it part or partial replication or even a constructive replication. Much research is partial replication.

- Your personal motivation is important so choose a topic that interests you – perhaps it is relevant to what you want to do in your future career. Prioritise your favourite topic and start reading the psychological literature relevant to it. If necessary, go on to the next topic once you understand why your first choice has not been productive.

- There is no single, foolproof way of generating a good idea for research. However, ideas are most likely to be generated as one reads and ponders over the research that other people have reported. New research is usually highly dependent on what went before and absolute originality is not typical of academic research.

- Carrying out a piece of original research is your opportunity to make a contribution to the topic that interests you. Make the most of this opportunity.

ACTIVITY

Think of three topics that you would like to do research on. Decide which of these three is the most promising for you, and start thinking about what you would like to know about it or what you think should be known about it. Do a literature search, preferably using an electronic database such as Web of Science or PsycINFO. Try to locate the most recent research on the topic and read it. When reading the research, adopt a critical and questioning attitude to what has been written. Try to read some of the references cited to see whether they have been accurately cited and are relevant to the point being made in the paper you are currently reading. Are the views in these references generally consistent with those in the paper? If they are not consistent, what seem to be the reasons for this? Which view do you generally support? In terms of the study, how were the main variables operationalised? Are there better ways of operationalising them? What suggestions were made for further research and do these seem worth pursuing? What questions remain to be answered? How would you design a study to test these?

CHAPTER 29

Managing your research project

- This chapter offers thoughts and ideas which may be helpful when preparing for and carrying out a research project for the first time.

- Planning is vital – make sure you give yourself enough time in the early stages to ensure you submit the best possible report or dissertation that you can.

- Your research topic needs to be feasible in terms of your resources and free from possible jams or delays. These include things like ethical problems or difficulties in recruiting appropriate participants.

- Research is not a sequential process. Assume that you will work on different aspects at the same time.

- The report or dissertation forms the basis of your assessment. Allocate plenty of time for writing, editing, and revising it.

- You probably have more resources available to you than you think. Think widely – your partner, friends and family may support you in a variety of ways.

29.1   Introduction

Have you ever tried to write a novel? Why not? After all you probably know just about every word to be found in all the top-selling books (even if your punctuation and spelling are a bit ropey!). Perhaps you don't know what to write about or how to tell a story. Maybe a novel seems like an awful lot of words to write. Your reluctance to begin writing your first novel, which might provide you with a livelihood for the rest of your life, is only a smidgeon different from the anxiety and trepidation you probably feel when faced with your first major research project at university. Don't worry, most of us have problems when conducting independent research for the first time. Being nonchalant and laid-back about the prospect is not the right attitude since this research project may affect your future tangibly. Do it badly and you may not get the grades you need for your degree. Do it well and you may even fall in love with research as your future career. In this chapter, we will make or repeat some suggestions which may help you make the best of the opportunity to conduct substantial research for the first time – or at any time.

Managing your own research project is a lengthy, complex and time-consuming undertaking as it involves a number of activities, beginning with the selection and development of an interesting research idea to the submission of a clear and concise research report. The project should be largely your own work, although you can expect a certain amount of support and guidance from your supervisor and from others who may be able to provide help or advice. Its purpose is your learning as well as an assessment of how well you can independently plan, conduct and write up research. Contrast this with the role of a research assistant who is employed to carry out and, possibly, write up someone else's research proposal. Although a research assistant may make an original contribution to the method and interpretation of the research, they are not usually expected to do so. They execute research as planned by senior staff with substantial research experience. Most likely, these senior staff have written a research proposal for which they have obtained funding. A good research proposal usually contains a timetable of when and how long the major activities should be expected to take. These activities include the literature review, developing the method, collecting data, analysing data and writing up the report. The work of the research assistant will be managed by the senior staff. As a student, you almost certainly will not have the luxury of a ready-made research proposal and you will be managing yourself.

29.2   Advice for consideration

Below are our suggestions for things that may help you manage your own research more effectively. They do not concern research methods as such – the previous chapters give you plenty to think about – but are things that textbooks leave out. They are intended to help you manage your project effectively and without trauma. To the extent that they do so, you may be spared some of the pain that managing your work poorly can bring. They should be read in the context of you needing to reach a satisfactory balance between your studies and the rest of your life. This involves compromises in both respects.

◼ Initial stages

- *Start as soon as possible*   Begin thinking about possible topics for your research project as soon as possible so that you give yourself the greatest amount of time to reflect on what you want to do. Most psychology degrees require students to carry out a research dissertation in their final year so ideally you should start thinking about your project in your first year. Choose a topic which interests you. Before your final year you may have opportunities to select essay titles or optional courses which allow you to study aspects of the topic in more detail.

- *Seek as much information as possible*   You don't have to wait until your department gives information out about your project. It may be useful to talk to students already in their final year about their projects and how they view the experience. Don't be afraid to ask members of staff in your department about final-year projects well ahead of time. They may have ideas that will help you choose a topic to pursue.

- *What is the weighting of your project?*   Sometimes but not always research projects are weighted by your university more than other courses that you take. You need to make sure that you allocate your time and efforts proportionate to this weighting.

- *Selecting a supervisor*   Typically you will be assigned a staff member to supervise your final-year dissertation. This may happen towards the end of your penultimate year so that you have an opportunity to meet them and discuss your ideas. You may have a choice as to who you would like your supervisor to be. If this is the case, find out which staff are available for supervision, and find out more about them. Not all staff have the same research interests or supervisory style. Indeed, they may have been given their academic post because they have different interests. You need to decide what you value most highly in your potential supervisor, such as similar research interests or a particular supervisory style. Ideally you should choose your supervisor as early as possible as some may be more popular than others and will fulfill their quota quickly. Try and find out from your supervisor what you can expect from them. It is possible that it is most convenient for you to collect your data in the summer vacation preceding your final year and that you are sufficiently ready to do so, in which case you may want to run through your proposed research with your supervisor before you collect your data. This includes ethics and other practical matters.

- *List a few research topics*   Don't restrict yourself to a single topic as you may find that what interested you initially no longer seems as important or relevant as it did when it first occurred to you. If this is the case, you can then move onto the second topic on your list without feeling that you have to start afresh. If you find that you are interested in a relatively large number of research topics, then it is useful to prioritise them in some way, such as their theoretical importance, feasibility or practical relevance.

- *Stuck for a research topic?*   If Chapter 28 did not solve this, remember that modern psychology is a broad church. Qualitative methods provide opportunities for addressing different sorts of research question from mainstream quantitative research. Qualitative research generally emphasises how people experience things which gives you scope for a whole raft of alternative research.

- *Make use of your social resources*   While your research project is your own work, consider using your partner, friends, and family to help you where this is appropriate. For example, they might be of help as unpaid research assistants for data collection or to read through your draft thesis for errors, typos, etc. Of course, you could just use them for social support when things are not running smoothly. Make it clear in your report where you have had help, in your acknowledgements or in the main body of the text if you 'employed' others as research assistants.

- *Make everyone aware*   You may become a freaked-out zombie at some stage when doing your research project – or something similar. It is a good idea to let your partner, friends, and family know that you may be burning the midnight oil all day long! Explain that you may be preoccupied, inattentive to them, or downright ratty, but that you will emerge from it all a fuller and better person – with a degree!

Keeping out of trouble

- *Your research project is not a small task*   Don't be tempted to think that your research project is only a few thousand words which you can easily knock out. You need to make each one of these words count so your draft work will require very careful honing and editing to present your efforts in the best possible light.

- *Stick to the rules*   Your department should have plenty of documentation about final-year projects. This will include things like deadlines, word lengths, structure, referencing, arrangements for supervision, etc. Adhere to all of these things as they should make the submission of your project report seamless.

- *Don't create bottlenecks*   Given your time constraints, it is imperative that you avoid inadvertently creating delays. These can happen in various ways. A good example is failing to anticipate ethical problems with your research. You may think that research on small children is a good idea but they are defined as a vulnerable group so you may have to produce documentation for your university's ethical committee before you can proceed. You should make sure that you have a good understanding of ethical and data protection rules so that you can avoid obvious no-go studies. Do not get into the mind-set that there is nothing that you can do until you have finished your literature review or collected your data. There is always something to be done and expect to be working on several aspects of your project at the same time.

- *Attend all meetings*   No matter how tempting to do otherwise, attend every meeting with the department and your supervisor about research projects. All such meetings will be profitable to you. Perhaps you may think that you have nothing new to discuss with your supervisor, nevertheless go along to the meeting since it will almost certainly be helpful.

- *Avoid the rumour mill*   University departments may be hotbeds for rumours especially for something as emotional and stressful as a dissertation. Take what you hear with a grain of salt. For example, you might be told that you may lose marks if you make too much use of your supervisor. If you avoided supervision as a consequence the likelihood is that this has a negative impact on the quality of your project and you will receive poorer marks because of this.

- *Treat deadlines positively*   Deadlines are there to help you structure your time. So treat them positively and work systematically towards them rather than having a last-minute panic.

- *Deadlines*   Make a note of important deadlines. There may be a number of these. The first may be for an outline of the research topic you want to work on – your broad research plan. This is usually set in the preceding year. The second deadline may be for a detailed research proposal and the ethics form. This may occur in the first term or semester of the final year. It is important to determine whether your supervisor is allowed to comment on a draft of this before it is submitted. If this is the case, you need to know how long they need to look at it. The final deadline is for the research dissertation itself. Once again you need to know whether your supervisor is allowed to comment on a draft before it is submitted. Make sure that you will have sufficient time to incorporate any changes they suggest.

● *Back up your digital media*   Back up your digital files in a secure way very frequently. A computer crash or worse without back up can be disastrous at any stage and cost a great deal of time. Whatever approach to backups you choose, always remember that memory sticks, etc., may be stolen along with your PC. Cloud or other external storage devices may be a better answer in most circumstances.

● *Be systematic*   Make sure that you make a full record of things which will eventually be part of your research project report. For example, keep full details of any references that you may eventually cite as you may struggle to find it again.

● *Time management*   It is essential to get the right balance in your work (and life in general). While doing your research project you will almost certainly have other pressures on your time such as the other modules you are taking at the same time. Most research projects cover two or three semesters or terms so it is tempting to think that you have plenty of time. Simply do not steal time from your research project in order to meet other deadlines. If you have problems in this area you might look for short courses on time management which might be of help.

Use your varied learning resources

● *Learn to read like a professional*   Reading research publications is not the same as reading a novel. So you may choose not to read every part of a research paper word by word. Your reading is really to obtain information primarily and enjoyment is essentially irrelevant. When you first start reading papers for your literature review you may well read most of its contents because everything is new to you. After a while, you will probably read only parts of a paper – some of it you are now familiar with and so you can skim through these. Don't get bogged down with overly technical details of the paper which you are struggling to understand. This may particularly be the case with statistics used in a paper. You may be unfamiliar with them. So long as you have got the gist of what the technical stuff achieves you can try later to understand some of these technicalities if necessary.

● *Writing a research proposal is a very good thing*   It may be a requirement that you submit a research proposal at some stage. Even if it is not required, you should commit yourself to producing one. The research proposal is an opportunity to express your thoughts coherently for the first time no matter how hard it may be. It is basically a plan for your research so will include your research questions or hypothesis, your justification for these, your literature review, the methodology that you will employ, your ideas about your method of analysis, etc. It will expose your weaknesses, of course, and these will need to be addressed. It may be appropriate to include some aspects of the research plan into the final research report with a little adaptation.

● *Keep talking*   It is very difficult to think through complex ideas simply in your own head. Although writing your thoughts down will certainly help, bouncing your ideas off other people is also essential. This includes everyone who will listen to your ideas. They need to be encouraged to respond to your ideas, ask questions and make suggestions. It does not matter whether or not they know anything about doing research. Of course, your supervisor and friends on your degree are essential people to talk to but your family, old friends, and virtual strangers may also be a valuable resource though theirs would be a different form of input. You must make it clear that you welcome criticisms and questions of clarification but not simply warm, encouraging words as nice as they may be which do not challenge you at all.

● *Use your supervisor shamelessly*   It is a mistake to think that you will be penalised in some way for using your supervisor. You will not. Students who disappear below the parapet while doing their research project are, however, quite problematic for staff. It is important to them to know that you are progressing satisfactorily.

● *Supervisory meetings*   It is usual to have regular meetings with your supervisor to discuss your progress. Make the most of these meetings. If you have been working on your project there should be plenty to talk about even though you may be reluctant to discuss your half-formed ideas. The topics for these meetings may follow the structure of the research report. Early on you can discuss what research possibilities you are working on and why these might be important. For example, what is the hypothesis you are interested in testing and what is the explanation behind this hypothesis. You could discuss key studies which are most similar or relevant to your own proposed study. This can then be followed up by the method you are using, the data analysis and the discussion of the study.

● *Keep making notes*   There is no way that your brain can remember everything you read or think about during the course of your research. It probably matters little the way in which you make your notes – in a notebook or on your tablet, laptop, or PC – though, of course, anything in digital form is easy to manipulate, copy, and read! Really make notes about everything as you just cannot anticipate just which notes will turn out to be important. For example, you may have problems writing up your procedure unless you have notes about what you have decided to do and how you are going to do it. Obviously, keeping notes is vital when conducting your literature search as it is so easy to forget essential details kept just in memory.

■ Face up to your demons

● *The demon statistics*   Few students, even at a late stage in their studies, are comfortable with statistics. Their actual ability in statistics is largely irrelevant to this. Do not adopt statistics evasion tactics no matter how tempted you are. Being able to do a satisfactory statistical analysis is not as difficult as you anticipate, especially if you plan.

● *Anticipate your statistical analysis*   You will probably have some idea of the appropriate way to analyse your data statistically once you know your hypotheses and the data you intend to collect. You may not be sure that you are correct. Don't forget that there is always more than one way of analysing your data. You may consider basing your analysis on what studies in the published literature have done. Bear in mind that you do not need fancy statistics in order to address a research question. Simple statistics often provide elegant analyses.

● *Qualitative research is not the answer to statistics phobia*   It is a big mistake to opt for a qualitative study simply because you dislike statistics. You may not have the skills, for example, to conduct a good qualitative study or you may not have satisfactory supervisory support.

● *Make sure that you are prepared if you plan a qualitative study*   Qualitative research is no less demanding than any other form of research. Data analysis involves exacting processes which you may have had little preparation for. Make sure that you are familiar with what is expected.

● *Practise data analysis*   If you are unfamiliar with the analyses you intend to carry out and you have not collected any data as yet, then it is useful to make up some data in the form it is to be collected and to practise analysis on this data.

● *Check quantitative data entry*   It is easy to make slips when entering data into a spreadsheet such as when using SPSS. Even one or two errors may make a big difference to your research findings if they are extremely large or small scores. While out-of-range values may be identified by requesting the frequencies of all values, this is less likely to be the case for values which fall within that range though they too can distort your findings. One way of checking whether your data entry is correct is to have the data entered into two separate files, preferably by different people, and to use a program to cross-check the values in the two files.

Data collection

● *Do not fall into the trap of thinking that it is easy to obtain participants*   Obtaining samples for your research is hard work and you need to put effort into getting the required sample. People who agree to take part may not turn up at agreed meeting places, for example. Collecting data is demanding in terms of time, so leave plenty for doing this. Quick and easy ways of collecting your data may not be ideal. Internet surveys, for instance, may not generate the sample size you require and it is difficult to know how representative your sample is.

● *Do not rely on agreements*   You may have plans to do research in a specific setting and discuss the possibility with a member of that organisation who says that they can help you. The problem is that such offers of help may be withdrawn when you come to take them up.

● *Efficient data collection*   In quantitative research the most time-consuming activity may be collecting data from participants. You may be able to save yourself some time if you can collect data from more than one participant at a time, if you can do this. Depending on your research, this may be done in a number of ways such as collecting data from people in groups or inviting people to participate by running your study on the Web. Some universities have appropriate software to enable Internet surveys.

● *Anonymity of participants*   When collecting data from participants, it is a legal requirement that that participants are anonymous and that they cannot be identified or otherwise data protection legislation applies. You do not need the complications that this brings. There is no need, for example, for you to have a record of their name. Where you need to match different data from the same participants, you need to allow participants to provide some information about themselves which will allow you to match the data but not to enable anybody to identify the participant.

■ Writing-up

- *That 'finally got it together' feeling*   It has been noted quite often that even the best researchers only get things totally together when they complete their final draft. This is because there is a complex and slow learning process happening at each stage you pass through in a research project. You may only find, for example, the best means of expressing your ideas at this late stage. Or you may only finally realise what your data mean when you are writing your abstract. This is a long-winded way of saying that a research project which seems easy and unproblematic is not much of a learning process.

- *Avoid bamboozling writing*   You have probably come across examples of unreadable academic writing which you have struggled to understand. Writing badly in this way is not recommended as it is likely to fool very few readers. Clarity and accessibility should be among your writing aims.

- *Exploit any weakness of your project*   While it would be silly to deliberately introduce flaws into your work, do not try to hide them in your writing when you notice them. Instead draw attention to them, evaluate their implications, and propose solutions.

- *Write the abstract last*   You probably will have a good few stabs at writing your abstract. If you write it early then you probably are still struggling a little with your ideas about what you are doing. Abstracts are short and pithy and it is difficult not to waffle on until you have the best possible clarity about your work.

29.3   Conclusion

Managing your research is a complex task because it generally involves you not only developing your own idea but also ensuring that it is carried out and written up appropriately. This task may be made more difficult by the fact that you have had little opportunity to practise doing this. However, while carrying out your own research may be daunting, you should be reassured that most students end up doing this successfully despite their initial anxieties. Although this may not be required, it is generally useful to write as detailed a research proposal as you can. As this usually takes the form of the final research report itself, it can be used as the basis for the report itself. Included in this proposal should be a timetable of when and how long the different activities comprising the research should be expected to occur.

It is impossible to learn to be a researcher just from a book. Research projects provide an in-depth opportunity to delve into your chosen topic and make a contribution, however modest, to our understanding of that topic. They allow you to show just what you are capable of intellectually. For many students, it will be the most fulfilling and possibly the most frustrating part of their studies. Almost certainly, your experience will help provide you with a sound understanding of research methods in practice allowing you to develop further if you so wish. Conducting research is a skill which requires practice. We would be delighted to know that this book has stimulated your appetite for research.

Alternatively, there is always Plan B!

Key points

- It is vital to carry out and complete on time the best research and research report you can produce.

- Managing research is primarily concerned with ensuring that this is done.

- Management for students' research stretches from conceiving a potentially fruitful idea to submitting an exemplary report.

- Effective management means giving yourself sufficient time to learn, practise and carry out a complex set of skills such as literature searching, data analysis and interpretation, and report writing.

- Although you think you may have a clear idea of what you need to do, it is usually helpful to write this down in the form of a research proposal and timetable.

- It is generally useful to discuss your research with interested others such as your supervisor and fellow students, which may help to clarify and elaborate your own thinking.

- Although the time constraints for conducting your research may already be tight, it is better to give yourself too much rather than too little time to complete tasks.

- Give yourself time to receive feedback from others and to be able to take it into consideration in any revision of your report.

GLOSSARY

a priori **comparison:** An analysis between two or more groups in which the direction of the difference has been predicted on the basis of strong grounds and before the data have been collected.

abstract: The summary of a publication.

action: Behaviour which is meaningful rather than reflexive.

adjacency pairs: A unit consisting of two turns in a conversation which follow a standard pattern.

alpha reliability (Cronbach's alpha): A measure of internal reliability (consistency) of items. It is effectively the mean of all possible split-half reliabilities adjusted for the smaller number of variables making up the two halves.

alternate forms reliability: The correlation between different versions (forms) of a measure designed to assess the same variable. The reliability coefficient indicates the extent to which the two forms are related. Alternate forms are used to avoid the practice effects which might occur if exactly the same measure is given twice.

alternate (or alternative) hypothesis: A statement or expression of a proposed relationship between two or more variables.

American Psychological Association (APA): The largest organisation in the USA of professional psychologists.

analysis of covariance (ANCOVA): An analysis of variance in which the relation between the dependent variable and one or more other variables is controlled.

analysis of variance (ANOVA): A parametric test which determines whether the variance of an effect differs significantly from the variance expected by chance.

analytic induction: The process of trying to develop working ideas or hypotheses to explain aspects of one's data. It is the opposite of deduction where ideas are developed out of theory.

ANCOVA: *see* analysis of covariance.

ANOVA: *see* analysis of variance.

APA: *see* American Psychological Association.

appendix: The section at the end of a publication or report which contains supplementary further information.

applied research: Research which has as its primary objective the search of solutions to problems.

archive: A collection of documents.

attrition: The loss of research participants during a study such as when they drop out or fail to attend.

basic laboratory experiment: A true or randomised experiment which is conducted in a controlled environment. Random assignment to the groups or conditions is an essential feature.

Behaviourist School of Psychology: An approach which holds that progress in psychology will be advanced by studying the relation between external stimuli and observable behaviour.

between-subjects design: A study in which subjects or participants are randomly assigned to different conditions or groups.

bias: The influence of pre-existing judgements on a research study.

big data: This refers to the massive amounts of data generated by digital media including Facebook, etc. The analysis of this data requires large amounts of computer power and, often, specialised statistics.

Bonferroni test: The significance level of a test multiplied by the number of comparisons to be made to take account of the fact that a comparison is more likely to be significant the more comparisons are carried out.

bracketing: The attempt to suspend normal judgements by the researcher/analyst.

British Crime Survey: A regular, nationally representative survey of people in Britain looking at their views and experience of crime. Since 2012 called the Crime Survey of England and Wales.

British Psychological Society: The largest organisation of professional psychologists in Britain.

British Social Attitudes Survey: A regular, nationally representative survey of adults in Britain about a variety of different social issues.

CAQDAS (Computer-Assisted Qualitative Data Analysis System): Computer software used to help carry out the analysis of qualitative data.

carryover, asymmetrical/differential transfer: The finding of a different effect depending on the order in which conditions are run in a within-subjects design.

CASCOT: *see* Computer-Assisted Structured COding Tool.

case: A specific instance of the thing chosen for study, such as a single research participant.

case study: A study based on a single unit of analysis such as a single person or a single factory.

categorisation: The classification of objects of a study into different groups.

category/categorical variable: *see* nominal variable.

causal explanation: An explanation in which one or more variables are thought to be determined (affected) by one or more other variables.

causal hypothesis: A hypothesis which states that one or more variables are brought about by one or more other variables in a cause-and-effect sequence.

causality: The idea that one or more variables affect one or more other variables.

cause: A variable that is thought to affect one or more other variables.

chance finding: A result or outcome which generally has a probability of occurring more than five times out of 100.

check on experimental manipulation: The process of determining whether a particular intervention has varied what it was supposed to have varied. It assesses whether the experimental manipulation has been effective in creating a particular difference between the experimental and control groups. It cannot be assessed simply by comparing means on the dependent variable.

Chicago School of Sociology: An approach to sociology which emphasised quantification and the study of large groups.

citation: A reference to another source of information such as a research article.

cluster sampling: The selection of spatially separate subgroups which is designed to reduce the time and cost to obtain a sample because members of each cluster are physically close together.

coding data: The process of applying codes or categories to qualitative data (or sometimes quantitative data).

coding frame: The list of codes which may be applied to the data such as in content analysis.

coefficient of determination: The square of a correlation coefficient, which gives the proportion of the variance shared between two variables.

comparative method: A comparison of one group of objects of study with one or more other groups to determine how they are similar and different in various respects.

Computer-Assisted Structured COding Tool (CASCOT): Software for assigning the occupations of participants according to the Standard Occupation Classification 2000.

computer grounded-theory analysis: The use of computer software to help carry out a grounded theory analysis.

concept: A general idea which is developed from specific instances.

conclusion: The final section of a publication in which the main arguments are restated.

concurrent validity: The extent to which a measure is related to one or more other measures all assessed at the same time.

condition: A treatment usually in a true experimental design which is part of the independent variable.

confidence interval: The range between a lower and a higher value within which a population estimate may fall with a certain degree of confidence, usually 95 per cent or more.

confidentiality: The requirement to protect the anonymity of the data provided by participants in research.

confounding variable: A variable which wholly or partly explains the relation between two or more other variables. It can bring about a misinterpretation of the relationship between the other two variables.

construct validity: The extent to which a measure has been found to be appropriately related to one or more other variables of theoretical relevance to it.

constructivism: The idea that people have a role in creating knowledge and experience.

content analysis: The coding of the content of some data such as television programmes or newspapers.

control condition: A condition which does not contain or has less of the variable whose effect is being determined. It forms a sort of baseline for assessing the effect of the experimental condition.

convenience sample: A group of cases which have been selected because they are relatively easy to obtain.

convergent validity: The extent to which a measure is related to one or more other measures to which it is thought to be related.

conversation analysis: The detailed description of how parts of conversation occur.

correlational research: *see* correlational/cross-sectional study.

correlational/cross-sectional study: Research in which all the measures are assessed across the same section or moment of time.

covert observation: Observation of behaviour when those being observed are not aware they are being observed.

crisis: the stage in the development of a discipline when commonly accepted ways of understanding things become untenable, thus motivating the search for radically new approaches to the discipline.

critical discourse analysis: A form of discourse analysis which is primarily concerned with observing how power and social inequality are expressed.

critical realism: The idea that there is more than one version of reality.

Cronbach's alpha: *see* alpha reliability.

cross-lagged relationship: The association between two different variables which have been measured at different points in time.

cross-sectional design: A design in which all variables are measured at the same point in time.

cross-sectional study: Research in which all variables are measured at the same point in time.

data: Information which is used for analysis.

data mining: Statistical techniques for the analysis of big data which are led by the data rather than the researcher's hypotheses and expectations.

data scraping: the use of computers to capture machine readable information from websites.

debriefing: Giving participants more information about the study after they have finished participating in it and gathering their experiences as participants.

deception: Deliberately misleading participants or simply not giving them sufficient information to realise that the procedure they are taking part in is not what it appears.

deconstruction: The analysis of textual material in order to expose its underlying contradictions and assumptions.

deduction: The drawing of a conclusion from some theoretical statement.

demand characteristics: Aspects of a study which were assumed not to be critical to it but which may have strongly influenced how participants behaved.

dependent variable: A variable which is thought to depend on or be influenced by one or more other variables, usually referred to as independent variables.

design: A general outline of the way in which the main variables are studied.

determinism: The idea that everything is determined by things that went before.

deviant instance: A case or feature which appears to be different from most other cases or features.

Dewey Decimal Classification (DDC) system: A widely-used scheme developed by Dewey for classifying publications in libraries, using numbers to refer to different subjects and their divisions.

dialogical: In the form of a dialogue.

dichotomous, binomial/binary variable: A variable which has only two categories such as 'Yes' and 'No'.

directional hypothesis: A hypothesis in which the direction of the expected results has been stated.

discourse analysis: The detailed description of what seems to be occurring in verbal communication and what language does.

discriminant validity: The extent to which a measure does not relate highly to one or more variables to which it is thought to be unrelated.

discussion: A later section in a publication or report which examines alternative explanations of the main results of the publication and which considers how these are related to the results of previous publications.

disproportionate stratified sampling: The selection of more cases from smaller-sized groups or strata than would be expected relative to their size.

Economic and Social Research Council (ESRC): A major organisation in Britain which awards grants from government funds for carrying out research and for supporting postgraduate research studentships and fellowships.

electronic database: A source of information which is stored in digital electronic form.

emic: The understanding of a culture through the perspective of members of that culture.

empiricism: The belief that valid knowledge is based on observation.

ESRC: *see* Economic and Social Research Council.

essentialism: The idea that things have an essential nature which may be identified through research.

ethics: A set of guidelines designed to govern the behaviour of people to act responsibly and in the best interest of others.

ethnography: Research based on the researcher's observations when immersed in a social setting.

etic: The analysis of a culture from perspectives outside that culture.

evaluation/outcome study: Research which is primarily concerned with the evaluation of some intervention designed to enhance the lives and welfare of others.

experimental condition: A treatment in a true experiment where the variable studied is present, or is present to a greater extent than in another treatment.

experimental control: A condition in a true experiment which does not contain or has less of the variable whose effect is being determined. It forms a baseline against which the effect of the experimental manipulation is measured.

experimental manipulation: The deliberate varying of the presence of a variable.

experimenter effect: The systematic effect that characteristics of the person collecting the data may have on the outcome of the study.

experimenter expectancy effect: The systematic effect that the results expected by the person collecting the data may have on the outcome of the study.

external validity: The extent to which the results of a study can be generalised to other, more realistic settings.

extreme relativism: The assumption that different methods of qualitative research will provide different but valid perspectives of the world.

face validity: The extent to which a measure appears to be measuring what it is supposed to be measuring.

factor analysis: A set of statistical procedures for determining how variables may be grouped together because they are more closely related to one another.

factorial design: A design in which there are two or more independent or subject variables.

feasibility study: A pilot study which attempts to assess the viability and practicality of a future major study.

fit: The degree to which the analysis and the data match.

focus group: Usually a small group of individuals who have been brought together to discuss at length a topic or a related set of topics.

Grice's maxims of cooperative speech: Principles proposed by Grice which he believed led to effective communication.

grounded theory: A method for developing theory based on the intensive qualitative analysis of qualitative data.

group: A category or condition which is usually one of two or more groups which go to make up a variable.

hierarchical or sequential multiple regression: Entering individual or groups of predictor variables in a particular sequence in a multiple regression analysis.

human participant: According to the British Psychological Society (2010), p. 5, 'a human participant is defined as including living human beings, human beings who have recently died (cadavers, human remains and body parts), embryos and foetuses, human tissue and bodily fluids and human data and records (such as but not restricted to medical, generic, financial, personnel, criminal or administrative records and test results including scholastic achievements)'.

hypothesis: A statement expressing the expected relation between two or more variables.

hypothetico-deductive method: The idea that hypotheses should be deduced from theory and tested empirically in order to progress scientific knowledge.

idiographic: The intensive study of an individual.

illocution: The effect of saying something.

illocutory act: The function that saying something may have.

independent variable: A variable which is thought and designed to be unrelated to other variables, thus allowing its effect to be examined.

in-depth interview: An interview whose aim is to explore a topic or a set of topics at length and in detail.

indicator: A measure which is thought to reflect a theoretical concept or construct which may not be directly observed.

induction: The development of theory out of data.

inferring causality: The making of a statement about the causal relation between two or more variables.

informed consent: Agreement to taking part in a study after being informed about the nature of the study and about being able to withdraw from it at any stage.

Institutional Review Board (IRB): A committee or board in universities in the United States which considers the ethics of carrying out research proposals.

interaction: When the relation between the criterion variable and a predictor variable varies according to the values of one or more other predictor variables.

internal reliability: A measure of the extent to which cases respond in a similar or consistent way on all the variables that go to make up a scale.

internal validity: The extent to which the effect of the dependent variable is the result of the independent variable and not some other aspect of the study.

interpretative phenomenological analysis (IPA): A detailed description and interpretation of an account of some phenomenon by one or more individuals.

intervening or mediating variable: A variable which is thought to explain wholly or partly the relation between two variables.

intervention manipulation: An attempt to vary the values of an independent variable.

intervention research: A study which evaluates the effect of a treatment which is thought to enhance well-being.

interview: Orally asking someone questions about some topic or topics.

introduction: The opening section of a research paper which outlines the context and rationale for the study. It is usually not titled as such.

item analysis: An examination of the items of a scale to determine which of them should be included and which can be dispensed with as contributing little of benefit to the measure.

item–whole or item–total approach: The relation between the score of an item and the score for all the items including or excluding that item.

Jefferson transcription: A form of transcription which not only records what is said but also tries to convey some of the ways in which an utterance is made.

known-groups validity: The extent to which a measure varies in the expected way in different groups of cases.

laboratory experiment: *see* basic laboratory experiment.

Latin squares: The ordering of conditions in which each condition is run in the same position the same number of times and each condition precedes and follows each other condition once.

levels of treatment: The different conditions in an independent variable.

Library of Congress Classification system: A scheme, developed for the library of the US Congress, that uses letters to classify main subject areas with numbers for their subdivisions.

Likert response scale: A format for answering questions in which three or more points are used to indicate a greater or lesser quantity of response, such as the extent to which someone agrees with a statement.

literature review: An account of what the literature search has revealed, which includes the main arguments and findings.

literature search: A careful search for literature which is relevant to the topic being studied.

locution: The act of speaking.

locutory: The adjective for describing an act of speaking.

longitudinal study: Research in which cases are measured at two or more points in time.

MANOVA: *see* multivariate analysis of variance.

margin of error: *see* sampling error.

matching: The selection of participants who are similar to each other to control for what are seen as being important variables.

materials/apparatus/measures: The subsection in the Method section of a research paper or report which gives details of any objects or equipment that are used, such as questionnaires or recording devices.

measurement characteristics of variables: A fourfold hierarchical distinction proposed for measures comprising nominal, ordinal, equal-interval and ratio scales.

mediating variable: *see* intervening or mediating variable.

memo-writing: The part of a grounded theory analysis in which a written record is kept of how key concepts may be related to one another.

meta-analytic study: Research which seeks to find all the quantitative studies on a particular topic and to summarise the findings of those studies in terms of an overall effect size.

metaphysics: Philosophical approaches to the study of mind.

method: The section in a research report which gives details of how the study was carried out.

moderating variable: A variable where the relation between two or more other variables seems to vary according to the values of that variable.

multidimensional scale: A measure which assesses several distinct aspects of a variable.

multi-method research: This refers to the use of two or more distinct types of research methods in the same study. Usually it specifically implies the mixing of qualitative and quantitative approaches together.

multinomial variables: A variable having more than two qualitative categories.

multiple comparisons: A comparison of the relation or difference between three or more groups two at a time.

multiple dependent variables: More than one dependent variable in the same study.

multiple levels of independent variable: An independent variable having more than two groups or conditions.

multiple regression: A parametric statistical test which assesses the strength and direction of the relation between a criterion variable and two or more predictor variables where the association between the predictor variables is controlled.

multi-stage sampling: A procedure consisting of the initial selection of larger units from which cases are subsequently selected.

multivariate analysis of variance (MANOVA): An analysis of variance which has more than one dependent variable.

national representative survey: A study of cases from a nation state which is designed to reflect all the cases in that state.

national survey: A study of cases which selects cases from various areas of a country.

naturalism: The belief that psychology and the social sciences should adopt the methods of the natural sciences such as physics and chemistry.

naturalistic research setting: A situation which has not been designed for a particular study.

Neyman–Pearson hypothesis testing model: The formulation of a hypothesis in the two forms of a null hypothesis and an alternate hypothesis.

nominal variable: A variable which has two or more qualitative categories or conditions.

nomothetic: The study of a sufficient number of individuals in an attempt to test psychological principles.

non-causal hypothesis: A statement of the relation between two or more variables in which the causal order of the variables is not specified.

non-directional hypothesis: A statement of the relation between two or more variables in which the direction of the relation is not described.

non-experiment: A study in which variables are not manipulated.

non-manipulation study: A study in which variables are not deliberately varied.

NUD*IST: Computer software designed to aid the qualitative analysis of qualitative data, now known as NVivo.

null hypothesis: A statement which says that two or more variables are not expected to be related.

NVivo: Computer software to aid the qualitative analysis of qualitative data.

objective measure: A test for which trained assessors will agree on what the score should be.

observation: The watching or recording of the behaviour of others.

Occam's razor: The principle that an explanation should consist of the fewest assumptions necessary for explaining a phenomenon.

odd–even reliability: The internal consistency of a test in which the odd-numbered items are summed together and then correlated with the sum of the even-numbered items with a statistical adjustment of the correlation to the full length of the scale.

one-tailed significance level: The significance cut-off point or critical value applied to one end or tail of a probability distribution.

Online Public Access Catalogue (OPAC): A computer software system for recording and showing the location and availability of publications held in a library.

open-ended question: One which does not constrain the responses of the interviewee to a small number of alternatives.

operationalising concepts/variables: The procedure or operation for manipulating or measuring a particular concept or variable.

panel design: A study in which the same participants are assessed at two or more points in time.

paradigm: A paradigm, in Thomas Kuhn's ideas, is a broad way of conceiving or understanding a particular research area which is generally accepted by the scientific/research community.

partial replication: A study which repeats a previous study but extends it to examine the role of other variables.

participant: The recommended term for referring to the people who take part in research.

participant observation: The watching and recording of the behaviour of members of a group of which the observer is part.

passive observational study: Research in which there is no attempt on the part of the researcher to deliberately manipulate any of the variables being studied.

PASW Statistics: The name of SPSS in 2008–09. PASW stands for Predictive Analytic Software.

Pearson correlation coefficient: A measure of the size and direction of the association between two score variables, which can vary from -1 to 1.

percentile: The point expressed out of 100 which describes the percentage of values which fall at and below it.

perlocution: The effect of the speaker's words on a hearer.

phenomenology: The attempt to understand conscious experience as it is experienced.

phi: A measure of association between two binomial or dichotomous variables.

piloting: The checking of the procedures to be used in a study to see that there are no problems.

placebo effect: The effect of receiving a treatment which does not contain the manipulation of the variable whose effect is being investigated.

plagiarism: The use of words of another person without acknowledging them as the source.

point-biserial correlation coefficient: A Pearson correlation between a binomial and a score variable.

point estimate: A particular value for a characteristic of a population inferred from the characteristic in a sample.

pool of items: The statements or questions from which a smaller number are selected to make up a scale.

positivism: A philosophical position on knowledge which emphasises the importance of the empirical study of phenomena.

***post hoc* comparison:** A test to determine whether two or more groups differ significantly from each other which it is decided will be made after the data have been collected.

postmodernism: Philosophical positions which are critical of positivism and which concentrate on interpretation.

postpositivism: Philosophical perspectives which are critical of positivism.

pre-coding: The assignment of codes or values to variables before the data have been collected.

predictive validity: A measure of the association between a variable made at one point in time and a variable assessed at a later point in time.

pre-test/post-test sensitisation effects: The effect that familiarity with a measure taken before an intervention may have on a measure taken after the intervention.

probability sampling: The selection of cases in which each case has the same probability of being selected.

procedure: The subsection of the Methods section in a research report which describes how the study was carried out.

prospective study: A study in which the same cases are assessed at more than one point in time.

protocol: A research protocol is a document kept on file which specifies the procedures to be employed in the research, such as the recruitment of participants and how the data are to be managed. Adherence to the protocol is important, as it forms the basis of documentation submitted for ethical review.

psychological test: A measure which is used to assess a psychological concept or construct.

PsycINFO: An electronic database produced by the American Psychological Association which provides summary details of a wide range of publications in psychology and which for more recent articles includes references.

purposive sampling: Sampling with a particular purpose in mind, such as when a particular sort of respondent is sought, rather than a representative sample.

qualitative coding: The categorisation of qualitative data.

qualitative data analysis: The analysis of qualitative data which does not involve the use of numbers.

qualitative variable: *see* nominal variable.

quantitative data analysis: The analysis of data which at the very least involves counting the frequency of categories in the main variable of interest.

quantitative variable: At its most basic, a variable whose categories can be counted.

quasi-experiment: A study in which cases have not been randomly assigned to treatments or the order in which they are given.

questionnaire item: A statement which is part of a set of statements to measure a particular construct.

quota sample: The selection of cases to represent particular categories or groups of cases.

random assignment: The allocation of cases to conditions in which each case has the same probability of being allocated to any of the conditions.

random sampling: *see* stratified random sampling.

randomised experiment: A study in which one or more variables have been manipulated and where cases have been randomly assigned to the conditions reflecting those manipulations or to the order in which the conditions have been run.

realism: A philosophical position which believes that there is an external world which is knowable by humans.

reference: A book or article which is cited in a publication.

register: A list of cases.

Registrar General's Social Class: A measure of the social standing of individuals which is used by the British civil service.

relativism: The philosophical view that there is no fixed reality which can be studied.

reliability: The extent to which a measure or the parts making up that measure gives the same or similar classification or score.

replication study: A study which repeats a previous study.

representative sample: A group of cases which are representative of the population of cases from which that group have been drawn.

representativeness of sample: The extent to which a group of cases reflects particular characteristics of the population from which those cases have been selected.

research: Systematic and disciplined enquiry which has as its aim contributing to knowledge and theory in an area of study.

research ethics: Moral principles governing the form and nature of research at every stage from the commencement of research to its publication.

Research Ethics Committee (REC): An interdisciplinary independent body which has the role within institutions such as universities, hospitals and so forth of reviewing research proposals for research on human participants in order to protect the participants and the institution.

retrospective study: A study in which past details of cases are gathered.

rhetoric: Language designed to impress or persuade others.

sampling: The act of selecting cases, unit or value.

sampling error (margin of error): The variability of groups of values from the characteristics of the population from which they were selected.

scale: A measuring instrument.

simple random sampling: A method in which each case has the same probability of being chosen.

snowball sampling: The selection of cases which have been proposed by other cases.

socio-demographic characteristic: A variable which describes a basic feature of a person such as their gender, age or educational level.

speech act: The act of making an utterance.

split-half reliability: The association of the two halves of a measure as an index of its internal consistency.

SPSS: *see* Statistical Package for the Social Sciences.

stability over time: The extent to which a construct or measure is similar at two or more points in time.

stake: The investment that people have in a group.

standard deviation: The square root of the mean or average squared deviation of the scores around the mean. It is a sort of average of the amount by which scores differ from the mean.

standard multiple regression: A multiple regression in which all the predictor variables are entered into or analysed in a single step.

Standard Occupational Classification 2000: A system developed in the UK for categorising occupations.

standardisation of a procedure: Agreement on how a procedure should be carried out.

standardised test: A measure where what it is and how it is to be administered are clear and for which there are normative data from substantial samples of individuals.

statistical hypothesis: A statement which expresses the statistical relation between two or more variables.

Statistical Package for the Social Sciences (SPSS): The name of a widely used computer software package for handling and statistically analysing data, which was called PASW Statistics in 2008–09.

statistical significance: The adoption of a criterion at or below which a finding is thought to be so infrequent that it is unlikely to be due to chance.

stepwise multiple regression: A multiple regression in which predictor variables are entered or removed one at a time in terms of the size of their statistical significance.

straight replication: The repetition of a previous study.

stratified random sampling: The random selection of cases from particular groups or strata.

structural equation modelling: A statistical model in which there may be more than one criterion or outcome variable and where the specified relations between variables is taken into account.

structured interview: An interview in which at least the exact form of the questions has been specified.

subject variable: A characteristic of the participant which cannot or has not been manipulated.

subjectivism: The philosophical position that there is not a single reality that is knowable.

suppressor variable: A variable which, when partialled out of the relation between two other variables, substantially increases the size of the relation between those two variables.

synchronous correlation: An association between two variables measured at the same point in time.

systematic sampling: The selection of cases in a systematic way, such as selecting every tenth case.

temporal change: The change in a variable over time.

temporal precedence/order of variable: A relation where the association between variable A assessed at one time and variable B assessed later is significantly stronger than the association between variable B measured at the earlier point and variable A at the later point.

test–retest reliability: The correlation between the same or two similar tests over a relatively short period of time such as two weeks.

theism: The belief in gods or a god.

theoretical sampling: A group of values in which each value has the same probability of being selected.

theory: A set of statements which describe and explain some phenomenon or group of phenomena.

third variable issue: The possibility that the relation between two variables may be affected by one or more other variables.

title: A brief statement of about 15 words or less which describe the contents of a publication.

transcription: The process of putting spoken words into a representative written format.

triangulation: The use of three or more methods to measure the same variable or variables.

true or randomised experiment: A study in which the variable thought to affect one or more other variables is manipulated and cases are randomly assigned to conditions which reflect that manipulation or to different orders of those conditions.

***t*-test:** A parametric test which determines whether the means of two groups differ significantly.

two-wave panel design: A panel design in which the same cases are assessed at two points in time or waves.

unidimensional scale: A measure which is thought to assess a single construct or variable.

universalism: The assumption that there are laws or principles which apply to all humans.

utterance act: The act of saying something.

validity: An index of the extent to which a measure assesses what it purports to measure.

variable: A characteristic that consists of two or more categories or values.

Web of Science: An electronic database originally developed by the Institute of Information which provides summary details and the references of articles from selected journals in the arts, sciences and social sciences.

web source: The address of information listed on the web.

within-subjects design: A research design in which the same cases participate in all the conditions.

REFERENCES

Adjerid, I., & Kelley, K. (2018). Big data in psychology: A framework for research advancement. *American Psychologist, 73,* 899–917.

Alcock, J. E. (2011). Back from the future: Parapsychology and the Bem affair. *Skeptical Inquirer,* from http://tinyurl.com/5wtrh9q

Allen, R. E. (Ed.) (1992). *The Oxford English dictionary* (2nd ed.). CD-ROM. Oxford, UK: Oxford University Press.

American Psychological Association (2010). *Publication manual of the American Psychological Association* (6th ed.). Washington, DC: APA.

American Psychological Association (2018). Summary report of journal operations, 2017. *American Psychologist, 73,* 683–684.

Anguera, M. T., Blanco-Villaseñor, A., Losada, J. L., Sánchez-Algarra, P., & Onwuegbuzie, A. J. (2018). Revisiting the difference between mixed methods and multimethods: Is it all in the name? *Quality and Quantity, 52,* 2757–2770.

Aronson, E., & Worchel, P. (1966). Similarity versus liking as determinants of interpersonal attractiveness. *Psychonomic Science, 5,* 157–158.

Arribas-Aguila, D. (2011). Psychometric properties of the TEA Personality Test: Evidence of reliability and construct validity. *European Journal of Psychological Assessment, 27,* 121–126.

Atkinson, D. R., Furlong, M. J., & Wampold, B. E. (1982). Statistical significance, reviewer evaluations, and the scientific process: Is there a (statistically) significant relationship? *Journal of Counseling Psychology, 29,* 189–194.

Austin, J. L. (1975). *How to do things with words.* Cambridge, MA: Harvard University Press.

Babcock, M. K. (1988). Embarrassment: A window on the self. *Journal for the Theory of Social Behavior, 18,* 459–483.

Barber, T. X. (1973). Pitfalls in research: Nine investigator and experimenter effects. In R. M. W. Travers (Ed.), *Second handbook of research on teaching* (pp. 382–404). Chicago, IL: Rand McNally.

Barber, T. X. (1976). *Pitfalls in human research: Ten pivotal points.* New York, NY: Pergamon Press.

Barlow, D. H., & Hersen, M. (1984). *Single case experimental designs: Strategies for studying behavior change* (2nd ed.). New York, NY: Pergamon Press.

Baron, R. M., & Kenny, D. A. (1986). The moderator-mediator variable distinction in social psychological research: Conceptual, strategic, and statistical considerations. *Journal of Personality and Social Psychology, 51,* 1173–1182.

Bartholomew, T. T., & Lockard, A. J. (2018). Mixed methods in psychotherapy research: A review of method(ology) integration in psychotherapy science. *Journal of Clinical Psychology. 74,* 1687–1709.

Baxter, B. (1941). Problems in the planning of psychological experiments. *American Journal of Psychology, 54,* 270–280.

Beaugrande, R. D. (1996). The story of discourse analysis. In T. van Dijk (Ed.), *Introduction to discourse analysis* (pp. 35–62). London, UK: Sage.

Beecher, H. K. (1955). The powerful placebo. *Journal of the American Medical Association, 159,* 1602–1606.

Belia, S., Fidler, F., Williams, J., & Cummings, G. (2005). Researchers misunderstand confidence intervals and standard error bars. *Psychological Methods, 10,* 389–396.

Bem, D. J. (2011). Feeling the future: Experimental evidence for anomalous retroactive influences on cognition and affect. *Journal of Personality and Social Psychology, 100,* 407–425.

Benneworth, K. (2004). A discursive analysis of police interviews with suspected paedophiles. Doctoral dissertation, Loughborough University, UK.

Berenson, M. L., Levine, D. M., & Krehbiel, T. C. (2009). *Basic business statistics: Concepts and applications* (11th ed.). Upper Saddle River, NJ: Prentice Hall.

Berkowitz, L. (1962). *Aggression: A social psychological analysis.* New York, NY: McGraw-Hill.

Bertero, C. (2012). Grounded theory methodology – has it become a movement? *International Journal of Qualitative Studies on Health and Well-Being, 7,* 1–2.

Bettanysalikov, J., & McSherry, R. (2016). *How to do a systematic literature review in nursing: A step-by-step guide.* London: McGraw-Hill.

Bezeau, S., & Graves, R. (2001). Statistical power and effect sizes of clinical neuropsychology research. *Journal of Clinical and Experimental Neuropsychology, 23,* 399–406.

Billig, M., & Cramer, D. (1990). Authoritarianism and demographic variables as predictors of racial attitudes in Britain. *New Community: A Journal of Research and Policy on Ethnic Relations, 16,* 199–211.

Binet, A., & Simon, T. (1904). Méthodes nouvelles pour le diagnostic du niveau intellectuel des anormaux. *L'Année Psychologique, 11,* 191–244. Reprinted in H. H. Goddard (Ed.) and translated by E. S. Kite (1916) as New methods for the diagnosis of the intellectual level of subnormals. In *The development of intelligence in children.* Baltimore, MD: Williams and Wilkins. http://psychclassics.yorku.ca/Binet/binet1.htm

Bodner, T. E. (2006a). Designs, participants, and measurement methods in psychological research. *Canadian Psychology, 47,* 263–272.

Bodner, T. E. (2006b). Missing data: Prevalence and reporting practices. *Psychological Reports, 99,* 675–680.

Boland, A., Cherry, G., & Dickson, R. (eds.) (2013). *Doing a systematic review: a student's guide paperback.* Sage: London.

Bolden, G. B. (2015). Transcribing as research: "Manual" transcription and conversation analysis. *Research on Language and Social Interaction, 48,* 276–280.

Bolles, R. C. (1962). The difference between statistical hypotheses and scientific hypotheses. *Psychological Reports, 11,* 639–645.

Braun, V., & Clarke, V. (2006). Using thematic analysis in psychology. *Qualitative Research in Psychology, 3,* 77–101.

Bridgman, P. W. (1927). *The logic of modern physics.* New York, NY: Macmillan.

British Psychological Society (2006, 2009). *Code of ethics and conduct.* Leicester, UK: BPS.

British Psychological Society (2007). *Guidelines for psychologists working with animals.* Leicester, UK: BPS.

British Psychological Society (2011). *Code of human research ethics.* Leicester, UK: BPS.

Brown, J. F. (1935). Towards a theory of social dynamics. *Journal of Social Psychology, 6,* 182–213.

Brown, J. F. (1936). On the use of mathematics in psychological theory. *Psychometrika, 1,* 7–15, 77–90.

Brown, J. F. (1937). Psychoanalysis, topological psychology and experimental psychopathology. *Psychoanalytic Quarterly, 6,* 227–237.

Brown, M. S. (2014). *Data mining for dummies.* Hoboken, NJ: John Wiley and Sons.

Bryman, A. (2006). Integrating quantitative and qualitative research: How is it done. *Qualitative Research 6,* 97–113.

Bryman, A. (2015). *Social research methods* (5th ed.). Oxford, UK: Oxford University Press.

Bryman, A., & Bell, E. (2015). *Business research method* (4th ed.). Oxford, UK: Oxford University Press.

Buss, A. R., & McDermot, J. R. (1976). Ratings of psychology journals compared to objective measures of journal impact. *American Psychologist, 31,* 675–678 (Comment).

Byrne, D. (1961). Interpersonal attraction and attitude similarity. *Journal of Abnormal and Social Psychology, 62,* 713–715.

Byrne, D., & Blaylock, B. (1963). Similarity and assumed similarity of attitudes between husbands and wives. *Journal of Abnormal and Social Psychology, 67,* 636–640.

Byrne, D., Gouaux, C., Griffitt, W., Lamberth, J., Murakawa, N., Prasad, M., Prasad, A., & Ramirez III, M. (1971). The ubiquitous relationship: Attitude similarity and attraction: A cross-cultural study. *Human Relations, 24,* 201–207.

Byrne, D., & Rhamey, R. (1965). Magnitude of positive and negative reinforcements as a determinant of attraction. *Journal of Personality and Social Psychology, 2,* 884–889.

Callaham, M. L., Baxt, W. G., Waeckerle, J. F., & Wears, R. L. (1998). Reliability of editors' subjective quality ratings of peer reviews of manuscripts. *Journal of the American Medical Association, 280,* 229–231.

Campbell, D. T. (1957). Factors relevant to the validity of experiments in social settings. *Psychological Bulletin, 54,* 297–312.

Campbell, D. T. (1969). Prospective: Artifact and control. In R. Rosenthal & R. L. Rosnow (Eds), *Artifact in behavioural research* (pp. 351–382). New York, NY: Academic Press.

Campbell, D. T., & Fiske, D. W. (1959). Convergent and divergent validation by the multitrait–multimethod matrix. *Psychological Bulletin, 56,* 81–105.

Campbell, D. T., & Stanley, J. C. (1963). *Experimental and quasi-experimental designs for research.* Boston, MA: Houghton Mifflin.

Campbell, M. L. C., & Morrison, A. P. (2007). The subjective experience of paranoia: Comparing the experiences of patients with psychosis and individuals with no psychiatric history. *Clinical Psychology and Psychotherapy, 14,* 63–77.

Canter, D. (1983). The potential of facet theory for applied social psychology. *Quality and Quantity, 17,* 35–67.

Centre for Reviews and Dissemination, University of York (2008). *Systematic reviews.* York: Centre for Reviews and Dissemination https://www.york.ac.uk/media/crd/Systematic_Reviews.pdf

Chan, A., Hróbjartsson, A., Haahr, M. T., Gøtzsche, P. C., & Altman, D. G. (2004). Empirical evidence for selective reporting of outcomes in randomized trials: Comparison of protocols to published articles. *Journal of the American Medical Association, 291,* 2457–2465.

Chan, L. M. (1999). *A guide to the Library of Congress classification* (5th ed.). Englewood, CO: Libraries Unlimited.

Chan, L. M., & Mitchell, J. S. (2003). *Dewey Decimal Classification: A practical guide*. Dublin, OH: OCLC.

Charmaz, K. (1995). Grounded theory. In J. A. Smith, R. Harré, & L. van Langenhove (Eds.), *Rethinking methods in psychology* (pp. 27–49). London, UK: Sage.

Charmaz, K. (2000). Grounded theory: Objectivist and constructivist methods. In N. K. Denzin & Y. S. E. Lincoln (Eds.), *Handbook of qualitative research* (2nd ed.) (pp. 503–535). Thousand Oaks, CA: Sage.

Chen, E. E., & Wojcik, S. P. (2016). A practical guide to big data research in psychology. *Psychological Methods, 21*, 458–474.

Cheung, M. W., & Jak, S. (2018). Challenges of big data analyses and applications in psychology. *Zeitschrift für Psychologie, 226*, 209–211.

Cicchetti, D. V. (1991). The reliability of peer review for manuscript and grant submissions: A cross-disciplinary investigation. *Behavioural and Brain Sciences, 14*, 119–186.

Clarivate Analytics (n.d.). Journal selection process. https:// clarivate.com/essays/journal-selection-process/

Clark-Carter, D. (1997). The account taken of statistical power in research published in the *British Journal of Psychology*. *British Journal of Psychology, 88*, 71–83.

Clarke, V., Burns, M., & Burgoyne, C. (2006). "Who would take whose name?": An exploratory study of naming practices in same-sex relationships'. Unpublished manuscript.

Clifford, G., Craig, G., & McCourt, C. (2019). "Am iz kwiin" (I'm his queen): Combining interpretative phenomenological analysis with a feminist approach to work with gems in a resource-constrained setting. *Qualitative Research in Psychology, 16*, 237–252.

Cohen, A. A., & Hyman, J. S. (1979). How come so many hypotheses in educational research are supported? (a modest proposal). *Educational Research, 8*, 12–16.

Cohen, J. (1988). *Statistical power analysis for the behavioural sciences* (2nd ed.). Hillsdale, NJ: Lawrence Erlbaum Associates.

Cohen, J. (1962). The statistical power of abnormal-social psychological research: A review. *Journal of Abnormal and Social Psychology, 65*, 145–153.

Cohen, J., & Cohen, P. (1983). *Applied multiple regression/ correlation analysis for the behavioral sciences* (2nd ed.). Hillsdale, NJ: Lawrence Erlbaum Associates.

Cohen, J., Cohen, P., West, S. G., & Aiken, L. S. (2003). *Applied multiple regression/correlation analysis for the behavioral sciences* (3rd ed.). Hillsdale, NJ: Lawrence Erlbaum Associates.

Coleman, L. M., & Cater, S. M. (2005). A qualitative study of the relationship between alcohol consumption and risky sex in adolescents. *Archives of Sexual Behavior, 34*, 649–661.

Condon, J. W., & Crano, W. D. (1988). Inferred evaluation and the relation between attitude similarity and interpersonal attraction. *Journal of Personality and Social Psychology, 54*, 789–797.

Cook, T. D., & Campbell, D. T. (1979). *Quasi-experimentation: Design and analysis issues for field settings*. Chicago, IL: Rand McNally.

Coover, J. E., & Angell, F. (1907). General practice effect of special exercise. *American Journal of Psychology, 18*, 328–340.

Cornelius, T. L., Alessi, G., & Shorey, R. C. (2007). The effectiveness of communication skills training with married couples: Does the issue discussed matter? *The Family Journal, 15*, 124–132.

Coulson, M., Healey, M., Fidler, F., & Cumming, G. (2010). Confidence intervals permit, but do not guarantee, better inference than statistical significance testing. *Frontiers in Quantitative Psychology and Measurement, 1*, 26. doi:10.3389/fpsyg.2010.00026. http://www.frontiersin. org/psychology/quantitativepsychologyandmeasurement/ paper/10.3389/fpsyg.2010.00026/

Coursol, A., & Wagner, E. E. (1986). Effect of positive findings on submission and acceptance rates: A note on meta-analysis bias. *Professional Psychology: Research and Practice, 17*, 136–137.

Cowen, E. L., Underberg, R. P., & Verrillo, R. T. (1958). The development and testing of an attitude to blindness scale. *Journal of Social Psychology, 48*, 297–304.

Cox, B. D., Blaxter, M., Buckle, A. L. J., Fenner, N. P., Golding, J. F., Gore, M., Huppert, F. A., Nickson, J., Roth, M., Stark, J., Wadsworth, M. E. J., & Whichelow, M. (1987). *The health and lifestyle survey*. London, UK: Health Promotion Research Trust.

Cramer, D. (1991). Type A behaviour pattern, extraversion, neuroticism and psychological distress. *British Journal of Medical Psychology, 64*, 73–83.

Cramer, D. (1994). Psychological distress and neuroticism: A two-wave panel study. *British Journal of Medical Psychology, 67*, 333–342.

Cramer, D. (1995). Life and job satisfaction: A two-wave panel study. *Journal of Psychology, 129*, 261–267.

Cramer, D. (1998). *Fundamental statistics for social research: Step-by-step calculations and computer techniques using SPSS for Windows*. London, UK: Routledge.

Cramer, D. (2003). A cautionary tale of two statistics: Partial correlation and standardised partial regression. *Journal of Psychology, 137*, 507–511.

Cramer, D., & Buckland, N. (1995). Effect of rational and irrational statements and demand characteristics on task anxiety. *Journal of Psychology, 129*, 269–275.

Cramer, D., & Fong, J. (1991). Effect of rational and irrational beliefs on intensity and 'inappropriateness' of feelings: A test of rational–emotive theory. *Cognitive Therapy and Research, 15*, 319–329.

Cramer, D., Henderson, S., & Scott, R. (1996). Mental health and adequacy of social support: A four-wave panel study. *British Journal of Social Psychology, 35*, 285–295.

Creswell, J. W., & Plano Clark, V. L. (2007). *Designing and conducting mixed methods research*. Thousand Oaks, CA: Sage.

Creswell J. W., & Plano Clark V.L. (2011). *Designing and conducting mixed methods research* (2nd ed.). Thousand Oaks, CA: Sage.

Cronbach, L. J. (1951). Coefficient alpha and the internal structure of tests. *Psychometrika, 16,* 297–334.

Cronbach, L. J., & Meehl, P. E. (1955). Construct validity in psychological tests. *Psychological Bulletin, 52,* 281–302.

Crowe, M., Inder, M., & Porter, R. (2015). Conducting qualitative research in mental health: Thematic and content analyses. *Australian and New Zealand Journal of Psychiatry, 49,* 616–623.

Crutchfield, R. S. (1938). Efficient factorial design and analysis of variance illustrated in psychological experimentation. *Journal of Psychology, 5,* 339–346.

Cumming, G. (2012). The new statistics: What we need for evidence-based practice. http://www.psychology.org.au/inpsych/2012/june/cumming.

Cumming, G. (2016). Confidence intervals and the new statistics. Retrieved 14 January 2016, from http://www?.apa.org/education/ce/confidence-intervals.pdf.

Cumming, G., Williams, J., & Fidler, F. (2004). Replication and researchers' understanding of confidence intervals and standard error bars. *Understanding Statistics, 3,* 299–311.

Danziger, K. (1985). The origins of the psychological experiment as a social institution. *American Psychologist, 40,* 133–140.

Danziger, K., & Dzinas, K. (1997). How psychology got its variables. *Canadian Psychology, 38,* 43–48.

Darley, W. K. (2000). Status of replication studies in marketing: A validation and extension. *Marketing Management Journal, 10,* 121–132.

Denscombe, M. (2002). *Ground rules for good research: A 10 point guide for social researchers.* Buckingham, UK: Open University Press.

Denzin, N. (1978). *The research act* (2nd ed.). Englewood Cliffs, NJ: Prentice Hall.

Denzin, N. K., & Lincoln, Y. S. E. (2000). Introduction: The discipline and practice of qualitative research. In N. K. Denzin & Y. S. E. Lincoln (Eds.), *Handbook of qualitative research* (2nd ed.) (pp. 1–28). Thousand Oaks, CA: Sage.

Dereshiwsky, M. (1999). The five dimensions of participant observation. http://jan.ucc.nau.edu/~mid/edr725/class/observation/fivedimensions/

Dewey Services (n.d.). http://www.oclc.org/en/dewey/

Dickersin, K., Min, Y. I., & Meinert, C. L. (1992). Factors influencing publication of research results: follow-up of applications submitted to two institutional review boards. *Journal of the American Medical Association, 263,* 374–378.

Dickson, J. M., Moberly, N. J., & Kinderman, P. (2011). Depressed people are not less motivated by personal goals but are more pessimistic about attaining them. *Journal of Abnormal Psychology, 120,* 975–980.

Diehl, H. S. (1933). Medicinal treatment of the common cold. *Journal of the American Medical Association, 101,* 2042–2049.

Dirnagl, U., & Lauritzen, M. (2010). Fighting publication bias: Introducing the Negative Results section. *Journal of Cerebral Blood Flow and Metabolism, 30,* 1263–1264.

Doyle, L., Brady, A.-M., & Byrne, G. (2009). An overview of mixed methods research. *Journal of Research in Nursing 14,* 175–185

Doyle, L., Brady, A.-M., & Byrne, G. (2016). An overview of mixed methods research – revisited. *Journal of Research in Nursing, 21,* 623 – 635.

Drew, P. (1995). Conversation analysis. In J. A. Smith, R. Harré, & L. van Langenhove (Eds.), *Rethinking methods in psychology* (pp. 64–79). London, UK: Sage.

Eagle, B. W., Miles, E. W., & Icenogle, M. L. (1997). Interrole conflicts and the permeability of work and family domains: Are there gender differences? *Journal of Vocational Behavior, 50,* 168–184.

Easterbrook, P. J., Berlin, J. A., Gopalan, R., & Matthews, D. R. (1991). Publication bias in clinical research. *Lancet, 337,* 867–872.

Eatough, V., & Smith, J. A. (2006). I feel like a scrambled egg in my head: An idiographic case study of meaning making and anger using interpretative phenomenological analysis. *Psychology and Psychotherapy: Theory, Research and Practice, 79,* 115–135.

Ebbinghaus, H. (1913). *Memory: A contribution to experimental psychology.* New York, NY: Teacher's College, Columbia University; Reprint edition, 1964, New York, NY: Dover.

Edley, N. (2001). Analysing masculinity: Interpretative repertoires, ideological dilemmas and subject positions. In M. Wetherell, S. Taylor, & S. J. E. Yates (Eds.), *Discourse as data: A guide for analysis* (pp. 189–228). London, UK: Sage.

Edwards, D., & Potter, J. (1993). Language and causation: A discursive action model of description and attribution. *Psychological Review, 100,* 23–41.

Edwards, W. (1965). Tactical note on the relation between scientific and statistical hypotheses. *Psychological Bulletin, 63,* 400–402.

Ellis, P. D. (2010). *The essential guide to effect sizes.* Cambridge, UK: Cambridge University Press.

Engstrom, L., Geijerstam, G., Holmberg, N. G., & Uhrus, K. (1963). A prospective study of the relationship between psycho-social factors and course of pregnancy and delivery. *Journal of Psychosomatic Research, 8,* 151–155.

Epley, N., & Huff, C. (1998). Suspicion, affective response, and educational benefit as a result of deception in psychology research. *Personality and Social Psychology Bulletin, 24,* 759–768.

EPPI Centre. *What is a systematic review?* http://eppi.ioe.ac.uk/cms/Default.aspx?tabid=67

Eysenck, H. J. (1980). *The causes and effects of smoking.* London, UK: Sage.

Falk, R., & Greenbaum, C. W. (1995). Significance tests die hard: The amazing persistence of a probabilistic misconception. *Theory and Psychology, 5,* 75–98.

Fanelli, D. (2012). Negative results are disappearing from most disciplines and countries. *Scientometrics, 90,* 891–904.

Fairclough, N. (1989). *Language and power.* London: Longman.

Fairclough, N. (1992). *Discourse and social change.* Cambridge: Polity Press.

Fairclough, N. (1995). *Critical discourse analysis.* Boston: Addison Wesley.

Farr, J., & Nizza, I. E. (2019). Longitudinal Interpretative Phenomenological Analysis (LIPA): A review of studies and methodological considerations. *Qualitative Research in Psychology, 16,* 199–217.

Farrington, D. P. (1996). Psychosocial influences on the development of antisocial personality. In G. Davies, S. Lloyd-Bostock, M. McMurran, & C. Wilson (Eds.), *Psychology, law and criminal justice: International developments in research and practice* (pp. 424–444). Berlin, FRG: Walter de Gruyter.

Feilzer, M. Y. (2010). Doing mixed methods research pragmatically: Implications for the rediscovery of pragmatism as a research paradigm. *Journal of Mixed Methods Research, 4,* 6–16.

Ferri, E. (Ed.) (1993). *Life at 33: The fifth follow-up of the National Child Development Study.* London, UK: National Children's Bureau.

Field, A. (2005). Effect Size. www.statisticshell.com/docs/effectsizes.pdf

Field, A. (2013). *Discovering Statistics using IBM SPSS Statistics* (4th ed.). London, UK: Sage.

Fincham, F. D., Beach, S. R. H., Harold, G. T., & Osborne, L. N. (1997). Marital satisfaction and depression: Different casual relationships for men and women? *Psychological Science, 8,* 351–357.

Fisher, R. A. (1925). *Statistical methods for research workers* (1st ed.). Edinburgh, UK: Oliver and Boyd.

Fisher, R. A. (1935). *The design of experiments* (1st ed.). Edinburgh, UK: Oliver and Boyd.

Fisher, R. A. (1936a). The use of multiple measurements in taxonomic problems. *Annals of Eugenics, 7,* 179–188.

Fisher, R. A. (1936b). "The coefficient of racial likeness" and the future of craniometry. *Journal of the Royal Anthropological Institute, 66,* 57–63. Retrieved 6 November 2019 from http://hdl.handle.net/2440/15228.

Forsyth, J. P., Kollins, S., Palav, A., Duff, K., & Maher, S. (1999). Has behavior therapy drifted from its experimental roots? A survey of publication trends in mainstream behavioral journals. *Journal of Behavior Therapy and Experimental Psychiatry, 30,* 205–220.

Frazier, K. (2013). Failure to replicate results of Bem parapsychology experiments published by same journal. *Skeptical Inquirer, 37.2,* March/April. Retrieved 6 November 2019 from https://skepticalinquirer.org/wp-content/uploads/sites/29/2013/03/p05.pdf

Galak, J., LeBoeuf, R. A., Nelson, L. D., & Simmons, J. P. (2012). Correcting the past: Failures to replicate psi. *Journal of Personality and Social Psychology, 103,* 933–948.

Garfinkel, H. (1967). *Studies in ethnomethodology.* Englewood Cliffs, NJ: Prentice Hall.

Gee, D., Ward, T., & Eccleston, L. (2003). The function of sexual fantasies for sexual offenders: A preliminary model. *Behaviour Change, 20,* 44–60.

Gergen, K. J. (1973). Social psychology as history. *Journal of Personality and Social Psychology, 26,* 309–320.

Gibbs, A. (1997). Focus groups. *Social Research Update, 19.* Retrieved 6 November 2019 from http://sru.soc.surrey.ac.uk/SRU19.html

Giorgi, A. (1985). Sketch of a psychological phenomenological method. In A. Giorgi (Ed.), *Phenomenology and psychological research.* Pittsburgh, PA: Duquesne University Press.

Giorgi, A. (2010). Phenomenological psychology: A brief history and its challenges. *Journal of Phenomenological Psychology, 41,* 145–179.

Glaser, B. G., & Strauss, A. L. (1967). *The discovery of grounded theory: Strategies for qualitative research.* New York, NY: Aldine de Gruyter.

Glass, G. V., & Hopkins, K. D. (1984). *Statistical methods in education and psychology* (2nd ed.). Englewood Cliffs, NJ: Prentice-Hall.

Gleser, G. C., & Dubois, P. H. (1951). A successive approximation method of maximizing test validity. *Psychometrika, 16,* 129–139.

Goffman, E. (1959). *The presentation of self in everyday life.* Garden City, NY: Doubleday.

Goffman, E. (1961). *Asylums: Essays on the social situation of mental patients and other inmates.* Garden City, NY: Anchor Books.

Goldthorpe, J. H. (1987). *Social mobility and class structure in modern Britain* (2nd ed.). Oxford, UK: Clarendon Press.

Gómez, O. S., Juristo, N., & Vegas, S. (2010). Replication types in experimental disciplines. *Proceedings of the 2010 ACM-IEEE International Symposium on Empirical Software Engineering and Measurement,* 1–10.

Gottfredson, S. D. (1978). Evaluating psychological research reports: Dimensions, reliability, and correlates of quality judgments. *American Psychologist, 33,* 920–934.

Gough, D., Oliver, S., & Thomas, J. (2017). *An introduction to systematic reviews.* Sage: London.

Graham, J. W. (2009). Missing data analysis: Making it work in the real world. *Annual Review of Psychology, 60,* 549–576.

Graphpad (2015). Interpreting the confidence interval of a mean. http://www.graphpad.com/guides/prism/6/statistics/index.htm?stat_more_about_confidence_interval.htm

Greene, E. (1990). Media effects on jurors. *Law and Human Behavior, 14,* 439–450.

Greene, J. C., Caracelli, V. J., & Graham, W. F. (1989). Toward a conceptual framework for mixed-method evaluation designs. *Educational Evaluation and Policy Analysis, 11,* 255–274.

Grice, G. R. (1966). Dependence of empirical laws upon the source of experimental variation. *Psychological Bulletin, 66,* 488–498.

Grice, H. P. (1975). Logic and conversation. In P. Cole & J. Morgan (Eds.), *Syntax and semantics 3: Speech acts* (pp. 41–58). New York, NY: Academic Press.

Grichting, W. L. (2011). Psychology and sociology in Australia: The published evidence. *Australian Psychologist, 24,*115–126.

Groom, R., Cushion, C., & Nelson, L. (2011). Delivery of video-based performance analysis by England youth soccer coaches: Towards a grounded theory. *Journal of Applied Sport Psychology, 23,* 16–23.

Groves, R. M., Couper, M. P., Presser, S., Singer, E., Tourangeau, R., Acosta, G. P., & Nelson, L. (2006). Experiments in producing nonresponse bias. *Public Opinion Quarterly, 70,* 720–736.

Groves, R. M., & Peytcheva, E. (2008). The impact of nonresponse rates on nonresponse bias: A meta-analysis. *Public Opinion Quarterly, 72,* 167–189.

Haggbloom, S. J., Warnick, R., Warnick, J. E., Jones, V. K., Yarbrough, G. L., Russell, T. M., et al. (2002). The 100 most eminent psychologists of the 20th century. *Review of General Psychology, 6,* 139–152.

Häggman-Laitila, A., Salokekkilä, P., & Karki, S. (2018). Transition to adult life of young people leaving foster care: A qualitative systematic review. *Children and Youth Services Review, 95,* 134–143.

Hahn, H. H., & Thorndike, E. L. (1914). Some results of practice in addition under school conditions. *Journal of Educational Psychology, 5,* 65–84.

Hall, N. S. (2007). R. A. Fisher and his advocacy of randomization. *Journal of the History of Biology, 40,* 295–325.

Hamby, S., & Turner, H. (2013). Measuring teen dating violence in males and females: Insights from the National Survey of Children's Exposure to Violence. *Psychology of Violence, 3,* 323–339.

Hare, R. D. (1991). *The Hare Psychopathy Checklist – Revised.* Toronto, ON: Multi-Health Systems.

Harlow, L. L., & Oswald, F. L. (2016). Big data in psychology: Introduction to the special issue. *Psychological Methods, 21,* 447–457.

Have, P. ten (2004). Methodological issues in conversation analysis. http://icar.cnrs.fr/ecole_thematique/contaci/documents/bonu/MethodologicalIssues.pdf

Hays, W. L. (1994). *Statistics* (5th ed.). New York, NY: Harcourt Brace.

Henriques, J., Hollway, W., Urwin, C., Venn, C., & Walkerdine, V. (1984). *Changing the subject: Psychology, social regulation and subjectivity.* London, UK: Methuen.

Hepburn, A. (2003). *An introduction to critical social psychology.* London, UK: Sage.

Hergenhahn, B. R. (2001). *An introduction to the history of psychology* (4th ed.). Belmont, CA: Wadsworth Thomson Learning.

Hoecht, A. (2011). Whose ethics, whose accountability? A debate about university research ethics committees. *Ethics and Education, 6,* 253–266.

Hoekstra, R., Morey, R. D., Rouder, J. N., & Wagenmakers, E.-J. (2014). Robust misinterpretation of confidence intervals. *Psychonomic Bulletin & Review, 21,* 1157–1164.

Hoinville, G., & Jowell, R. (1978). *Survey research practice.* London, UK: Heinemann Educational Books.

Holaday, M., & Yost, T.W. (1995). A preliminary investigation of ethical problems in publication and research. *Journal of Social Behavior & Personality, 10,* 281–291.

Horton-Salway, M. (2001). The construction of ME: The discursive action model. In M. Wetherell, S. Taylor, & S. J. E. Yates (Eds.), *Discourse as data: A guide for analysis* (pp. 147–188). London, UK: Sage.

Hotelling, H. (1931). The generalization of Student's ratio. *Annals of Mathematical Statistics, 2,* 360–378.

Howell, D. C. (2013). *Statistical methods for psychology* (8th ed.). Belmont, CA: Wadsworth.

Howitt, D. (1992a). *Concerning psychology: Psychology applied to social issues.* Milton Keynes, UK: Open University Press.

Howitt, D. (1992b). *Child abuse errors.* London, UK: Harvester Wheatsheaf.

Howitt, D. (1995). *Paedophiles and sexual offences against children.* Chichester, UK: Wiley.

Howitt, D. (2019). *Introduction to qualitative methods in psychology* (4th ed.). Harlow, UK: Pearson Education.

Howitt, D., & Cramer, D. (2011). *Introduction to SPSS statistics in psychology* (5th ed.). Harlow, UK: Prentice Hall.

Howitt, D., & Cramer, D. (2017). *Introduction to SPSS in psychology* (7th ed.). Harlow, UK: Prentice Hall.

Howitt, D., & Cramer, D. (2020). *Understanding statistics in psychology with SPSS* (8th ed.). Harlow, UK: Prentice Hall.

Howitt, D., & Owusu-Bempah, J. (1990). Racism in a British journal? *The Psychologist: Bulletin of the British Psychological Society, 3,* 396–400.

Howitt, D., & Owusu-Bempah, J. (1994). *The racism of psychology.* London, UK: Harvester Wheatsheaf.

Humbad, M. N., Donnellan, M. B., Klump, K. L., & Burt, S. A. (2011). Development of the Brief Romantic Relationship Interaction Coding Scheme (BRRICS). *Journal of Family Psychology, 25,* 759–769.

Hunter, M. A., & May, R. B. (1993). Some myths concerning parametric and nonparametric tests. *Canadian Psychology/Psychologie canadienne, 34,* 384–389.

Husserl, E. (1900/1970). *Logische Untersuchungen,* translated by J. N. Findlay as *Logical investigations.* London, UK: Routledge & Kegan Paul.

Husserl, E. (1913/1962). *Ideen zu einer reinen phänomenologie und phänomenologischen philosophie,* translated by W. R. Boyce Gibson as *Ideas: A general introduction to pure phenomenology.* London, UK: Collier.

Hutchby, I., & Wooffitt, R. (1998). *Conversation analysis: Principles, practices and applications.* Cambridge, UK: Polity Press.

Institute for Scientific Information (1994). The impact factor. *Current Contents,* 20 June. https://clarivate.com/essays/impact-factor/

Jang, S. J. (2018). Religiosity, crime, and drug use among juvenile offenders: A test of reciprocal relationships over time. *International Journal of Offender Therapy and Comparative Criminology, 62,* 4445–4464.

Jefferson, G. (1984). On stepwise transition from talk about a trouble to inappropriately next-positioned matters. In J. M. Atkinson & J. Heritage (Eds.), *Structures of social action: Studies in conversation analysis* (pp. 191–222). Cambridge, UK: Cambridge University Press.

Jesson, J. K. (2011). *Doing your literature review: Traditional and systematic techniques.* London: Sage.

John, L. K., Loewenstein, G., & Prelec, D. (2012). Measuring the prevalence of questionable research practices with incentives for truth telling. *Psychological Science 23,* 524–532.

Jones, H. (1981). *Bad blood: The Tuskegee syphilis experiment.* New York, NY: Free Press.

Jones, N. M., Wojcik, S. P., Sweeting, J., & Silver, R. C. (2016). Tweeting negative emotion: An investigation of Twitter data in the aftermath of violence on college campuses. *Psychological Methods, 21,* 526–541.

Jones, M. C., Bayley, N., MacFarlane, J. W., & Honzik, M. P. (1971). *The course of human development.* Waltham, MA: Xerox Publishing Company.

Keith-Spiegel, P., & Koocher, G. P. (1985). *Ethics in psychology: Professional standards and cases.* Hillsdale, NJ: Lawrence Erlbaum Associates.

Kelle, U. (2006). Combining qualitative and quantitative methods in research practice: Purposes and advantages. *Qualitative Research in Psychology, 3,* 293–311

Kelly, G. A. (1955). *The psychology of personal constructs. Volume 1: A theory of personality.* New York, NY: Norton.

Kempthorne, O., & Barclay, W. D. (1953). The partition of error in randomized blocks. *Journal of the American Statistical Association, 48,* 610–613.

Keppel, G., & Wickens, T. D. (2004). *Design and analysis: A researcher's handbook* (4th ed.). Upper Saddle River, NJ: Pearson Education.

Kerr, N. L. (1998). HARKing: Hypothesizing After the Results are Known. *Personality and Social Psychology Review, 2,* 196–217.

Kirk, R. C. (1995). *Experimental design* (3rd ed.). Pacific Grove, CA: Brooks/Cole.

Kitzinger, C., & Frith, H. (2001). Just say no? The use of conversation analysis in developing a feminist perspective on sexual refusal. In M. Wetherell, S. Taylor, & S. J. E. Yates (Eds.), *Discourse theory and practice: A reader* (pp. 167–185). London, UK: Sage.

Klein, O., Doyen, S., Leys, C., Magalhães de Saldanha da Gama, P. A., Miller, S., Questienne, L., & Cleeremans, A. (2012). Low hopes, high expectations: Expectancy effects and the replicability of behavioural experiments. *Perspectives on Psychological Science, 7,* 572–584.

Korn, J. H. (1997). *Illusions of reality: A history of deception in social psychology.* New York, NY: State University of New York Press.

Kottenkamp, R., & Ullrich, H. (1870). Versuche über den Raumsin der Haut der oberen Extremität. *Zeitschrift für Biologie, 6,* 37–52.

Kraemer, H. C., & Thiemann, S. (1987). *How many subjects?* Newbury Park, CA: Sage.

Lana, R. E. (1969). Pretest sensitisation. In R. Rosenthal & R. L. Rosnow (Eds), *Artifact in behavioural research* (pp. 119–141). New York, NY: Academic Press.

Landers, R. N., Brusso, R. C., Cavanaugh, K. J., & Collmus, A. B. (2016). A primer on theory-driven web scraping: Automatic extraction from the Internet for use in psychological research. *Psychological Methods, 21,* 475–492.

Latane, B., & Darley, J. M. (1970). *The unresponsive bystander: Why doesn't he help?* New York, NY: Appleton-Century-Crofts.

Lazarsfeld, P. F. (1948). The use of panels in social research. *Proceedings of the American Philosophical Society, 92,* 405–410.

Leahy, T. H. (2004). *A history of psychology: Main currents in psychological thought* (6th ed.). Upper Saddle River, NJ: Prentice Hall.

LeBel, E. P., & Peters, K. R. (2011). Fearing the future of empirical psychology: Bem's (2011) evidence of psi as a case study of deficiencies in modal research practice. *Review of General Psychology, 15,* 371–379. doi: 10.1037/a0025172

Levitt, H. M. (2019). *Reporting qualitative research in psychology: How to meet APA style journal article reporting standards.* Washington, D.C.: American Psychological Association.

Leyens, J. P., Camino, L., Parke, R. D., & Berkowitz, L. (1975). The effect of movie violence on aggression in a field setting as a function of group dominance and cohesion. *Journal of Personality and Social Psychology, 32,* 346–360.

Library of Congress Classification Outline (n.d.). http://www.loc.gov/catdir/cpso/lcco.

Loftus, E. F., & Palmer, J. C. (1974). Reconstruction of auto-mobile destruction: An example of the interaction between language and memory. *Journal of Verbal Learning and Verbal Behaviour, 13,* 585–589.

Lovering, K. M. (1995). The bleeding body: Adolescents talk about menstruation. In S. Wilkinson & C. Kitzinger (Eds.), *Feminism and discourse: Psychological perspectives* (pp. 10–31). London, UK: Sage.

Ludbrook, J., & Dudley, H. (1998). Why permutation tests are superior to *t* and *F* tests in biomedical research. *American Statistician, 52,* 127–132.

Lund, T. (2012). Combining qualitative and quantitative approaches: Some arguments for mixed methods research. *Scandinavian Journal of Educational Research, 56,* 155–165.

Lykken, D. T. (1968). Statistical significance in psychological research. *Psychological Bulletin, 70,* 151–159.

MacCorquodale, K., & Meehl, P. E. (1948). On a distinction between hypothetical variables and intervening variables. *Psychological Review, 55,* 95–107.

Mace, K. C., & Warner, H. D. (1973). Ratings of psychology journals. *American Psychologist, 28*, 184–186.

MacMartin, C., & Yarmey, A. D. (1998). Repression, dissociation, and the recovered memory debate: Constructing scientific evidence and expertise. *Expert Evidence, 6*, 203–226.

Maddock, J. E., & Rossi, J. S. (2001). Statistical power of articles published in three health-psychology related journals. *Health Psychology, 20*, 76–78.

Matar, H. E., Almerie, M. Q., Al Marhi, M. O., & Adams, C. E. (2009). Over 50 years of trial in *Acta Psychiatrica Scandinavica*: A survey. *Trials, 10*, 35.

Maxwell, S. E. (2004). The persistence of underpowered studies in psychological research: Causes, consequences, and remedies. *Psychological Methods, 9*, 147–163.

Mazzola, J. J., & Deuling, J. K. (2013). Forgetting what we learned as graduate students: HARKing and selective outcome reporting in I–O journal articles. *Industrial and Organizational Psychology, 6*, 279–284.

McArthur, T. (1992). *The Oxford companion to the English language*. Oxford, UK: Oxford University Press.

McGraw, K. O., & Wong, S. P. (1992). A common language effect size statistic. *Psychological Bulletin, 111*, 361–365.

McGuigan, F. J. (1963). The experimenter: A neglected stimulus object. *Psychological Bulletin, 60*, 421–428.

McGuire, W. J. (1997). Creative hypothesis generating in psychology: Some useful heuristics. *Annual Review of Psychology, 48*, 1–30.

McHugh, P. (1968). *Defining the situation: The organization of meaning*. Evanston, IL: Bobbs-Merrill.

McLeroy, K. R., Northridge, M. E., Balcazar, H., Greenberg, M. R., & Landers, S. J. (2012). Reporting guidelines and the *American Journal of Public Health*'s adoption of preferred reporting items for systematic reviews and meta-analyses. *American Journal of Public Health, 102*, 780–784.

Mead, M. (1944). *Coming of age in Samoa*. Harmondsworth, UK: Pelican.

Medway, C., & Howitt, D. (2003). The role of animal cruelty in the prediction of dangerousness. In M. Vanderhallen, G. Vervaeke, P. van Koppen, & J. Goethals (Eds.), *Much ado about crime: Chapters in psychology and law* (pp. 245–250). Brussels, BE: Politeia.

Merton, R., & Kendall, P. (1946). The focused interview. *American Journal of Sociology, 51*, 541–547.

Michelson, L., Mavissakalian, M., & Marchione, K. (1985). Cognitive and behavioral treatments of agoraphobia: Clinical, behavioral, and psychophysiological outcomes. *Journal of Consulting and Clinical Psychology, 53*, 913–925.

Milgram, S. (1974). *Obedience to authority*. New York, NY: Harper & Row.

Moser, C. A., & Kalton, G. (1971). *Survey methods in social investigation* (2nd ed.). London, UK: Gower.

Munley, P. H., Sharkin, B. S., & Gelso, C. J. (1988). Reviewer ratings and agreement on manuscripts reviewed for the *Journal of Counseling Psychology. Journal of Counseling Psychology, 35*, 198–202.

Murphy, P. M., Cramer, D., & Lillie, F. J. (1984). The relationship between curative factors perceived by patients in their psychotherapy and treatment outcome. *British Journal of Medical Psychology, 57*, 187–192.

Neyman, J., & Pearson, E. S. (1933a). On the problem of the most efficient tests of statistical hypotheses. *Philosophical Transactions of the Royal Society of London, Series A 231*, 289–337.

Neyman, J., & Pearson, E. S. (1933b). The testing of statistical hypotheses in relation to probabilities *a priori. Mathematical Proceedings of the Cambridge Philosophical Society, 29*, 492–510.

Norman G. (2014). Data dredging, salami-slicing, and other successful strategies to ensure rejection: Twelve tips on how to not get your paper published. *Advances in Health Science Education: Theory and Practice, 19*, 1–5.

Nunnally, J. (1978). *Psychometric theory* (2nd ed.). New York, NY: McGraw-Hill.

Ochs, E. (1979). Transcription as theory. In E. Ochs & B. Shieffelin (Eds.), *Developmental pragmatics* (pp. 43–72). New York: Academic Press.

O'Connell, D. C., & Kowal, S. (1995). Basic principles of transcription. In J. A. Smith, R. Harré, & L. van Langenhove (Eds.), *Rethinking methods in psychology* (pp. 93–105). London, UK: Sage.

Open Science Collaboration (2015). Estimating the reproducibility of psychological science. *Science, 349*, aac4716.

Orne, M. T. (1959). The nature of hypnosis: Artifact and essence. *Journal of Abnormal and Social Psychology, 58*, 277–299.

Orne, M. T. (1962). On the social psychology of the psychological experiment: With particular reference to demand characteristics and their implications. *American Psychologist, 17*, 776–783.

Orne, M. T. (1969). Demand characteristics and the concept of quasi-controls. In R. Rosenthal & R. L. Rosnow (Eds.), *Artifact in behavioural research* (pp. 143–179). New York, NY: Academic Press.

Orne, M. T., & Scheibe, K. E. (1964). The contribution of nondeprivation factors in the production of sensory deprivation effects: The psychology of the 'panic button'. *Journal of Abnormal and Social Psychology, 68*, 3–12.

Owusu-Bempah, J., & Howitt, D. (1995). How Eurocentric psychology damages Africa. *The Psychologist: Bulletin of the British Psychological Society, 8*, 462–465.

Owusu-Bempah, J., & Howitt, D. (2000). *Psychology beyond Western perspectives*. Leicester, UK: BPS Books.

Page, M., & Scheidt, R. J. (1971). The elusive weapons effect. *Journal of Personality and Social Psychology, 20*, 304–309.

Parker, I. (1989). *The crisis in modern social psychology*. London, UK: Routledge.

Parker, I. (Ed.) (1999). *Deconstructing psychotherapy*. London, UK: Sage.

Parker, I., Georgaca, E., Harper, D., McLaughlin, T., & Stowell-Smith, M. (1995). *Deconstructing psychopathology.* London, UK: Sage.

Patton, M. Q. (1986). *How to use qualitative methods in evaluation.* London, UK: Sage.

Pavlov, I. P. (1927). *Conditioned reflexes: An investigation of the physiological activity of the cerebral cortex,* trans. G. V. Anrep. London, UK: Oxford University Press.

Pearson, K. (1900). On the criterion that a given system of deviations from the probable in the case of a correlated system of variables is such that it can be reasonably supposed to have arisen from random sampling. *Philosophical Magazine, 5th Series, 50,* 157–175.

Pedhazur, E. J., & Schmelkin, L. P. (1991). *Measurement, design and analysis: An integrated approach.* Hillsdale, NJ: Lawrence Erlbaum Associates.

Peeke, S. C., Callaway, E., Jones, R. T., Stone, G. C., & Doyle, J. (1980). Combined effects of alcohol and sleep deprivation in normal young adults. *Psychopharmacology, 67,* 279–287.

Peters, D. P., & Ceci, S. J. (1982). Peer-review practices of psychological journals: The fate of published articles, submitted again. *Behavioral and Brain Sciences, 5,* 187–255.

Petticrew, M., & Roberts, H. (2006). *Systematic reviews in the social sciences: A practical guide.* Oxford, UK: Blackwell.

Pietschnig, J., Voracek, M., & Formann, A. K. (2010). Mozart effect–Shmozart effect: A meta-analysis. *Intelligence, 38,* 314–323.

Pitcher, J., Campbell, R., Hubbard, P., O'Neill, M., & Scoular, J. (2006). *Living and working in areas of street sex work: From conflict to co-existence.* Bristol, UK: Policy Press.

Popper, K. (1959). *The logic of scientific discovery.* London, UK: Hutchinson & Co. (Original work published 1935).

Poropat, A. E. (2009). A meta-analysis of the five-factor model of personality and academic performance. *Psychological Bulletin, 135,* 322–338.

Postal Geography (n.d.). https://www.ons.gov.uk/methodology/geography/ukgeographies/postalgeography

Potter, J. (1997). Discourse analysis as a way of analysing naturally occurring talk. In D. Silverman (Ed.), *Qualitative research: Theory, methods and practice* (pp. 144–160). London, UK: Sage.

Potter, J. (1998). Qualitative and discourse analysis. In A. S. Bellack & M. Hersen (Eds.), *Comprehensive clinical psychology,* Vol. 3 (pp. 117–144). Oxford, UK: Pergamon.

Potter, J. (2001). Wittgenstein and Austin. In M. Wetherell, S. Taylor, & S. J. Yates (Eds.), *Discourse theory and practice: A reader* (pp. 39–56). London, UK: Sage.

Potter, J. (2004). Discourse analysis. In M. Hardy & A. Bryman (Eds.), *Handbook of data analysis* (pp. 607–624). London, UK: Sage.

Potter, J., & Wetherell, M. (1987). *Discourse and social psychology: Beyond attitudes and behaviour.* London, UK: Sage.

Potter, J., & Wetherell, M. (1995). Discourse analysis. In J. A. Smith, R. Harré, & L. van Langenhove (Eds.), *Rethinking methods in psychology* (pp. 80–92). London, UK: Sage.

Povee, K., & Roberts, L. D. (2015). Attitudes toward mixed methods research in psychology: The best of both worlds? *International Journal of Social Research Methodology, 18,* 41–57.

Powell, L., Richmond, V. P., & Cantrell-Williams, G. (2012). The 'drinking-buddy' scale as a measure of para-social behavior. *Psychological Reports, 110,* 1029–1037.

Pratt, M. G. (2009). From the editors: For the lack of a boilerplate: tips on writing up (and reviewing) qualitative research. *Academy of Management Journal, 52,* 856–862.

PsycINFO Database Information (n.d.). https://www.apa.org/pubs/databases/psycinfo/

Ramo, D. E., Hall, S. M., & Prochaska, J. J. (2011). Reliability and validity of self-reported smoking in an anonymous online survey with young adults. *Health Psychology, 30,* 693–701.

Rauscher, F. H., Shaw, G. L., & Ky, K. N. (1993). Music and spatial task performance. *Nature, 365,* 611.

Rauscher, F. H., Shaw, G. L., Levine, L. J., Wright, E. L., Dennis, W. R., & Newcomb, R. (1997). Music training causes long-term enhancement of pre-school children's spatial–temporal reasoning. *Neurological Research, 19,* 2–8.

Reichardt, C. S., & Gollob, H. F. (1999). Justifying the use and increasing the power of a *t* test for a randomized experiment with a convenience sample. *Psychological Methods, 4,* 117–128.

Reinhart, A. (2015). *Statistics done wrong: The woefully complete guide.* San Francisco, CA: No Starch Press.

Reis, H. T., & Stiller, J. (1992). Publication trends in *JPSP*: A three-decade review. *Personality and Social Psychology Bulletin, 18,* 465–472.

Reysen, S. (2006). Publication of nonsignificant results: A survey of psychologists' opinions. *Psychological Reports, 98,* 169–175.

Ritchie, S. J., Wiseman, R., & French, C. C. (2012). Replication, replication, replication. *The Psychologist, 25,* 344–357.

Rivers, W. H. R. (1908). *The influence of alcohol and other drugs on fatigue.* London, UK: Arnold.

Rivers, W. H. R., & Webber, H. N. (1908). The influence of small doses of alcohol on the capacity for muscular work. *British Journal of Psychology, 2,* 261–280.

Robbins, B. D., & Parlavecchio, H. (2006). The unwanted exposure of the self: A phenomenological study of embarrassment. *The Humanistic Psychologist, 34*(4), 321–345.

Roediger III, H. L. (2012). Twist, bend, hammer your effect. *The Psychologist, 25,* 350–351.

Rogers, C. B., Webb, J. B., & Jafari, N. (2018). A systematic review of the roles of body image flexibility as correlate, moderator, mediator and in intervention science (2011–2018). *Body Image, 27,* 43–60.

Rokeach, M. (1960). *The open and closed mind*. New York, NY: Basic Books.

Rosenberg, M. (1968). *The logic of survey analysis*. London, UK: Basic Books.

Rosenthal, R. (1963). On the social psychology of the psychological experiment: The experimenter's hypothesis as unintended determinant of experimental results. *American Scientist, 51*, 268–283.

Rosenthal, R. (1969). Interpersonal expectations: Effects of the experimenter's hypothesis. In R. Rosenthal & R. L. Rosnow (Eds.), *Artifact in behavioural research* (pp. 181–277). New York, NY: Academic Press.

Rosenthal, R. (1978). How often are our numbers wrong? *American Psychologist, 33*, 1005–1008.

Rosenthal, R. (1991). *Meta-analytic procedures for social research* (rev. ed.). Newbury Park, CA: Sage.

Rosenthal, R., & Rosnow, R. L. (1969). The volunteer subject. In R. Rosenthal & R. L. Rosnow (Eds.), *Artifact in behavioural research* (pp. 59–118). New York, NY: Academic Press.

Rosenthal, R., & Rubin, D. B. (1978). Interpersonal expectancy effects: The first 345 studies. *Behavioral and Brain Sciences, 3*, 377–415.

Rosenthal, R., & Rubin, D. R. (1982). A simple, general purpose display of magnitude of experimental effect. *Journal of Educational Psychology, 74*, 166–169.

Rosnow, R. L. (2002). The nature and role of demand characteristics in scientific enquiry. *Prevention and Treatment, 5*, no page numbers.

Rosnow, R. I., & Rosenthal, R. (1989). Statistical procedures and the justification of knowledge in psychological science. *American Psychologist, 44*, 1276–1284.

Rossi, J. S. (1990). Statistical power of psychological research: What have we gained in 20 years? *Journal of Consulting and Clinical Psychology, 58*, 646–656.

Rossi, J. S. (1997). A case study in the failure of psychology as a cumulative science: The spontaneous recovery of verbal learning. In L. L. Harlow, S. A. Mulaik, & J. H. Steiger (Eds.), *What if there were no significance tests?* (pp. 175–197). Mahwah, NJ: Erlbaum.

Rousseau, A., & Eggermont, S. (2018). Media ideals and early adolescents' body image: Selective avoidance or selective exposure? *Body Image, 26*, 50–59.

Rousseau, M., Simon, M., Bertrand, R., & Hachey, K. (2012). Reporting missing data: A study of selected articles published from 2003–2007. *Quality & Quantity: International Journal of Methodology, 46*, 1393–1406.

Rushton, J. P., & Roediger III, H. L. (1978). An evaluation of 80 psychology journals based on the *Science Citation Index*. *American Psychologist, 33*, 520–523.

Sacks, H. (1992). Lecture 1: Rules of conversational sequence. In E. Jefferson (Ed.), *H. Y. Sacks lectures on conversation*, Vol. 1 (3rd ed.). Oxford, UK: Blackwell.

Sacks, O. (1985). *The man who mistook his wife for a hat*. London, UK: Picador.

Schlenker, B. R. (1974). Social psychology and science. *Journal of Personality and Social Psychology, 29*, 1–15.

Schulz, K. F., & Grimes, D. A. (2002). Generation of allocation sequences in randomised trials: chance, not choice. *Lancet, 359*, 515–519.

Searle, J. R. (1969). *Speech acts: An essay in the philosophy of language*. Cambridge, UK: Cambridge University Press.

Sedlmeier, P., & Gigerenzer, G. (1989). Do studies of statistical power have an effect on the power of studies? *Psychological Bulletin, 105*, 309–316.

Shadish, W. R., Cook, T. D., & Campbell, D. T. (2002). *Experimental and quasi-experimental designs for generalised causal inference*. New York, NY: Houghton Mifflin.

Shadish, W. R., & Ragsdale, K. (1996). Random versus nonrandom assignment in controlled experiments: Do you get the same answer? *Journal of Consulting and Clinical Psychology, 64*, 1290–1305.

Sharpe, D., & Faye, C. (2009). A second look at debriefing practices: Madness in our method? *Ethics & Behavior, 19*, 432–447.

Sharpe, D., & Whelton, W. J. (2016). Frightened by an old scarecrow: The remarkable resilience of demand characteristics. *Review of General Psychology 20*, 349–368.

Shaver, J. P., & Norton, R. S. (1980a). Randomness and replication in ten years of the *American Educational Research Journal*. *Educational Researcher, 9*, 9–15.

Shaver, J. P., & Norton, R. S. (1980b). Populations, samples, randomness, and replication in two social studies journals. *Theory and Research in Social Education, 8*, 1–20.

Sheldon, K., & Howitt, D. (2007). *Sex offenders and the Internet*. Chichester, UK: Wiley.

Sheldrake, R. (1998). Experimenter effects in scientific research: How widely are they neglected? *Journal of Scientific Exploration, 12*, 1–6.

Sherman, R. C., Buddie, A. M., Dragan, K. L., End, C. M., & Finney, L. J. (1999). Twenty years of *PSPB*: Trends in content, design, and analysis. *Personality and Social Psychology Bulletin, 25*, 177–187.

Shinebourne, P. (2011). The theoretical underpinnings of interpretative phenomenological analysis. *Existential Analysis, 22*(1), 16–31.

Shye, S., & Elizur, D. (1994). *Introduction to facet theory: Content design and intrinsic data analysis in behavioral research*. Thousand Oaks, CA: Sage.

Silverman, D. (1997). The logics of qualitative research. In G. Miller & R. Dingwall (Eds.), *Context and method in qualitative research* (pp. 12–25). London: Sage.

Simmons, J. P., Nelson, L. D., & Simonsohn, U. (2011). False-positive psychology: Undisclosed flexibility in data collection and analysis allows presenting anything as significant. *Psychological Science, 22*, 1359–1366.

Simons, D. J. (2014). The value of direct replication. *Perspectives on Psychological Science, 9*, 76–80.

Skinner, B. F. (1938). *The behavior of organisms*. New York, NY: Appleton-Century-Crofts.

Smart, R. G. (1964). The importance of negative results in psychological research. *Canadian Psychologist, 5a,* 226–232.

Smith, J. A. (1996). Beyond the divide between cognition and discourse: Using interpretative phenomenological analysis in health psychology. *Psychology and Health, 11,* 261–271.

Smith, J. A. (2011). "We could be diving for pearls": The value of the gem in experiential qualitative psychology. *Qualitative Methods in Psychology Bulletin, 12,* 6–15.

Smith, J. A. (2019). Participants and researchers searching for meaning: Conceptual developments for interpretative phenomenological analysis. *Qualitative Research in Psychology, 16,* 166–181.

Smith, J. A., & Eatough, V. (2006). Interpretative phenomenological analysis. In G. M. Breakwell, S. Hammond, C. Fife-Schaw, & J. A. Smith (Eds.), *Research methods in psychology* (3rd ed.) (pp. 322–341). London, UK: Sage.

Smith, J. A., & Eatough, V. (2019). Looking forward: Conceptual and methodological developments in interpretative phenomenological analysis: Introduction to the special issue. *Qualitative Research in Psychology, 16,* 163–165.

Smith, J. A., Flowers, P., & Larkin, M. (2009). *Interpretative phenomenological analysis: Theory, method and research.* London, UK: Sage.

Smith, J. A., & Osborn, M. (2003). Interpretative phenomenological analysis. In J. A. Smith (Ed.), *Qualitative psychology: A practical guide to research methods* (pp. 51–80). London, UK: Sage.

Smith, J. A., & Osborn, M. (2007). Pain as an assault on the Self: An interpretative phenomenological analysis of the psychological impact of chronic benign low back pain. *Psychology and Health, 22,* 517–534.

Smith, N. C. (1970). Replication studies: A neglected aspect of psychological research. *American Psychologist, 25,* 970–975.

Smith, S. S., & Richardson, D. (1983). Amelioration of deception and harm in psychological research: The important role of debriefing. *Journal of Personality and Social Psychology, 44,* 1075–1082.

Snyder, L. J. (1999). Renovating the *Novum organum:* Bacon, Whewell and induction. *Studies in History and Philosophy of Science, 30,* 531–557.

Solomon, R. L. (1949). An extension of control group design. *Psychological Bulletin, 46,* 137–150.

Solomons, L. M. (1897). Discriminations in cutaneous sensations. *Psychological Review, 4,* 246–250.

Steffens, L. (1931). *Autobiography of Lincoln Steffens.* New York, NY: Harper & Row.

Sterling, T. D. (1959). Publication decisions and their possible effects on inferences drawn from tests of significance—or vice versa. *Journal of the American Statistical Association, 54,* 30–34.

Sterling, T. D., Rosenbaum, W. L., & Weinkam, J. J. (1995). Publication decisions revisited: The effect of the outcome

of statistical tests on the decision to publish and vice versa. *American Statistician, 49,* 108–112.

Stevens, S. S. (1935). The operational definition of psychological concepts. *Psychological Review, 42,* 517–527.

Stevens, S. S. (1946). On the theory of scales of measurement. *Science, 103,* 677–680.

Straus, M., Harmby, S., Boney-McCoy, S., & Sugarman, D. (1996). The revised Conflict Tactics Scale (CTS2): Development and preliminary psychometric data. *Journal of Family Issues, 17,* 283–316.

Strauss, A., & Corbin, J. (1998). *Basics of qualitative research: Techniques and procedure for developing grounded theory* (2nd ed.). Thousand Oaks, CA: Sage.

Strauss, A., & Corbin, J. (1999). Grounded theory methodology: An overview. In A. Bryman & R. G. Burgess (Eds.), *Qualitative research,* Vol. 3 (pp. 73–93). Thousand Oaks, CA: Sage.

Stubbs, M. (1983). *Discourse analysis.* Oxford, UK: Blackwell.

Swann, W. B., Jr., Griffin, J. J., Predmore, S. C., & Gaines, B. (1987). The cognitive–affective crossfire: When self-consistency confronts self-enhancement. *Journal of Personality and Social Psychology, 52,* 881–889.

Tannen, D. (2007). Discourse analysis. Linguistic Society of America, https://www.linguisticsociety.org/resource/discourse-analysis-what-speakers-do-conversation

Tashakkori, A., & Creswell, J. W. (2007). The new era of mixed methods. *Journal of Mixed Methods Research, 1,* 3–7.

Taylor, S. (2001). Locating and conducting discourse analytic research. In M. Wetherell, S. Taylor, & S. J. E. Yates (Eds.), *Discourse as data: A guide for analysis* (pp. 5–48). London, UK: Sage.

Tomer, C. (1986). A statistical assessment of two measures of citation: The impact factor and the immediacy index. *Information Processing and Management, 22,* 251–258.

Torrance, H. (2012). Triangulation, respondent validation, and democratic participation in mixed methods research. *Journal of Mixed Methods Research, 6,* 111–123.

Trafimow, D., & Marks, M. (2015). Editorial. *Basic and Applied Social Psychology, 31,* 1–2.

Trochim, W. M. K. (2006). Positivism and post-positivism. http://www.socialresearchmethods.net/kb/positvsm.htm

Tversky, A., & Kahneman, D. (1971). Belief in the law of small numbers. *Psychological Bulletin, 76,* 105–110.

Tyler, D. B. (1946). The influence of a placebo, body position and medication on motion sickness. *American Journal of Physiology, 146,* 458–466.

VanBuren Trachtenberg, J., Anderson, S. A., & Sabatelli, R. M. (2009). Work–home conflict and domestic violence: A test of a conceptual model. *Journal of Family Violence, 24,* 471–483.

van Dijk, T. (2001). Principles of critical discourse analysis. In M. Wetherell, S. Taylor, & S. J. E. Yates (Eds.), *Discourse theory and practice: A reader* (pp. 300–317). London, UK: Sage.

Velten, E., Jr. (1968). A laboratory task for induction of mood states. *Behaviour Research and Therapy, 6,* 473–482.

Vernmark, K., Lenndin, J., Bjärehed, J., Carlsson, M., Karlsson, J., Öberg, J., Carlbring, P., Eriksson, T., & Andersson, G. (2010). Internet administered guided self-help versus individualized e-mail therapy: A randomized trial of two versions of CBT for major depression. *Behaviour Research and Therapy, 48,* 368–376.

Vuchinich, R. E., & Sobell, M. B. (1978). Empirical separation of physiologic and expected effects of alcohol on complex perceptual motor performance. *Psychopharmacology, 60,* 81–85.

Wampold, B. E., Furlong, M. J., & Atkinson, D. R. (1983). Statistical significance, power, and effect size: A response to the reexamination of reviewer bias. *Journal of Counseling Psychology, 30,* 459–463.

Watson, J. B., & Rayner, R. (1920). Conditioned emotional reactions. *Journal of Experimental Psychology, 3,* 1–14.

Weiss, R. L. (1980). Strategic behavioral marital therapy: Toward a model for assessment and intervention. In J. P. Vincent (Ed.), *Advances in family intervention, assessment, and theory,* Vol. 1 (pp. 229–271). Greenwich, CT: JAI Press.

West, S., Newsom, J., & Fenaughty, A. (1992). Publication trends in *JPSP:* Stability and change in topics, methods, and theories across two decades. *Personality and Social Psychology Bulletin, 18,* 473–484.

Westermann, R., Spies, K., Stahl, G., & Hesse, F. W. (1996). Relative effectiveness and validity of mood induction procedures: A meta-analysis. *European Journal of Social Psychology, 26,* 557–580.

Wetherell, M. S., & Taylor, S. (Eds.) (2001). *Discourse as data: A guide for analysis.* London, UK: Sage.

Wilkinson, L. (1999). Statistical methods in psychology journals: Guidelines and explanations. *American Psychologist, 54,* 594–604.

Wilks, S. S. (1932). Certain generalizations in the analysis of variance. *Biometrika, 24,* 471–494.

Wilson, V. L., & Putnam, R. R. (1982). A meta-analysis of pretest sensitization effects in experimental design. *American Educational Research Journal, 19,* 249–258.

Winston, A. S. (1988). *Cause* and *experiment* in introductory psychology: An analysis of R. S. Woodworth's textbooks. *Teaching of Psychology, 15,* 79–83.

Woodworth, R. S. (1934). *Experimental psychology* (3rd ed.). New York, NY: Holt.

Wooffitt, R. (2001). Researching psychic practitioners: Conversation analysis. In M. Wetherell, S. Taylor, & S. J. E. Yates (Eds.), *Discourse as data: A guide for analysis* (pp. 49–92). London, UK: Sage.

Woolston, C. (2015). Psychology journal bans P values. *Nature, 519* (7541), 9.

Yarkoni, T. (2011, 10 January). The psychology of parapsychology, or why good researchers publishing good articles in good journals can still get it totally wrong. Retrieved 6 November 2019, from http://www.talyarkoni.org/blog/tag/parapsychology/

INDEX